The Contemporary American Essay

Edited by Phillip Lopate

Phillip Lopate is the author of *To Show and to Tell: The Craft of Literary Nonfiction* and four essay collections: *Bachelorhood, Against Joie de Vivre, Portrait of My Body,* and *Portrait Inside My Head.* He is the editor of the anthologies *The Glorious American Essay, The Golden Age of the American Essay, The Art of the Personal Essay, Writing New York,* and *American Movie Critics.* He was awarded a John Simon Guggenheim Fellowship, a Cullman Center Fellowship, two National Endowment for the Arts grants, and two New York Foundation for the Arts grants. He is a professor of writing at Columbia University's nonfiction MFA program and lives in Brooklyn, New York.

The Contemporary American Essay

The Contemporary American Essay

Edited and with an introduction
by Phillip Lopate

ANCHOR BOOKS
A DIVISION OF PENGUIN RANDOM HOUSE LLC
NEW YORK

AN ANCHOR BOOKS ORIGINAL, AUGUST 2021

Pages 609–615 constitute an extension of this copyright page.

The Cataloging-in-Publication Data is on file at the Library of Congress.

Anchor Books Trade Paperback ISBN: 978-0-525-56732-5
eBook ISBN: 978-0-593-31497-5

Book design by Nicholas Alguire

www.anchorbooks.com

Printed in the United States of America
10 9 8 7 6 5 4 3 2

CONTENTS

INTRODUCTION

The first quarter of the twenty-first century has been an uneasy time of rupture and anxiety, filled with historic challenges and opportunities. In that close to twenty-five-year span, the United States witnessed the ominous opening shot of September 11, followed by the seemingly unending Afghanistan and Iraq wars, the effort to control HIV/AIDS, the 2008 recession, the election of the first African American president, the legalization of same-sex marriage, the contentious reign of Donald Trump, the stepped-up restriction of immigrants, the #MeToo movement, Black Lives Matter, and the coronavirus pandemic, just to name a few major events. Intriguingly, the essay has blossomed during this time, in what many would deem an exceptionally good period for literary nonfiction—if not a golden one, then at least a silver: I think we can agree that there has been a remarkable outpouring of new and older voices responding to this perplexing moment in a form uniquely amenable to the processing of uncertainty.

When the century began, essays were considered box office poison; editors would sometimes disguise collections of the stuff by packaging them as theme-driven memoirs. All that has changed: a generation of younger readers has embraced the essay form and made their favorite authors into bestsellers. We could speculate on the reasons for this growing popularity—the hunger for humane, authentic voices trying to get at least a partial grip on the truth in the face of so much political mendacity and information overload; the convenient, bite-size nature of essays that require no excessive time commitment; the rise of identity politics and its promotion of eloquent spokespersons. Rather than trying to figure out why it's happening, what's important is to chart the high points of this resurgence, and to account for the range of styles, subgenres, experimental approaches, and moral positions that characterize the contemporary American essay.

Of course, roping off a period like the year 2000 to the present and calling it "contemporary" is somewhat arbitrary, but one has to start somewhere. At least this artificial chronological box allows for the inclusion of older authors who made their mark in the twentieth century and had the temerity to keep producing significant work in the twenty-first (such as John McPhee, Joyce Carol Oates, Barry Lopez, Thomas Lynch). Just as set designers of period films make a mistake in choosing only articles of clothing or furnishings that were produced in that era, forgetting that we always live with the layered material objects of previous decades, so it would be wrong to restrict the literary flavor of an era to writers under forty. Indeed, what makes this period so interesting is the mélange of clashing generations and points of view. There are still tightly reasoned sequential essays being written in the classical mode, side by side with ones that resist that tidiness.

The essay has always been an adaptable, plastic, shape-shifting form: it may take the form of meditation, reportage, blog, humor piece, eulogy, autobiographical slice, diatribe, list, collage, mosaic, lecture, or letter. Contemporary practitioners seem bent on further testing its limits. For instance, Lia Purpura, Eula Biss, and Mary Cappello are drawn to the lyric essay, which stresses the essay's associational rather than narrative or argumentative properties. Cappello has shrewdly spoken about essay writing—"that nongenre that allows for untoward movement, apposition, and assemblage, that is one part conundrum, one part accident, and that fosters a taste for discontinuity." In line with modernist aesthetics, a mosaic essay with "a taste for discontinuity" may be constructed from fragments, numbered or not, with white space breaks between pieces that connect intuitively or emotionally if not logically. It is up to the reader to figure it out. The list essay, which is highly generative of disparate materials, by its very nature evades an argumentative through line, and can seem initially as random as a poetic inventory by Whitman, though it may deepen subtly and organically. (For example, Nicholson Baker's charming "One Summer," which crisscrosses periods of his life, nevertheless builds to a revealing self-portrait.)

While the influence of poetic technique on the lyric essay has been largely acknowledged, less recognized is the short story's impact on the contemporary essay. Many memoir essays exist in a kind of fictive space, progressing through scene and dialogue and a sensory-laden mood that stays tied to the moment by moment. The piece itself may be entirely factual, but the sentences give off a minimalist frisson that shows the influence of short story writers such as Lydia Davis, Amy Hempel, and Lorrie Moore.

Nonfiction has been agitated in recent years by certain ethical questions, such as, "How legitimate is it to insert fictional details in nonfiction?" or "Is it proper to appropriate the voice of someone of a different ethnicity, sex, or social class?" That both can be done successfully can be seen in Hilton Als's "I Am the Happiness of This World," which channels the silent film star Louise Brooks's ruminations, as though Brooks herself were dictating an essay to Als from the grave.

The role of technology—the Internet and social media—in altering our rhetorical lives may even affect the typography of an essay (as evidenced in Ander Monson's unshackled "Failure: A Meditation"). "Are we merging with our computers and turning into 'spiritual machines'?" wondered the essayist Meghan O'Gieblyn. The blog, once viewed as a debasement or poor relation of the essay, has proven itself a useful invitation to free-flowing, self-surprising displays of consciousness (see Ross Gay, Eileen Myles). Some feminist essayists have expressed a desire to arrive at a "post-patriarchal essay," implying that the very structure of linear argumentation is authoritarian and reinforces status quo sexist power relations. (Maggie Nelson's influential *Bluets* and *The Argonauts* offer clues for shaking up the old model.) Yet all these ways to challenge and subvert the classic essay are in the tradition of the essay itself, whose very name bespeaks an attempt, an experimentation, a stab in the dark. All this is to suggest that the essay remains the most open-ended of forms. (It has even spilled out into other media, as witness the essay film and the graphic essay, subjects for another day.)

Perhaps nothing has so shaped the contemporary practice of essay writing as the rise of the personal essay. It scarcely matters whether the subject be illness (Floyd Skloot), loitering (Charles D'Ambrosio), or prisons (Joyce Carol Oates): some insertion of authorial character is likely to invade the text. Much the way journalism has increasingly surrendered its claims of objective neutrality and allowed reporters room for subjective voice, so the essay has come to rely more and more on an "I." With that has come an infusion of raw honesty, vulnerability, and awkward admission such as would scarcely have been seen in earlier essays. Younger essayists are often willing to acknowledge confusion, psychological distress, thralldom to contradictory drives and uncontrollable desires. There is often a trade-off: more heat, urgency, diaristic excitement, less perspective. Younger essayists might struggle to resolve questions about their authentic nature and perplexing disparities, while older essayists might feel more at ease with the self's mutable, impure, self-betraying nature. Those who are entering middle age will often situate their I characters on a moving platform that begins in childhood or adolescence and transitions into adulthood and sometimes even parenthood. The personal essayist can accommodate these chronological shifts between life's passages more easily than the short story writer (unless you're Alice Munro). As the essayists age, they are less likely to be writing from the midst of distressed confusion and more from a place of wry self-mockery and detachment. The younger the essayist—not all, of course—the more likely an identification with a generational perspective. Popular culture, rock music, or TV programs may be convenient markers for that shared membership. The sense of being part of a generation tends to fade as one grows older: one sees one's unshakable limits and singularities, for better or worse.

It has long been the province of the personal essayist to turn one's narrator into a character by asserting defining autobiographical facts, eccentric or contrarian notions, odd tastes, behavioral tics, and so on. Having done so, the essayist might then wish to parry that Crusoe-like separateness by analyzing to what extent he or she belongs to a larger group or tribe. Ethnicity, gender, sexual preference, physical or mental disability, national origin, generational awareness, social class, and political alignment are some of the categories increasingly tempting contemporary essayists to situate themselves in the midst of a group or at an ambivalent angle from it. This is especially true when the minority to which you belong is asserting its rights or finds itself under attack—when the question becomes unavoidably topical.

The hyphenated American often experiences self-division: "One ever feels his twoness," in W. E. B. Du Bois's famous formulation. Thoughtful African American essayists such as Teju Cole, Darryl Pinckney, and Clifford Thompson, who have found broad acceptance in white academic circles, have felt called upon to reflect about the police actions visited on black people. Depression among minority groups is a subject taken up by Margo Jefferson and Yiyun Li. The tightrope situation of biracial individuals (Alexander Chee) or of immigrants who continue to inhabit two spheres (Aleksandar Hemon) guarantees a tension suitable for an essay's exploration. The outrage that the #MeToo movement produced regarding the sexual harassment, condescension, and mistreatment of women in the workplace is given sharp expression in Rebecca Solnit's "Cassandra Among the Creeps."

One dilemma for the contemporary essayist is how to tackle a social problem while avoiding self-righteousness or strident virtue signaling. To oversimplify: many younger essayists, armed with a checklist of deplorables (racism, sexism, ableism, ageism, homophobia, ethnocentrism, speciesism), set out to denounce these prejudices by recounting how they have witnessed or been victimized by them. They show a commendable sensitivity to the discomfort of minorities and a perhaps overactive desire to restrict any speech that might offend, in line with the trigger warnings, safe zones, and checking of privilege that many campuses now invite. There has been some pushback from older essayists, such as Lynn Freed and Camille Paglia, against the ideological policing of literature: these authors issue from a more skeptical, ironic tradition, and insist on the writer's and instructor's freedom to question, provoke, complicate, argue, and dispute orthodox ideas. Somewhere in the middle may be found, for example, Wesley

Yang's "We Out Here," which seeks to balance the stoical acceptance that life will always bring pain and indignity with an admiration for youth's idealistic opposition to such slights.

In times of calamity, it is only natural for writers to respond to the crisis as concerned citizens. "These days," observes the poet Gregory Pardlo, wistfully, "we feel pulled out of our private selves and called to perform our public accountability." On the other hand, Harold Bloom warns that, whatever the impulse writers might feel toward commitment to social change, "The pleasures of reading indeed are selfish rather than social. . . . I am wary of any arguments whatever that connect the pleasures of reading to the public good." So each essayist must find a way to navigate between commenting on the times, opportunistically or otherwise, and mining the secrets of the interior self for the reader's pleasure and enlightenment.

Of course, there are many impressive essays that have nothing to do with topical controversies or identity politics, but that grapple with eternal questions of life and death, suffering and illness, love and joy, family life. Religion and transcendence are examined in Anne Carson's brilliant analysis, "Decreation." The mortician-essayist Thomas Lynch displays an expert's take on death in "Bodies in Motion and at Rest." Love and loss are movingly explored by Bernard Cooper in "Greedy Sleep" and David Lazar's "Ann; Death and the Maiden," while relationship's perils are enumerated in Laura Kipnis's sardonic "Domestic Gulags." The complicated ties that bind parents and children are demonstrated in Rivka Galchen's "The Case of the Angry Daughter" and Meghan Daum's "Matricide." Then there are simply the pleasures of wasting time leafing through interior decorating magazines, as in Terry Castle's "Home Alone."

Humor will always have an honored place in the contemporary essay: David Sedaris (represented here by "This Old House") has mastered the form, as have Sloane Crosley and Samantha Irby. Finally, there is writing about one's own literary practice: Patricia Hampl assessing the guilt of writing about others, or veteran John McPhee taking us through his messy stages of composition in "Draft No. 4." In a world that often makes little sense, sometimes the only way to face down uncertainty is to write. What better vehicle to process shifting hunches and anxieties than the essay, the ideal form for tracking one's thoughts? If some larger pattern or resolution can be teased from the effort, so much the better. If they don't add up in the end, maybe that is its own valid truth, matching as it does the spirit of our deeply unsure and divided age.

A note on the selections: This is the third in a series of anthologies I have edited, the first one being *The Glorious American Essay: One Hundred Essays from Colonial Times to the Present,* and the second, *The Golden Age of the American Essay: 1945–1970.* Some of the essays included in the current volume I would have loved to place in the first one, but space limitations prevented me from doing so. All along, for the past five years of working on this three-volume project, I have been collecting newer essays with an eye toward curating the present scene. The reader is entitled to some skepticism: Is this selection truly representative of the contemporary essay in all its omnium-gatherum splendor, or is it merely one (elderly white man's) take? Both. Were I younger, in midcareer myself, I would probably have chosen more exclusively from among insurgent essayists. That is the case with other recent anthologies, such as the commendable *Touchstone Anthology of Contemporary Creative Nonfiction,* whose editors, Lex Williford and Michael Martone, assembled their contents in part by conducting a survey among creative writing teachers and practitioners, asking them which essays they favored the most. I have conducted no surveys, but have trusted, perhaps too arrogantly, my personal taste and gut instincts in finding well-crafted, high-quality essays, trying always to go beyond my comfort zone. The main principle that has guided me in these selections was aptly enunciated by Harold Bloom: "We read frequently, if unknowingly, in quest of a mind more original than our own." I was already familiar with the field of American essays, having edited an earlier historical anthology, *The Art of the Personal Essay,* judged many essay contests, and written a quartet of essay collections myself. I hope that background has given me a stronger link to the centuries-old traditions of the essay, and a clearer understanding of how the current array of essayists might be extending or resisting those traditions. (See, for instance, the way Teju Cole and Darryl Pinckney are each in conversation with James Baldwin's essays, specifically his "Stranger in the Village" and "Equal in Paris.")

I would like to acknowledge with gratitude the following friends and colleagues who helped me make these selections: Lisa Jobs, David Mikics, Shifra Sharlin, and Jaydra Johnson. Jaydra also assisted me immeasurably in assembling this manuscript. My talented graduate students in the Columbia MFA Writing Program, where I teach, helped me understand which contemporary essays spoke to younger readers. I am once again indebted to my editor, Diana Secker Tesdell, and my agent, Gail Hochman, for their support along the way. Finally, I'd like to thank my daughter, Lily Lopate, for reading so much of this material and telling me frankly what she thought, and my wife, Cheryl, for making my life so much easier and happier.

The Contemporary American Essay

I AM THE HAPPINESS OF THIS WORLD

Hilton Als

I am Louise Brooks, whom no man will ever possess. Photographed in profile, or three-quarter profile, or full front, photographed and filmed for as long as I can remember (before and after I was forgotten); slandered and revered for as long as I can remember—I remain Louise Brooks, whom no man will ever possess. There is my hair, as black as all that, and the crest of my eyebrows, as black as all that, too, but my eyebrows do not meet in the center of my forehead; instead, they nearly meet at the edge of my bangs, the enameled black of my bangs attached to the rest of my hair, which I wore less as a helmet than a shroud. There is my face and there are my eyes, implanted in that absolutely alabaster exterior known as my face, which was seen time and again in profile and three-quarter profile and full front, a face that did not convey the vitality of youth so much as it conveyed the dissatisfaction one might have with one's youth upon realizing one's youth is there to be ruined, capsized, and sometimes one simply wants to get on with it. In my face you did not see death at work but death at play, hence my film "character," the same one again and again, living in the mortuary of this world and knowing that Death, as an entity, has no regard for whether or not one takes one lover or sixteen, or seeks the ravages of gin to ravage and/or revenge one's beauty, to accelerate hate or disappoint love—in the end, we are all assassinated. My "character"—in everything from *Love 'Em and Leave 'Em* to *Pandora's Box* to *Prix de Beauté* to *Diary of a Lost Girl*—thinks of nothing beyond this moment, the moment of assassination ("It is Christmas Eve and she [Lulu] is about to receive the gift that has been her dream since childhood: death by a sexual maniac," as I wrote once, describing myself "acting"). No Christian ethic to speak of for "her." And yet I myself died a devout Catholic. I am Louise Brooks, whom no man will ever possess.

I am Louise Brooks, whom no man will ever possess—not the biographer, chronicler, or fan. We are all the product of someone else's dream. This I have known since childhood. It was then that a man, a neighborhood friend, did things to me that hurt and hurt. There was no Jesus for me then, just him, this man. And the things he did—my beauty was a conduit for violence against me. And yet I became "her," desired to be seen time and again.

There is nothing unusual in that. There was nothing, ever, to recommend myself to myself except my alabaster skin, the hair I wore as a shroud, the combined effect of which was to make men want to disappear in it. Again and again, I wanted them to absent themselves in the perfection of a beauty I never owned. Believe me in this: my distance from it was so great that I viewed my face as one would a misremembered dream featuring a face and a story I would never come to know, that of Louise Brooks, whom no man will ever possess.

And yet these men did seek to possess me, again and again, and primarily as authors of a text—biography, film criticism, memoirs—that features my name and descriptions of myself—or herself, the "star"—and sometimes photographs as well. But they did it for themselves. They did it by becoming authors of a text in which they are in control of me or herself, that thing that moves them to want to define and fix me through language that is not my own.

The least an object can do is shut up. Speech is impertinent. And yet, although it was, primarily, as a silent film actress that I was known, the complexity and ultimate failure of language was what I conveyed. As one critic wrote upon the 1929 release of

Pandora's Box: "Miss Brooks is attractive and she moves her head and eyes at the proper moment, but whether she is endeavoring to express joy, woe, anger, or satisfaction it is often difficult to decide." Words fail the author in this case because the language I conveyed was not prescriptive. Life is not made up of one word or one projected feeling. Nor was my face. There are those writer's words—joy, woe, anger—and there is my expression of them: in the face that appears under my hair, in my neck that seems to be carved out of any and all the space surrounding it, through my body, which was a complete style unto itself.

Again, I wrote once, elsewhere: "That I was a dancer and Pabst essentially a choreographer in his direction came as a wonderful surprise to both of us. . . . As I was leaving the set, he caught me in his arms, shaking me and laughing as if I had played a joke on him. 'But you are a professional dancer!' It was the moment when he realized that his choice of me for Lulu was instinctively right. He felt as if he had created me. I was his Lulu."

But in creating movement that matters, there is no need to invent a "character"—it is the self that we strive to express. In that early self, that early Louise Brooks, neither Pabst nor anyone else "created" me in a role—I was there myself, in it.

"Louise Brooks cannot act. She does not suffer. She does nothing," wrote yet another critic of one of my early performances. In this review, the language is more to the point, although it, too, conveyed little of what I actually did: it does not analyze why I chose not to "act" but, rather, to be, and was among the first of my kind to do so.

One of the essential rules of screen acting is not to "do" anything at all. This happens when, and only when, one is free or absent enough from one's self to believe we have nothing to lose. Which I did not: before I had lived, my life was lost to me at the hands of a man who did things to me that hurt and hurt. And about my "life" as it was lived: the biographer, Mr. Barry Paris, describes the events constituting it with such caution and at such a remove that my life, in the reading, becomes yet another experience of nonreading; I am less written about in his book than chronicled. There is nothing to suggest "How I Became Louise Brooks," yet another thing I should have written.

Several biographical details for the more documentary-minded among you: I was born in Cherryvale, Kansas, in 1906, and raised in Wichita, Kansas; from my father I inherited my eyebrows and love of scholarship; from my mother I inherited everything that was inattentive, moody, critical. I became interested in dance at an early age; I danced and danced; I left home to dance with Ruth St. Denis and Ted Shawn and their troupe, Denishawn, another member of which was Martha Graham; I left Denishawn at the insistence of Miss St. Denis (I was too critical of others, she said, and too lax with myself). I was asked to perform with the Ziegfeld Follies; I was the most hated Follies girl, ever (too well-read, too much attitude); I was loved then and only then by several lesbians of intellectual distinction and many fairy boys who drank and wrote; I left the Ziegfeld Follies to make films. I slept with Chaplin, Garbo, Pepi Lederer (Marion Davies's niece), William S. Paley, G. W. Pabst—in no particular order. I married twice but, by my own admission, loved only one man, George Marshall, who never restricted himself to the role of fan. I made a number of films, here and in Europe—twenty-four in all; was roundly hated for doing as I pleased and was regarded by many as a child to be cast out, especially in Hollywood—the studio system as fucked family. Many years of drinking; years of writing or not writing. Several people along the way fell in love with me for what I had been once: that image played in their minds as my self, old, stooped, a recluse, talked some to some and little or nothing to others.

There is something to be said for dropping out, saying no, the gin in bed, and books, reading those writers who probably didn't give a damn about their bodies and tried to write them away. Writers' bodies don't make sense in a place like Hollywood: soft and white, defenseless in a town where everyone's defended, right up to their celluloid tits. Maybe that's why I drank so much and did so little during at least part of the second part of my life: Did I lose my dancer's body and slowly acquire a writer's in preparation for writing? I could only be what I played, and for years before I started writing, I played the dropout. I saw little of my old friends and gradually withdrew my swinish behavior from the so-called pearls who wanted to convince me the world wasn't a sty after all, like Lillian Gish. Or Garbo, who saw me from her automobile once. I was living in another hole then, reading and drinking; I was maybe forty, through with being looked at, or so I thought. Me and Garbo shared a moment back in the day; what the hell, we both squandered her beauty. When she saw me from the car window, the sun was so sad; it slanted through the Third Avenue El train tracks; it was winter, I was growing older. I had on a black coat. I was carrying a bottle in a brown paper bag. I think she saw me before I saw her, but I knew it was her the minute I saw her car, and then I saw her face, that face, in a passenger seat, I saw her eyes, she wanted to offer me a ride, but just looking at me she could also see that I wasn't up for a reunion, or even her help, and so she drove right by, what grace.

Here's the thing: if you drop out you're not so much bottoming out but rising: above the mundane, above being anyone's wife. The pots and pans, kids, it's your call, honey, someone else's needs—they are beyond you. You float in your own thin air, your time is your own. Admittedly, I wouldn't have made it out of my little flat in New York, where I supported myself in my early forties as a kind of call girl sometimes, or (more disastrously) as a counter girl in a department store, who cares, I drank most of my earnings away, but I wouldn't have made it on those scullery-maid wages anyway were it not for the largesse of former lovers like William S. Paley, the CBS head, who gave me a monthly stipend that kept a roof over my head and in gin and books until I died. Sometimes I wonder when he wrote the check what he smelled like when he looked down the ledger of his life and saw my name. My pink skin, his hand imprinted on my neck, my black bangs?

It takes great courage to do nothing. You wear the world's tolerance down with your passivity and mind for nothingness. You have no season like spring in you to be reborn, because nothing has been planted. People leave you alone, because you are the face of that which they fear most: failing, not caring, doing nothing. In that freedom you have time, then, to face what most performers never face, and that I could face, with all that time on my hands: how little I wanted to be seen even as I longed to be seen. Back in Kansas, the same old story: the elderly man who finds me, a little girl, charming, and then his cunty fingers in my mouth; don't tell the folks; it's your fault; I have to lick myself off his fingers; this pleases him; I gag, but I do it because, after all, what's a body for? What does beauty mean? And I smile as I do it, and gag; and, after all, how different is that smile from smiling in toe shoes, standing on a block of wood, *en pointe,* smiling under the Ziegfeld brand or taking a movie light on the chin, the light like a fist assaulting the mug that launched a disappointment? Once you give up on trying to change any of that, which is to say, reversing your story so it jibes with the American way of health—I will be a beautiful and free and prosperous white woman, I know I am, you must work to deserve me—you can relax and sink into being as dull and monstrous as the mirrors you once plagued looking for someone called I am Louise Brooks, whom no man will ever possess.

What the mirror shows: your looks looking at you as you change. Your beauty becoming a memory. I am a woman and feast on memory, having had no children to feast on. I kept a scrupulously clean hovel as I worked my way down, always. Meanwhile, my heart beat for that which I couldn't help but respond to: a director. Whenever one showed up in the guise of a lover, I responded with all my being. I wanted nothing, and a director. Obliteration, and someone to tell me where to hit my mark.

James Card was the next-to-last man who gave me direction. In 1955 I received a letter from him; some people never give up. His letter said he was the director of the Eastman House in Rochester, New York; it housed one of the great film libraries, a place that contained, he told me, examples of my work, ha, if you want to call it that. Well, he did. In his first letter, he described how, on a recent visit to Paris, he sat with Henri Langlois, the venerable founder of the Cinémathèque Française, when Langlois screened *Pandora's Box* and *Diary of a Lost Girl*. Langlois was apparently knocked out by what he saw, he had no idea, and was moved to put my picture up, along with Falconetti's, at the entranceway to his exhibition, *60 Ans de Cinéma*. When people asked why me over Garbo or Dietrich, Langlois is reported to have said, "There is no Garbo! There is no Dietrich! There is only Louise Brooks!"

In response to Card's letter and attention, I wrote this:

> The mystery of life . . . that you should, after almost thirty years, bring me the first joy I ever tasted from my movie career. It's like throwing away a mask. All these years making fun of myself with everyone overjoyed to agree . . . away all false humility forever!

You see, they had to hog-tie me to get me into pictures. They didn't know what to do with me, I did not fit into any of it. After the day I went into the projection room with Walter Wanger and the director to my second picture, and they laughed and kidded me about my acting, I vowed that I would never see another picture that I was in—and I never have, not even my pictures made in Europe.

Save me from my past. I was living in grimy shade near the Queensboro Bridge when Card came running to me the first time. He was married, what did I care, it was impossible, I could care, he would never leave his wife for me, I could care less. The point was to hate him for what he did and did not give me: himself. The truth is, I wasn't interested in any man being there, not completely, and the minute I felt they wanted to be there, I accused them of being unavailable, which scared them off, of course: no one likes being told they don't exist. But the fact is, most of the men I was with were never smart enough to get the fact that when I accused them of not being available, I was talking about myself.

I moved to Rochester in '56, something like that, and Card got me writing about cinema by looking at films and thus memories. I looked at movies starring "her" myself—and bitterly despised the vomit that lodged in my throat: my sentimental streak. Whatever dream I had about her—myself—was stripped away by my writer's eyes. I couldn't pity her! And that's when I knew I could write about her for real, and give as good on the page as she gave me on the screen, which is to say no pity at all.

Card and I were through by '63. After him, I wrote and drank for sixteen years in that little room in Rochester. Loneliness is what every writer deserves for all their ruthless betrayals—telling other people's stories their way—and what every actress deserves for all the intimacies they're offered because of their beauty, and seductiveness, which the actress does or does not believe in. Either way, she'll treat you like shit for having fallen for any of it. It's true because I know it.

I thought I was on my own until the last director or translator or whatever showed up. That would be Kenneth Tynan. But that didn't last long. Once his *New Yorker* piece about me came out, and I saw what it was—fan-based, he couldn't be as critical of "her," as I learned to be; he couldn't discipline his ardor, but I could; I had to be the best, so vain, it's true—I jettisoned him from my life, forever. Again and again my dismissal of these men. What can it mean to any of you that that dynamic—the quivering male heart bent in gratitude at the unfeeling heel of my shoe—meant and can mean everything and nothing to someone like me, and that that ambivalence can consume a life? Or that that is all one's life sometimes becomes—what Proust called "reciprocal torture," or what Virginia Woolf called her "looking-glass shame"? Perhaps they did what I sought to do: to become the living embodiment of everything being nothing at all, this Death we live, this life the living never fully comprehend, or claim.

ONE SUMMER

Nicholson Baker

One summer I lived in a house that was being renovated, in a bright yellow room, with a mattress on the floor. I woke up late and tried to type in bed. I was working on a story about a man who by chance runs into his brain on the street. His brain is wearing a jaunty hat and is in a hurry. It has some kind of a sales job. At night I walked to a restaurant called Gitsis Texas Hots and ordered two hot dogs and a cup of coffee and reviewed the day's work on "My Brain." The story was never finished.

One summer my family went on a boat in Georgian Bay with another family. There was a girl who slept on the boat with her eyes open.

One summer a friend and I went on a bicycle trip. In a small town in New York State, somebody opened a car door and we both collided with it and fell down on the street. And we were fine. Later a flock of birds gathered in the tree above our sleeping bags in the early morning.

One summer in California I owned a hundred shares of stock in Koss Corporation, the headphone company. I bought a newspaper and discovered that the stock had doubled in value. I sold all my shares and bought a Honda Passport motor scooter. My girlfriend rode on the back, wearing a red helmet, and I had a blue helmet, and it was lots of fun except that she burned her leg on the muffler and had to go to the emergency room.

One summer my girlfriend and I got engaged and we went to Jordan Marsh and bought a mattress and a box spring from a salesman named Sam. Sam said his wife liked a softer mattress, but he liked a firmer mattress. He led us to a mattress that was both firm and soft. The thing about this mattress, he explained, was that on it the two of us could "sleep to the edge." If you got a cheap queen-size mattress, he said, it was really like only getting a full-size mattress, because you couldn't sleep to the edge. We bought the mattress Sam recommended and twenty years later we are still sleeping to the edge on it.

One summer I painted the floor and ceiling of a room in the same day. The paint didn't stick very well to the floor, however.

One summer I tried to write about a man I'd interviewed named Pavel Moroz. Mr. Moroz had invented something he called a microcentrifuge. He took tiny spheres of liquid and spun them at the highest speed he could spin them at, using a dentist's drill. Nothing spins faster than a dentist's drill, apparently. Mr. Moroz believed that ultracentrifugation would transform matter into new states of purity and enlightenment. But nobody paid attention to him. When I talked to him he was taking classes to become a licensed masseur.

One summer I had a paddleboard and I went up the side of a big wave to the top. Then I was under the wave looking up at its sunlit crest. Then I was turned some more, and I saw sand and gravel doing a little polka on the bottom. I had no idea there was so much going on inside a wave.

One summer there were several cars with trick horns installed that played "La Cucaracha."

One summer I heard someone next door typing on an electric typewriter while I sat outside in the sun. I listened to the swatting of the keys and thought how rare that sound was now. I tore an article out of the newspaper about the bankruptcy of Smith Corona.

One summer I sat at a table with Donald Barthelme, the short story writer, while he drank a Bloody Mary. He said he was planning to buy a new stereo system. I recommended that he go with Infinity loudspeakers.

One summer I worked for a company that made modems. I began working twelve hours a day. In the morning, driving to work, I held the coffee cup in my teeth when I was unwrapping a doughnut. Once, passing a truck, I forgot that the coffee cup was there and I whipped my head around to be sure a car wasn't in the next lane, sloshing coffee on my shirt and my seat belt. Another time a can of 7 Up exploded in the glove compartment. The car, a Dodge Colt, began to have a sweetish smell that I liked.

One summer my grandmother took us to visit a blind woman who lived by the sea. The woman told us that when she swam, she would listen for her dog, who barked whenever she drifted too far from shore. Once she went out to do errands and didn't come home till very late. Her dog had had a bathroom emergency under a knickknack shelf, away from where she would step, which she thought was very considerate. We agreed.

One summer I went on a bike trip through Quebec and Maine, eating four peanut butter and jelly sandwiches a day. The roads in Quebec are very straight and flat.

One summer I worked at a place where they stored old copying machines. I learned to drive a forklift, and I drove it around the old copying machines, beeping the horn, which made a plummy "meep meep." The second floor was filled with metal desks, and when it was break time, I would go up there to read spy novels. One of the people I worked with wandered around these desks drinking clear fluid from a bottle. That man sure drinks a lot of water, I thought. He opened and closed the drawers of the desks, checking to see if something of value had been left behind. I listened to the sound of drawers opening and closing, far away and nearer by, and fell asleep.

One summer a raisin stuck to a page I was writing on, so I drew an outline of it and wrote "A Raisin Stuck Here—Sunmaid."

One summer I went to Italy with my girlfriend and her family. My girlfriend's uncle brought a set of dissolvable capsules containing foam circus animals. Every night at cocktail hour we dropped one capsule into a glass of water. As each foam leg emerged, we would say, "There's another leg!"

One summer two of my friends and I found a loose door. We hauled it up to the top of the garage roof and positioned it there with some struts so that we could sit on the door and look out at the world. There wasn't much to do once we were up there except eat crackers, and the asphalt roof shingles were soft and easily torn, like pan pizza, we discovered. They overlapped unnecessarily, wastefully, so we tore off quite a number of them and flung them down. They glided like Frisbees. My parents were unhappy because they had to have the garage reroofed.

One summer my friend and I bought Corgi toys, about fifteen of them, and built a parking garage for them out of blocks. Then we had an argument, and my friend took the Corgis he owned back to his own house.

One summer I worked as a waiter in a fancy restaurant that had been owned by a reputed mobster. The mobster sold the restaurant to the head chef for a lot of money. But many of the people who'd gone to the restaurant had been friends and associates of the reputed mobster—when he stopped going, they stopped going. So business dropped, and I stood wearing a ruffle-fronted shirt with a black bow tie, looking out at the empty tables. Once a waitress told the chef that a patron wanted a simple chicken salad sandwich. The chef, whose specialty was veal dishes, was affronted. "Chicky salad?" he said. "Tell him to bring his dick in here. I'll make him some nice chicky salad."

One summer I converted all my old word processing files, written on a Kaypro computer, to DOS. And that was fun.

One summer a guy down the street got mad at the fact that people were allowing their dogs to poop every day in front of his yard. He took some white plastic forks and put them in the dog poops. They looked like little sailboats.

One summer we had four fans set up in the upstairs bedrooms. One fan started smoking and our alert dog barked to let us know. Then we had three fans.

One summer I read the Edmund Scientific catalog a lot of times and fantasized about owning a walkie-talkie and communicating with my friends with it. But they cost a hundred dollars.

One summer I was on the verge of making a baloney sandwich. I had the tomato in my hand and I'd opened the door of the refrigerator and I was looking down at the jar of mayonnaise on the bottom shelf, and then I thought, No, no baloney right now. And I closed the refrigerator door. I was able to resist that baloney and put it out of my mind.

One summer I read an old copy of *Confessions of an English Opium-Eater* with great fascination.

One summer my father put up a Tarzan swing in our backyard. My friend and I used an old refrigerator crate as the leaping-off point, with two smaller boxes on top of that for extra height. We swung so high that we could grab a branch in a spruce tree and hold on to it. Then one time the branch broke, and my friend fell. He lay on his back going "Orf orf." I was worried and got my mother. She said he'd had the wind knocked out of him, but that he would be fine. And he was fine.

One summer I got a crush on a girl who was eleven. I was eleven at the time as well.

One summer my father planted an herbaceous border in our yard. I helped him plant the *Santolina incana nana* and mix in the peat moss. On weekdays he would go out after dinner and water in the dark, so that if I went out to get him I could only see the spray from the hose reflecting the porch light, and hear his whistling.

One summer I went to see a new movie called *Annie Hall* with two women who played the harp. One harp player didn't like it, one harp player really didn't like it, and I liked it a lot.

One summer I spent a lot of time in my room trying to learn how to handstand. But one of my wrists was not flexible enough.

One summer a photographer was doing an ad for a bank and needed a woman to make a funny face. He called up my mother, because he had heard that she could make funny faces. The two of them went out onto the front porch, and he said to her, "Okay, now make a funny face." She grimaced, then laughed. He said, "Try not to laugh. Good. Now puff out your cheeks." So she puffed out her cheeks. The ad, announcing a higher interest rate on savings accounts, came out in the newspaper. The picture looked nothing like my mother. I spent a good deal of time making funny faces in the mirror in case a photographer called me.

One summer I went to a science camp called Camp Summersci. We were driven in a used hearse to places of scientific interest. In Herkimer, New York, we chiseled quartz crystals called Herkimer diamonds out of a rocky hillside. One of the campers was a kid who knew more about *The Lord of the Rings* than I did. We talked about *The Lord of the Rings* for many hours in the back of the hearse.

One summer my father and I put up a basketball hoop above the garage door, and I played basketball with myself for a week and then stopped.

One summer a new friend said we should learn taxidermy at home. He sent off for lesson one. The course instructed us to look around for dead squirrels to stuff. I told him I didn't know where any dead squirrels were. His voice was already changing and mine wasn't. He laughed: "Heh heh." I laughed nervously back. He shook his head and said, "See, I knew you'd laugh. All I have to do is pretend to laugh, and you laugh."

One summer my girlfriend was unhappy with me when we went out for dinner because I pulled the onions out of my salad with my fingers and put them on the bread plate along with a glob of salad dressing. Later I leapt up from the table to watch a brief fistfight between a waiter and a patron. I said I was sorry and she forgave me.

One summer my daughter learned how to read the word *misunderstanding*.

One summer I rode to the top of a hill and then coasted, and the wind came under the back of my neck and down in my shirt and cooled me down. It felt very good. This was somewhere in West Virginia, on my bike.

One summer my friend Steve and I went out to a movie. He was getting his medical degree then. He suggested we go buy some cheese at the Super Duper. That sounded like a good idea to me. We bought two large pieces of mozzarella cheese and got into his car and ate them, talking about the current state of science fiction.

One summer I worked at a job where we had to wash hundreds of Venetian blinds in a tall metal tank that stood in a loud room next to the air circulation fans. We dipped the blinds in soapy water in the tank, and then we moved them up and down. The dipping was supposed to remove the dust from the slats, but the dust had bonded with the paint and it stayed. So the man said we had to wash the slats by hand, with a rag. This made the white paint come off. We put all the blinds back in the windows, although they were bent and peeling and sorry-looking. Later I used a sledgehammer on a big piece of cement.

One summer I went to a Nautilus Fitness Center at the Americana Hotel in Rochester. I did various strenuous things on the machines, and then I crossed the street to McDonald's and ordered two Big Macs. My hand trembled so much from the exercise that I could barely push the straw through the little cross in the plastic lid of my root beer.

One summer my son and I built a tree house near the compost pile. We painted it green. We ate dinner up there a few times.

One summer after my wife and I spent all day packing boxes I had a dream in which I'd grown a split personality that snarled and lunged at me like a police dog. I woke up and lay perfectly still, too afraid to close my eyes or click on the light. After several minutes of motionless nostalgia for the days when I had been a sane person, I finally touched my wife and said, "Dear one?" She made a questioning noise from deep in her sleep. I said, "I'm sorry to wake you but I'm having some kind of unusual panic attack." She said, "I'm so sorry, baby." I said, "It's really bad, I'm scared about everything, I'm even scared to turn on the light." She said, "I'll hold you. Everything is good. Go back to sleep now." She held me and I turned a different way in the bed and the fear dissolved and I went back to sleep. I woke up feeling fine.

One summer I dropped a bowl of hot fudge that I'd warmed up in a microwave onto the kitchen floor of a Howard Johnson's and burned myself.

One summer my friend and I dug in his backyard using a hose to blast holes deep in the dirt. We made a series of small ponds and bogs. My friend's mother was unhappy with us because the water bill was very high.

One summer my family and I ate dinner at a restaurant that had a machine that made saltwater taffy. The machine had two double-forked prongs that folded and stretched the taffy ball onto itself until there were unimaginable numbers of layers. When the taffy had been stretched and folded enough times a man rolled it into a loaf and mounted it in a machine that cut it and wrapped the cut pieces with waxed-paper wrappers. The device that twisted the wrapper ends moved too fast for the eye to see. The taffy man looked at us without acknowledging us or smiling. He had no privacy—he was like a zoo creature. He had a small mustache.

One summer we moved from Boston, Massachusetts, to New York State. I was driving the old brown car and my wife was driving the new red car down Routes 5 and 20. There was a big hot blue sky and enormous trees. I rolled my window all the way down. Immediately the wind sucked a map of New York State off my dashboard. In my rearview mirror I saw the pale creased shape float on air for a moment, as if deciding what to do. Then it plastered itself to my wife's windshield, where she pulled it inside. She waved.

One summer when I was fourteen I took care of an orange cat at a house owned by two minimalist painters. All their walls were flat white, and they had many of their paintings up—long, narrow paintings, with silver metallic paint sprayed in from the ends, dripping subtly. The lonely cat roamed this minimalist house, meowing. I read issues of *Artforum* neatly stacked on their coffee table. There was an article about an artist who created an empty room with a sloping wooden floor. The artist, whose name was Vito Acconci, "pleasured himself" under the sloping floor, while visitors walked around the room overhead. I fed the cat, pleasured myself, and rode my bike home.

One summer I wrote "Truth wears sunglasses" in my notebook.

PORTRAIT OF THE BAGEL AS A YOUNG MAN

Thomas Beller

27 Years Old

His hands were large. My résumé lay flat on his desk. He had cleared a space amid the clutter, and he ran one of those big, sensitive, but also violent-looking hands over it again and again while he studied it, as though his hand were a scanner and would impart some key bit of information that reading never could. I later discovered that this was in fact what he was doing—he couldn't read very well, and seemed to place as much importance in a document's texture as in its contents.

The boss—sitting behind an impossibly cluttered desk, in an impossibly cluttered room, with the sound of the bagel factory in full swing upstairs, churning away with the noise of a ship's engine—looked down at the résumé and chewed thoughtfully on his lower lip. Then he abruptly looked up with the penetrating, profound, and fired-up expression of a prosecutor who is about to ask the question on which the whole case would turn. He said: "If someone buys three dozen bagels, and they get a free bagel for every dozen, how many would you give them?"

I thought I heard everyone else in the room collectively catch their breath. There were five of them crammed into the tiny space. They had given me a cursory once-over when I walked in, but now I could feel their eyes upon me. I had seen the ad in *The New York Times,* and it occurred to me that I was part of a long parade of applicants that had come through the office that day. I wondered whether it had been on this question that they had stumbled, one after another.

"Thirty-nine," I said.

Mr. H didn't respond. He went back to studying my résumé, chewing his lips and running that large hand over it again and again. Then he looked up at me.

"Are you Jewish?" he said.

I like bagels, but I never craved them, never viewed them as something special, out of the ordinary, or exotic. They were a fact of life, personified, when I was growing up, by the local store that baked and sold them, H&H Bagels, on Eightieth Street and Broadway, which was open twenty-four hours a day, seven days a week. Besides selling bagels, the store performed a kind of community service by perfuming the air in its vicinity with the smell of baking bread, which gave the chaotic stretch of Broadway north of Seventy-Ninth Street a neighborly, friendly feel. There is something about the smell of baking bread, in its diffuse form, that civilizes people.

Once, during an autumn college break, I was walking along Broadway late at night on the way home from a party when an unexpected snow began to fall. It was exhilarating and beautiful, and I rhapsodized about the beauty of the city and of the snow, paid careful attention to the little clumping sounds of my feet on the whitening sidewalk, and scarcely noticed that I was cold.

Then, after a few blocks, I noticed. I progressed very quickly through the various stages of cold until I felt on the verge of freezing to death. I walked faster. I had no money in my pocket for a cab, just a couple of quarters, and with each block the distance home seemed to increase.

And then, amid dark and shuttered Broadway, there appeared an oasis of light and warmth—H&H Bagels.

A lone cashier stood behind her register, white paper cap atop her head.

"What's hot?" I said.

Behind the cashier was the oven, and just then one of the bakers in his white uniform slid a wooden platter into the maw of the oven and removed a squadron of steaming plain bagels, which he dumped into a wire bin. My two cold coins were enough for a hot bit of sustenance. The bagel burned my numb fingers. I walked the rest of the way home with the warm dough permeating my senses.

It was this kind of memory—vague, nostalgic, innocent—that had sprung to mind that day in early September 1992 when, amid a bleak session of scanning *The New York Times* help-wanted ads, I came across an ad placed by a bakery that identified itself as being located on the Upper West Side.

I looked up and thought, What other bakery is located on the Upper West Side? And then I ran to a fax machine with my résumé.

At that time I was a fledgling writer with a graduate degree, a couple of publications, and a few jobs under my belt—bike messenger, gallery assistant, office temp. I took these jobs to make money, but there was also an aspect of penance to them. I don't know exactly for what sin I was repenting. Maybe the sin of having gone to graduate school for writing. On some level I saw these jobs as a kind of karma insurance. It was a way of testing myself: You want to be a writer? Can you handle this? How about *this*?

I wasn't so noble and pure-minded about literature that it was my only interest. I also played drums in a rock band, and I took these temporary jobs because it seemed that, on any given week, everything could change, we could sign a deal, record, go on tour. I wanted to pay the bills, take things a week at a time, and be ready for the big break. I was still high from a two-month road trip/tour the band had taken two years earlier. When that was over I only wanted to do it again. At the time it seemed inevitable, but two years later it was fading in the gauzy haze of fantasy, and I was descending into a panic.

I don't want to romanticize this panic. I think the breaking wave of the present tense is always accompanied by a whitecap of panic, as true of the moment of this writing as it was then, when I was looking for a job to pay the rent and wondering what the hell was going to happen next with everything that was important to me.

I got the job, in spite of being Jewish. Besides being the truth, this seemed to be the expedient answer when applying for a job at a kosher bagel factory, but it turned out that it was a minor liability. Mr. H was worried I might demand to be let off on each and every one of the many holidays—apparently some long-ago employee had given him all kinds of headaches on this matter.

My job didn't have a title, but I knew right away that it was special. I was to be in charge of inventory, which seemed a position of considerable gravity, as it included all sorts of items out of which the bagels were made (poppy seeds, raisins, sesame seeds, sourdough, salt, sugar), and I was to be paid ten dollars an hour, which I intuited was at the very high end of the pay scale at H&H. I was also to function as a kind of right-hand man to Mr. H, which meant, among other things, that I had to arrive at eight in the morning and call a series of automated voice-mail systems belonging to several different banks, get that day's balance on several different accounts, and write it all out for him so it was there as soon as he sat down at his desk at nine.

My immediate superior was a young man named Rick, a lapsed classical trumpet player from Buffalo, whose blond hair was cut Marine-short and whose glasses had small round rims that made him seem efficient and fastidious. His career had ground to a halt several years earlier when he stood backstage at a recital and found that he was incapable of going onstage. Rick had been at the bagel factory for three years and was in the midst of an extremely gradual exit. He had commenced exiting, as far as I could tell, almost as soon as he got there, and it seemed possible the process still had another year or so left in it.

Rick showed me around the ground floor, where the bagel-making took place, and the downstairs, a dungeonlike space illuminated by bare lightbulbs dangling from the ceiling. There was one long hallway, which led to a series of crevices that were used for storage, for locker rooms, for the mechanic's room.

Descending the stairs from the ground floor to the basement

felt like entering another world. Each stair had a rounded edge, worn down from years of use. At the bottom of the stairs was a long passageway where one was immediately in full view of Mr. H sitting behind his desk, way at the other end. The first time I went down those stairs, I was brought up short by a very peculiar image: a pipe leading straight down from the ceiling spewing water into a white porcelain sink. The water splashed into the sink, careened around the white porcelain, and disappeared down the drain.

"What the hell is that?" I asked Rick.

"It's water from the oven, to cool the engines. It just pours down twenty-four hours a day, seven days a week. It never stops." This was a metaphor. For something. I hoped not for my time at H&H bagels.

Rick taught me the ropes.

Concerning perks: All the bagels you want, for free.

Concerning theft: You cannot steal money, but you can steal food (tuna fish, lox, orange juice, soda, ice cream). It was tacitly acceptable for us—the exalted, white, downstairs-dwelling, Mr. H's right-hand men—to do it, but the Puerto Ricans who worked upstairs were strictly forbidden, so as a matter of courtesy we should make a point of being surreptitious.

Concerning Mr. H: Sporadically bighearted but for the most part a hard-ass in the mold of a boss who has worked his way up from the bottom. He was a Vietnam vet. A Puerto Rican from the Bronx, the youngest of eight kids, he had converted to Judaism when he got married. Some of his brothers and other relatives peppered the staff, but they got no preferential treatment, no extra pay. His oldest brother arrived at the factory in the small hours to load his truck with bagels for his delivery route. Mr. H himself had started out as a driver for the previous owners of the bakery.

There was a certain artistic quality to the precise movements of the bakers upstairs, the way they pushed slats of "doughs" into the ever-rotating carousel inside the ovens, and then flipped them, and then later removed them, but Rick assured me that

Mr. H was the best, fastest, most dexterous baker at H&H and that he had once stayed up for twenty-four hours helping bake a special order, which he then single-handedly drove down to Philadelphia on no sleep.

Days turned into weeks. I could feel myself falling, gleefully falling into H&H Bagels, into its reality, reveling in the sheer *physicality* involved in making such a delightfully tangible thing, the sensuous, arduous, choreographed world of the bagel factory.

And nothing entranced me more than the huge, ancient ledger book in which all the inventory details were recorded, a book that would come to dominate my days, and eventually my nights as well.

When I saw that huge, decrepit, almost biblical-looking ledger book in Rick's hands, filled with tiny numerical entries, my heart leapt with recognition.

The ledger book became my domain. I studied it. In the mornings I wandered around the factory with the thing open in my arms, a pencil behind my ear, counting. All around me was the chaos of the men in white uniforms making bagels—the roar of the oven and, at the other end of the floor, the dough mixer, a hilarious machine into which huge globs of dough were fed and which then spat out measured dough sausages. A conveyor belt took them to another machine, which grabbed these dough sausages, rolled them into a loop, and dropped the loops onto another conveyor belt. A team of men stood at the end of the conveyor belt and, with expertly Chaplinesque efficiency, plucked them off one at a time and placed them on wooden platters.

Other men took the platters to a boiling cauldron and dumped the dough loops in. Still other men fished them out with a wire scoop the size of a shovel. They flung the dough loops down a moist steel gully, a bit like shuffleboard, where another crew took the boiled rings and placed them on wooden slats. Then another group of men took the slats and expertly shoved them into the oven, which had within it a continuously rotating carousel, onto which slats were pushed or flipped, and from which bagels were removed and dumped into large wire bins. The bins were then placed next to an open side door, where a huge industrial fan blew on them to cool them off.

Thus: the bagel smell on Broadway.

I counted the fifty-pound bags of poppy seeds, sesame seeds, caraway seeds, sourdough, pretzel salt, and regular salt. I counted boxes of cinnamon and raisins. I counted the number of whitefish salads, the kippered salmon salads, the tuna fish salads, and the jars of pickled herring. I counted the number of sliced lox packages, nova packages, and the whole whitefish (complete with their head, and the one dead golden eye that stared at me while I counted).

I counted the Tropicana orange juice (Original, Homestyle, Grove) and the grapefruit juice and the sodas. I counted the frozen fruits and Häagen-Dazs in the freezer up front. I counted the number of mop heads, broom handles, Brillo pad boxes, and Ajax. I counted coffee cup lids, coffee cups, and the little plastic sticks people use to stir their coffee (a thousand to a box). I counted plastic forks and spoons and knives. I counted napkins, paper towels, and rolls of toilet paper. I counted the number of white paper bags, the ones that held two bagels and the ones that held four, and six, and a dozen (plus the free extra one). I put on a coat and a scarf and a hat and entered the walk-in freezer, which held a galaxy of cream cheese products so diverse my mind reeled. I searched out the smallest, most minute things and counted them, entered the number in the ledger, and later compared the current number to the one a few days ago to determine our rate of use and to figure out how much more to order. These long periods of contemplating the ledger book were probably the closest I've ever come to Talmudic study.

And then there was the brown sugar. Right in the middle of the bakery, like a huge chimney rising from the floor behind the cashiers, was a huge stack of fifty-pound bags of brown sugar. It sat there like a monument to its own importance.

The recipe for H&H bagels is, Mr. H informed me with a wink, top secret. But I feel, given the size and visibility of this sugar monument, that I am not betraying any trust in saying that each and every one of the bagels made there has a dollop (a pinch? a smidgen? a teaspoon?) of brown sugar in it. Twice a week a truck arrived and workers rebuilt that four-sided column of sugar from its diminished status to a magnificent, proud height. When the sugar stack was low, I felt a pang of fear in my heart; after a delivery, I could stare at it for ten straight minutes and feel all was well with the world.

Downstairs, in a small crevice off to the side of the main office, was a row of desks. I was given one. To my left was Jay, who had been hired the same day as me. He was a slightly built Hispanic man with a thin and neatly groomed mustache, and for the first few days he arrived at work in a long black leather coat, black pants, pointy black cowboy boots, and a huge black cowboy hat. He played trombone in a Latin band that performed regularly at S.O.B.'s and other dance halls around the city. I respected his outfits. They obviously meant a lot to him. He came all the way down from the Bronx, first on a bus and then by subway, and though he spent his days hunched next to me making calls to various delis and grocery stores around the city asking after unpaid bills, he seemed intent on retaining his image as a star trombonist.

But after the first week he started showing up in sweatpants and sweatshirts. It was not a question of self-esteem, but rather of flour.

Behind us, a few feet away, was a huge flour silo. Twice a week fifty thousand pounds of flour was pumped into it from a truck that drove down from somewhere in Pennsylvania, and several times a day an engine revved up to pump flour upstairs to the dough-mixing machine. The pipes leading upstairs often sprang a leak and a fine mist of flour would fill the air. Sometimes it was so fine we would work through it, and after half an hour all of us would be very lightly frosted, as though we'd all gone a little gray. Sometimes the leaks would be more serious, and we would suddenly be engulfed in a blizzard.

Jay's outfits were getting killed. And so he gave up wearing them and surrendered his identity, during that eight-hour stretch, to being an accounts receivable guy at a bagel factory.

The flour storms did not deter Shirley, who sat to my right.

She arrived at work dressed as though this were a brief stopover on her way to a shopping spree at Bergdorf Goodman. She was from one of the Caribbean Islands, had dark black skin, was very pretty, and conducted herself in a regal, aristocratic manner as though her presence at H&H were one of her good works. In fact she was putting herself through business school, which she attended at night. Shirley handled shipping, and one of my first delinquent acts was to start picking up Shirley's line and trying to engage whoever was on it in conversation. As it was early September, I encountered a large number of mothers who were shipping bagels off to their sons and daughters who had just started college. These mothers were, on the whole, extremely willing to discuss their children.

"Bucknell?" I would say. "Really? How interesting. And what do you think your daughter might major in?" And then I'd get a whole biography. But the most eager conversationalists were those New York expatriates who for whatever reason had moved away from the big city for more pastoral environs, but who were occasionally seized with longing for the old country, which manifested itself in the need for good bagels. "The bagels out here are terrible!" they would say, speaking (rather freely, because it was an 800 number) from Salt Lake City, Atlanta, or Portland. And it was amazing, even alarming, how willing these people were to take the next step and enter into a mild confessional about how much they missed New York, and all the ways their new home was disappointing them, as though to say it to someone who was actually physically on Broadway that very second would connect them more to the place they were missing.

My responsibilities were far-reaching. I drove out to the Brooklyn Navy Yard, where a huge shipment of plastic bags with the H&H logo on them had just arrived from China, and managed to get into an at once acrimonious but somehow friendly fight on the subject of Senator Al D'Amato with the religious Jew who owned the shipping firm.

A salesman from a seed company paid a visit and Mr. H summoned me to sit by his side while the salesman poured little piles of poppy and sesame seeds out on the desk. "Taste them!" he kept saying, while he talked about prices and volume and shipping schedules, and Mr. H did, nibbling the seeds with the blank, unemotive expression of a connoisseur who didn't need to act the part. I felt a surge of pride to be part of the whole operation, and was amazed at the parts of the world with which I now had contact. It seemed vital and alive in a way an office job never could. But at the same time I was worried. This bagel job wasn't what I wanted to be. But with every moment spent thinking about the pretzel salt, the coffee stirrers, and, always, the brown sugar, it became more and more what I was. In November an anthology came out with a story of mine in it, and Shakespeare & Company put it in their window up the block. I stared at it through the glass, and vaguely wondered if I should bring a copy to the office to let them know who I was. But then, they knew who I was. I was the inventory guy.

Shortly after I had begun working, Mr. H called me into his office and handed me a black canvas money belt. He instructed me to put it on and, seeing it was well fastened around my waist, handed me a wad of cash totaling seven thousand dollars. He instructed me to walk the six blocks down Broadway to his bank and deposit the money.

"Wear a jacket," he said, "so no one sees it."

"I don't have a jacket."

"Take mine."

I took his jacket.

All day and all night money flowed into the registers upstairs, and a good amount of time was spent counting it, storing it, and generally organizing it. The place was awash in cash, but this was the first time I had held any of it in my hand. Large sums of bills are so weird, just paper, but with personality. It was as though the green ink of the dollars had some chemical property that briefly stunned me, and for a moment I just stood there on the black and white tiles, staring abstractedly at the cash in my hand.

"Take Jay with you," he said.

"Are you worried I'll get robbed?" I said.

Mr. H gave me one of those penetrating stares through his wire-rimmed glasses. He was always in such a swirl of papers and phone cords that when he stared right at you for more than a second it seemed significant. Now it seemed clear that he had understood the true content of my question: *You don't trust me?*

"It's about insurance," he said. "My insurance says you gotta have two people if you're moving more than five thousand dollars."

Broadway was bright with sun and people. The outdoors always seemed especially great and open after a few hours in the dungeon-like confines of the basement office; walking past that porcelain sink, with its water pouring forever down, was like walking past some mythic animal guarding its gates, promising your return. Traffic careened down the avenue, and Jay and I bopped down the street with the bounce of truant schoolkids. The pouch of the money belt was nestled in that soft private place between the bottom of my stomach and my hip, a safe, comforting place. Mr. H's windbreaker fit pretty well. I wore it open.

These bank deliveries were a frequent occurrence. Sometimes I took Jay, once in a while Rick, and on occasion one of the workers upstairs. The tight bulge of the money belt under my shirt became familiar. I felt a certain honor that Mr. H trusted me with his cash. I wondered if he was tempting me. Maybe he was taunting me. Some free time on a crowded avenue with a wad of cash strapped to your gut is stimulating to the imagination. "Where do we want to go today?" I would say to myself as I hit the street, and toy with the idea all the way to the bank.

One day, shortly after Thanksgiving, when I had been on the job three months and the novelty was long gone, I arrived at the factory at an unusually early hour. The job's intensity had been increasing. "Don't forget about the holiday rush," Mr. H had said to me on a number of occasions. There had been a gradual increase in the general sense of frenzy; we had all the cash registers running upstairs and still the lines stretched out the door in the morning, and again during the after-work rush hour. Those lines made the place seem like a combination of a hit Broadway show and, with its worn linoleum floors on which people stood waiting for their bread, a Depression-era soup kitchen.

On that chilly November morning my thoughts occupied the

increasingly rare space in my mind that was not populated by bagels. During the previous weeks I had been on a few dates with a woman I liked. In addition to all the more familiar anxieties, I was careful to monitor her for her feelings about my current job. She seemed to think my bagel career was amusing and temporary. She thought it was an interlude, a funny story in the making. I kept my panic that this was no interlude to myself. I liked her attitude. And I liked her. And she liked me. And on the morning in question, I had woken up at her place.

I emerged from the subway into the cold air of Broadway in great spirits, triumphantly replaying certain moments from the night before, and looking forward to the calm stretch of time when I had the office to myself. It was early, and I bought a paper, got a cup of coffee, grabbed a bagel, and headed downstairs, where I gleefully sat down at Mr. H's desk and prepared for a pleasant half-hour interlude before everyone showed up. But first I made my bank calls. I had developed a weird attachment to the soft, tidy, mellifluous female voice on the automated account information line. I had come to look forward to starting my days with the sound of her voice. This placid image—the solitude, the breakfast, my paper spread out on Mr. H's desk—was so fixed in my imagination that I burrowed toward it single-mindedly, not pausing for my customary glance around the bakery floor to make sure all was well.

And so I had barely flattened the paper on the desk and taken a sip of coffee when Alberto, the night foreman who was just now coming to the end of his eight-hour shift, entered the room and, with the grave manner of a sergeant reporting bad news to an officer, removed the pointed white paper cap he and everyone else upstairs wore. He stared at me with his black eyes, which were always touched with a hint of violence.

"We're out of sugar," Alberto said.

He had worked as the night foreman for ten years and earned only a few cents an hour more than I. Like most of the workers upstairs, he was Puerto Rican. He understood my role at the company, my prerogatives and my perks. There was no sympathy in his eyes. I stared at them anyway.

"We ran out around five o'clock in the morning," he said. "I've had thirty guys sitting on their asses for two and a half hours." He ran a hand slowly over his slicked-back hair, as though this bit of information might have, in the very telling, unsettled it, put his paper cap back on, and went back upstairs.

I had underestimated the holiday rush. The ever-fluctuating but always formidable pillar of brown sugar had been vanquished.

I went into the blankly efficient mode of the deeply freaked out. I called my sugar supplier and begged him to let me have some of the inventory that he had already loaded onto a truck headed for other destinations. Then, having been promised enough to get me through the day, I sank into a numb state of dread. I felt a little like someone who had borrowed his father's car, driven around like a big shot for a while, and then crashed it. I monitored the approach of Mr. H like someone watching a hurricane on a weather monitor. I could only watch the clouds gather and hope the storm was brief.

The gale was of hurricane force. Mr. H just happened to arrive a bit late that day, so it took place in view of the whole office. Mr. H was a hands-on manager. Every one of the myriad details concerning the production and shipping and selling of his bagels was in his head—he delegated with reluctance. And now his worst fears had come true. He came barreling down that narrow alley that funneled right into the black-and-white-tiled room, his face a scrunched-up ball of red. This collapsed-in-rage face was an expression I recognized from my old basketball coach. By now Mr. H would have passed the empty platter where the sugar stack normally rose, he would have seen the idle workers sitting around, the machines all still. He started screaming at a distance of twenty feet. And as he screamed and yelled at me and waved his arms around—all this with his coat still on, his paper still in his hand, his scarf still wrapped around his neck—I could see in his angry features another, quieter and more complicated exasperation: One day I come in twenty minutes late and everything falls apart! he seemed to be thinking. He had a family, but his business was his baby. It consumed him even as it fed him.

He raged on until I pointed out that it was Tuesday. Tuesday was the day I did a massive inventory of the cream cheeses, and the order had to be in by ten-thirty. I put on my coat, my scarf, my gloves, and retreated into the cold humming silence of the old walk-in freezer, the ledger book open in my arms, and began the process of counting, and penance.

I overcompensated, and placed a mammoth sugar order. The next morning a crew of men carried it in from the truck on their shoulders. They made the stack in its customary place. It rose up like a very narrow log cabin, but there were still more bags. They found a place for them in the stairway. But there were still more bags. By the time they were done, the entire factory looked like a World War I trench. A bunker. The staircase, the hallways downstairs, every available space was lined with fifty-pound bags of brown sugar, as though we were sandbagging a river that threatened to flood. Getting to work downstairs meant that everyone now had to turn their shoulders sideways so as to fit through what little space remained. The complaints were endless, though curiously the only person who did not chastise me was Mr. H himself. His was a tunnel vision, and I suspected that the space his body was now compelled to move through was no larger than the space through which his mind always moved, and so he hardly noticed it. All he registered was that we had enough sugar; and perhaps he wanted to give me a break. I was a quantity to be burned through fast and then replaced; just as a basketball coach will drive his team hard at the start of the season and soften up toward the end, I think Mr. H was instinctively letting up on me in preparation for my departure.

Following the sugar disaster, I redoubled my efforts to get out of the bagel factory. I had been focusing my moneymaking energies in what was meant to be my profession—writing. I would make numerous phone calls from my desk to magazine editors, trying to scrounge up some freelance work. There were two obstacles to success in this endeavor. One was that other than a short story that I had published in *The New Yorker,* I had very little in the way of credentials.

The other problem was the dough mixer. With some regularity the enormous engine would switch on, making a sound similar in texture and volume to a big airplane getting ready to take off. This tended to complicate my phone conversations with editors.

"What's that?" they would say when the engine kicked in.

I'm at the airport? I'm at the heliport? I'm at the hairdresser's?

"I'm at work," I would reply, and usually, thinking that offense is better than defense, I would add, "I'm working at a bagel factory."

"Oh, how wonderful!" was a common reply.

At last I pulled my ace in the hole—I called my editor at *The New Yorker*. The flour silo's engine did not turn on. The call was brief. I told him about the bagel factory. He didn't seem to think it was such a bad thing. He was perilously close to joining the ranks of the "Oh, how wonderfuls!" I asked if the magazine needed someone to lick stamps or sweep the floor. He said they had those bases covered. He suggested that perhaps I could do a piece of nonfiction, something short, and asked if I had any ideas.

I blurted out the name of Esteban Vicente, an old painter with whom I was acquainted, who was having a ninetieth birthday coming up and an exhibit to go along with it. Vicente had once shared a studio with de Kooning and had become famous along with Jackson Pollock and all the other New York School painters, but his star had waned. Now he was obscure. But he had continued to paint, oblivious to his professional fluctuations, or at least not unmoored by them, and was now having something of a revival.

It was agreed that I would write a very short profile—more like a long blurb—to go along with a full-page reproduction of one of his paintings.

Suddenly Esteban Vicente became the focus of my existence, along with Euro-Disney, who had placed a mammoth order for our bagels. Every day for a week I drove a truck out to a warehouse in a desolate section of Long Island City. The truck was packed to the brim with boxes of bagels, each about fifteen pounds. I would throw each box into the arms of a scrawny black kid who stood on the loading dock and stacked them on a platter, which then was wrapped in a giant roll of Saran Wrap and finally driven by forklift into a monstrous freezer, from which they would be shipped to France for the consumption of European people looking at Mickey Mouse and Goofy. It was arduous physical labor. The boxes got heavier throughout the afternoon. My back was a mess. The skinny guy caught each one into his chest. We didn't have the energy to talk. I kept thinking: I'm killing myself for Euro-Disney!

I went to Vicente's studio on West Forty-Second Street to interview him. We sat and talked for a long time—I had called in sick, not entirely a lie because my back could not take another day of throwing boxes—and the longer I talked, the more I began to feel that it was a strange coincidence that I should be coming to know this man at this particular time.

There was something wonderfully impervious about him, and resilient. He had a self-worth that in someone else could become vanity, but vanity is always defining itself against the appreciation of others. The only compass Vicente was watching was his own. Vicente was an education in how much single-mindedness is necessary if you want to survive as an artist.

"Like every human being, I want to be loved, but I want to be loved on my own terms," he said. "No one told me to be a painter—it's my responsibility. Artists have a purpose in life, but you must make the effort. Through effort you have joy."

These rather grand emotions did not, however, mitigate my rather craven ambitions to get my piece in print, to get paid, to see my name published somewhere besides an H&H paycheck, and I faxed the article from the bagel factory in the spirit of someone buying a lottery ticket. I had worked on it all night. After I sent it in I put in a good day's work, buoyed by the thought that my days at H&H were numbered. I returned home that night ready to submerge myself in bed and sleep, but not before, just on cue, as my eyes closed heavily, the phone rang—it was my editor, who in his typical measured tones told me, "We liked the piece." He said he would call me later in the week. I slept deeply.

The next day was Tuesday, cream cheese day, and I went about my duties in the walk-in freezer in a state of elation. Wednesday went by quickly. Thursday, disaster struck. I received a call from my editor saying that there was a problem with the art department. Apparently someone somewhere had raised an objection to reprinting a full page of abstract art. Vicente had been asked for a self-portrait.

The man had been an abstract painter for over forty years, and this after a very considered decision to stop painting and exhibiting figurative work. I didn't think he was a prime candidate for a self-portrait. I amused myself with a mock speech I could deliver to him about how, maybe just a few dots with a mouth beneath it, it would mean so much to . . . me! To everyone! Hey, it's exposure! But if there was ever a nonpragmatist, it was Vicente. He didn't give a damn about exposure, and for this I admired him.

I drove my truck full of bagels out to Long Island City, parked it on a side street, and crawled back to lie among the boxes, warm and fragrant (they were all sesame bagels that day). I fell asleep. By now my job had thoroughly infiltrated my dreams: Every other night I had anxiety dreams about running out of whitefish salad. I had another anxiety dream amid the boxes of bagels. I dreamed that I slept in a bagel submarine that never came up for air. I opened my eyes, and the dream continued. This was my life. The fact that it was this beautiful moment of comfort and peace—all those boxes of bread around me muffling the outside world, warming me, the consoling smell—just made it more complicated. Vicente, I knew then, would never do a self-portrait.

Later that day I returned from the Euro-Disney job and called my answering machine. We were in the midst of one of the minor flour leaks, and I sat being slowly covered in white powder. I got a message saying that Esteban Vicente had done a self-portrait. I leapt to my feet. I floated through the flour-saturated air. I ran my hands through huge vats of poppy seeds and watched them pour through my fingers as though they were treasure. I went to an out-of-the-way crevice and threw punches at a sack of sourdough like it was a heavy bag, ducking and weaving, ready for my shot at the championship. I was outrageously happy! The piece was on! Vicente would do the self-portrait!

But gradually this elation gave way to something else. How could Vicente agree to such a thing? My elation turned to a kind of mild, sour grief. Had the voice of commerce lulled his artistic integrity? Had he been bullied into doing something for pragmatic reasons? Did he whip off lots of self-portraits all the time and not tell anyone?

And as I contemplated this, I came to realize that intertwined with all my admiration for the man was a little strand of resentment. This is the weird thing that often accompanies one's appraisal of the virtuous—I had regarded his integrity ever so slightly as a reproach. But now, as I considered that it might have faltered, I missed it. I was rooting for it and lamenting it. As much as I wanted the piece to run, I did not want Esteban Vicente to sell out.

The next day, clutching the phone as the flour silo roared in the background, I was told that Esteban had in fact handed in the self-portrait. The magazine had the self-portrait. It was a . . .

The roar of the flour silo drowned out the words. I waited twenty seconds and asked the person at the other end of the line to repeat herself. "The self-portrait was a splotch of red," she said.

The piece was killed. But my seven hundred words landed on the magazine's new editor-in-chief's desk entirely by accident, and found there a receptive audience. The piece was going to run, after all, and she wanted to meet me.

I lasted at H&H through the New Year. Other than a small pretzel-salt crisis there were no major mishaps. In late January I gave Mr. H my notice. He responded coolly to this, but did not seem too upset.

Later that afternoon he had a heart attack. I helped carry him up the stairs, still sitting in his chair, past the porcelain sink into which the endless waterfall poured. The place was in an uproar as we watched the paramedics put an oxygen mask on his face. Among the white-suited workers upstairs, the men Mr. H ruled with a strong hand (primarily by paying them little more than minimum wage, not giving them any vacation time until they worked there nine months, and not allowing so much as the scent of a union to enter the floor), there was a surge of genuine grief. Everyone spilled out of the side entrance to watch silently as the paramedics loaded him into the ambulance. They all took off their hats.

Downstairs, we had to deal with the fact that, at the time he had the heart attack, Mr. H was counting out a huge sum of cash, which lay untended on his desk. About five different people volunteered to be responsible for it. I prevailed. In my dreamy fantasies about theft and revenge I could not have conjured a more enticing scenario. But I counted the money out scrupulously, totaled it, and put it back in a white paper bag (the size for a dozen bagels) as was the custom, and dropped it in the ancient black safe in the corner.

I watched my replacement be interviewed. He had graduated from Deerfield, then Dartmouth. He was an aspiring actor. I showed him around the place, presented him with the ledger book, and informed him that when Mr. H asked him to read something, it didn't mean his expert opinion was being asked, you were just supposed to paraphrase. The rest was up to him to figure out.

Shortly before my last day, I found myself standing in the walk-in freezer wearing a suit. I had an appointment with *The New Yorker*'s editor-in-chief that morning, and I was racing through the cream cheese inventory so as to be on time. I stood in the walk-in freezer and slowly counted, enjoying the ritual, the strange environment, the privacy. As always the heavy door to the freezer was slightly ajar. And then, for the first time since I had been working there, someone bumped the door, and the ancient metal bolt clicked shut. I carefully put the ledger book on some boxes of olive and pimiento cream cheese and commenced to bang hysterically on the inside of that door, screaming at the top of my lungs to be let out. I was screaming in fear—that I would miss my appointment, that my big chance would be squandered because I was locked in the cream cheese freezer—but I was also laughing. The bagel factory was clutching me for one last moment in its absurd embrace. And when the door was pulled open at last and I was free to rise up out of that place forever, I felt a tiny pang of sorrow to have been released so soon.

BRAVE FACE

Sven Birkerts

The writer Lucy Grealy died in New York on December 18, 2002, of an apparent overdose of heroin. She was thirty-nine years old. "Death by misadventure" was a tag that was sometimes used in the old days when excessive spirits like Malcolm Lowry or Dylan Thomas fell to abrupt ruin, figurative if not literal suicides. But though I confess I thought of the phrase soon after I heard the news, it did not quite stick. There was no sense of the headlong in Lucy's case, just the dispiriting vacuum-suck of a life that had run out of hope. All of us who knew her were, of course, stunned, but I have not talked to anyone who was surprised.

The main outward thing, and inescapably a very big part of the inner life, was the fact of Lucy's facial disfigurement from cancer surgery when she was nine years old, just a few years after she moved to this country from Ireland with her family. The original operation removed part of her lower jaw, and long decades of successive reconstructive surgeries held her agonizingly poised between despair over what the public eye would unforgivingly declare as ugly and the hope, renewed again and again, that another operation could restore the face she'd been meant to have, and hand her a life in scale with her dreams.

"I spent a great deal of time looking in the mirror in private," she admitted in her 1994 essay "Mirrorings," written after innumerable surgeries, "positioning my head to show my eyes and nose, which were not only normal but quite pretty, as my friends told me often. But I could not bring myself to see them for more than a moment: I looked in the mirror and saw only the reasons why I would be alone for the rest of my life." This same pain, arising from the collision between outer and inner, between the public perception and the magnifications of her private sensibility, formed the core of her extraordinary 1994 memoir, *Autobiography of a Face,* which recounts with great candor Lucy's ordeals from girlhood through her college years.

But if this wound, this sense of fondest hopes persistently crushed, forms the central subject matter of her work (in 2000, Lucy published *As Seen on TV,* a beautifully diverse book of "provocations"), the countering thrust—of humor, of stubbornly independent spiritual searching, and of sheer writerly delight in the possibilities of expression—reminds us of the power and elasticity of the human soul. Reading Lucy's work we realize how vigorously we cling to the myth of redemptive inwardness, the idea that personal suffering can become a source of strength. When she died, we lost, along with the person, some of the consolation of that myth, though of course most of us will renew it elsewhere and in others. It is that essential.

I knew Lucy as a fellow nonfiction instructor at the Bennington MFA Writing Seminars, a program that twice a year brings students and teachers together for intensive ten-day residencies, at the heart of which are the workshop sessions in fiction, poetry, and nonfiction. Lucy and I taught together on three or four occasions over the years, usually sitting at opposite ends of a long conference table while our students filled out the sides, turning their heads—so I like to imagine—in synchronized unanimity as one or the other of us made some telling observation about the manuscript under discussion.

But in fact our dynamic was quite different. Where I was blustery and performative, Lucy would be coolly retracted, doodling jagged shapes until she found her pouncing point. I sometimes accused her in my mind of taking license. I, too, wanted to be the intuitive one, the impromptu truth-teller. I wanted to have the privilege of saying the hard thing that needed saying. Finally, though, I'm proud to say, my admiration trumped my pettiness.

Sitting in those workshops, hour after hour, I would look at Lucy, studying her face, pulled toward looking as by any enigma, working relentlessly at what felt like an equation, beauty on one side, disfigurement on the other, fascinated by the blurring together of the terms. For the moment we begin to know a person we can no longer entirely distinguish the outer aspect of the face from what that face expresses, and the more we know, the less we can "see" them in that most basic external sense. (Never is this more obvious than when we try to study our own reflection in the mirror.) To be around Lucy even slightly was to get tangled up with the quick of her spirit—comic, soulful, self-deflating, dead-on honest.

As I sat there, then, facing her across the length of the table, I saw less and less of what she herself in her more despairing moments called her ugliness. Ashamed as I am to admit it, I sometimes patted myself on the back for this. But maybe I shouldn't be ashamed: maybe we all did the same thing. I do know that over time I was increasingly able to see in past the face itself and connect with that elusive thing that touched me so directly in the writing.

Lucy was a brilliant essayist, a writer so attuned to the nuances of her perceptions and so true to the prompting of her own associations that nearly everything she wrote repays not only reading but, for the writer, careful study. The prose is balletic—elegant while holding tension—and charged with surprise. Not deliberate surprise, but the surprise, as in Orwell and Baldwin, of honesty—truthfulness delivered without a flinch of self-congratulation. In her piercing essay "My God," for instance, she wrote: "I read books about the Holocaust and imagined how I'd be so graceful there that I'd withstand oppression with such nobility that the Nazis would have to stop in their tracks. In my real life, I hated myself for being petty and shallow, because, try as I might, I could only manage my transmutation into benign understanding for just moments at a time. Acts of charity—these I only seemed to manage with animals, and even with them, whom I loved so much, I was often experimentally cruel." Maybe her long suffering made this directness possible, if not inevitable. A more literary essay would give this rarest of her artistic virtues the space it deserves.

Outside of workshop, I knew Lucy mainly from conversations at our various social gatherings, which always made her uneasy, probably for the expected reasons, and from the raucous poker games we conjured up mid-residency. Safe among trusted peers, she joked rudely and ventured bets with charming foolhardiness. Outside the danger zone of mere appearance, past the curse of the "first encounter," she could cut loose, venting an outrageousness that was pure performance. She was "Lu," drinking beers and bumming cigarettes. Cutting up. She loved the attention—for itself, naturally, but also because it was such a powerful antidote to her loneliness.

It was all the more sad, then, in recent years, to catch glimpses of what was happening in her hidden life. For the hopeless side of Lucy had found its way first to painkillers, then to heroin, and through heroin came the downward pull of oblivion. That her decline was as gradual as it was suggests to me that there were rallying surges of resolve, and renewals of her faith in the possibility of transformation, if not outward then inward. Certainly there was the care and attention of her many friends.

A year and a half ago came another heartbreak—the failure of a major reconstructive operation she had allowed herself to dream about. This was the big surgery, the one that would give her back the face she wanted, her face. But it didn't, the fates had betrayed her. And after this, Lucy's life began to come apart in more obvious ways. She lost two teaching jobs; she fell into a crisis over a book contract she could not fulfill; her debts mounted. Finally—who will ever know whether by intention or inadvertence—she overdosed and died.

I miss Lucy a great deal, more than our level of acquaintance might have warranted. I write this at the Bennington residency, where memories of casual interchanges will suddenly flare up into what feels like a larger profundity. I am not alone in experiencing this. Several of her friends and former students have said similar things to me. It's a strange legacy, this intensification. I can't explain how it works, but every day it seems to pull my thinking forward in some new way.

I find that I do dwell a great deal on the idea—the question—of beauty these days, and Lucy is very often the pretext and whetstone for my thoughts. Contemplating her—the person and her work, the face and the sensibility it both shaped and shielded—I keep registering the age-old opposition between "appearance" and "essence." With Lucy, far more readily than with most people I've known, I felt a quick passage from the one to the other. We all have our inwardness, of course, but Lucy had it right there, available, on tap. It was her genius. Maybe it was also her way of getting people quickly past the outer negotiation.

However it worked, this readiness served her well in the outside world, among those who paused to get to know her. Tragically, this intensity of self, this reservoir of awareness, could not prevail against her emotional pain, a failure which raises the redemption question, the hardest one on the exam.

EXCERPT FROM *ON IMMUNITY*

Eula Biss

The day before my son was born was the first warm day of spring. In labor, I walked out to the end of the pier, where the morning sun was breaking up the ice floes on Lake Michigan. My husband held up a video camera and asked me to speak to the future, but the sound did not record, so whatever I said has been lost to the past. What remains evident on my face is that I was not afraid. During the long labor that followed that sunlit moment I imagined myself swimming in the lake, which became, against my will, a lake of darkness and then a lake of fire and then a lake without a horizon. By the time my son was born late the next day a cold rain was falling and I had crossed over into a new realm in which I was no longer fearless.

That spring, a novel strain of influenza would begin spreading from Mexico to the United States to the rest of the world. I did not register those early reports, as I was too busy listening to my son breathe at night. During the day, I was entirely preoccupied by how much he did or did not nurse, and how much he did or did not sleep. I cannot now decipher the entries I made in a notebook then—long lists of times, some of them only minutes apart. Obscure notations next to the times indicate, I think, waking, sleeping, nursing, and crying. I was searching for a pattern, trying to determine what made my baby cry inconsolably. What made him cry, I would learn much later, was an intolerance to cow's milk. Offending proteins from the milk I drank passed through my milk to him—a possibility that had not occurred to me.

By the end of the summer, the evening news was running footage of people wearing white surgical masks in airports. The novel influenza virus was officially pandemic at that point. Churches were serving holy wafers on toothpicks, and airlines were removing pillows and blankets from their flights. What surprises me now is how unremarkable this seemed to me at the time. It all became part of the landscape of new motherhood, where ordinary objects like pillows and blankets have the power to kill a newborn. Colleges were daily sterilizing every "high-touch" surface, while I was nightly boiling every object my child put in his mouth. It was as if the nation had joined me in the paranoia of infant care. Like many other mothers, I had been informed of a syndrome affecting infants that had no warning signs and no symptoms other than sudden death. Perhaps this is why, despite everything, I do not remember feeling particularly scared of the flu—it was just one concern of many. There was lead paint, I knew, on my walls and hexavalent chromium in my water, and the books I was reading were telling me to run a fan while my baby slept because even stagnant air could suffocate him.

When I search now for a synonym for *protect,* my thesaurus suggests, after *shield* and *shelter* and *secure,* one final option: *inoculate.* This was the question, when my son was born—would I inoculate him? As I understood it then, this was not a question of whether I would protect him so much as it was a question of whether inoculation was a risk worth taking. Would I enter into a gamble, like Thetis dipping the infant Achilles into the River Styx?

The mothers I knew began debating whether or not to vaccinate our children against the novel influenza virus long before any vaccine became available to us. We were hearing that what made this particular strain of flu dangerous was that it was new to humans, like the virus that caused the Spanish flu epidemic of 1918 in which more than 50 million people died. But then we were also hearing that the vaccine had been produced hurriedly and that it might not have been fully tested.

One mother told us that she had miscarried while she was sick with the seasonal flu and, being wary of any flu now, she planned to vaccinate. Another mother said that her child had screamed frighteningly all night following her first vaccination and she would not risk another vaccination of any kind. Every exchange about the new flu vaccine was an extension of the already existing discussion about immunization, in which all that is known of disease is weighed against all that is unknown about vaccines.

As the virus spread, a mother I knew in Florida reported that her entire family had just had the H1N1 flu and it was not any worse than a bad cold. Another mother in Chicago told me that her friend's healthy nineteen-year-old son had suffered a stroke after being hospitalized with the flu. I believed both of these stories, but they told me nothing more than what the Centers for Disease Control and Prevention already seemed to be trying to tell me—the flu could be harmless in some cases and serious in others. Under the circumstances, vaccination began to seem prudent. My baby was just over six months old and I had just returned to work at a large university where the majority of my students would be coughing by the last week of classes.

That fall, *The New Yorker* ran an article in which Michael Specter noted that influenza is regularly among the top ten causes of death in the United States and that even relatively mild pandemics of influenza have killed in the millions. "And, though this H1N1 virus is novel," he wrote, "the vaccine is not. It was made and tested in exactly the same way that flu vaccines are always made and tested." Some of the mothers I knew did not like the tone of this article. They found it insulting for the same reason I found it reassuring—it did not acknowledge any good reason for doubt.

The fact that the press is an unreliable source of information was one of the refrains of my conversations with other mothers, along with the fact that the government is inept, and that big pharmaceutical companies are corrupting medicine. I agreed with all these concerns, but I was disturbed by the worldview they suggested: nobody can be trusted.

It was not a good season for trust. The United States was engaged in two ongoing wars that seemed to be benefiting no one other than military contractors. People were losing their houses and their jobs while the government was bailing out the financial institutions it deemed too big to fail and using taxpayer money to shore up the banks. It did not seem unlikely that our government favored the interests of corporations over the well-being of its citizens.

During the initial aftershocks of the economic crash there was talk of "restoring the public's trust," though even then the emphasis fell more often than not on consumer confidence. I disliked the term *consumer confidence,* and I bristled every time I was encouraged to trust myself as a mother. I had little confidence, consumer or otherwise, but I tended to believe that confidence was less important than the kind of trust that transcends the self. Even now, years after my son's birth, I remain interested in the precise meaning of *trust,* particularly in legal and financial terms. A trust—in the sense of a valuable asset placed in the care of someone to whom it does not ultimately belong—captures, more or less, my understanding of what it is to have a child.

By late October, the mothers who were still talking about the flu vaccine were mainly talking about how hard it was to get a child vaccinated. My son had been on a waiting list at his pediatrician's office for over a month. Other mothers were waiting in long lines outside community colleges and public high schools. While we waited, a mother who did not vaccinate her children mentioned that she had heard there was an additive called squalene in the H1N1 vaccine. No, another mother countered, squalene was used in flu vaccines in Europe, but it was not used here. The mother who had originally mentioned squalene was not so sure—the fact that U.S. vaccines did not contain squalene, she said, had been disputed elsewhere. "Where exactly is elsewhere?" one of my friends wondered. *What,* I wondered, *is squalene*?

The women with whom I debated the merits of the flu vaccine

possessed a technical vocabulary that was entirely unfamiliar to me at the time. They used words like *adjuvant* and *conjugate,* and they knew which vaccines were live virus vaccines and which were acellular. They were familiar with the intricacies of the vaccine schedules of other countries, and literate in an array of vaccine additives. Many of them were, like me, writers. And so it is not surprising that I began to hear metaphors behind the technical language and information we traded.

Squalene is found in a great many living things including the human body, where it is manufactured in the liver. It circulates in our blood and is left behind in our fingerprints. Some European flu vaccines do indeed contain squalene from shark liver oil, but squalene has never been added to U.S.-licensed vaccines. Squalene's presence in absence is something like the curious properties of thimerosal, the mercury-based preservative that was removed from every childhood vaccine except multidose flu vaccines by 2002. Well over a decade later, fear of mercury in vaccines persists.

My son finally got his flu vaccination in late November. We didn't know it yet, but the worst of the pandemic was already over—cases of H1N1 influenza had peaked in October. I remember asking the nurse if the vaccine my son was receiving contained thimerosal, but I was asking more out of due diligence than true concern. I already suspected that if there was a problem with vaccines it was not thimerosal, and it was not squalene.

TACTLESS

Mary Cappello

I've come to accept the fact that most people maintain an unthinking relationship to words; everyone uses language, but you can't expect people who aren't in the word trade to use language sensitively, ethically, radically, or well. Maybe that's why I'm continuously surprised and subsequently tortured by my own tactlessness. I'm at an awards ceremony intended to celebrate the fruits of our students' labor as writers at the university. I've served as judge for the creative nonfiction contest and am eager to meet the student writers who have won, as well as to congratulate winners whom I've played a part in mentoring and whose work has earned a prize. One woman's name appears several years in a row. I've never worked with her, though she always promises to take a course, and I am awed by the way her work repeatedly rises to the top with each year's new slate of judges. Here's a sheerly great writer, I think, destined for great things, and I want to tell her that. I remember last year she had her small son with her and between attempts to offer her effusive praise, I looked down on the small shy shuffling form beside her and said something wholly in-apropos, like "Maybe your mom will write something about *you* someday! Or, maybe you'll be a writer yourself!" This year, I immediately find the face of this writer in the buoyant, noisy, crowded room. She smiles and waves, and I yell "Congratulations!" She's taken first prize in the fiction competition and an honorable mention for a piece about her mother's battle with cancer. Her mother, all her life, had been the model of unflinching survivorhood, but now she appeared afraid, and the daughter had to face this—her mother's vulnerability. Across the heads of several people and a clanking bevy of voices and noise, I tilt my head toward the student, and ask, "Did you lose your mother?" She can't hear me and probably can't imagine that this would be a question that a person in her right mind would attempt to yell across a crowded room, maybe especially at an awards ceremony. I leave my seat and move closer to her, even though the ceremony is about to begin. "Did you lose your mother?" I ask. "No," she says, "she's still alive." The essay, submitted to the contest weeks ago, described the mother in ICU in a septic state. Nonfiction often puts us in touch with the intimate realities of people's lives. Should I have asked "How's your mother?" and risked the writer telling me she was dead? Or ignored the subject matter of the essay altogether and simply said "Once again, you've produced a fine piece of writing," and that's what we're here to celebrate after all: tact, craft. I didn't think much about the supreme tactlessness of yelling across a crowded room "Did you lose your mother?" until later. There was so much more to observe, so much to be nervous about: a mutual inability to get beyond small talk with one new colleague for four consecutive years; another aging male colleague's decision to lean forward and kiss the female award recipients as they received their awards; the fact that upon offering the briefest hug to one of my students who had won an award, she literally fled from the room. And how the act of her abrupt running made me feel that the hug was a deep and long embrace, how the announcement of awkwardness elongates time and makes the feeling of an untoward act linger, persist, abide.

I once knew a woman who was an obsessive reviewer of her own faux pas. She didn't seem in search of absolution but appeared to enjoy the confession and the self-aggrandizing fantasy that she was continuously transgressing the sensibilities of others. She was offensiveness incarnate, and it was hopeless to save her; she only bade you listen to the details of her latest embarrassment. "Oh, oh, oh," she would whimper, and the pores on her forehead would open with sweat, she would bite her nails, and in a sing-song voice, as though admitting self-irony, exclaim, "Ohhh, woe is me!"

Following the awards ceremony, I suffered my own share of writhing, a wringing of hands to the tune of the memory of my insensitive blurt. And then something strange happened. We were trying to leave, we were cleaning up the last dregs of coffee and cake crumbs, but my colleague who kissed the girls remained. He was sitting at a table alone, eating cheese squares and cream puffs. "Somebody has to eat it," he said when I asked him what he was doing. I was wondering why he was staying, why he wasn't leaving. Clearly we were cleaning up. Was he feeling the anticlimax of such events, did he want the party to go on, was he lonely and hopeful that something touching would emerge from this, a sweet inside his belly? I felt I understood, but my own impulse was to head home to my flagellation booth. On my way out the door, I spotted a credit card that obviously had fallen from someone's pocket unbeknownst to them. As I picked it up, the name of the outstanding writer whose mother was ill blinked back at me, as though a guardian angel had put a means of reparation in my path—I could help rather than harm her—as though a higher power required that contact be maintained: "Oh, woe is her to have to hear from me again!"

I am a writer. I wear mittens. They keep me warm but make things hard to grasp. I shake the hand of my dentist, as well as the man who gives me estimates on furnaces and occasionally the dry-cleaning man. I let a salesman selling plaster replicas of antiquities kiss me in the Roman forum again and again and again. I rarely wear hand coverings. I find them constricting, but if forced, in cold, I wear thin leather driving gloves that enable me to feel the wheel, and a bit of winter's bite, and something mean. I don't wish to be treated with kid gloves. I prefer a winded punch to the belly. Or so I say. The only way a gay male friend would let me touch him was to, Three Stooges–style, twist his arm in a monkey grip. Don't mind me—my people were touchers and they taught me to touch others warmly and with ease. Is there anything worse than being grabbed against one's will? Being clutched, dragged, and coiled? And then the refrain: “Please, release me, let me go.” I wear gardening gloves because inevitably I get scratched in the garden and then I fear that microbes will enter my open wounds. The gloves have raised polka dots meant to help a person grip a garden tool. Eventually they get drenched with water or with sweat and I ditch them, and then the earth beneath my skin embeds so fully no soap will wash it off.

What’s mysterious about contact is that it happens at all. Can contact ever become threadbare from overuse, or is its nature, its mystery, that it dissolves like candles or soap or water into air? I’m on fire with static electricity—my cat jumps back when a woolly spark accidentally ignites the touch of my finger to her sleek and lovely forehead. Don’t cling to it. Attach, detach; button, unbutton; tie, otherwise you will trip on your shoelaces, or over your own words, you will become tongue-tied.

The mystery of contact has unwound. How easily we get lost, or are tossed, released from touching. I stray. Let me finger this thread, let me gather loose ends together, or pretend to.

DECREATION: HOW WOMEN LIKE SAPPHO, MARGUERITE PORETE AND SIMONE WEIL TELL GOD

Anne Carson

This is an essay about three women and will have three parts. Part One concerns Sappho, a Greek poet of the seventh century B.C. who lived on the island of Lesbos, wrote some famous poetry about love, and is said to have organized her life around worship of the god Aphrodite. Part Two concerns Marguerite Porete, who was burned alive in the public square of Paris in 1310 because she had written a book about the love of God that the papal inquisitor deemed heretical. Part Three concerns Simone Weil, the twentieth-century French classicist and philosopher whom Camus called "the only great spirit of our time."

Part One

What if I were to begin an essay on spiritual matters by citing a poem that will not at first seem to you spiritual at all. Fragment 31 of Sappho says:

He seems to me equal to gods that man
whoever he is who opposite you
sits and listens close
to your sweet speaking

and lovely laughing—oh it

puts the heart in my chest on wings
for when I look at you, even a moment, no speaking
is left in me

no: tongue breaks and thin

fire is racing under skin
and in eyes no sight and drumming
fills ears

and cold sweat holds me and shaking

grips me all, greener than grass
I am and dead—or almost
I seem to me.

But all is to be dared, because even a person of poverty . . .[1]

This poem has been preserved for us by the ancient literary critic Longinus, who quotes four complete Sapphic stanzas and then the first line of what looks like a fifth stanza and then breaks off, no one knows why. But the first four stanzas seem to compose a unit of music and thought; let's consider the thought. It comes to us bathed in light but this is the weirdly enclosed light of introspection. Sappho is staging a scenario inside the little theater of her mind. It appears to be an erotic scenario but the characters are anonymous, their interrelations obscure. We don't know why the girl is laughing, nor what the man is doing there, nor how Sappho's response to them makes sense. Sappho seems less interested in these characters as individuals than in the geometric figure that they form. This figure has three lines and three angles. One line connects the girl's voice and laughter to a man who listens close. A second connects the girl to Sappho. Between the eye of Sappho and the listening man runs a third. The figure is a triangle. Why does Sappho want to stage this figure? Common sense suggests it is a poem about jealousy. "Lovers all show such symptoms as these," says Longinus. So let's think about what the jealousy of lovers is.

The word comes from ancient Greek *zelos* meaning "zeal" or "hot pursuit." A jealous lover covets a certain location at the center of her beloved's affection only to find it occupied by someone else. If jealousy were a dance it would be a pattern of placement and displacement. Its emotional focus is unstable. Jealousy is a dance in which everyone moves.

Sappho's poem sets the stage for jealousy but she does not dance it. Indeed she seems to forget the presence of her dancing partners entirely after the first stanza and shifts the spotlight onto herself. And what we see in the spotlight is an unexpectedly spiritual spectacle. For Sappho describes her own perceptual abilities (visual, aural, tactile) reduced to dysfunction one after another; she shows us the objects of outer sense emptying themselves; and there on the brightly lit stage at the center of her perception appears—her own Being: "I am . . . ," she says at verse 15 ("greener than grass I am").

This is not just a moment of revealed existence: it is a spiritual event. Sappho enters into ecstasy. "Greener than grass I am . . . ," she says, predicating of her own Being an attribute observable only from outside her own body. This is the condition called *ekstasis,* literally "standing outside oneself," a condition regarded by the Greeks as typical of mad persons, geniuses, and lovers, and ascribed to poets by Aristotle.

Ecstasy changes Sappho and changes her poem. She herself,

she says, is almost dead. Her poem appears to break down and stop. But then, arguably, both of them start up again. I say arguably because the last verse of the poem has a puzzling history and is regarded with suspicion by some scholars, although it appears in Longinus and is corroborated by a papyrus. Let us attempt to see its coherence with what goes before.

"All is to be dared because even a person of poverty . . . ," says the last verse. It is a new thought. The content of the thought is absolute daring. The condition of the thought is poverty. I don't want to give the impression that I know what this verse is saying or that I see where the poem is headed from here, I don't. Overall it leaves me wondering. Sappho sets up a scenario of jealousy but that's not what the poem is about, jealousy is just a figure. Sappho stages an event of ecstasy but that's not what the poem is about either, ecstasy is just a means to an end. Unfortunately we don't reach the end, the poem breaks off. But we do see Sappho begin to turn toward it, toward this unreachable end. We see her senses empty themselves, we see her Being thrown outside its own center where it stands observing her as if she were grass or dead. At which point a speculation occurs to me: Granted this is a poem all about love, do we need to limit ourselves to a reading of it that is merely or conventionally erotic? After all, Sappho is believed by some historians to have been not just a poet of love and a worshiper of Aphrodite on Lesbos but also a priest of Aphrodite's cult and a teacher of her doctrines. Perhaps Sappho's poem wants to teach us something about the metaphysics or even the theology of love. Perhaps she is posing not the usual lovesong complaint, *Why don't you love me?* but a deeper spiritual question, *What is it that love dares the self to do?* Daring enters the poem in the last verse when Sappho uses the word *tolmaton:* "is to be dared." This word is a verbal adjective and expresses a mood of possibility or potential. Sappho says it is an *absolute* potential:

pan tolmaton: all is to be dared.

Moreover she consents to it—or seems to be on the point of consenting when the poem breaks off. Why does she consent? Her explanation no longer exists. So far as it goes, it leads us back to her ecstatic condition. For when an ecstatic is asked the question, *What is it that love dares the self to do?* she will answer:

Love dares the self to leave itself behind, to enter into poverty.

Part Two

Marguerite Porete was burned at the stake in 1310 for writing a book about the absolute daring of love. *The Mirror of Simple Souls*[2] is a theological treatise and also a kind of handbook for people seeking God. Marguerite Porete's central doctrine is that a human soul can proceed through seven different stages of love, beginning with a period of "boiling desire,"[3] to an ecstasy in which the soul is carried outside her own Being and leaves herself behind. This departure from her own center is not passive. Like Sappho, Marguerite first discovers in reality a certain absolute demand and then she consents to it. Like Sappho she sees herself split in two by this consent and experiences it as a kind of "annihilation." Marguerite's reasoning is severe: she understands the essence of her human self to be in her free will and she decides that free will has been placed in her by God in order that she may give it back. She therefore causes her will to depart from its own will and render itself back to God with nothing left over. Here is how she describes this event:

> . . . a ravishing expansion of the movement of divine Light is poured into the Soul and shows to the Will [the rightness of what is . . . in order to move the Soul] from the place where it is now and ought not to be and render it back to where it is not, whence it came, there where it ought to remain. Now the Will sees . . . that it cannot profit unless it departs from its own will. And thus the Soul parts herself from this will and the Will parts itself from such a Soul and then renders itself and gives and goes back to God, there where it was first taken, without retaining anything of its own. . . .[4]

Now it is noteworthy, in light of Sappho's account of ecstasy and its consequences, that Marguerite Porete twice refers to herself at the moment when God's abundance overflows her as:

> I who am in the abyss of absolute poverty.[5]

She also describes her impoverishment as a condition of physical and metaphysical negation:

> Now such a Soul is nothing, for she sees her nothingness by means of the abundance of divine understanding, which makes her nothing and places her in nothingness.[6]

Throughout *The Mirror* she speaks of herself as null, worthless, deficient, deprived, and naked. But at the same time she recognizes her poverty as an amazing and inexpressible kind of repletion; and of this absolute emptiness which is also absolute fullness she speaks in erotic language, referring to God as "overflowing and abundant Lover" or as "the Spouse of my youth."[7] Even more interesting for our analogy with Sappho, Marguerite Porete twice proposes jealousy as a figure for her relationship with God. Thus she refers to God as "the most high Jealous One" and speaks of God's relation to her Soul in this way:

> Jealous he is truly! He shows it by his works which have stripped me of myself absolutely and have placed me in divine pleasure without myself. And such a union joins and conjoins me through the sovereign highness of creation with the brilliance of divine being, by which I have being which is being.[8]

Here is an unusual erotic triangle consisting of God, Marguerite, and Marguerite. But its motions have the same ecstatic effect as the three-person situation in Sappho's poem. Marguerite feels her self pulled apart from itself and thrown into a condition of poverty, to which she consents. Her consent takes the form of a peculiarly intense triangular fantasy:

> . . . and I pondered, as if God were asking me, how would I fare if I knew that he preferred me to love another more than himself? And at this my sense failed me and I knew not what to say. Then he asked me how would I fare if it could happen he should love another more than me? And here my sense failed me and I knew not what to say. . . . Beyond this, he asked me what would I do and how would I fare if it could be he preferred another to love me more than he. . . . And there I fainted away for I could say nothing to these three things, nor refuse, nor deny.[9]

Notice how Marguerite turns the fantasy this way and that, rotating its personnel and reimagining its anguish. Jealousy is a dance in which everyone moves. It is a dance with a dialectical nature. For the jealous lover must balance two contradictory realities within her heart on the one hand, that of herself at the center of the universe and in command of her own will, offering love to her beloved; on the other, that of herself off the center of the universe and in despite of her own will, watching her beloved love someone else. Naked collision of these two realities brings the lover to a sort of breakdown—as we saw in Sappho's poem—whose effect is to expose her very Being to its own scrutiny and to dislodge it from the center of itself. It would be a very high test of dialectical endurance to be able to, not just recognize, but consent to this breakdown. Sappho seems to be entering on a mood of consent when her poem stops. Marguerite faints three times before she can manage it. But then, with a psychological clarity as amazing as Sappho's, Marguerite pushes open the implications of her own pain. Here is her analysis of what she sees when she looks inside Marguerite:

> And so long as I was at ease and loved myself "with" him, I could not at all contain myself or have calm: I was held in bondage by which I could not move. . . . I loved myself so much along "with" him that I could not answer loyally. . . . Yet all at once he demanded my response, if I did not want to lose both myself and him. . . . I said to him that he must want to test me in all points.[10]

Marguerite reaches rock bottom here when she faces the fact that loyalty to God is actually obstructed by her love of him because this affection, like most human erotic feeling, is largely self-love: it puts Marguerite in bondage to Marguerite rather than to God. Her reasoning uses the figure of jealousy in two ways. She sees jealousy as an explanation of her own feelings of inner division; she also projects jealousy as a test of her ability to de-center herself, to move out of the way, to clear her own heart and her own will off the path that leads to God. For in order to (as she says) "answer God loyally" she cannot stay one with her own heart or with her own will, she cannot love her own love or love herself loving or love being loved. And insofar as she can "annihilate" all these—her term—she can resolve the three angles of the dance of jealousy into a single nakedness and reduce her Being from three to two to one:

> Now this Soul . . . has left three and has made two one. But in what does this one consist? This one is when the soul is rendered into the simple Deity, in full knowing, without feeling, beyond thought. . . . Higher no one can go, deeper no one can go, more naked no human can be.[11]

Part Three

Simone Weil was also a person who wanted to get herself out of the way so as to arrive at God. "The self," she says in one of her notebooks, "is only a shadow projected by sin and error which blocks God's light and which I take for a Being." She had a program for getting the self out of the way which she called "decreation." This word is a neologism to which she did not give an exact definition nor a consistent spelling. "To undo the creature in us" is one of the ways she describes its aim.[12] And when she tells of its method she uses language that may sound familiar. Like Marguerite Porete she expresses a need to render back to God what God has given to her, that is, the self.

> We possess nothing in this world other than the power to say "I." This is what we must yield up to God.[13]

And like Marguerite Porete she pictures this yielding as a sort of test:

> God gave me Being in order that I should give it back to him. It is like one of those traps whereby the characters are tested in fairy tales. If I accept this gift it is bad and fatal; its virtue becomes apparent through my refusal of it. God allows me to exist outside himself. It is for me to refuse this authorization.[14]

And also like Marguerite Porete she feels herself to be an obstacle to herself inwardly. The process of decreation is for her a dislodging of herself from a center where she cannot stay because staying there blocks God. She speaks of a need "to withdraw from my own soul" and says:

> God can love in us only this consent to withdraw in order to make way for him.[15]

But now let us dwell for a moment on this statement about withdrawal and consent. Here Simone Weil enters upon a strangely daring and difficult negotiation that seems to me to evoke both Marguerite Porete and Sappho. For Simone Weil wants to discover in the three-cornered figure of jealousy those lines of force that connect a soul to God. She does not, however, fantasize relationships with ordinary human lovers. The erotic triangle Simone Weil constructs is one involving God, herself, and the whole of creation:

> All the things that I see, hear, breathe, touch, eat; all the beings I meet—I deprive the sum total of all that of contact with God, and I deprive God of contact with all that insofar as something in me says "I." I can do something for all that and for God—namely, retire and respect the tête-à-tête. . . .

> I must withdraw so that God may make contact with the beings whom chance places in my path and whom he loves. It is tactless of me to be there. It is as though I were placed between two lovers or two friends. I am not the maiden who awaits her betrothed but the unwelcome third who is with two betrothed lovers and ought to go away so that they can really be together.
>
> If only I knew how to disappear there would be a perfect union of love between God and the earth I tread, the sea I hear. . . .[16]

If only she could become what Marguerite Porete calls an "annihilated soul," if only she could achieve the transparency of Sappho's ecstatic condition "greener than grass and almost dead," Simone Weil would feel she had relieved the world of an indiscretion. Jealousy is a dance in which everybody moves because one of them is always extra—three people trying to sit on two chairs. We saw how this extra person is set apart in Marguerite Porete's text by a canny use of quotation marks; remember her plaintive observation:

> I loved myself so much along "with" him that I could not answer loyally.[17]

When I read this sentence the first time, it seemed odd to me that Marguerite Porete puts the quotation marks around the "with" rather than around one of the pronouns. But Marguerite knows what she is doing: the people are not the problem here. Withness is the problem. She is trying to use the simplest language and the plainest marks to express a profoundly tricky spiritual fact, viz. that I cannot go toward God in love without bringing myself along. And so in the deepest possible sense I can never be alone with God. I can only be alone "with" God.

To catch sight of this fact brings a wrench in perception, forces the perceiver to a point where she has to disappear from herself in order to look. As Simone Weil says longingly:

> If only I could see a landscape as it is when I am not there. But when I am in any place I disturb the silence of heaven by the beating of my heart.[18]

As we saw, Marguerite Porete found a way to translate the beating of her own heart into a set of quotation marks around the word "with." And Sappho found a way to record the beating of her heart while imagining its absence—for surely this is the function performed in her poem by "the man who opposite you sits and listens close." This man, Sappho tells us, is "equal to gods"; but can we not read him as her way of representing "the landscape as it is when I am not there"? It is a landscape where joy is so full that it seems to go unexperienced. Sappho does not describe this landscape further but Marguerite Porete offers an amazing account of a soul in some such condition:

> Such a Soul . . . swims in the sea of joy—that is in the sea of delights flowing and streaming from the Divinity, and she feels no joy for she herself is joy, and swims and floats in joy without feeling any joy because she inhabits Joy and Joy inhabits her. . . .[19]

It seems consistent with Simone Weil's project of decreation that, although she too recognizes this kind of joyless joy, she finds in it not an occasion of swimming but one of exclusion and negation:

> Perfect joy excludes even the very feeling of joy, for in the soul filled by the object no corner is left for saying "I."[20]

Part Four

Inasmuch as we are now entering upon the fourth part of a three-part essay, we should brace ourselves for some inconsequentiality. I don't feel the cause of this inconsequence is me. Rather it originates with the three women we are studying and the cause of it is the fact that they are writers. When Sappho tells us that she is "all but dead," when Marguerite Porete tells us she wants to become an "annihilated soul," when Simone Weil tells us that "we participate in the creation of the world by decreating ourselves," how are we to square these dark ideas with the brilliant self-assertiveness of the writerly project shared by all three of them, the project of telling the world the truth about God, love, and reality? The answer is we can't. It is no accident that Marguerite Porete calls her book a *Mirror*. To be a writer is to construct a big, loud, shiny center of self from which the writing is given voice and any claim to be intent on annihilating this self while still continuing to write and give voice to writing must involve the writer in some important acts of subterfuge or contradiction.

Which brings us to contradiction and its uses. Simone Weil speaks plainly about these:

> Contradiction alone is the proof that we are not everything. Contradiction is our badness and the sense of our badness is the sense of reality. For we do not invent our badness. It is true.[21]

To accept the true badness of being human is the beginning of a dialectic of joy for Simone Weil:

> If we find fullness of joy in the thought that God is, we must find the same fullness in the knowledge that we ourselves are not, for it is the same thought.[22]

Nothing and something are two sides of one coin, at least in the mind of a dialectician. As Marguerite Porete puts it:

> Nothing is nothing. Something is what it is. Therefore I am not if I am something, except that which God is.[23]

She also says:

> Lord you are one goodness through opened out goodness, absolutely in you. And I am one badness through opened out badness, absolutely in me.[24]

Marguerite Porete's vision is dialectical but it is not tragic: she imagines a kind of chiastic immersion or mutual absorption by means of which these two absolute opposites—God and the soul—may ultimately unite. She uses various images of this union, for example, iron, which when placed in the furnace actually becomes fire; or a river that loses its name when it flows into the sea.[25] Her common images carry us beyond the dialectical account of God and soul. For dialectic is a mode of reasoning and an application of the intellectual self. But the soul that has been driven by love into God, the soul consumed as into fire, dissolved as if into water—such a soul has no intact intellect of the ordinary human kind with which to construe dialectical relationships. In other words such a soul passes beyond the place where she can *tell* what she knows. To tell is a function of self.

This situation is a big problem for a writer. It is more than a contradiction, it is a paradox. Marguerite Porete broaches the matter, early in her *Mirror,* with her usual lack of compromise:

> For whoever talks about God . . . must not doubt but must know without doubt . . . that he has never felt the true kernel of divine Love which makes the soul absolutely dazzled without being aware of it. For this is the true purified kernel of divine Love which is without creaturely matter and given by the Creator to a creature and *takes away absolutely the practice of telling.*[26]

Marguerite delivers herself of a writerly riddle here. No one who talks about God can have experienced God's Love, she asserts, because such Love "takes away absolutely the practice of telling." She reinforces this point later by arguing that, once a soul has experienced divine Love, no one but God ever understands that soul again (chapters 19 and 20). We might at this point be moved to question what Marguerite Porete thinks she is doing in the remaining chapters of her book, which number 139 in all, when she gives a step-by-step account of the soul's progress toward annihilation in God. We might wonder what all this telling is about. But we are unlikely to receive an answer from Marguerite Porete herself. Nor I think will any prudent writer on matters of God and soul venture to nail such things down. Quite the contrary, to leave us in wonder is just what such a writer feels compelled to do. Let us look more closely at how this compulsion works. We have said that telling is a function of self. If we study the way these three writers talk about their own telling, we can see how each of them feels moved to create a sort of dream of distance in which the self is displaced from the center of the work and the teller disappears into the telling.

Let's begin with Simone Weil, who was a practical person and arranged for her own disappearance on several levels. Among other things, she is believed to have hastened her own death from tuberculosis in 1943 by a regimen of voluntary self-starvation undertaken out of sympathy for people in France who didn't have enough to eat. However that may be, when her parents insisted on fleeing France for America in 1942 she briefly and reluctantly accompanied them, leaving behind in the hands of a certain Gustave Thibon (a farmer in whose vineyard she had been working) about a dozen notebooks of personal reflection (which now form a substantial part of her published work). She told him in a letter to use the thoughts in the notebooks however he liked:

> So now they belong to you and I hope that after having been transmuted within you they will one day come out in one of your works. . . . I should be very happy for them to find a lodging beneath your pen, whilst changing their form so as to reflect your likeness. . . .
>
> In the operation of writing, the hand which holds the pen and the body and soul attached to it are things infinitely small in the order of nothingness.[27]

Gustave Thibon never saw Simone Weil again, nor did he follow the instructions of this letter, to transmute her ideas into his own—at least not explicitly. Instead he went through the notebooks, extracted punchy passages, grouped these under headings like The Self, The Void, The Impossible, Beauty, Algebra, Luck, The Meaning of the Universe, and published them as a book with her name on the title page as its author.[28] That is, he made a serious effort to force her back into the center of herself, and the degree to which she nonetheless eludes this reinstallation is very hard for readers like you or me to judge from outside. But I admire the final, gentle piece of advice that she gives to him at the close of her letter of 1942:

> I also like to think that after the slight shock of separation you will not feel any sorrow about whatever may be in store for me and that if you should happen sometimes to think of me you will do so as one thinks of a book read in childhood. . . .[29]

When I think of books read in childhood they come to my mind's eye in violent foreshortening and framed by a precarious darkness, but at the same time they glow somehow with an almost supernatural intensity of life that no adult book could ever effect. I remember a little book of *The Lives of the Saints* that was given to me about age five. In this book the various flowers composing the crowns of the martyrs were so lusciously rendered in words and paint that I had to be restrained from eating the pages. It is interesting to speculate what taste I was expecting from those pages. But maybe the impulse to eat pages isn't about taste. Maybe it's about being placed at the crossing-point of a contradiction, which is a painful place to be and children in their natural wisdom will not consent to stay there, but mystics love it. So Simone Weil:

> Man's great affliction, which begins with infancy and accompanies him till death, is that looking and eating are two different operations. Eternal beatitude is a state where to look is to eat.[30]

Simone Weil had a problem with eating all her life. Lots of women do. Nothing more powerfully or more often reminds us of our physicality than food and the need to eat it. So she creates in her mind a dream of distance where food can be enjoyed perhaps from across the room merely by looking at it, where desire need not end in perishing, where the lover can stay, at the same time, near to and far from the object of her love.

Food and love were analogous contradictions for Simone Weil. She did not freely enjoy either of them in her life and was always uneasy about her imaginative relationship to them. But after all, eternal beatitude is not the only state where to look is to eat. The written page can also reify this paradox for us. A writer may tell what is near and far at once.

And so, for example, in Marguerite Porete's original terminology the writer's dream of distance becomes an epithet of God. To describe the divine Lover who feeds her soul with the food of truth, Marguerite Porete invents a word: *le Loingprés* in her Old French, or *Longe Propinquus* in the Latin translation: English might say "the FarNear." She does not justify this word, simply begins using it as if it were self-evident in chapter 58 of her book, where she is telling about annihilation. At the moment of its annihilation, she says, God practices upon the soul an amazing act of ravishing. For God opens an aperture in the soul and allows divine peace to flow in upon her like a glorious food. And God does this in his capacity as *le Loingprés,* the FarNear:

> For there is an aperture, like a spark, which quickly closes, in which one cannot long remain. . . . The overflowing from the ravishing aperture makes the Soul free and noble and unencumbered [and its] peace lasts as long as the opening of the aperture. . . . Moreover the peace is so delicious that Truth calls it glorious food. . . .
>
> And this aperture of the sweet movement of glory that the excellent FarNear gives is nothing other than a glimpse which God wants the soul to have of her own glory that she will possess without end.[31]

Marguerite Porete's concept of God as "the excellent FarNear" is a radical invention. But even more radical is the riddle to which it forces her:

> . . . where the Soul remains after the work of the Ravishing FarNear, which we call a spark in the manner of an aperture and fast close, *no one could believe . . . nor would she have any truth who knew how to tell this.*[32]

Inside her own telling Marguerite Porete sets up a little ripple of disbelief—a sort of distortion in the glass—as if to remind us that this dream of distance is after all just a dream. At the end of her book she returns to the concept one last time, saying simply:

His Farness is the more Near.[33]

I have no idea what this sentence means but it gives me a thrill. It fills me with wonder. In itself the sentence is a small complete act of worship, like a hymn or a prayer. Now hymns and prayers are the conventional way for lovers of God to mark God's FarNearness, for prayer lays claim to an immediate connection with this Being whose absence fills the world. But Marguerite Porete was a fairly unconventional lover of God and did not engage in prayer or credit its usefulness. Simone Weil, on the other hand, although she was never a Christian herself, had a profound attachment to that prayer Christians call the Our Father. During the summer of 1941 when she worked in the vineyard of Gustave Thibon she found herself repeating this prayer while she worked. She had never prayed before, she acknowledges in her notebook, and the effect was ecstatic:

> The very first words tear my thoughts from my body and transport it to a place outside space . . . filling every aspect of this infinity of infinity.[34]

Prayer seems to have been for her an experience of spatial contradiction—or perhaps a proof of the impossible truth of God's motion. In another passage she returns to the Lord's Prayer and its impossible truth:

> *Our Father who art in heaven.* There is a sort of humour in that He is your Father, but just try going to look for him up there! We are quite as incapable of rising from the ground as an earthworm. And how should he for his part come to us without descending? There is no way of imagining a contract between God and man which is not as unintelligible as the Incarnation. The Incarnation explodes unintel-

ligibility. It is an absolutely concrete way of representing impossible descent. Why should it not be the truth?[35]

Why should the truth not be impossible? Why should the impossible not be true? Questions like these are the links from which prayers are forged. Here is a prayer of Sappho's which will offer us one final example of the dream of distance in which a writer tells God:

. . . [come] here to me from Krete
to this holy temple where is
your graceful grove of apple trees and altars
smoking with frankincense.

And in it cold water makes a clear sound through apple branches

and with roses the whole place
is shadowed and down from radiant-shaking leaves
sleep comes dropping.

And in it a horse meadow has come into bloom

with spring flowers and breezes
like honey are blowing. . . .

In this place you Kypris having taken up

in gold cups delicately
nectar mingled with festivities:
pour.[36]

This fragment was scratched on a shard of pottery by a careless hand in the third century B.C. The text is corrupt and incomplete. Nonetheless we can identify it as a hymn of the type called "kletic," a calling hymn, an invocation to God to come from where she is to where we are. Such a hymn typically names both of these places, setting its invocation in between in order to measure the difference—a difference which it is the function of the hymn to *decreate*—not to destroy, but to decreate. Among the remarks on decreation in Simone Weil's notebooks is the statement:

> God can only be present in creation under the form of absence.[37]

For the writer of a kletic hymn, God's absence is something tricky, perhaps impossible, to tell. This writer will have to invoke a God who arrives bringing her own absence with her—a God whose Farness is the more Near. It is an impossible motion possible only in writing. Sappho achieves it by various syntactic choices: for example, suppression of the verb in the first stanza of her poem. In my translation I supply an imperative "Come!" in square brackets as the first word of the poem, and the sense may seem to require this, but the Greek text has no such verb. It begins with the adverb "Here." In fact the imperative verb for which the entire poem, with its slow and onomatopoeically accumulating clauses, seems to be waiting does not arrive until the very last word of our text: "Pour!" The effect of this suspension is uncanny: as if the whole of creation is depicted waiting for an action that is already perpetually *here*. There is no clear boundary between far and near; there is no climactic moment of God's arrival. Sappho renders a set of conditions that at the beginning depend on Aphrodite's absence but by the end include her presence. Sappho imitates the distance of God in a sort of suspended solution—and there we see Divine Being as a dazzling drop that suddenly, impossibly, saturates the world.

To sum up. Each of the three women we've been considering had the nerve to enter a zone of absolute spiritual daring. Each of them undergoes there an experience of decreation, or so she tells us. But the telling remains a bit of a wonder. Decreation is an undoing of the creature in us—that creature enclosed in self and defined by self. But to undo self one must move through self, to the very inside of its definition. We have nowhere else to start. This is the parchment on which God writes his lessons, as Marguerite Porete says.

Marguerite's parchment burned in 1310. To us this may seem an outrage or a mistake. Certainly the men who condemned her thought she was all wrong and referred to her in the proceedings of her trial not only as "filled with errors and heresies" but as *pseudo-mulier* or "fake woman."[38]

Was Marguerite Porete a fake woman?

Society is all too eager to pass judgments on the authenticity of women's ways of being but these judgments can get crazy. As a case in point, the book for which Marguerite Porete was burned in 1310 was secretly preserved and copied after her death by clerics who transmitted the text as an anonymous devotional work of Christian mysticism, until 1946 when an Italian scholar reconnected the *Mirror* with the name of its author. At the same time, it is hard to commend moral extremism of the kind that took Simone Weil to death at the age of thirty-four; saintliness is an eruption of the absolute into ordinary history and we resent that. We need history to remain ordinary. We need to be able to call saints neurotic, anorectic, pathological, sexually repressed, or fake. These judgments sanctify our own survival. By the same token, Sappho's ancient biographers tried to discredit her seriousness by assuring us she lived a life of unrestrained and incoherent sexual indulgence, for she invented lesbianism and then died by jumping off a cliff for love of a young man. As Simone Weil says:

> Love is a sign of our badness.[39]

Love is also a good place to situate our mistrust of fake women. What I like best about the three women we've been studying is that they know what love is. That is, they know love is the touchstone of a true or a false spirituality, that is why they play with the figure of jealousy. As fake women they have to inhabit this figure gingerly, taking a position both near and far at once from the object of their desire. The truth that they tell from this paradoxical position is also fake. As Marguerite says briskly:

> For everything that one can tell of God or write, no less than what one can think, of God who is more than words, is as much lying as it is telling the truth.[40]

So in the end it is important not to be fooled by fake women. If you mistake the dance of jealousy for the love of God, or a heretic's mirror for the true story, you are likely to spend the rest of your days in terrible hunger. No matter how many pages you eat.

NOTES

1. Sappho, fragment 31, in *Sappho et Alcaeus Fragmenta,* ed. Eva-Maria Voigt (Amsterdam: Standardausgabe, 1971).
2. Marguerite Porete, *Le Mirouer des simples âmes anienties et qui seulement demeurent en vouloir et désir d'amour,* ed. R. Guarnieri = *Archivio Italiano per la Storia della Pietà* 4 (1965), 513–635. The text was composed in Old French; there are two recent English translations which I have consulted and adapted: *Marguerite Porete: The Mirror of Simple Souls,* trans. E. Babinsky (New York: Paulist Press, 1993); *The Mirror of Simple Souls,* trans. E. Colledge, J. C. Marler, and J. Grant (Notre Dame, Ind.: Notre Dame Univ. Press, 1999). Henceforth this book = MP.
3. MP, chap. 118.
4. Ibid.
5. MP, chap. 38.
6. MP, chap. 118.
7. MP, chaps. 38, 118.
8. MP, chap. 71.
9. MP, chap. 131.
10. Ibid.
11. MP, chap. 138.
12. Simone Weil, *Gravity and Grace,* trans. A. Wills (Lincoln: Univ. of Nebraska Press, 1997), 81. Henceforth this book = SW. (The translation is somewhat adapted.)
13. Ibid., 71.
14. Ibid., 87.
15. Ibid., 88.
16. Ibid.
17. MP, chap. 131.
18. SW, 89.

19. MP, chap. 28.
20. SW, 77.
21. Ibid., 148.
22. Ibid., 84.
23. MP, chap. 70.
24. MP, chap. 130.
25. MP, chaps. 25, 82.
26. MP, chap. 18, emphasis added. The text of chapter 18 is controversial; the oldest extant manuscript of Marguerite Porete's book in Old French (made about 1450) does not contain the phrase in italics, while an older Latin translation (made about 1350) does. See Paul Verdeyen, "La premiere traduction latine du *Miroir* de Marguerite Porete," *Ons Geestelijk Erf* 50 (1984), 388–89.
27. SW, 11.
28. Simone Weil, *La pesanteur et la grâce* (Paris: Plon, 1948).
29. SW, 12.
30. SW, 153.
31. MP, 58, 63.
32. MP, 58, emphasis added.
33. MP, 135.
34. Simone Weil, *The Simone Weil Reader,* ed. G. Panichas (New York: David McKay, 1977), 492.
35. SW, 148.
36. Sappho, fragment 2, in *Sappho et Alcaeus Fragmenta,* ed. Eva-Maria Voigt (Amsterdam: Standardausgabe, 1971).
37. SW, 162.
38. Paul Verdeyen, "Le procès d'inquisition contre Marguerite Porete et Guiard Cressonesart (1309–1310)," *Revue d'histoire ecclésiastique* 81 (1986), 47–94.
39. SW, 111.
40. MP, 119.

HOME ALONE

Terry Castle

The late Mario Praz—dandy, scholar, eccentric chronicler of interior-decorating styles through the ages—once observed that human beings could be divided into those who cared about such things and those who didn't. An avid, even ensorcelled member of the first group, he confessed to finding people who were indifferent to décor both baffling and somewhat sinister. To discover that a friend was content to dwell in "fundamental and systematic ugliness," he wrote in *An Illustrated History of Interior Decoration: From Pompeii to Art Nouveau*, was as disturbing as "turning over one of those ivory figurines carved by the German artificers of the Renaissance, which show a lovely woman on one side and a worm-ridden corpse on the other." All the more macabre when the friend was otherwise refined:

> A venerated master of mine at the University of Florence used to say, from his lectern, many learned things about the Provençal poets. I hung on his every word. But it was a grim day when I first crossed the threshold of his house. As soon as the door was opened, I was confronted by a loathsome oleograph of a Neapolitan shepherdess (that same oleograph used to turn up often in the shops where unclaimed objects from the state pawnshop, the Monte di Pietà, are sold). The shepherdess, shading her eyes with her

hand, affected a simpering smile, while Vesuvius smoked in the background.

Granted, for the "loathsome oleograph" (which now sounds enchantingly kitsch) one might want to substitute any number of contemporary abominations: fur-covered kitty condos placed nonchalantly in the living room, embroidered sofa pillows that say things like "She Who Must Be Obeyed" or "Bless This Mess," Southwestern-style bent-willow furniture (barf), neoclassical wall sconces made out of glued and gilded polyurethane, monstrous sleigh beds from Restoration Hardware, Monet water-lily refrigerator magnets, fake "bistro" clocks, and just about any item of domestic ornament with an angel or a dolphin or a picture of Frida Kahlo on it. Yet even without a tchotchke update we can all sympathize with Praz's baffled revulsion: "It's curious, the squalor, the unnecessary and even deliberate squalor in which people who profess a sensitivity to the fine arts choose to live, or manage to adapt themselves."

Or at least *some* of us can. I think Praz is right: you either have the "interiors" thing going on or you don't. Sherlock Holmes would have no difficulty determining into which of Praz's categories I fall: a quick riffle through the contents of my mailbox—engorged each day to the point of overflowing—makes it comically clear.

The surreal monthly haul, I'm embarrassed to say, includes just about every shelter magazine known to man or woman, from *House and Garden*, *Elle Decor* (not to be confused with *Elle Decoration*, a British mag that I also get), *Metropolitan Home*, *House Beautiful*, and *Architectural Digest* to *Dwell*, *Wallpaper*, *Veranda*, the British *Homes and Gardens*, and—holy of holies—the epicene and intoxicating *World of Interiors*, a U.K. shelter mag so farcically upscale and eccentric that it might have been conceived by P. G. Wodehouse. (Until its recent demise I also subscribed to *nest*. More on that dark Manhattan cult mag later.) Add to these the innumerable glossy catalogues—from Pottery Barn, Crate & Barrel, Room and Board, Design Within Reach, Ikea, West Elm, Home Decorators Collection, Williams-Sonoma, Wisteria, Ballard Designs, Plow & Hearth, NapaStyle, Eddie Bauer Home, and the like—that regularly deluge anyone who has ever made the mistake (as I have) of ordering a distressed-teak milking stool or a kilim-covered ottoman online, and any residual doubt about my propensities will be removed.

The obsession, I confess, has its autoerotic dimension. At times, despite the ever-renewing bounty on hand, I still mooch down to an insalubrious foreign newsstand near where I live in San Francisco and peruse *Maison Française, Maisons Côté Sud,* or *Résidences Décoration*—just to practice my French, of course. (Though rather more arduous linguistically, the German *Elle Decoration* also sometimes beckons.) Paging through the offerings on display, I am aware of bearing a discomfiting resemblance to various male regulars furtively examining the dirty magazines across the aisle. An ex-girlfriend (we split up in part over closet space) informs me I am a "house-porn addict," and although the term is exactly the sort of metrosexual-hipster cliché, cheeky yet dull, that one finds every Thursday in the *New York Times* House & Home section, it does get at the curious feelings of guilt, titillation, and flooding bourgeois pleasure—relief delivered through hands and eyeballs—that such publications provide.

Yet more and more people, I've come to decide, must share my vice to some degree. The sheer ubiquitousness of interiors magazines—in airport terminals, supermarket checkout lines, big-box bookstores, doctors' offices, and other quintessentially modern (and often stressful) locations—suggests I am not the only person, female or male, gay or straight, experiencing such cravings. (Though hardly one of the more soigné publications, *Better Homes and Gardens,* owned by ABC Magazines, has an annual circulation of 7.6 million and generates nearly $173 million in revenue a year.) And lately the oddest people have started to confess to me their shelter-mag obsessions—including, a couple of weeks ago, a scary-looking young 'zine writer with a metal bolt through her tongue and Goth-style tattoos all over her neck, arms, legs, and back. Crystal meth would seem to have nothing on *House Beautiful*—and the latter won't turn your teeth into pulpy little black stumps.

How to understand such collective absorption? One might moralize, of course, and simply write off the phenomenon as yet another example of life in obscene America—home of the fat, spoiled, and imbecilic. How dare to broach such a subject when more than 2.6 billion people, or "more than 40 percent of the world's population," according to *The New York Times,* "lack basic sanitation, and more than one billion people lack reliable access to safe drinking water"? Easy enough to say that shelter mags are silly and odious—not worth even talking about—and leave it at that.

Yet while satisfying to the censorious, such judgmentalism in another way begs the question. Even the most embarrassing or guilt-inducing features of daily life, Freud famously argued, have their "psychopathology" and can be plumbed for truths about the human condition. One could as easily argue, it seems to me, that house porn, like the billion-dollar business of home improvement itself, is symptomatic of a peculiar disquiet now haunting ordinary American life. However callow it may seem to point it out, being middle-class these days means feeling freaky a lot of the time. *The heebie-jeebies are definitely a problem.* The issues here are deep ones. Home—no less than the cherished "homeland" of dismal fame—seems in desperate need of securing. The precariousness of All We Hold Dear is dinned into our heads daily. It's hardly feckless to feel scared or neurasthenic at times.

Might paging through a shelter mag be seen—in an analytic spirit and with a certain Freudian forbearance—as a middle-class coping mechanism? As a way of calming the spirit in bizarre and parlous times? House porn, I'm beginning to think, could best be understood as a postmodern equivalent of traditional consolation literature—Boethius meets Mitchell Gold. Though shamelessly of this world—and nowhere more so than in the glutted and prodigal U.S.A.—it's as spiritually fraught, one could argue, as the breviaries of old.

Which isn't to say that certain people aren't, for complex reasons, particularly susceptible to the shelter-mag jones. Décor-fixated individuals (and you know who you are), according to Praz, are usually "neurotic, refined, sad people," prone to "secret melancholy" and "hypersensitive nerves." Quaint language aside (he enlists the "mad, lonely spirit" of Ludwig II of Bavaria as a historical example of the syndrome), the claim is weirdly compelling. Readers with the obsessive-compulsive gene—the twenty-first-century version, perhaps, of "hypersensitive nerves"—will be familiar with the low-level yet troublesome anxiety produced when something in a room seems misplaced, askew, or somehow "wrong." I won't be surprised when brain scientists discover the odd little fold in the cerebral cortex that makes one agitate over slipcovers or jump up and rearrange the furniture.

But along with whatever innate disposition may exist, the typical interiors fanatic almost always has some aesthetic trauma looming up out of the past—a decorative primal scene, so to speak—exacerbating the underlying syndrome. For the legendary American designer Elsie de Wolfe (1865–1950), the so-called First Lady of Interior Decoration, just such a shock awaited her, she recalled in her memoirs, when she returned home one day from school to find that her parents—pious Scottish-Canadian immigrants otherwise deficient in fantasy—had repapered the sitting room of their New York City brownstone in a lurid "[William] Morris design of gray palm-leaves and splotches of bright green and red on a background of dull tan." Something "that cut like a knife came up inside her," de Wolfe recollected. "She threw herself on the floor, kicking with stiffened legs as she beat her legs on the carpet." The novelettish third person is a nice dramatic touch: Freud's Dora had nothing on Elsie in the girlish-hysteria department.

And indeed, there's just such a primal scene in my own childhood: the day my mother—faced with replacing our bedraggled old tweed sofa—decided, in a fit of desperate-divorcée economy, to spray-paint it instead. (When I succumb to rectal cancer, it will no doubt be the result of having sat on this unwholesome piece of furniture throughout my adolescence.) In a single sunny late-sixties San Diego afternoon—I can still hear the clack-clack of aerosol cans being shaken—our couch went from its normal faded-beige color to a lethal-looking southern California turquoise. That wasn't the end, though: overcome by a sort of decorative frenzy, she then sprayed the flimsy shelf unit separating the "kitchenette" from the living room in our tiny pink-and-green motel-style apartment—and after that two discarded toys of mine, a hapless pair of plastic palomino ponies. Resplendent in turquoise from forelock to hoof, Trigger and Buttermilk were subsequently elevated to the unlikely role of room-divider ornaments. No doubt my adult hankering after Zuber *papiers peints,* Omega Workshop textiles, and Andre Arbus escritoires germinated at just this moment.

Now, it's worth considering to what degree decorative trauma functions as a mental screen for more-troubling kinds of distress. Is the interiors mania rooted in deeper childhood travails? Elsie de Wolfe's Calvinist mother seems to have been gruesome enough: she made de Wolfe wear sackcloth pinafores and shipped her off at fifteen to a *Jane Eyre*–style boarding school in Edinburgh. In his notes to the elegant new Rizzoli reprint of de Wolfe's so-called design bible, *The House in Good Taste* (1913), Hutton Wilkinson, the president of the Elsie de Wolfe Foundation, suggests that the revolutionary decorating philosophy de Wolfe evolved in the first decade of the twentieth century—one favoring simplicity, creamy-white walls, natural light, informal furniture groupings, bright chintzes—had its psychic roots in juvenile pain and estrangement. (De Wolfe "simply didn't like Victorian," Wilkinson writes, because it was "the high style of her sad childhood.")

Again, no question but that family ructions—notably my parents' nuclear-war-style divorce when I was seven—left me, like de Wolfe, with a bit of a shelter neurosis. As soon as the papers were filed, my British-born mother yanked me and my little sister out of the standard-issue suburban West Coast middle-class home we had occupied for as long as I could remember and took us off to a dreary seaside bungalow in the U.K. Returning to San Diego three years later—my mother then in flight from British Inland Revenue—we landed in the aforementioned cheesy apartment, the best she could do on the child support she received from my father. I spent my mopey teenage years there like an exiled monarch, dolefully contemplating the spindly 1950s hibiscus-print bamboo armchairs and roll-up window blinds (courtesy of Buena Vista Apartments management) and lamenting the fate that had befallen us.

The real nightmare, however, was a squalid domicile across town that threatened off and on to become our future home:

the "snout house" (a boxy So-Cal tract house with garage and driveway dominating the frontage) owned by the man my mother would later marry—a hapless submariner named Turk, whose previous wife had dropped dead there of alcohol poisoning a few months before my mother met him. The place was my private House of Usher; I worried over the ghastly reality—maternal lack of cash—it represented. And as if to confirm its baleful role in my imaginative life, it was an abode of surpassing ugliness: dank and malodorous, with fake wood paneling and a tattered Snopes-family screen door at the front admitting numerous flies. The only decorative touches were the grimy ashtrays on every surface, a faded Navy photo of the U.S.S. *Roncador* surfacing, and, in one dim corner, a dusty assemblage of bronze baby shoes—one for each of Turk's five wildly delinquent children. Luckily, by the time my mother married him I had already left for college, so I—the female Fauntleroy—never had to live there. Staying overnight was bad enough, though: I have dreams to this day in which the mother who dropped dead emerges from the closet—here, now, in my grown-up bedroom in San Francisco—to enfold me in a noxious and crumbly embrace.

Which brings me back, by a somewhat gothic route, to shelter mags and their allure. One essential part of their appeal, it seems to me, lies precisely in the fact that they proffer—even brazenly tout—an escape from the parental. (The step-parental, too, thank God.) They do this in several ways—perhaps most conspicuously through a glib, repetitious, wonderfully brain-deadening "express the inner you" rhetoric. Now, supposedly no one actually "reads" shelter magazines; you just drivel over the pictures. Patently untrue in my experience: I devour all the writing, too—such as it is—no matter how fatuous and formulaic. I take special pleasure in the "editor's welcome"—usually a few brief paragraphs (next to a little picture of said editor) about new decorating trends, the need for beauty in one's life, how to create a private "sanctuary" for yourself, the meaning of "home," etc. It's always the same stupefying tripe, but soothing nonetheless.

Who is this editor? She (rarely he) might best be described as the Un-Mother. She is typically white, middle-aged yet youthful, apparently straight, and seldom much more ethnic-looking than the Polish-American Martha Stewart. She is often divorced, and may (paradoxically) have grown-up children. But her authority is of an oblique, seemingly nontoxic kind—more that of a benevolent older sister or a peppy, stylish aunt than any in-your-face maternal figure. And the therapeutic wisdom she dispenses—almost always in the cozy second person—is precisely that *you don't have to do what your mother tells you to do*. In fact, your ma can buzz off altogether. You can now buy lots of nice things and make "your own space," from which all signs of the past have been expunged.

Yay! No more U.S.S. *Roncador*!

If you enter the words "not your mother's" on Google, you'll get nearly 200,000 results, a huge number of which point you immediately toward shelter-mag articles. "Not your mother's [whatever]" turns out to be an established interiors trope, endlessly recycled in titles, pull quotes, advertisements, photo captions, and the like. "Not Your Mother's Tableware" is a typical heading—meant presumably to assure you that if you acquire the featured cutlery you will also, metaphorically speaking, be giving your mom the finger. (Other online items that are not your mother's: wallpaper, mobile homes, Chinette, faucet sponges, slow cookers, backyard orchards, and Tupperware parties. Beyond the realm of interior decoration—it's nice to learn—you can also avoid your mother's menopause, divorce, Internet, hysterectomy, book club, Mormon music, hula dance, antibacterial soap, deviled eggs, and national security. Thank you, Condi.)

"Your House Is You, So Start Reveling in It" is a virtual creed in Shelter-Mag Land, one derived from the holy books of interior design. "You will express yourself in your home, whether you want to or not," proclaimed the prophet Elsie in *The House in Good Taste*—best to "arrange it so that the person who sees [you] in it will be reassured, not disconcerted." In *The Personality of a House,* a rather more florid copycat volume from 1930, Emily Post was no less insistent: "[Your home's] personality should express your personality, just as every gesture you make—or fail to make—expresses your gay animation or your restraint, your old-fashioned conventions, your perplexing mystery, or your emancipated modernism—whichever characteristics are typically yours." Narcissism in a go-cup: the ladies say it's okay.

Now, in 2006, the message is ubiquitous, sloganized, inevitable. "Not Everything in Your Home Is All About You, You, You" reads an ad for flooring in a recent issue of *Elle Decor*. "Oh, Wait. Yes, It Is." Unsurprisingly, it is taken for granted that one's inner life—externalized in décor—will be an improvement on whatever has gone before. "What do you think you want?" asks *Elle Decoration* (September 2005). "A bigger house? A better view? Frette bedlinen? A matching set of original Saarinen dining chairs?" It seems that "you" have very expensive tastes. But that's fine too, because shelter literature is all about consumption, luxury goods, and the pipe dreams of upward mobility.

When one has pretensions to taste, such dreams can be hard to resist. Out of necessity my own decorating style has long been fairly down-market and bourgeois: your standard Academic-Shabby-Chic-Wood-Floors-Vaguely-Ethnic-Somewhat-Cluttered-Bohemian-Edith-Sitwell-Crossed-with-Pottery-Barn-Squeaky-Dog-Toys-Everywhere-Eccentric-Anglophile-Lesbian. (The last two elements being signified by various grubby Vita Sackville-West first editions on the shelves. No one else on the Internet seems to want them.) Yet raffishness notwithstanding, the entire visual scheme is as fraught with socioeconomic symbolism as any. Having been plucked out of the (semi-) prosperous middle class as a child, I have spent thirty years or so trying to wiggle my way back in. Indeed, to the degree that such mobility is possible on an academic salary, I've sought fairly relentlessly to upgrade to even higher status—1920s-Artistic-British-Boho-with-Inherited-Income has usually been the target look, as if Augustus John and Virginia Woolf had mated. (The "British" part has no doubt been a way of renegotiating childhood fiascos on my own terms.) Say the word "Bloomsbury" or "Charleston" and I become quite tremulous with longing.

That the "express yourself" ethos of the shelter mag is both illogical and manipulative should go without saying. While encouraging you to find your "personal style," the Un-Mother also wants to show you how. Even my own fanatically considered décor, I'm forced to admit, may be part of some greedy stranger's business plan—a version of that nostalgic "vintage" or "Paris flea market" style heavily promoted to urban college-educated women of my generation throughout the United States and Western Europe over the past decade or so. (Other incessantly marketed "looks" now vying for dominance in Shelter-Mag Land: "mid-century modern"—a variety of Baby Boomer Rat Pack retro distinguished by funky space-age design, Case Study houses, pony skins on the floor, and, if you're lucky, lots of Eames, Mies, and Corbu—and the more minimalist, Asian-inspired "W Hotel" look, involving wenge wood, stark-white walls, spa bathrooms, dust-mite-free bedding, solitary orchids in raku pots, etc. *Chacun à son goût* and all that, but the latter mode—like the frigid minimalism of the British cult architect John Pawson—always strikes me as simply the latest twist on twentieth-century fascist design.) But whether my never-ending quest for antique finials, faded bits of toile de Jouy, old postcards, and other quirky "flea-market finds" is a product of disposition or suggestion, I am, I realize, as much a slave to commodity fetishism as any McMansion-owning reader of *Architectural Digest*—hideous bible of parvenus from the Hamptons to Malibu.

Resentful, matriphobic, pretentious, gullible: could the shelter-lit addict be any less appealing? Unfortunately, yes, as a brief foray—into Shelter-Mag Land's heart of darkness, its paranoid psychic core—will reveal. Here the real-world rooms on display—static, pristine, and seemingly uninhabited—are key. To be "at home" in the World of Interiors, one rapidly gathers, is to bask in the privacy of your own space, serene and unabashed, while the rest of the world goes *kaboom* all around you. (Not for nothing does the industry term "shelter magazine" play subliminally on "bomb shelter." Self-fortification is one of the goals here; likewise the psychic eradication of other people.)

Some shelter-lit purveyors are tough-minded enough to cop to it—that the urge to "project the self" through décor can be deeply allied with misanthropy. "I live inside my head," the decorator Rose Tarlow declares in *The Private House* (2001), "often oblivious to the world outside myself. I see only what I wish to see." In her own home, she acknowledges, other people aren't really part of the scene:

> I know there are times when we plan our houses as much for the pleasure of our friends as for ourselves, because we wish for their enjoyment, and rely on their appreciation and praise—especially their praise. Thankfully that stage of my life has passed!

Having now become "interested in a home only for myself," she would like nothing better, she says, than to live in a "nun's cell"—a sort of little medieval crypt-world. ("I imagine a bed covered in a creamy, heavy hemp fabric in a tiny room that has rough, whitewashed plaster walls, a small Gothic window, a stone sink; outside a bird sings. Peace prevails.") The book's illustrations—chill, austere, and undeniably gorgeous—give form to the tomblike aesthetic: not one of the exquisite rooms shown (all designed by Tarlow) has a human being in it.

Shelter-Mag Land is a place in which other people are edited out—removed from the picture, both literally and metaphorically, so that one is free to project oneself, forever and a day, into the fantasy spaces on view. In any given interiors piece this "disappearing" of other people is usually a two-part process—beginning retrospectively, as it were, with the ritual exorcism of the last owner before the current one. Former owners invariably have atrocious taste, one discovers, and every trace of them must be removed. When the former owner is also the Mother in Need of Banishment, heroic measures are necessary. A 2004 article in *The New York Times Style Magazine* has a telling item about how Goldie Hawn's daughter, the actress Kate Hudson, bought "the Los Angeles house she grew up in" precisely in order to gut the interior and remodel it in "her own image." No Goldie vestiges will be allowed to remain. "Goldie's taste is more classic," notes a male designer assisting Hudson. "Kate wants to turn everything on its ear." Don't look now, Private Benjamin—the kid's just decoratively cleansed you.

But *other* people need cleansing too—most urgently the lucky oinkers now in possession. It is common for interiors magazines—higher-end ones like *World of Interiors* especially—to suppress the names and images of current owners. There are exceptions, of course: *Elle Decor,* for some reason, likes to run pictures of blissed-out property owners—usually Ralph Lauren–ish white people relaxing on patios, cuddling their French bulldogs, or flourishing salad tongs in a gleaming Corian-countertopped kitchen. In some cases, especially when he's gay and humpy, the designer responsible for the new décor will be shown lounging about the premises looking highly pleased with himself, like a porn star who's just delivered big-time.

And small children—especially if beautiful, blond, and under five—sometimes get a pass, though they are liable to appear in curiously fey and stylized ways. For several years now I've been keeping tabs on a shelter-mag cliché I call the Blurred Child Picture: a light-filled shot of some airy urban loft, all-stainless kitchen, or quaint Nantucket cottage in which the child of the house is shown—barefoot, pink, and perfect—either whizzing by in the background or bouncing joyfully on a bed. The face and limbs are often fuzzy, as if to suggest a sort of generic kidness in motion. These hallucinatory urchins usually turn out to bear excruciatingly hip names—Samantha, Cosmo, Zoe, and Miles are current favorites—and seem as branded and objectified as the furnishings around them. The ongoing reproductive anxieties of young, white, middle-class American professional women—a crucial segment of the shelter-magazine demographic—would seem to prompt such wish-fulfillment imagery: here's your new space and a designer child to put in it.

But the ideal room in Shelter-Mag Land is unpeopled—stark, impervious, and preternaturally still—like the haunted castle in Cocteau's *Beauty and the Beast*. As aficionados know, just about every room shown in a shelter magazine has been meticulously staged by unseen stylists: flowers placed just so; covetable objects illuminated; expensive art books arranged on tables; take-out menus, sex toys, and drug paraphernalia discreetly removed. The place is usually flooded with heavenly light—as if an angel had just descended outside, or a nuclear flash had irradiated the environs. When windows in a room are visible, one typically can't see through them: they remain opaque, like weirdly glowing light boxes. The unearthly illumination from without is mesmerizing. Whether or not one likes the space on view, one finds oneself absorbed, drawn in by the eerie promise of peace and immutability. It's seductive, sanitized, calm-verging-on-dead: mausoleum chic.

The standard interiors shot might be categorized as a degraded form of still life—a kind of iconography distinguished, traditionally, by the absence of human subjects. And as with the painted form, the viewer is faced with puzzles and paradoxes. Confronting the perfectly styled objects before us, are we, the spectators, in the presence of life or death? Where are the human beings? In the traditional *nature morte* (the French name for the mode is telling) the depiction of food and drink—fruit, bread, goblets of wine, limp game birds—alluded to organic processes (here's something good to eat), but a "life" inextricably dependent on the death and decay of other living things. In the most profound and unflinching still-life arrangements (Zurbarán's, say, or those of the seventeenth-century Dutch school) the viewer is suavely implicated in the cycle of mortality. A human skull sometimes appears, Hamlet-style, as an explicit and sobering memento mori.

There's one big problem here, and you don't need to rent old Ingmar Bergman movies to see it. There's a real skeleton at the door, and whoa—looks like he's aiming to get in. He was first spotted in Shelter-Mag Land, scythe in hand, one sunny September morning a few years ago, and recently he's turned up again—in true *Seventh Seal* fashion—in one of its favorite "style destinations." (Two days into the unfolding Katrina disaster, *New Orleans Style: Past and Present*, the most lavish of recent shelter books devoted to the doomed southern city, had sold out on Amazon.com. I know: I was trying to order it.)

It's fair to say that even while seeking to exploit readers' existential fears, the shelter-lit industry has itself been traumatized over the past five years, its Benday-dots dream world cracked open by explosions from without. The first shock to the system was 9/11, an event so cognitively strange, so incomprehensible according to shelter-mag logic, that what to do about it—rhetorically, psychically—remains unresolved in most interiors publications. What sort of high-gloss feature to run when other people not only won't go away but also want to blow your trendy "sanctuary" to bits? "Home," after all, is what terrorists set out to destroy: the everyday illusion of comfort and safety, the rolling-along-as-usual feeling that is bourgeois life. Floods and fire and civic breakdown in the Gulf Coast states put a further grisly spin on the problem. It's hard to focus on window treatments when bodies are floating by outside.

It's true that in the aftermath of 9/11 at least one gallant Un-Mother—to her credit—tried to address the matter as best she could. Dominique Browning, the melancholic editor of Condé Nast's *House and Garden* and a dead ringer for the Lady of Shalott, ran a number of columns in which she wrote awkwardly yet movingly about the effect of the attacks on her mental world. These columns were painful—I remember starting to cry while reading one—not least because one saw Browning struggling against the banality of the context in which she wrote. Such pathos in Shelter-Mag Land was a shock: like finding a dismembered corpse in a beautiful meadow. *Et in Arcadia ego* indeed.

A similar pathos suffused a *Metropolitan Home* essay by Emily Prager ("Safe as Houses," September 2004)—the only interiors article I've come across so far to tackle 9/11 at any length. Prager, a longtime Greenwich Village resident who witnessed the collapse of the South Tower, candidly recounted how the day's events left her "wounded in my sense of home." The piece ended with its author in a state of panicky ambivalence, wanting to flee New York yet unable to follow through on any of the fantastical moving plans she kept devising. Scarcely a comforting endpoint—but at least Prager seemed able to articulate her confusion.

Other responses, however, have been less honest and sometimes freakishly dissociated. For example, the editor of *Elle Decoration* (a publication aimed largely at fashion-conscious working women in their twenties and thirties) recently offered this schizoid hodgepodge of girl talk and carpe diem:

> Colour. Pattern. Decoration. Ornamentation. It's all coming back. I think it's to do with celebrating life—perhaps

> it's because, in these terrorist-aware times, we're more conscious than ever that this life isn't a rehearsal, it's the main event. And what simpler way to add some joy and pattern to your life than with flowers.

Though priding itself on being hip, even the House & Home section of *The New York Times* has gone a bit bipolar lately. Opposite a jaunty piece about co-op residents catfighting online (December 2, 2004), the editors ran a full-page public-service ad for a government disaster-readiness website, complete with a huge picture of a grim-faced FDNY firefighter and apocalyptic copy. ("After a terrorist attack your first instinct may be to run. That may be the worst thing you could do.") The emotional dissonance was nerve-jangling, corrosive, surreal. Maybe the best thing, after all, would be to go round to the neighbors and make up with them.

Yet the most disturbing case of 9/11 schizophrenia involves the now defunct *nest*. Often heralded as the most iconoclastic interiors publication since Fleur Cowles's short-lived *Flair*, in the 1950s, *nest* set out to be everything the ordinary shelter magazine was not: louche, sly, sexy, so dark and downtown in sensibility it was funny—an interiors rag for the John Waters set. Typical features had to do with Hitler's decorating tastes, the phallus-studded home of Miss Plaster Caster (she who once made plaster molds of rock-star penises), Lucy and Ricky's soundstage "apartment" on *I Love Lucy*, how to arrange kitty boxes when you live with 114 cats, and the joy of clear-plastic sofa covers. My all-time favorite piece was about the Toys "R" Us–style "playrooms" of "adult babies"—men and women who find sexual gratification by wearing diapers and lying in oversized baby cribs. Every now and then amid the camp one would encounter authentic blue-chip writing: Muriel Spark on "Bed Sits I Have Known," John Banville on Gianni Versace's Miami villa (outside which the designer was shot), the poet Eileen Myles on sleeping on a city sidewalk in a cardboard box.

The magazine was quite stupendously mannered—rather like Ronald Firbank trawling for hunky handymen at Home Depot. Yet manner proved bootless when *nest* fell victim to grotesque and unfortunate coincidence. Attached to the cover of the fatal thirteenth issue—Summer 2001—was a black silk mourning ribbon, the sort of thing one might find on a Victorian scrapbook or photo album. (*nest* regularly violated ordinary packaging conventions.) On the cover itself was a cleverly Photoshopped image of the U.S. Capitol wrapped in a huge white shroud with black-and-white funeral bunting. It transpired that Rei Kawakubo, the fashion force behind Comme des Garçons, had been asked by *nest*'s editor and presiding genius, Joseph Holtzman, to design a "mourning" dress for the Capitol building, precisely to ready it for "whatever calamity may befall us in the future." The shroud tarp and bunting were the result: Christo meets Edgar Allan Poe.

The "national grief" theme was playfully reflected in the issue's editorial content: one item had to do with the planning and decoration of Abraham Lincoln's funeral cortege, another with Sarah Bernhardt's coffin bed.

One can hardly overstate the spookiness of it all—for those morbid enough to notice—when the imagined "tragedy" came to pass a few weeks later. The Summer 2001 *nest* suddenly seemed ghoulishly prescient—akin to the British journalist W. T. Stead's uncanny 1892 short story about a White Star ocean liner's sinking in the ice fields of the North Atlantic (Stead would go down on the *Titanic* twenty years later), or "King's Cross," a melancholy Pet Shop Boys song of 1987 that seemed to predict the terrible Underground fire at that ill-starred station two months later. Odder still, however, was the official *nest* response to 9/11.

There wasn't one.

No comment on Kawakubo and the shrouded Capitol; no mention of the attacks; no nuttin'. Given *nest*'s Manhattan address and relentless downtown feel, the absence of immediate acknowledgment was creepy—as if the magazine had suffered a brain injury and been rendered selectively mute. The blankness and blockage never went away. *nest* carried on for several more years, through the Fall 2004 issue, but one couldn't help feeling that the debunking zest had gone out of it—the punkish will to provoke seemed tainted and damaged. I lost some of my enthusiasm for the magazine after the 9/11 watershed: *nest*, it seemed, was just too hip to be human.

In retrospect the aphasia seems part of a more pervasive syndrome. Despite the rad profile, *nest* was as knee-deep in bathos and bourgeois denial as any other shelter mag. But who among us isn't? How could anyone reconcile the scarifying truth—all men are mortal—with that illusion of calm and safety to which most of us still regularly aspire in everyday life? Regardless of means, status, or political investment, just about everyone craves warmth, light, four walls, and some bits of furniture—a *shelter,* in a word, from miseries we know are out there and others still to come. Our vulnerability is too extreme to be "integrated" in any supposedly therapeutic fashion.

So we devise psychic buffers. The habits of bourgeois life—first adumbrated in Northern Europe as early as the sixteenth century—have been for some time the buffer of choice, civilization's all-purpose comfort-and-happiness maximizer. But the bourgeois outlook could hardly be called valiant or hardheaded: it's all about *not* staring death in the face. Under its sway one seeks a world without pain. The search is doomed, of course—the "safe house" a house of cards. But maybe we needn't start thinking about *that* yet.

I find myself hung up on the predicament—how to strike a balance between the longing for security (that infantile need on which shelter mags batten) and the more grown-up recognition that any "serenity" to be achieved is illusory, or at best fleeting. I'm a dawdler on the road to unhappy consciousness. Yet there are signs—this essay among them, perhaps—that I've started to wean myself of the more brainless aspects of my addiction. I've let some of the crap subscriptions lapse—*Old House Interiors* (too boring-Berkeley-in-the-seventies) and the ludicrous, vamping *Architectural Digest. House Beautiful* had started to irk me: its former male editor—odd and smarmy—was always twaddling on in fake-folksy manner about his adorable daughter "Madison." But is he gay or straight?—that's what I want to know.

And I'm getting tired of the whole Let's-Pretend-There's-Nothing-Wrong trip; it's become so breathless and false. Death has lately been popping up rather explicitly in Shelter-Mag Land, but hidden in plain sight, as it were—like the purloined letter. Something one might call "taxidermic chic," for example, has become a huge fad: cow skulls, fossils, mounted "jackalope" heads, stuffed rodents in doll clothes, lizards embalmed in varnish or the like—all deployed as "edgy" urban décor. (Trendy rag-and-bone-cum-interiors shops like Evolution in SoHo and Paxton Gate in San Francisco make a bundle out of this strange and desiccated style.)

I've even had bouts of outright revulsion. The worst came not long ago as I was innocently paging through *Homes and Gardens*. I had found a feature—instantly mesmerizing—about a renovated English farmhouse built in 1604. My sort of wattle-and-daub thing exactly! One could just see Vanessa Bell in it, paintbrushes in hand. I was fascinated to read how the current owners, a handsome couple with children, had kept "the carcasses of the original kitchen" in the interest of authenticity. And I also loved the milky gray "period" color chosen for the drawing room: a Jacobean hue named "Silken Flank." But the pièce de résistance was undoubtedly the Vintage Hospital Bed—late-nineteenth-century and loaded with pricey Stieff teddy bears—taking pride of place in their daughter's bedroom.

A lovely white iron bedstead: funky, fresh-looking, impeccable shabby chic. I wanted it immediately. But suddenly I found myself imagining all the people who had slept, and possibly died, in this particular bed over the past hundred years. In fact, the more I looked at it, the more it reminded me of those metal beds you see lined up in haunting photographs of First World War military hospitals, in which a ward full of grievously injured young men—heads bandaged, empty pajama sleeves pinned up—lie propped against pillows and (if they can) glumly regard the camera. Teddy bears notwithstanding, one could almost smell the carbolic. How many blind or limbless soldiers, I wondered, had succumbed in little Scarlett's bed?

From there my thoughts went naturally on to the avian-flu epidemic of 1918–19. That appalling global contagion killed more than 20 million people: surely one or two of them must have expired in this particular bedstead? Bird-to-human influenza viruses have been in the news, of course, so the speculation was not unduly morbid. If the earthquakes, floods, or dirty bombs don't get us, I gather, the Asian poultry will.

In Hardy's *Tess of the d'Urbervilles,* there's an unforgettable passage in which the ill-starred heroine, brooding on mortality, wonders on what "sly and unseen" day she will die. "Of that day, doomed to be her terminus in time through all the ages, she did not know the place in month, week, season or year." Tess could have used www.deathclock.com, where you fill out a health questionnaire and get back your exact date of death. Having discovered when mine will be—January 28, 2038—I've found myself wondering lately where I will die. On a city street? In an overturned car? In some dark and fathomless polar sea into which my plane has crashed? But what about at home, in bed, Evian on the nightstand and Wally the mini-dachshund snoring stertorously under the covers? Given my "home" fixation, that would be an especially poetic fate. Will my 400-thread-count Egyptian-cotton bed linens be any comfort to me then? And what about the teak milking stool? If she ever knew—and I doubt she did—the Un-Mother isn't telling.

GIRL

Alexander Chee

Hair

The year is 1990. The place is San Francisco, the Castro. It is Halloween night. I am in my friend John's bathroom, alone in front of the mirror, wearing a black turtleneck and leggings. My face glows back at me from the light of twelve 100-watt bulbs. In high school I learned to do makeup for theater. I did fake mustaches and eyelashes then, bruises, wounds, tattoos. I remember always being tempted then to do what I have just done now, and always stopping, always thinking I would do it later.

This is that day.

My face, in the makeup I have just applied, is a success. My high cheekbones, large slanting eyes, wide mouth, small chin, and rounded jaw have been restrung in base, powder, eyeliner, lipstick, eyebrow pencil. With these tools I have built another face on top of my own, unrecognizable, and yet I am already adjusting to it; somehow I have always known how to put this face together. My hands do not shake, but move with the slow assurance of routine.

I am smiling.

I pick up the black eyeliner pencil and go back to the outer corners of my eyes, drawing slashes there, and, licking the edges of my fingers, I pull the lines out into sharp black points—the wings of crows, not their feet.

I have nine moles on my face, all obscured by base and powder. I choose one on my upper lip, to the right, where everyone inserts a beauty mark. I have one already, and it feels like a prophecy. I dot it with the pencil.

I pick up the lipstick and open my mouth in an O. I have always loved unscrewing lipsticks, and as the shining nub appears I feel a charge. I apply the color, Mauve Frost, then reapply it, and with that, my face shimmers—a white sky, the mole a black planet, the eyes its ringed big sisters. I press my lips down against each other and feel the color spread anywhere it hasn't gone yet.

The wig is shoulder-length blond hair, artificial—Dynel doll hair, like Barbie's, which is why I choose it. The cap shows how cheap the wig is, so I cut a headband out of a T-shirt sleeve and make it into a fall.

The wig I put on last. Without it, you can see my man's hairline, receding faintly into a widow's peak. You can see my dark hair, you can tell I'm not a blond woman or a white one, or even a woman. It is a Valkyrie's headpiece, and I gel it to hold it in place. The static it generates pulls the hairs out into the air one by one. In an hour I will have a faint halo of frizz. Blue sparks will fly from me when I touch people.

John knocks on the door. "Girl!" he says through the door. "Aren't you ready yet?" He is already finished, dressed in a sweater and black miniskirt, his black banged wig tied up with a pink bow. He has highlighted his cheekbones with rouge, which I forgo. He is wearing high heels; I have on combat boots. I decided to wear sensible shoes, but John wears fuck-me pumps, the heels three inches high. This is my first time. It is Halloween tonight in the Castro and we are both trying to pass, to be "real," only we are imitating very different women.

What kind of girl am I? With the wig in place, I understand that it is possible I am not just in drag, as a girl, but as a white girl. Or as someone trying to pass as a white girl.

"Come in!" I yell back. John appears over my shoulder in the mirror, a cheerleader gone wrong, the girl who sits on the back of the rebel's motorcycle. His brows rise all the way up.

"Jesus Mother of God," he says. "Girl, you're beautiful. I don't believe it."

"Believe it," I say, looking into his eyes.

I tilt my head back and carefully toss my hair over my right shoulder in the way I have seen my younger sister do. I realize I know one more thing about her than I did before—what it feels like to do this and why you would. It's like your own little thunderclap.

"Scared of you," John says. "You're flawless."

"So are you," I say. "Where's Fred?" Fred is my newest boyfriend, and I have been unsure if I should do this with him, but here we are.

"Are you okay?" Fred asks, as if something has gone wrong in the bathroom. "Oh, my God, you are beautiful." He steps into the doorway, dazed. He still looks like himself, a skinny white boy with big ears and long eyelashes, his dark hair all of an inch long. He hasn't gotten dressed yet.

He is really spellbound, though, in a way he hasn't been before this. I have never had this effect on a man, never transfixed him so thoroughly, and I wonder what I might be able to make him do now that I could not before. "Honey," he says, his voice full of wonder. He walks closer, slowly, his head hung, looking up at me. I feel my smile rise from somewhere old in me, maybe older than me; I know this scene, I have seen this scene a thousand times and never thought I would be in it. This is the scene where the beautiful girl receives her man's adoration, and I am that girl.

In this moment, the confusion of my whole life has receded. No one will ask me if I am white or Asian. No one will ask me if I am a man or a woman. No one will ask me why I love men. For a moment, I want Fred to stay a man all night. There is nothing brave in this: any man and woman can walk together, in love and unharassed in this country, in this world—and for a moment, I just want to be his overly made-up girlfriend all night. I want him to be my quiet, strong man. I want to hold his hand all night and have it be only that; not political, not dangerous, just that. I want the ancient reassurances legislated for centuries by mobs.

He puts his arms around me and I tip my head back. "Wow," he says. "Even up close."

"Ever kissed a girl?" I ask.

"No," he says, and laughs.

"Now's your chance," I say, and he leans in, kissing me slowly through his smile.

My Country

I am half-white, half-Korean, or, to be more specific, Scotch Irish, Irish, Welsh, Korean, Chinese, Mongolian. It has been a regular topic all my life, this question of what I am. People will even tell me, like my first San Francisco hairdresser.

"Girl, you are mixed, aren't you? But you can pass," he said, as if this was a good thing. He said this as he scrutinized me in the mirror, looking at me as if I had come in wearing a disguise.

"Pass as what?" I asked.

"White. You look white."

When people use the word "passing" in talking about race, they only ever mean one thing, but I still make them say it. He told me he was Filipino. "You could be one of us," he said. "But you're not."

Yes. I could be, but I am not. I am used to this feeling.

As a child in Korea, living in my grandfather's house, I was not to play in the street by myself: Amerasian children had no rights there generally, as they usually didn't know who their father was, and they could be bought and sold as domestic help or as prostitutes, or both. No one would check to see if I was any different from the others.

"One day everyone will look like you," people say to me all the time. I am a citizen of a nation that has only ever existed in the future, a nation where nationalism dies of confusion. I cringe whenever someone tells me I am a "fine mix," that it "worked well." What if it hadn't?

After I read Eduardo Galeano's stories in *Memory of Fire,* I mostly remember the mulatto ex-slaves in Haiti, obliterated when the French recaptured the island, the mestiza Argentinean courtesans—hated both by the white women for daring to put on wigs as fine as theirs, and by the Chilote slaves, who think the courtesans put on airs when they do so. Galeano's trilogy is supposed to be a lyric history of the Americas, but it read more like a history of racial mixing.

I found in it a pattern for the history of half-breeds hidden in every culture: historically, we are allowed neither the privileges of the ruling class nor the community of those who are ruled. To each side that disowns us, we represent everything the other does not have. We survive only if we are valued, and we are valued only for strength, or beauty, sometimes for intelligence or cunning. As I read those stories of who survives and who does not, I know that I have survived in all of these ways and that these are the only ways I have survived so far.

This beauty I find when I put on drag, then: it is made up of these talismans of power, a balancing act of the self-hatreds of at least two cultures, an act I've engaged in my whole life, here on the fulcrum I make of my face. That night, I find I want this beauty to last because it seems more powerful than any beauty I've had before. Being pretty like this is stronger than any drug I've ever tried.

But in my blond hair, I ask myself: Are you really passing? Or is it just the dark, the night, people seeing what they want to see? And what exactly are you passing as? And is that what we are really doing here?

Each time I pass that night, it is a victory over these doubts, a hit off the pipe. This hair is all mermaid's gold, and like anyone in a fairy tale I want it to be real when I wake up.

Angels

John and I are patient as we make Fred up. His eyelids flutter as we try to line and shadow them. He talks while we try to put on his lipstick. He feels this will liberate him, and tells us, repeats, how much he would never have done this before. I realize he means before me.

"Close your eyes," I tell him. He closes them. I feel like his big sister. I dust the puffball with translucent powder and hold it in front of his face. I take a big breath and blow it toward him. A cloud surrounds him and settles lightly across his skin. The sheen of the base is gone, replaced by powder smoothness. He giggles.

John pulls the wig down from behind him and twists it into place. He comes around beside me and we look at Fred carefully for fixable flaws. There are none. Fred opens his eyes. "Well?"

"Definitely the smart sister. Kate Jackson," John says, and turns toward me, smiling. "I'm the pretty one, the femmy one. Farrah. Which one are you, girl?"

I shake my head and pull the lapels of my leather trench coat. I don't feel like any of Charlie's Angels and I know I don't look like one. I look more like a lost member of the *Faster, Pussycat! Kill! Kill!* gang. Like if Tura Satana had a child with the blond sidekick. Or just took her hair out for a ride one day.

"You're the mean sister," John says with a laugh. "The one that makes you cry and breaks all your dolls."

Outside John's apartment, Eighteenth Street is full of cars, their headlights like footlights for the sidewalk stage in the early night. I can see my hair flashing around me in the dark as it catches the light. Doing drag on Halloween night in the Castro is an amateur but high-level competitive sport. Participating means doing drag in front of people who do drag on just about every other day of the year, and some of these people are my friends. I am most nervous at the thought of seeing them. I want to measure up.

According to the paper the next day, 400,000 people will come into the Castro tonight to see us. They will all try to drive down this street, and many will succeed. Some will have baseball bats, beer bottles, guns. Some of them hate drag queens, trans women, gender queers. They will tell you they want their girls to be girls. If they pick you up and find out the truth, they will beat and maybe kill you. Being good at a blow job is a survival skill for some of my friends for this very reason—though men are unpredictable at best.

"Most men, when they find out you have a dick, well, hon, they roll right over." This is something a drag-queen friend tells me early on in my life here. "Turns out, their whole lives all they ever wanted was to get fucked, and they never had the nerve to ask for it."

I think about this a lot. I find I think about it right now, on the street, in my new look.

John, Fred, and I walk out in front of the stopped cars. They are full of people I will never see again. John swivels on his heels, pivoting as he walks, smiling and waving. He knows he is why they are here from the suburbs, that he is what they have come to see. I smile at a boy behind a steering wheel who catches my eye. He honks and yells, all excitement. I twirl my hair and keep walking, strutting. In the second grade, the boys would stop me in the hall to tell me I walked like a girl, my hips switching, and as I cross this street and feel the cars full of people watching me, for the first time I really let myself walk as I have always felt my hips wanted to. I have always walked this way, but I have never walked this way like this.

The yelling continues from the car, and the boy's friends lean out the window, shouting for me. John is laughing. "Shit, girl, you better be careful. I'm going to keep my eye on you." Fred is walking quietly ahead of us. From behind, in his camouflage jacket, he looks like a man with long hair. His legs move from his thin hips in straight lines, he bobs as he steps, and the wig hair bounces gently at his shoulders. He has always walked like this also, I can see this, and here is a difference between us. I don't want him to be hurt tonight, however that happens—either for not being enough of a girl or for being too much, not enough of a boy.

The catcalls from the cars make me feel strong at first. Isn't beauty strong? I'd always thought beauty was strength, and so I wanted to be beautiful. Those cheers on the street are like a weightlifter's bench-press record. The blond hair is like a flag, and all around me in the night are teams. But with each shout I am more aware of the edge, how the excitement could turn into violence, blood, bruises, death.

We arrive at Café Flore, a few blocks from John's apartment. We run into Danny Nicoletta, a photographer friend. He sees us but does not recognize me. I see him every day at this cafe; I have posed for him on other occasions. He has no idea who I am. I wave at him, and as he looks at me, I feel him examine the frosted blond thing in front of him. I toss my hair. I already love the way this feels, to punctuate arrivals, announcements, a change of mood with your hair.

"Hi, Danny," I say finally.

He screams.

"Oh, my God, you look exactly like this girl who used to babysit for me," he says. He takes out his camera and snaps photos of me in the middle of the crowded cafe, and the flash is like a little kiss each time it hits my retinas.

We leave the café and I move through the Halloween night, glowing, as if all of the headlights and flashes have been stored inside me. I pause to peer into store windows, to catch a glimpse of myself. I stop to let people take my picture, and wave if they yell, I dance with friends to music playing from the tower of speakers by a stage set up outside the cafe. A parade of what look to be heavily muscled prom queens in glistening gowns and baubles pours out into the street from one of the gyms nearby. They glow beneath the stage lights, their shoulders and chests shaved smooth, their pectorals suitable for cleavage. They titter and coo at the people lining the streets, affecting the manner of easily shocked women, or they strut, waving the wave of queens. As they come by, they appraise us with a glance and then move on.

This power I feel tonight, I understand now—this is what it means when we say "queen."

Girl

My fascination with makeup started young. I remember the first time I wore lipstick in public. I was seven, eight years old at the time, with my mother at the Jordan Marsh makeup counter at the Maine Mall in South Portland. We were Christmas shopping, I think—it was winter, at least—and she was there trying on samples.

My mother is a beauty, from a family of Maine farmers who are almost all tall, long-waisted, thin, and pretty, the men and the women. Her eyes are Atlantic Ocean blue. She has a pragmatic streak, from being a farmer's daughter, that typically rules her, but she also loves fashion and glamour. When she was younger, she wore simple but chic clothes she often accessorized with cocktail rings, knee-high black leather boots, dark sunglasses with white frames.

I kept a secret from my mom, or at least I thought I did: I would go into her bathroom and try on her makeup, looking at myself in the mirror. I spent hours in front of that mirror, rearranging my facial expressions—my face at rest looked unresolved to me, in between one thing and another. I would sometimes stare at my face and imagine it was either more white or more Asian. But makeup I understood; I had watched the change that came over my mother when she put on makeup, and I wanted that for myself. So while she was busy at the makeup counter, I reached up for one of the lipsticks, applied it, and then turned to her with a smile.

I thought it would surprise her, make her happy. I am sure the reddish orange color looked clownish, even frightening, on my little face.

"Alexander," was all she said, stepping off the chair at the Clinique counter and sweeping me up. She pulled my ski mask over my head and led me out of the department store to the car, like I had stolen something. We drove home in silence, and once there, she washed the lipstick off my face and warned me to never do that again.

She was angry, upset, she felt betrayed by me. There was a line, and I had thought I could go back and forth across it, but it seemed I could not.

Until I could. Until I did.

I was not just mistaken for a member of other races, as a child. I was also often mistaken for a girl. What a pretty little girl you have, people used to say to my mother at the grocery store when I was six, seven, eight. She had let my hair grow long. I'm a boy, I would say each time. And they would turn red, or stammer an apology, or say, His hair is so long, and I would feel as if I had done something wrong, or she had.

I have been trying to convince people for so long that I am a real boy, it is a relief to stop, to run in the other direction.

Before Halloween night, I thought I knew some things about being a woman. I'd had women teachers and read women writers; women were my best friends growing up. But that night was a glimpse into a universe beside my own. Drag is its own world of experience—a theater of being female more than a reality. It isn't like being trans, either. It isn't, the more I think about it, like anything except what it is: costumes, illusion, a spell you cast on others and on yourself.

But girl, girl is something else.

My friends in San Francisco at this time, we all call each other "girl," except for the ones who think they are too butch for such nellying, though we call them "girl" maybe most of all. My women friends call each other "girl" too, and they say it sometimes like they are a little surprised at how much they like it. This, for me, began in meetings for ACT UP and Queer Nation, a little word that moved in on us all back then. When we say it, the word is like a stone we pass one to the other: the stone thrown at all of us. And the more we catch it and pass it, it seems the less it can hurt us, the more we know who our new family is now. Who knows us, and who doesn't. It is something like a bullet turned into something like a badge of pride.

Later that night we go to Club Uranus. John and Fred have removed their wigs and makeup. I have decided not to. Fred was uncomfortable—a wig is hot—and John wanted to get laid by a man as a man. I wasn't ready to let go. As we walked there, we passed heterosexual couples on the street. I walked with Fred, holding his arm, and noted the passing men who treated me like a woman—and the women who did also. Only one person let on that he saw through me, a man at a stoplight who leaned out his car window to shout, "Hey, Lola, come back here, baby! I love you!"

My friend Darren is at the club, a thin blond boy done up as Marie Antoinette, in hair nearly a foot tall and a professional costume rental dress, hoopskirts and all. On his feet, combat boots also. He raises his skirts periodically to show he is wearing nothing underneath.

Soon I am on the go-go stage by the bar. On my back, riding me, is a skinny white boy in a thong made out of duct tape, his body shaved. We are both sweating, the lights a crown of wet bright heat. The music is loud and very fast, and I roll my head like a lion, whipping the wig around for the cool air this lets in. People squeeze by the stage, alternately staring at and ignoring us.

I see very little, but I soon spot Fred, who raises his hand and gives me a little wave from where he is standing. I want to tell him I know the boy on my back and that it isn't anything he needs to worry about, but he seems to understand this. I wonder if Fred is jealous, but I tell myself he is not, that he knew what he was getting into with me—when we met, he mentioned the other stages he had seen me on around town. Tonight is one of those nights when I am growing, changing quickly, without warning, into new shapes and configurations, and I don't know where this all goes.

In that moment, I feel more at home than I ever have, not in San Francisco, not on earth, but in myself. I am on the other side of something and I don't know what it is. I wait to find out.

Real

I am proud for years of the way I looked real that night. I remember the men who thought I was a real woman, the straight guys in the cars whooping at me and their expressions when I said, "Thanks, guys," my voice my voice, and the change that rippled over their faces.

You wanted me, I wanted to say. You might still want me.

Real is good. Real is what you want. No one does drag to be a real woman, though. Drag is not the same as that. Drag knows it is different. But if you can pass as real, when it comes to drag, that is its own gold medal.

But mostly I'm still too aware of how that night was the first night I felt comfortable with my face. It makes me wary, even confused. I can feel the longing for the power I had. I jones for it like it's cocaine.

The little boy I used to be, in the mirror making faces, he was happy. But the process took so much work. I can't do that every day, though I know women who do. And that isn't the answer to my unhappiness, and I know it.

When my friend Danny gives me a photo from that night, I see something I didn't notice at the time. I look a little like my mom. I had put on my glasses for him—a joke about "girls who wear glasses"—and in that one picture, I see it all: the dark edges of my real hair sticking out, the cheapness of the wig, the smooth face, finally confident.

I send a copy to my sister and write, This is what I would look like if I was your big sister.

I can't skip what I need to do to love this face by making it over. I can't chase after the power I felt that night, the fleeting sense of finally belonging to the status quo, by making myself into something that looks like the something they want. Being real means being at home in this face, just as it is when I wake up. I am not the person who appeared for the first time that night. I am the one only I saw, the one I had rejected until then, the one I needed to see, and didn't see until I had taken nearly everything about him away. His face is not half this or half that, it is all something else.

Sometimes you don't know who you are until you put on a mask.

A few months after Halloween, a friend borrows my wig. He has begun performing in drag on a regular basis. I have not. I bring it to the bookstore where we both work and pass it off to him. It looks like a burned-out thing, what's left in the wick of a candle after a long night.

I go to see my friend perform in the wig. He has turned it into the ponytail of a titanic hair sculpture, made from three separate wigs. He is a hoopskirted vision beneath its impossible size, his face whited out, a beauty mark on his lip. Who was the first blonde to dot a beauty mark on her upper lip? How far back in time do we have to go? It is like some spirit in the wig has moved on, into him.

He never gives me the wig back, and I don't ask for it back. It was never really mine.

BLACK BODY

Teju Cole

Then the bus began driving into clouds, and between one cloud and the next we caught glimpses of the town below. It was suppertime and the town was a constellation of yellow points. We arrived thirty minutes after leaving that town, which was called Leuk. The train to Leuk had come in from Visp, the train from Visp had come from Bern, and the train before that was from Zurich, from which I had started out in the afternoon. Three trains, a bus, and a short stroll, all of it through beautiful country, and then we reached Leukerbad in darkness. So Leukerbad, not far in terms of absolute distance, was not all that easy to get to. August 2, 2014: it was James Baldwin's birthday. Were he alive, he would be turning ninety. He is one of those people just on the cusp of escaping the contemporary and slipping into the historical—John Coltrane would have turned eighty-eight in the same year; Martin Luther King, Jr., would have turned eighty-five—people who could still be with us but who feel, at times, very far away, as though they lived centuries ago.

James Baldwin left Paris and came to Leukerbad for the first time in 1951. His lover Lucien Happersberger's family had a chalet in a village up in the mountains. And so Baldwin, who was depressed and distracted at the time, went, and the village (which is also called Loèche-les-Bains) proved to be a refuge for him. His first trip was in the summer, and lasted two weeks. Then he returned, to his own surprise, for two more winters. His first novel, *Go Tell It on the Mountain,* found its final form here. He had struggled with the book for eight years, and he finally finished it in this unlikely retreat. He wrote something else, too, an essay called "Stranger in the Village"; it was this essay, even more than the novel, that brought me to Leukerbad.

"Stranger in the Village" first appeared in *Harper's Magazine* in 1953, and then in the essay collection *Notes of a Native Son* in 1955. It recounts the experience of being black in an all-white village. It begins with a sense of an extreme journey, like Charles Darwin's in the Galápagos or Tété-Michel Kpomassie's in Greenland. But then it opens out into other concerns and into a different voice, swiveling to look at the American racial situation in the 1950s. The part of the essay that focuses on the Swiss village is both bemused and sorrowful. Baldwin is alert to the absurdity of being a writer from New York who is considered in some way inferior by Swiss villagers, many of whom have never traveled. But, later in the essay, when he writes about race in America, he is not at all bemused. He is angry and prophetic, writing with a hard clarity and carried along by a precipitous eloquence.

I took a room at the Hotel Mercure Bristol the night I arrived. I opened the windows to a dark view in which nothing was visible, but I knew that in the darkness loomed the Daubenhorn mountain. I ran a hot bath and lay neck-deep in the water with my old paperback copy of *Notes of a Native Son.* The tinny sound from my laptop was Bessie Smith singing "I'm Wild About That Thing," a filthy blues number and a masterpiece of plausible deniability: "Don't hold it baby when I cry / Give me every bit of it, else I'd die." She could be singing about a trombone. And it was there in the bath, with his words and her voice, that I had my body-double moment: here I was in Leukerbad, with Bessie Smith singing across the years from 1929; and I am black like him; and I am slender; and have a gap in my front teeth; and am not especially tall (no, write it: short); and am cool on the page and animated in person, except when it is the other way around; and I was once a fervid teenage preacher (Baldwin: "Nothing that has happened to me since equals the power and the glory that I sometimes felt when, in the middle of a sermon, I knew that I was somehow, by some miracle, really carrying, as they said, 'the Word'—when the church and I were one"); and I, too, left the church; and I call New York home even when not living there; and feel myself in all places, from New York City to rural Switzerland, the custodian of a black body, and have to find the language for all of what that means to me and to the people who look at me. The ancestor had briefly taken possession of the descendant. It was a moment of identification. In that Swiss village in the days that followed, that moment guided me.

"From all available evidence no black man had ever set foot in this tiny Swiss village before I came," Baldwin wrote. But the village has grown considerably since his visits, more than sixty years ago. They've seen blacks now; I wasn't a remarkable sight. There were a few glances at the hotel when I was checking in, and in the fine restaurant just up the road; there are always glances. There are glances in Zurich, where I spent the summer, and there are glances in New York City, which has been my home for fourteen years. There are glances all over Europe and in India, and anywhere I go outside Africa. The test is how long the glances last, whether they become stares, with what intent they occur, whether they contain any degree of hostility or mockery, and to what extent connections, money, or mode of dress shield me in these situations. To be a stranger is to be looked at, but to be black is to be looked at especially. ("The children shout Neger! Neger! as I walk along the streets.") Leukerbad has changed, but in which way? There were, in fact, no bands of children on the street, and few children anywhere at all. Presumably the children of Leukerbad, like children the world over, were indoors, frowning over computer games, checking Facebook, or watching music videos. Perhaps some of the older folks I saw in the streets were once the very children who had been so surprised by the sight of Baldwin, and about whom, in the essay, he struggles to take a reasonable tone: "In all of this, in which it must be conceded that there was the charm of genuine wonder and in which there was certainly no element of intentional unkindness, there was yet no suggestion that I was human: I was simply a living wonder." But now the children or grandchildren of those children are connected to the world in a different way. Maybe some xenophobia or racism is part of their lives, but part of their lives, too, are Beyoncé, Drake, and Meek Mill, the music I hear pulsing from Swiss clubs on Friday nights.

Baldwin had to bring his records with him in the fifties, like a secret stash of medicine, and he had to haul his phonograph up to Leukerbad, so that the sound of the American blues could keep him connected to a Harlem of the spirit. I listened to some of the same music while I was there, as a way of being with him: Bessie Smith singing "I Need a Little Sugar in My Bowl" ("I need a little sugar in my bowl / I need a little hot dog on my roll"), Fats Waller singing "Your Feet's Too Big." I listened to my own playlist as well: Bettye Swann, Billie Holiday, Jean Wells, *Coltrane Plays the Blues,* the Physics, Childish Gambino. The music you travel with helps you to create your own internal weather. But the world participates, too: when I sat down to lunch at the Romerhof restaurant one afternoon—that day, all the customers and staff were white—the music playing overhead was Whitney Houston's "I Wanna Dance with Somebody." History is now and black America.

At dinner, at a pizzeria, a table of British tourists stared at me. But the waitress was part black, and at the hotel one of the staff members at the spa was an older black man. "People are trapped in history, and history is trapped in them," Baldwin wrote. But it is also true that the little pieces of history move around at a tremendous speed, settling with a not-always-clear logic, and rarely settling for long. And perhaps more interesting than my not being the only black person in the village is the plain fact that many of the other people I saw were also foreigners. This was the biggest change of all. If, back then, the village had a pious and convalescent air about it, the feel of "a lesser Lourdes," it is much busier now, packed with visitors from other parts of Switzerland, and from Germany, France, Italy, and all over Europe, Asia, and the Americas. It has become the most popular thermal resort in the Alps. The municipal baths are full. There are hotels on every street, at every price point, and there are restaurants and luxury-goods shops. If you wish to buy an eye-wateringly costly watch at forty-six hundred feet above sea level, it is now possible to do so.

The better hotels have their own thermal pools. At the Hotel Mercure Bristol, I took an elevator down to the spa and sat in the dry sauna. A few minutes later, I slipped into the pool and floated outside in the warm water. Others were there, but not many. A light rain fell. We were ringed by mountains and held in the immortal blue.

In her brilliant *Harlem Is Nowhere,* Sharifa Rhodes-Pitts writes, "In almost every essay James Baldwin wrote about Harlem, there is a moment when he commits a literary sleight-of-hand so particular that, if he'd been an athlete, sportscasters would have codified the maneuver and named it 'the Jimmy.' I think of it in cinematic terms, because its effect reminds me of a technique wherein camera operators pan out by starting with a tight shot and then zoom out to a wide view while the lens remains focused on a point in the distance." This move Rhodes-Pitts describes, this sudden widening of focus, is present even in his essays that are not about Harlem. In "Stranger in the Village," there's a passage about seven pages in where one can feel the rhetoric revving up, as Baldwin prepares to leave behind the calm, fabular atmosphere of the opening section. Of the villagers, he writes:

> These people cannot be, from the point of view of power, strangers anywhere in the world; they have made the modern world, in effect, even if they do not know it. The most illiterate among them is related, in a way I am not, to Dante, Shakespeare, Michelangelo, Aeschylus, Da Vinci, Rembrandt, and Racine; the cathedral at Chartres says something to them which it cannot say to me, as indeed would New York's Empire State Building, should anyone here ever see it. Out of their hymns and dances come Beethoven and Bach. Go back a few centuries and they are in their full glory—but I am in Africa, watching the conquerors arrive.

What is this list about? Does it truly bother Baldwin that the people of Leukerbad are related, through some faint familiarity, to Chartres? That some distant genetic thread links them to the Beethoven string quartets? After all, as he argues later in the essay, no one can deny the impact "the presence of the Negro has had on the American character." He understands the truth and the art in Bessie Smith's work. He does not, and cannot—I want to believe—rate the blues below Bach. But there was a certain narrowness in received ideas of black culture in the 1950s. In the time since then, there has been enough black cultural achievement from which to compile an all-star team: there's been Coltrane and Monk and Miles, and Ella and Billie and Aretha. Toni Morrison, Wole Soyinka, and Derek Walcott happened, as have Audre Lorde, and Chinua Achebe, and Bob Marley. The body was not abandoned for the mind's sake: Alvin Ailey, Arthur Ashe, and Michael Jordan happened, too. The source of jazz and the blues also gave the world hip-hop, Afrobeat, dancehall, and house. And, yes, by the time James Baldwin died, in 1987, he, too, was recognized as an all-star.

Thinking further about the cathedral at Chartres, about the greatness of that achievement and about how, in his view, it included blacks only in the negative, as devils, Baldwin writes that "the American Negro has arrived at his identity by virtue of the absoluteness of his estrangement from his past." But the distant African past has also become much more available than it was in 1953. It would not occur to me to think that, centuries ago, I was "in Africa, watching the conquerors arrive." But I suspect that for Baldwin this is, in part, a piece of oratory, a grim cadence on which to end a paragraph. In "A Question of Identity" (another essay collected in *Notes of a Native Son*), he writes, "The truth about that past is not that it is too brief, or too superficial, but only that we, having turned our faces so resolutely away from it, have never demanded from it what it has to give." The fourteenth-century court artists of Ife made bronze sculptures using a complicated casting process lost to Europe since antiquity, and which was not rediscovered there until the Renaissance. Ife sculptures are equal to the works of Ghiberti or Donatello. From their precision and formal sumptuousness we can extrapolate the contours of a great monarchy, a network of sophisticated ateliers, and a cosmopolitan world of trade and knowledge. And it was not only Ife. All of West Africa was a cultural ferment. From the egalitarian government of the Igbo to the goldwork of the Ashanti courts, the brass sculpture of Benin, the military achievement of the Mandinka Empire and the musical virtuosi who praised those war heroes, this was a region of the world too deeply invested in art and life to simply be reduced to a caricature of "watching the conquerors arrive." We know better now. We know it with a stack of corroborating scholarship and we know it implicitly, so that even making a list of the accomplishments feels faintly tedious, and is helpful mainly as a counter to Eurocentrism.

There's no world in which I would surrender the intimidating beauty of Yoruba-language poetry for, say, Shakespeare's sonnets, or one in which I'd prefer the chamber orchestras of Brandenburg to the koras of Mali. I'm happy to own all of it.

This carefree confidence is, in part, the gift of time. It is a dividend of the struggle of people from earlier generations. I feel little alienation in museums, full though they are of other people's ancestors. But this question of filiation tormented Baldwin considerably. He was sensitive to what was great in world art, and sensitive to his own sense of exclusion from it. He made a similar list in the title essay of *Notes of a Native Son* (one begins to feel that lists like this had been flung at him during arguments): "In some subtle way, in a really profound way, I brought to Shakespeare, Bach, Rembrandt, to the Stones of Paris, to the Cathedral at Chartres, and the Empire State Building a special attitude. These were not really my creations, they did not contain my history; I might search them in vain forever for any reflection of myself. I was an interloper; this was not my heritage." The lines throb with sadness. What he loves does not love him in return.

This is where I part ways with Baldwin. I disagree not with his particular sorrow but with the self-abnegation that pinned him to it. Bach, so profoundly human, is my heritage. I am not an interloper when I look at a Rembrandt portrait. I care for them more than some white people do, just as some white people care more for aspects of African art than I do. I can oppose white supremacy and still rejoice in Gothic architecture. In this, I stand with Ralph Ellison: "The values of my own people are neither 'white' nor 'black,' they are American. Nor can I see how they could be anything else, since we are people who are involved in the texture of the American experience." And yet I (born in the United States more than half a century after Baldwin) continue to understand, because I have experienced in my own body the undimmed fury he felt about racism. In his writing there is a hunger for life, for all of it, and a strong wish to not be accounted nothing (a mere nigger, a mere *neger*) when he knows himself to be so much. And this "so much" is neither a matter of ego about his writing nor an anxiety about his fame in New York or in Paris. It is about the incontestable fundamentals of a person: pleasure, sorrow, love, humor, and grief, and the complexity of the interior landscape that sustains those feelings. Baldwin was astonished that anyone anywhere should question these fundamentals—thereby burdening him with the supreme waste of time that is racism—let alone so many people in so many places. This unflagging ability to be shocked rises like steam off his written pages. "The rage of the disesteemed is personally fruitless," he writes, "but it is also absolutely inevitable."

Leukerbad gave Baldwin a way to think about white supremacy from its first principles. It was as though he found it in its simplest form there. The men who suggested that he learn to ski so that they might mock him, the villagers who accused him behind his back of being a firewood thief, the ones who wished to touch his hair and suggested that he grow it out and make himself a winter coat, and the children who, "having been taught that the devil is a black man, scream[ed] in genuine anguish" as he approached: Baldwin saw these as prototypes (preserved like coelacanths) of attitudes that had evolved into the more intimate, intricate, familiar, and obscene American forms of white supremacy that he already knew so well.

It is a beautiful village. I liked the mountain air. But when I returned to my room from the thermal baths, or from strolling in the streets with my camera, I read the news online. There I found an unending sequence of crises: in the Middle East, in Africa, in Russia, and everywhere else, really. Pain was general. But within that larger distress was a set of linked stories, and thinking about "Stranger in the Village," thinking with its help, was like injecting a contrast dye into my encounter with the news. The American police continued shooting unarmed black men, or killing them in other ways. The protests that followed, in black communities, were countered with violence by a police force that is becoming indistinguishable from an invading army. People began to see a connection between the various events: the shootings, the fatal choke hold, the stories of who was not given life-saving medication. And black communities were flooded with outrage and grief.

In all of this, a smaller, much less significant story (but one that nevertheless signified) caught my attention. The mayor of New York and his police chief have a public-policy obsession with cleaning, with cleansing, and they decided that arresting members of the dance troupes that perform in moving subway cars was one of the ways to clean up the city. I read the excuses for this becoming a priority: some people feared being seriously injured by an errant kick (it has not happened, but they sure feared it), some people considered the dancing a nuisance, some policymakers believed that going after misdemeanors is a way of preempting major crimes. And so, to combat this menace of dancers, the police moved in. They began chasing, and harassing, and handcuffing. The "problem" was dancers, and the dancers were, for the most part, black boys. The newspapers took the same tone as the government: a sniffy dismissal of the performers. And yet these same dancers are a bright spark in the day, a moment of unregulated beauty, artists with talents unimaginable to their audience. What kind of thinking would consider their abolition an improvement in city life? No one considers Halloween trick-or-treaters a public menace. There's no law enforcement against people selling Girl Scout cookies or against Jehovah's Witnesses. But the black body comes prejudged, and as a result it is placed in needless jeopardy. To be black is to bear the brunt of selective enforcement of the law, and to inhabit a psychic unsteadiness in which there is no guarantee of personal safety. You are a black body first, before you are a kid walking down the street or a Harvard professor who has misplaced his keys.

William Hazlitt, in an 1821 essay entitled "The Indian Jugglers," wrote words that I think of when I see a great athlete or dancer: "Man, thou art a wonderful animal, and thy ways past finding out! Thou canst do strange things, but thou turnest them to little account!—To conceive of this effort of extraordinary dexterity distracts the imagination and makes admiration breathless." In the presence of the admirable, some are breathless not with admiration but with rage. They object to the presence of the black body (an unarmed boy in a street, a man buying a toy, a dancer in the subway, a bystander) as much as they object to the presence of the black mind. And simultaneous with these erasures is the unending collection of profit from black labor and black innovation. Throughout the culture, there are imitations of the gait, bearing, and dress of the black body, a vampiric "everything but the burden" co-option of black life.

Leukerbad is ringed by mountains: the Daubenhorn, the Torrenthorn, the Rinderhorn. A high mountain pass called the Gemmi, another twenty-eight hundred feet above the village, connects the canton of Valais with the Bernese Oberland. Through this landscape—craggy, bare in places and verdant elsewhere, a textbook instance of the sublime—one moves as though through a dream. The Gemmi Pass is famous for good reason, and Goethe was once there, as were Byron, Twain, and Picasso. The pass is mentioned in a Sherlock Holmes adventure, when Holmes crosses it on his way to the fateful meeting with Professor Moriarty at Reichenbach Falls. There was bad weather the day I went up, rain and fog, but that was good luck, as it meant I was alone on the trails. While there, I remembered a story that Lucien Happersberger told about Baldwin going out on a hike in these mountains. Baldwin had lost his footing during the ascent, and the situation was precarious for a moment. But Happersberger, who was an experienced climber, reached out a hand, and Baldwin was saved. It was out of this frightening moment, this appealingly biblical moment, that Baldwin got the title for the book he had been struggling to write: *Go Tell It on the Mountain*.

If Leukerbad was his mountain pulpit, the United States was his audience. The remote village gave him a sharper view of what things looked like back home. He was a stranger in Leukerbad, Baldwin wrote, but there was no possibility for blacks to be strangers in the United States, or for whites to achieve the fantasy of an all-white America purged of blacks. This fantasy about the disposability of black life is a constant in American history. It takes a while to understand that this disposability continues. It takes whites a while to understand it; it takes nonblack people of color a while to understand it; and it takes some blacks, whether they've always lived in the United States or are latecomers like myself, weaned elsewhere on other struggles, a while to understand it. American racism has many moving parts, and has had enough centuries in which to evolve an impressive camouflage. It can hoard its malice in great stillness for a long time, all the while pretending to look the other way. Like misogyny, it is atmospheric. You don't see it at first. But understanding comes.

"People who shut their eyes to reality simply invite their own destruction, and anyone who insists on remaining in a state of innocence long after that innocence is dead turns himself into a monster." The news of the day (old news, but raw as a fresh wound) is that black American life is disposable from the point of view of policing, sentencing, economic policy, and countless terrifying forms of disregard. There is a vivid performance of innocence, but there's no actual innocence left. The moral ledger remains so far in the negative that we can't even get started on the question of reparations. Baldwin wrote "Stranger in the Village" more than sixty years ago. Now what?

GREEDY SLEEP

Bernard Cooper

I knew I had a problem when I woke up in a Motel 6 in Fresno. I'd driven there from Los Angeles late the previous afternoon, barreling for hours through the Central Valley, its furrowed green farmland rippling out on either side of the interstate. Humid wind blew through the windows, heavy with the smell of fertile earth. I checked into my room after dark and went straight to bed.

Fresno State University had invited me to appear on a panel at their annual writer's conference—at least I remembered that much when I opened my eyes the next morning. Still bleary from a long night's sleep, I had a harder time recalling the panel's title: "The Memoir: Unforgotten Recollections of the Past," or some such redundancy. In which direction was the lobby, I wondered? Where had I parked my car? Every moment of disorientation turned out to be temporary and could easily be blamed on the effects of waking up in a strange place. But the same couldn't be said of what happened next.

As I sat up in bed, I heard a faint rustling and looked down to see dozens of foil and paper wrappers cascade off my chest and land in my lap. Cookie crumbs had gathered in the folds of my T-shirt. Around me lay several half-eaten crackers and a cube or two of cheddar cheese. Gummy bears were strewn across the blanket like colorful, rubbery carnage.

My heart started racing. It was as if someone had snuck into the room while I'd slept and smashed a piñata above the bed. I scanned the room for evidence of an intruder—the year was 1996, and "home invasion robberies" had started making national headlines—but the door to my room was closed and bolted, and the placard requesting PRIVACY PLEASE, in both Spanish and English, dangled from the knob. My wallet lay untouched on the nightstand along with my car keys, eyeglasses, an amber vial of Ambien, and the book I'd been reading. Nothing had been disturbed except for me. I considered calling the front desk, though exactly how to phrase my complaint presented a challenge: pretty much any words I chose—*I'm in room 103, covered in crumbs!*—would make me sound crazy.

As I sat there, baffled, an image slowly formed in my mind, perhaps a scene from a dream I'd had the night before. I'm standing at the intersection of four long hallways. Before me rises a monolith that glows from within. I stare through its huge glass window at metal coils arranged in rows like the innersprings of a luminous mattress. One of the coils corkscrews toward me, pushing before it a foil-wrapped package that drops into a shallow trough near my knees and lands with a thud. The sound fills me with satisfaction; I want more thuds. I press a bunch of numbered buttons and another coil begins to turn, and still another, the bounty piling up.

The shadowy figure of a man approaches. We exchange a few words. Paper money is traded for coins. I quickly pivot back toward the machine, but my face now burns with embarrassment; I've been dressed in boxer shorts and a threadbare T-shirt this whole time. The man who gave me change is gone, but he's left me with the realization that my dream is peopled. While shoving quarters into the slot, I become dimly aware of comings and goings along the corridors. At the rounded sound of a nearby bell, several strangers walk out of the wall. Although some remote part of me realizes that the phenomenon of people emerging from the wall can be explained by the word "elevator," the word is elusive and, once I've found it, hard to retain. Still, none of this is alarming enough to send me scurrying back to my room; that people rise and descend inside a box is a fact that belongs to the physics of my waking life, about which I seem to possess a faint knowledge. What is alarming is how the people who land in the hallway turn and glance at the holes in my T-shirt, at my hairy legs and bare feet. I attempt, with great effort, a nonchalant smile. I can barely keep hold of all the junk food gripped in my fists.

Back in Los Angeles, I told myself that my raid on the vending machine was an anomaly. I didn't bother mentioning the incident to my partner, Brian, though he was a psychotherapist and no stranger to aberrations in human behavior. Before I'd left for Fresno, there'd been a precipitous drop in his T-cell count (he was HIV+ and I was HIV–) edging him closer to a diagnosis of full-blown AIDS, and so, in the larger scheme of things, my having gorged on gummy bears hardly seemed worth his concern.

My tale of gluttony might also have been an unpleasant reminder to Brian that the primary symptom of his failing immune system was his growing inability to metabolize food, no matter how much he ate, no matter how rich or frequent his meals. We'd learned of the difference in our HIV status in 1986, two years into our twenty-three-year relationship—soon after the HIV antibody test became available and national trials were being planned to determine the efficacy of a promising new drug called azidothymidine, or AZT. We'd discussed at length the risks involved in Brian's decision to try and become a participant in the trial. He had majored in psychology and minored in statistical research; he believed that his grasp of the methodology behind "blind" scientific studies would render him a candidate able to articulate the effects of AZT in both medical and anecdotal terms, which in turn would give him a slightly better than fifty-fifty chance of not only being chosen for the study, but being placed in the control group who received the drug instead of a placebo.

He was right on both counts. Waves of nausea offered him reassurance that he was ingesting the real thing, as did the neuropathy that stung his hands and feet like needles. In a world turned inside out, side effects were a harbinger of hope. Knowing that he would be called upon to describe these side effects allowed him a kind of dominion over their existence; he had to stand outside of himself and assume the observant, clinical distance he practiced when listening to his clients. This obliged Brian to find words for what might otherwise have been a kind of misery he could neither name nor escape. That year, the Centers for Disease Control estimated that 50,378 AIDS cases had been reported worldwide and 40,849 deaths had occurred since the epidemic had hit.

What no one involved with the AZT study could have foreseen was that the high dose prescribed to Brian's cohort resulted in all sixty men developing a resistance to the drug, which the virus rapidly mutated to reject. It was learned in a subsequent trial that AZT is effective only when administered at lower doses and in conjunction with other drugs, the combinations of which had to be switched like shells in a shell game in order to constantly trick the virus. During the trial, the tissue lining Brian's intestinal walls had been damaged, which meant he then absorbed fewer nutrients from food. Unable to benefit from the drug cocktail or reverse the effect on his intestines, Brian's wasting became difficult to stop. The lower his T-cell count, the more weight he lost, as if the absence of the cells themselves was measurable on a bathroom scale. At five nine, Brian had been 135 pounds when we'd first met at a local bar, and although he'd jokingly referred to himself that night as a "runt," I saw his remark for what it was: a ploy to elicit the compliments I was glad to offer if they paved the way to sex. I told him I'd never met a runt with such well-developed pecs and biceps. Now veins became prominent on his calves and forearms. His collars grew roomy, his belt loops too few.

I hadn't sidestepped the Fresno story solely to spare Brian's feelings. That night of snacking nagged at me with its utter surrender to impulse. I hadn't consciously made the decision to leave my room and look for food, and for the first time in my life I imagined the shock and indignity a somnambulist might feel when he wakes up and finds himself somewhere other than where he went to sleep, suddenly confronted with the understanding that his urges have a life of their own. The bout of morning amnesia had particularly unnerved me, reliant as I am on memory in my writing; the sheer amount of food I'd devoured was proof of a powerful craving I'd obeyed yet couldn't recall. Still, no matter how hungry I might have been, I'm too shy a person to walk into a public place wearing boxer shorts and a tattered T-shirt (a shirt I couldn't bring myself to throw away because its over-laundered softness held the very promise of sleep), though neither am I the kind of person who'd have to put on dress shoes before fleeing a burning house. I suspected that Ambien might have played a role in all this, but at that point I'd been taking it regularly for over a year and had enjoyed a run of predictable, restorative sleep without any episodes of nocturnal bingeing. In the end, the simplest explanation for what happened at the Motel 6 seemed to be this: disinhibited by a sleeping pill, I'd gone in search of something to eat, having found myself far hungrier after the long drive than I'd realized.

My doctor, after all, had instructed me not to take Ambien with food. The drug's active ingredient, zolpidem tartrate, is absorbed into the bloodstream through the stomach, so the emptier one's gut, the faster the medication works. I'd been fairly disciplined about not eating close to bedtime because I wanted the drug to metabolize as quickly as possible; I've experienced chronic insomnia since my late twenties, and I was never the kind of stayer-awake who could make those late hours productive by doing the laundry, say, or paying bills. Instead, I'd lie there and worry about how groggy and out of sorts I'd be the next day.

Under the influence of Ambien, however, I was knocked unconscious by what I'd come to think of as the chemical equivalent of a velvet sledgehammer. I could be turning the last, engaging pages of a novel, or watching a forensic expert explain blood-spatter patterns from a double homicide, when the need to sleep abruptly trumped every reason to stay awake.

Ambien doesn't work for everyone, but for the twenty-six million who make it America's most prescribed sleeping aid, its effectiveness is unequivocal. It acts as a central nervous system depressant and within about twenty minutes of ingestion, it relaxes muscles and slows brain activity by increasing gamma-Aminobutyric acid, a naturally occurring chemical in the brain that regulates messages between neurotransmitters. It allows me to turn off the whirring thought-machine—an occupational hazard for many writers—and to stop strip-mining the day's events, images, and snippets of conversation for potential insights into human nature in general, or my own nature in particular, all the while wondering how I might make use of these ruminations in my work. Consciousness may be sublime, but it's also exhausting. Six hours later, Ambien's targeted molecules are flushed from the bloodstream, which is why relatively few users experience fogginess or lingering fatigue the next morning.

My raid on the vending machine was the first instance of a sleep-related eating disorder (sleep researchers refer to this phenomenon by its acronym: SRED) that has dogged me ever since. The second instance occurred several months after my trip to Fresno. On my way to the kitchen one morning to make coffee, I was stopped in my tracks by two nearly identical orange stains on the hallway carpet. I bent over for a closer look, and there, at the perimeter of each stain, lay a wooden Popsicle stick. Since I had no recollection of eating Popsicles the night before, and since I don't even like Popsicles, I wondered if Brian, still in the bedroom dressing for work, had eaten a midnight snack. I went to ask him about it, but before I could open my mouth he asked, "What's with your T-shirt?" For the second time in my life, I looked down at my favorite threadbare T-shirt to discover indisputable evidence, writ in sticky orange, of a meal I didn't remember. "It's time," Brian added, cinching his tie, "to throw that ratty thing away."

I am an Ambien eater. I don't mean I eat the medication itself—I mean that taking Ambien causes me to feel, in the five-minute window before I conk out, a visceral and urgent hunger. Regardless of how hearty my dinner was, regardless of how unhungry I am when I turn out the light and slide beneath the covers, something shifts as I'm drifting off to sleep. First, the sharp contours of consciousness begin their predictable softening. It's not that the object of my concentration grows blurry—the printed words in a book, for example, remain typographically distinct—but the complex mental and physiological mechanisms for understanding those words and caring about what they say evaporate like water in the sun. Then, like clockwork, I'm encompassed by hunger, an emptiness swelling to the size of night itself. Next thing I know, I'm up and searching for something to eat, or more precisely, I'm asleep on my feet and hoarding provisions against what I sense is the coming of some endless dark, the earth a lifeless chunk of ice, the firmament stripped of planets and stars. What must I eat to delay or escape it? I'm rummaging through cupboards, ransacking the refrigerator, pondering the salvageability of bruised fruit, scrutinizing use-by dates, sniffing cartons of milk and Chinese takeout. What do I want? What do I want? All I need is a slice of bread. Or two, or ten. I'll harvest the fields of wheat myself. I'll wrestle with mountains of rising dough. I'll fill a yawning, infernal oven with loaf after yeasty loaf.

For the sake of gaining weight, Brian's physician advised him to supplement his meals with cans of Ensure, a viscous nutritional drink whose artificial chocolate or vanilla flavoring barely masked an insipid chemical odor that bore so little connection to the smell of any actual foodstuff that Brian sometimes held his nose as he swigged it. (Having once taken a whiff myself, I completely bypassed the shelf of Ensure during my raids on the kitchen.)

The two of us began a campaign to stock the house with food likely to whet Brian's appetite, including his own personal manna: the peanut butter we bought by the giant jarful from a bulk-food discount store that sold juice boxes by the pallet and bags of potato chips the size of bed pillows, amounts so formidable that buying a supply of chewing gum, say, became a commitment comparable to marriage. When Brian and I paused in an aisle to deliberate over a particular purchase, I sometimes asked, "Do we want to eat X for the rest of our lives?" The question hastened our decision—several foods seemed tempting in the moment but intolerable over the long haul—while also expressing my supposed certainty regarding his long-term survival, about which I felt anything but certain; the man was starving before my eyes despite continued advances in drug therapies and research. Still, voicing this question, with its implication of a future, offered me a fleeting relief from the almost continual dread of losing him, for I was the one who could better afford to contemplate for long, obsessive stretches of time—especially at night—the terrifying possibility of his death, while he permitted himself only rare, dizzying glimpses at his own demise, firmly believing that a steady diet of fear would harm his mental and physical health; "statistics show," he insisted, citing a study about anxiety's detrimental effect on the immune system.

This is not to suggest Brian was fearless, but rather to say that, of the two of us, he had always been the more logical; he was professionally trained, after all, to achieve empathy and insight through the practice of detachment. A statistician at heart, he loved the data that proved the rule, whereas I argued that literature proved the exception to the rule, and I loved it when norms were thrown into doubt. What was inarguable was the fact that I lived with a man who, while remaining fully aware of the severity of his illness, could successfully forestall thoughts of his own mortality in the name of a greater, self-preserving calm. I marveled at his self-control because it was utterly unlike the sloshing sea of emotional flotsam I found myself constantly tossed upon. Deep within me, a superstitious reflex demanded that I imagine the worst in great detail as a way to trap catastrophe in the realm of idea instead of event. It sometimes seemed to me that, by picking up the slack of Brian's worry, he would be free to fret even less, and the less he fretted—if statistics were correct—the longer he'd live.

"How do you manage to stay so optimistic?" I once asked him. I realized with a start that this question sounded like a measure of my pessimism rather than my admiration. We were in the bathroom, the mirror fogged with steam from the shower, and Brian, a towel wrapped around his waist, was applying to his shoulder the twenty-four-hour sub-dermal testosterone patch that was a new part of his routine, a hormonal prod to gain muscle mass and the weight that came with it.

"You're the optimist," he said matter-of-factly, "not me."

I must have looked puzzled.

"You're the optimist," he persisted, "because you hold out

hope that things will get better. That's what makes you afraid they won't."

Brian swiped his palm across the mirror and frankly assessed his own reflection. "Some treatment might eventually come along to break through my resistance," he said. "Or it might not. I'm walking a fine line between hopelessness and hope, and that's the line I'm going to stay on until there's a reason to move to either side."

Brian and I hated it when a friend or acquaintance referred to one of us as the other's "better half," which demoted both of us from whole. But standing beside him in the bathroom that day, I found myself so shaken by the prospect of his absence that I couldn't help but say, "I know we're autonomous and all that crap, but no matter how I try to look at it, I'm afraid I'd be nothing without you."

"*You'd* be nothing without me?" He laughed a single, propulsive laugh, then clamped the patch to his shoulder and held it there until it stuck.

Every weekday morning, Brian made three or four peanut butter and jelly sandwiches, taking them to work and forcing himself to eat one whenever he had a few extra minutes between clients. To call them snacks would be an understatement. These were the opposite of the dainty triangular tea sandwiches his mother made for her bridge club, a layer of pimento cream cheese spread as thin as tissue on crustless bread. Brian's PB&Js were glistening bricks of protein on whole wheat. They retained their shape and thickness thanks to hydrolyzed vegetable oil and artificial stabilizers. More than mere sandwiches, they were edible testaments to his will to live, cornerstones of a monument dedicated to the wonders of nut butter. They necessitated the toothbrush he kept in a desk drawer at his office in order to make sure that his mask of psychotherapeutic neutrality wouldn't be ruined by traces of Jif on his lips or teeth. He might have been especially careful in this regard after witnessing firsthand the telltale orange streaks on my now discarded T-shirt.

Although Brian told our friends that dealing with HIV was a

prolonged exercise in relinquishing control, he wrested control wherever he could. With what rigor he stuck to his drug regimen, a complex, ever-changing list of pills that he and his physician had chosen as admittedly iffy substitutes for the more potent antiviral properties of the AZT cocktail. Then there were the prophylaxis against oral thrush, pneumocystis pneumonia, and the purple skin lesions of Kaposi sarcoma, just to name a few of the life-threatening assaults one's compromised immune system could fall prey to in those days. He actually read the inserts that came with every prescription, a novel's worth of fine print folded like origami into an improbably small square. He closely monitored the compartments of his translucent blue pill case, each labeled with the day of the week.

Brian was such a dedicated advocate for his own health that I had little to do but worry on his behalf and listen to his answers when I asked how he was doing. True, I performed household tasks such as doing the laundry and cooking, but they were tasks that benefited us both; I would have done these things if I were single, and so they hardly seemed like a sacrifice on my part and didn't adequately reflect the extent of my love and concern. Nor were they proportional to the impending loss that became palpable in the dark of night, a boundless void that the Ambien eater within me believed he could shrink to the size of his stomach as long as he tried to fill himself with food.

Perhaps in my frustration at not playing a more direct role in Brian's fight against the virus, of not being even more intimate with the physical particulars of his illness—in short, because I wasn't HIV positive—I found an oblique way to know more closely what he was going through. In those days, along with Ambien, I took a common blood pressure medication called Tenormin as well as a multivitamin. To this regimen I added an amber gelcap containing ten essential minerals, as well as a chalky, almost unswallowable chondroitin and glucosamine tablet to ease the joint pain that came from working out as often as possible in order to offset the weight I stood to gain from eating in the wee hours and then falling asleep without any activity to burn off the glut. Although I'd put on a few pounds, a strange sense of bodily decorum prevented me from gaining an amount of weight conspicuous enough to make Brian even more aware of his physical diminishment. Although Brian never suggested that I needed to be more understanding of his status—although he in fact wanted to spare me an even greater sense of identification than I already possessed—taking more pills made me a kind of compatriot and justified buying a translucent blue pill case of my own. Brian suggested that my late-night eating might also indicate the early stages of an "exogenous" depression, i.e., a depression created by the circumstance of his deteriorating health in particular and the AIDS crisis in general, and he advised me to talk to the psychopharmacologist who'd first given me a prescription for Ambien. On my next visit to Dr. Hammond, a soft-spoken colleague of Brian's, I explained how my Ambien eating had become a nightly occurrence.

"I start off eating at the kitchen sink," I told him, "but I often find food on my side of the bed when I wake up the next morning."

The doctor waited.

"Bits of potato chips. I once woke up with a bagel on my chest. A trail of raisins . . ."

"This doesn't sound especially unhealthy."

"I'm not eating coffee grounds or raw meat, if that's what you mean."

"Do you stop when you're full?"

"I'm not sure I'm either hungry beforehand or full when I'm finished."

The doctor touched his pen to his lips and thought a minute. "You don't look like you're gaining weight."

"I'm exercising a lot."

"Purging?"

"Never."

"And you sleep about how long?"

"Six hours. Seven. But I have to take an Ambien every night now. I'm afraid I'm addicted."

"I have patients who've been taking Ambien every night for several years."

I shifted in my chair. "That's what I'm trying to tell you," I said. "I need it every night."

"You may be dependent at present, but the drug isn't physically addictive, and I think you'd agree with me when I say that sleep is essential, especially given the stress of Brian's illness."

"Do any of your other patients experience this eating thing?"

"Not to my knowledge."

He told me that a ten-minute window of amnesia occurs as the medication takes effect, and the best advice he could give me was to get straight into bed once I'd swallowed the pill. I didn't have the presence of mind to tell him that getting into bed wasn't the problem. The problem was getting into bed and then, with my eyes at half-mast, lurching up for the hunt as if I'd heard a trumpet.

I returned home not only with three refills on my prescription for time-release Ambien, but with a starter pack of Effexor, a selective serotonin reuptake inhibitor. Brian assured me that my concerns about taking an antidepressant and becoming a contented but affectless zombie incapable of entertaining a creative impulse or complex thought were completely unfounded.

"Besides," he reminded me, "if you don't like the way it makes you feel, you can always stop taking it."

"But what if I can't tell that I've been robbed of some essential part of my being?"

Brian rested his hand on my shoulder. "I'll be sure to let you know if that happens."

"Suppose you like me better when I'm drugged up?"

"Bernard," he said.

Effexor gave a glass floor to my night terrors; it was as if I could look down and see the abyss beneath my feet, as infinite as ever, but I stayed suspended above it without the fear of falling. While gradually ramping up my dosage as per Dr. Hammond's plan, my mood steadied and I became aware of what I can only describe as a kind of psychic insulation, soft as excelsior, that buffered me from the uncertainties of Brian's illness, from the vicissitudes of life itself. I remained a person susceptible to worry, but I knew, for perhaps the first time since the epidemic began, the kind of courage one associates with strength of character, and though

I also knew this strength was chemical in nature—from palm to mouth to bloodstream to brain—I didn't much care where it came from.

Only three side effects were worth mentioning to the doctor in our follow-up talk, and all of them turned out to be temporary: 1) although I didn't feel sleepy, I yawned dozens of times a day; 2) while I didn't suffer the erectile dysfunction I later learned is a common side effect, I did experience difficulty reaching a climax; 3) Effexor, like Ambien, had a disinhibiting effect.

As far as I could tell, the increased disinhibition that came from combining Effexor with Ambien had only one serious drawback: the peanut butter we'd stocked specifically for Brian and which I'd thus far managed to leave untouched was now fair game. Well, not *fair,* exactly; somewhere in the greedy, twilight state that propelled my forays into our kitchen, there existed the knowledge that Jif was off-limits, then to eat it was to deplete Brian's supply of the most tempting, fat-rich food in our house, and if I sleepily reamed it to the bottom, I'd have to go to the store the next morning and buy another jar. Yet the night was so immense and my sense of emptiness so distressing that ethics were muffled by existential dread. If I couldn't imagine life without Brian, wasn't his dying also mine? Wasn't his death a precipice we'd both step over?

There may have been a trace of guilt as I twisted off the lid, but it vanished when a tablespoon heaped with Jif glistened in the kitchen light. The salty-sweet glob took effort to swallow, displacing the lump of fear in my throat. For one blessed second, I believed my stomach would never be empty. For one blessed second my taste buds were eternal, the aftertaste filling my senses as an echo fills a canyon.

Not until the March 14, 2006, issue of *The New York Times* was a link between Ambien and sleep eating reported, when sleep researchers from both the Minnesota Regional Sleep Disorders Center and the Mayo Clinic had reason to suspect that something in the chemical composition of the drug made a subset of users confuse the urge to eat and the urge to sleep. The exact cause of the phenomenon eluded the medical community, but as far as I was concerned, the anecdotal data rang true.

One woman in the Minnesota study claimed to have gained one hundred pounds in a year without knowing why. Her nightly amnesia prevented her from believing her husband and sons' claims that she routinely masticated her way through their pantry late at night. For a while she blamed them for planting the empty wrappers and scraps of food she found scattered on the floor. Neither she nor her family had realized that Ambien was a contributing factor.

"These people are hell-bent to eat," said one researcher, perhaps referring to the son who found his mother, a woman otherwise bedridden from back surgery and unable to walk without assistance, standing at the stove in her full-body cast, blithely frying eggs and bacon in the middle of the night. For me, though, it was Helen Carry of Dickson, Tennessee, who most memorably described the primal, dreamlike urge to eat. "I got a package of hamburger buns and I tore it open like a grizzly bear and just stood there and ate the whole package," the fifty-seven-year-old labor and delivery nurse told researchers. Ms. Carry's husband, roused from his sleep by sounds in the kitchen, watched from the doorway, his jaw gone slack. She awoke only after her husband regained his power of speech.

Not until I read the article did I have evidence that Ambien caused me to sleep-eat, a side effect that no other Ambien user I knew (and I knew several by then) had experienced. Nor would I have guessed that, across the country, others plundered the contents of their kitchens in an urgent search they'd forget by morning, a feral pack of amnesiacs foraging through the same dark woods.

I put down the *Times* and went to check on Brian. He lay beneath the covers, eyes closed, body barely forming the raised shape of a man in repose. He wore layers of sweat clothes, a woolen toque, and two pairs of socks; since he hardly possessed any insulating fat, Brian shivered, cold to the bone. He weighed thirty-five pounds less than he had when he volunteered for the AZT study. There was nothing left to buffer the friction of bone against bone. His scalp gleamed through sparse hair. The virus had recently crossed the blood-brain barrier, and although he sometimes used the wrong words, or mistook the floor for a set of stairs, he was able to draw from his fund of lucidity when he needed it the most, or when I did.

"Here we are at the end," he said one day, "and the learning curve is steep." On another: "We're dismantling an entire life." Mostly though, silence settled between us, as meaningful as speech.

In a few weeks he'd refuse food in the hope of hastening his own death. He had warned me he would do this. He needed neither my protests nor approval. Until then, I spoon-fed him bowls of incongruous broth—incongruous because, despite his shivering, it was an unseasonably hot March in Los Angeles. The nights were as warm and sultry as the days. Sunlight and darkness grew strangely interchangeable, charged with the terrible patience of our waiting. I'd begun to take my Ambien with ice water and every night, much later in the kitchen, I'd hear ice clinking as I lifted my glass and washed down all the food I consumed, the food that couldn't sustain him.

THE DOCTOR IS A WOMAN

Sloane Crosley

I used to subscribe to a magazine that came with a postcard crammed in the spine of each issue. On one side of the postcard was a famous work of art, on the other a thin line, splitting the negative space. Standard postcard protocol. I liked the postcards mostly because I like to avoid clutter and they gave me something to throw out. Except for one. A photograph of a tent called *Everyone I Have Ever Slept With,* by the British artist Tracey Emin. Inside a camping tent, Emin had stitched the names of anyone she'd ever shared a bed with, from friends to relatives to lovers. The tent's reproduction on a postcard whittled its meaning down to the provocative title, but that was enough to save it from the trash. I put it on the mantel of my defunct fireplace, where I kept other precious keepsakes, like crumpled receipts, votive candles, and free-floating sticks of gum.

One night, as I was making dinner, I smelled something burning in the living room. Somehow the postcard had migrated near one of the lit candles and begun to smoke. I rushed to blow it out, thinking only of the vulnerability of my own belongings. But the next morning, on the cover of the arts section of *The New York Times,* was the headline "London Warehouse Fire Destroys Artworks." At 2 A.M., right around when my postcard went up in flames in New York, a fire blew through a warehouse in East London, destroying millions of dollars' worth of artwork, including the tent. I couldn't believe my eyes but then, in an instant, I could. An instant is how long it takes to convince yourself of anything—that a banging shutter is an intruder, that you could live off juice for a week, or, in my case, that I was a full-blown witch.

In the wake of my latent powers, I looked into seeing a psychic. Game recognize game and all that. I had never been to a psychic before. I figured if I want to throw my money away, I'd be better served buying six-dollar lattes. Or curling up cash into little tubes and shoving it down the drain. As far as I'm concerned, the psychics on the sidewalk are hucksters: the ones with the neon signs tell you what you want to hear and the good ones tell you what you already know. *You have a fraught relationship with your mother.* Oh, do I? Go on. They're also notoriously poor marketers. Once I walked past a door that read PSYCHIC WITHIN, which I took to mean "within me" and kept walking.

Eventually, I settled on a psychic who came recommended by a rational friend whose only point of earthly disconnect was a nonsensical aversion to gluten. She sold me on this guy using the one guaranteed pressure point for any skeptic: our own skepticism. How could I be sure that my conception of the universe is the absolute one? I could not. Technically, this fellow was an "intuitor," which I found less hubristic than "psychic." And he had an actual office, which was encouraging. The office was located in a building in the Flatiron, behind a wavy glass door. Gold lettering on the door read PLEASE KNOCK. This was less encouraging. What kind of intuitor requires a knock at the door?

He welcomed me inside, sat me down, dumped a shot of ginger into his tea, and informed me that I would have many children.

"You will have many children," he said.

"Don't you need to see my palm first or something?"

He seemed insulted. He doesn't come to my house and tell me how to turn the computer on.

"No," he said, shuffling a pack of tarot cards.

When I told him about the postcard, he was unimpressed.

For me, it was one of the crazier things that had ever happened, one of the few life events that did not fall under the purview of coincidence. I was like one of those out-of-control mutant school brats. For him, it was as if I wanted a parade for flushing the toilet.

"You are not a destroyer," he assured me, trying to rid me of an idea that had never occurred to me. "Energy is like a giant sweater. All you did was tug on a thread. And by doing that, you have created something."

"I know," I agreed. "A five-alarm fire."

"No," he said, "not that."

There were tiny bells sewn into the seam of his head scarf. They chimed as he shook his head back and forth.

"You have created the children."

"What children?"

"Yours."

"Whose?"

"Yours."

I looked over my shoulder.

"The children inside you," he clarified, pointing at my belly.

I did not sign up for this Ray Bradbury shit. It's one thing to predict the future, it's quite another to alter its course. How could I possibly have made children, nay, "many children," simply by coming here? If this were feasible, he should change his business cards and become the richest man in America.

"I don't think about children," I said.

This came out chillier than I meant it, like I was snubbing a street canvasser. It's not that I was against children. I was not one of those women who felt the need to stress how much she never played with baby dolls as a child. As if the budding embracement of the power to procreate is somehow shameful. You're not one of *those* girls. Not you. It's just that I was still in my early twenties and against participating in a version of my life in which I wound up crediting a stranger for calling my motherhood in advance.

I explained that, as a literate female, it's difficult to control the flow of stories debating the merits of motherhood, pumping women full of anxiety and presumptive regret, yammering on about the inflexibility of biological time if you want to have kids and the inflexibility of actual time after you have them. As if it's entirely in your hands anyway, which it's not if you're single or poor or both. So I had opted to turn the faucet off entirely.

Even the articles about how one is permitted to forgo babies only added to the pressure. One or two in isolation, okay. I might have read those. I'm sure they're very good. But there were just too many. The more they screamed about a woman's right to make her own stigma-free decision, the more they kept the topic in circulation. So, at the risk of remaining ill-informed about my own desires and thus engaging in the kind of self-suppression that has haunted women for centuries, I closed my eyes and tried to think of nothing. Sometimes it worked. Other times I saw a giant uterus with fallopian tube arms, terrorizing the city, ripping the crown off the Statue of Liberty before sinking into the Hudson.

"It doesn't matter," the intuitor said. "The children think about you."

Okay, I thought. Good for them. Can we get back to me being a witch?

"They're coming," he stressed.

I told him I didn't want the kind of children who show up to places uninvited. He took a sip of his tea, smiling at me as if I, too, had taken a sip of the tea. Then he shouted:

"And I'm sure your tent didn't want to be set on fire but—poof!"

For this, I gave him sixty dollars and left the building. I briefly wondered if I should tip him. Does one tip an intuitor? A retroactive tipping system might be the way to go. *Tell you what: Turns out I get eaten by that anaconda, there's a ten-dollar bill in an envelope with your name on it*. I waited in line at the coffee shop downstairs. Where was this army of babies going to come from? I had no plans to get artificially inseminated, was bothered by the mere sound of it, and, even if I did, I wasn't going to start that afternoon. At the time, I didn't have a boyfriend or even a guy friend whom I could see as the father of my child, if only he'd take off his glasses and undo his ponytail. The only thing I was expecting was a six-dollar latte.

Most children are okay once you get to know them. They're like your flakiest, least employable friend who sleeps through brunch, makes terrible art, and name-drops characters you've never heard of. They're also easy to beat at tag. Personally, I like my child friends to be at least seven years old, as there is little difference between what amuses me and what amuses a seven-year-old. But the idea of pushing a whole person through my major organs has always been simultaneously too abstract and too horrible. As someone who has met pregnant women, I can tell you that babies pound your bladder into a pancake and put your stomach level with your heart. This would be funny if women were men because the joke with men is that the way to their hearts is through their stomachs. But women are not men.

Deep down, I thought it was a moot point anyway. I secretly thought that if I ever wanted to become pregnant, a doctor would tell me that my uterus was not broken, but absentee. There's just a bunch of insulation foam where a uterus might go. The one time I had reason to purchase a pregnancy test, I peed on the stick and waited for one blue line or two blue lines. When the timer went off, I went to check on the stick. The window was blank. Like a Magic 8 Ball without the magic. I consulted the box. "Blank" was not an option. I tried again with a second stick. Same deal. So I called my mother, who is generally useless on such matters but had recently knocked it out of the park after I lamented that a guy I was dating had never heard of Gloria Steinem.

"Eh," she had said, "find out if his mother doesn't know who she is. Then you're really screwed."

I thought perhaps this comment had ushered in a new era of wisdom. I was mistaken.

"This is a good thing," she assured me about the test. "Clearly, you're not pregnant!"

"I'm not 'not pregnant,'" I said. "I'm nothing."

"Which would you rather be?" she asked. "Pregnant or nothing?"

Those were my options? For so much of history, to not be pregnant was to be nothing. And while we have mostly sloughed off such beliefs, some animal part of me was speaking up, making a strong case for "pregnant." Another minute passed before a solitary blue line appeared in the window. I sighed, relieved. But we will never know who was the remedial one, me or the stick.

As I got older, I was surprised to find it was not my fellow women who were pressuring me to have a baby or even to have an opinion. You'd think a group of people who dress for one another would also have babies for one another. Not so. While I'm acquainted with a few status moms who believe what the world really needs is more Americans, and who ask, "What are you waiting for?" as if I have—whoops!—lost track of time, none of my actual girlfriends pressed the topic. They knew better. As for the question of immortality, of pushing my bloodline into the future, well, this is not the primary preoccupation of my gender.

Yet just about every guy I dated assumed that children were at the forefront of my brain. They became increasingly vocal about this, ridding me of my need to ignore the mountain of trend pieces—they brought the mountain to me. One guy was forever sniffing out my DNA-hustling agenda. He shoehorned the topic into conversations about guacamole. *You ever try to put toothpicks through an avocado pit? If only that's how babies were made!* His lack of verbal agility hit rock bottom as we lay on the beach one summer, chatting with our chins resting on our fists. I asked him if my back was getting red and he asked me what I would do if I got pregnant.

"What are you going to do if you go bald?" I shot back.

"That's totally different," he said.

"Biologically," I agreed, "not topically."

By this time, I was thirty-four. I told him that I wasn't sure what I would do. Because I wasn't. Furthermore, I resented what I perceived to be the weaponization of my own vulnerability for the purposes of this conversation. I could tell it would have been preferable if I had sprung to my feet and drawn ABORTIONS 4EVA in the sand. Looking back, it's clear that he was building a case for himself, a verbal paper trail in which the reason it didn't work out with us was because I was in a hurry to procreate. When the truth was he just wasn't sure he wanted to have kids with *me*. Which was fair. I wasn't sure I wanted kids with me either.

There's an old riddle that goes like this: A father and son are in a car accident. The father dies instantly, and the son is taken to the nearest hospital. The doctor comes in and exclaims, "I can't operate on this boy!"

"Why not?" the nurse asks.

"Because he's my son," the doctor replies.

How is this possible?

The riddle is a good litmus test for how we're doing as a society. How quickly does the person being riddled register that the doctor is a woman? It's hard to imagine a grown individual being confounded by this brain buster—even the language, "nearest," hints that everyone in the riddle has a familiarity with one another—but I remember being stumped by it as a kid. Probably because my coterie of medical advisers consisted of a pediatrician, an allergist, and an orthodontist, all of whom were men. I was too busy cracking my teeth on hard candies, oblivious to the patriarchy.

But even knowing what I know now, I still don't understand the doctor's reaction. I don't get the setup. Why can't a mother operate on her son? Obviously, it's not ideal. Her judgment could be obscured by emotion. Someone else really should do it. But I always picture the riddle taking place in a rural town, where she is the only doctor on duty. I imagine her pacing the hall while her son bleeds out on a gurney. All because she can't pull it together. She just seems like a bad doctor and a hysterical woman, which transforms the riddle from feminist to sexist. Was this lady responsible enough to have a child in the first place? Or did she absorb so many outside opinions that she failed to develop one of her own?

By thirty-six, I was expending more energy avoiding the topic than it would have taken to address it. Like leaving instructions for houseguests about a "tricky" showerhead when all parties would be better served by a new showerhead. But by ignoring the conversation, I had put myself in conversation with the conversation. I was tired of maintaining the protective cloak of apathy I had once valued. There's a term for this in economics: *diminishing marginal utility.* It's the only economics term I know and I probably retained it for times like this, for understanding the moment when more of what used to make you happy no longer does.

Which is how I found myself, on an idle Wednesday, at a fertility center located high above Columbus Circle. I came in for a general check on my fecundity, a medical morsel to tide me over. Was I broken or not broken? This was not a debate. This was a quiz. I could take a quiz.

I sat in a waiting room with a nice view of Central Park, staring at a woman across from me as she knitted a baby blanket. At first, I dismissed this as wearing the band's T-shirt to the show. But as I watched her needles go back and forth, clacking over each other, I became hypnotized. Her pain was so palpable, it was as if the needles were the one thing tethering her to polite society. If she dropped them, she might start screaming. I felt as if I could walk over, press my finger against her forehead, and sit back down. Even as I pitied her, I was jealous. She knew what she wanted and thus had the capacity to be disappointed when she didn't get it. Whereas I was afraid that by the time I knew, there would be nothing to hope for.

More women came in with husbands or partners or mothers, each pair looking more solemn than the last. This whole place was a six-word Hemingway story. The receptionist handed the newly arrived their informational folders. On the cover of the folder were tiny baby pictures arranged to form the face of one giant baby. This struck me not only as a Chuck Close rip-off, but as poor folder design. For patients like me, pictures of babies were intimidating and foreign. For patients like the blanket knitter, pictures of babies should come with a trigger warning. The whole reason I had selected this place to begin with was because their website featured the words *Let us help you meet your family goals* superimposed over a young couple playing with a Labrador. Turns out they lure you in with the promise of puppies right before they stick an ultrasound wand up your vagina.

An ultrasound screen is something you just don't see outside of a doctor's office. You have never owned a TV shaped like the trail of a windshield wiper. So it's no wonder we cross-stitch meaning with the image before us. Ultrasounds are the place where gender makes itself known, where one heartbeat becomes two, where one heartbeat becomes none. It's package tracking for your unborn child. It was therefore unsettling to look at mine and see a wasteland of static. I was a healthy woman who wasn't pregnant, so seeing anything in there, even an extra set of house keys, would have been disturbing. But how strange to look at a live cam of one's own uterus and confront emptiness.

The technician left me in the dark as I got dressed. I felt a hollow ball of grief expand in my body, but I couldn't say what for. I couldn't even say if it was real. Should I cry at the frozen tundra of my insides? Where had I put my underwear?

After the exam, I sat across from the fertility doctor in her office while, stone-faced, she reviewed my test results. On the doctor's desk were three glass sculptures, each with a colored jellyfish blown into the center.

"Those are funny," I said.

"Oh," the doctor deadpanned, "they were a gift."

Their bright tentacles so clearly resembled fallopian tubes; I was sad for this woman who surrounded herself by people who had failed to point this out to her. She closed my chart. Then she began explaining the reproductive process from scratch. As in from conception. I nodded the way I nod when a waiter details the steak special even though I don't eat meat. At long last, she alighted upon the reason for my visit. On a Post-it note, she drew a graph, pitting age against biology. Her pen marked the precipitous late-thirties fertility drop-off so sharply, she drew on her own desk.

"You look okay," she said, "but you might want to consider freezing your eggs."

I promised her I would think about it, intending to drop the idea into my vast bucket of denial.

In the elevator, I received a "What are you up to?" text from my boyfriend. I had not told him about this appointment, not because he would get squeamish but because he wouldn't. My main purveyor of external pressure—the opposite sex—had temporarily, perhaps permanently, closed for business. Here was a man who was open with his emotions, receptive to mine, and initiated casual discussions about the future. It was extremely disorienting. I wasn't sure I knew how to have an opinion about this without blaming everyone else for making me have it.

"At doctor's appt," I texted.

"Because you're totally knocked up?" he wrote back.

I smacked straight into the elevator doors before they had opened, like a bird who hasn't figured out how to get out of its cage.

In addition to being a questionably necessary procedure—contrary to popular belief, one's uterus does not spontaneously turn into a bag of stale tortilla chips at age forty—freezing your eggs costs a fortune. The cost is so high, I hesitate to state it here because I have worked hard to suppress the pain. You can easily find out for yourself by reading one of the many articles I refused to read. The best way I can describe the financial impact is this: I had a friend in college who had two hundred CDs stolen from his dorm room during our freshman year. He had learned to accept this loss but each time he heard a song he'd forgotten he once owned, he'd crumple into a depressed lump. For years, he basically couldn't go anywhere music might be played. This is exactly how I feel about the egg-freezing bill.

What egg freezing does is give you the illusion of a plan. An expensive illusion. I've paid far less to eat mushrooms and stare at a bedspread for an hour. But the women with the resources to pony up the cash are buying themselves time, which is, arguably, the most valuable commodity on the planet. Waylaying the inevitable doesn't come cheap. For me, time was the side dish. The entrée was brain space, the ability to release the pressure of making a decision that would impact the rest of my life and, potentially, the life of an additional human. When I looked at it this way, it almost seemed like a bargain.

Before you embark on the egg-freezing process, you have to take a class. The class is mandatory but you have to pay for it, which is a bit of a boondoggle. We arrived in the order of what kind of parent we would be. Women who got there early and sat up front would be the kind of moms who put notes in their children's lunch boxes. Women who sat in the second row would remember it was Purple Shirt Day the night before and do a stealth load of laundry. Women who sat in the back would let their kids drink in the basement. I consoled myself that at least I was not the very last person to arrive. I was the second to last. But then I had to borrow a pen from my neighbor, which set me back.

We were each given flesh-colored cushions reminiscent of ergonomic mouse pads. We had to practice pinching them as if they were our own skin, and injecting them with empty vials of medication. All the cushions were Caucasian. I don't know the exact statistics regarding the racial profile of women who get their eggs frozen but I can guess. I suppose there's an argument to be made, albeit a weak one, that it's easier for beginners to practice on something pale, to see the contrast of the needle on a mound of white-girl pseudo-flesh. But since such a creature does not exist in nature, I don't see the harm in manufacturing them all in violet or mint green.

The women in my class were advanced fertility chess players. I couldn't understand how they knew so much already. They were eight moves ahead, their hands flying skyward as they asked questions about dosages and hormone levels and how soon they could pop their frozen eggs back from whence they came. One lady asked if it was okay to have sex during the process, which is just showing off. Overwhelmed by the naked want they all shared, I stress-pinched my flesh wad. My heart raced from peer pressure. In the weeks to come, as I laid out needles like a mad scientist, consulting YouTube videos for each injection, experiencing foul moods that dripped down to my heart like black syrup, I would amuse myself by saying, "The real bitch of this whole thing is that they made us take that fucking class."

The only useful tidbit I learned is that the female reproductive system is just as dog-eat-dog as a man's. Every month, all the eggs vie to be the power egg. This queen-bee egg forces the other eggs to sulk in the corner, presumably with such bad self-esteem issues you wouldn't want one of them as your kid anyway. I had no idea that eggs were competitive like sperm. This is something we should toss into middle school health curriculums, if only for the sociological implications. My entire life, I have assumed that eggs were passive creatures, inert trophies to be earned by ambitious sperm. I blame Woody Allen.

The first step in egg freezing is to hormonally democratize this dictatorship. You inject vials of drugs into your abdomen to persuade that one egg to let everyone have a chance. At the end of two weeks, you are briefly knocked out while your eggs are popped in a freezer. And that's that . . . with one tiny snag. Whatever symptoms of PMS a woman has when she normally gets her period exist in proportion to that one egg. One egg's worth of headaches. One egg's worth of bloating. One egg's worth of wondering why everyone in your life is such a goddamn disappointment.

The average egg-freezing cycle produces between eight and fifteen eggs.

You do the math.

But first, the drugs.

The hormones alone can cost up to two thousand dollars. When I unleashed this information on my therapist, she told me she had another patient who had just undergone the process and had leftover medication. I was delighted. Especially given how much therapy costs. I had always assumed that if I bought mass quantities of drugs on the black market, they would be recreational in nature, but here we were. My therapist—our therapist—introduced us over email and we arranged a time for me to come pick up the stuff.

The woman was an Indian lawyer who lived in an apartment in Chelsea, a large doormanned co-op with aggressive lobby art and confounding elevator buttons. The interior of her apartment could only be described as palatial. No wonder she was giving away drugs like candy. When I stepped inside, I was asked to remove my shoes and handed a pair of "guest slippers." In my house, I only have "guest hotel shampoos." She had changed into leggings and a T-shirt after a long day of deploying her expensive education. We stood on either side of her kitchen island.

"So, how long have you lived here?" I asked.

"About three years," she said. "I know it doesn't look like it."

"No, no," I said, "it definitely looks like it."

Visible through her open bedroom door was a large flat-screen television. *The Bachelor* was on.

"I moved in after my divorce."

"Oh," I said. "Cool."

It's hard enough to make small talk with a stranger without knowing you have the same therapist. There's a subtle jockeying for sanest. What you're both really thinking is: What are you in for?

"So you need three boxes of the Menopur and two of the Follistim, right?"

The top half of her body was obscured by the open refrigerator door as she stood on her tippy-toes.

"Yes," I said. "Thank you so much."

"You're aware that I'm selling these, right?"

"No," I said, "I was not aware of that."

"It's at least a thousand dollars' worth of medication." She stated the facts.

"That's why I was so grateful," I said, trying to laugh it off. "This is awkward."

"I couldn't figure out why you were being so nice about it," she mused.

"Nice" didn't begin to describe it. In our emails, I had referred to her as a "lifesaver" and a "saint." I told her she was "doing her good deed for the year." I was in for a financially and physically arduous ride, and the idea that a stranger with a heart of platinum would be so generous had renewed my faith in the capacity of women to support each other.

Later that evening, I went back and examined our correspondence. Sure enough, she had clearly listed prices next to the name of each medication. The numbers were unmistakable. The issue was, she had left the dollar signs off. That's how many boxes of drugs there are—it takes real time to type the dollar signs. Because I had never done this before, I assumed all those numbers were milligrams or micrograms or marbles. But the emails were not the point. Why would I assume a total stranger would part with such expensive items for free?

I wanted so badly to find just one loophole of ease, my subconscious made it so. I immediately began making justifications to myself about how I was right and she was wrong. She had found something incongruous about my appreciation and had ample opportunities to clarify the situation before I was standing in her kitchen. Not to mention the fact that these drugs had been in her possession for almost a year and would expire in a month, which meant she needed to find a buyer pronto. Selling them online would be illegal. If I knew that, she definitely knew that. Would she rather consign them to the dumpster or donate them to a clinic than give them to me? Absolutely she would.

I explained that if I was going to pay full price for nearly expired drugs, I might as well just be an upstanding citizen about it and go through a pharmacy.

"Well," she said and shrugged. "Good luck with it."

No negotiation. Case closed. She wasn't doing it to be spiteful. She wasn't even annoyed, as I surely would have been if the slipper were on the other foot. She was doing it because it was time to draw a line in the sand. She had gone through two rounds of egg freezing with negligible results. Her husband had left her for a younger woman. She was forty-four, spent her days thinking about fairness on behalf of other people, and she felt owed. And she was owed. Just as every woman who smiles through a lifetime of complicated biology and double standards is owed. But tonight, I was going to be the one to pay her.

On the television in the bedroom, a tearful girl told the camera how much she regretted "putting herself out there." I wondered if I should tell my therapist about this incident or if this woman would beat me to it.

Only the Upper West Side, a neighborhood that caters to the yet-to-be-born and the on-their-way-out, would be host to a pharmacy that specializes in both fertility meds and compression socks. I stood in line, eyeing bars of Reagan-era soap and a stunning variety of pastel candies. I tried to imagine the woman who had spent the past nine decades figuring out exactly which flavor of pastel candy she liked the best. When it was my turn, I relinquished my credit card to a cashier, who had to pry it from my fingers. As money had apparently ceased to have any meaning, I selected a couple of overpriced hair clips while he filled a supermarket bag. A few customers cast sympathetic looks in my direction. What would have to be so wrong with you that you'd walk away from a prescription counter with a shopping bag full of drugs?

"You want me to throw an ice pack in there?" asked the cashier.

"Why not?" I said. "Go crazy."

None of the medication required refrigeration unless you were going to store it for an extended time, and so long as you didn't do anything brilliant like rest it on a radiator. But at this juncture, I would take anything I didn't have to pay for. *Do you want me to throw a patty of petrified horse shit in there? Sure, why not? You only live once.*

I went straight home, put the bag on my kitchen counter, tossed the ice pack in the freezer, and threw on a dress. It was New Year's Eve. I was putting the "new year, new you" diets to shame. I would start the year as a grown-up card-carrying member of my gender, as someone who makes proactive health decisions and cowers before the reality of the future, as woman-shaped flesh wad.

The next day, I decided to familiarize myself with the drugs. I stood in my kitchen across from the bag, staring at it. But when I got up the nerve to peer inside, there were no drugs. Just the syringes, the needles, and a portable toxic waste container for disposing of them. I touched the bottom of the paper, thinking vaguely of trapdoors. I could feel the anger spread across my skin. The cashier had forgotten to put my entire order of medication in the bag. Naturally, such a thing had never happened with a five-dollar prescription but of course it had with the fifteen-hundred-dollar one.

I had all of New Year's Day to stew and pace. I called when the pharmacy opened the following day, displaying a kind of barely contained rage for which I expected to be rewarded. Anything short of murder warranted a gold star. But their records showed I had picked up the medication. I explained the difference between paying for something and leaving with it. I was not trying to swindle them. I don't need the extra needles for my side gig as a methadone addict. I barely wanted these needles. I threatened to take pictures of the empty bag. Still, they maintained the drugs were in there.

"There's nothing here," I said. "There was only an ice pack and I put it in—"

There are moments in life when one literally stops in one's tracks. Usually you have to see a wild animal or a celebrity you thought was dead.

"Will you please hold?"

I opened my freezer and removed the foil pack. For the first time, I noticed a seam at the top. I ripped it open. Inside was a packet of ice the size of a playing card and boxes of medication stickered with the words HUMAN HORMONE, DO NOT FREEZE.

The reality of what I had done took no time to sink in. I, who only four nights prior had registered the wasted cab fare to Chelsea, had just destroyed fifteen hundred dollars' worth of medication by tossing it into the freezer like a bag of peas.

One wonders what I would do with an actual child.

The pharmacy had neglected to sticker the foil pouch itself and kindly agreed to send me new drugs. My case was easy to make. Improperly labeling medication is not an offense I came up with. Still, how could *two* of these misunderstandings have occurred in forty-eight hours? Has anyone's ambivalence ever run so deep? Before we hung up, I asked the pharmacist how many functioning adults had ever done what I did. He pretended to scan his memory. The answer was none. I was the "hot coffee" case of the reproductive-medicine world. Next time you think to yourself, "What kind of idiot doesn't understand that coffee is hot?" know that the answer is: This kind.

In order to freeze your eggs, you must give yourself two different types of shots, one in the morning and one in the evening, always within an hour of the time you gave yourself the first shot. This is as elaborate as it sounds. Especially compared with every other medication I'd ever taken, for which I needed only a working esophagus. My boyfriend offered to do the injections for me.

"It'll be a good bonding experience," he said, afflicted as he is with a fondness for the bright side.

"It's not like I have to take them in the ass," I reasoned.

"I'm not even touching that rationale," he said and backed off.

Some of the shots burn, others bruise, all of them force you to abandon your squeamishness around needles. The margin of error is significant. One day I didn't mix in all the saline. Another day I managed to go through all the steps and somehow wound up with an unused needle, which is a bit like winding up with extra IKEA dresser parts, but slightly worse because you're injecting the dresser into your body. Another day I sliced my finger open removing the sheath from a mixing needle. It was such a precise cut, it took a second to get comfortable with its existence before bleeding all over the place. Freezing your eggs is essentially a cheap way to become a registered nurse. But by the time you know what you're doing, you don't need to do it anymore.

Meanwhile, I went into the fertility center every day to get reacquainted with the wand. One morning, as I lay back and put my feet in the stirrups, I announced that it was the darnedest thing—the hormones were having zero effect on me. No tears, no mood swings, no irrational behavior. Finally, I was excelling at something. Then the doctor on duty turned off the lights as I was in the middle of reading from a list of questions. I cleared my throat.

"Can you just ask me during the exam?"

Perhaps I have mentioned that the exam entails a wand being shoved into your body. Not the ideal time for a Q&A.

"But you turned the lights out."

"Don't you have them memorized?" she asked.

"No," I said, feeling my voice crack. "That's why I wrote them down."

I started crying. Hysterically. Inconsolably. People outside the door probably thought I'd lost a whole baby. The doctor removed the wand and flicked the lights back on.

"It's the hormones."

I sat up. I shook my head but was too busy sobbing to speak. It was, most definitely, not the hormones. The Venn diagram of financial, psychological, and physical strain was more of a total eclipse. What's worse, I had subjected myself to all this voluntarily. I had reasons to cry. My problem was that, once triggered, I couldn't seem to get it under control. And for argument's sake, let's say it was the hormones. It seemed borderline dangerous to point it out. Try asking a pregnant woman if she's in a bad mood because of the hormones and see what happens.

My boyfriend was out of town but offered to come back early for the procedure. As a longtime mostly single person, I appreciated this relationship perk. This was right up there with going to the bathroom at the airport without having to drag your luggage into the stall with you. That and the general reprieve from being viewed by society as either threatening or pitiable. But I discouraged him. It's fifteen minutes, I explained. A power nap. People go back to work afterward. I did, however, inform my parents that I was going under anesthesia. Which meant I had to tell them why.

"I told you so," said my mother. "You *do* have a uterus!"

I asked my friend Sara to retrieve me. Hospitals won't let you walk out the door by yourself, which really makes you wonder if they're fixing people in there. Before I went under, I asked the anesthesiologist what would happen if I didn't fall asleep. Most people, she said, wondered what would happen if they never woke up. I told her this seemed like a nonsense question. Who cares? You'll be dead. Your concerns are minimal.

Again, one wonders how I would speak to an actual child.

I don't remember waking up from the procedure—"harvesting," if you'd like to lose your lunch—but apparently I was less than pleasant. When Sara tried to force-feed me a saltine, I told her to "eat it." From a padded chair, I watched other women sign their discharge papers and go, flying away to their lives. Eventually, a doctor came over and pulled a chair up next to mine. I lolled my head in her direction, waiting for her to do something insidious like ask me to take a sip of apple juice.

The doctor was younger than I was. Triangular pink diamonds swayed from her earlobes. Definitely a gift, but from whom? She was young enough for the answer to be "Daddy." As she scooted forward, the concern on her face came into focus. She looked like the kind of lady who might refuse to operate on her son.

I *knew* it, I thought. I knew that my body would not behave as it should, that all my inklings about not being a real woman had been correct.

"Something a bit unusual happened during the procedure," said the doctor.

Unusual? I rolled the word around the padded walls of my brain. Like they had to give me more drugs than expected "unusual" or they staged a revival of *Gypsy* over my unconscious body "unusual"?

Evidently, my eggs were fine, now crowded cozily together in a petri dish. But at sixty-seven, the club was at capacity.

"What?!"

I was awake now. I looked at Sara to make sure she had heard the same thing. Sixty-seven is not within the range of numbers listed in pamphlets. It's a gaudy amount of eggs for a human to produce. On some core level, I was thrilled. To go through all this and get three eggs is like reading all of *Ulysses* only to discover the last page has been ripped out. But I was also disturbed. I felt disconnected from my body, as if it had been trying to tell me something for years and I hadn't been listening. Or I had been listening but had heard the wrong thing. Because I was right. I am not a woman—I am a fish.

Sara promptly told me that I had "ruined caviar" for her.

"How often are you sitting around, eating caviar?"

"Often enough."

How, I wondered, had the daily wand molestings failed to see this coming?

"Because they were so packed in," explained the doctor, cupping her hands to approximate the shape of an egg, "like a vending machine."

"Gross," Sara and I said in unison.

One of the benefits of having gone through something so specific is the ability to rehash the details with other people who have gone through that same specific thing. We may be done with our subcutaneous injections but our subcutaneous injections are not done with us. But I learned quickly to keep my mouth shut about my egg number. If it came up, I changed the subject or indicated that the procedure had gone fine. It's a pass/fail world and I passed. Number disclosure is considered as gauche as bragging about your massive pay increase for doing the exact same job as your coworker. Many women find it insensitive. It's how I feel about straight-haired beauties who get a thrill out of humidity. Know your audience, I think, tallying up a lifetime of hair products, keeping my hands in my pockets so I don't throttle these shaggy-banged bitches. Seeing as how we're dealing with the potential for human life, the throttling urge is that much stronger.

To so badly want a baby and not be able to have one is a peerless brand of devastating. Everyone knows this. Fictionally, it turns women deranged (*The Hand That Rocks the Cradle*) and men monstrous (*The Handmaid's Tale*). In real life, it just makes everybody sad. I am not in the habit of making people feel bad about themselves when they can do that on their own. And if it were just about hurt feelings, I'd continue to stay mum. I wouldn't even have revealed my number here. But there was something rotten in the state of Denmark.

By freezing my eggs, I had stuck my toe into the world of competitive female biology. Women who had plenty of eggs retrieved (but still within the realm of reason) confessed something like pride in their number. They flaunted their results under the guise of relief. I want to distinguish myself from them. I was not so lucky as I looked, I explained. My big payout had come at a high cost. Mo' eggs, mo' problems. After the procedure, I was treated to a panoply of medical complications including a *Tales from the Crypt*–style syndrome in which one's abdominal region retains multiple liters of water in ten hours. For me, this also resulted in a bonus surgery. Boy, had I been through the wringer!

I listened to myself recite all this, trying to fend off judgment. Was it really necessary for me to drag out stories of additional specialists in order to justify telling the truth? *I won the lottery but my dog exploded, so, you know.*

But even the complications couldn't get me out of jail. When I told a friend who'd always been dyspeptic about having kids, she was unable to hide her disgust.

"See?" she said, assured of her own choices. "This is why it's not worth it."

Which is a bit like critiquing someone's email to their ex after they've sent it.

When I told one mother of three, she replied with: "Well, now you know what it feels like to be pregnant." Not quite. Being pregnant is a natural occurrence. You don't become six months pregnant over ten excruciating hours. It is my understanding that you also get a baby out of it. Now whose turn was it to be offended?

This was getting ugly.

The thing is, even if I had produced two eggs, I like to believe I would have been forthright about it. It's impossible to say. But I know for certain that focusing on the math as the defining moment of one's life only perpetuates the idea of fertility as identity. This isn't the seventeenth century. Nor is it the dystopian future. There doesn't have to be social meaning. There only has to be personal meaning. Tell everyone, tell no one. Read the articles, don't read the articles, find kinship or alienation in them, it doesn't matter. By virtue of them being written by someone else, none of them are prescribed for you and you alone. When it comes to your own life, there is only one location in the world where the right decisions are being kept. Which, come to think of it, is the kind of thing I would tell an actual child.

The children are coming, the children are coming. I would have sent that intuitor his tip if I hadn't just broken the bank proving him right. My transcendental Paul Revere had succeeded where a magic wand had failed. But his prophecy felt less ominous now.

The children are en route, okay, but they could always change their minds. My eggs are frozen in a cryobank in Midtown—they don't have any travel plans. For months after the procedure, I would get automated updates from the cryobank using language that made me feel as if I'd arranged to freeze my head.

Then one day I was walking up my apartment stairs, flipping through junk mail, when I came across an envelope with the cryobank's logo. My eggs had never sent me actual mail before. *Camp is fun. We are cold.* The letter explained that enclosed was "a representative photomicrograph of your oocytes frozen during the cryopreservation cycle." I mean, they really go out of their way to make it sound like you're freezing your head. I moved the letter aside to reveal a piece of paper with a black-and-white photograph of my eggs. They looked like the marks that would appear if you pressed a pen cap into your skin sixty-seven times. Or craters on the surface of some very distant moon.

They are just floating fractions of an idea. I know that. But I had never seen a part of my body exist outside my body before. I felt such gratitude. My eggs had held up their end of the bargain. They had saved me from having to think about them, which, for the first time in my life, made me want to think about them. This doesn't mean I know what will become of them. Maybe I have a baby. Maybe none. Maybe eight. Maybe I sell them all on the black market, buy a townhouse, and forget this whole thing ever happened. But sometimes when I'm alone, I run my fingers over the photo, even though it doesn't feel like anything. I focus on one egg at random, imagining this will be the one my body uses to make a person, a person that grows up and reads this, and I think—Oh girl, I hope you set the world on fire.

LOITERING

Charles D'Ambrosio

> *In the manner of the police blotter: On the night of July 8 a call was received saying a man was beating his girlfriend at 110 Vine Street in Belltown. Police responded and a hostage situation ensued. The man gave himself up, after an all-night standoff, at ten in the morning. . . .*

This is totally false, but for the sake of the story let's say the events in question begin around 2:00 A.M., just because that's when I show up on the scene. The events as I find them are fairly meaty by big-league journalistic standards, involving domestic violence, assault and battery, a hostage, a gunman—all of which, I realize, could easily (and most often does) play itself out in lonely, tragic, and unobserved ways—but there's also, this night, cordons of yellow police ribbon closing off several blocks in Belltown, maybe fifty cops, a spooky antiterrorist vehicle the color of some nightmare rodent, plus a ruck of TV news reporters and their retinue of technicians. This guy—the Bad Guy—apparently thought he was just going to drink a few beers and bounce his girlfriend against the walls and go to sleep, but instead of a little quiet and intimate abuse before bed he's now got major civic apparatus marshaling for a siege outside his window. No sleep for him tonight, and no more secrets, either, not at this unholy intersection of anomie and big-time news. The story's been taken away from him, and other people are now trying to affect the plot. The police have a story they'd like to tell and so do the media folks and so, I suppose, do I, although in the hierarchy of things I suspect I'm just as clueless as the Bad Guy. When I arrive at First and Vine he's busy negotiating by phone. He wants to know what kind of trouble he's in.

The falling rain makes a pleasant hum on the asphalt, but barely a block away the whole city gives out, dissolved in a granular fog, and I dreamily sense that out there, out beyond the end of the avenues and streets where right now the only destination I see is murk, there might be silence again, a silence we might enter and lose ourselves in and thereby forget all this cowboy business of guns and women. Meanwhile, back in the real world, my first instinct is a sort of stupid ducking motion I've learned from the movies, and I have the sure sense I'm going to be shot in the neck, where I feel particularly exposed and vulnerable. At first I don't know in which building the guy's holed up, and I assume it's one of the high-rise Miami Beach–style architectural monstrosities that distort the human scale of this, the north end of Belltown. But this assumption is just pure cornball stuff, and I'm instantly aware that everything I feel and think is little more than the coalescence of certain clichés, that the Bad Guy isn't a madman barricaded in the top floor of the tallest building, that he doesn't necessarily plan to take potshots at pedestrians and commuters on their way to work, that he might just be drunk and deranged and wondering how he came to this strange pass on an ordinary evening that began normally enough and is now in the wee hours rapidly going to hell. In short, I don't know anything about him, beginning with the most fundamental thing, like where he is.

Not knowing where he is translates pretty soon into a polymorphous fear, and now it's not just my neck constricting, but also my shoulders and my stomach and my balls, the fear having spread practically right down to my toes as I vividly imagine all the places a bullet can enter the body, and I try to squat casually behind a cement wall—casually because I don't want to embarrass myself in front of the gathering pack of seasoned hard-core TV news journalists, who frankly seem, with all their unwieldy equipment and their lackadaisical milling around, like sitting ducks—until it occurs to me that the whole notion of being "behind" anything is a logistical matter I can't quite coordinate, since I don't know where the Bad Guy is. A ballistic line from point A (Bad Guy) to point B (author's neck) can't be established just yet, and for all I know I might actually be casually squatting right in front of him, cleanly fixed between his sights. In deer and elk hunting there's a moment when you sight your quarry, when everything is there, and you feel the weighty potential of the imminent second in your every nerve, and this weight, this sense of anticipation, this prolepsis, can really screw up your shot. It's as if the moment were vibrating, taking on static interference from the past and the future, and success depends on your ability to still it, to calm yourself through careful breathing right back into the singular present. The condition is variously called buck or bull fever, and I'm now feeling a variant of that, imagining myself notched neatly in the iron sights of the Bad Guy's gun. My fear is as vaporous and real and enveloping as the rain and fog, and I have this not-unfamiliar feeling of general and impending doom.

This might seem unnecessarily preambular, but I also want to say my pants are falling down and I'm sopping wet. I came back from salmon fishing in Alaska with a severe case of atopic dermatitis primarily caused by contact with neoprene. I had what's called an "id" reaction—pretty much systemic—and all week my fingers and neck and feet and legs were puffy and disgusting, with weeping sores. I think my condition even freaked the dermatologist. My hands were so raw and inflamed I wasn't able to type, hold a pen, or turn the pages of a book. Because I don't own a television my week of forced zombiism passed without distraction and nothing to gnaw on but my own increasingly desperate thoughts. I lay in bed, staring at the ceiling, the walls. It was a new kind of aloneness for me, being imprisoned in my own skin. It was easy to imagine never being touched by another human being ever again. The dermatitis made my skin crawl, and I was taking forty milligrams of prednisone, a steroid that cruelly kept me awake so as, it seemed, to fully and consciously experience my suffering in a state of maximum alertness. I mention all this to establish a certain oblique connective tissue between observer and observed, between myself as witness and the thing witnessed. Half the reason I'm at the crime scene is I haven't had any human contact for a while, and besides I can't sleep with my skin prickling (and the other half of why I'm standing in the rain at two in the morning is I'm probably some kind of tragedy pervert). When I got back from Alaska my hands were already painfully suppurating and I couldn't carry all my bags and grabbed only the expensive stuff, the rods and reels, leaving a duffel of clothes in my truck. The next time I could put on shoes and walk, three days later, the neighborhood crackheads had stolen my clothes, including my only belt and my only raincoat, and that's why my drawers droop and I'm soaked and starting to shiver a little in this mellisonant humming rain.

But I didn't come to this crime-scene-in-progress innocently. Before leaving the apartment I put a pen in my pocket, along with a stack of three-by-five cards and a tape recorder, thinking that if this thing got real hairy, if there was actually some shooting, then I might jot a few notes and make of an otherwise blank night a bona fide journalistic story, full of who, what, where, when. Like a lot of my aspirations, this one, too, was internally doomed and hopeless long before I realized it. My main problem vis-a-vis journalism is I just don't have an instinct for what's important. I realize that now, looking over my notes. My first note was about the old alleys in Seattle, those island places where sticker bushes flourish and a man can still sleep on a patch of bare earth, where paths are worn like game trails and leave a trace of people's passing, and how these naturally surviving spots are systematically vanishing from the city, rooted up and paved over mostly because they house bums—an act of eradication that seems as emotionally mingy as putting pay slots on public toilets, but is probably cost-effective in terms of maintenance, since bums generate a lot of garbage in the form of broken glass and wet cardboard. Then I started another note about how, in contrast to these hardscrabble plots, the flower beds and parking strips of lush grass and manicured shrubs and trees are pampered and how, currently, it's maybe three in the morning and all up and down the street automatic sprinklers spit and hiss in the rain, redundantly watering.

Also my notes bleed black ink and blur in the rain as I write them. I don't write a note about that.

But after investigating the alley it occurs to me there's a whole parking lot full of highly paid professional journalists just loafing around and that some of them might answer a few questions. I'm not properly credentialed and I'm feeling a little timid because, with my falling-down pants, my soaking wet waxed-cotton coat, and my sore, swollen, hideous, raw red fingers, I don't look nearly so crisp and ready to report news as these people, and in fact, the way I look, I might be an escapee from the other side, I might just *be* a piece of news myself, but I need to approach them and find out what's going on and, if nothing else, I'd really like to fix on a location for the Bad Guy. Certainly these journalists know the scoop, otherwise they wouldn't look nearly so bored and unconcerned. Watching them from a distance, I have the feeling we're all waiting for dawn and that dawn, in turn, will bring us death; the atmosphere is straight out of an old Western, where the man gets hanged at sunup. I mean this whole aimless scene badly needs a plot, and nothing emphasizes that more than these journalists, these TV people, standing around in a parking lot scattered with expensive equipment that now waits idly for . . . *something*. All this inaction is underscored and made emphatic by the sheer number of journalists flocking in the lot, which creates a sense of collective anticipation, a weird hope. Really it would be a relief if that gun would go off.

In a kind of illustrated food chain of journalism there are big white vans representing every major TV station in Seattle and then several shrimpy economy cars, also white, with the names of radio stations printed on the doors. I notice every journalist is wearing a particularly nice raincoat, with team colors. Then I notice other things, like the cameras, the monitors, they too are covered in specially made rain bonnets. And a couple of people are walking around with umbrellas the size of parachutes. All these dry people are from another tribe. This kind of hard-hitting, high-level journalism obviously requires neat hair, which partly explains all the first-rate rain gear, and that equipment can't be cheap, not like three-by-five cards. One of the TV reporters is wearing navy-blue pants and a red coat, an outfit that resembles the unsexed uniform of a reservations clerk for a national hotel chain. Another TV guy is practicing a look of grave concern in his monitor, a look that, live at least, seems woefully constipated. It's weird to watch what amounts oxymoronically to a rehearsal of urgent news, especially without sound, emptied of content, because this pantomime of immediacy is patently fake, a charade, a fine-tuning, not of emotions, but the reenacted look of emotions. It's method acting or something. In a curious twist, I realize I always knew TV news seemed full of shit, but I never knew it was, in fact, full of shit. Previously I thought the TV news had a certain endemic phoniness because all the reporters were sorority girls who'd majored in communications, but it never occurred to me that the fakery was intentional. These people do this on purpose, and realizing that stunned me, because all my life I'd generously overlooked the canned quality of broadcast journalism, thinking it was, like other infirmities, something these people couldn't help. I thought they were just naturally corny people and no more deserving of scorn than cripples, and in fact were entitled, because of their impairment, to an extra helping of tolerance and understanding on my part. And now this morning I'm learning that that peculiar phony quality really is phony.

It's all big-time wrestling.

It occurs to me I'm not supple enough of an ironist to be alive and freely moving around in public anymore. With my skin practically leprous I might just hang a cowbell off my neck and clang around town the rest of my days. I'm not going to mention the name of the big-league TV journalist I finally talked to because later in the morning, in between taping the twenty-five seconds of filler that feeds into the national show, he tried on a couple occasions to pick up secretaries who'd come out on the sidewalk to gawk. Every time I turned around he was chatting up another secretary, then he'd rush in front of the camera and morph into the face of a slightly panicked and alarmed person nevertheless manfully maintaining heroic control while reporting nearby horrors. To look at his on-camera face you'd think Godzilla was eating lawyers off the Winslow ferry. It was clear to me that sometime in the past the putative luster of his job had landed him in bed with bystanders.

But before that, I thought he might be a reliable source of information.

"Hey," I said, "what do you think of this?"

"It's wet," the guy said, and then, I kid you not, he lit up a cigarette and squinted at the sky—just like a hero of some sort.

In a study of poetics you'd call that kind of rhetorical understatement "meiosis." In its most simple metalogical form it works by deadpanning the ostensive situation (the Bad Guy with the gun, the hostage, homicidal intent) by rerouting it through the bluntly obvious and uninteresting observation that it is raining. This kind of locution can be found in *King Lear* and some of Auden's poetry, and it's nearly a national mental disease in England, plus it's pretty common in war, where the irony functions as an anodyne against other, more painful emotions.

Putting moves on secretaries, phony-faced reports, meiosis—you can't finally penetrate the pose to anything real.

I walk off and get my story by eavesdropping on a wondrously cute black woman wearing a blue coat, the back of which quite clearly states, in reflective block letters, her purpose: SEATTLE POLICE MEDIA RELATIONS. She's exactly what I've been looking for, maybe all my life. She's the unambiguous source of everybody else's story anyway. The most interesting thing I learn is there's no hostage.

"Is there a reporter here?" some guy demands to know.

His voice wavers with anger but his question floats unanswered and hangs ignored in a rude silence until, unnerved, I point to the parking lot and say, "Yeah, there's tons of them. They're all over the place."

Even as I watch the guy walk off I know in a low-frequency animal-to-animal way that he's the one, the man I need to talk to. Some part of this story is lodged inside him. In terms of clothing alone he's way worse off than I am, and what he's wearing, jeans and a T-shirt, shows he's been rudely expelled from one cozy circumstance and dragged against his will into the rain. He's now caught in between, trapped in some place I recognize as life itself. It's obvious he hasn't been sober in hours and maybe years. If it could be said that these big-deal journalists have control of the story, and therefore, in a fundamental sense, are liars, albeit professional and highly compensated, then this guy is the anti-journalist because in his case the story is steering him, shoving him around and blowing him willy-nilly down the street. The truth is just fucking with him and he's suffering narrative problems. He began the night with no intention of standing in this rain, and his exposure to it is pitiful. As he moves unheeded like the Ancient Mariner through the journalists I feel a certain brotherly sympathy for him, and I'm enamored of his utter lack of dignity. He's moved beyond all poses. I know he'll come back to me, that it's just a matter of a little more rejection, and when he returns, when he settles on me, I'll welcome him like a prodigal.

He doesn't know it yet, but I'm the only one who will listen to him.

Meanwhile we're at the edge of dawn, a first feathering of gray light that brings a bum stampede to the streets of Belltown. I live down here, and every morning at roughly five o'clock bums pour out of the missions and shelters and alleys in a kind of shabby and shadowy pre-commute, followed by the real thing an hour or two later. They pool up and briefly form a chorus. They fish around in squashed packs of GPC cigarettes, fire up. "Look at these news-media dicks," they say. Lights have come on in the IBEW Local 46 building and a few guys with lunch buckets are standing outside the Labor Temple Restaurant and Lounge. More and more people are standing around, trying to figure out what's going on. When the bums ask what's happening the question sounds yearningly metaphysical or like a child stirring from a dream. Their need to know, at any rate, is tonally different than that of a big-league journalist. And still we've got beaucoup reporters doing their insane pantomime of sincerity in the parking lot. It's like the Hitler tryouts in that Mel Brooks movie *The Producers*. None of the TV people have budged from encampment in the parking lot, and I realize they're operating under the strictest criterion of relevance—every camera is focused in the same direction—and that their sense of the narrative is, generally, in sync with the police, that is, their reason for being here will end in a roughly coincident moment.

The guy's back. No one will listen to him, he's just learned.

"These fucking cops," he starts right up. "These goddamn pigs! They said there's no room on the bus. Me and my friend been standing in the rain all night. I'm a vet and he's an American Native. That ain't right. And these fucking assholes—you don't believe me? Here's my card."

He shows me his veterans ID, establishing his credentials, his suprapatriotic right to feel and also express his grievous outrage.

"That's some real shit," he says. "Dennis R. Burns. U.S. Army Retired."

I tell him my first name.

"You know anybody?" he asks.

"You mean, like, somebody that could do something? Like Jesus Christ?"

"You a Born Again?"

"I was just joking."

"I know somebody," Dennis says.

I ask him if he knows what's going on.

"Yeah, got a guy with a gun, big black guy, 110 Vine Street, apartment #210. L. was throwing furniture at his girlfriend. This was about midnight. I'm the one that called the police, stupid me. I'm the maintenance man. L.'s generally a quiet guy, a little hypertensive, but nice. Very intelligent, well spoken."

"So he has a gun?"

"He's got two, a 9mm and something else, like a .357. I hope they don't hurt the man. Are you a journalist?"

"I'm really wet. You want some coffee?"

"What happened to your hands?"

"They're all fucked up. It's not contagious or anything."

"Are you a reporter?"

"Yeah," I say.

"7-Eleven's open. We could get coffee at 7-Eleven."

On the way there I pull out my Olympus Pearlcorder S803—*testing, one, two, three*—and discover the batteries are dead.

"You sure you're a journalist?" Dennis says. "Hey, my son's an editorial cartoonist for the *Albuquerque Times*. He makes fun of everything—politicians, everything. He's always got a shitty fucking look on his face—like you."

On the way back from 7-Eleven with our coffees we hook up with Tom, who's drinking something throttled in a brown bag. He tells me, "I been up all night and I'm getting kinda moody. We were just gonna get drunk and listen to Elton John or some Asian music. But this gunman kept me up all night."

"And they wouldn't let us on the bus," Dennis says. And then he asks, "You ever write about Veterans Affairs?"

I feel bad I've led him on. "No," I say.

"There's prejudice on the bus," Tom says. "Those that like to drink and raise hell can't get on the bus. I tried to sleep on the sidewalk but it didn't feel right."

I ask about the gunman again.

Tom says, "I don't like L., but he's a human being. I live right above him and he's always yelling, 'I don't like white music!' I'm reservation Indian, but I'm part white too. I'm glad he's gone. He's gone now. He's not a tenant. Soon as he gives up, I mean."

I really want to know who the gunman is but certain elements of life in what's essentially an SRO conspire against the ready flow of this kind of information. In the main you're talking about people at the tail end of a trajectory, people who aren't any longer carrying around much of the baggage by which we're known to each other—family, jobs, schools, common aspirations, sundry memberships and affiliations, political grievances, etc.—and so asking for anything in the way of remotely biographical material brings scarcely more than vagaries. Dennis, for instance, insisted several times that the Bad Guy, L., was nice, a nice guy—but I don't get what kind of very elastic notion of "nice" he's talking about, given what's going on. And while of course everyone, even the most wrecked and destitute among us, has a unique personal history, the problematic nature of trying to gather information about people who've severed too many basic ties is this—that in a sense we truly have history only in so far as it's shared, and too much uniqueness really leads away from individuality to anonymity, the great sea of the forgotten. And because the Bad Guy is busy and I can't talk to him, I've got to rely on people who might reasonably be expected to know him, and in fact don't. I suppose it could also be said we're known to the extent that we're dull and orbital about our life, that what's quotidian about us is more easily shared than the exuberances and passions that push us out of the predictable.

And something like this is further confirmed when Dennis, Tom, and I arrive at the bus. Apparently the deal is that Metro brings around a bus for all the folks who've been forced to evacuate in situations like this, an ordinary accordion-style city bus where people can sleep and keep warm. Inside this bus what you see is pretty much a jackpot of social and psychic collapse, a demographic of bad news. Everybody in there's fucked up in some heavy way, dragged out of history by alcohol, drugs, mental illness, physical decrepitude, crime, old age, poverty, whatever. Riding this bus in your dreams would give you the heebie-jeebies big-time. There are maybe ten or fifteen people on the bus but between them if you counted you'd probably come up with only sixty teeth. In addition to dental trouble, there are people leaning on canes, people twitching and barefoot with yellow toenails curled like talons, gray-skinned people shivering in gauzy nightgowns, others who just tremble and stare. They've been ripped out of their bedrooms and are dressed mostly in nightwear, which is something to see—not because I have any fashion ideas or big thesis about nighties and pj's, but rather because, this surreal dawn, the harsh, isolated privacy of these people is literally being paraded in public. The falling rain, the bus going nowhere, the wrecked-up passengers dressed for sleep, the man with the gun—these are the wild and disparate components of a dream, and I haven't slept, and it's just weird.

And meantime that rodent-like anti-whatever vehicle has parked in the street below the Bad Guy's window and there's a super highly trained SWAT guy launching tear gas canisters. We hear the dull pop report like a distant shotgun blast, and then a rainy sprinkling of broken glass on the sidewalk.

"There goes the windows," Dennis says. "Those are double pane, $145 a piece. I got a very secure job."

"Look how fast I left," Tom says. He pulls a TV remote control out of the pocket of his sweats and clicks at the sky. "It's pitiful, I know. It's pitiful."

"What are the rooms like?" I ask, kind of trying to figure the size of the rooms and calculate how fast the pepper spray or tear gas or whatever will take effect.

Dennis says, "You got one room. You got a stove in the room. You got a fridge in the room. You got a bed."

After hearing Dennis describe the Bad Guy's room, the story, the night, everything, starts to end for me. I know they haven't got him and maybe things will go crazy an hour from now, two hours from now, and people will die or some other TVish sort of scenario will play itself out, but I don't care. I've been out here for seven-plus hours and I'm really wet and can't hardly bend my fingers anymore. My feet ache and swell inside my boots, even though I've removed the laces. But that room! I'm starting to feel all buggy imagining that man in that room. It sounds so simple, so stripped, so precariously close to nothing, yet outside all this complication is whirling around, cops and meter maids and a SWAT guy and a crisis negotiator and TV and spectators, everyone focused on this man in a room with a stove, a fridge, and a bed.

What would you do? How would you end this story?

I walk back to my place, change into dry pants, and feed the dog a bowl of kibble. I sit on the edge of my bed. To keep my feet from cracking I've bought a lot of fancy lotions, the labels of which make outlandish, existential promises. One offers itself as "cruelty-free"; another says it will rid my skin of the toxins that are an inescapable part of modern life. The thing is, over the last couple weeks my desire to believe has collapsed into actual belief, and I slather the stuff on like holy water at Lourdes.

I ease my feet into my boots and head back to First and Vine. In my mind I'm turning over the possibility that this whole strange night is a love story, and that if it is, if in fact there's some kind of romance at the heart of it all, then the entire event will elude me. Also I wonder, in an idle, academic way, why the police alone are so refreshingly without irony. Then I wonder why I find it refreshing. Then I think about the crackheads who stole my belt and raincoat and how the economics of addiction might connect up with this event. Then I go back to considering the love angle, how it's nearly impossible to convey our deepest passions yet damned easy to share what's dullest and worst about ourselves. I'm already composing the story in my head, but when I get back to First and Vine everyone's gone. The crime scene is no longer officially a scene because the yellow ribbon has been rolled up and taken away. The Bad Guy has surrendered. The police have left. The TV people are off on other assignments. Dennis is gone. Tom is gone. The bus is gone. The window is bashed to hell, the blinds mangled, but otherwise there's no sign of the siege and the night's dreamy drama; the workaday world is beginning and all of life is back to pumpkins and mice, and I feel like I'm just waking up, standing there on the sidewalk, all alone, loitering.

MATRICIDE

Meghan Daum

People who weren't there like to say that my mother died at home surrounded by loving family. This is technically true, though it was just my brother and me and he was looking at Facebook and I was reading a profile of Hillary Clinton in the December 2009 issue of *Vogue*. A hospice nurse had been over a few hours earlier and said my mother was "very imminent." She was breathing in that slow, irregular way that signals that the end is near. Strangely, I hadn't noticed it despite listening for the past several weeks (months earlier, when her death sentence had been officially handed down but she was still very much alive, my mother had casually mentioned that she'd noticed this breathing pattern in herself and that I should be prepared to walk into the room and find her gone at any moment) but apparently it was here now and when I reached the third paragraph of the second page of the Hillary Clinton article (this remains imprinted on my brain; I can still see the wrap of the words as my eye scanned the column; I can still see the Annie Leibowitz photo on the previous page) I heard her gasp. Then nothing more.

"Mom?" I called out.

My brother got off the couch and called her name, too.

Then I said, "Is that it?"

That was it. I found that I wasn't quite sure suddenly how to identify a dead person—it didn't occur to me in that moment that not breathing was a sure sign—so I picked up her hand. It was turning from red to purple to blue. I'd read about this in the death books—*Final Gifts, Nearing Death Awareness, The Needs of the Dying*—that I'd devoured over the last few months. Medically speaking, I'd found these books to be extremely accurate about how things progressed, though some put a lot of emphasis on birds landing on windowsills at the moment of death or people opening their eyes at the last minute and making amends or saying something profound. We weren't that kind of family, though, and I harbored no such expectations. I had been slightly worried that when my mother actually died I'd be more grief-stricken than I'd anticipated, that I'd faint or lose my breath or at least finally unleash the tears that I'd been unable to shed all this time. I thought that in my impatience to get through the agonizing end stages I'd surely get my comeuppance in the form of sneaky, shocking anguish. Perhaps I would rage at the gods, regret all that had gone unsaid, pull an article of clothing from her closet and hold it close, taking her in. But none of that happened. I was as relieved as I'd planned to be. I picked her hand up a few more times over the next two hours while we waited for another hospice worker to come over and fill out the final paperwork and then the men from the funeral home to take her away. I did this less for the sake of holding it than to make sure she still had no pulse. She'd chosen cremation but had said once that she feared being burned alive.

A woman worked for us during the last two months of my mother's illness. She must have found us appalling. A week or so before my mother died, my brother and I started packing up the apartment right in front of her. I know this sounds grotesque, but we were hemorrhaging money and had to do whatever we could to stem the flow. It was late December and her lease was up at the first of the year. If she died before then and we didn't have the place cleared out, we'd not only have to renew the lease and pay another month of sizable rent, but we'd also have to then go on to break the lease and lose her sizable security deposit. She was unconscious, so "right in front of" is a matter of interpretation, but her hospital bed was in the living room and we had to crouch behind it to remove books from shelves. My mother had a set of George Kovacs table lamps that I liked very much, and every time I look at them in my own house now, three time zones away in a living room she's never seen, I think about how I had to reach around her withering body to unplug them, after which I packed them into their original boxes, which I'd found deep in her coat closet, walked them over to the UPS Store, and mailed them off to California.

"You have to start sometime," said Vera, the woman who worked for us. I'm almost certain she said this because she had no idea what to say but felt some obligation to validate our behavior since we were paying her seventeen dollars per hour. Vera was a professional end-of-life home health care aide, referred to us by hospice. She was originally from Trinidad and spent a lot of time listening to Christmas music on headphones. I assumed she'd known every kind of family and witnessed every iteration of grief, though later I learned she'd worked for only one other terminal patient in New York, a man who was dying of something other than cancer and whose daughter apparently cried all the time and threw herself on his empty hospital bed after he was taken away. Our family, as my mother might have said, had "a significantly different style."

My mother died the day after Christmas. She was sixty-seven years old. She lived on the Upper West Side of Manhattan, where she'd moved three years earlier after retiring from her job as a high school theater teacher and director in New Jersey. She had an exquisitely decorated one-bedroom apartment that she couldn't really afford, though, true to her nature, she had a number of business and creative projects in the works that she trusted would change her financial equation. These included theater coaching for Broadway hopefuls as well as potentially mounting a play she'd written (her first literary endeavor) that she told me she felt could hit the big time if only she got it in the right hands. But in January 2009, after months complaining of pain in her side and being told by her doctor it was probably a pulled muscle, she was found to have gallbladder cancer. This sounds like the kind of thing you could easily cure by just removing the gallbladder, which everyone knows is a nonessential organ, but it turns out the disease is not only extremely rare but barely treatable. Not that they weren't going to try.

The week of my mother's diagnosis, her own mother died at age ninety-one. This wasn't as calamitous as you might think. "I don't really feel anything," my mother said when she told me the news. "I lost her so long ago." Technically she was referring to the dementia my grandmother had suffered for several years but we both knew that the real loss existed from the very beginning. My grandmother was tyrannical in her childishness. She was stubborn, self-centered, and often seemingly willfully illogical. Though she didn't overtly mistreat my mother, I'm fairly certain that my mother saw her as a neglecter. Not in the sense of failing to provide food and shelter but in the sense that is knowable only to the neglectee, and even then maybe never entirely. I'm tempted to say that my grandmother damaged my mother on an almost cellular level. But then again maybe some of my mother's damage was her own. She freely admitted that from the age of fourteen until she left her parents' house after college, she stopped speaking almost entirely when she was at home. In the outside world, she won piano competitions and twirled the baton, but inside the house she offered nothing more than an occasional mumble. I think the idea was that her mother was so unwilling to listen to her that she was no longer going to waste her breath.

As a very young child I'd taken the requisite delight in my grandparents; they had candy dishes and cuckoo clocks; plus they lived far away and I saw them only once a year at the most. But as I grew older and my grandfather died and my mother lost what little buffer had once stood between her and her adversary, the more I came to see the pathology that swarmed around my grandmother like bees. She was a mean little girl in a sweet old woman's body; she spoke about people behind their backs in ghastly ways, sometimes loudly just seconds after they'd left the room. She spoke in a permanent whine, sometimes practically in baby talk. My mother, whose life's mission was to be regarded as serious and sophisticated, recoiled from this as though it were a physical assault. She often said she believed her mother had an "intellectual disability." For my mother's entire life, her mother was less a mother than splintered bits of shrapnel she carried around in her body, sharp, rusty debris that threatened to puncture an organ if she turned a certain way.

We didn't need to have the funeral right away, my mother said. It would require travel to Southern Illinois, a ragged, rural place out of which my grandmother had rarely set foot and from which my mother, despite having left at twenty-three, never felt she could totally escape. Like me, my brother lived in Los Angeles, though unlike me, it was hard for him to get away from work and no one expected him to just drop everything to attend his grandmother's funeral. My father, though sort of in the picture in that he also lived in Manhattan and was still married to my mother, was not in any picture that would have required him to make this trip. My parents had been separated for nearly twenty years, beginning around the time my mother began to self-identify as a theater person and potential single person, though they'd never bothered to divorce. The rest of us, though, would go the following month, when my brother could request a few days off and after my mother was recovered from her surgery and had gotten in a round or two of chemotherapy. It would turn out to be the last trip she ever took. At the memorial service, she addressed the small crowd of mostly eighty- and ninety-somethings about how far she'd moved beyond Southern Illinois but how she still appreciated it as a good place to have grown up. This was entirely untrue, since as far back as I can remember she'd blamed a large portion of her troubles on her hometown as well as her mother. Also untrue was the notion, which my mother had let grow in her hometown some years earlier and never bothered to tamp down, that she was single-handedly responsible for the career of a famous actor that had gone to the high school where she'd taught. In fact, the actor had dropped out before she began working there, but my brother and I nodded and went along with it.

In our family, being good children did not have to do with table manners or doing well in school but with going along with my mother's various ideas about herself and the rest of us. Mostly they amounted to white lies, little exaggerations that only made us look petty if we called her out on them so we usually didn't.

Or at least we didn't anymore. There was a period of at least fifteen years, from approximately age eighteen to age thirty-four, when every interaction I had with my mother entailed some attempt on my part to cut through what I perceived as a set of intolerable affectations. The way I saw it, she had a way of talking about things as though she wasn't really interested in them but rather imitating the kind of person who was. What I always felt was that she simply didn't know how to *be*. She reminded me a bit of the kind of college student who's constantly trying on new personalities, who's a radical feminist one day and a party girl the next, who goes vegan for a month and doesn't let anyone forget it, who comes back from a semester in Europe with a foreign accent. Not that she actually was or did any of these things. It was more that she always felt to me like an outline of a person, a pen-and-ink drawing with nothing colored in. Sometimes I got the feeling she sort of knew this about herself but was powerless to do anything about it. She wanted to be a connoisseur of things, an expert. She wanted to believe she was an intellectual. Once, among a group of semistrangers, I heard her refer to herself as an academic. Later when I called her on it she told me she appreciated college towns and academic-type people and therefore was one herself. When I asked her what she thought an intellectual was, she said it was someone who "valued education" and preferred reading to sports.

What was my problem? Why couldn't I just let it go, laugh it off, chalk it up as quirkiness rather than a legitimate source of rage? For starters, her need for praise was insatiable. And around the time of her emancipation from her old self, when she moved out of the house and seemingly took up permanent residence in the high school theater, that need redoubled. We never gave her any credit, she said. We always put her down, didn't take her seriously. And now that she "felt really good" about herself (for dressing better, for going blond, for losing weight, for having a career), we couldn't bring ourselves to be happy for her. That she was completely right about all of this only added to my rage. We couldn't give her any credit, at least not enough. She just wanted it too badly. She'd ask for it outright. In heated moments, she'd practically order me to praise her as though I were a child being told to clean my room. "It would be nice if just once you'd just say 'Hey, Mom, you're really good at what you do,'" she'd tell me. "If you said, 'You do that *so very* well.'"

If you asked me what my central grievance with my mother was, I would tell you that I had a hard time not seeing her as a fraud. I would tell you that her transformation, at around age forty-five, from a slightly frumpy, slightly depressed, slightly angry but mostly unassuming wife, mother, and occasional private piano teacher into a flashy, imperious, hyperbolic theater person had ignited in her a phoniness that I was allergic to on every level. I might try to explain how the theater in question was the one at my very high school, a place she'd essentially followed me to from the day I matriculated and then proceeded to use as the training ground and later backdrop for her new self. I might throw in the fact that she was deeply concerned with what kind of person I was in high school because it would surely be a direct reflection of the kind of person she was.

Thanks to my own need to please others and draw praise, my life in high school became a performance in response to my mother's performance. When I saw her approaching in the hall I'd grab a friend by the elbow and throw my head back in laughter so she'd perceive me as being popular and bubbly. When I did poorly on a test I followed her advice and didn't let on to anyone. Meanwhile she copied my clothes, my hair, my taste in jewelry, so much so that I started borrowing her things (they were exaggerated versions of my things; skirts that were a little too short, blazers with massive shoulder pads, dangling, Art Deco–inspired earrings) because it seemed easier than trying to pull together my own stuff. In the years to come, my mother would become the go-to teacher for the sexually confused and the suddenly pregnant. But in the nascent stages of her coolness, I wasn't allowed out past ten o'clock. She found it embarrassing that I had a boyfriend. This was beneath me, an unserious pursuit, especially since he wasn't involved in the arts. She didn't want to be known as someone whose daughter would have a boyfriend in high school. She liked when I waited for her at the end of the day so she could drive me home, even (perhaps especially) if it meant pacing around the theater while she finished up her business.

Kids whose parents are teachers in their schools are members of a special club. They have to build invisible fences. They have to learn to appear to take it in earnest when their classmates tell them how cool the parent is. They have to learn not to take it personally when they aren't privy to the pot smoking in the boiler room. I never considered myself a member of that club. In those years, my mother seemed to have just slipped through the door as I walked through it on the first day of school. It was never entirely clear what she was doing. She had no theater experience; her background was in music. It made sense that she was volunteering as a piano accompanist, playing in the pit orchestra, coaching singers. It made less sense that she always seemed to be there even after the musicians went home. Hanging out with the set builders, feigning disapproval when kids banged out pop songs instead of the assigned show tunes on the piano, giving more and more orders until everyone just assumed she was in charge.

In all the years that came before, when I was three and six and ten and fourteen, my mother had cautioned me not to be dramatic, not to overaccessorize, not to be "the kind of kid who's always *on*." "That doesn't show a lot of substance," she'd say. *Substance* was one of her all-time most used words; in both of her incarnations she used it liberally, though her powers of appraisal were questionable. A man we knew who was brilliantly insightful, well read and well spoken—a true intellectual—came across to her as lacking in substance because he told hilarious stories about what a screwup he'd been in college. She believed Barbara Walters showed substance on *The View* when she hushed the other ladies up and spoke her mind.

In the last twenty years of my mother's life, I think I can count on one hand the times when she did not have a delicate, artisan-woven scarf tossed around her neck. In her entire lifetime I don't think I ever once heard her laugh out loud.

There was no more clothes sharing after I left for college. During that time my mother moved out of our house and into her own place and I came home as infrequently as possible, staying with my father when I did. Her career in full throttle, she was usually too busy for family time anyway. She was out late rehearsing summer stock productions of *Sweeney Todd*. She had close friends whose names I didn't know and would never learn. Still, my assignment from there on out was clear. For the rest of her life, what I was supposed to do was celebrate what little resemblance my mother bore to her own mother. I was supposed to accept that her old personality had been nothing more than a manifestation of various sources of oppression (her mother, her husband, the legacy of 1950s Southern Illinois) and that what we had on our hands now (the fan club of gay men, the dramatic hand gestures, the unsettling way she seemed to have taken on the preening, clucking qualities of a teenage girl, almost as if to make up for skipping over that phase the first time) was the real deal.

I could not, however, manage to do those things. Even more cruelly, I couldn't even fake it. She had a habit of picking up the phone in her office inside the high school theater and letting the receiver hang in the air for several seconds as she continued whatever in-person conversation she was already having. When she did this to me I usually just hung up. On the rare occasions when I visited the theater, I smiled silently when her students gushed about her superfabulousness. Several times I told her flat out that if I, as a kid (who had been instructed at the age of six to answer the phone, "Hello, this is Meghan Daum," and then "professionally" field the call to the appropriate parent), had for even one second exhibited the traits of her new personality, her former personality would have sent me to my room for three months.

"I wish you'd been raised by the new me," she said more than once.

The last time I saw my grandmother was almost ten years before she died. Arriving at her apartment, which was in a sterile two-story complex near the main highway of the town she'd never left, my mother and I were immediately taken into her bedroom and shown her latest collection of teddy bears. They were dressed in clothing that said things like "God Bless America" and "I Hate Fridays." My grandmother's speech had the thick, Ozarks-influenced twang endemic to Southern Illinois—a "hillbilly" accent, my mother always called it—and as she cooed over the bears and pronounced this one "real purdy" and another one "cute as can be," I saw my mother's hands curling into tight, livid little fists. They were the same fists I made whenever I heard the outgoing message on my mother's answering machine, which for the nearly twenty years she lived alone had somehow rubbed me as the most overarticulated and high-handed version of "leave a message after the tone" in the history of human speech.

(My mother told me that when she was a girl she secretly unwrapped her Christmas presents ahead of time and then rewrapped them and placed them back under the tree. The reason for this was that she didn't trust herself to react appropriately to them. She had to plan in advance what she was going to say.)

My grandmother's infractions went deeper than stuffed animals, of course; and while I might be able to cite my mother's central grievance—that her mother didn't recognize her accomplishments, didn't appreciate the person she was, didn't, in fact, see her at all—I'd be a fool to think I had any real grasp of the terrain of their relationship. During that last visit, while my mother was describing in detail the complexities of her latest theater production, my grandmother interrupted her mid-sentence and asked, "Honey, do you ever wish you'd been a career gal?"

You'd think something like that maps out the terrain pretty well—"Jesus Christ, what do you think she's been talking about?" I snapped as my mother fumed silently—but no one can ever truly read that map, maybe especially not even those occupying its territories. A lot of people knew my grandmother to be as nice as pie, just as a lot of people knew my mother as an incredibly talented theater arts administrator and overall fun person to be around. Neither of those observations was objectively wrong, they just weren't the whole story. But there again, what can you say to that? In the history of the world, a whole story has never been told. At my grandmother's burial site, my mother broke away from the crowd and stood alone at the headstone looking mournful and pensive. I recognized my cue and walked over and put my arm around her, knowing this would create a picture she wanted people to see and would therefore console her. Not that anyone could see the real source of our grief, which was not my grandmother's absence but the limited time my mother now had to enjoy that absence. My mother would die nine months later, and what most people don't know is that of all the sad things about this fact, the saddest by far is that she did not have one day on this earth where she was both healthy and free of her mother. All her life she'd waited to be relieved of the burden of being unseen, only to have that relief perfectly timed with her own death sentence.

My father was one person who understood this cruel twist, though at times he seemed to understand little else. He did not, at least to my knowledge, bother to look up *gallbladder cancer* on the Internet when it first entered our family lexicon and see that the average life expectancy after diagnosis is five months and that fewer than 2 percent of patients make it to the five-year mark. Since he lived a twenty-minute cab ride away and since their relationship, for all its animus, still extended to things like hospital visits and accompaniment to chemotherapy appointments, he did do his share of emptying buckets when she vomited and showing up at the emergency room when she had a crisis of pain or hydration. Our family was not one to shirk its duties, even if we did not always perform them warmly.

Curiously, though, my father did not seem particularly affected when, after eight months of aggressive chemotherapy at a major cancer center that prided itself on beating the odds, the news was delivered that the treatment was no longer working—"longer" referring to the three months beyond the average my mother had survived. She would likely die within half a year's time (it turned out to be two months). There were many ways my mother could have chosen to tell my father she was dying and there were many ways he could have chosen to respond. Their choices, as my mother lay in her hospital bed and I sat nearby in my usual visitor's chair, playing around on my laptop computer as usual, were these:

"The timeline has been moved up," my mother said.

"I see," said my father.

"So they're talking months at this point."

"Hmm. Okay."

"So what else is going on?" my mother finally asked when it was clear he wasn't going to say anything more.

"Well, actually I have done something to my foot," my father said. "I somehow stumbled when I got out of bed and stepped down on it the wrong way. And it's been killing me."

My mother said maybe he should have it looked at.

"He's happy," she hissed after my father left the hospital on his aching foot. I told her that wasn't true, that he was scared. I said this not because I believed it but because it seemed like the kind of thing you should say.

I could try to go into the reasons why my parents never got divorced but I suspect that would fall into the category of trying to explain fully how things were between my mother and my grandmother or even my mother and myself, and that would be: overreaching, moot, a fool's errand. I could try to explain all the ways that my father is a good person who behaved the way he did partly because he lacked the "emotional vocabulary" to face the situation and partly because my mother, who'd hired a van and moved out of the house on a humid summer day in the early nineties, could never make up her mind about what she wanted from him. For years, she'd summoned him when she needed him—to mark holidays, to suggest to out-of-town guests that their marriage was not exactly over but simply had "a different style"—and shunned him pretty much the rest of the time. When she got sick, a few ferociously loyal friends from her old personality came in from New Jersey whenever they could, though no one would have held it against them if they hadn't. But the gay man posse, not to mention the friends my mother had claimed to have made since moving into the city ("a costume designer who has many inroads to theater producers," "a *very* interesting museum curator," "so many former students who live here now but still want my advice"), were largely absent and so it was that she was forced to call on my father for help and he obliged, though not as graciously as she would have liked. When I hopped on a red-eye flight at a moment's notice because it was clear she needed to go to the famous cancer center's urgent care unit but didn't want my father to take her, my presence was tacitly understood as a polarizing force. My mother felt grateful and vindicated. My father felt snubbed.

"You didn't have to come out here, you know," he told me as we loitered around the vending machines. "I've taken her before. I'm capable of it."

He wasn't capable of it. He didn't know the code. Or, if he did, he refused to abide by it. I can't blame him. The code had to do with not just showing up but actually being there, which was no longer really a part of their social contract. My mother didn't want my father to be her husband but she still wanted him to impersonate one when the occasion arose. All around us were family members of other patients, people who sobbed in the hallways or set up camp at bedsides or emerged from the elevators carrying piles of blankets and needlepoint pillows and framed photos from home. One afternoon, en route to the visitors' kitchenette to get coffee, I passed a man clutching the door handle of a utility closet and crying. He looked to be in his sixties. He looked weathered and hammered down, as if he'd spent his life doing manual labor. I assumed he was crying over his wife, though I had no idea. No one was crying like that for my mother. Occasionally I'd overhear family members of other patients using words like *gift* and *blessing,* words they seemed to be able to use without apologizing for sounding sentimental. Our family had a significantly different style. We weren't bringing anything up in the elevator except our own lunch. Occasionally I brought up flowers or a book I knew she'd never read, which is to say I understood the code enough to fake it.

The best line in this whole saga goes to my mother's oncologist, who broke the bad news like this:

"Our hope for this treatment was that it would give you more time. Some of that time has now passed."

One day back in the summer I had entertained a passing fantasy that my mother would get hit by a bus. The oncologist had just delivered the news that the chemotherapy was working. This came as a surprise, since an earlier therapy had failed and this was plan B, which I'd assumed stood even less chance. My mother was elated and shifted at once into one of her more dramatic gears, calling friends and telling them she was on the road to recovery, that it appeared she was a special case, that the doctors "were so pleased." She was so happy that day that she actually ventured outside the apartment on her own to buy a Frappuccino and I remember thinking to myself how great it would be if she were hit by, say, the M7 express on Columbus Avenue and killed instantly and painlessly. I knew from the Internet that chemotherapy for gallbladder cancer works (when it works at all) for about one cycle before the body develops immunity and the disease resumes the process of ravaging it. She would never have a better day than this day. She would never again walk down the street feeling as hopeful and relieved and exceptional as she had when she strode out of the doctor's office that morning, past the throngs of chemo patients and their families sprawled out in the lounge like stranded airline passengers, past the ever-friendly lobby personnel (trained, no doubt, to greet each visitor as if it were the last greeting they'd ever receive) and on to the street, where for the first time in weeks she actually hailed a cab herself and announced her desire for a Frappuccino.

That night she drank half a vodka gimlet to celebrate and regretted it for the next several days. She vomited from the chemo through the rest of the summer until she landed back in the hospital with severe intestinal and bowel trouble. It was September. Autumn, New York's most flattering season, was preparing to make its entrance. I had just gotten engaged to my longtime boyfriend, which had made my mother very happy.

"Our recommendation would be to transfer to another level of care," the oncologist said.

Hearing this, I moved my chair closer and grabbed my mother's hand under the blanket. I did this because I felt that if we were in a play this would surely be part of the stage directions. I was also afraid the doctor would judge me if I didn't. If I just sat there with my arms crossed against my chest, as I was inclined to, the doctor would make a note in the file suggesting that I might not be capable of offering sufficient support to the patient.

I retrieved her hand from under the blanket and squeezed it in my own. She did not reciprocate. She didn't pull away, but there was enough awkwardness and ambivalence coming from both sides that it was not unlike being on a date at the movies and trying to hold hands with someone who'd rather not. I think we were both relieved when I let go. The doctor said she would most likely make it through Christmas, so we should feel free to go ahead with any holiday plans.

For three nights in a row, my mother made me stay in her hospital room. She was dealing with incontinence (if you learn nothing else from these pages, learn that gastrointestinal cancer is not the kind of cancer to get; get any other kind, even lung, even brain, but don't get carcinoma of the gut) and it had grown so severe that she was up every few minutes and sometimes didn't make it to the bathroom in time. The people who came to clean her up were terse and tired and spoke mostly in heavy Caribbean accents. A few times she lay there in her own shit before they could get there. I know this because I was in the sleeping chair on the other side of the room, listening to it all while pretending to be asleep.

I tell myself now, as I told myself then, that if things had gotten really bad, if she had cried out in pain or called my name or if a serious amount of time had passed before a staff member came, I'd have gotten up and helped her. I tell myself that I closed my eyes to protect her dignity, that if she could step back from the situation she'd never want me wiping her shit, that there are some daughters in the world who would do this for their mothers but that we had never been that kind of mother and daughter and trying to pretend to be so now would only make both of us feel inexpressibly and inerasably violated. I tell myself I did it out of compassion but the truth is I also did it, as I had done so many other things where she was concerned, out of rage. I was enraged at her for her lifetime of neediness that she'd disguised as a million other things—independence, fabulousness, superiority—and demanded praise for. I was enraged at how this bottomless longing encircled her like barbed wire and that now that she genuinely and rightfully needed me I just couldn't deliver. I was enraged that what I was doing struck me as so unspeakably cowardly that when I was finally allowed to return to her apartment and order Chinese food and drink from the wine stash she hadn't touched in ten months I wouldn't even be able to call my fiancé in Los Angeles and say what I'd done.

Later, when the horror of those nights had been eclipsed by other horrors—patient proxy forms, calls to an attorney, wrenching phone conversations with her friends—my mother was discharged from the hospital and my father and I took her back to her apartment in a taxi. I'd been in taxis countless times with my mother since her ordeal had begun, mostly taking her to or from a chemo session, and it seemed that invariably the driver was playing a talk radio station sponsored heavily by cancer treatment centers. This day was no exception. "I got my life back," a voice earnestly intoned. "So say goodbye to cancer and hello to a front-row seat at your granddaughter's wedding." My mother would have no grandchildren. Neither my brother nor I ever had shown an interest in reproducing. I had a dog, which she sometimes called her granddog. The three of us sat in silence through this advertisement and several others—for weight loss, for acne scar removal, for adjustable mattresses. It was a cold, gusty day and tree branches scraped the car while we waited at red lights.

Back at the apartment, my father stood around awkwardly for a while, and finally left.

"Would you do all this for him?" my mother asked me. "Would you take care of him?"

One thing I did for my mother that I would not have done for my father was get married. That is to say, I got married pretty much right then and there, less than six weeks after getting engaged, so she could be in attendance. We spent three weeks discussing the wedding and five days actually arranging for it, which in retrospect I think is the perfect amount of time to plan a wedding. During the time we were discussing it my mother became fixated on hosting the event in her apartment and inviting her friends and associates. Due to limited space, this would exclude many of my and my fiancé's friends and associates. She also made it clear she did not want children in her apartment for fear of knocking over her pottery or damaging her art. My fiancé made it clear he didn't want to get married in a dying woman's apartment. He did not make this clear to the dying woman herself but to me during the countless hours I sat with my cell phone in the lobby of the famous cancer center's hospital trying to figure out how to handle the situation of a dying woman (a woman dying brutally and prematurely) who effectively wanted to turn her only daughter's wedding into a funeral she could orchestrate and attend herself. Meanwhile my mother, who'd heretofore thought my fiancé walked not only on water but on some magical blend of Evian, Pellegrino, and electrolyte-enhanced Smartwater, began to say things like "Well, now I'm seeing a different side of him." When I pointed out to her that he'd like the wedding to include his sister's small children she told me he had to realize he couldn't always get what he wanted.

The discussion period ended when my mother realized she was too sick to orchestrate anything. She told me to wait and get married after she was gone—"it happens all the time," she said, crying. This was one of our more authentic conversations because it so happened that I authentically wanted her there. My father, as far as I could tell, regarded marriage as a fatuous institution. In moments, he seemed to regard my wedding plans as yet another complication that had been thrown into the mix of our crisis. My mother was the only person on earth for whom my getting married really meant something. She was the only one for whom it wasn't a take-it-or-leave-it kind of thing. I felt like it wouldn't count if she weren't there. It was the first thing I'd needed her for in a long time and the last thing I'd need her for from there on out. So on a Sunday in late October we rounded up everyone we could and walked from my mother's apartment to the park across the street, where we were married by a close friend who'd been ordained online the day before. Photos taken by another close friend later suggested my mother was in an extraordinary amount of pain. Wearing a wig, being humiliatingly pushed along in a wheelchair by my brother (with whom, a month later, at Thanksgiving, I would trade earsplitting obscenities as she lay in the next room after vomiting at the dinner table), she is wincing in every shot. In some, she's not only wincing but staring into space. After seeming relatively alert during the preshow (champagne at her apartment, compliments on the decor), she appeared to unravel throughout the ceremony, shifting from barely living to officially dying in the time it took me to slip from lack of official attachment into wedlock. The next day, the four members of the hospice team came to the apartment to introduce themselves. When they asked her to describe her level of pain on a scale from one to ten—one being no pain, ten being unbearable—she told them eight. When we asked if she was really sure about that she said she wasn't sure. She said she had never in her life been able to answer that sort of question.

A few times I saw Vera kneeling by my mother praying. I ducked away and pretended not to see but I appreciated the gesture nonetheless. Bedside praying wasn't something I'd ever done myself, though when my mother was still cogent I'd told her a secret I've told maybe two other humans ever. I'd told her that I'd prayed most nights since I was nine years old (prompted by extreme guilt over a schoolyard incident in which I'd caused another child to burst into tears) and found it a useful tool for, if not speaking to a higher power per se, articulating that for which I was most grateful and that for which I most hoped ("thank you for letting me pass the French test; please get me through math class tomorrow"). I added that I usually tried to send out a special prayer to someone who probably needed it (the girl I'd inadvertently made cry, the stray animals of the world), at least if I didn't fall asleep first.

Given our belief system (atheist) and overall family dynamic (cynical, avoidant of confrontation yet judgmental behind people's backs), this was an extremely vulnerable thing to share. It didn't entirely pay off. "That sounds like a nice ritual," my mother said before going back to staring at the television (in an echo of her own mother that would have horrified her, she never changed the channel and watched anything that came on: the news, the weather, *The Price Is Right*). Other times, when she seemed particularly aware of the irreversibility of her situation, I'd turn off the TV and try to get philosophical. I told her that as presumptuous as it might be to believe in an afterlife it was equally presumptuous to deny the possibility of one. Then, at the risk of mockery or at least disapproval, I said that I felt like reincarnation was at least something worth thinking about, that it felt clear to me that souls existed and that you could just tell from knowing people that some souls had been around longer than others. Plus, dogs obviously had souls, so there you had it.

"Maybe you'll have a whole new life and it'll be even better than this one," I said.

"But I don't want to be a baby again," she said. Her voice sounded genuinely worried.

Ironically, she was in adult diapers. Women's Depends, size small. I'd been sent to the drugstore to buy them on numerous occasions, especially when she was in the hospital and didn't like the brand they had there. I suspected she'd been using them for several months now, actually. Back in the summer, when she was still thinking she might be cured, I'd walked into her apartment and thought odors from the young children who lived upstairs were somehow migrating downward. Months later I realized those children were all too old for diapers.

"Maybe you won't have to be a baby again," I told her. "Maybe you'll be a bird. You'll fly around and look at everything from up high."

"I don't want to be a bird," she said.

It's amazing what the living expect of the dying. We expect wisdom, insight, bursts of clarity that are then reported back to the undying in the urgent staccato of a telegram: *I have the answer. Stop. They're waiting for me. Stop. Everyone Who Died Before. Stop. And they Look Great. Stop.* We expect them to reminisce over photos, to accept apologies and to make them, to be sad, to be angry, to be grateful. We expect them to clear our consciences, to confirm our fantasies. We expect them to be excited about the idea of being a bird.

My mother's official date of death was December 26 but the day she actually left was December 5. This was the day her confusion morphed into unremitting delirium, the day the present tense fell away and her world became a collage of memory and imagination, a Surrealist canvas through which reality seeped in only briefly through the corners. Suddenly she seemed no longer in pain. She was mobile, even spry, and given to popping out of bed as if she'd forgotten to take care of some piece of essential business. When I walked into her bedroom that morning, a painting had been removed from the wall and clothes she hadn't worn in months were strewn across the floor. She'd thrown up, of course, and the green-brown vomit was dribbling down her pajamas and onto the bed. Whereas the day before she'd have been flustered and embarrassed, she now seemed unfazed, unapologetic, even ecstatic. She wanted her purse, she told me. She needed to put some things in it. I recognized this impulse from my death books. Dying people often pack suitcases and retrieve their coats from the closet because they're overcome with the idea that they're going somewhere. My mother had a cane she used for the rare occasions when she got up—a tasteful wooden thing; she'd refused the walker sent over from the medical supply company—and now she had it in bed with her and was waving it around so it threatened to knock over the lamp and yet more pictures. When I leaned over the bed to wipe up the vomit she put the end of the cane on my head and began rubbing my hair. She was smiling a crazy smile, her tongue hanging from her mouth like an animal's. The gesture struck me as something an ape might do if you were sitting across from it trying to make it play nicely with blocks, a helpless molestation, a reaching out from behind a cage. When I managed to grab the cane she resisted for a moment before letting it go.

"Meghan," she said solemnly. Her voice over the last few weeks had grown faint, her speech slurred and monotone. It was the sound of fog rolling in over a life.

"What, Mom?" I chirped. She could hear just fine but I'd taken to talking loudly, as if she were an old person who couldn't. It drove her crazy. She was always shushing me.

"We need to figure something out here."

"What's that?"

"I need to ask you something."

"What?"

"How did we get kidnapped?"

The dying have their own version of dementia. They drift not only between the real and the not real, the past and the present, but also the living and the dead—and not just the dead they appear to be seeing but the dead the living want to believe they're seeing. It's like they're living in six dimensions, at least two of which exist solely for the benefit of the people standing around watching and listening to them. ("Folks with dementia say the darnedest things!") "Is that Grandpa you're talking to?" we ask when they murmur at an empty chair. "Is there someone up there? Tell me!" we plead when they lift their arms in the air and curl their hands over invisible shapes. Science says the grasping gestures are related to changes in brain chemicals as the body shuts down but my death books said it's because dying people reach up to greet those who died before them. A cat visited my mother regularly in her final weeks, at one point jumping on her bed and lying at the foot of it like every cat we had when I was growing up. In the beginning, I'd laughed and told her there was no cat, but with the dying you soon learn the folly of raining on a parade, especially one that might produce that holy grail of darnedest things: insight into the afterlife.

"What kind of cat is it?" I asked, finally. "Is it orange?"

"Black," she rasped.

We'd had two orange cats, both named Magnificat and called Niffy for short. Niffy One and Niffy Two, both of which were friendly and affectionate. In between we'd also had a black tomcat that was an asshole. My mother softened in senility. She developed a childlike quality she probably hadn't had even as an actual child. Her head seemed perennially cocked to one side, her eyes wide, and with her hair now growing back in soft white tufts she looked like a perfect white frosted truffle. For the first time in years, she was without affectation. There was no trace of the drama queen. As feathery and ephemeral as she was, she seemed like a real person rather than someone impersonating her idea of a person. Though I never would have said it, she looked almost exactly like her mother, who, despite her fleshiness and thick glasses and suspected intellectual disability, everyone, even my mother herself, had recognized as being very pretty. For the first time in years, I didn't merely love her. I actually liked her.

"Do you know why you're here?" the hospice nurse asked her gently one day (unlike me, she knew not to shout). This was turning out to be a day of particularly acute agitation. There was a lot of picking at the sheets and furious murmuring. I'd long given up my philosophical lectures. My new best friend was Haldol, which was supposed to keep her calm and which I administered under her tongue through a syringe. There was a perverse, momentary pleasure in this act; it made me feel like I was a stern, efficient nurse, like someone who knew what they were doing.

Her words, barely intelligible, were like soft formations carved from her teeth and lips. Her breath could scarcely carry them an inch.

"Because," she said, "my mother was here."

Ten months after my mother died, twenty months after my grandmother died, I nearly died myself. Oddly enough, this was a scenario that had crossed my mind a time or two over the preceding year. Talk about a morbid trifecta: three generations of women in one family, each of them almost physically repelled by the one before, wiped out in less than two years' time. This wasn't a recurring thought, more like the kind of thing that crosses your mind two or three times and then convinces you that the sheer act of thinking about it at all converts it from a mere implausibility to an almost total impossibility. This is what doomsday scenarios are for. They protect us from disaster by playing out the disaster ahead of time. They're the reason the plane doesn't crash and the bomb doesn't drop. They're the reason we will almost certainly not die in childbirth. That I almost died despite having entertained the thought of dying, that my organs began to fail despite having walked down the snowy sidewalks in the days after my mother's death thinking, *Maybe you're next, maybe there are no coincidences, maybe you were right about it being presumptuous not to believe in an afterlife and maybe the afterlife of this matriarchal line is a group entry kind of deal,* still feels at once too overwhelming and too silly to fully contemplate. And yet it became relevant to the story of my mother's death and my grandmother's death before that. In fact it's part of the same story, a third act that got rewritten at the last minute, a narrowly dodged bullet from the gun that went off in the first.

It started with a fever. Actually it started before that. Of course it did. Nothing ever begins when you think it does. You think you can trace something back to its roots but roots by definition never end. There's always something that came before; soil and water and seeds that were born of trees that were born of yet more seeds. The fever may have been the first thing I bothered to pay attention to but there was so much before that. It's possible I'd been getting sick all along, that my immunity had begun slowly eroding from the week my grandmother died and my mother became a cancer patient. Throughout it all, I hadn't so much as gotten a cold. But in October 2010, right around the one-year mark of the wedding and the screaming at Thanksgiving and the buying of Depends and the administering of the morphine and then the Haldol and then the methadone, I returned to New York for a visit. I wanted to attend a friend's wedding, see the leaves, escape the taunting, pitiless heat of autumn in Southern California. It was my first time back in New York since my mother had died and I thought it might be possible to claim the streets as my own again, to seal the preceding eighteen months in plastic and toss them in a trash can where they could await collection alongside the Greek paper coffee cups and the dog shit.

The fever was perplexing, as I am rarely sick, so rarely in fact that I didn't have a primary care doctor at home in Los Angeles, much less in New York, where I'd lived during my entire twenties without health insurance. Not that there seemed any need for one. It was the flu, obviously. The only cure was time and fluids. For three days I staved off the fever with aspirin, huddling under blankets in a friend's Brooklyn apartment and canceling one plan after another. But time was curing nothing. Each day I woke up to more weakness and more fever, body aches that felt like I'd been thrown down the stairs the day before, thirst that no amount of orange juice could quench.

The day after returning to Los Angeles I went to a walk-in

clinic, where I was put on an IV for rehydration, told I had a nasty virus, and sent home. The next day I couldn't stand up and my eyes were yellow. I returned to the clinic and was put on another IV and then in an ambulance to the nearest hospital, where I was asked what year it was and couldn't think of the answer. Formless, meaningless words rolled out of my mouth like worms. There was no grabbing on to them. They had no edges, no consonants, no meaning. A doctor came and held his fingers up and asked me to follow them. He furrowed his brow as he wrote notes in his chart. When my husband showed up from work I was suddenly compelled to express grave concern for a friend back in New York. She was the last person I'd seen before I got the fever. We'd had dinner in Carroll Gardens and then I'd stopped at a drugstore for vitamin C pills. Now, after closing my eyes in a hospital bed and then waking from a half sleep involving some half dream in which this friend was being held against her will (metaphorically speaking, that is; it was as if I were witnessing her life from afar and seeing all the ways in which she was an indentured servant—to her husband, to the publishing business, to New York City itself), the words fell from my mouth like food dribbled down a baby's chin. Somewhere in my mind there was a concept; an urgent, hulking, planetlike idea that I had to get out. But it seemed composed of invisible gases. It was an abstraction within an abstraction and now it was sliding out of my line of vision the way the landmarks drift past the windows of an airborne plane. Still, I had something to say.

"Listen to me," I slurred. "I need to tell you something. We have to help Sara."

The words came out as *lishen to me* and *we hava help Shara*.

I do not recall being in any pain or even being terribly anxious. Instead, I was mortified. I sounded exactly like my mother. The voice coming from my parched mouth might as well have been a recording of her voice on the day she rubbed her cane in my hair. Even in my delirium, I cringed the way adult children cringe when they look down and realize the hands sticking out of their arms are actually their parents' hands. I remember thinking that everyone was on to me now. My husband, the doctor, whoever else was there: they all knew not only that I was my mother's daughter but that I was no different from her. Just as she had outlived her own mother by less than a year, I, too, would be denied a life outside of her shadow. The message was so obvious it might as well have been preordained: no woman in this matriarchal line would escape punishment for not loving her mother enough, for not mourning her mother enough, for not missing her enough, for refusing to touch her. None of us would be allowed out in the world on our own.

Apparently this had all happened on a Wednesday. It's the last thing I remember before waking up on what I was told was Sunday. It would be several more days before I understood that they'd put me in a medically induced coma and I'd almost taken things a step further by dying.

People who'd been milling around the hospital, bringing my husband food he couldn't eat and asking questions no one could answer, would later want me to tell them what had happened during the four days I was out. Had there been a white light? Had I encountered any dead relatives? Had I experienced anything that would move me to radically change my life? When I couldn't come up with anything interesting I started to wonder if the random thoughts I'd had in the half-awake state of the postcatatonic, prelucid days that followed my transfer out of the ICU were actually remnants of a near-death narrative. In those days I'd started to think, for instance, that if I survived whatever had happened (and we didn't know what had happened until my ninth day in the hospital) I'd get my act together and behave like an adult. I would, for instance, stop being so bratty about finding the perfect piece of real estate. (My last conversation with my husband, before I grew too sick to converse, had been yet another argument over how much we were willing to overpay to remain living in the inflated, rapidly gentrifying neighborhood where we'd recently sold my tiny, rather ramshackle single-girl house and which I believed to be the only neighborhood in the continental United States where I could be happy.) I'd forgive my father (who'd gotten on a plane for L.A. around the time I'd been put in the coma) for complaining about his foot. I'd make an effort to be closer to my in-laws, who I'd heretofore never thought to call on my own volition. (My father, for his part, had managed to go his entire married life without ever initiating a conversation with my mother's mother or even addressing her by name.)

I even, to my great shock, entertained the thought of having a baby. I'd never really wanted one. For about a million reasons, it had barely scraped the bottom of my to-do list since approximately the seventh grade. My husband knew this, but I'd always suspected that one of the pacts of our marriage was an unspoken belief that I might change my mind. And the more I learned about how sick I'd been—it seemed I'd had swelling of the brain, multiple organ failure, and a severe platelet disorder that required several transfusions; it seemed my wrists were bruised not because of medication, as I'd suspected, but because I'd tried to pull my breathing and feeding tubes out; it seemed there'd been a very real possibility that I'd die and an even greater possibility that, if I didn't die, I'd have brain trauma that would require long-term rehabilitation; it seemed throughout all this, my husband had left my side only to use the bathroom and to phone anyone he could think of that might know of the best brain trauma specialists—the more I thought that refusing to have a child was fatuous at best and gratuitously defiant at worse. After all, who says I'd be as negative and judgmental a parent as I'd always assumed I'd be? Who says I'd shudder at the sight of toys in my quiet, spare, grown-up rooms? Who says I'd be as nervous and angry as my own mother had been, that the damage incurred by her own mother would trickle down and sting my eyes just enough to blind me to the damage I myself was inflicting? Who says my old maxim on this subject would turn out to be right, that if I had a child I would certainly love it but not necessarily love my life. Who was saying this but me? No one, of course. And who was I to be trusted?

Miraculously (this was the word they used), I got better fast enough to leave the hospital after eleven days. The diagnosis, in a nutshell, was freak illness. A bacterial infection gone terribly awry. I went home and slept for two weeks. Two months later my husband and I bought a house in a neighborhood other than the one I'd insisted on living in. It had twice as many bedrooms as we had people in our household; it was owned by the bank and we got it for cheap. Within a month of moving in, a few weeks after my forty-first birthday, I was pregnant.

I was neither excited nor dismayed. I told myself that now that my mother wasn't around to make me feel guilty for not being sufficiently impressed with her, I could find it within myself to be impressed with a child. I told myself there was plenty of room in the house, that I wouldn't have to give up my study if we could combine the den and the guest room, that it was perfectly acceptable to be sixty years old by the time your kid graduated high school. I told myself I'd raise the kid to be strong and independent and to not need me. I'd send it to summer camp and maybe to boarding school. I'd encourage it to make the kind of friends who stick around, to find a community and stay there, maybe even to marry young. I'd ensure that if I died at sixty-seven the kid would be able to pack up those George Kovacs lamps around my decaying body and not feel too bad about it. I thought of it as "it" even though I was sure it was a boy. I was also sure all these provisions were unnecessary because the thing itself wasn't going to stick around.

It didn't. It was gone after eight weeks. I was neither relieved nor devastated. There'd been an element of impostordom to the whole thing, as though I'd spent two months wearing the wrong outfit. The lab results came back the way they usually do for forty-one-year-olds who miscarry: chromosomal abnormalities, totally nonsurvivable, nothing that could have been done. When I asked the doctor if it was possible to know what sex it would have been, she told me that it would have been a girl. I was shocked for a moment but then not. Of course it was a girl. It was a girl and of course it was dead, another casualty of our fragile maternal line, another pair of small hands that would surely have formed furious fists in the presence of her mother. Except this one was gone before she even got here. Maybe she'd joined the others somewhere. Maybe she'd already become a bird. Maybe she'd circle back to me someday and reattempt her landing. Or maybe, better yet, she was the quick, quiet epilogue at the end of our story. Not that I'll ever know what this story is about. I know only that I'll probably never finish telling it and it most certainly will never be whole.

JOYAS VOLADORAS

Brian Doyle

Consider the hummingbird for a long moment. A hummingbird's heart beats ten times a second. A hummingbird's heart is the size of a pencil eraser. A hummingbird's heart is a lot of the hummingbird. *Joyas voladoras,* flying jewels, the first white explorers in the Americas called them, and the white men had never seen such creatures, for hummingbirds came into the world only in the Americas, nowhere else in the universe, more than three hundred species of them whirring and zooming and nectaring in hummer time zones nine times removed from ours, their hearts hammering faster than we could clearly hear if we pressed our elephantine ears to their infinitesimal chests.

Each one visits a thousand flowers a day. They can dive at sixty miles an hour. They can fly backward. They can fly more than five hundred miles without pausing to rest. But when they rest they come close to death: on frigid nights, or when they are starving, they retreat into torpor, their metabolic rate slowing to a fifteenth of their normal sleep rate, their hearts sludging nearly to a halt, barely beating, and if they are not soon warmed, if they do not soon find that which is sweet, their hearts grow cold, and they cease to be. Consider for a moment those hummingbirds who did not open their eyes again today, this very day, in the Americas: bearded helmetcrests and booted racket-tails, violet-tailed sylphs and violet-capped woodnymphs, crimson topazes and purple-crowned fairies, red-tailed comets and amethyst woodstars, rainbow-bearded thornbills and glittering-bellied emeralds, velvetpurple coronets and golden-bellied starfrontlets, fiery-tailed awlbills and Andean hillstars, spatuletails and pufflegs, each the most amazing thing you have never seen, each thunderous wild heart the size of an infant's fingernail, each mad heart silent, a brilliant music stilled.

Hummingbirds, like all flying birds but more so, have incredible enormous immense ferocious metabolisms. To drive those metabolisms they have race-car hearts that eat oxygen at an eye-popping rate. Their hearts are built of thinner, leaner fibers than ours. Their arteries are stiffer and more taut. They have more mitochondria in their heart muscles—anything to gulp more oxygen. Their hearts are stripped to the skin for the war against gravity and inertia, the mad search for food, the insane idea of flight. The price of their ambition is a life closer to death; they suffer more heart attacks and aneurysms and ruptures than any other living creature. It's expensive to fly. You burn out. You fry the machine. You melt the engine. Every creature on earth has approximately two billion heartbeats to spend in a lifetime. You can spend them slowly, like a tortoise, and live to be two hundred years old, or you can spend them fast, like a hummingbird, and live to be two years old.

The biggest heart in the world is inside the blue whale. It weighs more than seven tons. It's as big as a room. It *is* a small room, with four chambers. A child could walk around in it, head high, bending only to step through the valves. The valves are as big as the swinging doors in a saloon. This house of a heart drives a creature a hundred feet long. When this creature is born it is twenty feet long and weighs four tons. It is waaaaay bigger than your car. It drinks a hundred gallons of milk from its mama every day and gains two hundred pounds a day, and when it is seven or eight years old it endures an unimaginable puberty and then it essentially disappears from human ken, for next to nothing is known of the mating habits, travel patterns, diet, social life, language, social structure, diseases, spirituality, wars, stories, despairs, and arts of the blue whale. There are perhaps ten thousand blue whales in the world, living in every ocean on earth, and of the largest animal who ever lived we know nearly nothing. But we know this: the animals with the largest hearts in the world generally travel in pairs, and their penetrating moaning cries, their piercing yearning tongue, can be heard underwater for miles and miles.

Mammals and birds have hearts with four chambers. Reptiles and turtles have hearts with three chambers. Fish have hearts with two chambers. Insects and mollusks have hearts with one chamber. Worms have hearts with one chamber, although they may have as many as eleven single-chambered hearts. Unicellular bacteria have no hearts at all; but even they have fluid eternally in motion, washing from one side of the cell to the other, swirling and whirling. No living being is without interior liquid motion. We all churn inside.

So much held in a heart in a lifetime. So much held in a heart in a day, an hour, a moment. We are utterly open with no one in the end—not mother and father, not wife or husband, not lover, not child, not friend. We open windows to each but we live alone in the house of the heart. Perhaps we must. Perhaps we could not bear to be so naked, for fear of a constantly harrowed heart. When young we think there will come one person who will savor and sustain us always; when we are older we know this is the dream of a child, that all hearts finally are bruised and scarred, scored and torn, repaired by time and will, patched by force of character, yet fragile and rickety forevermore, no matter how ferocious the defense and how many bricks you bring to the wall. You can brick up your heart as stout and tight and hard and cold and impregnable as you possibly can and down it comes in an instant, felled by a woman's second glance, a child's apple breath, the shatter of glass in the road, the words *I have something to tell you,* a cat with a broken spine dragging itself into the forest to die, the brush of your mother's papery ancient hand in the thicket of your hair, the memory of your father's voice early in the morning echoing from the kitchen where he is making pancakes for his children.

OTHERWISE KNOWN AS THE HUMAN CONDITION

(with Particular Reference to Doughnut Plant Doughnuts)

Geoff Dyer

For many years I lived in various flats either on or just off Brixton Water Lane. So I was always walking, cycling, or taking a bus down Effra Road. How many times did I walk down Effra Road? How many hours did I spend walking down Effra Road? If I was going to Brixton Rec to play squash, or to Franco's for a pizza or a cappuccino (this was before I acquired the refinement of taste in cappuccinos that, in the years since then, has invariably been a source of torment and frustration rather than enhanced satisfaction), or to the aptly named Effra to meet friends for drinks, or just to take the tube to some other part of London, I always had to trudge or cycle down Effra Road. Wherever I was going, the journey began and ended on Effra Road. One of the reasons I moved away from Brixton was that I could not face trudging, cycling, or taking the bus down Effra Road again. Effra Road was so deeply lodged in my muscle memory that I could have made my way home blind or after some kind of seizure or stroke had completely wiped out part of my brain. Assuming I was able to walk, I could have made my way down Effra Road when I was no longer capable of going anywhere—or doing anything—else.

The route never varied, but, in small and large ways, the experience changed over time. In the mid-1980s, when a lot of my friends lived in the area, the fact that I was always bumping into someone I knew as we made our respective ways up and down Effra Road added to the cozy sense that this was exactly where I most wanted to be in the world. Over time, the road itself changed also. The disused Cool Tan plant was co-opted for various alternative ventures: pre-rave-type parties; a sensory-deprivation flotation tank. My friend Heather Ackroyd grew the first of her grass sculptures there in the 1980s. Then it became the European Business Centre or something like that. Then branches of Halfords and Currys opened (very handy for the one time I needed to buy a fridge). What struck me about this was how completely each new development obliterated the previous one. At first you would notice that the Cool Tan plant had been knocked down, that something was being built in its stead. But once that new thing was completed it was as though the previous thing had never been there. It was the opposite of the model of the unconscious offered by Freud: a version of Rome in which all successive stages of construction are preserved simultaneously. I struggle to remember the Cool Tan factory. To all intents and purposes, Currys and Halfords have been there forever, even if they are no longer there. I don't know. I haven't been to check, haven't walked down Effra Road for ages (thank god) and I hope I never have to do so again.

I say Effra Road but it could be any road. We are always taking the same routes through cities. The tube forces us to do this, and so—less claustrophobically—do buses. Even on a bike, when we can take any route, we allow ourselves to get funneled along familiar paths, preferring the often slightly longer but nicer cycle lanes because they are ostensibly safer even though they can actually be more dangerous because one is in a state of less than heightened alert. As pedestrians, too, we not only stick to the same routes but prefer to cling to the same side of the road (north side of Effra Road going into Brixton, south side coming home, in the same direction as the traffic). This tendency to the habitual expresses in linear terms the way that, in a vast city like London, we avail ourselves of only a fraction of the numerous other opportunities—all those concerts, films, and lectures listed in *Time Out,* a magazine that I stopped buying years ago—and alternative routes open to us. As the routes prescribed by habit grow more and more familiar, so we become increasingly oblivious to them. Alex, the protagonist of Alan Hollinghurst's *The Spell,* lives in Hammersmith but he speaks for all of us when his immediate environment gets reduced to "a block or two worn half-invisible by use."

We tend always to approach a given place from the same direction, via the same route. I am always surprised how thoroughly disorienting it is if I arrange to meet someone at a café I know well but, for whatever reason—an earlier appointment somewhere else—end up approaching it from an unusual direction. It's completely bewildering, as if the place we are supposed to be meeting at has disappeared. What's happened to it? Where did it go? Psychologically, the location of a place is not fixed. It is determined not by *where* it is but by *how* we get to it.

Even though I was unhappy and lonely for much of my time there, I always think of the period when I lived on rue Boulle in the eleventh arrondissement of Paris as an idyllic phase of my life. Partly this was because I liked the *quartier* so much, partly it was because I was able to leave and approach my apartment in so many ways. Depending on where in the city I was going I could use one of three Métro stops served by three different lines. I could get buses at the Bastille. If I was walking somewhere I could set off in all sorts of directions. Now, obviously, your home is always the hub from which you branch out, but when I lived off or on Brixton Water Lane, 90 percent of the time I would be heading east, into Brixton, along the Effra Road. Whereas when I lived on rue Boulle, my routes were divided equally between the ten options that were available. All points of the compass were equally alluring. There was always some reason to go in a new direction. Having said that, being a creature of habit, I did tend to go to the same place every morning for my coffee and croissant—a café on rue de la Roquette—and I always took the same route there, just as I always took the same route to the same café—the Croissant d'Or—when I lived on Esplanade in New Orleans, or as I did when I trudged down Effra Road for a cappuccino in Franco's (or Franca Manca, as it has now become).

I am like Michael Hofmann in his poem "Guanajuato Two Times":

> I could keep returning to the same few places
> till I turned blue, till I turned into
> José José
> on the sleeve of his new record album
> "What is love?"

I like to go back to the same few places all the time—then, as soon as I break free of the prison of routine, I am left wondering why I kept going to a place I had stopped enjoying years earlier. For many years, whenever I had errands to run or meetings to attend in Soho, I would have a cappuccino at the Cappuccetto. Then, for reasons I can no longer remember, I started going to Patisserie Valerie a hundred yards down the road, on Old Compton Street, and wondered why I'd wasted so many years in the Cappuccetto, which, by comparison, was a dismal and unatmospheric place. I kept going to Patisserie Valerie for years after it had stopped being any good, for years after it had become a source of constant and terrible disappointment, for years after the nice Spanish waitress, Maria (who worked there for years, who always flirted a bit with my friend Chris and me), had left so that instead of this nice unchanging waitress-customer relationship we were faced with such a rapid turnover of staff as to suggest that Valerie might not be an entirely happy ship. The pastries got bigger and bigger, I no longer liked the coffee, and the staff, though rapidly changing, seemed always to be drawn from the same ex-Soviet republic where the idea of service or charm was anathema. On the larger stage, meanwhile, Valerie began opening new branches across London, thereby undermining the idea that you were at a unique quasi-bohemian hangout and creating the feeling that you were part of a mini-empire, a Starbucks in the process of formation. But I kept going anyway, even though I ranted to anyone who would listen about how terrible the service, coffees, and pastries had become.

Nietzsche loved what he called "brief habits" but so hated "enduring habits" that he was grateful even to the bouts of sickness or misfortune that caused him to break free of the chains of enduring habit. (Though most intolerable of all, he went on, would be "a life entirely devoid of habits, a life that would demand perpetual improvisation. That would be my exile and my Siberia.") Unlike Nietzsche, I succumb all too easily to enduring habits. Programmed by habit, I kept going to Patisserie Valerie until I met the woman who became my wife. She persuaded me to meet her in the Monmouth Street Coffee Shop or, later, at Fernandez & Wells on Beak Street, one of the new wave of antipodean cafés that is revolutionizing the coffee scene in Soho. Once I had taken my custom to Fernandez & Wells or to Flat White (on Berwick Street), I never thought of Patisserie Valerie again except with regret for all the years I had loyally wasted there. I would like to claim I am now in a state of bliss, but the truth is that the pastries at Fernandez & Wells and Flat White could be a lot better, are actually a bit on the dismal side.

Which brings me to the thing I really want to talk about, namely doughnuts of New York.

In September 2004 I rented a studio apartment on Thirty-Seventh Street between Park and Lex, in Manhattan. It was a very busy period for me; all sorts of things had to be sorted out with some urgency, but although there were other, ostensibly more serious things to sort out, nothing was more urgent than the need to find a local café I could go to every day for my elevenses.

Given that so many conditions had to be met, this was easier said than done. First, the coffee had to be exactly as I liked it, although I would have been hard-pressed to define exactly how this was. Second, the pastry had to be exactly as I liked it. By pastry I mean a croissant or doughnut—I don't like those American staples, muffins or bagels. Third, I would never drink coffee out of a paper cup; the coffee had to be served in a proper china cup. This is not as easy as you might think. There are plenty of places in Manhattan where, although the coffee is good, it is only served in a paper or Styrofoam cup. Fourth, when I said cup I meant cup (i.e., cup, not mug) and, fifth, it had to be the right size cup. This question of size is not simply a matter of size; I have never ever had a nice cappuccino in a place where they serve them in those jumbo-size cups; all you get is a great bucket of foam.

In the excited hope that it might be possible to fulfill these conditions I began to explore the neighborhood, which turned out to be far more promising than I'd initially thought, especially if you walked east a couple of blocks to Third Avenue. I went into a place called Delectica on the corner of Third and Thirty-Eighth. It looked like the kind of place where people had a quick lunch or picked up a coffee on the way to work—but they did at least have proper cups. It wasn't atmospheric, but I saw that as well as proper cups they had a wide selection of pastries. I ordered a cappuccino and it was okay—a bit too frothy, but it came in a cup the right size. I also ordered a croissant. It wasn't up to much, but great croissants are quite rare in Manhattan (and, increasingly, in Paris too). When I'd stayed for a few weeks on Prince Street near Mott, I went to Gitane, a very cool café, but the croissants, as is so often the case, were just a species of bun. I once commented on this to the dreadlocked waitress, who said, in explanation, that they came from Balthazar, as though the fact that they hailed from this swish restaurant transformed them from soggy buns into something crisp and fluffy.

I went back to Delectica the following day and ordered another cappuccino and a doughnut. The doughnut I ordered that day was a ring doughnut, and it was an amazing doughnut. This was a major turning point in my New York life. As such, it will feature prominently in my forthcoming book *Great Pastries of the World: A Personal View*. It will be autobiography, odyssey, and testament. It will be a tale of epic disappointments and giddy successes, one of which, undoubtedly, is the discovery of the doughnut in Delectica. It had a slight glaze of icing—but not too much—and this icing wasn't too sweet. And the texture . . . what can I say about the texture except what I said to myself on that fateful morning: "Wow-ee," I said, "this is really something, this is a *major doughnut experience* I'm having here." The doughnut experience was perfectly complemented by the cappuccino experience, which had been quite nice the day before but today was right on the money. It wasn't a coffee with a scum of foam floating on the top; no, the foam was *integrated* with the coffee. Foam and coffee were one. It had been made by a different person, and she had made it perfectly. I had not made any specific requests but this waitress, quite by chance, had made my cappuccino exactly as I liked it and had, in the process, made something much more than that—namely, my day. And not just *that* day, because from then on, if I was in the queue and the other waitress offered to serve me, I would say I was still making up my mind—even though I had exactly the same thing every day—and wait until the waitress who made my cappuccino exactly as I liked it was free.

It's funny, even though I ended up going there every day for six weeks, I never achieved any great rapport with this waitress who brought me so much happiness each day. We never chatted or flirted in the way that I had eagerly flirted with the dreadlocked waitress in Gitane as she brought me my soggy—frankly soul-destroying—croissant each day; in fact, after a very short time the waitress in Delectica would prepare my cappuccino and serve my doughnut without my saying a word, but in its austere, functional way it was a perfect relationship. Part of the reason for this silence—at least on my part—was that the stakes were so high. Every day—except Mondays, when they didn't have any doughnuts, so I had, as they say, to take my custom elsewhere—the coffee and doughnut were perfect. Anything less than perfection would have been disappointing, and disappointment would, in this context, have been devastating. It's quite possible that disappointment could have made me go completely to pieces or completely berserk. I could have ended up throwing the coffee in her face and then breaking down in tears of self-pity. But it never happened—each day this standard of unparalleled excellence was maintained.

And so my life fell into the unvarying routine I crave and need. I would wake up, have my muesli at home, work for a bit, and then go to Delectica for my elevenses. I say "unvarying," but gradually, as my eagerness to go to Delectica increased, I found it impossible to concentrate on my work because all I could think about was my doughnut and coffee, and so I started having my elevenses earlier and earlier until I ended up skipping breakfast and having my elevenses at nine. At the latest. I went to bed at night looking forward to my nineses and then, as soon as I woke up, I stumbled out of bed, dressed, and went to Delectica before I was even properly awake. I got dressed in a hurry, I hurried down there, and then although I loved them and should have savored them, I started gobbling my doughnut and drinking my coffee in a hurry, gobbling and slurping them down in such a frenzy that I barely tasted a thing. Before I knew it, this, the high point of my day, was over with. It was only eight forty-five and there was nothing to look forward to. I also found it increasingly difficult to keep my rapture to myself. One morning, as I gobbled my doughnut and slurped my coffee, thinking to myself, *What a fantastic doughnut, what an amazing coffee,* I realized that I had not just thought this but was actually saying aloud, "What a fantastic doughnut! What a totally fantastic experience!" and that this was attracting the attention of the other customers, one of whom turned to me.

"You like the doughnuts, huh?" he said.

"And the coffee!" I said. "The doughnut would be nothing without the coffee—and vice versa."

"Where you from?" he said.

"England."

"Don't they have doughnuts like that in England?"

"Not like this they don't," I said. "I've spent twenty years searching for just such a doughnut. Now that I've found it I can go to my grave a happy man. I've achieved everything I wanted from life."

"Well, enjoy," he said, as though I had been making a joke.

"Sure will," I said, and resumed my chewing.

The problem of going to Delectica earlier and earlier for my elevenses was eventually resolved in a very simple way—by going there for lunch as well. It turned out that they made very nice roasted vegetable sandwiches, but I don't intend dwelling on these sandwiches because what's important in this parable is me and my state of mind, otherwise known as the human condition. I'd moved into what I thought was a non-neighborhood in quite desperate circumstances in a thoroughly distraught frame of mind. Basically I was on the brink of total nervous collapse but gradually, largely through the discovery of Delectica, my state of mind improved and I regained my appetite for life, of which my appetite for doughnuts might best be seen as a metaphor or symbol.

Time passed. I was only subletting this apartment for six weeks. I arranged to sublet another place, for another six weeks, in the heart of the East Village, on Ninth Street between First and A. As the time for moving grew close, I realized that I had actually come to love my apartment and my neighborhood and that I was blissfully happy there. No sooner had I realized this than I realized I was in countdown mode, that I only had five mornings left to take my coffee and doughnut in Delectica. Then I had just four, then three. . . . It wasn't just the thought of leaving that was terrible; it was the knowledge that as soon as I moved into my new place I'd have to start over again. Eventually I had no more days left. I moved into my new place and once again began rolling the stone up the steep hill of consumer choice. The problem here was almost the opposite of the one I'd faced on Thirty-Seventh Street—there were too many cafés. I hardly knew where to start so I sought guidance from my friend Jaime, who lived a couple of blocks away and who explained that the doughnuts I loved at Delectica came from a place called the Doughnut Plant and that the aptly named Doughnut Plant distributed their doughnuts to quite a few places, one of which was on the corner of Third and A, opposite 2 Boots, the Cajun pizza place that I had been completely obsessed by and utterly dependent on when I lived in New York in the late 1980s. They did have the doughnuts at this place on the corner of Third and A, but the coffee came in a mug and wasn't so nice. It was too frothy and rather bland. After a while I discovered that I could get Doughnut Plant doughnuts even closer to home, on my street, on the corner of

Ninth and A, but the coffee there was really not up to much so I preferred to go down to Third and A. Well, it was okay, and I trudged down there every day but with nothing like the spring in my step that had characterized my trips to Delectica. In every other respect this was a perfect neighborhood, it was full of cool people, there were tons of cheap places to eat, and the St. Mark's bookstore was only a five-minute walk away. . . .

Yes, it was a great neighborhood, but in my cups I often fell to thinking about Delectica and although I never walked up there just for coffee, if I had any excuse, however flimsy, to go up that way, I would stop off at Delectica. Delectica had been my base, it was the point from which my sense of familiar and localized happiness had spread. It was the epicenter of my well-being, what Marx, in a non-pastry-related context, termed the heart of a heartless world. I've always been dependent on places like this wherever I've lived. In New Orleans it was the Croissant d'Or, in Rome it was the bar San Calisto in Trastevere, in Brixton it was Francos. Even if I am only in a place for a short while I quickly build up a routine: I want not just to visit a city but to *inhabit* it as rapidly as possible. A few years ago I was in Turin for a conference. I was only there three days, but, in a classic instance of the Nietzschean "brief habit," I came to love having my coffee and *cornetto* in the café across the road from my hotel. (Turin, of course, is where Nietzsche suffered his final breakdown—a desperately successful attempt to break free of the habit of sanity?) If I were in Turin tomorrow I would return to that same café immediately and it would be a completely satisfactory experience, but when you've had an ongoing relationship with a place, when you've built your life around it as I had built mine around Delectica, there is no going back.

Sometimes this is literally the case: places close or change hands, the disused Cool Tan factory where Heather grew her grass sculptures turns into a branch of Halfords; the lease runs out or the management changes or a new chef comes along and where previously you found delight now there only lurks the grim specter of the kind of disappointment that haunted my last years at Patisserie Valerie when I kept going back there even though I knew, in my heart, that it was time to move on. But even if nothing changes, even if the place and the food and the staff remain unchanged, there is still no going back even though, of course, one does exactly that: one goes back.

When we went to New Orleans for a wedding earlier this year, I took my wife to see my old apartment on Esplanade (I could not find it exactly, was not sure whether the building that seemed in roughly the location was actually my building or was a new building that had been built on the same site), and then we took exactly the walk that I used to take to the Croissant d'Or. It was still there and we ordered cappuccinos and croissants, and the croissant, while it was just about tolerable, was nowhere near as good as I remembered and the coffee was pretty terrible (too milky and the foam was all bubbly, and although it seemed okay at first, by the halfway stage I decided it was totally revolting). That was nothing, though, compared to the disappointment of my return to Delectica about a year and a half after first discovering it.

I was staying at a hotel on Forty-Eighth Street and Seventh Avenue but, such is my compulsion to repeat experiences, I trudged across town and went to Delectica. It took about forty minutes to get there. They still had the doughnuts but I recognized none of the staff. I ordered a cappuccino. When it was prepared I looked in horror: it was like a knickerbocker glory or something with foam piled high like cream in a tall glass.

"What on earth is that?" I demanded.

"A cappuccino," the waitress said proudly.

"Well, that's where you're wrong," I said. "It's not a cappuccino. It's an abominaccino! If you knew how much this place meant to me . . ." I couldn't go on. I felt so angry and so sorry for myself that I stormed out of the door and into the street, where I began asking people, randomly, if they knew any cafés where they stocked Doughnut Plant doughnuts, getting myself into more and more of a frenzy as I did so. Obviously, most people had not heard of Doughnut Plant doughnuts, and the few who had heard of them did not know of a café that stocked them, but eventually someone said that they thought Oren's Daily Roast stocked Doughnut Plant doughnuts and he thought that there was a branch of Oren's in Grand Central Station. And so, like a commuter hurrying for a train, I made my way to Grand Central Station. Finding Grand Central Station was easy enough, but finding Oren's Daily Roast within the vast station complex was extremely difficult. Eventually I found it, saw it, saw a line of people queuing up, saw that although it was essentially just a stall, they did indeed stock Doughnut Plant doughnuts but that only one vanilla doughnut remained. I joined the queue. If anyone had taken the last doughnut I would have pleaded with her and put my case—"If you knew what I have been through this morning . . ." If, after pleading with her to take something else, she had refused, I would have snatched the doughnut from her hand and started chewing on it frantically, but no one wanted this last doughnut and so I ordered it together with a cappuccino and although I had to drink my cappuccino out of a paper cup, standing, like a commuter who has missed the train he had been hurrying for, I was grateful, in the circumstances, to have got a coffee and a doughnut at all.

Thereafter, whenever I was in New York, I checked online at the Doughnut Plant website to find a Doughnut Plant outlet close to wherever I was staying. When I was staying at the Maritime in Chelsea for a week, the best bet seemed Joe's Art of Coffee on Waverly Place. A fifteen-minute walk, often in terrible weather, but it was well worth it. The coffee was amazing, they had the doughnuts, though it was often touch and go whether they had *enough* doughnuts. On two occasions there was only one doughnut left and as had happened at Oren's Daily Roast, I found myself in a state of great tension, waiting to see if someone would take the last doughnut, girding my loins to say, "Excuse me, sir/madam, but I wonder if there is anything else that takes your fancy because, frankly, I *must* have that doughnut." It never came to that; miraculously, there was always at least one doughnut left for me, and the combination of doughnut and excellent coffee was bliss, even better, in a way, than Delectica, because unlike Delectica this was a cool and atmospheric place in a fun neighborhood. I went there so often in the course of my week-long stay that I took out a loyalty card and, on my last morning, my loyalty was rewarded with a free coffee: a perfect example of Nietzsche's ideal of the brief habit.

My last trip to New York was nothing like as happy. I was staying at a hotel on Fifty-Fifth Street and Broadway, very near the N and R subway lines, so I took the train down to Joe's Art of Coffee on Thirteenth Street near Union Square. They had Doughnut Plant doughnuts all right, but not the ones I like, only the more exotic flavors and so, thinking quickly—I had a hectic schedule, was pressed for time, should not really have been schlepping down all this way just for a coffee and a doughnut—I decided to walk back to the Waverly Place branch. I got there and it was the same story except it was even worse than the same story because in addition to not having doughnuts I wanted, the coffee was too milky and the doughnut I opted for—coconut glaze, filled with coconut cream—was actually a bit horrible and as I sat there chewing I found it hard to fathom what could lead anyone to abandon the basic doughnut, the default doughnut from which all others are derived, in favor of the more elaborate versions that may appeal to some tastes. To be honest, I made my way to the subway with my tail between my legs, wishing, at some level, that I was not forced to live this way, was not compelled to seek out things I have decided I like in the face of terrible odds. Sitting in the subway car as it clanged and hurtled back to Midtown, I reflected on the way that wherever we live we are always compelled to repeat the same thing over and over, that at some level, perhaps every level, all we ever do is trudge up and down Effra Road and that whatever we are talking about, whether it is something pleasurable (like finding the supreme doughnut) or something onerous (like taking the subway or the tube), when we talk about life we might just as well talk about trudging up and down Effra Road, irrespective of where we are in the world.

The story could have ended there—I intended ending it there—on a note of glum resignation, but to present a truly global picture of how things stand, mention must be made of a recent trip to Tokyo. It seems to me that we are always trying to re-create our particular ideal of a city in whichever actual city we happen to find ourselves. Before going to Tokyo I remembered reading, on the Doughnut Plant website, that they had opened a branch in

Tokyo, not a concession in the sense of a place where Doughnut Plant doughnuts cooked in New York were available for purchase in Tokyo but an actual doughnut-producing Doughnut Plant. As in New York, these doughnuts were available at a number of locations throughout the sprawling megalopolis that is Tokyo. We were staying at the Peninsula in Marunouchi and by studying the Doughnut Plant website carefully we saw that the nearest location was a branch of Dean & DeLuca, a mere fifteen minutes' walk away.

There were other reasons for going to Japan, of course. There were ancient temples and carp ponds, there were geishas and cherry blossoms, there were incredible feats of retail architecture, and there was the sci-fi neon of Shinjuku, but at the back of my mind, in contrast to the untranslatable otherness of Japan, was the familiar prospect of Doughnut Plant doughnuts, which, far from being reminders of home, were, for most of the year—the part of the year spent in London—site-specific New York treats, edible emblems of everything that New York was and London was not. So that what I was looking for was not *London*-in-Tokyo but *New York*-in-Tokyo.

Ryszard Kapuściński claimed that whereas in the past an encounter with "the Other" meant an encounter between a European (white) and an Easterner (non-white), increasingly there would be contacts between these Others and *other* Others (Indians and South Americans, say, or Chinese and Africans). That, it seemed to me, was what we had here. The doughnut as Other (i.e., not England) being consumed in Dean & DeLuca (the quintessential upmarket New York deli) in a part of Tokyo (the quintessential urban Other) that looked incredibly like downtown Chicago. I am not quite sure what I mean by this, am worried slightly that I am using "Other" in the sense of "Same," but it doesn't matter because we went kind of insane in Tokyo.

Because it was not New York (home of the doughnut), because it was a kind of double treat (a place where one did not expect to find doughnuts, *where doughnuts were miraculously available*), my wife and I ordered two doughnuts each and two coffees each, each and every day. We would sit there with vanilla ice stuck to our faces and noses, smiling and chewing. In a sense this was everything that was bad about the homogenizing effect of globalization, an upmarket equivalent of finding a McDonald's in every city on earth, or a branch of Patisserie Valerie in every area of London, but the thing, the point I want to emphasize, is that I love doughnuts and I wouldn't mind if there were a Doughnut Plant outlet on every city block in London—the world would be a better place.

We arrived at Dean & DeLuca at ten on the dot every day. One day it wasn't open, would not be open until eleven, because, we discovered, this was a Japanese national holiday. We stood outside. There was nowhere to sit but there was a keen wind that made standing even more irksome. There was nothing to do but wait. We were in a pedestrian version of the London double bind whereby if we walked back to the hotel—and we had already begun to find this walk onerous; in less than five days Naka Dori had taken on some of the qualities of Effra Road, stroll had turned to trudge—we would have had to set out again the moment we got back there. So we had pure dead time to kill. We were in this strange, strangely familiar city, and we stood there as time congealed around us on the nearly deserted, litterless street. We stood and waited and it was like being one of the undead, because whatever we thought of doing, there was nothing to do and so we just stood there in the keen wind, wishing time would pass, wanting one thing and one thing only: for time to pass, to get out of the wind and into Dean & DeLuca so that we could order our doughnuts and coffees and sit down, eating and drinking them in this distant part of the world that, at this moment, at the moment that was not yet at hand but that was drawing closer at an agonizingly slow pace, contained everything that we wanted from a city, namely, *doughnuts.*

Eventually Dean & DeLuca opened, we scoffed our doughnuts and swilled our coffees, and then, when we had finished scoffing and swilling, walked back to the hotel, noticing, as we had failed to on the way down (I was blind to everything except the prospect of doughnuts), the Japanese flag—the red circle on a field of white—flying from many buildings. It seemed that although there were many nice flags in the world, none was nicer than the Japanese flag, even though when I was growing up, reading about Japanese atrocities in the Pacific War, it had seemed a symbol of pure evil. It did not seem like that at all now; now it became a symbol of the healing potential of the doughnut, of a world community of doughnut lovers living in peace and harmony, bound together by the vision and ambition of a Czech immigrant who went to New York, opened his Doughnut Plant, and then forged a doughnut empire, extending from New York to Tokyo while regrettably bypassing London, where we still have to make do with croissants that are like stale buns so that at times the whole of London seems like nothing else so much as an interminable extension of Effra Road.

CID–LAX–BOG

Lina Ferreira

Any minute now a message from the Offices of International Students and Scholars Services will appear in my inbox.

Please read this email carefully.

And I will. Though, of course, I don't have to.

It is the same email I've read dozens of times before, and like every time before I will find—listed at the very top—my full name. Official, personalized. With the strange precision and familiarity of automated bureaucracy.

My name. Long and unpronounceable. Too many *R*s. "So many *R*s! Am I saying this right? *Fuh-ruh-rah*?" But the name is Portuguese, so technically, I'm not saying it right either. *Feh-rrrrr-eee-rah*.

Dear Lina Maria Ferreira Cabeza-Vanegas.

Like my mother would say when I'd made her truly mad. "Lina Maria," number of names directly proportional to the heat of her rage, "Ferreira Cabeza-Vanegas." Personal, precise. Though the email itself will be pocked with the generalities of mass-generated messages.

Some students may not need to respond. Your legal status may be impacted.

A list of self-selecting "if's" cascading down the page like an immigration Choose Your Own Adventure.

If you plan to apply for an extension . . .

If you plan to change your legal status . . .

If you believe you have received this message in error . . .

I don't. I can't. I haven't.

The eleventh of May is my last day here. Then sixty courtesy days to exit the country, during which—the email informs me—I'm not allowed to work or drive.

If you fail to apply for a necessary extension . . .

Though I most certainly will do both. Sixty days. *Ticktock.*

So I hit refresh. MLA, NWP, HigherEd Jobs, the Higher Education Recruitment Consortium. *Click-click, tick-tick.* I send out letters and emails like braids down tower walls and corked bottles into high tide. Like that kid in grade school who would catch beetles and ladybugs to write his name across their shells with marker, in case they ever came back. "This way I'll know they're mine."

Reinstatement requires approval, a minimum of $290 in fees, several months of processing, and does not have guaranteed approval.

I feel sweat stream down my back as the summer presses itself up against the windows. I listen to the ambulances driving past my apartment and a sound I can't quite make out inside the walls. Something shifting between rooms, like the creaking of wet ropes, or the turning of a crumbling wind wheel. As if I were living inside the rotting belly of whaling shipwreck.

By following these instructions, you will avoid that difficulty.

Hickory Moby Dickory Dock. *Tick-tick, tock-tock.*

You are responsible for your own legal status.

"Welcome to the Unmmm . . . of . . . Ammrr . . . May I please have you Immm . . . frmmmm . . . ?" The second time I entered the United States on my own I was greeted by an exhausted, middle-aged immigration officer with a three-fingered hand. He slurred his words like a drunk sailor and thumbed through my passport pages before looking at the blue immigration form I'd filled while flying over Mexico, and then he sighed. "Wrrrng."

"I'm sorry?"

He cleared his throat. "Wrong. Got to do it over."

I stand at a barely roller-coaster-permissible five feet two inches. Three inches below average and scarcely another three above the Atlanta airport immigration counter. Eight hours on a plane, a sleepless night before, and a desperate need to rest my head on the sticky counter beside the immigration officer's hand. So, it was hard to concentrate. A counter whispering promises of primordial sleep. But then, that hand. Bull's-eye center counter. A thumb, an index, a middle finger, and two sprawling knuckle-knot scars like a tarp laid over copper pipes.

If I could have only laid my head down for a second, I thought, everything would have faded into a self-solving haze. "Got to do it over. Understand?" But it would not move. His hand would not give an inch. It sat firmly on the counter, unmoving and unmovable. Skin and scar and anchor, full of bones full of stones. "Hey!" So, I tried to picture it in motion. A three-finger cancan, then a hermit crab shuffle, and finally one long sweep across the surface of the counter. Fingers and knuckles striking my forehead and nose, brushing me off as if he were sweeping crumbs from a table. "You listening?"

It's not complicated. Not really, not at all. A dozen little fill-in-the-blank boxes. I went through them quietly in my head, trying to find my error. *Name,* right, *birth date,* right, *address,* right.

"Which," I started, while the officer began waving the next person over, "part?"

"What?"

"Which . . ." Three-fingered hand on a lovely flat counter. "Which is the wrong one? Where's the one . . . the not right one?"

He looked down at me and I looked up at him. He had a reddish white face and eyebrows like prickly patches of gray grass. I remember hearing knuckle bones turning like gears inside his hand, but that memory can't be true, can it? "Residence."

Below the blue eagle inside the blue circle at the top left corner. About three inches down. Question number seven: *Country of residence.* So, *right,* I thought, *right.*

Country of residence, in mid-flight turbulence penmanship. *USA. Country,* I thought. *Residence,* I thought. Rolodex bilingual brain loop. *To reside, to live, to inhabit, to dwell, to settle, to occupy. To nest, endure, sojourn.* Re-side. Re-sident. *Where do I settle-dwell-nest-endure? Where do I lay down my head?*

So, *right,* I thought. *That's right, right?* So, "That's right," I told him. "Right?"

The immigration officer straightened his back, spine like the string in a trap. "Like, what's the wrong part of it?" Thinking, perhaps, that I should have written out the whole thing, *The United States of . . .*

"The," he said, taking a breath as if he were loading a gun, "the part that says, 'country of residence.'" Then he lifted that three-fingered hand from the counter. I stared at the ghost mark of condensation it left behind, thinking of how vast it really was, that short distance between my head and the counter. "Do it," words, lead-heavy and lead-slow, "over," he said pointing at a table against the very back wall of the room.

"But . . ." I tried again.

"Please." Taut spine-trap snap and tall immigration officer like a leaning tower of Babel as he bent low to meet my eye. "Do it over."

"But, what's the right answer?"

I visit a friend's apartment and look at all the shiny surfaces and upholstered things in her home. I lay my hand on an end table and it feels electrified, charged and sticky with days and dust. I dream of shapes falling into place and rooms full of sun-dried amulets to ward off impermanence.

I set aside some books I don't want to part with: my great-grandfather's dictionaries, a green book with a dedication, and a leaning-tower stack of books on Colombian history. In the morning I pack all these things along with my passport and computer in a duct-taped canvas bag and go out. I drive around town with the windows down. I buy apples and kimchi and oatmeal in a corner store, and no one I meet so much as suspects. I could have kept driving, leapt onto a train or the back of someone's pickup truck. I walk in and out of bookshops and 7-Elevens, I fall asleep in someone's front yard, and I stay out until the insects descend on me as if I'm covered in sugar, blood, and neon light. And then, because there's nowhere else to go, I go back home.

Hi Lina,

Open tabs, single digits, scrolling advertisements, and the sound of me clicking away on a hundred-dollar computer I bought in a garage sale two months ago.

You are due for the Imaging study here in Psychiatry.

Two years ago, I responded to a mass-generated email sent out by the University of Iowa Hospital and Clinics.

You will need to do a 0.5 hour brain scan and 1.5–2 hours of cognitive testing.

A week later I rode my bike to the hospital through sprinklers and joggers and puffy brown birds mimicking the sound of speeding ambulances. I made my way past well-lit lobbies, waiting rooms, and hallways, and I got lost twice before finally finding the wing reserved for researchers and their research subjects.

Payment is $120. Scanning times are generally between 8:30–3:30. I will contact you closer to the time to set up an appointment.

A woman in white sneakers holding a clipboard met me by the elevators and explained that before the initial brain scan some tests needed to be administered. So, "Of course," I said, and, "makes sense," I said, as she led me into a small room where two more women sat waiting for me. I tried to fix my posture and smile like those charming people in sport-themed airport bars, swiping their cards and checking their watches. But the woman in the sneakers was already gone and the two new women were clicking their pens and scribbling notes. *Come in, sit down*. The younger of the two explained that the other was only there to attest to the scientific standards of the evaluation. So, "Of course," I said. "Makes sense," I said, and sat down. I glanced over at the older woman who called herself the monitor, and who instructed me to ignore her completely because she was "Not important" and "Only there to observe the observer," whom she then instructed to begin the study, and who in turn instructed me to pay close attention because this was "very important," and the whole reason for being there. "Find your way through," she said, handing me a pencil and placing a piece of paper on the table. "Nothing too complicated. Just a maze. Easy, right?"

I looked at the monitor whom I was not supposed to look at and then back at the grad student. "Easy."

"Do you have any questions for me?"

Sometimes the tests start before the tests have started. The study that you are taking part in is not the study you thought you were taking part in. So, "Is there," I asked, turning to the woman who wasn't important, "anything I should be asking?"

"Oh." The younger seemed confused. She turned to the monitor. "Is . . . is there something? I'm just supposed to ask. People don't usually ask anything."

Then silence while we both waited for the woman who wasn't important to shake her head and tell us that that wasn't important either, and that it was okay to keep going.

"Okay, then. Ready?" the younger woman asked.

"Ready."

And she clicked the start buttons on the chronometer hanging from her neck. *Ready.* Six two-dimensional tunnels, through which my pencil sprinted. Beginning to end within five or so seconds. "Done!"

"Okay, now this one." She laid out the next sheet with a maze about twice the size of the previous one, and I fought the urge to start from the heart of it and draw the line back out because it always seems easier to find your way back than to find your way in. "Ready?"

"Ready." I dug the lead into the page like a knife. My full weight against the pencil and I feared it might snap. Feared it would burst into splinters, lightning-split and wooden sparks. Partly to mask my overeagerness for the first maze—which maybe I had thought would be the only maze—*What? This is how I always do mazes. Do mazes all the time, me.* And partly because this is a rare definite problem I can rarely definitely solve.

One, two, three. Each maze doubling in size from the last. Four, five. A wild-rabbit pencil leaping and crashing through printer-ink tunnels, searching desperately for a way through. "How many more?"

"This'll be the last one."

Iowa City is a quasi-transient town. Of seventy thousand residents nearly thirty thousand are students who come and go as they please. From house to house, and state to state, counties and countries, study abroads and jobs and stupors and fogs, like semi-domesticated animals, the tumbleweed people of tumbleweed towns.

I sit on my doorstep and watch them pack the trunks of their cars with coolers and grills, sometimes for tailgating, sometimes for barbeques, sometimes for nearby lakes full of golden fish and black-green frogs. Drive out, drive back. I watch them pack backpacks and purses and clutch bags full of loose pens and change and lip gloss. Sometimes for class, sometimes for fun. Go out, come back. Watch them pack large Penske trucks full of Hawkeye memorabilia and sidewalk furniture. Drive out—always, eventually—never come back. And I like the summer solitude of half-deserted college towns. I like walking at three in the morning when the earth has finally cooled and nothing awake can speak any language I can understand. I like watching them drive away. And I like it when they don't come back.

"So where are ya off to now? PhD? Home? Vacation?" Some days it seems like I know every single one of the remaining forty thousand people left in Iowa City. And it's always the same question.

"Not that much of a choice," I say, in the middle of the Iowa City Public Library, waiting for my next tutoring job to start. "Government says I gotta go—so I gotta go."

"Oh, right. That." The woman turns her head to a sympathetic angle, and she really does seem sincere. "Tough. Well you can always—"

"I'm thinking about having a deportation party." I cut her off before she has a chance to finish her sentence.

When I was a kid, my father's sister—who worked as a nanny for rich gringos—sent us Betamax tapes of recorded U.S. television. *Frosty the Snowman, A Pink Panther Christmas, The Dark Crystal,* and *The Blue Lagoon,* like whole rotisserie chickens, skin and bones, magnetic-strip static and seasonal Sears commercials.

"Oh yeah?"

And though neither Paula nor I spoke English, we watched them on a loop on my family's brand-new, twelve-inch, color TV.

"Sure. People could come dressed to fit the theme. It could be great." I see the woman shuffling and know she has somewhere to go, something to do, she works here—of course she does. But I don't stop talking either.

"It really could be, you should come." Apart from *The Dark Crystal,* however, we loved one commercial above the rest. A man driving through the white howl of a winter storm, a thing neither of us could really imagine, snow is a concept only fully understood knee-deep, barefoot, and hungry. On the screen a man sat in his car outside a closed garage while the white wind engulfed the vehicle, then pressed a single-red-button remote and watched as the garage door raised itself like Lazarus from his grave. "I've never thrown a theme party before . . . or a party ever, really. But how hard can it be?"

I remember rewinding the tape and watching the commercial over and over and over again. My parents said winter was brutal. *Up there? Brutal. En los Estados Unidos.* That we couldn't begin to imagine. *They pay to make their buildings feel like our weather.* The man pressed the button, the wind howled. *Bogotá isn't cold. We don't know real cold. We're lucky like that.* The door raised itself—all on its own, miraculous mechanical. *We went there once. We took our galoshes. Useless. Cold that stays with you your whole life.* The man drives in, single-red-button push, the door closes behind him. *But it's like* Star Trek, *too. You can't imagine. Doors open all on their own.* And when they said my father's sister might come back to Colombia, I couldn't imagine it either. Who would turn down *Star Trek*?

"And the theme?"

"Deportation."

The woman in the library raises an eyebrow and turns her head a little. "Like," a pause, "immigration officers?"

"No. Well, I don't know. Could be." I have not thought this through. I hear automatic doors sliding open and the AC fighting the Iowa heat. "More like, get a baby, tie an anchor to it. Wet your back, bring a green card bouquet. Maybe something to do with Home Depot?"

"Oh my!" She is smiling but she straightens her spine like someone has just dropped an ice cube down the back of her shirt. "That could be fun."

"And everyone can take something on their way out. Like a lamp, or a chair, or a book, or my TV. That way I don't have to drive that stuff to the Goodwill. Right?"

"Do you mean . . ." She plays with her name tag. "Like a baby doll, or a real baby?"

Are you feeling healthy and well today?

Are you currently taking any antibiotics?

I walk through the empty hallways of the normally undergrad-filled plasma center, and it's like a cracked maraca. The normal noise of the rolling crowds, shaking donors, and grumbling phlebotomists is now reduced to a few hollow *plicks* and *placks* inside a nearly empty building. I alone stand before the row of touch-screen computers, halfheartedly answering the prescreening questionnaire.

Have you been pregnant in the last 12 months or are you pregnant now?

Black Dynamite plays in the background, as a frat boy falls asleep in his chair and an older man in a grease-stained coat rocks back and forth while whispering into a paper cup as if it's one half of a tin-can telephone.

In the past 8 weeks have you had any vaccinations?

The frat boy catches himself right before falling off his folding chair and on to a freshly disinfected tile floor, but then he stumbles to his feet, pulls his sweatpants up and his T-shirt sleeves down, while the older man taps the side of his cup gently as if to keep the heavier words from pooling at the bottom, and I try to hear what he is whispering. The frat boy manages only two or so steps out of his chair before a beautiful, blond phlebotomist walks past us, and he pulls his pants back down and his sleeves back up, exposing a pair of black and gold basketball shorts and a pink Band-Aid on his shoulder.

In the past 12 months were you the recipient of a transplant such as organ, tissue, or bone marrow?

On-screen, Black Dynamite finds out his murdered brother had been working undercover for the CIA, and off-screen the frat boy goes into one of the screening rooms. As he walks by, he flashes his pink Band-Aid one more time and I immediately know that floating in his bloodstream, like backwash in a can of Coke, there are traces of the rabies virus.

In the past 12 months have you come into contact with someone else's blood?

I know, because I have them, too. A couple of shots a week and more than double the money for each "donation." Two shots, seven times, and one cheap, pink, fluorescent Band-Aid that always falls off within the hour, leaving a sticky outline around a swollen patch of skin.

I touch my shoulder where the Band-Aid used to be as the next question flashes on the screen.

In the past 12 months have you had a tattoo?

"You kinda have to sign it here while I watch. It's weird, I know. But, you know. Just to make sure, you know?" The Phys Sub pointed at a line that read *I understand the risks involved in participating in this study.* Which I didn't, because I barely glanced at the document before signing above the dotted line. What I did know was this: first, you were paid four times a month; second, reporting "adverse reactions" would get you booted from the program. And what's a little headache, dizziness, muscle pain, nausea, stomach pain, vomiting, diarrhea, lightheadedness, and fainting, anyway?

The Phys Sub rubbed my left shoulder with a cotton swab soaked in alcohol and asked me where I was from. "*Fu-ruh-rah?* Am I pronouncing that right?" The question implies only one correct pronunciation; it implies authority and authenticity I may not have.

"Oh, it's a Portuguese name. I'm not pronouncing it right either."

She took out a small glass vial of clear liquid and shook it like a kid with a soda can. "So, Portugal then?"

"Oh. No. Colombia. The Portuguese just got around. Colonial thing."

She ripped a new syringe out from its packaging and pulled off the plastic cap. "And your family is still out there?" I nodded. "I bet you miss them tons." I smiled. "You gonna go back after this? Or they gonna follow you up here?"

My aunt Chiqui is not long for this world and she knows it. She sits on her bed all day, staring out at Bogotá from her window. What cancer didn't take, chemo wrecked. She can barely see, barely walk, and she never leaves her apartment. She holds the oxygen mask to her face and feels a deep crumbling rot, which the doctors cannot account for, spreading through her back, so she turns to my mother and says, "Vilma, please don't go." She knows my mother has not seen her daughters all together in well over a decade, and I believe she empathizes, but she also does not want to die alone. Not in her country, not in her bedroom. Not anywhere. The rot feels deep and ancient. Like wooden beams that rot turns into moldy peach meat, fat, white worms chewing holes in her muscles and filling them back up with squirming egg sacs. The pain holds my aunt tight, and she holds my mother tighter still, but she promises that she will die soon and my mother won't have to take care of her anymore. "But please don't leave me yet."

"Probably not," I said, watching the Phys Sub stick the needle in the vial's plastic cap, a white-hot knife into a tub of vanilla ice cream.

"So," she said, "how do *you* say it then?" What does staying imply? What does going back?

"Oh, um. *Ferreira*." I rolled my tongue, overenunciating as I held up my sleeve and watched her stick the needle into my shoulder.

"Oh, wow," she said, pushing on the plunger head and pumping me full of iced rabies. Then she winked. "That's sexy." And asked, "What do you miss the most from back home?"

The second I stepped out of the air-conditioned plasma center I felt it. I scratched around the Band-Aid and felt the swollen vaccine-knot growing under my skin. Then three steps into the wafting curtains of heat and humidity of an Iowa City summer and the sky began to flicker. A white-blister sun and lemon-juice light suddenly dimmed and watered down. Translucent rabies termites crawled through my wood-rot veins, and I made it three blocks before stumbling on to a bench and fainting. And I sank, I did not swim. Something held me tight and pulled under.

So, I scratch at the scab on my left arm while I wait to be called in for my intake interview. Twice a week they stick a needle into my left arm like a spigot into a maple tree. Over the years scar tissue has built up like sap, like grime at the lip of my open vein, like barnacles, like gold flakes in a pan. Sometimes enough builds up that when a phlebotomist pierces the scab, it crumbles like a sugar cookie, warm blood drips down my forearm and pools in my palm while a man or woman in a white lab coat frantically dabs it with cotton swabs and white gauze.

While I wait to be called in a young phlebotomist tries to calm the man speaking into his paper cup. He tries to place his hand on the man's shoulder, but the man shakes it off and his whispers suddenly become audible. "I'm not going anywhere," the man says, pacing and shaking his head. "Not going anywhere. Can't make me. Can't make me. Stay right here, I'll stay right here." Sometimes speaking into his paper cup and sometimes directly at me and the young phlebotomist. "I'm staying right here."

And as a thin thread of blood drips down my forearm, I picture my veins like great cylindrical halls lined with all the willing and unwilling participants of my mixed heritage. The rabies virus pumped in as if through the vents, weaving in and out, drifting over and under all the bodies inside my body, all the mixed blood in my blood.

I sit in the Iowa City Public Library across from Sung Ho as he pulls out torn pieces of paper from a bag.

"I was watching a commercial Monday and in it they said . . . the man said . . . the voice . . . *it* said: 'Come down and test drive one . . .' Wait." He is a man of constant reiterations and interruptions. "Let me find it. I have it somewhere." I feel my neck like a rusted hinge as I watch Sung Ho pull out torn scraps of paper as if he's been gathering bread crumbs all night and now lays them out on the table so I can draw him a map of the woods. "Right. Here. 'Come on down and test drive the new Toyota Camry.' "

He turns his head and places the piece of paper between us like the last hand of the night. We've talked about this before.

"Why test drive 'the'?" He says, "You are only driving one car. You said 'an' is an old spelling for 'one.' One car. Right?"

"Right."

"And there are so many Camrys in so many of these car shops . . . malls . . . lots?"

"Lots."

"So why 'the'? Why not, 'Come test drive *a* Toyota Camry?"

We've been talking about this for weeks upon weeks for eighteen dollars an hour, but it doesn't seem to matter how many times I tell him that it doesn't *really* matter. "You *could* test drive *a* Toyota Camry too." That it's all about exposure. That if you are in the tropics you develop a tan, and if you're in Iowa you learn to drive in the snow, and you can't help it. It'll seep into you and *you'll know like they know, eventually—you'll be like them*. It doesn't matter. He wants to know now. So, I repeat, "It's mostly usage, Sung Ho," and I watch him sigh and pull out more indefinite-definite sentences from his bag.

"Does that make sense, Sung Ho?"

He nods. "Yes." Then he shakes his head. "Sort of. Not yet. I . . ." He scribbles in English with tiny Hangul notes between words. "I will think on it." And as he's pulling out another scrap of paper, his phone rings.

"Sorry, sorry," he says, "it's my wife," and he begins speaking in a fast-paced, whispered Korean. He holds the blue flip phone to his ear and cups his hands around his mouth as if he is afraid the words might spill out and soak the carpet.

"Hey, Sung Ho?" I say as he hangs up. "You are almost done, right?"

"Yes, only a few more questions."

"No." I rub my eyes and lean forward. "I mean with school."

He looks up for a brief moment and returns to the pages of commercial snippets and overheard bus conversations. "Yes, a year."

"A year is nothing," I say, and I mumble to myself that I could hold my breath for a year, *if I really needed to*. "When you're done," I start again, "will you go back?"

Sung Ho straightens his spine and narrows his eyes. He looks confused. Like I should know better, and I wish I did.

"I have a son," he says unsentimentally. "There is nothing to go back for." South Korea underwater, like a city at the bottom of a lake, and then he pulls out another piece of paper. " 'The McRib.' "

"There are other ways, you know," a friend tells me at a local bar while I scratch under the adhesive gauze wrapped around my elbow. "We can go do it first thing in the morning." Whatever Iowa City summer heat the night dispels we summon back with bodies and shouting and music and alcohol and anxiety. "Just say the word."

I laugh. There is something to be said about the kindness of inebriation offers of marriage fraud. "Done! I'll meet you at the courthouse, I'll be the one wearing a Colombian flag."

A pound of fries is set down on the table, and I begin to pull off the neon-colored, plasma-center gauze as if I'm unraveling myself by a thread. I check my inbox on my phone. *Please read this email carefully.*

"My sister married a U.S. Marine, you know?" I say while scrolling through emails and job postings.

The first time my sister went back to Colombia as a U.S. citizen, she was greeted by a blond immigration officer sitting at a folding-table desk.

She stood in line feeling the communal sweat rising and mixing in the air while sweat-stained maps sprawled across tucked-in polo shirts and white linen blouses, until, finally, the immigration officer waved her over. *Documentos y pasaportes.* "Documents and passports."

Claro. "Of course," she responded in her flat Bogotá accent, and she set down three identical blue U.S. passports—Paula, husband, and daughter. The officer picked up each one and riffled through them like an animated flip-book while heavy white foundation dripped down her forehead and down the sides of her face. She glanced at one and picked up the next while all the other crumpled-uniform officers repeated the same motions beside her.

But then she broke from the rest.

"And your passport?" she asked, looking up at my sister.

"What do you mean?" Paula asked. "Right there." But instead of a quick *oh-right-so-sorry-of-course-right-here!* The immigration officer sighed. This was a woman whose sole job was to meet travelers from all across the blue-speck world and who surely would have met other Colombians married to other foreigners by then—surely. And yet.

A sigh like steam from a pressure cooker. And she said, "No," with that mix of annoyance and disappointment usually reserved for children and dirty-pawed animals on white sofas. "You are *Colombian.* Where is your *Colombian* passport? Don't you know you can't travel without a passport?"

"Really?" My friend orders another drink. "Did she do the . . . what's it called? The swearing-in thing?"

I put my phone on the table and take an ice cube from my glass. "Yeah." I hold it between my index finger and thumb until they feel numb. "Whole thing. She even renounced her allegiance to Colombia."

"Hm. Must be true love then." My friend raises her glass as if to make a toast.

"Must be."

"So how does that work then?"

"Which part?" I scratch the terra-cotta skin ruts on my arm that the tight gauze leaves behind.

"The whole forsaking your country thing." Handfuls of fries

and mouthfuls of alcohol, and the sound of billiard balls and ice striking the edges of tables and glasses. "How does it work?"

"Oh, umm. I don't know."

"But I have a passport," Paula replied. "It's a U.S. passport because I am a U.S. citizen. And it's right there."

Documents and credentials lay scattered on the officer's table like bread crumbs. Paula changed her hair color, changed her haircut, and—much worse, for the officer—she changed her last names to match her husband's. Switched her maternal "Cabeza-Vanegas" and her paternal "Ferreira" for a single all-encompassing name, which Colombians generally don't do. So what was the officer to do? "Where is your passport?"

"Right there!" Paula points.

"No," the officer responds, "*your* passport."

"That one, that's *mine*."

"No. You are Colombian." But that is not what Paula calls herself any longer, or not what the U.S. government calls her, and maybe this isn't the point anyway. "So why don't you just give me your *Colombian* passport?"

I wonder if that is the moment when it occurred to Paula that all her shiny new documents were in English, and that the immigration officer with strands of bleach-burnt blond hair may not have been able to read any of it. Maybe this was the moment the officer became acutely aware of more than mere location inscribed in my sister's accent, because all houses stand divided, and there is privilege, education, and colonial heritage locked inside our voices and drawn on our skins. Later Paula tells me of a moment I have now forgotten, our mother, of whom I am the spitting image, in a quiet panic standing in the corner of an airport while we stood with our father across the way. "The U.S. immigration officer said there was no way to prove she was our mother, said that families have the same last name, don't you remember?" So maybe this was the moment the Colombian officer realized the similarity, the physical closeness, how the baby clung to this foreign Colombian. More likely, that's when both my sister and the officer felt the crowd growing around them, pushing in on them, inhaling the air others exhaled and exhaling it right back into their nostrils, until the room was a mist of continuous breath and sweat and human heat. And in the end, there is no more compelling argument than that.

"I really shouldn't let you in, but . . . ," said the woman who had likely never left her own country, never flown, and never had much of a choice to leave or to stay. "If you don't get a new passport," she continued as she stamped, and typed, and finally let the woman before her into the country where they were both born, "you won't be able to leave again," while white beads of makeup and sweat dripped off her dark skin. *You are Colombian.*

"Maybe," I tell my friend as the waitress sets a drink down before her, "you just say the words, 'I renounce my allegiance, I renounce my allegiance . . . ,' and it's done. Like that whole saying 'I divorce you' three times thing."

She raises an eyebrow. "I don't know." And tilts her head. "I've never renounced anything."

"Me either," I say, though I'm sure that's not true.

"What is there to renounce anyway?" She laughs and takes a sip from her drink. Half the fries are gone, and more rounds are ordered.

"Don't know," I say, flipping through emails and looking for jobs. "Satan and Colombia."

"So," a man across the table asks, "you actually leaving?"

"Looks like it," I say, suddenly remembering that there is a Colombian waitress in this bar. One of whom I often think of as more sincerely Colombian than I'm capable of being. "Unless a job comes through last minute." Reasoning that it's because she lived there longer, or lived there better, or at more important ages. Maybe she has more cousins—she cooks, she dances, she drinks *aguardiente* and goes to mass. "But that seems kinda unlikely right now." Though it might be as simple as her long black hair and dark eyes. Because I am no descendant of *indigenas,* or the drowned queens of a sacred lake. I am no true daughter of the Muisca nation, but I've no interest in moving to Europe either.

"Bummer," the person across the table says. "Do you know when you'll leave?"

"Soon," I say, still looking for the Colombian waitress. "I just gave away my books. I've only to pack up and hand my car over."

"You sold it already?"

"Mm-hmm, yesterday." I look behind the pillar, behind the bar, by the pool tables.

"Have you then," the friend beside me interrupts, "have you already bought the ticket back?"

I pause. "No . . . my father," I say, and clear my throat because it suddenly feels like I have lake water in my lungs. "He insisted on buying the ticket himself." And I leave out the bit about how he cannot really afford it and hasn't been able to afford it for a good long while now, and how sometimes I pay his credit cards. "I think maybe it's symbolic, or something." And how I'll be moving in with my parents into their one-bedroom apartment in Bogotá after nearly eight years of education in this foreign country of plenty.

"It'll be good though," she says nonchalantly, "to see them again. Right?"

I think I see the Colombian waitress coming down from a wooden staircase with a tray under her arm, and I want to speak Spanish again. I want to hear that history-heavy accent, speak in that slang. Feel like I *don't* have an "accent," and just as she turns the corner, I feel myself turn, too. Away from the staircase, away from her, sliding down my chair and pulling up my hood, because I want to say something in Spanish, but I also realize I don't have much to say.

The position has been filled thank you for your interest. . . .

We received an unexpectedly large number of applications this year. . . .

Please read this carefully.

Walking out of the bar is like sticking your head into an open chest cavity. Stagnant air and pulsing heat, and I miss the snake-jaw snap of chilly Andean nights. I miss the rain. I brush my hair behind my ear and imagine while miles away in Bogotá, my dark-skinned aunt Chiqui feels a crumbling rot inside her back and my grandmother loses the last of her memories. I think of them both in that small apartment. How my grandmother ranked her daughters and granddaughters according to the paleness of their skin. "No, Lina, you are wrong. Paula is whiter than you!" And how my aunt ranked last, and how she was the one who stayed with her all her life.

I think about talking to my mother on the phone earlier in the week.

"I don't think," I stumbled, "it's just . . . I don't think anyone is gonna hire me."

I walk through crowds of wailing undergrads, short-skirted girls sitting on the curb and vomiting in convulsive fits. "I know, Lina. I know," my mother said.

"It's just . . . I don't think." I picture myself, learning to speak the language of an overstayed visa, undocumented, illegal, thing afraid and thing to fear.

"Just consider," my mother said, "just consider . . . just staying."

There are other ways, you know.

"Just . . . ," I paused. My mother is a woman who believes in laws and fairness and holy lands and divine intent. "What do you mean?"

"Just," she said, and I could hear my grandmother's nurses shuffling in the background and my aunt moan in pain. "Lina," she said, "don't come back."

Three months after that night in the bar, a plane lands in the El Dorado airport runway in Bogotá, Colombia, and I am on it.

It lands on time but then neither docks nor moves toward any gate or walkway, as if it is struggling with indecision. Instead it veers into a far-off corner of the strip, where it sits quietly in darkness as if at the bottom of a lake, while I stare out the window at the red lights flashing through a black-fog night like the eyes of sacred snakes swimming in the deep.

Inside the cabin people wearing various assortments of Disneyland memorabilia begin to wake up tangled in cables and drool-soaked blankets. A woman tries to wake up her little girl; a man tries to look up her skirt; and my father rushes for the aisle with a return ticket in my name in his breast pocket. Because, "You'll be back in no time," he says. *Del ahogado el sombrero, de tripas corazón, donde uno menos piensa salta la liebre.* "When God closes a door . . ." *That's what this story is about,* he tells me. But I'm not sure.

"It's okay," my mother says, sitting beside me, trying to console me as she clutches my forearm. "It's okay." Though I can tell she is on the verge of tears and my return marks her failure to keep me away from a country she is convinced is a kingdom of ravenous things which will either blow me up, tear me down, or "much worse"—she says—"turn you into me."

But now she holds the tears back. I should tell her that that is not what I am afraid of, but instead I say nothing, and I feel her pat me on the arm and say, *Ya llegamos, Linita*. "We're back, now. We're home."

DOING NO HARM: SOME THOUGHTS ON READING AND WRITING IN THE AGE OF UMBRAGE

Lynn Freed

During the darkest days of apartheid, I was invited onto a morning television talk show in the San Francisco Bay Area, to appear there with a black South African writer. His memoir had recently been brought into the light by Oprah Winfrey, and he was now on the circuit with the mass-market paperback. It seemed obvious to me as to why they wanted me on the show: I was white; I'd grown up under apartheid, and I was to be held to account for its injustices and sufferings.

"I can't do it," I said to my editor.

"But you *must,*" she said. "It's wonderful exposure. And it's been far too long since your last book."

My last book, published three years before, had been an autobiographical novel about a Jewish girl growing up in a rather eccentric theatrical family in South Africa in the fifties and sixties. The book had garnered respectable reviews and caused outrage in South Africa, where the government considered a few semi-sexual scenes between white and black dangerously provocative. So they'd canceled my appearances at local universities, and on radio and television.

To be put on display again, now that all that was behind me—to be paraded out this time as the child of privilege, having to face off against a victim of such privilege—well, no, I wouldn't do it.

"Do you know," said the editor, "how many millions watch this show?"

Thousands or millions, it would only make the thing worse. "Can't they find someone else?" I said.

She sighed. "We'd like you to do this," she said impatiently, "and we'll be disappointed if you don't. But, if you're adamant, of course there's nothing we can do."

At 6 A.M., I arrived at the television station and was ushered quickly into the greenroom. The other writer was there already, staring at a television monitor on which a gerontologist was chatting amiably about geriatric incontinence. In a ribbon along the bottom of the screen ran, A WORLD OF DIFFERENCE: BLACK HISTORY MONTH, and then, NEXT: A JEWISH WOMAN DESCRIBES HER EXPERIENCES GROWING UP UNDER APARTHEID IN SOUTH AFRICA.

Jewish woman? I leaned forward to look more closely. But the gerontologist was winding up now, shaking hands, leaving the screen. And a young man had arrived to shepherd us both from the greenroom and out into the blinding light of the stage.

There I sat, hardly breathing, as the microphone was clipped on, tested, reclipped. For over a week, my friends had been rehearsing me: If they ask you this, say that. If they accuse you of that, just say this. I'd written it all down, read it in the bath every night, and then again before going to bed. But, somehow, neither the questions nor the answers would stick. The minute I read them, I forgot them.

As it happens, I am at my most useless when rehearsed. Had I gone in without trying so hard to be prepared—straining for phrases, ideas, arguments that were not my own—I might have saved myself at least this terror. But, in the event, I sat as if carved in rock, my back straight, and a look of gravity on my already-grave face.

The interviewer gave a practiced smile. She held up first the other writer's book, and then my own. "Ongoing racial injustices faced by those who grew up in South Africa," she was saying. "Devastating poverty, horrors of growing up under apartheid rule—these made for difficult, if not impossible childhoods as our next guests know firsthand. They both survived growing up in this country—she, a white Jewish female, and he a black male."

Survived? I tried to take the words in, but they only seemed to hum around my head like flies. And the stage was a furnace. This must be what a stroke is like, I thought, looking around for someone, some sort of audience to give me my bearings. From the stage, however, it was impossible to work out just who the real audience was—the live audience out there, somewhere in the dark? the interviewer? the enormous eye of the camera turning this way and that like a cyclops?

And then, suddenly, I remembered. One of my friends, a woman entirely comfortable on television shows, had already given me the answer. The camera is the real audience, she'd said, but you must *never* look at it, never. You look only at the interviewer, as if you don't even see a camera.

The trouble with this was that the interviewer was ever more painful to look at. She was a hopeless actress—opening her eyes too wide, scrinching and scrunching her face into an exaggerated look of sorrow as the other writer talked.

"We slept on pieces of cardboard under the kitchen table," he was saying. "Sirens blaring, dogs barking . . . We had to scavenge for half-eaten sandwiches—"

He wasn't much good at this himself, delivering the lines too quickly, and in a high-pitched, self-righteous singsong.

The interviewer sighed. She shook her head.

"The only solace we children had," he went on, "was that each night my mother would gather us around the fire and tell some beautiful stories."

"And we," the interviewer broke in, "go home and watch television." She held his book sadly up to the camera.

I'd seen this sort of show before, usually while flipping through channels in hotel rooms. Regardless of the offenses being aired, there was something in the parading of suffering as entertainment—the bid for sympathy, the performance of the sympathy itself—shallow, sentimental, short-lived—something in all this that left the heart defiant.

Considering this now, as they talked, I was thinking that the paradox applied in just the same way to self-pity or self-righteousness on the page. And, for a moment, I almost managed to forget what I was there for myself.

"Lynn?"

I looked up.

"You were growing up in South Africa at the same time," said the interviewer, the smile back in place.

Here we go, I thought.

"Yes," I said, trying not to look at the camera. But there, on a small monitor attached to it, was my face staring back at me—sober, somber, worthy of Mount Rushmore—and LYNN FREED, RAISED IN SOUTH AFRICA running beneath it.

She sat forward. "But certainly, it couldn't have been as horrible?"

"No, of course not," I said. "It couldn't have been more different. I grew up in a large house, with loving parents, servants, a measure of ease and freedom—"

"But you also experienced some *difficulties*?" she cut in quickly.

"Difficulties?" I said.

"Because you are Jewish?"

I frowned at her. Never mind that I couldn't conjure up any of the answers I'd tried to memorize; this was entirely the wrong question.

"No," I said. "Whatever difficulties I experienced were trivial in comparison with his." And then, because this didn't seem to satisfy her, I added, "Probably much the same as those of any Jewish child growing up in an Anglo-Saxon society."

She blinked. She reached for my book and held it up. LYNN FREED, RAISED IN SOUTH AFRICA ran again along the bottom of the screen. But her smile seemed to have frozen in place and she with it. I saw that she was wearing an earphone, and that beads of sweat were beginning to stand out on her forehead.

I glanced at the other writer. He, too, was sweating under the heat of the lights. So was I.

"Okay!" said the interviewer suddenly. "Back in a moment!"

With that, the lights went up in the auditorium and, yes, there was the real audience out there. They were raked almost to the ceiling—a sea of women chatting, shuffling, gazing down at the stage.

"*Lynn!*" A large blond woman with a clipboard had rushed at me out of nowhere, hair and eyes wild.

I looked up at her.

"This was not *at all* what we *expected* you to say!" she hissed, panting.

"What?"

"I'm the *producer*!" she said.

The producer? For the moment, I couldn't think what a producer was, or why this should matter to me. But, whatever she was, I felt as if I were failing my orals. Or had been stopped for speeding on the highway.

"What *did* you expect me to say?" I whispered urgently.

"We want you to talk about being *discriminated* against, as a *Jewish* girl!" she said furiously, very flushed in the face.

"But that was not at *all* the case!" I was reddening in anger now myself. "It was *my* sort of parents who employed *his* sort of parents, for God's sake! It's all in the book."

"Agh!" she said, consulting the clipboard. "*We don't have time to read the books!*"

Recently, in a creative writing course I was teaching, I found myself facing a standoff between two of the students. One was a rather beefy athlete and the other, whom I'll call Alice, a woman who had once been a man. The contention was over a story the athlete had written, in which men have been magically turned into women, dogs stand up on their hind legs and talk, and so forth. At a certain point in this story, one of the newly minted women looks down disconsolately to where once had been the pride of his (or her) manhood and feels disempowered, "empty," airy.

The class, most of whose members were devotees of fantasy fiction, was quite taken with it all. But then up spoke Alice. She was offended, she said, *very* offended. What's more, she had compiled a list of the offenses, which she then proceeded to work through, taking over the class.

Over the years, I have had to defuse any number of such standoffs in the face of offended sensibilities, although never until now on the score of sex. Usually I would do this by fiat: No grandstanding! The story will be discussed on its own merits, and the author not held to account for writing about racists, idiots, perverts, and so on.

All this the students knew. They knew, too, how I felt about the stranglehold of political correctness in a creative writing class, or in any class, for that matter—that it had no place there, trigger warnings and safe spaces notwithstanding. They would have heard me quote E. L. Doctorow, who said, "I believe nothing of any beauty or truth comes of a piece of writing without the author's thinking he has sinned against something—propriety, custom, faith, privacy, tradition, political orthodoxy, historical fact, or indeed, all the prevailing community standards together."

In this case, however, Alice clearly considered the sin to lie so far out of bounds, and herself so qualified to address it from both sides of the issue, that she felt entitled to teach us all a lesson in right thinking. Indeed, as she worked through the points on her list—empowerment, disempowerment, victimization, and so forth—the class fell into a sort of guilty silence, casting down their eyes or glancing, occasionally, over at me. The athlete, in the meanwhile, bleated weakly, here and there, that he hadn't meant to offend anyone; it was just an idea he'd had, a sort of joke—

Some years ago, the New York State Regents English Exams were discovered to contain excerpts from the works of well-known writers, almost all of which had been sanitized wholesale, and without permission. This had been done, explained a commissioner, to comply with "sensitivity guidelines," and in order that no student be "uncomfortable in a testing situation."

To these ends, the word *hell* had been changed to *heck, skinny* to *thin, fat* to *heavy;* whole sections of a Chekhov story had been removed; Isaac Bashevis Singer cleansed of all references to Jews and Gentiles, and so on.

Is it any wonder then that, in such a world, my student, working down her list of offenses, should have felt so entitled to her discomfort? Or the writer himself so obliged to apologize?

"Okay," I said, breaking into the litany, "that's quite enough."

They looked up, startled. Generally, I would let them have their say before taking over.

"I am a Jew," I said. "And if I chose to be offended by every writer who describes Jews unflatteringly, I'd have to avoid Chaucer, Shakespeare, Dickens, Trollope, Pound, T. S. Eliot, Dostoevsky, and any number of others, not to mention Isaac Bashevis Singer and Philip Roth."

Silence, dead silence. What shocked them, I knew, was not Chaucer, Shakespeare, etc., but the word *Jew,* unsoftened by an *ish*. To be Jewish in this new world of ours is one thing, but to be a Jew—well, no, that was far too close to the ghetto.

"So now," I said, "we'll simply discuss this story."

Almost immediately, things loosened up. Someone pointed out that it's all very well to switch genders—I had failed completely in getting them to use the words sex and gender correctly—but the dogs in the athlete's story all seemed to talk like teenage boys. The discussion lightened into laughter. In fact, for the rest of our weeks together, a sort of lightness took hold of the whole class, Alice included. She laughed along, seeming to forget entirely the heavy role in which she'd cast herself. And, in so doing, she became rather beloved of the others.

They were young, most in their early twenties, and few, if any, I thought, would become writers. The issue of corruption—the corruption of the imagination by the constraints of right-mindedness—posed little danger to literature from them. And, anyway, their imaginations, their thinking, their use of the language itself, was already well on the way to corruption. They were students at an English-speaking university, in a country of English-speaking universities, where talks such as the following were commonly on offer in the humanities:

"Women's Self-Perpetuated Oppression: Complicity and Moral Responsibility in Collective Action Problems."

"The 'Illegal Alien': Intersectionality, Biopolitical Racism, and the Construction of Immigrant Subjectivity."

"Quasi-Metaphoricity and the Turning Force of Alterity."

Comedy Central? *Saturday Night Live*? Not at all. These conglomerations are what passes for the language of scholarship. And, as it turned out, the students themselves seemed quite well versed in it. Perhaps they took its meaning on faith, not expecting to be able to understand it in any standard way. What they also understood quite well, I found, was the value of oppression in their cultural universe. And so the subjects of their stories were often victims—of bullying, of incest, of poverty, racism, unfairness of every sort. It was difficult to convince them that life is unfair, and that the *intention* of the writer, moral or otherwise, is irrelevant to the success of the story. That the real currency of value, the moral currency of literature, if you will, lies in the just use of the words themselves in the quest for truth.

I was not, of course, making a plea for the sort of language to be found in the self-conscious, carefully crafted prose that can seem to pass for high literary achievement. Seldom, when reading such prose, do I find myself able to forget the writer. In fact, I suspect, one is not meant to be able to forget him or her. There she is behind every clever phrase or metafictional trick—there he is delivering careful photographic descriptions of an attic, a train circa 1939, an American suburban street. Look at me! the writing shouts. See how observant I am? How significant? How clever?

And then I think yet again of Thomas Mann saying, "There are many forms of stupidity, and cleverness is the worst."

And so I try to find stories that seem to leap into existence off the half shell—stories in which the writer seems so inextricably woven into the fabric of the fiction that one can forget, as Somerset Maugham puts it, that it is a story one is reading and not a life one is living. I try to find stories that neither sanctify victimhood nor labor to serve received standards of rectitude.

So I might suggest Marguerite Duras—in particular, the way she explores the story of her first love affair as a very young, very poor white girl in French Indochina with a much older, very rich

Chinese man. In many books, over her entire writing life, Duras wrote versions of this story, most recently in *The North China Lover,* published in 1992 when she was seventy-eight:

> He's Chinese. A tall Chinese. He has the white skin of the North Chinese. He is very elegant. He has on the raw silk suit and mahogany-coloured English shoes young Saigon bankers wear.

In *The Lover,* her forty-eighth book, published to great acclaim when she was seventy, she describes him thus:

> He smells pleasantly of English cigarettes, expensive perfume, honey, his skin has taken on the scent of silk, the fruity smell of silk tussore, the smell of gold, he's desirable. I tell him of this desire.

But, thirty years before that, when she was thirty-six, Duras wrote a far-less-flattering portrait of him in *The Sea Wall:*

> His face was certainly not handsome, nor was his figure. His shoulders were narrow, his arms were short. . . .
>
> When he stood up, his ugliness became apparent.

And, in one of her notebooks, begun when she was almost thirty, she went even further:

> [He] was perfectly laughable. . . . He looked ridiculous because he was so short and thin and had droopy shoulders. . . . Not once did I agree to walk a hundred yards with him in a street. If a person's capacity for shame could be exhausted, I would have exhausted mine with [him]. . . . The mouth, the saliva, the tongue of that contemptible creature had touched my lips.

Does it matter, I ask, which depiction is most just to the original experience? Does the original experience—*if,* indeed, the notebooks are faithful to that experience—matter at all? Of course it does not, I say. What matters here—what matters in all writing, in any genre—is not the life of the writer that may or may not lie behind the work at hand, but the life *in* that work, with all its inbuilt contradictions, its "significant irrelevancies," as Henry Green put it. And for this there is no formula.

In all these books, Duras herself seems to be on a voyage of discovery, moving around and through the central experience of her life, realizing it in fiction most magnificently in *The Lover*—wild, furious, oblique, contradictory, true.

"The writer," wrote Flannery O'Connor, "sees his obligation as being to the truth of what can happen in life, and not to the reader—not to the reader's taste, not to the reader's happiness, not even to the reader's morals."

I read this to the students.

But never mind O'Connor; at least one of them is bound to be offended by Duras. In a culture of grievance, they have found, the victim walks at the front of the parade. And so offense will be taken on behalf of the lover, whether flatteringly or unflatteringly described. Is Duras entitled to his character? they want to know. After all, he is Chinese and the girl is white. And what about the family of impoverished white colonials, clinging ruthlessly to their last shreds of status among the natives? Racism there, too? And the domestic abuse? The mother virtually prostituting her own child? The avaricious, opium-addicted, violent brother who beats the girl up? Even the girl herself, both victim and perpetrator? Shouldn't she be judged complicit? Or is she simply the sad prey of an evil system run by evil, evil human beings?

Looked at through the prism of offense, literature is rich in subjects for discussion. It is the rare writer who hasn't found himself, at some point in his career, drawn into discussing his work in terms of its social or political significance. Making a feint toward truth-on-the-page reflecting truth-in-life can seem deliberately to be veering things off the path of righteousness. Anyway, for those with a firm toehold on the moral high ground, the complexities and contradictions inherent in the truth are not particularly interesting.

"[Political correctness]," said Doris Lessing, "is a continuation of Communist party doctrine. It's the same attitude—the need to control literature by an ideology. But the interesting thing is the people who are politically correct don't seem to recognize this. . . . They haven't, as far as I can make out, taken the trouble to find out what terrible results it's had in the past, like destroying literature all over the Communist world."

Destruction apart, writing "correctly"—which is to say, endeavoring to eliminate all cause for offense—is by far the most difficult sort of writing to undertake. It is to run the story, or the essay, or the memoir—or whatever one is attempting—through an ever more crowded minefield, a crooked path at best. And this metaphor does not take into account the skill it takes to negotiate a real minefield. What it takes to write the sort of bland, flat, predictable, charmless prose that tells the reader only what she approves of already is a deadening of the mind and heart, a stilling of the desire for truth, without which desire nothing good can ever be written.

Once, in the mid-eighties, riding on a bus down Fifth Avenue with my editor, I was telling her about a book I had found recently in a bookstore in South Africa. It was entitled *An Easy Zulu Vocabulary and Phrase Book,* and subtitled, *Simple Sentences for Use in the Home and Garden and on Other Everyday Occasions.* The book had been published in 1938 by a respectable publisher of textbooks in South Africa and was now in its fourth edition, umpteenth printing.

"The primary object of this little work," said the preface, "is to help newcomers in their common contacts with Zulus." To this end, the phrases provided were mostly in the imperative: *Come here, Answer when I call you, Wipe the table, Do not smear your clothes with blood,* etc.

The editor was predictably outraged. "You *must* write this up!" she said.

And, as soon as I returned to California, I sat down to do so. Day after day I struggled. After a while, just *thinking* about how to find my way into a subject with what I knew to be the appropriate tone of outrage seemed to guarantee that nothing would take life. Still, I persevered, draft after draft of predictable, lifeless, self-righteous nonsense.

And then, one day, just as I was about to give up, I landed on an opening sentence. "White South Africans," I wrote, "are convinced that having servants is no easy matter." Away went all thoughts of pleasing the editor—and, behind her, the whole, vast outrageable audience whom I had hoped to serve.

From then on, I wrote quickly, one ironic leap to the next, as if in the interests of explaining that world to this. Taking this tone, coming at the thing from behind, allowed the book, those commands, and that whole complicated world to speak for themselves. It also, and not incidentally, allowed the reader to laugh.

The piece built up to a finale in a picnic vignette from a section in the book entitled "Motoring."

We will stop here.
We will have some lunch.
Make a fire.
Put the kettle on.
Spread the rug in the shade.
Get out the lunch basket.
See how deep the river is.

"Useful Zulu Phrases" was my first publication in *Harper's Magazine*.

Some years ago, a poet I knew told the story of a class she was teaching in Southern California. In this class was an old woman who had survived Auschwitz. She was writing about it, but her poems were a failure. They were simply litanies of horror, suffering, misery, all in the abstract, all sounding as if they had been told many times before. In one poem, the survivor wrote of children being led to their deaths. And, indeed, the members of the class responded with phrases of horror and outrage. But nothing in the poem seemed more real than the idea itself—no images, no phrases, nothing that made the blood run cold.

"Tell me," said the teacher, "what you saw when those children were being led past you. Tell me what you heard."

The survivor shook her head. "We couldn't see because there was a wall," she said. "And we couldn't hear because of the geese."

"Geese?" said the teacher.

"Oh yes," said the survivor. "The Germans kept a flock of geese. They beat them so that they would honk, and we couldn't hear the children crying as they led them to the gas chamber."

So, there was the poem. And the class was, at last, in tears.

THE CASE OF THE ANGRY DAUGHTER

Rivka Galchen

My five-year-old daughter had been called the Buddha baby. Not by me, but by many a stranger and friend—reliable observers. But when she starts kindergarten, she becomes, abruptly, no longer the Buddha baby. At night, she weeps and begs not to go to school. In the morning, the same. She is sad but also enraged. She kicks me for not having a banana. She punches me in the stomach for not being able to find her bumpy red ball. She says repeatedly that she is leaving to find a new family.

These moods and feelings, I'm told, are normal, a transition. But it doesn't seem normal for her. At the preschool she attended for two years, she ran into her classroom in the morning; at most she wanted me to draw a turtle on a Post-it for her to wear during the day. She is still a loving and expressive girl, but suddenly I am in one moment "the best mama in the world" and then, seconds later, "the very worst mama in the whole wide world."

It is around this time, late September, that the first of her detective-agency signs go up. There will be more to come, though I don't know that then. "How do you spell 'solves'?" G. asks me. "How do you spell 'until'?" I don't know what she is doing until she shows me: "GDOESCASESSOLVESUNTIL 8."

The letters go across the page left to right, then take the corner and return, backward, right to left. Beneath them is a spooky figure drawn in black marker who is holding . . . a lollipop? No, she says: a magnifying glass. In the upper corner of the page, there is a red rectangle with an X through it and another dark and mysterious figure standing by. "That means I'm not available when I'm playing the piano," G. says. She tapes her sign onto the wall of the living room—something she's never done before.

This G., the calm detective and maker of informative signs, is a change from minutes earlier, when she slammed her door, wept, and shouted, "If that ever happens again, you're going to be eaten by fish!"

The "that" in this case was that I hadn't yet gotten her a pumpkin for Halloween. The "being eaten by fish" imagery came to her from I have no idea where.

G. loves detective stories for kids, and over the coming weeks, she shows that she has become attached to the idea of being a detective—she finds keys and wallets, she follows prints—but what her detective-agency-and-rage phase really does is turn *me* into a detective: the reluctant, inept kind, who is never even sure if there's been a crime.

At G.'s elementary school, kids have to walk into the building alone. There's not much choice in the matter; it's a crowded public school, and there's not enough space for both kids and parents. So by the second week of kindergarten, when G. is still unwilling to walk into the school, she is dragged in by her armpits by an officer of the law. A kind, maternal officer of the law, sure, but maybe that is a mistake I make, letting that happen. But the other kids—hundreds of them—are simply walking into the building, no problem.

It's a sunny, friendly school, so far as I can tell. The worst anecdote G. brings home—"It is so bad, I can't tell you," she says, before telling me—is that someone at lunch said grapes make you fat. Also, a second grader told her "to shoo." The art center, she complains, is often already full when she wants to go there. Surely these setbacks are insufficient explanation for her feelings. I need a better clue to her personality change, to her distress.

As the weeks go by, G.'s anger, dread of school, and fear of separation don't ease; they intensify. I ask friends and family for advice; I ask them often, sometimes texting after 11 P.M. To a one, they respond with the tolerance of an unusually nice pediatrician being woken from sleep with a phone call about an earache: It's only kindergarten! But from the inside, it feels overwhelming. Is it because she doesn't like "girlie" things? Is it math? Is it a tumor? Are the other kids terrible people who should be taught how to treat my child?

One afternoon, in her backpack, I find a drawing she made at school: an orange "I," a red heart, a blue "U" and then a scary, frowning stick person with wild black hair pointing in every direction. "Oh, that," G. says. "That means I love you even when I'm mad at you."

The one other durable clue G. has provided is her ongoing, and unceasing, interest in detective stories. She makes me and her father tell her detective stories on the subway. She asks to have detective stories read to her in the evening: the Nate the Great series, the High-Rise Private Eyes series, "The Case of the Hungry Stranger," "The Case of the Scaredy Cats," "Aunt Eater's Mystery Christmas," "Detective Dinosaur." I have googled to find pretty much any detective series written for kids, which often means I'm ordering used children's books in library bindings. Most are from the late 1970s and early 1980s, when the genre seems to have been in full bloom, in tandem with the heyday of Scooby-Doo. "I'm available to solve a case," she keeps telling us. "Do you have any cases for me?" We try to come up with cases. "A real one," she says. "Not like a lost pen." Maybe I need to take her game more seriously.

As a genre, the detective story has often found popularity at moments of great social upheaval, as if it somehow helps to make overwhelming trauma more manageable. The wild popularity of Agatha Christie novels in England followed swiftly the deaths of hundreds of thousands of young British men in the First World War. Detective Hercule Poirot, who first appears in a Christie novel in 1920, is a Belgian refugee from the war, arrived to the English countryside. Of her Tommy and Tuppence detective duo, introduced in her 1922 novel *The Secret Adversary,* the reader learns that Tuppence and Tommy both served in "the Great War" and that Tommy was injured. Christie herself famously disappeared—when her first husband was having an affair. She left the disappearance out of her autobiography, though at the time it was an international news story. Her husband attributed it to amnesia.

The Sherlock Holmes stories, which preceded Christie's, grew to prominence after the Industrial Revolution. The lower classes were coming into new roles; the old order was being shaken. The archnemesis of Holmes is the criminal Moriarty—an Irish, and therefore lower-class, name. Holmes, meanwhile, is an aesthete who meets his assistant, Watson, when he needs someone to share the rent. Sir Arthur Conan Doyle, the author of the series, attended posh British schools but had Irish-Catholic roots, his heart on both sides. Instead of facing the changing fortunes of whole social classes, the stories let the contemporary reader confront disguised fears one tidy plot at a time.

Mysteries are a comforting narrative structure for managing social shifts and loss. Kindergarten is clearly a battle on a much tinier scale. But any life from the inside can feel like *The Iliad,* especially when you're a child. Maybe G. is telling me, or herself, something about a tremendous battle, an overwhelming fear.

We carve that first pined-for pumpkin too many weeks in advance of Halloween. Sitting in our humid, hurricane-weather hallway, it turns moldy within three days. Now it's scary in the wrong way. G. is furious. "I am losing more than my temper," she screams. Then she weeps. We go buy another pumpkin. We go that afternoon. She is overjoyed. Back home, I tell her to be careful holding the carving tool. "You ruin everything!" she yells at me. She storms away to hide under her blanket and weep again.

Eventually we carve off a lid from the pumpkin. G. pulls it up by the stem. The stringy squash strands and gooey seeds hang down, and G. exclaims joyfully: It looks like a chandelier!

Has she ever seen a chandelier? Her observation weirdly throws me. Her inner life is more than what I myself have populated it with—a bittersweet shift. I should be glad, I tell myself, that she is growing. That she knows about, for example, fish eating people. And about chandeliers.

I go to the bathroom to wash pumpkin goo off my hands. Now she is furious again, at my "leaving" her to wash my hands. "If you ever do that ever, ever again," she shouts about my hand-washing, "I'm going to lose more than my love. You are breaking more than my heart." I hurry out of the bathroom, hands still wet.

A close intellectual cousin of the detective is the psychoanalyst. Someone has a dream about strawberries or about wolves sitting in a tree—what does it really mean? People knock analysis, or revere it, which either way obscures the field's gift for offhand illumination. One kind of clue in analysis is a mésalliance—a mismatch. It can be a sign that something meaningful is being disguised, lies in wait in an association. The mésalliance here, I'm suspecting, is the mismatch between the intensity of feeling and the referenced event that provoked the feeling. Why does a Halloween pumpkin matter so much? What overwhelming story or fear or feeling has been Trojan-horsed inside?

I don't know.

In G.'s Nate the Great books, the breaks in cases often occur when Nate is not thinking about the case *directly;* the breaks come when he is taking a break, usually by eating pancakes. That indirect form of searching is also what Freud, and Proust, and even Poe present with their searches after the unconscious, or lost time, or the criminal.

Chandelier, Chandler. G.'s dad sometimes tells her "Chandler stories." It's Chandler, Girl Detective, like Encyclopedia Brown, Boy Detective. In the stories, Chandler lives next door to the trio of boys who featured in the core stories that G.'s dad told to her three older brothers, when they were around her age. Part of the thrill of these stories for G. is that they are a secret from me. They are just for her and her dad to know. That's the running family bit—that I'm desperate to know what happened, but they're not going to tell me.

I file Chandler/chandelier away. Some flowers bloom in shadow—impatiens, fuchsias—and maybe G. is asking for some shadow, for some benign neglect. Maybe kindergarten is somewhat difficult for her, but what's even more difficult is that I can tell it's difficult for her. Part of what is frustrating as a child is that everyone knows your business.

Or maybe not.

The next morning, a Tuesday, G. announces that it's Saturday.

I counter that it is Tuesday.

She insists: No, it's Saturday.

I don't yield on the Tuesday point. Nor does she yield on the Saturday point.

She refuses to get dressed for school. Because it's Saturday! This escalates, and maybe I raise my voice and say, "OK, I'm going to school by myself." A weak strategy. She storms off straight to . . . her markers. She takes a black Sharpie and a sheet of paper. She draws another large, scary frowning stick person with wild hair. This time the figure also has big, club hands; in the corner, she draws a smiling, smaller stick figure, holding a magnifying glass, examining a shoe print. She then draws a large black X across the whole drawing.

I hesitate to inquire what it means.

She doesn't wait for me to inquire. She tapes it onto the wall, next to her earlier sign. "This means the detective does not see people who are very rude."

We go to school that Tuesday. It's the worst school in the world, she tells me on the way there. You are the worst mama in the world.

Then on the block of her school, her tone abruptly changes. Mama, I love you to the moon and back and back again, she says. (It is terrible to be put in touch with the unconscionable amount of power you have over your child.) You are the best girl in the world, she says. Please, Mama, please don't make me go. Please. Please. She cries. OK. Pick me up as soon as possible.

In *The Murder of Roger Ackroyd,* by Agatha Christie, the reader eventually discovers that it is the narrator—the voice we have come to trust—who has been the murderer all along. Am I the guilty party in the mystery of my daughter's unhappiness? I am dimly aware that the thinking on the kind of separation anxiety that G. is experiencing—the anxiety and its accompanying rage—is that children who feel safe and loved are able to separate easily. Only the children who do not feel safe and loved and attached have trouble being away from their caregiver when the time comes.

I dismiss this line of thinking. One, because it is unflattering. But also, I am the mother who is altogether too around. Before G. was born, I had planned to drop her off at day care as soon as possible; I found a place that would take her at two months old. I was surprised that no one would take her after, say, a week. I read only one book about babies before she was born—a book about getting babies to sleep. But then G. was born. If someone else held her, I felt empty and wrong. If ever I had to be away for a day for work, the way it felt inside of me was as if I had been posted in a distant port for a season of war. I felt this way even as at the same time I knew that my being away was an opportunity for her to bond more closely with her dad. Which is to say: from birth, we had been together nearly all the time. I took her to school most days; I picked her up from school most days; I brought her on work trips; I brought her to dinner with friends.

If this baby (now child) needs something, the one thing she can't possibly need is more time with me. And though it feels wrong to say it out loud, I feel confident that my daughter knows I love her, and that we are attached. And though I'm as prone to melancholy as every other person I know, I don't find it plausible that I am withholding, or absent on account of mood—another favored theory.

The famous British pediatrician and analyst D. W. Winnicott, most famous for his concept of "the good-enough mother," argued that children live in two worlds: a rich, imaginative one and a more prosaic one; a mother's job is to let the more ordinary world come through in small doses. Have I somehow dosed out kindergarten, or life before kindergarten, all wrong? Had I chosen too tender and beautiful a preschool? Have I been around too much?

It can feel powerful to find yourself at fault. And I will always be a prime suspect. But these first notions sound off-key.

Maybe have her dad drop her off? my brother suggests. Which helps. A tiny bit.

She rages and weeps through September, she rages and weeps through October, she rages and weeps into November. I cancel any plans with friends. I cancel work trips. She begs me to always be there. My acceding to her demand must only confirm her belief that what is happening between us—that every now and again we are apart—is catastrophic. But the case remains cold.

Then at the first parent-teacher conference, I am given an essential clue. Maybe.

G. is easygoing, her teacher tells me. She's happy. She talks to lots of her classmates. She often has something she wants to share or say.

Really? I ask.

Yes.

She's happy during the day? I ask again.

Yep.

Does she have friends in class?

The teacher explains that there's a rash of so-and-so-is-my-best-friend, and G. doesn't have her one person, but, the teacher says, not all kids need that, right?

So she's happy during the day, I ask again.

Her teacher laughs: "And she's always saying to me, 'You're the best girl in the world!' I try to explain to her, I make mistakes; no one needs to be the best."

I think about that one. G. is still crying about going to school in the morning. She is still crying about going to school at night. Sunday is a particularly horrible day, anticipating the week ahead. But is G. angry and terrified of separation from me because she . . . is having such a great time without me? Maybe learning that she can be happy without me is distressing.

I think of the Frog and Toad stories by Arnold Lobel. Frog and Toad are best friends, and other characters hardly even exist in their world. A snail helps deliver a letter; some robins laugh when Toad tries to fly a kite; but Frog and Toad are everything to each other, and no one else, and nothing else, much matters.

Frog is the bigger and more confident and steady of the pair. Toad is more anxious and clingy and lovable and small. In one story, "The Dream," Toad dreams that he is on a stage, doing amazing things. He plays the piano. He walks a high wire. He is cheered and hurrahed. All the while his best friend, Frog, sitting in the audience, is shrinking. Clapping and shrinking. And shrinking more. Until finally he disappears altogether. Toad panics, calling out for Frog again and again. Frog wakes a terrified Toad from his dream. "I'm right here," Frog says.

I should feel good about this, I tell myself.

"I really am a detective, even if you don't believe me," G. tells me, apropos of nothing I can myself detect. But when did I tell her she wasn't a detective? She finds my lost keys in the hallway. She is triumphant in discovery. I am the one who is losing things, not her.

Sir Arthur Conan Doyle used to say, of the creation of his Holmes stories, that he had wanted to write mysteries whose solution did not rely upon chance discoveries over time. He wanted, instead, scientific thinking to lead to the solutions. Conan Doyle trained as a physician, and he modeled Holmes in part on a doctor under whom he had studied, Dr. Joseph Bell. An observant physician can deduce pulmonary disease from ridges on fingernails, hypertension from an eye exam, a heart problem from a gentle shake of the hand. That was what Conan Doyle wanted for Holmes: a detective who could read a person's profession and nationality from the color of dirt on his shoe at the moment that he came knocking at 221B Baker Street. The drama of detection is not one of action but of thought. The most important clues for solving the mystery are there from the very beginning, rather than revealed, by chance discovery, over time.

What if all the clues to the changes in G.'s mood were there from the beginning of her story? The *very* beginning? What if they didn't come out over time; what if the ever-present clue was time itself?

It's early pickup. I go to get G. Another day of feeling it's nearly impossible for me to get my work done. I'll let her watch videos when we come home, I think, so that maybe I can finish. G. draws a heart on my hand in pink pen. She wants to play checkers at the coffee shop around the corner. I say today we'll have to play checkers at home. She says she's going to kick me in the face if we don't play checkers Right Now. I say that I promise we can play a round first thing when we get home. She wants a chocolate stick. I say we're not getting a chocolate stick. She says if she doesn't get a chocolate stick, then she's not taking one more step toward the subway. She says I ruin everything. She's going to tell Papa that I ruined everything.

She has her fists up, in a fighting stance. She wants the chocolate and the checkers right now. Our checkerboard at home is black and white, and the one at the coffee shop is black and red. She tells me she will be so mad at me unless we play checkers "on the red board" and get a chocolate stick. I pick her up to walk the half block to the subway. She is only five, and one day I won't be able to carry her anymore, but for now I can move her through space against her will.

On the subway, she asks me to tell her a detective story. I say I don't have any stories in my head. She suggests Mickey Mouse and the case of the missing trophy. I say when people shout at a person all the stories go out of her head, and it takes a little time for them to come back.

We sit there in the moving subway car. The man across from us indicates to me that my daughter is crying. "I want you to tell me the Mickey Mouse and the case of the missing trophy story right now!" she says. I don't tell a story. She lies down on my lap and says she's tired. When we get off the subway, she asks me to carry her again, and I carry her the last four blocks home. She is smiling. She is kissing my cheek, now she's sucking on my cheek and nearly giving me a hickey.

"Someone's coming home in a good mood," her dad says to her when we get home.

"More like a tired mood," she says.

A third detective-agency sign goes up. The detective is large and smiling at the center, again near a shoe print and holding a lollipop/magnifying glass. Next to the detective's head is a backward "S" followed by an "H." Then in the upper-left-hand corner is a smaller stick figure, next to a box with many circles in it. Then the whole page has a large X through it, like the second detective-agency sign.

Hesitantly, I ask her what the sign means.

"It means the detective agency is closed on Saturdays and Sundays."

I ask, "What is the box and the person in the corner?"

"That's lost treasure. It can't be found."

Conan Doyle killed off his famous detective in "The Final Problem" but was coerced by public pressure to bring his detective back to life again. Conan Doyle devoted the later years of his life not to writing but to defending the claims of spiritualists. He would defend the veracity of photographs of ghosts and of fairies. Conan Doyle's son died of influenza shortly after the war. The author believed the dead could speak to the living, as did his wife, Jean, who became a medium and an automatic writer. The family communicated regularly with a spirit guide named Pheneas, who advised the Conan Doyles on various things, such as when and where to travel.

Conan Doyle needed at once to be the man of science he had dreamed up and also have a way to believe his son's spirit was still within reach; he went to great lengths to defend as real photographs of fairies taken by children. The couple once invited their friend Harry Houdini to a séance; Lady Conan Doyle contacted Houdini's beloved dead mother. Lady Conan Doyle took dictation of a lengthy letter from Houdini's mother. Houdini went on to denounce mediums vociferously; the friendship ended. Conan Doyle cared too much for his child to let him go, and Houdini cared too much for his mom to take false comfort.

By December, G. remains out of sorts and still protests going to school, but something is shifting. She says it's fine for this year, but next year she will be returning to her preschool. Another afternoon, she tells me she's thinking about something so, so, so, so sad. It's so sad she can't say it. She can't tell me, she just can't: She is thinking about the song about the five little ducks, do I know it? I do know it. One by one the little ducks fly away from mother duck. Another day she asks me if I have a jacket that has thumb holes like her jacket's. I did once have a jacket with thumb holes like that, I say. It was a beautiful and cozy jacket; I really loved it. Where did it go, what happened to it? she asks of my old jacket. I don't remember, I say. I guess it got old.

"I am thinking about your jacket, and there are tears in my eyes," she says, shaking her head at the tragedy of it all.

When her dad is out of town for a week, she becomes even more gentle, even though she still doesn't want to go to school. She can intuit that the resources in the home are diminished, that there's less room for trouble. Winnicott says it's terrible for a child to accommodate to reality too early; isn't it too early? "If I had a tiger, I would name him Fierce But Love," she announces on the walk home from school. "Is there a housefly tooth fairy?" she asks me later, over a slice of pizza at a corner shop where a housefly buzzes around. When I say I don't know if houseflies have teeth, she doesn't yell at me and tell me how wrong I am; she says, "Of course houseflies have teeth." I am probably a "worse" mom than usual that week, while her father is briefly away, but maybe I am a better "good enough" mom—which is to say, a better mom. Or maybe not, maybe I need too much from her that week. G. and I sleep in the same bed, more for me than for her.

"Mama, your head is hot," she says. "But don't worry, I like hotheads."

After she falls asleep, I find myself thumbing through some

of the (admittedly thousands) of photos of G. on my phone. I make a minor unwelcome discovery: I often take photos of five-year-old G. from an angle that makes her look like three-year-old G. I could scroll through years of photos of her and somehow maintain the illusion that she is not getting bigger or older. When she was really little, I used to bend down and photograph her eye to eye. Over time, I seem to have done less and less of that. The more recent photos are often taken from an angle that leaves her head as oversize as a toddler's, her legs foreshortened, her feet like a doll's not too far away from her waist.

Am I not letting her grow up? Or worse: Am I dropping clues for her to interpret that her growing up is not OK with me? Is she angry and confused because, on some level, she feels that to get older is to put our bond at risk? Maybe her rages are experiments to make certain that she can trespass my will—that she can be independent—and that I will still be there. That I will still think and feel that she is, of course, the best girl in the world.

I had started to love the detective-agency signs G. made, even though I was a monster in them. But the next morning, G. takes them off the wall and throws them in the garbage. She seems embarrassed, as if she realized that they revealed something about her, that they weren't simply useful announcements about her agency.

Discreetly, I rescue the signs from the garbage.

I hadn't noticed before what all the signs had in common: None of them announced when the detective was available. They all announced when she was not. They specified not when the agency was Open, but when it was Closed.

It is January, late on the night before school starts again after the long winter break. G. is again weeping and begging me not to send her to school; or if she does go to school, then I have to be in the classroom with her the whole time. The anger and fear is more intense than ever. "You have two choices!" she shouts through tears. Falling asleep is impossible. "I am losing more than my temper! You are breaking more than my heart!" This goes on for more than two hours. Her father, level as any Chandler, Girl Detective narrator ought to be, confirms to me that it really has been two hours. He can't get her to sleep, either. All the old standbys fail. Someone has sent us a book in the mail about a tiger, a beautiful book, which looks too serious for G.'s taste, but at least it's new and unfamiliar. As a late and nine hundredth resort, I try reading it to her.

On the first page of the story, I discover that the tiger is angry because her cubs have been killed. I think about putting the book away. Instead, I warn G. that some parts of the story will be sad and ask her if she still wants to read it.

"But in the end it's OK?" she asks.

I say I think so, yes.

In her rage and mourning, the mother tiger has been attacking villages. Her violent rage seems unending, and unstoppable. The king, in desperation, turns to a wise woman for advice. She tells him: You must give your child to the tiger. The king is afraid and angry. The queen is afraid and angry. The child is quietly courageous and ready. He goes to the tiger without hesitation.

The tiger raises the prince as her own. The prince faces dangers, shows courage, learns the tiger's ways. The tiger stops attacking villages.

But meanwhile the king and queen don't know if their son, who has grown so much, is still alive. They are devastated. They send soldiers to destroy the tiger.

The prince defends the tiger with his life. At that moment, the queen emerges from the crowd, to reunite with her beloved child. The story then flashes forward to the boy, now a man, bringing his own child out to the mother tiger. Once the full cycle is depicted, the story is over.

At the end of the book, there is a drawing of a bronze vessel from the eleventh century B.C. that references the story of the Tiger Prince, confirming that the drama of leaving home is one of the oldest stories around.

G. wants to read *The Tiger Prince* again. And again. She stops crying and shouting. She calms down, falls asleep, and goes to school the next day with some, but not too much, trouble. I'm still playing with the toys the story has set out. The rage is the tiger's, not the child's; the rage is frightening and destructive but also reassuring—a symptom of how powerfully children are loved. The child's leaving home is not an abandonment; it is heroic—he is saving the village. The child grows up—it's not avoidable—but he grows up well.

The writer Joy Williams once observed in a novel that children vanish without dying. G. has not vanished, yet, but by spring, she does start to anticipate rather than dread going to school. She goes from finding recess and lunch the "worst" part of the day—because her teacher is not there—to "the best." She starts reassuring me that she will never leave me, she will stay at home even when she grows up, which must mean she knows she will one day leave. When spring break comes, she wants to be reassured that she is not missing any days of school—that all the kids are not there. She is still interested in mysteries but now wants to alloy them with "spooky" stories. She wants to be told mystery stories about zombies, vampires, witches, ghosts, and werewolves. Chandler, Girl Detective, has already faced several vampires, though I'm not supposed to know about that. Though she tells me about it. "But vampires don't really exist, right?" she asks. She wants to be reassured about that. Then told more stories about them.

Often with mysteries, people remember the setups but forget the resolutions. A storied diamond goes missing and . . . other stuff happens. A decapitated body is found by a canal in Paris, and . . . someone was responsible, not the person you first thought. The not-knowing part is more essential than the knowing. The not-knowing is the cozy feeling the reader seeks.

I never really solve the mystery of G. and kindergarten. The anxiety rises and falls a few more times, but by summer, I drop her off at a summer camp, in a different city, in a different language, where she knows nobody, and on the first day, she simply smiles and waves goodbye.

G.'s grandmother, who has four children and twelve grandchildren, once told me that raising children is like being moved around in a theater. When children are very young, you are the director of the play of their life. Later you have front-row seats for what is happening with them. Then maybe fourth-row seats. They get older, and you, the parents, get to watch from the front of the mezzanine. But you keep getting moved farther back. Eventually you're so far, you're in the seats they used to call paradise.

SCAT

Ross Gay

Cleaning out the shed today, what remains of my shed, roofless with half of the framing rotted out, I noticed two fingers of black shit bejeweled throughout with mulberry seeds. I was so delighted at the turds, delighted at what I figured was one of the neighborhood deer hunkering down in my not-quite-shed beneath the starry night to gobble mulberries dropped from the tree above, that I snagged a thick leaf from the pokeweed plant growing in my not-quite-shed and scooped the less coiled of the nuggets for further inspection, for further delighting upon. I was going to write a delight about the turd, I'm saying. With some kind of moral, I'm sure, about finding delight even in dookie.

The first clue that I'm a novice naturalist, some of you are already noting it, is that deer scat is not loggish or fingerish. It is pelletish. Once I remembered that, walking toward the tomato beds I was weeding, I tossed the turd to the ground nervous it might be raccoon shit. I was trying to remember if raccoons were among the more avid transporters of rabies, and if that might fester in dookie, and if so, if it might permeate my skin, and if so, if it might leave me writhing and foaming at the mouth beneath the blueberries, so different from the romantic way I sometimes imagine keeling over in my garden.

Looking at the late-day light gleaming in the seeds in the shit, my tiny reflection winking in every one of them, I remembered

Galway Kinnell's poem "The Bear," in which the speaker, tracking a bear he's tricked into eating a blade whittled of a wolf's rib, eats some of its bloody scat. He calls it a *turd*. It is a bafflement that people, myself included, did not immediately consider the poem goofy, or even, at the very least, scatological. It somehow managed to elevate itself into the mythic, the profound. You can imagine the twentysomething boys in a poetry circle-jerk reading that poem, none of them cracking the least smile so immersed in the presence of transcendent knowledge were they. My friend Dave lifted the veil for me, showed me the poem was serious *and* goofy, which doesn't in the least diminish my love for many of Kinnell's poems, a couple of which I've kind of plagiarized. Anyhow, it often delights me when a grave thing is revealed to be, also, kind of silly.

The first time I saw *The Exorcist* I was nine years old. My mom, flipping through the *TV Guide,* saw that it was coming on HBO, and she wanted to see it because my dad, a very reasonable man, asked her to hold off when it first came out. She was pregnant with my brother and people watching the movie were having miscarriages and heart attacks in the theater, both of which used to be evidence of a good movie. In twenty minutes or so, when little Linda Blair disrupts the socialite party by peeing on the rug in her white nightgown, I was very frightened, and I asked my mother if we might watch *Falcon Crest* instead. *It's a rerun,* she said. *Just go to bed if you don't want to watch it.*

(Dear Reader, I am here going to leap a boundary I shouldn't, like some of your childless ex-friends before me, to tell you how to raise your children. My brother's and my bedroom was, maybe, twenty feet from this television. It was maybe three or four seconds by foot away. But my imagination was vast. By which I mean to tell you not to watch *The Exorcist* with your children. Or *The Shining*. Or *Rosemary's Fucking Baby*.)

Damn right I was already too scared to do anything by myself, and when little Linda Blair was stabbing herself with a crucifix and vomiting in the faces of priests, I was doomed. I sat on the couch pretending to read the *Bucks County Courier Times* as I heard the girl, about my age, panting and growling. I peeked beneath the business section to see little Linda Blair write, from inside of her Lucifer-ravaged tummy, HELP. Of course, my dad, the one person in the world who could for sure beat up Evil, was down at Roy Rogers on Cottman, slinging burgers.

When I did finally go to bed, I sobbed, certain I, too, would be possessed by Satan, which my brother didn't go the extra mile to discourage me from thinking.

ME: Matt, am I going to be possessed?

MATT: I don't know.

ME: Am I possessed?

MATT (pulling the covers over his head): I don't know. Maybe.

For the record, my mother now knows this was an instance of heroically poor parenting, in part because I rub her face in it often. She puts her forehead in her hand and shakes her head, while I bask in her shame.

When I mustered up the courage to see *The Exorcist* again, the redux, I was about twenty-six. I went with my friend Joanna to the theater between Eighteenth and Nineteenth on Chestnut in Philadelphia. When Linda Blair peed on the rug this time someone said to the screen, "Oh no she didn't!" And when her head spun around, someone yelled, "That girl is trippin'!" At which point I realized this movie, which had occupied for years a grave space in my imagination, was actually silly. I was freed from the grave. Or rather, I was offered another version of the grave—laughter in its midst.

ON REVENGE

Louise Glück

When I was a child, I was enormously sensitive to slights; my definition of slights was as broad as my sensitivity was deep. I trust my memory on this point because the child I describe corresponds so exactly to the evolved adult. I was also, then as now, rigidly proud, unwilling to show hurt or admit need. Pride governed my behavior. It precluded, to my mind, all show of anger (which seemed obviously retaliatory—by confirming the slight or wound, it gave satisfaction, I thought, to the tormentor). Anger was the show of blood that proved the arrow had penetrated. Moral or ethical anger (of the kind provoked by concentration camps) was exempt from these inhibitions. But most such focuses, like the camps, aroused terror rather than rage. I had, if I can judge by my vast catalogue of slights and my icily theatrical self-protective disdain, a vast suppressed rage.

It is hardly surprising that my fantasy life consisted mainly of dreams of triumphant ascendance. None of these fantasies involved action. My revenge fantasies were founded on contempt for action, for any show of effort. Damage occurred without my apparent agency and perpetuated itself indefinitely: to need to wound or—as in the books I read—murder the enemy was to display the insufficiency of self, just as action proved the existence of hurt. My idea of revenge was to prove that I had not been hurt, or had somehow exacted hurt, which (as my fantasies repeatedly demonstrated) I had miraculously transformed into something intensely to be envied. My dream was to create envy: my idea of revenge depended on the object's remaining conscious and fully aware.

Mainly, I thought about the poems I would write. In my imagination, these poems would be of a greatness that compelled, in throngs of readers, a uniform amazement, the only disagreements arising out of attempts to describe this greatness or account for it. At some point, I became aware that such response had never, in the history of literature, occurred. But I continued to feel it would occur, it had to occur, because my own response to the literature I revered was so intense, so absolute. I was in such moments suffused with awe, which seemed to me utterly different from opinion (the latter garrulous, the former dumbstruck). I felt myself in the presence of an incontestable truth or universal law. Curiously, I was not annihilated by this awe, as I expected the enemies in my fantasies to be. In them, awe would combine with feelings of horrified shame, an awareness of wrongs that could never be made right, a sense of their own lacks and misjudgments. My revenge fantasies equipped my adversaries with sophisticated and discerning literary taste; they punished themselves while I simply and transcendently existed.

This scenario was always to some degree present in my imaginative life. It became my immediate response to all public and private failure, to scorn, to betrayal, but also to much smaller events and embarrassments to which such fantasies were wildly disproportionate. But they were not simply balm. They were also fuel. They fed an existing desire to write poetry, transforming that desire into urgent ambition. They could not replace inspiration, or bribe it into existence, but they augmented inspiration with a driving sense of purpose or necessity; they animated me when I might easily have been paralyzed. It was for many years intensely pleasurable to anticipate the leisurely unfolding, over time, of revenge, with its just and glorious reversals of existing judgments and power relations.

Crucial to these fantasies was a premise of spacious or expansive time, in which the distance from the humiliated present self to the triumphant innate self could be bridged. The language of revenge depends wholly on the future tense: they'll see, they'll be sorry, and so on. Because time always seemed to me imperiled or in short supply, I did not expect age to influence what, in my fantasy life, must have been a theoretical attitude. And yet something has changed. The fantasies have vanished, and with them the tremendous surges of energy and stamina.

Something about actually attaining those ages at which, in every possible sense, time is likely to be short (or certainly rapidly diminishing) seems different from feeling constantly that one would be cut off unfairly or prematurely. In addition to that sense of expansive time, my fantasies required that my adversaries remain immutable, stable, frozen in my infinite future: the person soon to be devastated by my virtuosity and spiritual depth must be identical to the person who held an object about to be thrown at me. But my rivals and judges, like my friends and colleagues, have all been chastened and battered by time. Pity and fellow feeling have weakened vengefulness, or replaced it with a sense of collective, as opposed to hierarchical, experience, substituting an unexpected mildness and generosity for my earlier sternness and violence. These shifts have made the fixation on new targets a far less vigorous act—briefly rancorous but capable of generating no real energy.

I sometimes miss them, those immutable enemies and the power they conferred, as well as the myth of generous time on which the little raft of self seemed likely to be supported for many decades. But my fascination now with this subject is more pragmatic and anxious: how to supply those energies that were, all my life, fed by the passion for revenge.

FACULTY WIFE

Emily Fox Gordon

They're nearly gone now, victims of attrition and destruction of habitat. The sociology of academic life may never record their dwindling and extinction.

I speak of the faculty wives of my mother's generation. Rare as they have become, I still spot them occasionally. That near-elderly woman I see on my walks, for example, out in the swampy fields gathering grasses: there is a diffuse benevolence of her aspect that marks her. And the museum docent leading a group of grade school children through the Gainsboroughs; surely she's one too. "Children," she whispers, leaning down to address them intimately, draping her arms around the necks of two representatives, "look at the lady's shoulders. Aren't they just like two scoops of vanilla ice cream?"

I. The Kangas

Once, at age ten, on my way home from school, I stood watching as two dogs mated in Mrs. B's yard. Neither of these belonged to anybody I knew—they were members of a pack of yellow, dingo-like dogs that roamed our small New England college town in those unregulated days. As I stood, ashamed and riveted, the strap of my bookbag cutting into my shoulder, watching the conjoined vibrating of these curs, Mrs. B emerged from the door of her house and padded out to join me. Mrs. B was a small woman who wore her glasses on a velveteen rope around her neck, walked on the balls of her feet, and hummed airs from Mozart. "Isn't it fascinating!" she stage-whispered as she joined me, taking my arm while the glazed-eyed dogs shuddered to stillness and decoupled, the female, once released, twisting to snarl and snap at the male.

Mrs. B was insufferable, but she was happy and virtuous. She belonged to the subspecies of faculty wife that I've privately named the Kangas, after the intrusively maternal kangaroo in *Winnie-the-Pooh*. They were the super-competent elite. Their gardens spewed healthy produce; their homemade bread rose high and evenly pocked; their children were born gifted and raised according to psychoanalytically sound principles which the Kangas felt no compunction about applying to the children of others whenever possible. That was what Mrs. B was doing on that fall afternoon when she mortified me so; she was demonstrating that I need feel no shame about my curiosity. She was commending to me an attitude of appreciative detachment toward all the processes of nature. Instead, of course, she opened up to me the true depth of my shame, acquainted me with the reek of my horrified arousal. I will always associate that experience with the sulfurous smell of the egg salad sandwich remnant lying smashed in the bottom of my bookbag.

Did she consider me capable of the detachment she modeled for me? Or was she deliberately shaming me? I remember her profile as we watched the dogs hump, the enlightened elevation of her chin, her lower lip slightly pursed. She lacked only a pair of opera glasses.

The Kanga households were a grid of interlocking fiefdoms circling the college campus. Their shaggy backyard gardens abutted one another brandishing sunflowers and booby-trapped with monstrous zucchinis in August, still bearing frost-blighted brussels sprouts in October. My brother and I tromped a zigzag path through those gardens like bear cubs, foraging for tomatoes and beans.

On my way to school I heard snatches of violin and flute, also the whirr and thump of the kiln in Mrs. R's mudroom. I saw the sparks of Mrs. L's blowtorch as she worked in the garage she had converted into a sculptor's studio. And silent work was going on all around me; in the long spaces of school day afternoons sestinas and novellas were being composed.

This was the era of the Feminine Mystique, of women languishing in suburban isolation, manifesting their unhappiness somatically with ulcers and rashes. But Kangas (a demographically insignificant group, I'm sure, a tiny powerless elite) seemed immune to the general malaise. They were a vigorous bunch, highly educated and accomplished. Their musical consorts, book discussion groups, charitable and political activities all served to confirm these women in their conviction that their lives were beautiful and useful, even if their work was unpaid.

The Kangas consciously resisted the domestic cleanliness obsession that gripped American women in the fifties. The big Victorian houses they rented from the college were cluttered with evidence of their enthusiasms. Unwieldy arrangements of dried flowers spilled out of giant hand-thrown pots; surfaces were littered with children's collections of seashells and butterflies. Sometimes a harp or a loom occupied a corner of the living room. With Kangas, the rule was accretion; where they nested, culture thickened and deepened. Unpressed by the mold of employment, they grew into all the eccentric spaces of their differently cultivated leisure.

At the top of Kanga society was a select group of the older wives, the permanent staff of the Women's Exchange, a consignment shop that supported the local Visiting Nurses' Association. These were Kangas of an earlier generation, less educated than the postwar faculty wives and even more tightly bonded as a group. I spent many hours at the Exchange while my mother worked there as a volunteer; I remember lying on my back in a litter of snowsuits in the back room, inhaling dry-cleaning fumes and staring up at a buzzing, blinking fluorescent light. I listened, on and off, to the conversation between the women working there. Sometimes they would exclaim over the quality of a new consignment—a clutch of the Rudolph girls' cashmere sweaters, perhaps, in six pastel shades, never worn—and their voices would lower and hover together deploringly as they allowed themselves the pleasure of touching the soft wool. Or they would speak more softly yet—this was always my cue to listen hard—about failed marriages, illnesses, birth defects. The older wives were amateur eugenicists, shrewd judges of the health and viability of newborns. Often I heard them speak about "good" and "bad" faces, and when a local doctor's daughter dropped dead at age nineteen of an undiagnosed heart ailment they all swore that they had privately predicted it.

The most benign of the Kangas was my parents' friend M. She was a big, soft woman with a heap of disordered hair worn in an outsize twist. Her voice was more than musical; she was the only person I've ever known who consistently sang their speech.

M's house was full of dhurries, woven baskets, brass bowls, batik hangings—things commonplace enough nowadays, but exotic then. Here I'm reminded of an interesting generalization I can make about the faculty wives of my youth: their tastes and interests were culturally prophetic. As I've grown up and then older I've watched various customs and items of cuisine and decoration favored by my mother and her friends which were odd and singular at the time become trendy and widely disseminated. The Kangas grew their own herbs, ground their own coffee, cut up their own chickens and cooked them in olive oil, drank wine with meals, made sure that their children's diets included fiber, or "roughage" as they called it, inquired about the availability of endive at the A&P. They favored earth colors and matte surfaces. Now that I find these provisions and proclivities all around me, it's as if my mother had been writ large and faint upon the culture.

M was a Californian exiled in a cold New England town where her expansiveness of spirit could never quite find room. The other Kangas viewed her enthusiasms—during a Polynesian phase she hosted a cocktail party in a grass skirt and a lei—with affectionate irony. I was grateful to her because she was kind to me in a way I could have found acceptable only in somebody whose air of breezy dissociation made her incapable of intrusiveness. Once when she was giving me a ride somewhere in her big rattling station wagon, she began to muse about me and my prospects. "How wonderful," she sang, "to get taller and stronger and just grow out of all the misunderstandings and fears. How wonderful to have all that time and to know that things will get better and better." She gestured extravagantly, but she kept her shining eyes turned forward toward the road and toward a vague and glorious vision of me and the transforming future. I felt a slight mortification at being reminded that for me there was nowhere to go but up. Even so, as she spoke I began to feel buoyed, like a grounded ship slowly lifted by the tide. She had goodwill by the gallon, and the impersonal banality of what she said served to dilute it enough so that I could absorb it.

In those days I was busy with a complicated internal project; at the same time I was trying to assimilate my mother's aesthetic (which contained her ethic) and casting about for alternatives to it. I had to do both simultaneously, because the more I attempted to apprentice myself to my mother, and the more I learned about her through this effort, the more I saw that her worldview would ultimately exclude me. So M and her big loose enthusiasms became significant to me; she lodged in the back of my mind and stayed. When I think of the future she imagined for me—and suffer the attendant shock of realizing that for me any such future is past—the picture that accompanies my thoughts is a Polynesian landscape, a stylized palm tree against a mauve and black sky.

II. The Princeton Party

A faculty wife remnant seems to have survived into my own generation as well, but this group hardly recognizes itself as such. I would not have acknowledged myself as one of their number if my husband and daughter and I had not spent his sabbatical year seven years ago at the Institute for Advanced Study in Princeton.

There the "members" lived with their families in a housing complex on the grounds of the institution. The wives—or spouses, as the administration took pains always to call us—were mostly a self-selected group, or at least the Americans among us were. These were women who had chosen to accompany their husbands on leave. Absent were the professionals, the lawyers, businesswomen, doctors, tenure-track academics. Present were the potters, the painters, the jewelry makers, the academic "part-timers," the writers. Also present were some particularly enterprising and devoted mothers of small children. Kangas, in other words, were everywhere. My daughter, then five, tore around the grounds with her cohort of faculty brats, safe and free and watched over as she would never be again. For a year, she lived my childhood.

The institute, where Einstein and von Neumann once worked, was a weird place, full of cultural contradictions. The receptions we attended in the vine-covered administration building were high-toned, chilly affairs. White-coated waiters circulated with flutes of champagne and nest-baskets of deviled quail eggs. Life in the housing units was another, humbler story: too poor to use the communal laundromat, the peasant mothers of young Chinese physicists stumped out of the units every morning to string hand-washed towels and sheets from tree to tree across the grounds.

The institute was a reservation for faculty wives. We gathered daily at the school bus stop, a multicultural group wearing our coats over our pajamas, herding our children and breathing steam, shuffling in place to keep warm. We loaded the children onto the bus and then dispersed into our days of solitary unpaid busyness, our grocery shopping, house cleaning, reading, translating, flute playing, novel writing. We gathered again at three when the bus returned.

I had found myself so isolated in my daughter's early years that at first the daily bus stop ritual seemed a reassuring emblem of community. I felt the novelty of knowing that I was among my own kind. But soon I began to understand that it would be difficult to make friends among the wives. I looked at them more carefully and I saw all the stigmata of shyness. This generation of Kangas had been affected by some curious attenuation. Except for a few loud, hale, natural-leader types—and only a month or two were required to reveal these as even more deeply insecure than the rest of us—we were a self-doubting, introspective group, abashed and reproachful, accustomed to solitude. We wore our graying hair in long ponytails; we favored wrap-around skirts with commodious pockets and Birkenstocks with knee socks. Our noses were raw from the continuous colds our children brought home from school. Many of us had suspended the connections to the world we had established back home—the part-time job in the library, the graduate program, the circle of supportive friends—and we resented the loss. I did some internal thrashing around that year, anxious that I was being left out of something and yet baffled about what that could be, eager both to identify myself with this group and to distance myself from it. I also began, haltingly, to work on a novel, the first really serious and sustained literary project I had ever attempted. I think I picked up something confirming in the air, just enough to get me started.

Early in the fall semester, some of the institute fellows and their spouses were invited to a Sunday brunch at the home of a Princeton professor, a gathering of academics, mostly philosophers with an interest in politics and the social sciences. In spite of the well-meaning efforts of our hosts, themselves both philosophers, to put everyone at ease, this was an intimidating occasion. Guests arranged themselves through the book-lined spaces of that house in the mysteriously nonrandom and meaningful way that guests always do. The pattern here was established early, and it was striking. One room reserved itself for the wives, who huddled together in a semicircle, softly discussing vaccination reactions and orthodontia. Two of them were nursing babies.

In an adjoining room there was loud lively talk, punctuated by the laugh of sudden, delighted insight that philosophers seem particularly prone to. Perhaps a third of these disputatious intellectuals were female, but they seemed a different species from the wives in the other room: they were upright, mobile, angular, assertive, expressive. They were, I was thinking from my place among the Female Women in the other room, the Female Men.

To move from one of these rooms to the other was to feel a change in emotional weather so extreme that a kind of physical barrier seemed to erect itself. I noticed a few of the male academics hovering at the doorway, sending two-fingered waves and guilty smiles to their wives. But somehow they seemed to balk at the prospect of actually entering the room. This scene was too primitively female for comfort, and I suspect the sight of breast-feeding made these men shy.

The only person who traveled freely between the two zones was our hostess, a woman far too gracious not to make an effort. She stood over us and offered anecdotes about her daughter's infancy, but these stories soon began to sputter in the face of our assembled passivity. (I think we were exaggerating the bovine act out of hostility.) She had been careful to acquaint herself with our interests, and several times she leaned into the Female Women's room in an effort to coax one or another of us out. "Julia," she would call, "didn't you write your dissertation on the social contract in a Nepalese village? Why don't you come out here and tell us about it?" But I was the only one to take the bait and follow her. "Emily," said my hostess, drawing me into the ambit of a famous intellectual whose books I had read and admired, "wrote a doctoral dissertation on Kafka."

"Master's thesis," I corrected. "Ah," said the famous intellectual, giving me a faint, bilious smile and turning back to his eager interlocutors. I had no choice but to return to the welcoming circle of round-shouldered women, remarking to myself on the wild irony of this situation. Of all places and times, I thought, to be relegated to the prison of gender, the home of two distinguished married academics in Princeton, New Jersey, in 1989 seemed the least likely.

In one room, a scene of vigorous free intellectual exchange, apparently genderless. In the other, like atavistic phantoms, a group of females, babies, and small children who might as well have been huddled on an earthen floor in a thatched hut, poking at a fire with sticks. (Two or three of the small children being monitored by the Female Women at the Princeton party actually belonged, I should add, to Female Men.) But, of course, strictly speaking, the dividing line here was not gender, because women stood on either side of it. Nor was it education or aptitude. Most of the Female Women had advanced degrees; all were highly intelligent. Instead, it was something more like temperament. For whatever reasons, and if only temporarily, the Female Women lacked the assertiveness and ambition of the Female Men. Or perhaps, to put it more positively, they felt the nurturing imperative more strongly. And of course, the Female Women lacked one thing essential in order to be taken seriously these days at a faculty party—a university affiliation.

Maybe the odd nature of this gathering was a product of the artificial situation from which it sprang—guests were chosen from the roster of the institute's members, academics spending a year among strangers and forming bonds on the basis of shared intellectual interests and accomplishments. So perhaps the wives, along for the year's ride, were unduly thrown back on one another and on the common denominator of baby and child talk. But this is not an adequate explanation; I've seen the same dilemma many times since, plausibly diluted, at various faculty functions.

Our hosts' dismay and embarrassment were obvious; it couldn't have been comfortable for them to preside over this apartheid-riven afternoon. What was happening? Why were the wives so sullenly resistant to the efforts of our hostess to integrate us into this gathering? I think we were unconsciously reaching back into our sixties arsenal of passive-resistance ploys, playing that trump card of postmodern ideology, the claim to authenticity. We had lost the respect we felt was our due; we had been marginalized, and so we arranged ourselves in a tableau which we knew would instantly evoke a shock of guilty recognition. We were far too liberated to plant ourselves at our husbands' sides to smile artificially until the ordeal of the party ended. We would revert instead to a more primitive, more compelling set of images. We would act the part of Woman—the burdened, the earthbound, the oppressed.

Which was ridiculous, of course. Whatever room we occupied, we were all of us members of a class of people who take for granted unprecedented comfort and liberty. We had freely chosen our roles. Even so, the Female Women had reason to feel defensive and depressed. We had lost access to the protective environmental niche that an earlier generation of faculty wives had enjoyed. Gone was the set of understandings and expectations which established the idea that a wife and mother could enrich and decorate her family life by bringing to it the benefits of her education, festooning it with her art and learning. She lived outside the real-world economy, but inside a private economy that rewarded her efforts with validation and approval. Some of this reward came from her husband and children, but perhaps, even more of it issued from the sisterhood of faculty wives. Without this reward, the latter-day Faculty Wife's efforts come to seem pointless to her, cranky and anachronistic.

III. Bad Wives

I recall no such separation at my parents' parties, which were frequent. There was an absolute gender divide along professional lines, of course, no females at all among the faculty members. The men talked shop and the wives talked babies, but only at the beginning. As the evening progressed and the guests became more lubricated, the room integrated itself; groups of fours and fives, only a few of them single sex, began to form, dissolve, re-form. When viewed directly from above, high up on the stair landing (children were expected to perform one turn with the hors d'oeuvres tray and then vanish), these human constellations looked like blossoms or starfish drawn in rough outline.

With experience I was able to recognize the stages of the party: after an awkward half hour, the manic yammer began to build, the conversational groups slowly contracting, then flaring outward in reaction to the punch line of the joke or the point of the anecdote. At this moment the party would feel to me like something single and organic, a breathing beast.

The noise would begin to modulate and steady until it had attained a raga-like drone. Then began a gradual migration toward the periphery of the room and a slow trickling into other parts of the house. The convivial roar was replaced by intelligible words and phrases, spoken softly and with a new earnestness. Now that the guests were seated I could see that they had arranged themselves in pairs and threesomes, and that many women were talking to men who were not their husbands and many men were talking to women who were not their wives. The hectic flirtation, the explosion of Dionysian energy and noise in the earlier stages of the party: all that had been in the service of this scattering and rearranging, and finally, this coming to rest. Conversations during this latter phase of the party had a relaxed intimacy, a quality I would later come to recognize as postcoital. During this magic interval—the hour of the coffee cups—men and women got to know one another as equals. Real talk went on, or so it seemed to me from my post on the landing.

The element of flirtation is utterly absent at the academic gatherings of today. (Let me disarm the reader's suspicion that I draw this conclusion only because nobody is flirting with me. Believe me, nobody is flirting with anybody at these functions.) Children are often present; alcohol is far less central than it was in my parents' day. These parties—mostly potluck suppers and Sunday open houses—usually begin with the establishment of zones: wives and small children gather on the couch, recapitulating in less dramatic form the pattern of the Female Women at the Princeton party. The older wives cluster in the kitchen, overseeing the food, while young faculty and graduate students congregate near the beer cooler; senior members of the department find nooks in which to lean together talking serious shop. Thus the party continues until it reaches its sober, sensibly early end. It is all very cozy and wholesome, but to my mind it is as much like a party as a shopping mall is like a town square.

Some devil gets into me on these occasions and makes me behave badly, or want to. I'm irritated by the sight of these men and women with their innocent eyes, their gentle and slightly fuddled manners, helping themselves moderately to drink and grazing among the raw vegetables. Where is their aggression? I ask myself. Where is their lust? I feel cheated of my childhood expectation that adult life would be charged with violent emotion, and all the more aggrieved because it happens to be true that I would be content to enjoy violent emotion vicariously, if only somebody would provide me that gratification.

They seem capable, these academics, of peevishness and spite, but none of the forthright, elemental energy that people on the outside have in abundance. Especially as we all grow older, they begin to seem marsupial to me. They have lived too long in an unevolved paradise; no wonder they were unprepared when conditions changed and a horde of young theory mongers, red in tooth and claw, dropped from the trees and ate or colonized them.

I don't mean to imply that what went on at my parents' parties was seamy, that it was anything like the suburban adultery clusters one encounters in Updike's early fiction. My parents' parties served to acknowledge and release sexual tension in a socially sanctioned way, and for the most part they were harmless. Only a few guests seemed unable to resist the temptation to ride the beast of the party out the door.

Among these the most memorable was J, the wife of a distinguished sociologist, the mother of a large brood of children and overseer of a big messy ambitious Kanga household full of musical instruments, books, baskets of rotting apples and unfolded laundry. She was a plump, busty woman with a slightly overblown Celtic prettiness. I disliked her, partly because my mother did, but also because I dreaded her temper. She had a terrifying way of moving from a fugue-like state of dreamy preoccupation to sudden quivering rage with no intermediate steps. I have a vivid memory of her small feet in scuffed flats, planted on dusty floorboards. As I tilt the memory upward I can see her face, broad and rosy with anger as she berates me for dropping her son's violin.

J took pains to preserve appearances; she volunteered at the Women's Exchange and played the cello in a local quartet, but she was very promiscuous. I remember watching her from my top-of-the-stairs vantage point at a party. She stood on tiptoe as she talked animatedly with a much taller man, one hand flattened with spread fingers against her breastbone in the classic flirting position, the other flung across her half-open mouth and flaming cheek in feigned amazement. Her high color—it frightened me to look into the oven of her face—her insinuating smirks and roguish smiles: how all this amazed and repelled me. Rumors circulated about her affairs, at least one of which was certainly true: she served as the mistress of a disreputable townie, a figure of fear to faculty children, a big rough man with picket teeth and a perpetual five o'clock shadow who once clambered drunkenly onto a float at a football rally to imitate a woman wriggling into her girdle. Eventually J's marriage broke up. Later she married a wealthy widower within a month of his wife's death; the two could often be seen downtown, J clutching her frail husband's arm tightly and steering him from store to store. My mother and her friends clenched their teeth and rolled their eyes at the mention of her name.

J was one of the cautionary tales of my childhood, but she was also a kind of inspiration. I didn't like to think about, nor did I know enough to imagine, the couplings of J and the disreputable townie. (Today I can picture them spilling out of a parked car on a rural road late at night. I can hear her coy shriek and his laughing growl as he pursues her through the long grass of a field and brings her down with a thump.) But she gave me a sense for the parameters of adult passion; even as I recoiled at her gaminess I marveled at the power of what burned in her. "She thinks with her glands," I overheard my mother say, and I wondered how she had mastered that trick and whether one day I might be able to do it too.

I believe that what J did in her life would be impossible for a similarly situated woman today. She lived out a specifically female destiny, one fated to end in low comedy or in tragedy, or in some mixture of the two. Such a destiny is no longer available to a woman of J's socioeconomic class. While a woman might be just as compulsively unfaithful as J, society is no longer configured so as to register her actions, to mirror her back to herself as anything but unhappy. And nobody has time or energy to go in for promiscuity as a calling. My own daughter has no such bad examples to watch and wonder at. It would be hard to imagine the mothers of her friends in the role of courtesan or harlot. They are lean and healthy and tense; they wear beepers on their belts and carry daily planners in their bags. My daughter gets her notions more efficiently than I got mine: she watches MTV, where Salt-N-Pepa do squats and point at their vulvas.

One often hears the African folk saying that it takes a village to raise a child. True enough, but it also takes a village to produce a first-class adulteress.

IV. Femina Ludens

At least for a while, our small-town college society provided J just the combination of reluctant tolerance and steady, mild disapprobation that she required.

It was not so kind to R, a painter who looked like a dancer past her prime. She dressed in leotards and calf-length skirts. Her face was as pale as Anaïs Nin's, her hair a bleached, broom-shaped helmet. She drank heavily even by the standard of that place and those days, when two stiff drinks before dinner and wine with it were a daily ritual. I can summon up a clear image of R drinking publicly—in front of people and at somebody's house—straight out of a bottle of gin. But that picture may come from the vault of apocrypha that occupies half my memory.

R was married to a historian, a tall man whose wry insouciance was undercut by weariness. She seemed constantly in a rage—I remember making way for her on the sidewalk as she swept by, black cloak flaring, pulling her two pale daughters behind her, her mouth written into an angry slash with red lipstick. Eventually her marriage broke up and she moved to Cambridge with the two girls.

I knew that my mother and her friends disapproved of R even more intensely than they did of J, and so, as usual, I followed suit. When, on a school trip, I saw R walking across Harvard Square, thinner now and more raddled, I felt a frisson of horror. How unseemly that R should continue to exist, I thought, when by now it should surely all be over for her (she was forty or so). For her, continued animation could be only a hideous reflex, like the galvanic twitching of a dead frog's legs.

The wives never sanctioned R's high bohemian style. They looked askance at her railroad flat with good light in the back room, which she furnished minimally with low-slung couches and Japanese paper-moon lamps. Casual to the point of negligence about their own children's hygiene, they clucked at the wax visible in the ears of R's lovely, solemn, conscientious daughters.

When R persuaded the art department to let her display her paintings in the college gallery—and that must have taken some doing—her husband played a practical joke on her. He sneaked in after hours and tacked up his own primitive crayon drawing of a horse and barn, priced at $14.95, between two of her big abstract canvases. I'm not sure whether this was the proximate cause of her removal to Cambridge, but I know that it delighted the Kangas, particularly my mother, who told the story at dinner tables for decades.

R had offended faculty-wife society with her pretension, her incivility, and her flagrantly excessive drinking. But what the Kangas really held against her was her ambition to be professional. This brought out all the latent clannish nastiness that enlightened training had taught them rigorously to suppress. There was something dangerous about the violation of this taboo, as if the placing of a real price tag on a painting put the private Kanga economy itself at risk. I believe that it was the Kangas who exiled R, who ran her out of paradise.

And they were prescient: it was the linked forces of professionalization and feminism that were to bring about the extinction of the role of faculty wife. As a result of these developments, a great undifferentiated space was opened up for women—a kind of savannah, a wide-open plain on which one could wander and hunt. What was lost was shade, cover, protection, a place to hide. But this is nothing new; more and more of these niches have disappeared as institutionalized hiding places like the clergy and the military have lost their protective status for men, and the solid walls of bourgeois marriage, behind which women found privacy, have become transparent.

Some fit, keen-eyed people are well equipped for the savannah. Others, weaker and slower, are soon picked off by predators. Still others, deprived not only of habitat but of fixed points of reference, wander into the place where the savannah becomes desert and perish slowly of thirst and exposure. The savannah is no place for reverie or distraction. Passive people, dreamy and contemplative people, don't do well there.

I'm a faculty wife by default, because I'm married to an academic, whose salary supports me. We live in the great diaspora that academic life has become. I'm no potter, no gardener, no musician, and I've never been a particularly resourceful or inventive mother. What I am is a writer, and during the twenty years when I was producing nothing, covering my existential nudity with an inadequate garment composed of patches of housewife/graduate student/mother, I was serving the writer's apprenticeship, letting the world trickle through me to leave behind sedimented layers of impression. All through my protracted apprenticeship I felt anomalous and apologetic, subject to fits of self-loathing and panicky self-consciousness, inclined to take refuge in the comfort of grandiose fantasies. The fact is that for years I was a social parasite, the same years when dependency has been a condition of shame for a woman of my class and station. In my case, the absence of shade has meant the absence of a secure and secluded vantage point, a place from which I could observe without being observed. How can I hide where there is no shade?

My apprenticeship might have been shortened if I had been a faculty wife of my mother's generation. I might have been happier surrounded by other amateurs, other experimenters, in an atmosphere that encouraged artistic endeavor for its own sake. But what would have happened when my apprenticeship was complete, when I was ready for metamorphosis? Would the wives have turned on me as they turned on R?

Faculty-wife culture was healthiest in the late fifties, just at the time when bohemia was flowering. I think the two social phenomena are interestingly similar. Kangas and beatniks: both lived out, demonstrated in their lives, the vital link between art and the gratuitous, between art and play. Postwar affluence floated these groups for a while. Then, like the tadpole societies that spring up briefly in puddles after storms, they disappeared.

Would I then wish myself back forty years, in my mother's place? Like all arcadians, all unreconstructed lovers of the past who ask themselves that question, I have to reluctantly admit that the answer is no. I would not wish myself back. Faculty wives were free spirits only to a very limited degree. In spite of their educated backgrounds, their enlightened views, they were also those anachronistic things called ladies, which few of us today could imagine ourselves to be. We wear looser, rougher clothing now; our language is fouler, our patience shorter as we slouch toward the millennium. I would be unable, of course, to accept the circumscription of their lives. Like R I would trespass, and like R I would be expelled.

But how I envy their playfulness! In high summer, when the inevitable zucchini glut overtook their gardens, they drew faces on the outsized squashes, wrapped them in christening robes, put them in bassinets, and left them on one another's doorsteps like foundlings.

How I envy their sense of community, the long deep friendships they maintained through days and years of steady, uneventful proximity, and continue to enjoy in their dotage.

How I envy them their safety, that lost prerequisite for so much else. But here perhaps I'm falling into confusion; perhaps I'm confounding their safety with the safety I felt as a child, protected and fostered by those many mothers. Perhaps I'm remembering them wrongly, with a deceiving, simplifying clarity. Perhaps I'm projecting my wish for protection onto the past, as people are often said to do. Can the wives have been so tightly banded, so consciously what they seem to me to have been? Can the trees have been as deeply leaved, the shade as thickly dappled as I remember?

OTHER PEOPLE'S SECRETS

Patricia Hampl

The river is still now. Nighttime, and I have come here to sit alone in the dark in the wooden boat under its canvas roof, to tally up, finally, those I have betrayed. Let me count the ways. Earlier, white herds of cloud, way up there and harmless, buffaloed across the sky. A beautiful day, and everyone, it seemed, was on the water.

But now the pleasure craft that tooled back and forth all day, plying the marina's no-wake zone, are gone. Only a flotilla of linked barges rides high and empty, headed downriver to Lock Number Two at Hastings, intent on the river's serious business. The massive lozenges look strangely sinister as they part the dark water. By day these barges seem benign—riverine trucks, floating grain or ore or gravel between Saint Paul and the great Elsewhere. But now they pass by spectrally, huge and soundless.

Spotlights from the county jail send wavering columns of moon-colored light across the water from that side of the river to the marina on this side. I once saw a woman, standing on the Wabasha Bridge, lean as far over the guardrail as she could, and blow kisses toward the jail while traffic rushed around her. I followed her gaze and saw a raised arm clad in a blue shirt, indistinct and ghostly, motioning back from a darkened window. The loyal body, reaching even beyond bars to keep its pledge.

The boat groans in its slip, the lines that hold it fast strain as they absorb the wake from the barges. Boat, dock, ropes rub companionably against each other, sending out contented squeaks and low, reassuring moans that sound as if they're saying exactly what they mean—*tethered, tethered.*

This is the location in between, not solid land, not high seas. Just a boat bobbing under a covered slip, the old city of my life laid out before me—the cathedral where my parents were married, the great oxidized bulb of its dome looking like a Jules Verne spaceship landed on the highest hill of the Saint Paul bluffs; on the near shore of Raspberry Island, an elderly Hmong immigrant casting late into the night for carp poisoned by PCBs; and downtown, in the middle distance, the bronze statue of the homeboy, Scott Fitzgerald, a topcoat flung over his arm even in summer, all alone at this hour in Rice Park, across from the neoclassical gray of the Public Library where it all began for me. "You'll like this place," my mother said, holding my hand as we entered—impossible luck!—a building full of books.

Let's start with mother, then, first betrayal.

It was all right to be a writer. In fact, it was much too grand, a dizzy height far above the likes of us. "Have you thought about being a librarian instead, darling?" At least I should get my teaching certificate, "to fall back on," she said, as if teaching were a kind of fainting couch that would catch me when I swooned from writing. But I knew I mustn't take an education course of any kind. Some wily instinct told me it is dangerous to be too practical in this life. I read nineteenth-century novels and Romantic poetry for four years, and left the university unscathed by any skill, ready to begin what, already, I called "my work."

I knocked around a jumble of jobs for ten years, working on the copy desk of the Saint Paul newspaper, recording oral histories in nursing homes around town—Jewish, Catholic, Presbyterian. I edited a magazine for the local public radio station. I lived in a rural commune on nothing at all, eating spaghetti and parsley with others as poetry-besotted as I, squealing like the city girl I was when a field mouse scurried across the farmhouse floor.

I went to graduate school for two years—two more years of reading poetry. A decade of this and that.

Then, when I was thirty-two, my first book was accepted for publication, a collection of poems. My mother was ecstatic. She wrote in her calendar for that June day—practically crowing—"First Book Accepted!!" as if she were signing a contract of her own, one which committed her to overseeing an imaginary multiple-book deal she had negotiated with the future on my behalf.

She asked to see the manuscript out of sheer delight and pride. My first reader.

And here began my career of betrayal. The opening poem in the manuscript, called "Mother/Daughter Dance," was agreeably imagistic, the predictable struggle of the suffocated daughter and the protean mother padded with nicely opaque figurative language. No problem. Only at the end, rising to a crescendo of impacted meaning, had the poem, seemingly of its own volition, reached out of its complacent obscurity to filch a plain and serviceable fact—my mother's epilepsy. There it was, the grand mal seizure as the finishing touch, a personal fact that morphed into a symbol, opening the poem, I knew, wide, wide, wide.

"You cannot publish that poem," she said on the telephone, not for once my stage mother, egging me on. The voice of the betrayed, I heard for the first time, is not sad. It is coldly outraged.

"Why not?" I said with brazen innocence.

Just who did I think I was?

A writer, of course. We get to do this—tell secrets and get away with it. It's called, in book reviews and graduate seminars, courage. *She displays remarkable courage in exploring the family's . . . the book is sustained by his exemplary courage in revealing . . .*

I am trying now to remember if I cared about her feelings at all. I know I did not approve of the secrecy in which for years she had wrapped the dark jewel of her condition. I did not feel she deserved to be so upset about something that should be seen in purely practical terms. I hated—feared, really—the freight she loaded on the idea of epilepsy, her belief that she would lose her job if anyone "found out," her baleful stories of people having to cross the border into Iowa to get married because "not so long ago" Minnesota refused to issue marriage licenses to epileptics. The idea of Iowa being "across the border" was itself absurd.

She had always said she was a feminist before there was feminism, but where was that buoyant *Our Bodies, Ourselves* spirit? Vanished. When it came to epilepsy, something darkly medieval had bewitched her, making it impossible to appeal to her usually wry common sense. I rebelled against her horror of seizures, though her own had been successfully controlled by medication for years. It was all, as I told her, no big deal. Couldn't she see that?

Stony silence.

She was outraged by my betrayal. I was furious at her theatrical secrecy. Would you feel this way, I asked sensibly, if you had diabetes?

"This isn't diabetes," she said darkly, the rich unction of her shame refusing my hygienic approach.

Even as we faced off, I felt obscurely how thin my reasonableness was. The gravitas of her disgrace infuriated me partly because it had such natural force. I was a reed easily snapped in the fierce gale of her shame. I sensed obliquely that her loyalty to her secret bespoke a firmer grasp of the world than my poems could imagine. But poetry was everything! I knew that. Her ferocious secrecy made me feel foolish, a lightweight, but for no reason I could articulate. Perhaps I had, as yet, no secret of my own to guard, no humiliation against which I measured myself and the cruelly dispassionate world with its casual, intrusive gaze.

I tried, of course, to make *her* feel foolish. It was ridiculous, I said, to think anyone would fire her for a medical condition—especially her employer, a progressive liberal arts college where she worked in the library. "You don't know people," she said, her dignified mistrust subtly trumping my credulous open-air policy.

This was tougher than I had expected. I changed tactics. Nobody even reads poetry, I assured her shamelessly. You have nothing to worry about.

She dismissed this pandering. "You have no right," she said simply.

It is pointless to claim your First Amendment rights with your mother. My arguments proved to be no argument at all, and she was impervious to any blandishment.

Then, when things looked lost, I was visited by a strange inspiration.

I simply reversed field. I told her that if she wanted, I would cut the poem from the book. I paused, let this magnanimous gesture sink in. "You think it over," I said. "I'll do whatever you want. But Mother . . ."

"What?" she asked, wary, full of misgivings as well she might have been.

"One thing," I said, the soul of an aluminum-siding salesman rising within me, "I just want you to know—before you make your decision—it really is the best poem in the book." Click.

This was not, after all, an inspiration. It was a gamble. And although it was largely unconscious, still, there was calculation to it. She loved to play the horses. And I was my mother's daughter; instinctively I put my money on a winner. The next morning, she called and told me I could publish the poem. "It's a good poem," she said, echoing my own self-promoting point. Her voice was rinsed of outrage, a little weary but without resentment.

Describe it as I saw it then: She had read the poem, and like God in His heaven, she saw that it was good. I didn't pause to think she was doing me a favor, that she might be making a terrible sacrifice. This was good for her, I told myself with the satisfied righteousness of a nurse entering a terrified patient's room armed with long needles and body restraints. The wicked witch of secrecy had been vanquished. I hadn't simply won (though that was delicious). I had liberated my mother, unlocked her from the prison of the dank secret where she had been cruelly detained for so long.

I felt heroic in a low-grade literary sort of way. I understood that poetry—my poem!—had performed this liberating deed. Mother had been unable to speak. I had spoken for her. It had been hard for both of us. But this was the whole point of literature, its deepest good, this voicing of the unspoken, the forbidden. And look at the prize we won with our struggle—for doesn't the truth, as John, the beloved apostle, promised, set you free?

Memory is such a cheat and privacy such a dodging chimera that between the two of them—literature's goalposts—the match is bound to turn into a brawl. Kafka's famous solution to the conundrum of personal and public rights—burn the papers!—lies, as his work does, at the conflicted heart of twentieth-century writing, drenched as it is in the testimony of personal memory and of political mayhem.

Max Brod, the friend entrusted to do the burning, was the first to make the point in his own defense which has been taken up by others ever since: Aside from the unconscionable loss to the world if he had destroyed the letters and the journals with their stories and unfinished novels, Brod, as his good friend Kafka well knew, was a man incapable of burning a single syllable. Kafka asked someone to destroy his work whom he could be sure would never do so. No one seriously accuses Brod of betraying a dying friend. Or rather, no one wishes to think about the choice in ethical terms because who would wish he had lit the match?

But one person did obey. Dora Diamant, Kafka's final and certainly truest love, was also asked to destroy his papers. She burned what she could, without hesitation. She took Kafka at his word—and he was alive to see her fulfill his command. She was never wife or widow, and did not retain any rights over the matter after Kafka's death, but even Brod, Kafka's literary executor, felt it necessary to treat her diplomatically, as late as 1930, and to present his case to her when he set about publishing the work.

As she wrote to Brod during this period when they tried to come to an understanding about publication of Kafka's work:

> The world at large does not have to know about Franz. He is nobody else's business because, well, because nobody could possibly understand him. I regarded it—and I think I still do so now—as wholly out of the question for anyone ever to understand Franz, or to get even an inkling of what he was about unless one knew him personally. All efforts to understand him were hopeless unless he himself made

> them possible by the look in his eyes or the touch of his hand. . . .

Hers is the austere, even haughty claim of privacy, a jealous right, perhaps. She knew it: "I am only now beginning to understand . . . the fear of having to share him with others." This, she freely admits to Brod, is "very petty." She does not claim that her willingness to destroy the work was a wholly noble act. She is surprisingly without moral posturing.

Still, she could not bear to give the world those works she had not destroyed. As Ernst Pawel says in *Nightmare of Reason: A Life of Franz Kafka,* she denied that she had them until, after her marriage to a prominent German Communist, their house was raided by the Gestapo in 1933 and every piece of paper, including all the Kafka material, was confiscated, never to be located to this day. She was, finally, distraught, and as Pawel says, "confessed her folly" to Brod.

Pawel, an acute and sensitive reader of Kafka and his relationships, puzzles over this willful act of secrecy. "The sentiment or sentimentality that moved this otherwise recklessly truthful woman to persist in her lie," he writes, clearly perplexed, "may somehow be touching, but it led to a tragic loss."

Yes—but. The lie Dora Diamant persisted in was a simple one—her refusal to admit to Kafka's editors or friends that she still possessed any of his papers. But her letter to Brod (written three years before the Gestapo raid) is not the document of a woman who is simply "sentimental." She is adamantly antiliterary. The papers she refused to hand over—and that, terrible irony, were swept away by the Gestapo into that other kind of silence, the wretched midcentury abyss—were, no doubt quite literally to her, private documents. After all, most of Kafka's works were written in—or as—journals. There is no more private kind of writing. The journal teeters on the edge of literature. It plays the game of having its cake and eating it too: writing which is not meant to be read.

The objects Kafka asked Dora Diamant to destroy and those she later refused to hand over to editors did not have the clear identity of "professional writing" or of "literature." They were works from a master of prose writing, but they were still journals and letters. They must have seemed, to her who had lived with them, intensely personal documents. If it is understood even between lovers that a journal is "private," off-limits, not to be read, it doesn't seem quite so outrageous that Dora Diamant, who loved the man, would choose to honor his privacy as she did. In fact, it is not a mystery at all, but quite in keeping with her character as a "recklessly truthful woman."

Privacy and expression are two embattled religions. And while the god of privacy reigns in the vast air of silence, expression worships a divinity who is sovereign in the tabernacle of literature. Privacy, by definition, keeps its reasons to itself and can hardly be expected to borrow the weapons of expression—language and literature—to defend itself. To understand the impulse of privacy that persists against every assault, as Dora Diamant's did, her position must not call forth the condescension of seeing her adamant refusal as being merely "touching."

In her 1930 letter to Brod, Dora Diamant is trying to express what she maintains—against the institutional weight and historical force of literature—is a greater truth than the truth that exists in Kafka's papers. She is determined to remain loyal to his appalling absence and to the ineffable wonder of his being, "the look in his eyes," "the touch of his hand."

This is not sentimentality. She speaks from a harsh passion for accuracy—nothing but his very being is good enough to stand as his truth. Literature at best is a delusion. It is the intruder, the falsifier. She makes an even more radical claim—it is unnecessary: "The world at large does not have to know about Franz." Why? Because their "knowing" (possible only through the work now that he is dead) is doomed to be incomplete and therefore inaccurate. A lie, in other words. In her terms, it is a bigger lie, no doubt, than her refusal to admit to those eager editors that she did indeed have the goods stashed away in her apartment.

No writer could possibly agree with her. Except Kafka, of course. But maybe Kafka wasn't "a writer." It may be necessary to call him a prophet. In any case, Dora Diamant wasn't a writer.

She belonged to the other religion, not the one of words, but the human one of intimacy, of hands that touch and eyes that look. The one that knows we die, and bears silently the grief of this extinction, refusing the vainglorious comfort of literature's claim of immortality, declining Shakespeare's offer:

So long as men can breathe or eyes can see,
So long lives this, and this gives life to thee.

The ancient religions all have injunctions against speaking the name of God. Truth, they know, rests in silence. As Dora Diamant, unarmed against the august priests of literature who surrounded her, also knew in her loneliness: What happens in the dark of human intimacy is holy, and belongs to silence. It is not, as we writers say, material.

There is no betrayal, as there is no love, like the first one. But then, I hadn't betrayed my mother—I had saved her. I freed her from silence, from secrecy, from the benighted attitudes which had caused her such anguish, and from the historical suppression of women's voices—and so on and so forth. If Dora Diamant was someone who didn't believe in literature, I was one who believed in nothing else.

This defining moment: I must have been about twelve, not older. A spring day, certainly in May because the windows and even the heavy doors at St. Luke's School are open. Fresh air is gusting through the building like a nimble thief, roller shades slapping against windows from the draft, classroom doors banging shut. The classrooms are festooned with flowers, mostly drooping masses of lilac stuck in coffee cans and Mason jars, placed at the bare feet of the plaster Virgin who has a niche in every classroom: *Ave, ave, Ma-ree-ee-ah,* our Queen of the May.

For some reason we, our whole class, are standing in the corridor. We are waiting—to go into the auditorium, to go out on the playground, some everyday thing like that. We are formed in two lines and we are supposed to be silent. We are talking, of course, but in low murmurs, and Sister doesn't mind. She is smiling. Nothing is happening, nothing at all. We are just waiting for the next ordinary moment to blossom forth.

Out of this vacancy, I am struck by a blow: I must commemorate all this. I know it is just my mind, but it doesn't feel like a thought. It is a command. It feels odd, and it feels good, buoyant. Sister is there in her heavy black drapery, also the spring breeze rocketing down the dark corridor, and the classroom doorway we are standing by, where, inside, lilacs are shriveling at the bare feet of Mary. Or maybe it is a voice that strikes me, Tommy Howe hissing to—I forget to whom, "OK, OK, lemme go."

These things matter—Tommy's voice, Sister smiling in her black, the ricochet of the wind, the lilacs collapsing—because I am here to take them in.

That was all. It was everything.

I have asked myself many times about that oddly adult word—*commemorate*—which rainbows over the whole gauzy instant. I'm sure that was the word, that in fact this word was the whole galvanizing point of the experience because I remember thinking even at the time that it was a weird word for a child—me—to use. It was an elderly word, not mine. But I grabbed it and held on. Perhaps only a Catholic child of the fifties would be at home with such a conception. We "commemorated" just about everything. The year was crosshatched with significance—saints' feast days, holy days, Lent with its Friday fasts and "Stations of the Cross." We prayed for the dead, we prayed *to* the dead.

How alive it all was. Commemoration was the badge of living we pinned on all that happened. Our great pulsing religion didn't just hold us fast in its claws. It sent us bounding through the day, the week, the month and season, companioned by meaning. To honor the moment, living or dead, was what "to commemorate" meant. This, I sensed for the first time, was what writers did. Of course, being a Catholic girl, I was already sniffing for my vocation. Sister was smiling, her garments billowing with the spring wind, and here was "the call," secular perhaps, but surely a voice out of the whirlwind.

The sense of the fundamental goodness of the commemorative act made it difficult to believe "commemoration" could be harmful. Beyond this essential goodness I perceived in the act of writing, I felt what I was up to was a kind of radiance, a dazzling shining-forth of experience. I never liked the notion that writers "celebrated" life—that was a notion too close to boosterism and the covering-over of life I thought writers were expressly commissioned to examine. But who could be hurt by being honored—or simply noticed? Who could object to that?

A lot of people, it turned out. My mother was only the first. "You can use me," a friend once said, "just don't abuse me." But who, exactly, makes that distinction?

"You're not going to use this, are you?" someone else asked after confiding in me. She regarded me suddenly with horror, as if she had strayed into a remake of *Invasion of the Body Snatchers,* where she played a real human who has just discovered I'm one of *them.*

Later, I strayed into a scary movie myself. I'd become friendly one year with a visiting writer from one of the small, indistinct countries "behind the Iron Curtain," as we used to say. It was a year of romantic upheaval for me—for her too. God knows what I told her. We met for coffee now and again, and regaled each other with wry stories from our absurdist lives. Then she went back where she had come from.

A year later I received in the mail a book in a language completely unknown to me. When I saw her name on the cover I realized this was the book she had been writing in Minnesota. "Just wanted you to have my little American book!" the cheery note said. An American publisher was interested in releasing an English translation, she added. I flipped through the incomprehensible pages. Suddenly, two hideous words cleared the alphabet soup with terrible eloquence: *Patricia Hampl.* Then I saw, with increasing alarm, that my name—me!—popped up like a ghoulish gargoyle throughout the text, doing, saying, I knew not what.

"I don't think you'll be too upset," someone who could read the incomprehensible language told me, but declined to translate. "It's a little sticky," she said vaguely. Sticky?

Later still, at a workshop with a Famous Novelist, I raised

my hand and posed the question. "You've said in interviews that your fiction is autobiographical," I began, notebook ready to take down his good counsel. "I'm wondering what advice you might have on writing about family or close friends?"

"Fuck 'em," he said. And I shivered the body-snatcher shiver. So you *do* have to become one of them?

Over the years, as other books followed my first, I told the story of how I had spoken for my mother who could not speak for herself. I had all my ducks lined up in a row—my belief in the radiance of the commemorative act, my honorable willingness to let my mother decide the fate of the poem, her plucky decision to let me publish the poem which at first she had seen as a cruel invasion but which—the real miracle—she came to recognize was nothing less than a liberation for her. She and I, together, had broken an evil silence. See what literature can do?

Then one day I got a call from a poet who was writing a piece about "personal writing." She had been in an audience where I had told my mother-daughter story—there had been many by this time: I had my patter down. It was a wonderful story, she said. Could she use it in her essay as an example of . . . ?

The words "wonderful story" hung above me like an accusation. The blah-blah-blah of it all came back and stood before me, too contemptuous even to slap me in the face. I felt abashed. I told her I wanted to check the story first with my mother.

She answered the phone on the first ring. She was still working, still at her library job. *Remember that poem in my first book,* I said, *the one that has the seizure in it and you and me?*

Oh yes.

Remember how I told you I wouldn't publish it if you didn't want me to, and you said I could go ahead?

Yes.

Well, I was just wondering. Is that something you're glad about? I mean, do you feel the poem sort of got things out in the open and sort of relieved your mind, or—I sounded like a nervous teenager, not the Visiting Writer who had edified dozens of writing workshops with this exemplary tale—*or . . .*

What *was* the or? What was the alternative?

Or did you just do it because you loved me?

Without pausing a beat: *Because I loved you.*
Then the pause: *I always hated it.*

Bobbing again on the water in the old boat, still in between. A nightly ritual, but now, as if on cue for the climax, lightning has begun to knife the sky, and thunder has started its drumrolls. Hot summer night, waiting to break open the heat, and spill.

No wonder I like to come down here, this floating place. I was attracted too to the in-between position of the writer. More exactly, I was after the suspended state that comes with the act of writing: not happy, not sad; uncertain of the next turn, yet not lost; here, but really there, the there of an unmapped geography that, nonetheless, was truly home—and paradisal.

The elusive pleasure to be found in writing (and only in it, not the *before* of anticipation, not the *after* of accomplishment) is in following the drift, inkling your way toward meaning. My old hero, Whitman, that rogue flaneur, knew all about it: "I'm afoot with my vision!" he exulted. It was an ars poetica I too could sign up for, basking in the sublime congruence of consciousness "afoot" in the floating world.

There are, it is true, memoirists who are not magnetized by memory. They simply "have a story to tell." They have the goods on someone—mother, father, even themselves in an earlier life, or on history itself. "Something" has happened to them. These stories—of incest or abuse, of extraordinary accomplishment or exceptional hardship, the testimonies of those who have witnessed the hellfire of history or the anguish of unusually trying childhoods—are what are sometimes thought of as the real or best occasions of autobiography.

Memory, in this view, is a minion of experience. It has a tale to tell. Its job is to witness the real or to reveal the hidden. Sometimes the impulse to write these accounts is transparently self-serving or self-dramatizing. But at least as often, and certainly more valiantly, this is the necessary literature of witness. Historic truth rests on such testimony. The authority of these personal documents is so profound, so incriminating, that whole arsenals of hatred have been arrayed in mad argument for half a century in a vain attempt to deny the truth of a little girl's diary. These kinds of memoir count for a lot. Sometimes they are the only history we can ever hope to get.

Still, memory is not, fundamentally, a repository. If it were, no question would arise about its accuracy, no argument would be fought over its notorious imprecision. The privacy of individual experience is not a right, as Dora Diamant tried to argue with Max Brod, or as my mother begged me to see. Not a right, but something greater—it is an inevitability that returns no matter what invasion seems to overtake it. This privacy is bred of memory's intimacy with the idiosyncrasy of the imagination. What memory "sees," it must regard through the image-making faculty of mind. The parallel lines of memory and imagination cross finally and collide in narrative. The casualty is the dead body of privacy lying smashed on the track.

Strangely enough, contemporary memoir, all the rage today as it practically shoves the novel off the book review pages, has its roots not in fiction, which it appears to mimic and tease, but in poetry. The chaotic lyric impulse, not the smooth drive of plot, is the engine of memory. Flashes of half-forgotten moments flare up from their recesses: the ember-red tip of a Marlboro at night on a dock, summer of '54, the lake still as soup, or a patch of a remembered song unhinged from its narrative moorings—"*Glow little glow worm, glimmer, glimmer,*" and don't forget the skinned knuckle—Dad's!—turning a dead ignition on a twenty-below winter day. Shards glinting in the dust.

These are the materials of memoir, details that refuse to stay buried, that demand habitation. Their spark of meaning spreads into a wildfire of narrative. They may be domesticated into a story, but the passion that begot them as images belongs to the wild night of poetry. It is the humble detail, as that arch memorialist Nabokov understood, which commands memory to speak: "Caress the detail," he advised, "the divine detail." And in so doing, he implicitly suggested, the world—the one lost forever—comes streaming back. Alive, ghostly real.

Kafka called himself "a memory come alive." His fellow townsman, Rilke, also believed that memory, not "experience," claims the sovereign position in the imagination. How strange that Kafka and Rilke, these two giants who preside as the hieratic figures, respectively, of The Writer and The Poet for the modern age, were both Prague boys, born barely eight years apart, timid sons of rigid fathers, believers in the word, prophets of the catastrophe that was to swallow their world whole and change literature forever. Canaries sent down into the mine of history, singing till the end.

In *Letters to a Young Poet,* the little book it is probably safe to say every young poet reads at some point, Rilke wrote to a boy who was a student at the very military academy where he himself had been so notoriously miserable. He wrote, no doubt, to his younger self as well as to this otherwise unknown student poet, Franz Zaver Kappus. Though the boy was only nineteen, Rilke sent him not forward into experience, but deeply inward to memory as the greatest "treasure" available to a writer.

"Even if you found yourself in some prison," Rilke says in the first letter, "whose walls let in none of the world's sounds—wouldn't you still have your childhood, that jewel beyond all price, that treasure house of memories."

This is not an invitation to nostalgia—Rilke had been painfully unhappy as a boy, stifled and frightened. He was not a sentimentalist of childhood. He is directing the young poet, rather, to the old religion of commemoration in whose rituals the glory of consciousness presides. He believes, as I cannot help believing as well, in the communion of perception where experience does not fade to a deathly pale, but lives evergreen, the imagination taking on the lost life, even a whole world, bringing it to the only place it can live again, reviving it in the pools and freshets of language.

I have gone to visit my mother. She is in the hospital, has been there now many weeks. "It's hell to get old," she says, barely voiced words escaping from the trach tube from which she breathes. Almost blind, but still eager to get back to her email at home. She smiles from her great charm, a beatific smile, when I say "email," when I say "home." There is a feeding tube in her stomach. There was a stroke, then her old nemesis, a seizure, a heart attack, respiratory this, pulmonary that—all the things that can go wrong, all the things that have their high-tech solutions. She is surrounded by beeps and gurgles, hums and hisses. She'll get home. She's a fighter. At the moment, fighting her way out of the thick ether of weeks of sedative medicines.

She is glad I have come. She has been, she tells me, in a coffin at Willwersheid's Mortuary. Terrible experience, very confining.

I tell her she has not been in a coffin, I assure her she has not been at a funeral parlor. I tell her the name of the hospital where she is.

She looks at me as at a fool, not bothering to conceal her contempt. Then the astonishing firmness that kept me in line for years: *I have been in a coffin. Don't tell me I have not been in a coffin.*

Well, I say, you're not in a coffin now, are you?

No, she says, agreeing with vast relief, *thank God for that.*

The trip, she says animatedly, trying to express the marvel of it all, has been simply *amazing*. Shipboard life is wonderful. Skirting Cuba—that was beautiful. But the best part? The most beautiful, wonderful black woman—a real lady—came to her cabin with fresh linens. The ironing smelled so good! That was what made Port-au-Prince especially nice. People everywhere, she says, have been so lovely.

Why not? It's better than the coffin at Willwersheid's. Then, the air, saturated by weeks of medication, suddenly clears, and we're talking sensibly about people we know, about politics—she knows who's running for governor, and she wouldn't vote for Norm Coleman if he were the last man on earth. We see eye to eye. She asks about my father, she asks about my work—our usual subjects.

"Actually," I say, "I'm writing about you. Sort of."

She's in a wheelchair, the portable oxygen strapped to the back. We have wheeled down to the visitors' lounge and are looking out the big picture window that has a view of the capitol building and the cathedral, and even a slender curve of the Mississippi in the distance where I will go when I leave here, to sit again to brood in the little boat under the canvas slip. She can see the capitol and the cathedral. Storms grizzle the sky with lightning, and her good eye widens with interest.

I say I am trying to tell the story again of the poem about the seizure. "I'm trying to explain it from your point of view," I say.

She nods, takes this in. "Yes," she says slowly, thoughtfully. "That's good you're doing that finally. It's very important to . . . to my career." Her smile, the great rainbow that the nurses have remarked on, beams in my direction, the wild sky behind us, flashing.

Her career. Yes. Her own passage through this life, the shape she too has made of things, her visions, the things she alone knows. The terrible narrowness of a coffin and the marvels of Port-au-Prince, the astonishing kindness of people, the pleasure of sweet-smelling linen. I can see now that she was standing up for the truth of her experience, the literal fact of it, how it jerked and twisted not only her body but her life, how it truly seized her. My poem and I—we merely fingered the thing, casually displaying it for the idle passerby. What she knows and how she knows it must not be taken from her.

I never understood the fury my desire to commemorate brought down upon me. The sense of betrayal—when I thought I was just saying what I saw, drawn into utterance, I truly believed, by the buoyancy of loving life, all its strange particles. I didn't have a dark story of abuse to purvey or even a horde of delicious gossip. I was just taking pictures, I thought. But then, doesn't the "primitive" instinct know that the camera steals the soul? My own name skittering down the pages of a foreign book, sending alarms down my spine. The truth is: The constraining suit of words rarely fits. Writers—and readers—believe in the fiction of telling a true story. But the living subject knows it as the work of a culprit.

Years ago, when I was living in the poetry commune, eating spaghetti and parsley, I had a dream I knew would stay with me. A keeper, as my father says of fish. I was behind the wheel of a Buick, a big improbable Dad car I couldn't imagine driving in real life. I was steering with my eyes shut, traveling the streets of my girlhood—Linwood, Lexington, Oxford, even Snelling with its whizzing truck traffic. It was terrifying. I understood I must not open my eyes. And I must not turn the wheel over to the man sitting beside me in the passenger seat though he had his eyes wide open. If I wanted to reach my destination (murky, undefined), I must keep driving blind. My companion kept screaming, "You'll kill us all!"

I've lost quite a few people along the way. And not to death. I lose them to writing. The one who accused me of appropriating her life, the one who said he was appalled, the poet miffed by my description of his shoes, the dear elderly priest who said he thought I understood the meaning of a private conversation, this one, that one. Gone, gone. Their fading faces haven't faded at all, just receded, turned abruptly away from me, as is their right.

I have the letters somewhere, stuffed in a file drawer I never open. The long letters, trying to give me a chance to explain myself, the terse ones, cutting me off for good. The range of tone it is possible for the betrayed to employ—the outrage, the disgust, the wounded astonishment, the quiet dismay, the cold dismissal. Some of them close friends, some barely known, only encountered. All of them "used," one way or another, except for the baffling case of the friend who wrote to complain because I had not included her.

Mother and I are safe inside, staring out the big hospital window as our city gets lost in sheets of gray. "Is it raining?" she asks. The storm is wild, bending old trees on Summit Avenue, snapping them easily, taking up clots of sod as they go down. Down at the river the boat must be banging against the dock.

My mind scrolls up the furious swirl of phrases in those letters from people who no longer speak to me. And me, surprised every time. "*I cannot believe that you would think . . .*" "*Maybe it seemed that way to you, but I . . .*"

But I'm getting too close again, hovering at their sides where they don't want me, trying to take down the dialogue. Better not. Leave the letters in their proud silence. No quotes, no names. Or else, someone, in a dream or elsewhere, is likely to rise up in fury, charging with the oracular voice of the righteous dead that I've killed again.

THE AQUARIUM

Aleksandar Hemon

On July 15, 2010, my wife, Teri, and I took our younger daughter, Isabel, to the doctor for a regular checkup. She was nine months old and appeared to be in perfect health. Her first teeth had come in, and she was now regularly eating with us at the dinner table, babbling and shoveling rice cereal into her mouth. A cheerful, joyous child, she had a fondness for people, which she had not, the joke went, inherited from her congenitally grumpy father.

Teri and I always went together to our children's doctor's appointments, and this time we also took Ella, Isabel's big sister, who was almost three. The nurse at Dr. Armand Gonzalzles's office took Isabel's temperature and measured her weight, height, and head circumference, and Ella was happy that she didn't have to undergo the same ordeal. Dr. G., as we called him, listened to Isabel's breathing and checked her eyes and ears. On his computer, he pulled up Isabel's development chart: her height was within the expected range; she was a little underweight. Everything seemed fine, except for her head circumference, which was two measures of standard deviation above her last measurement. Dr. G. was concerned. Reluctant to send Isabel for an MRI, he scheduled an ultrasound exam for the following day.

Back at home that evening, Isabel was restless and cranky; she had a hard time falling and staying asleep. If we hadn't gone to

Dr. G.'s, we would have assumed that she was simply overtired, but now we had a different interpretative framework, one founded on fear. Later that night, I took Isabel out of our bedroom (she always slept with us) to calm her. In the kitchen, I sang her my entire repertoire of lullabies: "You Are My Sunshine," "Twinkle, Twinkle, Little Star," and a Mozart piece I'd learned as a child, whose lyrics in Bosnian I miraculously remembered. Singing the three lullabies in a relentless loop usually worked, but this time it took a while before she laid her head on my chest and quieted down. When she did this, it felt as though she were somehow comforting me, telling me that everything would be all right. Worried as I was, I imagined a future in which I would one day recall that moment and tell other people how Isabel had calmed *me* down. My daughter, I would say, took care of me, and she was only nine months old.

The following morning, Isabel underwent an ultrasound exam of her head, crying in Teri's arms throughout the procedure. Shortly after we got home, Dr. G. called to tell us that Isabel was hydrocephalic and we needed to go to an emergency room immediately—it was a life-threatening situation.

The examination room in the ER at Chicago's Children's Memorial Hospital was kept dark, as Isabel was about to have a CT scan and the doctors were hoping she'd fall asleep so that they wouldn't have to drug her. But she wasn't allowed to eat, because there was the possibility of a subsequent MRI, and she kept crying from hunger. A resident gave her a colorful whirligig and we blew at it to distract her. She finally fell asleep. As the scan was performed, we waited for something to reveal itself, too afraid to imagine what it might be.

Dr. Tadanori Tomita, the head of pediatric neurosurgery, read the CT scans for us: the ventricles of Isabel's brain were enlarged, full of fluid. Something was blocking the draining channels, Dr. Tomita said, possibly "a growth." An MRI was urgently needed.

Teri held Isabel in her arms as the anesthetics were administered, then we handed her over to the nurses for an hour-long MRI. The cafeteria in the hospital's basement was the saddest place in the world, with its grim neon lights and gray tabletops and the diffuse foreboding of those who had stepped away from suffering children to have a grilled cheese sandwich. We didn't dare speculate about the results of the MRI; we were anchored in the moment, which, terrifying as it was, hadn't yet extended into a future.

Called up to medical imaging, we ran into Dr. Tomita in the overlit hallway. "We believe," he said, "that Isabel has a tumor." He showed us the MRI images on his computer: right at the center of Isabel's brain, lodged between the cerebellum, the brain stem, and the hypothalamus, was a round *thing*. It was the size of a golf ball, Dr. Tomita suggested, but I'd never been interested in golf and couldn't envision what he meant. He would remove the tumor, and we would find out what kind it was only after the pathology report. "But it looks like a teratoid," he said. I didn't comprehend the word "teratoid," either—it was beyond my experience, belonging to the domain of the unimaginable and incomprehensible, the domain into which Dr. Tomita was now guiding us.

Isabel was asleep in the recovery room, motionless, innocent. Teri and I kissed her hands and her forehead and wept through the moment that divided our life into *before* and *after*. *Before* was now and forever foreclosed, while *after* was spreading out, like an exploding twinkle-star, into a dark universe of pain.

Still unsure of the word that Dr. Tomita had uttered, I looked up brain tumors on the Internet, and found an image of a tumor that was nearly identical to Isabel's. Its full name was, I read, "atypical teratoid rhabdoid tumor" (ATRT). It was highly malignant and exceedingly rare, occurring in only three in a million children and representing about 3 percent of pediatric cancers of the central nervous system. The survival rate for children younger than three was less than 10 percent. There were even more discouraging statistics available for me to ponder, but I recoiled from the screen, deciding instead to talk to and trust only Isabel's doctors; never again would I research her condition on the Internet. Already I understood that it would be necessary to manage our knowledge and our imaginations if we were not to lose our minds.

On Saturday, July 17, Dr. Tomita and his neurosurgical team

implanted an Ommaya reservoir in Isabel's head, to help drain and relieve the pressure from the accumulated cerebrospinal fluid. When Isabel was returned to her hospital room on the neurosurgery floor, she kicked off her blanket, as she was wont to do; we took this as an encouraging sign, a hopeful first step on a long journey. On Monday, she was released from the hospital to wait at home for the surgery that would remove the tumor, which was scheduled for the end of the week. Teri's parents were in town, because her sister had given birth to her second son on the day of Isabel's checkup—too concerned about Isabel, we had hardly paid attention to the new arrival in the family—and Ella had spent the weekend with her grandparents, barely noticing the upheaval or our absence. Tuesday afternoon was sunny, and we all went out for a walk, Isabel strapped to Teri's chest. That night, we rushed to the emergency room, because Isabel had developed a fever; it was likely that she had an infection, which is not uncommon after the insertion of a foreign object—in this case, the Ommaya—in a child's head.

She received antibiotics and underwent a scan or two; the Ommaya was removed. On Wednesday afternoon, I left the hospital and went home to be with Ella, as we'd promised to take her to our neighborhood farmers' market. It was essential, in the ongoing catastrophe, that we keep our promises. Ella and I bought blueberries and peaches; on the way home, we picked up some first-rate cannoli from our favorite pastry shop. I talked to Ella about Isabel's being sick, about her tumor, and told her that she would have to stay with Grandma that night. She didn't complain or cry; she understood, as well as any three-year-old could, the difficulty of our predicament.

As I was walking to the car, cannoli in hand, to go back to the hospital, Teri called. Isabel's tumor was hemorrhaging; emergency surgery was required. Dr. Tomita was waiting to talk to me before going into the operating room. It took me about fifteen minutes to get to the hospital, through traffic that existed in an entirely different space-time, where people did not rush while crossing the street and no infant's life was in danger, where everything turned quite leisurely away from disaster.

In the hospital room, the box of cannoli still in my hand, I found Teri weeping over Isabel, who was deathly pale. Dr. Tomita was there, images of our daughter's hemorrhage already pulled up on the screen. It seemed that, once the fluid had drained, the tumor had expanded into the vacated space and its blood vessels had begun to burst. Immediate removal of the tumor was the only hope, but there was a distinct risk of Isabel's bleeding to death. A child of her age had just over a pint of blood in her body, Dr. Tomita told us, and continuous transfusion might not suffice.

Before we followed Isabel into the pre-op, I put the cannoli in the fridge that was in her room. The selfish lucidity of that act produced an immediate feeling of guilt. Only later would I understand that that absurd act was related to a desperate form of hope: the cannoli might be necessary for our future survival.

The surgery was expected to last between four and six hours; Dr. Tomita's assistant would keep us updated. We kissed Isabel's parchment-pale forehead and watched her being wheeled into the unknown by a gang of masked strangers. Teri and I returned to Isabel's room to wait. We alternately wept and were silent. We shared some cannoli to keep ourselves going—for days, we'd had very little food or sleep. The lights in the room were dimmed; we were on a bed behind a curtain, and for some reason no one bothered us. We were far away from the world of farmers' markets and blueberries, where children were born and lived, and where grandmothers put granddaughters to sleep. I had never felt as close to another human being as I did that night to my wife.

Sometime after midnight, Dr. Tomita's assistant called to say that Isabel had made it through the surgery. Dr. Tomita thought he'd removed most of the tumor. Isabel was doing well and would soon be transferred to the intensive care unit, he said, where we could see her. I remember that moment as a relatively happy one: Isabel was alive. Only the immediate outcome was relevant; all we could hope for was to reach the next step, whatever it was. In the ICU, we found her entangled in a web of IVs, tubes, and wires, paralyzed by Rocuronium (called "the rock" by everyone there), which had been administered to prevent her from ripping out her breathing tubes. We spent the night watching her, kissing the fingers on her limp hand, reading or singing to her. The next day, I set up an iPod dock and played music, not only in the willfully delusional belief that music would be good for a painful, recovering brain but also to counter the soul-crushing hospital noise: the beeping of monitors, the wheezing of respirators, the indifferent chatter of nurses in the hallway, the alarm that went off whenever a patient's condition abruptly worsened. To the accompaniment of Bach's cello suites or Charles Mingus's piano pieces, I registered every dip of Isabel's heart rate, every change in her blood pressure. I couldn't take my eyes off the cruelly fluctuating numbers on the monitors, as though the sheer act of staring could influence the outcome.

There's a psychological mechanism, I've come to believe, that prevents most of us from imagining the moment of our own death. For if it were possible to imagine fully that instant of passing from consciousness to nonexistence, with all the attendant fear and humiliation of absolute helplessness, it would be very hard to live. It would be unbearably obvious that death is inscribed in everything that constitutes life, that any moment of your existence may be only a breath away from being the last. We would be continuously devastated by the magnitude of that inescapable fact. Still, as we mature into our mortality, we begin to gingerly dip our horror-tingling toes into the void, hoping that our mind will somehow ease itself into dying, that God or some other soothing opiate will remain available as we venture into the darkness of nonbeing.

But how can you possibly ease yourself into the death of your child? For one thing, it is supposed to happen well after your own dissolution into nothingness. Your children are supposed to outlive you by several decades, during the course of which they live their lives, happily devoid of the burden of your presence, and eventually complete the same mortal trajectory as their parents: oblivion, denial, fear, the end. They're supposed to handle their own mortality, and no help in that regard (other than forcing them to confront death by dying) can come from you—death ain't a science project. And, even if you could imagine your child's death, why would you?

But I'd been cursed with a compulsively catastrophic imagination, and had often involuntarily imagined the worst. I used to picture being run over by a car whenever I crossed the street; I could actually see the layers of dirt on the car's axle as its wheel crushed my skull. When I was stuck on a subway with all the lights out, I'd envision a deluge of fire advancing through the tunnel toward the train. Only after I met Teri did I manage to get my tormentful imagination somewhat under control. And, after our children were born, I learned to quickly delete any vision I had of something horrible happening to them. A few weeks before Isabel's cancer was diagnosed, I'd noticed that her head seemed large and somewhat asymmetrical, and a question had popped into my mind: What if she has a brain tumor? But I banished the thought almost immediately. Even if you could imagine your child's grave illness, why would you?

A couple of days after Dr. Tomita had operated to remove the tumor, an MRI showed that there was still a piece left in Isabel's brain. The more cancer was taken out, the better the prognosis would be, so Isabel had to undergo another surgery, after which she returned to the ICU. Then, after she was transferred from the ICU to neurosurgery, it was discovered that her cerebrospinal fluid was still not draining: an external ventricular drain was put in, and a passage for drainage was surgically opened in her brain. She had a fever again. The EVD was taken out; her ventricles were enlarged and full of fluid, to the point of endangering her life, and her blood pressure was dropping. Undergoing yet another emergency scan, face upward in the MRI tunnel, she nearly choked, the vomit bubbling out of her mouth. Finally, a shunt was surgically implanted, allowing the fluid to drain directly into her stomach.

In less than three weeks, Isabel had undergone two brain resections—in which her cerebral hemispheres were parted to allow Dr. Tomita to access the region between the stem, the pineal gland, and the cerebellum and scoop out the tumor—and six additional surgeries to address the failure of the fluid to drain. A tube had been inserted into her chest so that chemotherapy drugs could be administered directly into her bloodstream. To top it all off, an inoperable peanut-size tumor was now detected in her frontal lobe, and the pathology report confirmed that the cancer was indeed ATRT. Chemo was set to start on August 17, a month after the diagnosis, and Isabel's oncologists, Dr. Jason Fangusaro and Dr. Rishi Lulla, did not wish to discuss her prognosis. We did not dare press them.

Teri and I spent most of the first few weeks after the diagnosis at the hospital. We tried to spend time with Ella, who wasn't allowed in the ICU, though she could visit Isabel in the neurosurgery ward and always made her smile. Ella seemed to be handling the situation pretty well. Supportive family and friends came through our house, helping us to distract her from our continual absence. When we talked to Ella about Isabel's illness, she listened, wide-eyed, concerned, and perplexed.

It was sometime in the first few weeks of the ordeal that Ella began talking about her imaginary brother. Suddenly, in the onslaught of her words, we would discern stories about a brother, who was sometimes a year old, sometimes in high school, and occasionally traveled, for some obscure reason, to Seattle or California, only to return to Chicago to be featured in yet another adventurous monologue of Ella's.

It is not unusual, of course, for children of Ella's age to have imaginary friends or siblings. The creation of an imaginary character is related, I believe, to the explosion of linguistic abilities that occurs between the ages of two and four, and rapidly creates an excess of language, which the child may not have enough experience to match. She has to construct imaginary narratives in order to try out the words that she suddenly possesses. Ella now knew the word "California," for instance, but she had no experience that was in any way related to it; nor could she conceptualize it in its abstract aspect—in its *California-ness.* Hence, her imaginary brother had to be deployed to the sunny state, which allowed Ella to talk at length as if she knew California. The words demanded the story.

At the same time, the surge in language at this age creates a distinction between exteriority and interiority: the child's interiority is now expressible and thus possible to externalize; the world doubles. Ella could now talk about what was here and about what was elsewhere; language had made *here* and *elsewhere* continuous and simultaneous. Once, during dinner, I asked Ella what her brother was doing at that very moment. He was in her room, she said matter-of-factly, throwing a tantrum.

At first, her brother had no name. When asked what he was called, Ella responded, "Googoo Gaga," which was the nonsensical sound that Malcolm, her five-year-old favorite cousin, made when he didn't know the word for something. Since Charlie Mingus is practically a deity in our household, we suggested the name Mingus to Ella, and Mingus her brother became. Soon after that, Malcolm gave Ella an inflatable doll of a space alien, which she subsequently elected to embody the existentially slippery Mingus. Though Ella often played with her blown-up brother, the alien's physical presence was not always required for her to issue pseudoparental orders to Mingus or to tell a story of his escapades. While our world was being reduced to the claustrophobic size of ceaseless dread, Ella's was expanding.

An atypical teratoid rhabdoid tumor is so rare that there are few chemotherapy protocols specifically designed for it. Many of the available protocols are derived from treatments for medulloblastomas and other brain tumors, modified, with increased toxicity, to counter ATRT's vicious malignancy. Some of those protocols involve focused-radiation treatment, but that would be detrimental to the development of a child of Isabel's age. The protocol that Isabel's oncologists decided on consisted of six cycles of chemotherapy of extremely high toxicity, the last of which was the most intense. So much so, in fact, that Isabel's own immature blood cells, extracted earlier, would have to be reinjected after that cycle, in a process called stem-cell recovery, to help her depleted bone marrow to recover.

Throughout the chemo, she would also have to receive transfusions of platelets and red blood cells, while her white-blood-cell count would need to reach normal levels by itself each time. Her immune system would be temporarily annihilated, and, as soon as it recovered, another chemo cycle would begin. Because of her extensive brain surgeries, Isabel could no longer sit or stand, and would have to undergo occupational and physical therapy, between bouts of chemo. Sometime in the uncertain future, it was suggested, she might be able to return to the developmental stage expected of a child of her age.

When her first chemo cycle began, Isabel was ten months old and weighed only sixteen pounds. On her good days, she smiled heroically, more than any other child I've known. Few though they may have been, those days enabled us to project some kind of future for Isabel and our family: we scheduled her therapy appointments; we let our friends and family know which days would be good for visits; we put things down on the calendar for the upcoming couple of weeks. But the future was as precarious as Isabel's health, extending only to the next reasonably achievable stage: the end of the chemo cycle, the recovery of her white-blood-cell count. I prevented myself from imagining anything beyond that. If I found myself envisioning holding her little hand as she was dying, I would erase the vision, often startling Teri by saying aloud to myself, "No! No! No! No!" I blocked thoughts of the other outcome, too—her successful survival—because some time ago I'd come to believe that whatever I wanted to happen would not happen, precisely because I wanted it to happen. I'd therefore developed a mental strategy that consisted of eliminating any desire for good outcomes, as if the act of wishing would expose me to the ruthless forces that drive this universe and spitefully effect the exact opposite of what I hoped for. I did not dare to think of anything but Isabel's present, torturous but still beautiful life.

A well-intentioned friend of mine called shortly after the start of Isabel's first chemo cycle, and the first thing she asked was, "So have things settled into some kind of routine?" Isabel's chemotherapy did, in fact, offer a seemingly predictable pattern. The chemo cycles had an inherent repetitive structure. The drugs were administered in the same order and were followed by the same reactions—vomiting, loss of appetite, collapse of the immune system—after which intravenous TPN (total parenteral nutrition, which is given to patients who are unable to eat), antinausea drugs, antifungal drugs, and antibiotics were administered at regular intervals. Then there were the transfusions, visits to the emergency room due to fever, gradual recovery measured by rising blood counts, and a few bright days at home, before beginning the next cycle.

If Isabel and Teri, who seldom left her side, were in the hospital for the chemo, I'd spend the night at home with Ella, drop her off at school the next day, then take coffee and breakfast to Teri, and, while she was having a shower, sing to or play with Isabel. I'd clean up her vomit or change her diapers, keeping them for the nurse so they could be weighed. In pseudo-expert lingo, Teri and I would discuss the previous night, what was expected that day. We'd wait for the doctors to make their rounds, so that we could ask our difficult questions.

The human sense of comfort depends on repetitive, familiar actions—our minds and bodies strive to become accustomed to predictable circumstances. But no lasting routine could be established for Isabel. An illness like ATRT causes a breakdown of all biological, emotional, and family order: nothing goes the way you expect, let alone want, it to. In addition to the sudden disasters and emergency-room visits, there was the daily hell: Isabel's coughing seldom ceased, and often led to vomiting; she had rashes and constipation; she was listless and weak; we were never able to tell her that things would get better. No amount of repetition can inure you to these things. The comfort of routines belonged to the world outside.

One early morning, driving to the hospital, I saw a number of able-bodied, energetic runners progressing along Fullerton Avenue toward the sunny lakefront, and I had a strong physical sensation of being in an aquarium: I could see out, the people outside could see me (if they chose to pay attention), but we were living and breathing in entirely different environments. Isabel's illness and our experience of it had little connection to, and even less impact on, their lives. Teri and I were gathering heartbreaking knowledge that had no application whatsoever in the outside world and was of no interest to anyone but us: the runners ran dully along into their betterment; people reveled in the banality of habit; the torturer's horse kept scratching its innocent behind on a tree.

Isabel's ATRT made everything in our lives intensely weighted and real. Everything outside was not so much unreal as devoid of comprehensible substance. When people who didn't know about Isabel's illness asked me what was new, and I told them, I'd witness them rapidly receding to the distant horizons of their own lives, where entirely different things mattered. After I told my tax accountant that Isabel was gravely ill, he said, "But you look good, and that's the most important thing!" The world sailing calmly on depended on platitudes and clichés that had no logical or conceptual connection to our experience.

I had a hard time talking to well-wishers and an even harder time listening to them. They were kind and supportive, and Teri and I endured their expressions of sympathy without begrudging them, as they simply didn't know what else to say. They protected themselves from what we were going through by limiting themselves to the manageable domain of vacuous, hackneyed language. But we were far more comfortable with the people who were wise enough not to venture into verbal support, and our closest friends knew that. We much preferred talking to Dr. Lulla or Dr. Fangusaro, who could help us to understand things that mattered, to being told to "hang in there." (To which I would respond, "There is no other place to hang.") And we stayed away from anyone who we feared might offer us the solace of that supreme platitude: God. The hospital chaplain was prohibited from coming anywhere near us.

One of the most common platitudes we heard was that "words failed." But words were not failing Teri and me at all. It was not true that there was no way to describe our experience. Teri and I had plenty of language with which to talk to each other about the horror of what was happening, and talk we did. The words of Dr. Fangusaro and Dr. Lulla, always painfully pertinent, were not failing, either. If there was a communication problem, it was that there were too many words, and they were far too heavy and too specific to be inflicted on others. (Take Isabel's chemo drugs: vincristine, methotrexate, etoposide, cyclophosphamide, and cisplatin—creatures of a particularly malign demonology.)

We instinctively protected our friends from the knowledge we possessed; we let them think that words had failed, because we knew that they didn't want to learn the vocabulary we used daily. We were sure that they didn't want to know what we knew; we didn't want to know it, either.

There was no one else on the inside with us (and we certainly didn't wish that any of our friends' children would suffer from ATRT so that we could talk to them about it). In "A Resource Guide for Parents of Children with Brain or Spinal Cord Tumors," which we were given at the hospital, ATRT was "not discussed in detail," because it was so rare; in point of fact, it was entirely elided. We could not communicate even within the small group of families with children who were beset by cancer. The walls of the aquarium we were hanging in were made of other people's words.

Meanwhile, Mingus allowed Ella to practice and expand her language. He also gave her the company and comfort that Teri and I were barely able to provide. On the mornings when I drove her to school, Ella would offer run-on tales of Mingus, the recondite plots of which were sunk deep in her verbal torrent. Now and then, we'd witness her playing with Mingus—the alien version or the imaginary one—administering fictional medicine or taking his temperature, using the vocabulary she had collected on her visits to the hospital or from our discussions of Isabel's illness. She'd tell us that Mingus had a tumor and was undergoing tests, but was going to get better in two weeks. Once, Mingus even had a little sister named Isabel—entirely distinct from Ella's little sister—who also had a tumor and was also going to get better in two weeks. (Two weeks, I recognized, was just about the length of the future that Teri and I could conceive of at the time.) Whatever accidental knowledge of Isabel's illness Ella was accumulating, whatever words she was picking up from our experience, she was processing through her imaginary brother. And she clearly missed her sister, so Mingus gave her some comfort in that respect as well. She longed for us to be together as a family, which was perhaps why, one day, Mingus acquired his own set of parents and moved out with them to a place around the corner, only to return to us the next day. Ella externalized her complicated feelings by assigning them to Mingus, who then acted on them.

One day at breakfast, while Ella ate her oatmeal and rambled on about her brother, I recognized in a humbling flash that she was doing exactly what I'd been doing as a writer all these years: the fictional characters in my books had allowed me to understand what was hard for me to understand (which, so far, has been nearly everything). Much like Ella, I'd found myself with an excess of words, the wealth of which far exceeded the pathetic limits of my own biography. I'd needed narrative space to extend myself into; I'd needed more lives. I, too, had needed another set of parents, and someone other than myself to throw my metaphysical tantrums. I'd cooked up those avatars in the soup of my ever-changing self, but they were not me—they did what I wouldn't, or couldn't, do. Listening to Ella furiously and endlessly unfurl the Mingus tales, I understood that the need to tell stories was deeply embedded in our minds and inseparably entangled with the mechanisms that generate and absorb language. Narrative imagination—and therefore fiction—was a basic evolutionary tool of survival. We processed the world by telling stories, produced human knowledge through our engagement with imagined selves.

Whatever knowledge I'd acquired in my fiction-writing career was of no value inside our ATRT aquarium, however. Unlike Ella, I could not construct a story that would help me comprehend what was happening. Isabel's illness overrode any form of imaginative involvement on my part. All I cared about was the firm reality of her breaths on my chest, the concreteness of her slipping into slumber as I sang my three lullabies. I did not want to extend myself in any direction but hers.

Isabel received the last drug of her third chemo cycle on a Sunday afternoon in October. We were hoping that she could return home that Monday morning, at least for a few days. Ella came to see her that afternoon and, as always, made her laugh by pretending to grab little chunks of her cheeks and eat them. After Ella left, Isabel was agitated as I held her. I recognized a pattern in her restlessness: watching the second hand on the big clock in the room, I realized that she was twitching and whimpering every thirty seconds or so. Teri summoned the nurse, who talked to the oncologist on call, who talked to the neurologist, who talked to someone else. They thought she was having microseizures, but it was not clear why this was happening. Then she went into a full-blown seizure: she stiffened, her eyes rolled back, her mouth foamed as she twitched. Teri and I held her hands and talked to her, but she was not aware of us. Urgently, she was transferred to the ICU.

The names of all the drugs she was given and all the procedures she underwent in the ICU are obscure to me now, as is most of that night—what is hard to imagine is hard to remember. Isabel's sodium levels had dropped precipitously, and this had caused the seizure; whatever the doctors did to her stopped it. Eventually, breathing tubes were inserted and the rock was administered again. Isabel would have to stay in the ICU until her sodium levels stabilized.

But they never did. Though she was taken off the rock and the breathing tubes were removed a couple of days later, sodium solution had to be constantly administered, at the expense of her TPN, and her levels still didn't return to normal. On Halloween, while Teri was taking Ella trick-or-treating in our neighborhood, as she had promised to do, Isabel was restive again in my arms. The night before, which I'd spent at home with Ella, I'd had a dream in which Isabel jerked violently backward as I held her, as if in sudden pain, and I dropped her. I'd snapped out of the dream with a scream before she hit the floor. In the ICU, I desperately looped through my lullabies, trying to calm her. When she finally managed to fall asleep, I could feel her breathing stopping only to start again a frighteningly long moment later. The nurse on duty told me that sleep apnea was common in babies, and his obvious bullshit scared me even more than it annoyed me. He informed the doctor on duty, and what needed to be noted was duly noted. Soon afterward, Teri and I traded places, and I went home to be with Ella.

The phone rang in the middle of the night. Teri put Dr. Fangusaro on the line and he told me that Isabel was having "a really hard time" maintaining her blood pressure. I needed to come to the hospital as soon as possible.

After dropping Ella off with my sister-in-law, I sped to the hospital. I found a crowd of the ICU staff looking into Isabel's room, where she was surrounded by a pack of doctors and nurses. She was bloated, her eyelids swollen. Her little hands were stabbed with needles, as liquid was pumped into her to keep her blood pressure up. Dr. Fangusaro and Dr. Lulla sat us down to tell us that Isabel's state was dire. Teri and I needed to tell them whether we wanted them to try everything they could to save her. We said yes. They made it clear that we would have to be the ones to tell them when to stop trying.

And now my memory collapses.

Teri is in the corner weeping ceaselessly and quietly, the terror on her face literally unspeakable; the gray-haired attending doctor (whose name has vanished from my mind, though his face stares at me daily) is issuing orders as residents take turns compressing Isabel's chest, because her heart has stopped beating. They bring her back, as I wail, "My baby! My baby! My baby!" Then there is another decision that Teri and I have to make: Isabel's kidneys have stopped functioning, she needs dialysis, and an immediate surgical intervention is necessary to connect her to the dialysis machine—there is a good chance that she will not survive the surgery. We say yes to it. Her heart stops beating again; the residents are compressing her chest. In the hallway outside, people unknown to me are rooting for Isabel, some of them in tears. "My baby! My baby! My baby!" I keep howling. I hug Teri. Isabel's heart starts beating again. The gray-haired doctor turns to me and says, "Twelve minutes," and I cannot comprehend what he is saying. But then I realize: what he is saying is that Isabel was clinically dead for twelve minutes. Then her heart stops beating again, a young resident is halfheartedly compressing her chest, waiting for us to tell her to stop. We tell her to stop. She stops.

In my hastily suppressed visions, I'd foreseen the moment of my child's death. But what I'd imagined, despite my best efforts, was a quiet, filmic moment in which Teri and I held Isabel's hands as she peacefully expired. I could not have begun to imagine the intensity of the pain we felt as the nurses removed all the tubes and wires and everyone cleared out and Teri and I held our dead child—our beautiful, ever-smiling daughter, her body bloated with liquid and battered by compressions—kissing her cheeks and toes. Though I recall that moment with absolute, crushing clarity, it is still unimaginable to me.

And how do you step out of a moment like that? How do you leave your dead child behind and return to the vacant routines of whatever you might call your life? Eventually, we put Isabel down on the bed, covered her with a sheet, signed whatever papers needed to be signed, packed our stuff: her toys, our clothes, the iPod dock, the food containers, the debris of the before. Outside the room, somebody had put up a screen to give us privacy; all the good people who had rooted for Isabel were now gone. Carrying, like refugees, our large plastic bags full of things, we walked to the garage across the street, got into our car, and drove on the meaningless streets to my sister-in-law's apartment.

I don't know what mental capacity is required for comprehending death, but Ella seemed to possess it. When we told her that her little sister had died, there was a moment of clear understanding on her face. She started crying in a way that could only be described as unchildlike, and said, "I want another little sister named Isabel." We're still parsing that statement.

Teri, Ella, and I—a family missing one—went home. It was November 1, the Day of the Dead. A hundred and eight days had passed since the diagnosis.

The next day, we took Ella to school. At pickup time, her best friend ran to his mother and said, "Mommy, Mommy! Ella's little sister died!"

One of the most despicable religious fallacies is that suffering is ennobling—that it is a step on the path to some kind of enlightenment or salvation. Isabel's suffering and death did nothing for her, or us, or the world. We learned no lessons worth learning; we acquired no experience that could benefit anyone. And Isabel most certainly did not earn ascension to a better place, as there was no place better for her than at home with her family. Without Isabel, Teri and I were left with oceans of love we could no longer dispense; we found ourselves with an excess of time that we used to devote to her; we had to live in a void that could be filled only by Isabel. Her indelible absence is now an organ in our bodies, whose sole function is a continuous secretion of sorrow.

Ella talks about Isabel often. When she talks about her death, she does so cogently, her words deeply felt; she is confronted by the same questions and longings that confront us. Once, before falling asleep, she asked me, "Why did Isabel die?" Another time, she told me, "I don't want to die." Not so long ago, she started talking to Teri, out of the blue, about wanting to hold Isabel's hand again, about how much she missed Isabel's laughter. A few times, when we asked her if she missed Isabel, she refused to respond, exhibiting an impatience that was entirely recognizable to us—what was there to talk about that was not self-evident?

Mingus is still going steadily about his alternative-existence business. He lives around the corner yet again, with his parents and a variable number of siblings, but he does stay with us a lot. He has had his own children now—three sons, at one point, one of whom was called Andy. When we went skiing, Mingus preferred snowboarding. When we went to London for Christmas, Mingus went to Nebraska. He plays chess ("chest," in Ella's parlance) pretty well, it seems. He is also a good magician. With his magic wand, Ella says, he can make Isabel reappear.

THE TERROR OF LOVE

Samantha Irby

I am missing the first bicuspid on the upper right side of my mouth. Eight years ago I got a root canal. It was routine, I guess? How the shit can you know unless you have a skull X-ray machine in your living room? Anyway, I hadn't seen a dentist in fucking forever because dental care is super expensive and while teeth are easily the thing a person is most afraid to fucking lose, ain't nobody got hundreds of dollars just lying around for annual X-rays and cleanings. Besides, I was twenty-five; was I really expected to worry about my goddamned teeth?! I AM YOUNG AND I AM GOING TO LIVE FOREVER BECAUSE HOT POCKETS ARE TOTALLY NUTRITIOUS.

Okay, so I woke up one morning in the gigantic apartment I had stupidly rented at the insistence of my then boyfriend who SWORE TO GOD that he would come over and spend the night more if he didn't have to tiptoe around to avoid pissing off my roommate (he hadn't yet fulfilled this promise, but four months isn't really that long is it? GAH, fuck that guy), and my mouth was hurting. Like, really hurting. Like, I walked past the fan in the kitchen window and almost collapsed in pain when a cool spring breeze hit the raw, exposed nerve also known as my goddamned mouth. I called a dentist from the phone book—because eight years ago there was still such a thing as a fucking phone book—and she called a pharmacist and two hours later I was on the bus clutching a bag filled with antibiotics and Tylenol 3 on my way home to "take it easy" and "try not to eat anything sweet or cold." A couple of days after that? On my back squinting into a blinding fluorescent light while this very nice woman talked to me about her toddler in a soothing voice as she drilled an access hole into my infected tooth and removed all the pulp and rot and mildewing beef gristle.

Last summer I was eating my lunch alone in the darkened conference room at work, crying softly to myself in ecstasy at the deliciousness of the pulled pork wrap I had just purchased from Pret a Manger, when suddenly I felt something hard and jagged on my tongue. Undeterred by what I assumed were the lost fingernails of a careless fast-food worker, I continued to eat that glorious sandwich, gulping down the gritty ends of some teenaged sandwich maker's stray hairs with fervor. But then the tip of my tongue grazed a sharp stalactite of broken tooth protruding from my upper gum. I dropped my sandwich on the floor (I mourn to this very day) and covered my face while run-walking to the bathroom before anyone could see that I had obviously just tried to EAT MY OWN FUCKING FACE. I pulled up my lip to reveal the dentition of a feral street beast: broken shards of mangled tooth and bone littering a tongue that oozed fresh blood and bits of partially chewed slow-roasted pork. My new dentist took an X-ray of my skull and informed me that the dark gray rain cloud I'd thought was a lazy hygienist resting her thumb on the machine was in fact a fist-size clot of bacteria slowly eating its way through my upper jaw.

After googling what "endodontist" meant, I went and saw one and then immediately decided I was too fucking poor to afford three thousand dollars in root therapy (or whatever the shit is called), and I went back to the regular dentist and let him stand with one foot on my chest and the other braced against the chair while he blackened my right eye trying to break what was left of my busted tooth loose from my skull. That is the worst sound I have ever heard, the crack and separation of bone from *inside my own fucking head*. Tears slid from my eyes involuntarily; I am convinced that this is what hell feels like, the soundtrack of a continuous loop of your head bones breaking in surround sound.

I was sent home with a leaky maw packed with gauze stained pink by blood and mouth goo, instructed not to drink anything from a straw for several hours. I iced my face with a tub of pineapple sherbet and texted my friends to bring me soup while gingerly probing my facehole's tender new vacancy with the tip of my tongue.

I'm sitting in Metropolis on Granville at a table in the back near the bathroom so that in case I have sudden-onset diarrhea or drop my three-fourths-full latte in my lap and the MOST DESPERATE THIEF IN THE HISTORY OF EARTH needs to steal the netbook I am borrowing from my boss and the approximately $3,875 worth of lip gloss I have on my person at all times I can, ostensibly, hear him doing so and burst through the door with my pants around my ankles and waddle after him, dripping liquid waste along the way in a fruitless attempt to recover my belongings. I have a date, A REAL DATE, with an actual human. A human who suggested this bustling coffee shop full of college kids and hipster mamas and all I can think about is why I've chosen today of all days to wear my fake tooth. It's something the dentist called a "flipper," a molded piece of plastic that looks like gum tissue with a little bit of tooth poking out.

I get self-conscious about the hole. Hyperaware that when I am laughing really hard and my eyes are crinkled and my belly is shaking that there is this missing piece of my mouth's puzzle. I am glad to be rid of it, for sure, because how lame would it be to drop dead from toxic-blood brain poisoning courtesy of a rotten *tooth* in the twenty-first fucking century? But then I think about meeting this new person, this new person who doesn't know me and might not forgive that six months ago my face was a flesh wound, and I think, LOVE IS TERRIFYING.

The flipper makes me slur my words, badly. And it hurts; the parts that connect it to my upper jaw dig into my gum and it fucking kills. In the mirror it seems totally obvious, almost distracting enough to make me forget the thieves plotting the theft of my two-hundred-dollar virus-riddled computer. The (soy) chai latte I'd ordered was already cold because the flipper didn't rest flush against my jaw and I didn't trust that I could have a normal conversation while dribbling hippie tea from the corner of my mouth. He was scheduled to arrive in three minutes, and I was sweating in the bathroom, using both hands to try to pry this tiny piece of pink-and-white plastic loose from my headbone.

I wear a maxi pad on dates because I am a crazy person and adult human males scare the shit out of me and I'm pretty sure I peed in it a little as a result of the force I was exerting on my poor fucking teeth. They'd already been through so much! I wiped my face with a cold paper towel and pulled my shit together enough to artfully arrange the smart-person books and magazines I just *happened* to be carrying around in my bag. I squinted at my computer screen, at this very essay, wondering how he's going to feel when the book comes out and he realizes that all of this sweaty panic was because of him. We would laugh, obviously, because that's seven months from now and we will already have exchanged house keys and "I love yous" by that point.

He will have already seen the gross, dark line worn into my torso from years of hauling these tits up to my chin with the strength of an underwire; he will already know that I don't really read *The New Yorker* as much as I would like him to believe today. By that point my missing tooth will just be a thing we chuckle about as I scrape together my royalties to pay for an implant. So that if this thing doesn't work, and inevitably it won't, I won't have to be terrified ever again. At least not about what my mouth looks like. But he never showed up, so I will never know.

I can't tie a man's necktie. And I love love love that lovely and romantic visual: the adoring wife or girlfriend, face upturned to the glowing sun that is her man's; his body slightly damp and smelling of the shower, of deodorant, of aftershave; white-collared shirt undone at the neck as she playfully tugs at the bolt of brightly colored shiny fabric she had stood in the bedroom doorway watching him struggle with moments before, a smile playing at the corners of her mouth.

Downstairs, there is breakfast made. Maybe not breakfast, because she has to work, too, and who has time for perfectly fried sunny-side-up eggs when there is a management meeting at nine-thirty? But the coffee is started and the bialys are defrosting on the counter and the lox from Kaufmans is on the second refrigerator shelf tucked next to the low-fat cream cheese she started buying when his cholesterol numbers came back elevated at his last physical. He showers first, always, because she likes to hit the snooze three or four times, clinging desperately to those precious extra minutes of sleep. She listens to him peeing; she listens to him humming as he lathers shaving cream across the sharp angle of his jaw, carefully and methodically dragging the razor across his cheeks and chin. His slacks and dress shoes have been laid across the overstuffed reclining chair he sometimes likes to watch *The Daily Show* in, after the bottle of wine but before the twenty minutes of reasonably inspired lovemaking. When she hears him fumbling with his toothbrush she takes that as her cue to hustle downstairs and put the coffee on.

This is, like, my fantasy. MY ROMANTIC FANTASY. I don't sit around fucking daydreaming about a dude going down on me for nine hours (BARF) or about riding some massive titanium cock for days at a time (GROSS). What gets *me* hot is all the *other* shit. Dreaming about someone whose allergies I need to remember when I'm at the grocery store: that's where the *real* romance is. Because I've *had* sex before. What a fucking snooze, my dude. Sex is so dumb and boring and unless you're in really incredible shape or you have a ridiculous imagination and are into some really freaky shit, what you do and what I do is limited to a handful of very similar things. Even your grandmother has been choked and spit on and handcuffed. Why don't we instead dream up some motherfuckers who will set up the automatic renewal on our magazine subscriptions?

I've dated approximately one man who had to wear a tie every day to work. And once I spent the night at his apartment and, after bolting upright in horror because homeboy had "space issues" and didn't like for me to fall asleep in his bed after sex, I ran into his kitchen and splashed some water on my face and then tried to make some coffee. Except I'd never used a French press before and I totally fucked the shit up, coffee grounds everyfuckingwhere, and then I burned him in the shower because

I flushed the toilet while he was directly under the stream after I'd snuck in to pee in the first place. I was watching MTV in the living room at an obnoxious volume as he called and called my name, asking if I could pack him a lunch because he was running late. I didn't fucking do it because I was too busy watching Usher videos and attempting to emulate his sweet dance moves. Ten minutes later I was straining weak coffee through a sieve into a travel thermos and wrapping random leftovers in plastic wrap for his lunch (one bruised kiwi, a quarter of a dried-out rotisserie chicken, a handful of cashews, most of a brownie) while he grumbled in the bedroom. A box of new dress socks? No, I hadn't seen it. The bag from the dry cleaner with his pale blue shirt in it? Nope, can't remember which closet I'd hung it in. I was virtually useless. BUT . . .

I'd practiced tying a Windsor knot with the help of some YouTube videos and my roommate Joseph's least favorite tie, and I was ready. I was ready to redeem myself in the eyes of my go-to fantasy, I was ready to be that woman who wrapped her hair in a towel so that she could apply her makeup and fetch her man's tweed jacket from the cedar closet without dripping leave-in conditioner all over his nice carpet (because, of course, he owns this condo and this carpeting was so expensive and when I dropped that sloppy joe in the hallway last weekend he really did look like he was actually contemplating slitting my actual throat), and even though I was scared, I WAS READY. There was bitter, gritty coffee in a busted travel mug and a crumpled plastic Jewel bag on the counter containing the kind of lunch you wouldn't feed your worst enemy and he isn't going to marry me, but goddamn it I was going to tie the shit out of that tie even if it killed me. He was wearing cufflinks, and a heady cloud of aftershave hung over the room, and he smiled when I asked if I could help with his tie and handed it over.

"Wide end on the right," I murmured to myself. "Cross the wide end over the narrow end, or is it the narrow end over the wide? Then bring the wide end up through the loop between the collar and the tie, no, wait, then bring the wide end back down?" I stepped back to survey my handiwork so far. My eyes widened in horror. "I'm just going to do this when I get to the office," he sighed, yanking loose the merit badge–worthy Boy Scout bowline knot I'd made from his necktie. He was so annoyed that he left his lunch on the counter. So I ate the brownie. And the kiwi. Okay, fine, I ate the whole fucking thing. Stress eating is a real thing.

I'm not going to have a baby. Not a biological one, at least, and that is a big deal to a lot of people. No, I have not done exhaustive research and I have not undergone extensive tests; I haven't harvested any eggs or thought about in vitro fertilization, because the first time I had that up-the-nose down-the-throat tube threaded UP MY NOSE and DOWN MY THROAT by a twelve-year-old medical student whose hands were shaking like a leaf during a torrential downpour while he reassured me that I should remain calm, I decided that whatever evil was brewing in the pit of my belly was never going to ever have to compete with a baby. A burrito? Probably, if I could ever stop shitting. Two gametes that would become a zygote that would then become a human life-form? Decidedly not. And that is a motherfucking deal breaker for a lot of these dudes.

A few years ago I was taking classes at community college because I hadn't quite yet given up all hope. There was a tall African dude with a deep, melodious voice in the class, and he was sexy. He carried a briefcase to community college, people: DUDE WAS OBVIOUSLY A WINNER. I spent the entire summer semester wondering when this asshole was going to ask me out on a goddamned date. Not kidding. Two and a half legit months making sure my hoodies were clean and my flip-flops weren't covered in street puke because I just knew that this dude was head over heels in love with me and was going to whisk me off to midlevel-management, associate-degree paradise. The last day of class I was in line turning in the final group project that only I had worked on when he grabbed my hand and said, "Let's get a drink to celebrate the end of the term?" And that was incredibly romantic, but my dumb ass still had three more classes to sit through that afternoon (what the fuck . . . ?) and I didn't want to miss my African history final fucking around in a bar with my

African future. I aced my multiple-choice final and met Frank at a bar near my apartment because I am lazy and I just don't feel like trying very hard anymore. He got a beer, I got a shot, and we spent half an hour making fun of most of our classmates, all total goddamned idiots. He was funny and smart and he wore polo shirts in earnest, and he even let me see what was inside his briefcase: bundles of paperwork from his job as a manager at Hollywood Video. "I love videos," I swooned, flagging down the bartender for another Jameson. He asked me about my job (it's the best) and my educational goals (none whatsoever) and then he asked if I wanted to have children. I felt the fear creeping up the back of my neck. "Today?" I asked, stalling. "It's kind of late in the day, don't you think?" OH, HA-HA-HA LOLZ.

Frank explained to me that having several strapping young sons to carry on his bloodline was the thing he wanted in life more than anything else and that adoption, or saving all that kid money to spend our golden years traveling abroad and trying not to die from a heart attack during sex, was totally out of the question. And then I explained to him that the only thing I planned on giving birth to in the near future was a roast beef sandwich with horseradish mayo and that fostering seventeen kids was pretty much the only reason I would ever want to get rich. "We wouldn't even need a maid, see?" I said, diagramming our adopted family on the back of a menu. "If we space out the ages just right, neither of us would have to wash a single dish, for like, the next thirty years. It's fucking genius. Also: CHILD ARMY." He signaled for the check.

"Can I still get a discount on my membership?" I asked as he politely handed the bartender his credit card. He rolled his eyes and nodded, digging a coupon out of his briefcase. I never did take that *Steel Magnolias* DVD back. Because fuck him.

I can't make pancakes. I feel like pancakes are these fundamental things that all good, husband-snagging women are capable of making. What is a Sunday morning for if not the sizzle of hotcakes on the griddle and bacon in the pan? What is that age-old tradition of "breakfast for dinner" if it doesn't include a fluffy stack of buttermilk silver dollars? There are lots of things I can cook, and there are a handful of things I make exceptionally well. But I have lived alone for a really long fucking time, long enough to be satisfied with a handful of microwaved Lit'l Smokies and a gluten-free cupcake for dinner. I made a big, fancy dinner a couple of weeks ago, mushroom bourguignon because I was going through a vegetarian cleanse thing, but don't worry, I'm over that brief bout of mental illness and eating so much sausage again. I spent an afternoon in my kitchen slicing and washing baby portabellas, making a roux and boiling wine and beef broth to make gravy, and when it was all done I got in bed and watched *The Mindy Project* on Hulu.

There are all of these recipes that I make and sometimes eat and I usually wish someone handsome was around to make sure they taste good, and someone who won't just eat the whole pot because he's spent half his paycheck on fancy spices to make it. But what if he doesn't want rogan josh or roasted skate wing? What if dude just wants a homemade apple pie?!

I cannot properly fold a fitted sheet. My whites often turn out dishwater gray. I have no household tips or tricks that involve apple cider vinegar. I needed to change that humidifier filter three months ago. And while these aren't the things someone notices upon making your acquaintance, I am way more scared of a dislocated button or a bee-stung appendage than I am a text that reads, "Where should we go for dinner?" That is the easy shit, the restaurant/the hot new bar/the spot with the best undiscovered rock band. I could write you a list of the best places to bat your eyelashes in a dimly lit room in the company of a dashing paramour, but if I needed to make an omelet for the hot naked body still wrapped in my sheets, I'd have no idea. This is why we need places that deliver breakfast. And why my next paycheck is going into my tooth-implant savings fund.

THE EMPATHY EXAMS

Leslie Jamison

My job title is medical actor, which means I play sick. I get paid by the hour. Medical students guess my maladies. I'm called a standardized patient, which means I act toward the norms set for my disorders. I'm standardized-lingo SP for short. I'm fluent in the symptoms of preeclampsia and asthma and appendicitis. I play a mom whose baby has blue lips.

Medical acting works like this: You get a script and a paper gown. You get $13.50 an hour. Our scripts are ten to twelve pages long. They outline what's wrong with us—not just what hurts but how to express it. They tell us how much to give away, and when. We are supposed to unfurl the answers according to specific protocol. The scripts dig deep into our fictive lives: the ages of our children and the diseases of our parents, the names of our husbands' real estate and graphic design firms, the amount of weight we've lost in the past year, the amount of alcohol we drink each week.

My specialty case is Stephanie Phillips, a twenty-three-year-old who suffers from something called conversion disorder. She is grieving the death of her brother, and her grief has sublimated into seizures. Her disorder is news to me. I didn't know you could convulse from sadness. She's not supposed to know, either. She's not supposed to think the seizures have anything to do with what she's lost.

STEPHANIE PHILLIPS

Psychiatry
SP Training Materials

CASE SUMMARY: You are a twenty-three-year-old female patient experiencing seizures with no identifiable neurological origin. You can't remember your seizures but are told you froth at the mouth and yell obscenities. You can usually feel a seizure coming before it arrives. The seizures began two years ago, shortly after your older brother drowned in the river just south of the Bennington Avenue Bridge. He was swimming drunk after a football tailgate. You and he worked at the same miniature-golf course. These days you don't work at all. These days you don't do much. You're afraid of having a seizure in public. No doctor has been able to help you. Your brother's name was Will.

MEDICATION HISTORY: You are not taking any medications. You've never taken antidepressants. You've never thought you needed them.

MEDICAL HISTORY: Your health has never caused you any trouble. You've never had anything worse than a broken arm. Will was there when you broke it. He was the one who called the paramedics and kept you calm until they came.

Our simulated exams take place in three suites of purpose-built rooms. Each room is fitted with an examination table and a surveillance camera. We test second- and third-year medical students in topical rotations: pediatrics, surgery, psychiatry. On any given exam day, each student must go through "encounters"—their technical title—with three or four actors playing different cases.

A student might have to palpate a woman's ten-on-a-scale-of-ten abdominal pain, then sit across from a delusional young lawyer and tell him that when he feels a writhing mass of worms in his small intestine, the feeling is probably coming from somewhere else. Then this med student might arrive in my room, stay straight-faced, and tell me that I'm about to go into premature labor to deliver the pillow strapped to my belly, or nod solemnly as I express concern about my ailing plastic baby: "He's just so quiet."

Once the fifteen-minute encounter has ended, the medical student leaves the room, and I fill out an evaluation of his/her performance. The first part is a checklist: Which crucial pieces of information did he/she manage to elicit? Which ones did he/she leave uncovered? The second part of the evaluation covers affect. Checklist item 31 is generally acknowledged as the most important category: "Voiced empathy for my situation/problem." We are instructed about the importance of this first word, *voiced*. It's not enough for someone to have a sympathetic manner or use a caring tone. The students have to say the right words to get credit for compassion.

We SPs are given our own suite for preparation and decompression. We gather in clusters: old men in crinkling blue robes, MFAs in boots too cool for our paper gowns, local teenagers in hospital ponchos and sweatpants. We help each other strap pillows around our waists. We hand off infant dolls. Little pneumonic Baby Doug, swaddled in a cheap cotton blanket, is passed from girl to girl like a relay baton. Our ranks are full of community-theater actors and undergrad drama majors seeking stages, high school kids earning booze money, retired folks with spare time. I am a writer, which is to say: I'm trying not to be broke.

We play a demographic menagerie: Young jocks with ACL injuries and business executives nursing coke habits. STD Grandma has just cheated on her husband of forty years and has a case of gonorrhea to show for it. She hides behind her shame like a veil, and her med student is supposed to part the curtain. If he asks the right questions, she'll have a simulated crying breakdown halfway through the encounter.

Blackout Buddy gets makeup: a gash on his chin, a black eye, and bruises smudged in green eye shadow along his cheekbone. He's been in a fender bender he can't even remember. Before the encounter, the actor splashes booze on his body like cologne.

He's supposed to let the particulars of his alcoholism glimmer through, very "unplanned," bits of a secret he's done his best to keep guarded.

Our scripts are studded with moments of flourish: Pregnant Lila's husband is a yacht captain sailing overseas in Croatia. Appendicitis Angela has a dead guitarist uncle whose tour bus was hit by a tornado. Many of our extended family members have died violent midwestern deaths: mauled in tractor or grain-elevator accidents, hit by drunk drivers on the way home from Hy-Vee grocery stores, felled by big weather or Big Ten tailgates (firearm accident)—or, like my brother Will, by the quieter aftermath of debauchery.

Between encounters, we are given water, fruit, granola bars, and an endless supply of mints. We aren't supposed to exhaust the students with our bad breath and growling stomachs, the side effects of our actual bodies.

Some med students get nervous during our encounters. It's like an awkward date, except half of them are wearing platinum wedding bands. I want to tell them I'm more than just an unmarried woman faking seizures for pocket money. *I do things!* I want to tell them. *I'm probably going to write about this in a book someday!* We make small talk about the rural Iowa farm town I'm supposed to be from. We each understand the other is inventing this small talk, and we agree to respond to each other's inventions as genuine exposures of personality. We're holding the fiction between us like a jump rope.

One time a student forgets we are pretending and starts asking detailed questions about my fake hometown—which, as it happens, is his real hometown—and his questions lie beyond the purview of my script, beyond what I can answer, because in truth I don't know much about the person I'm supposed to be or the place I'm supposed to be from. He's forgotten our contract. I bullshit harder, more heartily. "That park in Muscatine!" I say, slapping my knee like a grandpa. "I used to sled there as a kid."

Other students are all business, they rattle through the clinical checklist for depression like a list of things they need to get at the grocery store: *sleep disturbances, changes in appetite, decreased concentration*. Some of them get irritated when I obey my script and refuse to make eye contact. I'm supposed to stay swaddled and numb. These irritated students take my averted eyes as a challenge. They never stop seeking my gaze. Wrestling me into eye contact is the way they maintain power—forcing me to acknowledge their requisite display of care.

I grow accustomed to comments that feel aggressive in their formulaic insistence: *that must really be hard* [to have a dying baby], *that must really be hard* [to be afraid you'll have another seizure in the middle of the grocery store], *that must really be hard* [to carry in your uterus the bacterial evidence of cheating on your husband]. Why not say, *I couldn't even imagine*?

Other students seem to understand that empathy is always perched precariously between gift and invasion. They won't even press the stethoscope to my skin without asking if it's okay. They need permission. They don't want to presume. Their stuttering unwittingly honors my privacy: *Can I . . . could I . . . would you mind if I—listened to your heart?* No, I tell them. I don't mind. Not minding is my job. Their humility is a kind of compassion in its own right. Humility means they ask questions, and questions mean they get answers, and answers mean they get points on the checklist: a point for finding out my mother takes Wellbutrin, a point for getting me to admit I've spent the last two years cutting myself, a point for finding out my father died in a grain elevator when I was two—for realizing that a root system of loss stretches radial and rhizomatic under the entire territory of my life.

In this sense, empathy isn't just measured by checklist item 31—*voiced empathy for my situation/problem*—but by every item that gauges how thoroughly my experience has been imagined. Empathy isn't just remembering to say *that must really be hard*—it's figuring out how to bring difficulty into the light so it can be seen at all. Empathy isn't just listening, it's asking the questions whose answers need to be listened to. Empathy requires inquiry as much as imagination. Empathy requires knowing you know nothing. Empathy means acknowledging a horizon of context that extends perpetually beyond what you can see: an old woman's gonorrhea is connected to her guilt is connected to her marriage is connected to her children is connected to the days when she was a child. All this is connected to her domestically stifled mother, in turn, and to her parents' unbroken marriage; maybe everything traces its roots to her very first period, how it shamed and thrilled her.

Empathy means realizing no trauma has discrete edges. Trauma bleeds. Out of wounds and across boundaries. Sadness becomes a seizure. Empathy demands another kind of porousness in response. My Stephanie script is twelve pages long. I think mainly about what it doesn't say.

Empathy comes from the Greek *empatheia*—*em* (into) and *pathos* (feeling)—a penetration, a kind of travel. It suggests you enter another person's pain as you'd enter another country, through immigration and customs, border crossing by way of query: *What grows where you are? What are the laws? What animals graze there?*

I've thought about Stephanie Phillips's seizures in terms of possession and privacy—that converting her sadness away from direct articulation is a way to keep it hers. Her refusal to make eye contact, her unwillingness to explicate her inner life, the way she becomes unconscious during her own expressions of grief and doesn't remember them afterward—all of these might be a way to keep her loss protected and pristine, unviolated by the sympathy of others.

"What do you call out during seizures?" one student asks.

"I don't know," I say, and want to add, *but I mean all of it*.

I know that saying this would be against the rules. I'm playing a girl who keeps her sadness so subterranean she can't even see it herself. I can't give it away so easily.

LESLIE JAMISON

Ob-Gyn
SP Training Materials

CASE SUMMARY: You are a twenty-five-year-old female seeking termination of your pregnancy. You have never been pregnant before. You are five and a half weeks but have not experienced any bloating or cramping. You have experienced some fluctuations in mood but have been unable to determine whether these are due to being pregnant or knowing you are pregnant. You are not visibly upset about your pregnancy. Invisibly, you are not sure.

MEDICATION HISTORY: You are not taking any medications. This is why you got pregnant.

MEDICAL HISTORY: You've had several surgeries in the past, but you don't mention them to your doctor because they don't seem relevant. You are about to have another surgery to correct your tachycardia, the excessive and irregular beating of your heart. Your mother has made you promise to mention this upcoming surgery in your termination consultation, even though you don't feel like discussing it. She wants the doctor to know about your heart condition in case it affects the way he ends your pregnancy, or the way he keeps you sedated while he does it.

I could tell you I got an abortion one February or heart surgery that March—like they were separate cases, unrelated scripts—but neither one of these accounts would be complete without the other. A single month knitted them together; each one a morning I woke up on an empty stomach and slid into a paper gown. One depended on a tiny vacuum, the other on a catheter that would ablate the tissue of my heart. *Ablate?* I asked the doctors. They explained that meant burning.

One procedure made me bleed and the other was nearly bloodless; one was my choice and the other wasn't; both made me feel—at once—the incredible frailty and capacity of my own body; both came in a bleak winter; both left me prostrate under the hands of men, and dependent on the care of a man I was just beginning to love.

Dave and I first kissed in a Maryland basement at three in the morning on our way to Newport News to canvass for Obama in 2008. We were with an organizing union called Unite Here. *Unite Here!* Years later, that poster hung above our bed. That first fall we walked along Connecticut beaches strewn with broken clamshells. We held hands against salt winds. We went to a hotel for the weekend and put so much bubble bath in our tub that the bubbles ran all over the floor. We took pictures of that. We took pictures of everything. We walked across Williamsburg in the rain to see a concert. We were writers in love. My boss used to imagine us curling up at night and taking inventories of each other's hearts. "How did it make you feel to see that injured pigeon in the street today?" etc. And it's true: we once talked about seeing two crippled bunnies trying to mate on a patchy lawn—how sad it was, and moving.

We'd been in love about two months when I got pregnant. I saw the cross on the stick and called Dave and we wandered college quads in the bitter cold and talked about what we were going to do. I thought of the little fetus bundled inside my jacket with me and wondered—honestly wondered—if I felt attached to it yet. I wasn't sure. I remember not knowing what to say. I remember wanting a drink. I remember wanting Dave to be inside the choice with me but also feeling possessive of what was happening. I needed him to understand he would never live this choice like I was going to live it. This was the double blade of how I felt about anything that hurt: I wanted someone else to feel it with me, and also I wanted it entirely for myself.

We scheduled the abortion for a Friday, and I found myself facing a week of ordinary days until it happened. I realized I was supposed to keep doing ordinary things. One afternoon, I holed up in the library and read a pregnancy memoir. The author described a pulsing fist of fear and loneliness inside her—a fist she'd carried her whole life, had numbed with drinking and sex—and explained how her pregnancy had replaced this fist with the tiny bud of her fetus, a moving life.

I sent Dave a text. I wanted to tell him about the fist of fear, the baby heart, how sad it felt to read about a woman changed by her pregnancy when I knew I wouldn't be changed by mine—or at least, not like she'd been. I didn't hear anything back for hours. This bothered me. I felt guilt that I didn't feel more about the abortion; I felt pissed off at Dave for being elsewhere, for choosing not to do the tiniest thing when I was going to do the rest of it.

I felt the weight of expectation on every moment—the sense

that the end of this pregnancy was something I *should* feel sad about, the lurking fear that I never felt sad about what I was supposed to feel sad about, the knowledge that I'd gone through several funerals dry-eyed, the hunch that I had a parched interior life activated only by the need for constant affirmation, nothing more. I wanted Dave to guess what I needed at precisely the same time I needed it. I wanted him to imagine how much small signals of his presence might mean.

That night we roasted vegetables and ate them at my kitchen table. Weeks before, I'd covered that table with citrus fruits and fed our friends pills made from berries that made everything sweet: grapefruit tasted like candy, beer like chocolate, Shiraz like Manischewitz—everything, actually, tasted a little like Manischewitz. Which is to say: that kitchen held the ghosts of countless days that felt easier than the one we were living now. We drank wine, and I think—I know—I drank a lot. It sickened me to think I was doing something harmful to the fetus because that meant thinking of the fetus as harmable, which made it feel more alive, which made me feel more selfish, woozy with cheap Cabernet and spoiling for a fight.

Feeling Dave's distance that day had made me realize how much I needed to feel he was as close to this pregnancy as I was—an impossible asymptote. But I thought he could at least bridge the gap between our days and bodies with a text. I told him so. Actually I probably sulked, waited for him to ask, and then told him so. *Guessing your feelings is like charming a cobra with a stethoscope,* another boyfriend told me once. Meaning what? Meaning a few things, I think—that pain turned me venomous, that diagnosing me required a specialized kind of enchantment, that I flaunted feelings and withheld their origins at once.

Sitting with Dave, in my attic living room, my cobra hood was spread. "I felt lonely today," I told him. "I wanted to hear from you."

I'd be lying if I wrote that I remember what he said. I don't. Which is the sad half-life of arguments—we usually remember our side better. I think he told me he'd been thinking of me all day, and couldn't I trust that? Why did I need proof?

Voiced concern for my situation/problem. Why did I need proof? I just did.

He said to me, "I think you're making this up."

This meaning what? My anger? My anger at him? Memory fumbles.

I didn't know what I felt, I told him. Couldn't he just trust that I felt something, and that I'd wanted something from him? I needed his empathy not just to comprehend the emotions I was describing, but to help me discover which emotions were actually there.

We were under a skylight under a moon. It was February beyond the glass. It was almost Valentine's Day. I was curled into a cheap futon with crumbs in its creases, a piece of furniture that made me feel like I was still in college. This abortion was something adult. I didn't feel like an adult inside of it.

I heard *making this up* as an accusation that I was inventing emotions I didn't have, but I think he was suggesting I'd mistranslated emotions that were actually there, had been there for a while—that I was attaching long-standing feelings of need and insecurity to the particular event of this abortion; exaggerating what I felt in order to manipulate him into feeling bad. This accusation hurt not because it was entirely wrong but because it was partially right, and because it was leveled with such coldness. He was speaking something truthful about me in order to defend himself, not to make me feel better.

But there was truth behind it. He understood my pain as something actual and constructed at once. He got that it was necessarily both—that my feelings were also made of the way I spoke them. When he told me I was making things up, he didn't mean I wasn't feeling anything. He meant that feeling something was never simply a state of submission but always, also, a process of construction. I see all this, looking back.

I also see that he could have been gentler with me. We could have been gentler with each other.

We went to Planned Parenthood on a freezing morning. We rummaged through a bin of free kids' books while I waited for my name to get called. Who knows why these books were there?

Meant for kids waiting during their mothers' appointments, maybe. But it felt like perversity that Friday morning, during the weekly time slot for abortions. We found a book called *Alexander,* about a boy who confesses all his misdeeds to his father by blaming them on an imaginary red-and-green-striped horse. *Alexander was a pretty bad horse today*. Whatever we can't hold, we hang on a hook that will hold it. The book belonged to a guy named Michael from Branford. I wondered why Michael had come to Planned Parenthood, and why he'd left that book behind.

There are things I'd like to tell the version of myself who sat in the Planned Parenthood counseling room. I would tell her she is going through something large and she shouldn't be afraid to confess its size, shouldn't be afraid she's "making too big a deal of it." She shouldn't be afraid of not feeling enough because the feelings will keep coming—different ones—for years. I would tell her that commonality doesn't inoculate against hurt. The fact of all those women in the waiting room, doing the same thing I was doing, didn't make it any easier.

I would tell myself: maybe your prior surgeries don't matter here, but maybe they do. Your broken jaw and your broken nose don't have anything to do with your pregnancy except they were both times you got broken into. Getting each one fixed meant getting broken into again. Getting your heart fixed will be another burglary, nothing taken except everything that gets burned away. Maybe every time you get into a paper gown you summon the ghosts of all the other times you got into a paper gown; maybe every time you slip down into that anesthetized dark it's the same dark you slipped into before. Maybe it's been waiting for you the whole time.

STEPHANIE PHILLIPS

Psychiatry
SP Training Materials (Cont.)

OPENING LINE: "I'm having these seizures and no one knows why."

PHYSICAL PRESENTATION AND TONE: You are wearing jeans and a sweatshirt, preferably stained or rumpled. You aren't someone who puts much effort into your personal appearance. At some point during the encounter, you might mention that you don't bother dressing nicely anymore because you rarely leave the house. It is essential that you avoid eye contact and keep your voice free of emotion during the encounter.

One of the hardest parts of playing Stephanie Phillips is nailing her affect—*la belle indifference,* a manner defined as the "air of unconcern displayed by some patients toward their physical symptoms." It is a common sign of conversion disorder, a front of indifference hiding "physical symptoms [that] may relieve anxiety and result in secondary gains in the form of sympathy and attention given by others." *La belle indifference*—outsourcing emotional content to physical expression—is a way of inviting empathy without asking for it. In this way, encounters with Stephanie present a sort of empathy limit case: the clinician must excavate a sadness the patient hasn't identified, must imagine a pain Stephanie can't fully experience herself.

For other cases, we are supposed to wear our anguish more openly—like a terrible, seething garment. My first time playing Appendicitis Angela, I'm told I manage "just the right amount of pain." I'm moaning in a fetal position and apparently doing it right. The doctors know how to respond. "I am sorry to hear that you are experiencing an excruciating pain in your abdomen," one says. "It must be uncomfortable."

Part of me has always craved a pain so visible—so irrefutable and physically inescapable—that everyone would have to notice. But my sadness about the abortion was never a convulsion. There was never a scene. No frothing at the mouth. I was almost relieved, three days after the procedure, when I started to hurt. It was worst at night, the cramping. But at least I knew what I felt. I wouldn't have to figure out how to explain. Like Stephanie, who didn't talk about her grief because her seizures were already pronouncing it—slantwise, in a private language, but still—granting it substance and choreography.

STEPHANIE PHILLIPS

Psychiatry
SP Training Materials (Cont.)

ENCOUNTER DYNAMICS: You don't reveal personal details until prompted. You wouldn't call yourself happy. You wouldn't call yourself unhappy. You get sad some nights about your brother. You don't say so. You don't say you have a turtle who might outlive you, and a pair of green sneakers from your gig at the minigolf course. You don't say you have a lot of memories of stacking putters. You say you have another brother, if asked, but you don't say he's not Will, because that's obvious—even if the truth of it still strikes you sometimes, hard. You're not sure these things matter. They're just facts. They're facts like the fact of dried spittle on your cheeks when you wake up on the couch and can't remember telling your mother to fuck herself. *Fuck you* is also what your arm says when it jerks so hard it might break into pieces. *Fuck you fuck you fuck you* until your jaw locks and nothing comes.

You live in a world underneath the words you are saying in this clean white room, *It's okay I'm okay I feel sad I guess.* You are blind in this other world. It's dark. Your seizures are how you move through it—thrashing and fumbling—feeling for what its walls are made of.

Your body wasn't anything special until it rebelled. Maybe you thought your thighs were fat or else you didn't, yet; maybe you had best friends who whispered secrets to you during sleepovers; maybe you had lots of boyfriends or else you were still waiting for the first one; maybe you liked unicorns when you were young or maybe you preferred regular horses. I imagine you in every possible direction, and then I cover my tracks and imagine you all over again. Sometimes I can't stand how much of you I don't know.

I hadn't planned to get heart surgery right after my abortion. I hadn't planned to get heart surgery at all. It came as a surprise that there was anything wrong. My pulse had been showing up high at the doctor's office. I was given a Holter monitor—a small plastic box to wear around my neck for twenty-four hours, attached by sensors to my chest—that showed the doctors my heart wasn't beating right. The doctors diagnosed me with SVT—supraventricular tachycardia—and said they thought there was an extra electrical node sending extra out signals—*beat, beat, beat*—when it wasn't supposed to.

They explained how to fix it: they'd make two slits in my skin, above my hips, and thread catheter wires all the way up to my heart. They would ablate bits of tissue until they managed to get rid of my tiny rogue beat box.

My primary cardiologist was a small woman who moved quickly through the offices and hallways of her world. Let's call her Dr. M. She spoke in a curt voice, always. The problem was never that her curtness meant anything—never that I took it personally—but rather that it meant nothing, that it wasn't personal at all.

My mother insisted I call Dr. M. to tell her I was having an abortion. What if there was something I needed to tell the doctors before they performed it? That was the reasoning. I put off the call until I couldn't put it off any longer. The thought of telling a near-stranger that I was having an abortion—over the phone, without being asked—seemed mortifying. It was like I'd be peeling off the bandage on a wound she hadn't asked to see.

When I finally got her on the phone, she sounded harried and impatient. I told her quickly. Her voice was cold: "And what do you want to know from me?"

I went blank. I hadn't known I'd wanted her to say *I'm sorry to hear that* until she didn't say it. But I had. I'd wanted her to say something. I started crying. I felt like a child. I felt like an idiot. Why was I crying now, when I hadn't cried before—not when I found out, not when I told Dave, not when I made the consultation appointment or went to it?

"Well?" she asked.

I finally remembered my question: did the abortion doctor need to know anything about my tachycardia?

"No," she said. There was a pause, and then: "Is that it?" Her voice was so incredibly blunt. I could only hear one thing in it:

Why are you making a fuss? That was it. I felt simultaneously like I didn't feel enough and like I was making a big deal out of nothing—that maybe I was making a big deal out of nothing because I didn't feel enough, that my tears with Dr. M. were runoff from the other parts of the abortion I wasn't crying about. I had an insecurity that didn't know how to express itself; that could attach itself to tears or else their absence. Alexander was a pretty bad horse today. When of course the horse wasn't the problem. Dr. M. became a villain because my story didn't have one. It was the kind of pain that comes without a perpetrator. Everything was happening because of my body or because of a choice I'd made. I needed something from the world I didn't know how to ask for. I needed people—Dave, a doctor, anyone—to deliver my feelings back to me in a form that was legible. Which is a superlative kind of empathy to seek, or to supply: an empathy that rearticulates more clearly what it's shown.

A month later. Dr. M. bent over the operating table and apologized. "I'm sorry for my tone on the phone," she said. "When you called about your abortion. I didn't understand what you were asking." It was an apology whose logic I didn't entirely follow. (*Didn't understand what you were asking?*) It was an apology that had been prompted. At some point my mother had called Dr. M. to discuss my upcoming procedure—and had mentioned I'd been upset by our conversation.

Now I was lying on my back in a hospital gown. I was woozy from the early stages of my anesthesia. I felt like crying all over again, at the memory of how powerless I'd been on the phone—powerless because I needed so much from her, a stranger—and at a sense of how powerless I was now, lying flat on my back and waiting for a team of doctors to burn away the tissue of my heart. I wanted to tell her I didn't accept her apology. I wanted to tell her she didn't have the right to apologize—not here, not while I was lying naked under a paper gown, not when I was about to get cut open again. I wanted to deny her the right to feel better because she'd said she was sorry.

Mainly, I wanted the anesthesia to carry me away from everything I felt and everything my body was about to feel. In a moment, it did.

I always fight the impulse to ask the med students for pills during our encounters. It seems natural. Wouldn't Baby Doug's mom want an Ativan? Wouldn't Appendicitis Angela want some Vicodin, or whatever they give you for a ten on the pain scale? Wouldn't Stephanie Phillips be a little more excited about a new diet of Valium? I keep thinking I'll communicate my pain most effectively by expressing my desire for the things that might dissolve it. Which is to say, if I were Stephanie Phillips, I'd be excited about my Ativan. But I'm not. And being an SP isn't about projection; it's about inhabitance. I can't go off script. These encounters aren't about dissolving pain, anyway, but rather seeing it more clearly. The healing part is always a hypothetical horizon we never reach.

During my winter of ministrations, I found myself constantly in the hands of doctors. It began with that first nameless man who gave me an abortion the same morning he gave twenty other women their abortions. Gave. It's a funny word we use, as if it were a present. Once the procedure was done, I was wheeled into a dim room where a man with a long white beard gave me a cup of orange juice. He was like a kid's drawing of God. I remember resenting how he wouldn't give me any pain pills until I'd eaten a handful of crackers, but he was kind. His resistance was a kind of care. I felt that. He was looking out for me.

Dr. G. was the doctor who performed my heart operation. He controlled the catheters from a remote computer. It looked like a spaceship flight cabin. He had a nimble voice and lanky arms and bushy white hair. I liked him. He was a straight talker. He came into the hospital room the day after my operation and explained why the procedure hadn't worked: they'd burned and burned, but they hadn't burned the right patch. They'd even cut through my arterial wall to keep looking. But then they'd stopped. Ablating more tissue risked dismantling my circuitry entirely.

Dr. G. said I could get the procedure again. I could authorize them to ablate more aggressively. The risk was that I'd come out of surgery with a pacemaker. He was very calm when he said this. He pointed at my chest: "On someone thin," he said, "you'd be able to see the outlines of the box quite clearly."

I pictured waking up from general anesthesia to find a metal box above my ribs. I remember being struck by how the doctor had anticipated a question about the pacemaker I hadn't yet discovered in myself: How easily would I be able to forget it was there? I remember feeling grateful for the calmness in his voice and not offended by it. It didn't register as callousness. Why?

Maybe it was just because he was a man. I didn't need him to be my mother—even for a day—I only needed him to know what he was doing. But I think it was something more. Instead of identifying with my panic—inhabiting my horror at the prospect of a pacemaker—he was helping me understand that even this, the barnacle of a false heart, would be okay. His calmness didn't make me feel abandoned, it made me feel secure. It offered assurance rather than empathy, or maybe assurance was evidence of empathy, insofar as he understood that assurance, not identification, was what I needed most.

Empathy is a kind of care but it's not the only kind of care, and it's not always enough. I want to think that's what Dr. G. was thinking. I needed to look at him and see the opposite of my fear, not its echo.

Every time I met with Dr. M., she began our encounters with a few perfunctory questions about my life—*What are you working on these days?*—and when she left the room to let me dress, I could hear her voice speaking into a tape recorder in the hallway: *Patient is a graduate student in English at Yale. Patient is writing a dissertation on addiction. Patient spent two years living in Iowa. Patient is working on a collection of essays.* And then, without fail, at the next appointment, fresh from listening to her old tape, she bullet-pointed a few questions: *How were those two years in Iowa? How's that collection of essays?*

It was a strange intimacy, almost embarrassing, to feel the mechanics of her method so palpable between us: *engage the patient, record the details, repeat*. I was sketched into Cliffs-Notes. I hated seeing the puppet strings; they felt unseemly—and without kindness in her voice, the mechanics meant nothing. They pretended we knew each other rather than acknowledging that we didn't. It's a tension intrinsic to the surgeon-patient relationship: it's more invasive than anything but not intimate at all.

Now I can imagine another kind of tape—a more naked, stuttering tape; a tape that keeps correcting itself, that messes up its dance steps:

Patient is here ~~for an abortion~~ for ~~a surgery to burn the bad parts of her heart for~~ a medication to fix her heart because the surgery failed. Patient is staying in the hospital for ~~one night three nights~~ five nights until we get this medication right. Patient ~~wonders if people can bring her booze in the hospital~~ likes to eat graham crackers from the nurses' station. Patient cannot be released until she runs on a treadmill and her heart prints a clean rhythm. Patient recently got an abortion but we don't understand why she wanted us to know that. Patient didn't ~~think she~~ hurt at first but then she did. Patient ~~failed to use protection and~~ failed to provide an adequate account of why she didn't use protection. ~~Patient had a lot of feelings. Partner of patient had the feeling she was making up a lot of feelings.~~ Partner of patient is supportive. Partner of patient is spotted in patient's hospital bed, repeatedly. Partner of patient is caught kissing patient. Partner of patient is charming.

Patient is ~~angry disappointed~~ angry her procedure failed. Patient does not want to be on medication. Patient wants to know if she can drink alcohol on this medication. She wants to know how much. She wants to know ~~if two bottles of wine a night is too much~~ if she can get away with a couple glasses. Patient does not want to get another procedure if it means risking a pacemaker. Patient wants everyone to understand that this surgery ~~is~~ isn't a big deal; wants everyone to understand she is stupid for crying when everyone else on the ward is sicker than she is; wants everyone to understand her abortion is ~~also about~~ definitely not about the children her ex-boyfriends have had since she broke up with them. Patient wants everyone to understand ~~it wasn't a choice~~ it would have been easier if it hadn't been a choice. Patient understands it was her choice to drink while she was pregnant. She understands it was her choice to go to a bar with a little plastic box hanging from her neck, and get so drunk she messed up her heart graph. Patient is patients, plural, which is to say she is multiple—mostly grateful but sometimes surly, sometimes full of self-pity. Patient ~~already understands~~ is trying hard to understand she needs to listen up if she wants to hear how everyone is caring for her.

Three men waited for me in the hospital during my surgery: my brother and my father and Dave. They sat in the lounge making awkward conversation, and then in the cafeteria making awkward conversation, and then—I'm not sure where they sat, actually, or in what order, because I wasn't there. But I do know that while they were sitting in the cafeteria a doctor came to find them and told them that the surgeons were going to tear through part of my arterial wall—these were the words they used, Dave said, *tear through*—and try burning some patches of tissue on the other side. At this point, Dave told me later, he went to the hospital chapel and prayed I wouldn't die. He prayed in the nook made by the propped-open door because he didn't want to be seen.

It wasn't likely I would die. Dave didn't know that then. Prayer isn't about likelihood anyway, it's about desire—loving someone enough to get on your knees and ask for her to be saved. When he cried in that chapel, it wasn't empathy—it was something else. His kneeling wasn't a way to feel my pain but to request that it end.

I learned to rate Dave on how well he empathized with me. I was constantly poised above an invisible checklist item 31. I wanted him to hurt whenever I hurt, to feel as much as I felt. But it's exhausting to keep tabs on how much someone is feeling for you. It can make you forget that they feel, too.

I used to believe that hurting would make you more alive to

the hurting of others. I used to believe in feeling bad because somebody else did. Now I'm not so sure of either. I know that being in the hospital made me selfish. Getting surgeries made me think mainly about whether I'd have to get another one. When bad things happened to other people, I imagined them happening to me. I didn't know if this was empathy or theft.

For example: one September, my brother woke up in a hotel room in Sweden and couldn't move half his face. He was diagnosed with something called Bell's palsy. No one really understands why it happens or how to make it better. The doctors gave him a steroid called prednisone that made him sick. He threw up most days around twilight. He sent us a photo. It looked lonely and grainy. His face slumped. His pupil glistened in the flash, bright with the gel he had to put on his eye to keep it from drying out. He couldn't blink.

I found myself obsessed with his condition. I tried to imagine what it was like to move through the world with an unfamiliar face. I thought about what it would be like to wake up in the morning, in the groggy space where you've managed to forget things, to forget your whole life, and then snapping to, realizing: *Yes, this is how things are*. Checking the mirror: still there. I tried to imagine how you'd feel a little crushed, each time, coming out of dreams to another day of being awake with a face not quite your own.

I spent large portions of each day—pointless, fruitless spans of time—imagining how I would feel if my face was paralyzed, too. I stole my brother's trauma and projected it onto myself like a magic-lantern pattern of light. I obsessed, and told myself this obsession was empathy. But it wasn't, quite. It was more like *in*pathy. I wasn't expatriating myself into another life so much as importing its problems into my own.

Dave doesn't believe in feeling bad just because someone else does. This isn't his notion of support. He believes in listening, and asking questions, and steering clear of assumptions. He thinks imagining someone else's pain with too much surety can be as damaging as failing to imagine it. He believes in humility.

He believes in staying strong enough to stick around. He stayed with me in the hospital, five nights in those crisp white beds, and he lay down with my monitor wires, colored strands carrying the electrical signature of my heart to a small box I held in my hands. I remember lying tangled with him, how much it meant—that he was willing to lie down in the mess of wires, to stay there with me.

In order to help the med students empathize better with us, we have to empathize with them. I try to think about what makes them fall short of what they're asked—what nervousness or squeamishness or callousness—and how to speak to their sore spots without bruising them: the one so stiff he shook my hand like we'd just made a business deal; the chipper one so eager to befriend me she didn't wash her hands at all.

One day we have a sheet cake delivered for my supervisor's birthday—dry white layers with ripples of strawberry jelly—and we sit around our conference table eating her cake with plastic forks while she doesn't eat anything at all. She tells us what kind of syntax we should use when we tell the students about bettering their empathy. We're supposed to use the "When you . . . I felt" frame. *When you forgot to wash your hands, I felt protective of my body. When you told me eleven wasn't on the pain scale, I felt dismissed*. For the good parts also: *When you asked me questions about Will, I felt like you really cared about my loss.*

A 1983 study titled "The Structure of Empathy" found a correlation between empathy and four major personality clusters: sensitivity, nonconformity, even-temperedness, and social self-confidence. I like the word *structure*. It suggests empathy is an edifice we build like a home or office—with architecture and design, scaffolding and electricity. The Chinese character for *listen* is built like this, a structure of many parts: the characters for ears and eyes, the horizontal line that signifies undivided attention, the swoop and teardrops of heart.

Rating high for the study's "sensitivity" cluster feels intuitive. It means agreeing with statements like "I have at one time or another tried my hand at writing poetry" or "I have seen some things so sad they almost made me feel like crying" and *dis*agreeing with statements like: "I really don't care whether people like me or dislike me." This last one seems to suggest that empathy might be, at root, a barter, a bid for others' affection: *I care about your pain* is another way to say *I care if you like me*. We care in order to be cared for. We care because we are porous. The feelings of others matter, they are like matter: they carry weight, exert gravitational pull.

It's the last cluster, social self-confidence, that I don't understand as well. I've always treasured empathy as the particular privilege of the invisible, the observers who are shy precisely because they sense so much—because it is overwhelming to say even a single word when you're sensitive to every last flicker of nuance in the room. "The relationship between social self-confidence and empathy is the most difficult to understand," the study admits. But its explanation makes sense: social confidence is a prerequisite but not a guarantee, it can "give a person the courage to enter the interpersonal world and practice empathetic skills." We should empathize from courage, is the point—and it makes me think about how much of my empathy comes from fear. I'm afraid other people's problems will happen to me, or else I'm afraid other people will stop loving me if I don't adopt their problems as my own.

Jean Decety, a psychologist at the University of Chicago, uses fMRI scans to measure what happens when someone's brain responds to another person's pain. He shows test subjects images of painful situations (hand caught in scissors, foot under door) and compares these scans to what a brain looks like when its body is actually in pain. Decety has found that imagining the pain of others activates the same three areas (prefrontal cortex, anterior insula, anterior cingulate) as experiencing pain itself. I feel heartened by that correspondence. But I also wonder what it's good for.

During the months of my brother's Bell's palsy, whenever I woke up in the morning and checked my face for a fallen cheek, a drooping eye, a collapsed smile, I wasn't ministering to anyone. I wasn't feeling toward my brother so much as I was feeling toward a version of myself—a self that didn't exist but theoretically shared his misfortune.

I wonder if my empathy has always been this, in every case: just a bout of hypothetical self-pity projected onto someone else. Is this ultimately just solipsism? Adam Smith confesses in his *Theory of Moral Sentiments:* "When we see a stroke aimed and just ready to fall upon the leg or arm of another person, we naturally shrink and draw back our own leg or our own arm."

We care about ourselves. Of course we do. Maybe some good comes from it. If I imagine myself fiercely into my brother's pain, I get some sense, perhaps, of what he might want or need, because I think, *I would want this. I would need this*. But it also seems like a fragile pretext, turning his misfortunes into an opportunity to indulge pet fears of my own devising.

I wonder which parts of my brain are lighting up when the med students ask me: "How does that make you feel?" Or which parts of their brains are glowing when I say, "the pain in my abdomen is a ten." My condition isn't real. I know this. They know this. I'm simply going through the motions. They're simply going through the motions. But motions can be more than rote. They don't just express feeling; they can give birth to it.

Empathy isn't just something that happens to us—a meteor shower of synapses firing across the brain—it's also a choice we make: to pay attention, to extend ourselves. It's made of exertion, that dowdier cousin of impulse. Sometimes we care for another because we know we should, or because it's asked for, but this doesn't make our caring hollow. The act of choosing simply means we've committed ourselves to a set of behaviors greater than the sum of our individual inclinations: *I will listen to his sadness, even when I'm deep in my own*. To say *going through the motions*—this isn't reduction so much as acknowledgment of effort—the labor, the motions, the dance—of getting inside another person's state of heart or mind.

This confession of effort chafes against the notion that empathy should always rise unbidden, that *genuine* means the same thing as *unwilled,* that intentionality is the enemy of love. But I believe in intention and I believe in work. I believe in waking up in the middle of the night and packing our bags and leaving our worst selves for our better ones.

LESLIE JAMISON

Ob-Gyn
SP Training Materials (Cont.)

OPENING LINE: You don't need one. Everyone comes here for the same reason.

PHYSICAL PRESENTATION AND TONE: Wear loose pants. You have been told to wear loose pants. Keep your voice steady and articulate. You are about to spread your legs for a doctor who won't ever know your name. You know the drill, sort of. Act like you do.

ENCOUNTER DYNAMICS: Answer every question like you're clarifying a coffee order. Be courteous and nod vigorously. Make sure your heart stays on the other side of the white wall behind you. If the nurse asks you whether you are sure about getting the procedure, say yes without missing a beat. Say yes without a trace of doubt. Don't mention the way you felt when you first saw the pink cross on the stick—that sudden expansive joy at the possibility of a child, at your own capacity to have one. Don't mention this single moment of joy because it might make it seem as if you aren't completely sure about what you're about to do. Don't mention this single moment of joy because it might hurt. It will feel—more than anything else does—like the measure of what you're giving up. It maps the edges of your voluntary loss.

Instead, tell the nurse you weren't using birth control but wasn't that silly and now you are going to start.

If she asks what forms of birth control you have used in the past, say condoms. Suddenly every guy you've ever slept with is in the room with you. Ignore them. Ignore the memory of that first time—all that fumbling, and then pain—while Rod Stewart crooned "Broken Arrow" from a boom box on the dresser. *Who else is gonna bring you a broken arrow? Who else is gonna bring you a bottle of rain?*

Say you used condoms but don't think about all the times you didn't—in an Iowan graveyard, in a little car by a dark river—and definitely don't say why, how the risk made you feel close to those boys, how you courted the incredible gravity of what your bodies could do together.

If the nurse asks about your current partner, you should say, *We are very committed,* like you are defending yourself against some legal charge. If the nurse is listening closely, she should hear fear nestled like an egg inside your certainty.

If the nurse asks whether you drink, say yes to that too. Of course you do. Like it's no big deal. Your lifestyle habits include drinking to excess. You do this even when you know there is a fetus inside you. You do it to forget there is a fetus inside you; or to feel like maybe this is just a movie about a fetus being inside you.

The nurse will eventually ask, *How do you feel about getting the procedure?* Tell her you feel sad but you know it's the right choice, because this seems like the right thing to say, even though it's a lie. You feel mainly numb. You feel numb until your legs are in the stirrups. Then you hurt. Whatever anesthesia comes through the needle in your arm only sedates you. Days later you feel your body cramping in the night—a deep, hot, twisting pain—and you can only lie still and hope it passes, beg for sleep, drink for sleep, resent Dave for sleeping next to you. You can only watch your body bleed like an inscrutable, stubborn object—something harmed and cumbersome and not entirely yours. You leave your body and don't come back for a month. You come back angry.

You wake up from another round of anesthesia and they tell you all their burning didn't burn away the part of your heart that was broken. You come back and find you aren't alone. You weren't alone when you were cramping through the night and you're not alone now. Dave spends every night in the hospital. You want to tell him how disgusting your body feels: your unwashed skin and greasy hair. You want him to listen, for hours if necessary, and feel everything exactly as you feel it—your pair of hearts in such synchronized rhythm any monitor would show it; your pair of hearts playing two crippled bunnies doing whatever they can. There is no end to this fantasy of closeness. *Who else is gonna bring you a broken arrow?* You want him to break with you. You want him to hurt in a womb he doesn't have; you want him to admit he can't hurt that way. You want him to know how it feels in every one of your nerve endings: lying prone on the detergent sheets, lifting your shirt for one more cardiac resident, one more stranger, letting him attach his clips to the line of hooks under your breast, letting him print out your heart, once more, to see if its rhythm has calmed.

It all returns to this: you want him close to your damage. You want humility and presumption and whatever lies between, you want that, too. You're tired of begging for it. You're tired of grading him on how well he gives it. You want to learn how to stop feeling sorry for yourself. You want to write an essay about the lesson. You throw away the checklist and let him climb into your hospital bed. You let him part the heart wires. You sleep. He sleeps. You wake, pulse feeling for another pulse, and there he is again.

NEGROLAND

Margo Jefferson

In Negroland boys learned early how to die. They started in their teens, dying in period rec rooms with wood paneling and pool tables, train sets, golf clubs, liquor cabinets.

Did Father keep a rifle on the wall there, or did the son find his old army gun in the bedroom closet and sneak it downstairs? There, in the rec room, an amiable, well-mannered doctor's son shot himself. Motive, unknown; verdict, accidental death; time, not long after his father was arrested for assaulting his second wife.

A few years later, in another rec room, a sweet-faced doctor's son with a soft voice did the same. Suspected motive: he feared going the way of his father, sweet-faced, soft-voiced, seductively effusive, and (suspiciously) no longer married.

Vietnam opened other routes to self-extinction. A Negro boy could drop out of college, enlist, and come home a junkie. He could drink, shoot up, steal for several years, pawn his grandmother's silver, assault a homeless man, and evade a jail sentence because his parents, both doctors, knew the judge. He could retire to the family homestead in Virginia, decline steadily in health, and die of kidney failure.

Negroland children were warned by their parents that few Negroes enjoyed their privilege or plenty; that most non-Negro Americans would be glad to see their kind of Negro returned to indigence, deference, and subservience.

Their parents made sure to supply them with well-appointed homes and apartments, tasteful clothes and plenty of them, handsome cars, generous allowances, sailboats, summer camps, music and dance lessons, flying lessons, private schools, tutors, and an array of clubs where other children exactly like them met for sports and directed plays, cultural excursions, and Christmas visits to old people's homes to sing carols.

Nevertheless, life in Negroland meant that any conversation could be taken over by the White Man at any moment. He dominated dinner party army stories about the brown-skinned Negro officer who'd had to escort his angry unit to the shabby back cars of a segregated train; the light-skinned Negro officer who'd been given the last seat in the white section of a train until he said he was a Negro, whereupon a porter (another brown-skinned Negro) was sent to find a curtain that could separate him from the Caucasian in front and join him to the Negro behind.

When he's not lynching you, he's humiliating you, said the men at the dinner table. They leaned forward and raised their voices, then subsided into their chairs, shook their heads, let out a *hmmmm. He keeps you out of his hospitals, his law firms, his universities. Even his damn cemeteries. He never lets you forget you're a second-class citizen.*

Strategic privilege and flagrantly displayed prosperity let you forget. Cocktail parties and dinner dances urged you to forget. Season tickets to the opera, summer trips to the Caribbean and Mexico. The family together watching Ed Sullivan, watching *Gunsmoke* and *Maverick,* watching *Playhouse 90* and outstanding cultural productions like *Peter Pan* and *The Nutcracker.*

Suavely complicated marriages and urbane extramarital liaisons; hushed quarrels at the breakfast table. Fathers at the office, at the club, coming home late so many nights.

Mothers picking the children up from school, shopping, planning meals, lunching with friends, working to safeguard their marriages.

La Vie Bourgeoise.

Round up the usual Oedipal conflicts and divided loyalties. Fathers, insist that your sons become high-achieving Negroes, prepared, like you, to push their way manfully past every obstacle.

How are they to do this? Force of will. You did.

But the boys had started dying.

Negroland girls couldn't die outright. We had to plot and circle our way toward death, pretend we were after something else, like being ladylike, being popular, being loved. Between the late 1940s and the early 1960s, Good Negro Girls mastered the rigorous vocabulary of femininity. Gloves, handkerchiefs, pocketbooks for each occasion. Good diction for all occasions; skin care (no ashy knees or elbows); hair cultivation (a ceaseless round of treatments to eradicate the bushy and nappy). Manners to please grandparents and quell the doubts of any white strangers loitering to observe your behavior in schools, stores, and restaurants.

We were busy being pert, chic, cool—but not fast. Fast meant social extermination by degrees, because the boys who'd sampled a fast girl would tell another girl they'd taken up with (who was desirable but not fast) that the first girl was a slut.

The boys knew this because she'd made the mistake of being fast with more than one boy, so they'd talked about her with each other.

And then her girlfriends talked about her with each other. They were still cordial to her at parties. She wasn't put out of her clubs. But if she wasn't already in the Etta Quettes or the Co-Ettes, she wasn't asked in.

Occasionally, a daughter who'd been silly enough to get herself pregnant would actually drop out of college, have the child, and marry its father. That meant she had disgraced herself and her family.

In fact, she had committed matricide: she had destroyed the good reputation her mother, her grandmothers, and her grandmothers' grandmothers had fought for since slavery.

Premature sexual activity and pregnancy out of wedlock? She was just another statistic to be held against the race.

The world had to upend itself before shades of possibility between decorum and disgrace could emerge. Suddenly, people like us were denouncing war and imperialism, discarding the strategic protocol of civil rights for the combat aggression of

Black Power. We unmade our straightened hair, remade our pristine diction, renounced our social niceties and snobberies.

The entitlements of Negroland were no longer *relevant*.

We were not the best that had been known and thought in black life and history. We were a corruption of The Race, a wrongful deviation. We'd let ourselves become tools of oppression in the black community. We'd settled for a desiccated white facsimile and abandoned a vital black culture. Striving to prove we could master the rubric of white civilization that had never for a moment thought us the best of anything in their life or history.

You grilled yourself: Do I still like—love—too many white writers, musicians, artists? Have I immersed myself enough in African history and culture? Do my principles show in my work? And principles notwithstanding, in my heart am I still a snob? At meetings, in political conversations, class—your *background*, your *advantages*—weasels its way in. Purge it from your intellectual pronouncements; it pops up in how you expressed them. The preemptory tone that you tell yourself is rigorous. The way of seeming to listen politely when you aren't listening because you are so sure you know better.

And even when you didn't think you knew better, you'd get those looks at community poetry readings or concerts, once a nationalist heard your diction or watched your mannerisms . . . watched until you felt his gaze and had to return it; then he'd slowly curl his lip.

And the comments:

You have to understand: you can't be trusted. You've always insulted people like me.

Yeah, you Chicago folks' Scotch budget could fund a year's research at the Institute of the Black World.

When the Revolution comes, people like you will be lined up against the wall and shot.

Are you black enough became essential to style preening and sexual intimidation.

Good Negro Girls in search of lives their parents hadn't lived often sought men their parents didn't know and didn't care to know.

Naturally, errors were made. The doctor's daughter studying architecture married a man with suspected ties to the drug trade: within the year, she was shot in the head from behind and left beside her murdered husband, a large pool of blood widening in what *Jet* magazine called their "affluent South Side home."

The dark-skinned daughter of a socially responsible educator, who left her Paris career as a provocatively keen-featured model with exorbitant long limbs to teach early childhood education at an Illinois community college, was stabbed multiple times in the head and neck by an estranged husband who then drove her body to the police station and turned himself in, telling the officer, "I just went crazy."

Average American women were killed like this every day. But we weren't raised to be average women; we were raised to be better than most women of either race. White women, our mothers reminded us pointedly, could afford more of these casualties. There were more of them, weren't there?

There were always more white people. There were so few of us, and it had cost so much to construct us. Why were we dying?

The first of the dying boys had succumbed to the usual perils of family life—the unkind, philandering father, the kind but closeted father, the absent or insufficient mother. After them came the boys who threw off privilege and lusted for street life, imitating the slipslide walks of the guys who lounged on street corners in caps and leather coats, practicing the raucous five-stage laugh (clap, fold at the waist, run forward, arms in loose boxing position, squat, and return to loose standing position); working as hard as any white boy at a frat party to sound like Bo Diddley and Otis Redding.

Striving ardently to be what they were and were not. Behold the Race Flaneur: the bourgeois rebel who goes slumming, and finds not just adventure but the objective correlative for his secret despair.

I won't absolve the girls. We played ghetto too, rolled and cut our eyes to show disdain, smacked our gum and loud-talked.

But the boys ruled. We were just aspiring adornments, and how could it be otherwise? The Negro man was at the center of the culture's race obsessions. The Negro woman was on the shabby fringes. She had moments if she was in show business, of course; we craved the erotic command of Tina Turner, the arch insolence of Diana Ross, the melismatic authenticity of Aretha.

But in life, when a Good Negro Girl attached herself to a ghetto boy hoping to go street and compensate for her bourgeois privilege, if she didn't get killed with or by him, she usually lived to become a socially disdained, financially disabled black woman destined to produce at least one baby she would have to care for alone.

What was the matter with us? Were we plagued by some monstrous need, some vestigial longing to plunge back into the abyss Negroes had been consigned to for centuries?

Was this some variant of survivor guilt?

No, that phrase is too generic. I'd call it the guilty confusion of those who were raised to defiantly accept their entitlement. To be more than survivors, to be victors who knew that victory was as much a threat as failure, and could be turned against them at any moment.

I'm still obsessed with James Weldon Johnson's 1933 diagnosis of this condition. It deserves repeating.

Awaiting each colored child are cramping limitations and buttressed obstacles in addition to those that must be met by youth in general. How judicious he is. Yet, implacably, this dilemma approaches suffering, *in exact proportion to the parents' knowledge of these conditions, and the child's ignorance of them. Some parents try to spare their children this bitter knowledge as long as possible. Less sensitive parents (those maimed by their own bitterness) drive it into the child from infancy on.*

At each turn, Johnson forgoes high rhetorical drama. He chooses "this dilemma" over "our burden," prefers our "condition" to our "fate," and comes at last, with stately tread, to this: *And no parent may definitely say which is the wiser course, for either of them may lead to spiritual disaster for the child.* Tragedy has arrived and is content to wait quietly. In time it may be able to claim both parent and child.

Those of us who avoided disaster encountered life's usual rewards and pleasures, obstacles and limitations. If we still had some longing for death, we had to make it compatible with this new pattern of living.

In the late 1970s, I began to actively cultivate a desire to kill myself. I was, at that time, a successful professional in my chosen field of journalism. I was also a passionate feminist who refused to admit any contradiction between, on the one hand, her commitment to fighting the oppression of women and, on the other, her belief that feminism would let her draft a death commensurate with social achievement and political awareness.

A little background is needed here. The women's movement was controversial in the black community at this time. Many men and all too many women denounced feminism as a white woman's thing, an indulgence, even an assertion of privilege, since she was competing (and stridently) for the limited share of benefits white men had just begun to grant non-whites.

Black feminists responded that, thanks to sexism, women of color regularly got double blasts of discrimination and oppression. And, anyway, we had our own feminist history. Relations between white and black women had been wary, inequitable, or bluntly exploitative. Alliances between them had been scant and fraught.

Nevertheless, social and cultural progress through the decades had made interracial cooperation and friendship available to my generation. I'd had white friends since kindergarten. And I was willing to acknowledge this irony: the rituals of bourgeois femininity had given the girls of Negroland certain protections the boys lacked.

That vision of feral, fascinating black manhood possessed

Americans of every race and class. If you were a successful upper-middle-class Negro girl in the 1950s and '60s, you were, in practice and imagination, a white Protestant upper-middle-class girl. Young, good-looking white women were the most desirable creatures in the world. It was hard not to want to imitate them; it was highly toxic too, as we would learn.

Still, these rituals allowed girls the latitude to go about their studies while being pert and popular, to stay well-mannered and socially adaptable, even as they joined the protests of the sixties and seventies.

So, when the black movement and the women's movement offered new social and cultural opportunities, we were ready to accept them.

But one white female privilege had always been withheld from the girls of Negroland. Aside from the privilege of actually being white, they had been denied the privilege of freely yielding to depression, of flaunting neurosis as a mark of social and psychic complexity. A privilege that was glorified in the literature of white female suffering and resistance. A privilege Good Negro Girls had been denied by our history of duty, obligation, and discipline. Because our people had endured horrors and prevailed, even triumphed, their descendants should be too strong and too proud for such behavior. We were to be ladies, responsible Negro women, and indomitable Black Women. We were not to be depressed or unduly high-strung; we were not to have nervous collapses. We had a legacy. We were too strong for that.

I craved the right to turn my face to the wall, to create a death commensurate with bourgeois achievement, political awareness, and aesthetically compelling feminine despair. My first forays in this direction were petty. I conducted my own small battle of the books, purging my library of stalwart, valorous titles by black women and replacing them, wherever possible, with morbid, truculent ones by my sisters. Out with *This Child's Gonna Live*, up with *There's Nothing I Own That I Want*. Goodbye *My Lord, What a Morning* by Marian Anderson; hello *Everything and Nothing* by Dorothy Dandridge. As for Mari Evans's iconic sixties poem,

I am a black woman
. . . .
strong
beyond all definition still
defying place
and time
and circumstance
assailed
impervious
indestructible
Look
on me and be
renewed

I tore it out of an anthology and set fire to it in the bathroom sink.

I found literary idols in Adrienne Kennedy, Nella Larsen, and Ntozake Shange, writers who'd dared to locate a sanctioned, forbidden space between white vulnerability and black invincibility.

A Negro girl could never be purely innocent. The vengeful Race Fairy always lurked nearby; your parents' best hope was that the fairy would show up at someone else's feast and punish their child. Parents had to protect themselves too, and protect you from knowing how much danger you all were in.

And so arose one variation on the classic Freudian primal scene in which the child sees or imagines her parents having sex and finds it stirringly violent. Here the child sees and imagines her parents having fraught encounters with white people who invade their conversation and shadow their lives beyond the boundaries of home or neighborhood.

Work hard, child. Internalize the figures of your mother, your father, your parents (one omnipotent double-gendered personage). Internalize The Race. Internalize both races. Then internalize the contradictions. Teach your psyche to adapt its solo life to a group obbligato. Or else let it abandon any impulse toward independence and hurtle toward a feverishly perfect representation of your people.

DOMESTIC GULAGS

Laura Kipnis

What follows is a brief sample of answers to the simple question: "What can't you do because you're in a couple?" (This information is all absolutely true; nothing was invented. Nothing needed to be.)

You can't leave the house without saying where you're going. You can't not say what time you'll return. You can't stay out past midnight, or eleven, or ten, or dinnertime, or not come right home after work. You can't go out when the other person feels like staying home. You can't go to parties alone. You can't go out just to go out, because you can't not be considerate of the other person's worries about where you are, or their natural insecurities that you're not where you should be, or about where you could be instead. You can't make plans without consulting the other person, particularly not evenings and weekends, or make decisions about leisure time usage without a consultation.

You can't be a slob. You can't do less than 50 percent around the house, even if the other person wants to do 100 to 200 percent more housecleaning than you find necessary or even reasonable. You can't leave your (pick one) books, tissues, shoes, makeup, mail, underwear, work, sewing stuff, or pornography lying around the house. You can't smoke, or you can't smoke in the house, or you can't leave cigarettes in cups. You can't amass more knickknacks than the other person finds tolerable—likewise sports paraphernalia, Fiestaware, or Daffy Duck collectibles.

You can't leave the dishes for later, wash the dishes badly, not use soap, drink straight from the container, make crumbs without wiping them up (now, not later), or load the dishwasher according to the method that seems most sensible to you. You can't use dishes directly out of the dishwasher without unloading the whole thing. You can't accumulate things that you think you just might use someday if the other person thinks you won't. You can't throw wet clothes in the laundry hamper even though there's no logical reason not to—after all, they're going to get wet eventually. You can't have a comfortable desk because it doesn't fit the decor. You can't not notice whether the house is neat or messy. You can't not share responsibility for domestic decisions the other person has made that you've gone along with to be nice, but don't really care about. You can't hire a housecleaner, because your mate is a socialist and can't live with the idea. (Or as this respondent put it: "He said, 'I couldn't live with it'; I did the math.")

You can't leave the bathroom door open, it's offensive. You can't leave the bathroom door closed, they need to get in. You can't enter without knocking. You can't leave the toilet seat up. You can't read on the john without commentary. You can't leave bloody things in the bathroom wastebasket. You can't leave female hygiene products out. You can't wash your dirty hands in the kitchen sink. You have to load the toilet paper "over" instead of "under." You're not allowed to pay no attention to what you'd simply rather ignore: your own nose hair, underarm hair, or toenails. You can't not make the bed. You can't not express appreciation when the other person makes the bed, even if you don't care. You can't sleep apart, you can't go to bed at different times, you can't fall asleep on the couch without getting woken up to go to bed. You can't eat in bed. You can't get out of bed right away after sex. You can't have insomnia without being grilled about what's *really* bothering you. You can't turn the air conditioner up as high as you want—think of the environment instead of yourself all the time. You can't sleep late if the other person has to get up early. Or you can't sleep late because it's a sign of moral turpitude.

You can't watch soap operas without getting made fun of.

You can't watch infomercials, or the pregame show, or Martha Stewart, or shows in which men are humiliated in front of women or are made to play the buffoon. You can't watch porn. You can't leave CNN on as background. You can't pathologically withdraw into sports even if it's your only mode of anxiety release. You can't listen to Bob Dylan or other excesses of your youth. You can't go out to play pinball, it's regressive. You can't smoke pot. You can't drink during the day, even on weekends. You can't take naps when the other person is home because the mate feels leisure time should be shared. You can't work when you're supposed to be relaxing. You can't spend too much time on the computer. You can't play *Dungeons and Dragons*. And stay off those chat rooms! You can't have email flirtations, even if innocent. You can't play computer solitaire because the clicking drives the other person crazy. You can't talk on the phone when they're home working. You can't be rude to people who call on the phone for the mate. You can't just hang up on telemarketers, you must be polite. You can't talk on the phone when they're in the room without them commenting on the conversation, or trying to talk to you at the same time. Your best friend can't call after ten. You can't read without them starting to talk, and you're not allowed to read when they're talking to you. You can't not pay attention to their presence.

You can't be impulsive, self-absorbed, or distracted. You can't take risks, unless they're agreed-upon risks, which somewhat limits the concept of "risk." You can't just walk out on your job or quit in a huff. You can't make unilateral career decisions, or change jobs without extensive discussion and negotiation. You can't have your own bank account. You can't make major purchases alone, or spend money on things the other person considers excesses, you can't blow money just because you're in a really bad mood, and you can't be in a bad mood without being required to explain it. You can't have secrets—about money or anything else.

You can't eat what you want: goodbye marshmallow fluff, hello tofu meatballs. You can't not eat meals. You can't not plan these meals. You can't not have dinner together. You can't not feel like eating what the other person has cooked. You can't bring

Ding Dongs into the house. You can't break your diet. You can't eat garlic because they can't stand the smell. You can't eat butter if they're monitoring your cholesterol. You can't cook cauliflower even if you don't expect the other person to eat it. You can't use enough salt to give the food some flavor without it being seen as a criticism of their cooking. You can't refuse to share your entrée when dining out, or order what you want without negotiations far surpassing the Oslo accords. The question of which eating implement you use (or don't), the employment of the napkin, the placement of bones, pits, and other detritus, are all subject to commentary and critique. You can't blow your nose at the table. You can't read the newspaper at meals. You can't eat things that give you gas. You can't make jokes about gas.

You can't say the wrong thing, even in situations where there's no right thing to say. You can't use the "wrong tone of voice," and you can't deny the wrong-tone-of-voice accusation when it's made.* You can't repeat yourself; you can't be overly self-dramatic; you can't know things the other person doesn't know, or appear to parade your knowledge. You can't overly celebrate your own accomplishments, particularly if the mate is less successful. You can't ask for help and then criticize the mode of help, or reject it. You can't not produce reassurances when asked for, or more frequently, when they're not asked for yet expected. You can't begin a sentence with "You always . . ." You can't begin a sentence with "I never . . ." You can't be simplistic, even when things are simple. You're not permitted to employ the Socratic method in an argument. You can't have the wrong laugh: too loud, too

---

*Another striking linguistic feature of couple languages is the distinctive use of tone. As in other spoken languages such as Chinese, changes in intonation will completely change the meaning of an utterance. Listen carefully to the inflection of sentences such as "How many times do I have to *say* it?" or "Could you *please* not do that." The meaning of the communication isn't in the content, it's in the intonation. In fact, a phrase like "What did you mean by *that*?" conveys nothing less than the story of the relationship itself, a virtual catalogue of disappointments or rejections or ruffled egos: even the most tone-deaf observer can re-create a couple's entire history based solely on the particular inflection of "*that*."

explosive, too inappropriate, too silly. You can't say "cunt." You can't make penis size jokes, or laugh when others do. You can't say what you think about the mate's family. You also can't compare the mate to any of their family members, especially not the same-sex parent. You can't hold up your own family's preferable customs in anything as a model. You can't be less concerned with the other person's vulnerability than with expressing your own opinions. You can't express inappropriate irony about something the other person takes seriously. Or appropriate anger at something the other person takes casually. You can't call a handyman to repair something if they consider themselves to be "handy." You can't not be supportive, even when the mate does something insupportable. You can't analyze the cinematography in a movie that they were emotional about. You can't not participate in their minidramas about other people's incompetence, or rudeness, or existence. You can't make a joke that the other person could potentially construe as unconsciously aimed at them. You can't talk about (choose one): religion, politics, Germany, Israel, the class struggle. You can't tell Polish jokes. You can't make puns or tell dirty jokes, or relate overly lengthy anecdotes. You can't make jokes about bald spots, ear shape, fat, or any other sensitivity, even if you didn't know until that moment that it was an area of sensitivity. You can't talk about your crush on your shrink. You can't talk about past relationships. Or you can't not talk about past relationships, and can't refuse to reveal all the long-forgotten details when asked. You can't refuse to talk about what you talked about in therapy. But you can't "overanalyze" either, or import psychological terminology into the relationship. You can't not "communicate your feelings." Except when those feelings are critical, which they should not be.

You can't say anything that makes the other person too aware of their own incompetence or failures, reflects them back to themselves in a way that is not flattering, or pulls the rug out from any of their self-idealizations. You can't question their self-knowledge, or their reading of a particular situation. You can't issue diagnoses, even when glaringly obvious. You can't be cynical about things the other person is sincere about, or indifferent to the things they're deeply interested in that seem trivial to you: style, haute cuisine, electoral politics, office gossip, the home team.

You can't have friends who like one of you more than the other, or friends one of you likes more than the other. You can't be rude to houseguests, or leave the house when houseguests are around. You can't criticize the mate to others. You can't talk about their depression in public. You can't ignore the mate when out. When the mate is having an argument with someone, you must not take the other person's side. You can't be too charming in public, especially to persons of the opposite sex (or same sex, where applicable). You can't spend more than X amount of time talking to such persons, with X measured in nanoseconds. You can't provoke the mate's jealousy. You can't talk to people who make the mate feel insecure or threatened. You can't socialize with your exes, even if you swear it's really over. You can't transgress the standards or degree of honesty or bluntness that the other person feels is appropriate in social situations. You can't not have the other person's degree of perfectionism when entertaining. Or you can't not have their degree of casualness. You can't not laugh at their jokes in public. You can't laugh at their politics in public or in private. You can't talk about politics with their relatives, or with your own, because you're not allowed to be rude in social situations even when you think rudeness is called for, unless they also think rudeness is called for. You can't be argumentative. When playing mixed doubles you can't argue about line calls.

You can't wear mismatched clothes, even in the interests of being perversely defiant. You're not allowed to wear cowboy hats. You're not allowed to make fun of your mate's cowboy hat, despite it being a ridiculous form of headwear. You can't wear sloppy clothes at home without hearing some sort of comment on it. You can't sleep in the T-shirt you've had since college, it's ratty. You can't wear plaid, even though it's bohemian. You can't go clothes shopping alone if the other person doesn't trust your taste. You can't underdress for an occasion. If known to be indifferent to such things, you're not allowed to leave the house without passing inspection. You can't wear something that makes you look too sexy (or too dumpy, or not age appropriate). You can't dress up more than the partner is dressed up; you can't be more casual. You can't wear jeans if they think jeans are tacky.

You can't drink more than X amount when out together, even if you know you can "handle it." You can't drink without the other person counting your drinks. You can't bum cigarettes because it embarrasses the mate, even though you explain about the unspoken fraternity between smokers. You can't not "fit in." You must not dance because you're a terrible dancer (according to the mate; you happen to disagree). You can't leave a place before they're ready to go. You can't be late, even if you prefer being late. You can't dawdle. You can't lose track of time, especially when engaged in something that doesn't involve the mate, like your email. You can't forget things and then go back in the house for them once the door is closed. You can't drive too fast, or faster than the mate defines as fast. You can't tailgate, you can't honk. You may not criticize the other person's driving, signaling, or lane-changing habits. You can't listen to talk radio in the car. You can't get angry when driving, or swear at other drivers. You can't return the rent-a-car without throwing out the garbage because the mate thinks it looks bad, even if you insist that cleaning the car is rolled into the rates.

Thus is love obtained.

Such commands may be acceded to voluntarily, they may be negotiated settlements, or they may be the subject of ongoing friction. You go along with them to make your partner happy, or maybe you pick your battles, but primarily you go along (and they with you) because that's how best to preserve the couple. The less reconciled either party is to "being part of the team," the more of a loner or renegade anyone might be, the more friction in the household. The point isn't to pronounce judgment on whether or which such demands are "reasonable"—because the content doesn't matter. What matters is the form. What matters is that the operative word is *can't,* and that virtually no aspect of everyday life is not subject to regulation and review, and that in modern love acceding to a mate's commands is what constitutes intimacy, and that the "better" the couple the more the inhabitants have successfully internalized the operative local interdictions. What were once commands are now second nature. But once again, it's your choice. Or would be, if any of us could *really* choose not to desire love.

Certainly domesticity offers innumerable rewards, this we all know: companionship, shared housing costs, child-rearing convenience, reassuring predictability, occasional sex, insurance against the destabilizing effects of non-domestic desire, and many other benefits too varied to list. But if modern love has power over us, domesticity is its enforcement wing: the iron dust mop in the velvet glove. Historian Michel Foucault has argued that modern power made its mark on the world by inventing new types of enclosures and institutions—factories, schools, barracks, prisons, asylums—where individuals could be located, supervised, processed, known, subjected to inspection, order, and the clock. Although Foucault did not get around to the subject in his lifetime unfortunately, what current social institution is more enclosed than modern domesticity? What offers greater regulation of movement and time, or more precise surveillance of body and thought to a greater number of individuals?*

Exchanging obedience for love comes naturally—we were all once children after all, whose survival depended on the caprices of love. And thus you have the template for future intimacies: if you love me, you'll do what I want or need or demand to make me feel secure and complete and I'll love you back. Thus we grow to demand obedience in our turn, we household dictators and petty tyrants of the private sphere, who are in our turn, dictated to, *"If you love me you won't argue about it."* But as we all know (far too well), the fear and pain of losing love is so crushing, and so basic to our natures, that just about any trade-off to prevent it can seem reasonable. And thus you have the psychological signature of the modern self: defined by love, an empty vessel without it, the threat of love's withdrawal shriveling even the most independent spirits into complacency (and, of course, *ressentiment*).

---

*Considering that he'd already dealt with asylums, prisons, and sex, what could have been next? (There were intimations he was getting there—he did once remark that the best moment of love is riding home in the taxi afterward.)

And why has modern love developed in such a way as to maximize submission and minimize freedom, with so little argument about it? No doubt a citizenry schooled in renouncing desires—and whatever quantities of imagination and independence they come partnered with—would be, in many respects, advantageous: note that the conditions of lovability are remarkably convergent with those of a cowed workforce and a docile electorate. But if the most elegant forms of social control are those that come packaged in the guise of individual needs and satisfactions, so wedded to the individual psyche that any opposing impulse registers as the anxiety of unlovability, who needs a policeman on every corner? How very convenient that we're so willing to police ourselves and those we love, and call it living happily ever after.

Perhaps a secular society needed another metaphysical entity to subjugate itself to after the death of God, and love was available for the job. But isn't it a little depressing to think we're somehow incapable of inventing forms of emotional life based on anything other than subjugation?

ANN; DEATH AND THE MAIDEN

David Lazar

When O. J. Simpson was leading the police on the errant chase on that freeway in L.A., I was in Madison Square Garden in New York, at the famous Knicks playoff game where the monitors switched to the chase, to our astonishment, but it didn't register as surreally or wildly as it might have otherwise because I had been in the middle of telling my brother about Ann.

I was a young professor, thirty-seven, and she was an older doctoral student, thirty-four, and we had fallen for each other, and I thought it was going to be a big deal, in the way you know that someone is going to come into your life and the tectonics are going to change. I thought she might just be the girl for me, excuse the language, and was all aquiver in telling my brother the news, must have felt, I suppose in thinking back on it now, rather certain about my feelings, and about it, which is to say the prospects of where this new thing was headed.

Ann killed herself about a year and a half ago. The details are vague because no one seems terribly willing to yield them up. She had attempted suicide a few years before, slitting her wrists, but she was discovered or didn't quite go through with it—I'm not quite remembering which. It was serious enough for hospitalization—terrible, terrible, but not life-threatening, at least not the cuts.

She had been on a downward trajectory for years.

I haven't been able to quite stop thinking about her or to quite think about her since I heard about her death: the once promising career, writing about Virginia Woolf, that heavy eastern Kentucky accent, laden with irony and graceful goodwill. Her extraordinary recklessness. Her generosity. A bit like Zelda Fitzgerald gone in self-immolation. She was manic-depressive, as probably was Zelda. She looked a bit like Zelda, gamine and dark eyed. When I say I haven't been able to quite think about her, I mean that as much as she comes into my mind, a kind of creaturely sharp pain accompanies the thought of her, and I jump away as though I had laid my hand on a hot stove.

Twenty years ago an affaire de coeur between a professor and a graduate student not her or his own was not much of a deal in many places. In some places, geographical outposts, even encouraged. Younger, post-Internet readers perhaps won't quite understand the human urgencies of being alone and being isolated among rolling hills and aging colleagues in the earlier days of academe. To this sector of audience, the emotional premise of my memory might seem politically nauseating. What can I say except I understand, times change, etc. People communed where possible, even when the tincture of taboo tinted the edges of relation. They still do.

We met furtively at first, after a series of notes she had sent me toward the end of a seminar. We did meet, I must stress, after the seminar ended. But, and I suppose this is among the reasons I turn to writing these things, to see what repressed details show their hoary heads, I remember now that she was actually separated and moving toward a divorce from her third husband. But they hadn't actually, which is to say formally, made plans to divorce yet. That, no doubt, was part of our film noirish meetings in back alleys and cheap motels. It was one thing to date an available graduate student of one's own age. Quite another to be perceived (albeit wrongly) as a homewrecker, sharpest edge of a triangle.

We decided to go for a road trip. We would go to Louisville, Kentucky, to see George Carlin and stay in the Brown Hotel. What could be more alluring: how could I refuse a hotel whose history contains Lily Pons, Al Jolson, Marie of Romania, and Joan Crawford? I was hooked. I remember nothing of the drive there. And I do remember George Carlin then (this would have been around 1995) as harsh, funny, brilliant. I loved all his phases, even his dark, more existentially accusatory last phase. The drive back from Louisville to Athens, Ohio, was kaleidoscopically strange. Ann talked, virtually without pause, for the entire ten hours. I remember trying, at various times, to get a word, a question, a pithy aside, in, to virtually no avail. She was the Louisville Southern Railroad, and nothing was going to derail her. At the end of ten completely confusing hours, I felt like my head was going to explode; we finally made it back to my house in Ohio. Ann crashed, badly. Inconsolable, on my bed, she could only speak about the blackness of the world and how miserably unnecessary most things in life were.

Well, the virtue of love, one supposes, is sympathy. I didn't bail as she told me that she was bipolar since of course that was beyond her control, and she had been the person I had fallen for, which the scary blip in the car didn't seem to have altered. But a second item concerned me more: she had been prescribed lithium but didn't want to take it because she put on weight on lithium. As she put it in her eastern Kentucky accent, "Honey, it makes my stomach all poochy." I never liked that last word; it sounded like she had a small dachshund in there.

This was before the flood of memoirs, articles, etc., . . . about bipolarity, so I was only vaguely aware of what it meant. I imagine I looked it up. I know we talked about it quite a bit, Ann and me. I also know that she was adamant about not treating it clinically, despite her own misgivings about doing so. Like many manic-depressives, she was more than a little addicted to her mania, despite the price she paid with her depression. I have hundreds of pages of letters that she wrote to me—this was still the era of physical correspondence, and Ann was both intellectually and emotionally engaged with the epistle, Woolf's, Millay's, her own, and would pour out letter after letter to me, really lovely missives at first, before, over the three years we spent together, they turned first melancholy, then accusatory, occasionally incoherent, at times, rarely, strange, spooky. While never explicitly self-threatening, there was a just-wasn't-made-for-these-times, shouldn't-be-here note she would hit, which would give me chills. When we would reconcile, she would laugh it all off: "Honey, don't make too much of it."

It's almost too painful to admit this, but I had a glimmer that she was dead from Facebook. This was about two years ago, and she and I hadn't spoken for about a year but had thrown a few messages back and forth about how we were overdue, as though we were desultory library books that someone had forgotten to levy fines on. A post on her web page had struck a valedictory note that gave me pause, and there hadn't been any other posts for a long time. I'll tell you exactly what I did: I went to Google and typed in Ann ________ obituary, and it came right up, the details of her death, the service in Ashland, Kentucky, at the Lazar funeral home. I really did think I had snapped for a moment. Then, what's a Lazar doing in Ashland, Kentucky? As they say, as we say, you can't write this stuff. But more to the point, there was that sudden feeling that something is missing in the world that you suspected had been missing in the world. It isn't quite confirmation; it's more like a very sudden and ruthless sense that your teenaged angst-ridden feeling that absolutely nothing mattered was completely to the point. A feeling of nothingness, absolute degree zero.

Things started to fall apart between us rather quickly. Rather than take her lithium, Ann self-medicated with drinking. And I'll tell you, I joined the party. We drank like the proverbial fishes. There were wonderful nights. Lots of sex, lots of talk. Lots of music and dancing. But also: lots of *Who's Afraid of Virginia Woolf?* After a while I think we refined bitter repartee down to the point where Albee had nothing on us. We even had the missing child, since I very much wanted one, and she couldn't have one and refused to consider the idea of adopting one. And what would any relationship purgatory be without a parade of others?

I think Ann knew, fairly early, that her instability was difficult for me to hold on to. So, like any R(r)omantic, she went all out to make things impossible.

Polymorphous Ann, in a state you'd kiss a telephone pole while looking over your shoulder to see if I were witnessing it in sorrow or pain. Can you imagine the scenes? Have you versions of your own? They were intense and recriminatory and full of a sense of the inevitable. I remember trudging off to a party one night after a particularly cute ronde of accusations, whose against whose escapes me, but we were determined to socialize in the way that younger people think that socializing while miserable is part of some dark gospel of experience. Our general dark economy of failure and heartbreak meant that I could usually get the better of her (though just) through daggers of insinuation and insult, whereas she would always one-up me through behavioral outrageousness. In short, no matter what I would *say* to try to let some of the blood drain from my wounds (and in the process from her heart), she could *do* something to wound me further, deeper, more painfully. At this particular party (which could have been Anyparty) no sooner did I have my coat off, reaching, rather desperately, for my first drink of the night—there, I should specify—than I noted one of my colleague's arms around her, stroking her back, her head leaning toward or into him. Feeling my gaze—the point, of course—she turned and gave me one of those looks, or rather, not one of, because I think of it as distinctly hers, so heartbreaking was it, so incapable was I of responding to it at the time, a look that would have done Henry James proud, part hopeful and part self-loathing, part pleading and part lower-grade spite. In the spirit of sinking to the occasion, I shrugged a shoulder and turned away, walked off. Is there such a thing as having the final gesture? What's final, after all? I suppose when I spotted them making out in his car later that night I might have asked the same question.

Writing this makes me queasy, I hope for obvious reasons. Not because I care particularly about giving details about my own brazen bad behavior. Well, brazen? I was in the middle of an insoluble dilemma, seeing a wild, wonderful woman who wouldn't control her demons, her mis-chemistry.

If ever anyone I've known had a sense of determinism, a fatalistic sense that things were going to go badly, it was Ann. In this, however, or the way she carried this, she was very nouvelle vague-ish, very light on the *we're all damned so let's all have a damn good time.* She managed to pull it off because she meant it, because she was sincere. It didn't come across as a superficial quality, her carpe diem. And I'm not reading backward from her death. I'm reading backward from a closely remembered sense that her death was waiting up ahead, not very far up ahead, for her to be cast in its light. She was a postmortem avant la lettre but with a kind of wicked gaiety. It you've never been around anyone who created that kind of dark vortex, of wit and energy, of the world as our own small apocalypse just waiting to collapse on us, of the contradictory pressures of having to actually succeed at something colliding with a sense of the utter temporal meaninglessness of trying to do much of anything, you may have some sense of the cosmic charge of their pull, why that hand of theirs reaching out of the whirlpool seems more attractive as a way to be pulled in than as a moral imperative to save the drowning, though that, too, is listed on your day's list of things to do. But when they hand you your glass of bourbon and sit in your lap and say, "So, honey, let's talk about us and *Orlando* and the end of the world," you're hard-pressed not to set your stopwatch to Finis. This was her effect on me, a sense of not caring about consequence or time. It was liberating and horrifying, destructive, intense.

We really liked each other. We were quite hot for each other. After some dark night of the relational soul, when things were said that never should have been thought and one of us had threatened to leave for our cars, after three or seven martinis or shots of Jack Daniel's—rather vain threat, or was it? those were the days when I still might have done something that stupid—she would break the tension with a sexual tease, some honey-dripped request to scratch her back, or she would merely start laughing, which would infect my infected rage and break it.

One time she came with me back to New York, a family visit, and we planned a day walking around the city, museums and such. She wore high black heels, which I suggested was a bad idea. "Honey, I can't walk around New York in anything less than stylish shoes." By the end of the day, she couldn't walk, feet cramped, I—well, I was younger and full of reasons to be pissed off. You can be angry about anything if you're tending toward anger with someone. Nothing much will make you angry if you don't want to be angry. Oh, the delightful perquisites of age. I was annoyed as she walked barefoot down Sixth Avenue toward Penn Station, an image I now find equally winsome, delightful, heartbreaking. My own inability, at the time, to be charmed, though I haven't the slightest doubt I wanted to be and wouldn't let myself, is beyond unnerving. And you can't reminisce apologetically with her. But to whom am I speaking, other than a sentimentally guilty conscience?

One year I gathered my family in Ohio for Thanksgiving, the only time we've been together for the holiday in the thirty-five years since my mother's death. This detail overweighs the story from the outset, but that was my experience. I cooked everything, for fifteen people. I should have known trouble lay ahead. I mean, how many movies had I seen? My father and his wife arrived first, and a freak snowstorm hit. They decided to walk in the picturesque paths near my house; except that five feet away from the house, my father's wife slipped and broke her wrist. Emergency room. Weekend in pain.

Ann arrived with a good head start on being pickled. That part's okay—drink during the holidays. Sometimes I think the best thing about the holidays is an excuse for having a drink in the afternoon. Sometimes I don't need an excuse for having a drink in the afternoon, but during the holidays it's like a free pass. But Ann started hitting the bourbon hard after that. My most vivid memory of the day was of being in the kitchen, adjacent to the dining room, where everyone had started gathering, and cracking the door to see what was up. Ann was sitting astraddle a chair, skirt hitched up, and I caught her saying, to my father, REALLY LOUDLY, "I don't see the problem with my dating a Jew."

I closed the door and grabbed a bottle myself. The only other thing I remember is getting her a ride home early and a slightly wounded expression she gave me—kind of toasted, sardonic and hurt.

Why am I writing about Ann? Why am I thinking about Ann? Guilt is a privilege of the living. And it's certainly one of my defaults, one of the feelings I leap toward, or is it crawl into? whenever pressed, even when or perhaps especially when the pressing is internal. An old familiar and, yes, in some ways an easy one. I've always argued that going toward darker feelings too quickly, too easily, is just as sentimental as Hallmark brightness. Why do I feel so automatically guilty about Ann, why, for example, in this essay, while mentioning her wildness, her mania, skimming over what became a kind of tic toward betrayal ("I only fuck you over because I love you so much, and I'm afraid I can't really have you"), do I feel like I betrayed *her,* that I'm somehow responsible for the hole I feel in the world, the absence of her, even though we were not so much in touch?

It isn't that we were not so much in touch. Nor do I think I'm suffering from the delusion that I could have "saved" her, though I may be in a bit of denial about that. After we broke up, I had one of my scariest dreams ever. I was in my house, with the woman I was going to marry (rather quickly) and later divorce (rather belatedly), and dreamed that Ann was something like a witch, or perhaps a daemon, a very powerful and dark spirit who was trying to break into, or gain entry into, the house. The entire house was surrounded by the suffocating air of her presence, and the door was creaking at her hot breath, which would melt the locks. Should she enter, terrible things would happen. That's what was so awful about the dream, the lack of specificity—terrible, terrible things would happen, like I had never experienced before, and all would become horror and loss.

Just as the door was giving way, I woke up. And the house was quiet, and the woman next to me was quietly sleeping. Ann was miles away, presumably in her bed. The woman next to me would cause me much more harm than the figure in my dreams.

But Ann figured for me . . . as a loss of control. I have managed, barely, to keep things together through the years of my adult life—doing all the things one needs to do. And I think the face I show to the world is a very functional one. Yet I frequently feel as though I were a breath away from losing it, and I've wondered all my adult life what it would be like to let all caution, all responsibility, all care for self and public esteem, go. I seem to have gravitated frequently to people who were very irresponsible. My dear friend Tony, dead this spring of a heart attack—and he just a month younger than I—spent much of the last thirty years wearing down his body with vodka. First he was just drinking a lot. Then he was married with kids and was passing out in the street. There were interventions, rehabs, and he couldn't keep a job or finish his degree, and he just kept falling and falling and breaking things and turning his insides into a stew. And he died alone of a heart attack in a motel in Vermont a few months ago. He called me drunk all the time. He called all his friends drunk all the time. We stopped taking the calls because who had the time to hear Tony go on and on and not listen to a word you'd said? But he'd sober up, and we'd talk, and I'd see him when I went to New York, at his apartment on Ninth Street.

Once I tried to surprise him on New Year's Eve. The doorman shook his head and waved me in. Tony's doorway was ajar, and I found him naked on the floor, moaning like Caliban, looking like Caliban, bloated and dirty. I got him covered and over to the sofa. We talked for a bit. And I said, "Tony, you have to clean up." That was it. As messed up as he was, he threw me out.

But we talked a few days later. When you know someone for decades, it's like that.

Have I been a flaneur of some of my own darkest impulses with some of my friends and a woman I've loved, being close enough to my own worst-case scenarios to feel their hot breath while watching others take the heat? That would be too hard on myself, and thus too easy, though it's also not completely untrue as my own psychic précis.

After Ann and I moved into a *post-relationship but still who knows what's going on* state, I was in a rather dark place. I may have left a lot of bottles at her place, but I hardly left the bottle. Trying not to hit something in the road (like a projection of her face over Myrna Loy's? or a vision of her walking into a room with her cheekbones flaring?), I flipped my car three times and almost died. I was on my way to a liaison with another woman, but I had them call her and my best friend from the hospital. Apparently, I do have a bit of a problem with guilt. When the doctor came to sew up the cut over my eye, I told him not to use any anesthesia (I was still in shock). They all looked at me like I was mad.

Occasionally, after a cooling-down period, while I still lived in Ohio, I would meet Ann for lunch. And then she moved back to Kentucky, too distracted to keep working on the PhD, got a job at a high school, was fired. We talked on the phone occasionally. She was funny, incredibly sweet, every time sounding a little more broken. She'd always say that her craziness with me was her biggest regret, which was, I think, supposed to make me feel better but somehow always made me feel worse.

Ann, I think, felt the sting of her lost promise. As I and a few of the people who loved her do. But disappointing oneself is worse than anything else. She fled to Florida, was seeing a considerably older physician, in whose bathroom, apparently, she attempted to cut her wrists. She survived with a sense of ignominy added on to everything else.

She would always ask about my son and with a genuine interest and sweetness that made me think of her insistence that she didn't want children. But then I have to remind myself that there is a difference between not wanting children and thinking oneself incapable of raising them. Most of the people I know who are choosing childlessness are doing so because they simply do not want children, a perfectly respectable choice, if one inimical to my own essential emotional character. If anything in my life has given me consistent joy and satisfaction, it's child rearing. I've arguably been a bit of a washout at relationships, at least romantic relationships. But I seem to be pretty good at the parenting thing.

Ann, however, thought herself an impossible mother. I forget that. And I think at the time of our relationship I fused or confused that belief with her having some hostility to kids. Absurd. She was lovely with kids. But in her imagination she would have ended up the crazy mother, incapable of caring for her charge or charges. Who knows which of our decisions are sane, self-knowing appraisals of our shortcomings, and which are self-rationalizing justifications of what we really want? Half the time they overlap. Or as Yogi Berra might say, "Half the time they're 75 percent the same thing."

We talked, but then there were gaps. I'm sure you can traipse through your own spotty relational paths, filled with friendship sinkholes in which people you care about manage nevertheless to disappear, drop away for periods of time as you attend to your children, your books, your winter clothes, and your mortgages. It was during a fall, a winter, when I was listlessly trying to get in touch with her that I found out there would be no more getting in touch with her. This is a new category of social experience, the Facebook memento mori, and it makes me queasy, I must say, the way pages linger on after death like newspaper stories from the past that people can make continual addenda to, but why? . . . I understand the argument that they remain as monuments of a sort, although, I think, of a rather desultory sort. An editor of mine lingers on in my contacts after death, as do Ann and one or two others, their pages a form of accidental literary cryogenics.

Someone had written something on Ann's page about not forgetting her. That's what sent me racing to the obituaries, marked with my own name.

I've been listening to "Death and the Maiden" as I write this. I listen to Schubert a reasonable amount, the *Winterreise,* the *Impromptus* . . . and I was reminded of how much I loved the Quintet in D Minor recently when I was watching *Crimes and Misdemeanors* with my son. It's so muscular in its tragic overtones and so unrelenting in its oceanic grief, its continually enlarging beauty of unknowing that signifies the end, which is the end of music. The motif began as early as 1517, in Hans Baldung Grien's "Death and the Maiden," a mournful young woman pulled by her hair by the skeleton of doom, and then there are countless variations through the Renaissance, in the Romantic era. . . . One of my favorites is Adolf Hering's "Death and the Maiden" (1900), in which the scantily clad fin de siècle nymph is in a swoon, about to be romantically devoured by the black-shrouded figure, the Ur-mourner who devours what he wants, Death as Dracula, an obvious connection, turning our fears of dissolution into, ironically, a gothic nightmare of endless life. Talk about displacement.

Speaking of displacement, in *Crimes and Misdemeanors* the difficult woman, the troubled woman, is killed by Martin Landau, the Jewish man, to the strains of "Death and the Maiden." Unlike the character of Judah, I haven't killed anyone, but ironically, while Judah realizes that he can shake off his burden of guilt in a godless world, continue with his life, his family, I find my own sense of guilt less labile, more burdensome. The older I get, the less interested I find myself in changing feelings that, even if harrowing, are still somehow true to my essential nature or some part of a series of experiences that jibe with my sense of emotional necessity. One could say I want to keep feeling them because feeling them seems emotionally right, even if neurotic in a classic sense, and thus truer to me. Does this classify them as "sentimental" according to my earlier definition? Perhaps.

I feel responsible for Ann's death, as though if she hadn't met me, she would have been better off. Yes, who can possibly know this kind of thing? Who can rewind and untangle the currents of necessity and self-determination? Who can predict the pitiless fortunes or absurd graces of those who come into and out of our orbits? Who can keep friends and lovers alive when they won't take their medicine or won't put down their bottles? Who can forgive in just the right measure and with transcendent language? Seriously, tell me—I mean it. I'm easy to find. I spend half my days sitting around waiting for a knock on the door, someone standing there with a paper full of accusations. They would always all be just.

DEAR FRIEND, FROM MY LIFE I WRITE TO YOU IN YOUR LIFE

Yiyun Li

1.

My first encounter with *before and after* was in one of the fashion magazines my friends told me to subscribe to when I came to America. I duly followed their advice—I had an anthropologist's fascination with America then. I had never seen a glossy magazine, and the print and paper quality, not to mention the trove of perfumes waiting to be unfolded, made me wonder how the economics of the magazine worked, considering I paid no more than a dollar for an issue.

My favorite column was on the last page of the magazine, and it featured celebrity makeovers—hairstyle and hair color, for instance—with two bubbles signifying before and after. I didn't often have an opinion about the transformation, but I liked the definitiveness of that phrase, *before and after,* with nothing muddling the in-between.

After years of living in America, I still feel a momentary elation whenever I see advertisements for weight-loss programs, teeth-whitening strips, hair-loss treatments, or plastic surgery with the contrasting effects shown under *before* and *after*. The certainty in that pronouncement—for each unfortunate or inconvenient situation, there is a solution to make it no longer be—both attracts and perplexes me. Life can be reset, it seems to say; time can be separated. But that logic appears to me as unlikely as traveling to another place to become a different person. Altered sceneries are at best distractions, or else new settings for old habits. What one carries from one point to another, geographically or temporally, is one's self. Even the most inconsistent person is consistently himself.

2.

I was leaving to teach class when an acquaintance who lived across the country in New Hampshire called my office. She had traveled to a nearby city. I talked to her for no more than two minutes before telling my husband to go find her. He spent twelve hours with her, canceled her business appointments, and saw to it that she flew back home. Two weeks later her husband called and said she had jumped out of her office on a Sunday evening. He asked me to attend her memorial service. I thought for a long time and decided not to.

Our memories tell more about now than then. Doubtless the past is real. There is no shortage of evidence: photos, journals, letters, old suitcases. But we choose and discard from an abundance of evidence what suits us at the moment. There are many ways to carry the past with us: to romanticize it, to invalidate it, to furnish it with revised or entirely fictionalized memories. The present does not surrender so easily to manipulation.

I don't want the present to judge the past, so I don't want to ponder my absence at her memorial service. We had come to this country around the same time. When I told her that I was going to quit science to become a writer, she seemed curious, but her husband said that it was a grave mistake. Why do you want to make your life difficult? he asked.

3.

I have had a troublesome relationship with time. The past I cannot trust because it could be tainted by my memory. The future is hypothetical and should be treated with caution. The present—what is the present but a constant test: in this muddled in-between one struggles to understand what about oneself has to be changed, what accepted, what preserved. Unless the right actions are taken, one seems never to pass the test to reach the after.

4.

After the second of two hospital stays following a difficult time, I went to a program for those whose lives have fallen apart. Often someone would say—weeping, shaking, or dry-eyed—that he or she wished to go back in time and make everything right again.

I wished, too, that life could be reset, but reset from when? From each point I could go to an earlier point: warning signs neglected, mistakes aggregated, but it was useless to do so, as I often ended up with the violent wish that I had never been born.

I was quiet most of the time, until I was told I was evasive and not making progress. But my pain was my private matter, I thought; if I could understand and articulate my problems I wouldn't have been there in the first place.

Do you want to share anything, I was prompted when I had little to offer. By then I felt my hope had run out. I saw the revolving door admitting new people and letting old people out into the world; similar stories were told with the same remorse and despair; the lectures were on the third repeat. What if I were stuck forever in that basement room? I broke down and could feel a collective sigh: my tears seemed to prove that finally I intended to cooperate.

I had only wanted to stay invisible, but there as elsewhere invisibility is a luxury.

5.

I have been asked throughout my life: What are you hiding? I don't know what I am hiding, and the more I try to deny it, the less trustworthy people find me. My mother used to comment on my stealthiness to our guests. A woman in charge of admission at the public bathhouse often confronted me, asking what I was hiding from her. Nothing, I said, and she would say she could tell from my eyes that I was lying.

Reticence is a natural state. It is not hiding. People don't show themselves equally and easily to all. Reticence doesn't make one feel as lonely as hiding does, yet it distances and invalidates others.

6.

There are five time zones in China, but the nation uses a unified time—Beijing time. When the hour turns, all radio stations sound six beeps, followed by a solemn announcement: "At the last beep, it is Beijing time seven o'clock sharp." This memory is reliable because it does not belong to me but to generations of Chinese people, millions of us: every hour, the beeping and the announcement were amplified through loudspeakers in every People's Commune, school, army camp, and apartment complex.

But underneath this steadfastness, time is both intrusive and elusive. It does not leave us alone even in our most private moments. In every thought and feeling about life, time claims a space. When we speak of indecision, we are unwilling to let go of a present. When we speak of moving on—what a triumphant phrase—we are cutting off the past. And if one seeks kindness from time, it slips away tauntingly, or worse, with indifference. How many among us have said that to others or to ourselves: if only I had a bit more time. . . .

7.

One hides something for two reasons: either one feels protective of it or one feels ashamed of it. And it is not always the case that the two possibilities can be separated. If my relationship with time is difficult, if time is intrusive and elusive, could it be that I am only hiding myself from time?

I used to write from midnight to four o'clock. I had young children then, various jobs (from working with mice to working with cadaver tissue to teaching writing), and an ambition to keep writing separate from my *real* life. When most people were being ferried across the night by sleep, unaware of time, unaware of weather, I felt the luxury of living on the cusp of reality.

Night for those sound sleepers was a cocoon against time. For me, I wanted to believe, it was even better. Time, at night, was my possession, not the other way around.

8.

A friend came to see me when I visited Beijing in 2008. We talked about her real estate investments and our old schoolmates. Half an hour after she left my parents' apartment, she called. She hadn't wanted to mention it in person, but a boy who had been close to me when we were teenagers had committed suicide, along with a lover.

My first reaction was wonderment, that my friend would wait until we were out of each other's sight to tell me. My next reaction was still wonderment, as though I had always been waiting for this news.

Our dead friend had had an affair, and both he and the woman had gone through difficult divorces only to be ostracized as adulterers.

It'd have been better had he gone to America, my friend said.

Why, I asked. In college he had already been doing well as a self-taught designer. Often he would include with his letters cut-out ads from newspapers and magazines: brand-name garments, imported mints, cashmeres. He was someone who would have made a good life in the country's developing economy.

My friend sighed. You're the only one more impractical than he was, she said; you should know this is not a country for dreamers.

My friendship with the boy existed largely in correspondence. It was a different era, thoughts and feelings traveling by mail, urgency conveyed by telegrams. My family did not have a telephone until I was in college; email came much later, when I was in America. I still remember the days when the engine of a motorcycle disturbed the quietest night—only a telegram announcing a death or a looming one would permit such an intrusion. Letters, especially those bearing too many stamps, carried the weight of friendship.

I can recall only a few things from those letters: a crush on the girl sitting next to him in class; a Chekhovian political satire he wrote, featuring Gorbachev and an East German general and a pistol going off in act three—this was in 1988, and Communism still retained its hold on part of Europe. It was in that year too that we last saw each other.

But I do remember that before he found an outlet for his artistic obsession and sent those profitable ads, he had dreamed up, designed, and named endless car models; there had also been odd assortments of pistols, rifles, spacecraft, and household appliances, as well as abstract graphics. All the drawings were meticulously done, sometimes in their fifth or sixth drafts, and their detail used to fill me with awe and impatience.

Perhaps when I say I was expecting his suicide, it is only memory going back to revise itself. There is no reason an artistic and sensitive boy could not grow into a happy man. Where and how things went amiss with him I do not know, though even as a teenager, I recognized his despondency when at school the production of his play earned him jeers and a special exhibition of his car designs estranged him from his classmates. He was the kind of person who needed others to feel his existence.

9.

A dreamer: it's the last thing I want to be called, in China or in America. No doubt when my friend in Beijing used the term, she was thinking of traits like persistence, single-mindedness, willfulness, and—particularly—impracticality, which she must have seen plenty of in me. Still, that one possesses a dreamer's personality and that one has dreams do not guarantee that one knows how to dream.

The woman in New Hampshire and I, and many like us, came to this country with the same goal—to make a new life here. I wouldn't call it a dream, not even an ambition. She had followed the scientist's path and had a secure job at a biomedical company. I had drifted away, choosing a profession that makes hiding less feasible, if indeed I am a habitual hider.

I don't wonder what my life would have been had I stayed in China: not leaving had never felt like an option. For a decade there had been a concrete *after* ingrained in everything I did. The day I arrived in America I would become a new person.

But there is the possibility that I might never have taken up writing. Had I remained a scientist, would I have turned out differently—calmer, less troubled, more sensible? Would I have stopped hiding, or become better at it?

10.

A few months before my friend's suicide, he had found me on the Internet. In his email he told me about his divorce, and I told him about giving up science for writing. He wrote back, "I congratulate you. You've always been a dreamer, but America has made your dream come true."

Someone described me onstage as an example of the American dream. Certainly I have done that too, putting myself on a poster of *before* and *after*. The transformation, however, is as superficial and deceitful as an ad placed on the back of a bus.

Time will tell, people say, as though time always has the last word. Perhaps I am only hiding from time as I have been hiding from those who want the power to have the last word about others.

11.

I would have liked to be called a dreamer had I known how to dream. The sense of being an impostor, I understand, occurs naturally, and those who do not occasionally feel so I find untrustworthy. I would not mind being taken as many things I am not: a shy person, a cheerful person, a cold person. But I do not want to be called a dreamer when I am far from being a real one.

12.

What I admire and respect in a dreamer: her confidence in her capacities, her insusceptibility to the frivolous, and her faith that the good and the real shall triumph and last. There is nothing selfish, dazzling, or preposterous about dreamers; in everyday life they blend in rather than stand out, though it's not hiding. A real dreamer has a mutual trust with time.

Apart from feeling unqualified to be called a dreamer, I may also be worrying about being mistaken for one of those who call themselves dreamers but are merely ambitious. One meets them often in life, their ambitions smaller than dreams, more commonplace, in need of broadcasting and dependent on recognition from this particular time. If they cause pain to others, they have no trouble writing off those damages as the cost of their dreams. Timeliness may be one thing that separates ambitions from real dreams.

13.

The woman in New Hampshire was neither a dreamer nor an ambitious person. She had hoped for a solid and uneventful life in an American suburb, but loneliness must have made her life a desert.

My dead friend in Beijing was ambitious because he understood his talents; he had dreams, too. I must have been part of his dreams once—why else would he have written if not to seek kinship with another dreamer.

14.

I came to this country as an aspiring immunologist. I had chosen the field—if one does not count the practical motives of wanting a reason to leave China and of having a skill to make a living—because I had liked the working concept of the immune system. Its job is to detect and attack nonself; it has memories, some as long-lasting as life; its memories can go awry selectively, or, worse, indiscriminately, leading the system to mistake self as foreign, as something to eliminate. The word *immune* (from the Latin *immunis, in- + munia,* services, obligations) is among my favorites in the English language, the possession of immunity—to illnesses, to follies, to love and loneliness and troubling thoughts and unalleviated pains—a trait that I have desired for my characters and myself, knowing all the while the futility of such a wish. Only the lifeless can be immune to life.

15.

One's intuition is to acquire immunity to those who confirm one's beliefs about life, and to those who turn one's beliefs into nothing. The latter are the natural predators of our hearts, the former made into enemies because we are, unlike other species, capable of not only enlarging but also diminishing our precarious selves.

16.

I had this notion, when I first started writing this, that it would be a way to test—to assay—thoughts about time. There was even a vision of an after, when my confusions would be sorted out.

Assays in science are part of an endless exploration. One question leads to another; what follows confirms or disconfirms what comes before. To assay one's ideas about time while time remains unsettled and elusive feels futile. Just as one is about to understand one facet of time, it presents another to undermine one's reasoning.

To write about a struggle amid the struggling: one must hope that this muddling will end someday.

17.

But what more do you want? You have a family, a profession, a house, a car, friends, and a place in the world. Why can't you be happy? Why can't you be strong? These questions are asked, among others, by my mother.

There was a majestic mental health worker in the second hospital where I stayed who came to work with perfect lipstick, shining curly hair, and bright blouses and flats of matching colors.

Young lady, she said every time she saw me, don't lose that smile of yours.

I had liked her, and liked her still after she questioned my spiritual life. I could see that the godless state of my mind concerned her, and that my compliance made me a good project. Don't mind her, my roommate, a black Buddhist, said; she has an evangelical background. I don't, I assured my roommate; being preached to did not bother me.

Then I had a difficult day. At dinnertime, the majestic woman asked, Young lady, why did you cry today?

I'm sad, I said.

We know you're sad. What I want to know is, what makes you sad?

Can't I just be left alone in my sadness? I said. The women around the table smiled into their plates. The good girl was having a tantrum.

18.

What makes you sad? What makes you angry? What makes you forget the good things in your life and your responsibilities toward others? One hides from people who ask these unanswerable questions only to ask them oneself again and again.

I know you don't like me to ask what's brought you here, my roommate said, but can you describe how you feel? I don't have words for how I feel.

I had several roommates—another revolving door—but I liked the last one. Raised in a middle-class African American family, she was the only adopted child among her siblings. She married for love, and on her wedding day, she realized she had made the mistake of her life. For the whole first dance he didn't look at me once, she said; he looked into every guest's face to make sure they knew it was his show.

By the time she told me this story, her husband was confined to bed and blind from diabetes. She took care of him along with a nurse. She watched TCM with him because he remembered the exchanges in old movies. Still, she said she was angry because everything in their life was about him.

Have you ever thought of leaving him? I asked.

She said she had throughout the marriage, but she would not. I don't want my children to grow up and think a man can be abandoned in that state, she said.

Yet she had tried to kill herself—an attempted abandonment of both her husband and her children. But this I did not say because it was exactly what many people would say to a situation like that. One has to have a solid self to be selfish.

19.

There is this emptiness in me. All the things in the world are not enough to drown out the voice of this emptiness that says: you are nothing.

This emptiness does not claim the past because it is always here. It does not have to claim the future as it blocks out the future. It is either a dictator or the closest friend I have ever had. Some days I battle it until we both fall down like injured animals. That is when I wonder: What if I become less than nothing when I get rid of this emptiness? What if this emptiness is what keeps me going?

20.

One day my roommate said she noticed I became quiet if she talked about Buddhism with me. I don't mean it as a religion, she said; for instance, you can try to meditate.

I did not explain that I had read Buddhist scriptures from the ages of twelve to twenty-three. For the longest time they offered the most comforting words. The teaching of nothingness diluted the intensity of that emptiness.

My father taught me meditation when I was eleven. Imagine a bucket between your open arms, he told me, and asked me to listen to the dripping of the water into the bucket and, when it was full, water dripping out from the bottom. "From empty to full, and from full to empty." He underlined the words in a book for me. "Life before birth is a dream, life after death is another dream. What comes between is only a mirage of the dreams."

21.

My father is the most fatalistic person I have ever known. He once admitted that he had not felt a day of peace in his marriage and expressed his regret that he had never thought of protecting my sister and me from our mother, who is a family despot, unpredictable in both her callousness and her vulnerability.

But the truth is, he tried to instill this fatalism in us because it was our only protection. For years I have been hiding behind that: being addicted to fatalism can make one look calm, capable, even happy.

22.

For a while I read Katherine Mansfield's notebooks to distract myself. "Dear friend, from my life I write to you in your life," she wrote in an entry. I cried when I read the line. It reminds me of the boy from years ago who could not stop sending the designs of his dreams in his letters. It reminds me too why I do not want to stop writing. The books one writes—past and present and future—are they not trying to say the same thing: *Dear friend, from my life I write to you in your life?* What a long way it is from one life to another, yet why write if not for that distance, if things can be let go, every *before* replaced by an *after*.

23.

It's not fatalism that makes one lose hope, I now understand. It's one's rebellion against fatalism; it's wanting to have one's time back from fatalism. A fatalistic person cannot be a dreamer, which I still want to become one day.

24.

"The train stopped. When a train stops in the open country between two stations it is impossible not to put one's head out of the window and see what's up," Mansfield wrote at the end of her life. This is the inevitability of life.

The train, for reasons unknown to us, always stops between a past and a future, both making this now look as though it is nowhere. But it is this nowhereness that one has to make use of. One looks out the window: the rice paddies and alfalfa fields have long been the past, replaced by vineyards and almond groves. One has made it this far; perhaps this is enough of a reason to journey on.

EXPERIENCE NECESSARY

Phillip Lopate

> There is nothing so beautiful and legitimate as to play the man well and properly, no knowledge so hard to acquire as the knowledge of how to live this life well and naturally; and the most barbarous of our maladies is to despise our being.
>
> —Montaigne, "Of Experience"

1.

"Of Experience" is Montaigne's last and, I insist, greatest essay. It inspires us with its wisdom and balance. Montaigne, like Goethe, had the knack—some would say the bad taste—of benefiting from his experience at every stage of life and achieving a calm, benign perspective with age. Which I can't entirely seem to do. I am approaching my seventieth birthday: three score and ten, the alleged fulfillment of a life span. I am still agitated, perplexed. I look back at all that has happened to me and it seems as though it were practically nothing. To quote the last line of Borges's poem on Emerson: "I have not lived. I want to be someone else."

2.

On the other hand, I want to be only myself. I think I know what I am about, am comfortable with that person, can distinguish good writing from bad, and decent human beings from jerks. Less and less do I feel the need to justify my conclusions. I carry myself in public with impervious self-confidence. (In private is another story.) My students look to me for answers, and I improvise—something that passes for adequate. Most of the dilemmas that shake these young people, their existential, religious, or romantic doubts, their future professional prospects, their worries that someone won't like them, roll off my back. It could be that I am just numbed, unable to summon the urgency behind what to them constitutes a crisis. Mine is the questionable wisdom of passivity. What I cannot change, I no longer let myself be insanely bothered by. Even the latest political folly elicits from me only a disgruntled shrug. I am more upset when my favorite sports team loses; but then I remind myself that it wasn't, technically, my fault since I lacked magical powers to alter the outcome.

3.

"Are you experienced?" asked Jimi Hendrix, tauntingly. Does he mean: have I slept with fifty groupies, humped a guitar onstage before adulating thousands, taken so many drugs that I risked dying from an overdose? In that sense, no I am not experienced.

4.

Otherwise, are you experienced? Hell, yes. I know the score. I wasn't born yesterday. I've been around the block a few times.

I can tell which way is up. You can't pull a fast one on me. You can't pull the wool over my eyes. I'm from Missouri; show me. I know a thing or two. I know which side my bread is buttered on. I'm hip. I'm sadder but wiser. I'm no fool. I have eyes in the back of my head. I can tell my left from my right. I know my ass from my elbow. I can see which way the wind blows. I have a pretty good idea. I've been through the mill. I've been around the world in a plane. I've seen it all. Now I've seen it all.

5.

"Detachment . . . is one of the forms that engagement with experience can take: things seen at a remove, appearing strange and so more clearly seen," writes the art historian Svetlana Alpers. Experience can mean plunging into dangerous war zones, witnessing tragedies under fire, like George Orwell at the Spanish front and Susan Sontag in Bosnia, or it can mean staying on the sidelines, exercising watchful prudence. Then there is the experience of ordinary humdrum life, what Virginia Woolf calls cotton wool, those moments of "nonbeing." Bring it on. As Bartleby might say, I prefer not to live at the highest pitch. I have always been a fan of bemused detachment. I am rather attached to the notion of detachment. I accept in advance the guilt for being detached, should any such guilt attach.

6.

"Of Experience" was, as I said, Montaigne's last essay. I wonder if this will be my last essay. I am running out of things to say. Moreover, I feel I have done my life's work as a writer. I have nothing more to prove. It is strange to have come to such a pass and be surrounded by friends and colleagues still pressing on, unsure whether they will have time enough to fulfill their appointed destinies. I have fulfilled a modest destiny modestly. I have done what I set out to do, and now linger on past my assignment. I can still visit museums and relish new movies or old books, can still enjoy a walk through unfamiliar parts of the city, can still participate in the delights, follies, and chagrins of family life, can still teach the young and hold forth in AWP panel discussions, but I don't want to work so hard at writing anymore. It's as if I have a form of post-traumatic stress disorder: all those years trying to meet the challenge of writing well have left me trembling, with a desire for peace and inactivity.

7.

There is an abundance of things I can't do now, and so probably will never do. I can't change a tire to save my life (although if it were a matter of life and death perhaps I could). I can't read sheet music or play the piano. I used to be able to read Hebrew but now I can't without committing lots of errors. I am a poor swimmer and can barely stay alive in the water. I don't run marathons, not because I couldn't, physically speaking, but because I can't *make* myself run a marathon. What I can't do and what I don't care to do are connected at the hip. I don't know Latin. I can't tell one tree or flowering shrub from another. I am at a loss as to how to identify the stars; in fact, my grasp of astronomy is so scant that I could say, with Charles Lamb, "I guess at Venus only by her brightness—and if the sun on some portentous morn were to make his first appearance in the West, I verily believe, that, while all the world were gasping in apprehension about me, I alone should stand unterrified, from sheer incuriosity and want of observation." My understanding of the way things work, including the laws of physics, is so pathetic it's a wonder I can navigate the world at all. I specialize in ignorance. "What *do* I know?" as Michel would say. It looks as though I won't have sex with a man in this lifetime. Experience has taught me to honor my indifference and my cowardice both. Put it this way: Experience has finally proved to be a school that trains me to limit my concerns and tolerate my limitations.

8.

One privilege of growing older is that you do not have to adjust to the new, or even wax excited about it. I remain a man of the twentieth century. Reluctantly dragged into the new millennium, I stay loyal to the previous one, hewing to the patterns I established then. For instance, I still read the print versions of newspapers and magazines, and dress respectably when I take an airplane. I avoid thinking about Facebook, Twitter, or texting or any such innovations—not that I deplore them, I have no high-minded objections to the new technology, I simply refuse to engage mentally with it. When I happen to glance at op-ed essays about the evolutionary danger these new forms of communication pose to humanist values, I stop reading the article forthwith, because I don't want to care enough about the phenomena even to be alarmed by them. I refuse to be topical. I am thus spared much wasted effort trying to write ingenious think pieces about the latest splash or gizmo.

Experience has also taught me to recognize that much of what passes for innovation is simply puffery, the product of public relations and short memories. In pop or high culture, the "edgy" turns out usually to be the recycling of a tired trope. Take androgyny: Marlene Dietrich wore her tux and kissed a woman on the lips; now Madonna or Lady Gaga does the same. Similarly S/M and black leather, fragmentation, jettisoning of narrative, scrambling of chronology, self-reflexive loops, Artaudian stage ritual, Khlebnikovian nonsense syllables, neo-Dadaist anti-art, Brechtian-Marxist alienation effects, and politically correct consciousness-raising of all stripes.

In my youth, I would read the pages of the *New York Times* Arts & Leisure section (it was called something different then, but no matter) with avid credulity, thinking I must make it a point to catch up with this filmmaker, painter, opera conductor, or theater production. Now I scan the bylines, and, knowing most of these arts journalists, whose opinions I don't particularly trust nor do I value their prose styles, hardworking though they may be, I spend more time musing about how they got the assignment than reading through their articles. Does that sound merely snotty, or qualify as a sign of experience?

9.

I have experienced enough in the way of people's strange behaviors not to be surprised by sudden breakouts of kindness, brutality, tenderness, betrayal, inconsistency, vanity, rigidity, schadenfreude and its opposite. What does surprise me is current events. When 9/11 happened I was taken aback by such a freakish thing. (It was, to me, no accident that 9/11 occurred on the other side of the millennium, in 2001: no good, I thought, can come of the twenty-first century. Not that the twentieth did not have its share of nasty surprises.) I continue to marvel at Republicans' seeming willingness to shut down the federal government, and allow the United States to default rather than negotiate with the president. I don't understand my country anymore: how, after a century of federal programs such as the New Deal, Social Security, bank regulation, public housing and food stamps, a large swath of the population can still take umbrage at the government's minimal efforts to protect the weak and the poor, or indeed to have a presence in any aspect of life beyond the maintenance of a military force. Nothing prior has prepared me for this frightening swerve. I grew up in the postwar atmosphere of a modestly progressive welfare state, where problems such as racial segregation and poverty were expected to be addressed at the governmental level, and I assumed naively that we were marching at best or creeping at worst toward a more just society. What I took for an inevitable historical progression turned out to be an anomalous blip. I might better have looked to Nietzsche's theory of eternal recurrence. Today I am less experienced, less able to adapt to this harshly selfish environment than the average twenty-year-old, who has grown up without my New Deal–Great Society set of expectations.

10.

Newspapers were once enormously important; now they're not. I am a creature of newspaper culture, therefore I'm no longer important. I'm redundant. I must learn to accept my redundancy, like Turgenev's superfluous man. Fortunately, I've had plenty of practice. I always anticipated I would be redundant, a cultural throwback, which is why I prepared by steeping myself in the antiquarian tomes of ages past, whose authors' names I suspected would mean next to nothing to future generations. When my writer friends in college were reading Beckett, Burroughs, and Pynchon, I was poring over Fielding, Machado de Assis, and Lady Murasaki. Later, when I discovered the joys of the personal essay, I clung to the fustian charms of Lamb, Hazlitt, Stevenson, and Beerbohm, with scarcely a side glance at Sedaris, Wallace, and Vowell. I have cheerfully morphed into the type whose idea of a fun movie, as my teenage daughter scoffingly reminds me, is a restored black-and-white silent film.

So what good is experience if the experience I have managed to acquire no longer applies to the new era's challenges, except as the contrarian stiffening of my stubbornness in the face of novelty, and the embrace of the antedated and rarefied?

11.

Emerson rebukes me: "But the man and woman of seventy assume to know all, they have outlived their hope, they renounce aspiration, accept the actual for the necessary, and talk down to the young. Let them, then, become organs of the Holy Ghost; let them be lovers; let them behold truth; and their eyes are uplifted, their wrinkles smoothed, they are perfumed again with hope and power. This old age ought not to creep on a human mind. In nature every moment is new; the past is always swallowed and forgotten; the coming only is sacred. Nothing is secure but life, transition, the energizing spirit. . . . People wish to be settled; only as far as they are unsettled is there any hope for them."

Yeah, yeah; so you say. I do wish to be settled; perhaps I have outlived my hope. When Emerson wrote this passage it must have sounded fresh, rebellious, positively electric. Now it sounds dated. I realize that even in choosing to let Ralph Waldo Emerson rebuke me, I am indulging in an antiquarian longing.

12.

These are the last six lines of that beautiful Borges poem about Emerson:

> He thinks: I have read the essential books
> And written others which oblivion
> Will not efface. I have been allowed
> That which is given mortal man to know.
> The whole continent knows my name.
> I have not lived. I want to be someone else.

Well, the whole continent does not know my name, but I am . . . respected. I have read a good many essential books (alas, forgetting most of what was in them, so that I find I have to read them again from scratch) and have written more than a dozen books which, if not guaranteed to escape oblivion, have given some pleasure to some readers. More than that I will not, must not ask: the gods get angry at ingratitude. I am not grandiose enough, like Emerson or Borges, to think it even my place to want to be someone else. (This reminds me of the old Jewish joke: The rabbi and the synagogue bigwigs are beating their breasts on Yom Kippur, the Day of Atonement, and crying out "I'm a worm, I'm nothing, I'm nobody." The janitor, a goy, decides it looks like a good idea, and starts beating his chest too and moaning, "I'm nobody, I'm nobody!" They stare at him with alarmed disdain, until one of them says: "Look who thinks he's Nobody!") Is it faux-naive and presumptuous to consider myself a nobody, a mere minute speck under the stars, or is the larger geological perspective of looming environmental catastrophe the only proper and responsible one?

13.

What is the nature of experience? What is the connection, if any, between experience and knowledge? What is the relationship between knowledge and wisdom? Can one acquire wisdom passively? Can one live and not acquire experience? Is experience only "experience" if it has been converted into self-conscious thought, or do we count the unconscious in our stock of experience? Our dreams, for instance; are they not part of our experience? By the way, is there really such a thing as the unconscious? Is wisdom principally an intellectual or an emotional property? Can wisdom bypass the heart and lodge only in the brain? Or does it ever work vice versa? What is the difference in value between a shady experience consciously undertaken and one prudently avoided? Does prudence, meaning the wise avoidance of certain sketchy paths, result in a shallower or deeper soul? Is there even such a thing as the soul? If not, what is the point of gaining experience?

14.

"We are great fools. 'He has spent his life in idleness,' we say; 'I have done nothing today.' What, have you not lived? That is not only the fundamental but the most illustrious of your occupations. 'If I had been placed in a position to manage great affairs, I would have shown what I could do.' Have you been able to think out and manage your own life? You have done the greatest task of all. . . . To compose our character is our duty, not to compose books, and to win, not battles and provinces, but order and tranquility in our conduct. Our great and glorious masterpiece is to live appropriately."

So said Montaigne, who wrote "Of Experience" at fifty-six,

and died when he was fifty-nine. We'll say sixty, for the sake of rounded numbers. Since seventy is the new sixty, I should be reaching that point of ripe wisdom that Montaigne attained at the end of his life, no? But since the average young person today has so protracted an adolescence, compared to a youth in sixteenth-century France (see Philippe Ariès's *Centuries of Childhood,* which demonstrated that children were treated as little adults and expected to work from age seven on), we would have to subtract an additional twenty years from my maturity index, bringing me down to age forty. Then take another ten years off for the syndrome that Hemingway contemptuously called the "American boy-man," meaning that there was something uniquely arrested-development about the males in this particular land, which would reduce my emotional age even further, so I should probably be considered the equivalent of a thirty-year-old. No wonder I am still blinking my eyes like a hatched chick and pondering what's what.

15.

The problem of solipsism: not believing that others are as real as you are would seem to put a lid on acquiring wisdom. On the other hand, maybe we are all narcissists, and if narcissism proves to be the universal law, then we need to reexamine all the high-minded inveighing against narcissism and ask if it is a hypocritical form of social coercion. Why should we feel guilty about something we cannot avoid?

I don't think I'm really a narcissist of the first order. Unlike Montaigne, I'm not even terribly interested in myself. When I'm alone, in my study or walking the streets, I am usually thinking not about me but about other people, trying to figure them out, though that could just be another form of narcissistic self-protection: trying to anticipate what they might do, so as to parry it effectively when the situation arises. In any case, I am something of a literalist when it comes to reality. I assume that the people around me are real, the tree outside my window is real, etc. I have never understood that notion put forward by Jean

Baudrillard or David Shields, that we less and less feel our lives to be real, that the simulacra incessantly produced by the media have robbed us of the sense of our own authenticity, and therefore we hunger for the real. I don't hunger for the real. I don't have the foggiest notion what that means. I just want to get by, I just want to enjoy what years are left to me on earth, and most of all, I want to watch my daughter Lily turn into the amazing adult she is fast becoming, want to watch her embrace her full potential and her destiny. I worry about her fretting too much. Amor fati, I want to tell her. Love your fate—which I also tell myself constantly, for all the good that it does.

16.

I wake up between six and six-thirty each morning, having to pee. My cats know this about me and begin to rummage about the bed at that hour, to make sure I will get up and feed them. I put glaucoma-controlling drops in my eyes the first thing in the morning and the last thing at night. I have no problem dropping off to sleep, but I wake up in the night more often than I used to, sometimes roused by noisy neighbors, sometimes by snoring (mine or my wife's), sometimes by a dream, or for no discernible reason whatsoever. I wake up and start picking my nose, to clear the breathing passageways. This is particularly true in winter, when the heat goes on at night and dries out the bedroom air. Because I don't get enough sleep, in the late afternoon I find my eyes drooping when I read, and many times when I am at the movies or listening to an opera I start nodding off. It's outrageous to pay so much for opera tickets and then doze, but I can't help myself. Sometimes, just to keep awake, I rub my scalp above my forehead where there used to be hair, and often find bumps that I try to smooth out by picking off the loose flesh. When I am in a public place such as the subway or at the movies I am always worrying about bedbugs latching on to me, ever since we had an infestation of them a few years back and had to take extreme measures to rid ourselves, hauling all our clothing off to the dry cleaners and wrapping the books. Every time my skin itches I think it must be bedbugs returning.

17.

I hate to lie, and will do almost anything to avoid telling a lie, even if it means sneaking out of a poetry reading the moment it's over or, if directly accosted, blurting out something undiplomatic and giving offense. This resistance to lying stems not so much from an ethical principle as a superstitious dread, as though, if I ever started to lie glibly, my core self would dissolve and I would become a creature of multiple personalities. When you lie you split yourself into two selves, and then a third self has to keep watch and adjudicate the first two. Hence, adultery has never been much of an option for me. Of course I have lied, on some occasions, but I am not going to tell you where or when. That experienced I am. Most of my lies are sins of omission, like keeping my mouth shut when I could get in trouble by saying what I actually thought. If someone tells me that he loved a movie I found abysmal, I smile and nod enthusiastically, though with a slight catch of the head, so that if God is watching, He will understand and forgive my deception. Why should we be transparent, though? Is art transparent? Better to honor the mysteries. There is so much we will never be able to understand that we do not need to go in search of mystery, it will come to us regardless.

18.

Coda

In responding to Montaigne's great last essay, I attempted to gather my own notions and hunches about experience. I began writing my piece before rereading Montaigne's, telling myself that I would get a head start in this way; but in the end I could not bring myself to reread his text carefully—though I skimmed it for underlined passages—because it was too depressing. I felt too inadequate next to his bold, life-embracing manner. He was the master, he was the Father, and I could not engage him in Oedipal struggle because I owed him everything as an essayist, and knew it. The most I could do in the way of resisting his domination was to evade rereading his essay while writing my own. Mind you, I had read "Of Experience" at least fifteen times before, having taught it often over the years; and it was during one of these readings that I came to the definitive conclusion that it was his best, so much so that I second-guessed myself for including "On Some Verses from Virgil," his sexual meditation which I hoped would be popular with young readers, in my anthology *The Art of the Personal Essay,* instead of his more conclusive one on experience.

This was my third attempt to use Montaigne self-consciously as an influence. I had tried to appropriate his aphoristic manner in my essay "Against Joie de Vivre," and his listing of anatomical quirks in "Portrait of My Body." But when it came to approximating his robust final summations on life experience, I could not. I found my own grasp on experience much more tentative. And here we come to my apprehensions about the unitary self. I have been maintaining for quite a while that personal essayists assert a cohesive self and, in this respect, are more traditional than the postmodernists or French theorists who question the whole idea of the individual self. Now the fact is that I don't know whether my self is unitary, cohesive, or even that it exists—only that it profits me in my essay-writing to proceed according to the assumption that it is. I pretend that I have a unitary self, and that is good enough to get me started. Montaigne, for all his proclamations about doubt and the ever-changeable, undulating inconstancy of the human animal, does have, it seems to me, a single, self-confident, fracture-proof self. Or maybe it is his voice that seems so all-of-a-piece to me. He manages to sustain that self, that drily mellifluous voice, through lengthy essays that digress and return to the main matter over and over. I, on the other hand, could only sustain an essay on experience that came to fewer than twenty pages by breaking it into seventeen measly sections. I did the mosaic thing, wrote it in fragments with space breaks surrounding each discontinuous piece, which is not the way I usually compose essays. Usually I get a good head of steam up and follow it to the end. But I found myself fragmenting in the face of the Gascon's cliff-like certitude. Actually, what brought him to his nobly stoical awareness that "We must learn to endure what we cannot avoid," and what held together that last essay of his was his kidney stones. That disease was the central teacher of his final years: "But is there anything so sweet as that sudden change, when from extreme pain, by the voiding of my stone, I come to recover as if by lightning the beautiful light of health, so free and so full, as happens in our sudden and sharpest attacks of colic?" No thanks. I will take my prolonged, unresolved immaturity over his enlightenment via kidney stones.

THE INVITATION

Barry Lopez

When I was young, and just beginning to travel with them, I imagined that indigenous people saw more and heard more, that they were overall simply more aware than I was. They were more aware, and did see and hear more than I did. The absence of spoken conversation whenever I was traveling with them, however, should have provided me with a clue about why this might be true; but it didn't, not for a while. It's this: when an observer doesn't immediately turn what his senses convey to him into language, into the vocabulary and syntactical framework we all employ when trying to define our experiences, there's a much greater opportunity for minor details, which might at first seem unimportant, to remain alive in the foreground of an impression, where, later, they might deepen the meaning of an experience.

If my companions and I, for example, encountered a grizzly bear feeding on a caribou carcass, I would tend to focus almost exclusively on the bear. My companions would focus on the part of the world of which, at that moment, the bear was only a fragment. The bear here might be compared with a bonfire, a kind of incandescence that throws light on everything around it. My companions would glance off into the outer reaches of that light, then look back to the fire, back and forth. They would repeatedly situate the smaller thing within the larger thing, back and forth. As they noticed trace odors in the air, or listened for birdsong or the sound of brittle brush rattling, they in effect extended the moment of encounter with the bear backward and forward in time. Their framework for the phenomenon, one that I might later shorten just to "meeting the bear," was more voluminous than mine; and where my temporal boundaries for the event would normally consist of little more than the moments of the encounter itself, theirs included the time before we arrived, as well as the time after we left. For me, the bear was a noun, the subject of a sentence; for them, it was a verb, the gerund "bearing."

Over the years traveling cross-country with indigenous people I absorbed two lessons about how to be more fully present in an encounter with a wild animal. First, I needed to understand that I was entering the event as it was unfolding. It started before I arrived and would continue unfolding after I departed. Second, the event itself—let's say we didn't disturb the grizzly bear as he fed but only took in what he or she was doing and then slipped away—could not be completely defined by referring solely to the physical geography around us in those moments. For example, I might not recall something we'd all seen a half hour before, a caribou hoofprint in soft ground at the edge of a creek, say; but my companions would remember that. And a while after our encounter with the bear, say a half mile farther on, they would notice something else—a few grizzly bear guard hairs snagged in scales of tree bark—and they would relate it to some detail they'd observed during those moments when we were watching the bear. The event I was cataloging in my mind as "encounter with a tundra grizzly" they were experiencing as a sudden immersion in the current of a river. They were swimming in it, feeling its pull, noting the temperature of the water, the back eddies and where the side streams entered. My approach, in contrast, was mostly to take note of objects in the scene—the bear, the caribou, the tundra vegetation. A series of dots, which I would try to make sense of by connecting them all with a single line. My friends had situated themselves within a dynamic event. Also, unlike me, they felt no immediate need to resolve it into meaning. Their approach was to let it continue to unfold. To notice everything and to let whatever significance was there emerge in its own time.

The lesson to be learned here was not just for me to pay closer attention to what was going on around me, if I hoped to have a deeper understanding of the event, but to remain in a state of suspended mental analysis while observing all that was happening—resisting the urge to define or summarize. To step away from the familiar compulsion to understand. Further, I had to incorporate a quintessential characteristic of the way indigenous people observe: they pay more attention to *patterns* in what they encounter than to isolated objects. When they saw the bear they right away began searching for a pattern that was resolving itself before them as "a bear feeding on a carcass." They began gathering various pieces together that might later self-assemble into an event larger than "a bear feeding." These unintegrated pieces they took in as we traveled—the nature of the sonic landscape that permeated this particular physical landscape; the presence or absence of wind, and the direction from which it was coming or had shifted; a piece of speckled eggshell under a tree; leaves missing from the stems of a species of brush; a hole freshly dug in the ground—might individually convey very little. Allowed to slowly resolve into a pattern, however, they might become revelatory. They might illuminate the land further.

If the first lesson in learning how to see more deeply into a landscape was to be continuously attentive, and to stifle the urge to stand *outside* the event, to instead stay *within* the event, leaving its significance to be resolved later; the second lesson, for me, was to notice how often I asked my body to defer to the dictates of my mind, how my body's extraordinary ability to discern textures and perfumes, to discriminate among tones and colors in the world outside itself, was dismissed by the rational mind.

As much as I believed I was fully present in the physical worlds I was traveling through, I understood over time that I was not. More often I was only *thinking* about the place I was in. Initially awed by an event, the screech of a gray fox in the night woods, say, or the surfacing of a large whale, I too often moved straight to analysis. On occasion I would become so wedded to my thoughts, to some cascade of ideas, that I actually lost touch with the details that my body was *still gathering* from a place. The ear heard the song of a vesper sparrow, and then heard the song again, and knew that the second time it was a different vesper sparrow singing. The mind, pleased with itself for identifying those notes as the song of a vesper sparrow, was too preoccupied with its summary to notice what the ear was still offering. The mind was making no use of the body's ability to be discerning about sounds. And so the mind's knowledge of the place remained superficial.

Many people have written about how, generally speaking, indigenous people seem to pick up more information traversing a landscape than an outsider, someone from a culture that no longer highly values physical intimacy with a place, that regards this sort of sensitivity as a "primitive" attribute, something a visitor from an "advanced" culture would be comfortable believing he had actually outgrown. Such a dismissive view, as I have come to understand it, ignores the great intangible value that achieving physical intimacy with a place might provide. I'm inclined to point out to someone who condescends to such a desire for intimacy, although it might seem rude, that it is not possible for human beings to outgrow loneliness. Nor can someone from a culture that condescends to nature easily escape the haunting thought that one's life is meaningless.

Existential loneliness and a sense that one's life is inconsequential, both of which are hallmarks of modern civilizations, seem to me to derive in part from our abandoning a belief in the therapeutic dimensions of a relationship with place. A continually refreshed sense of the unplumbable complexity of patterns in the natural world, patterns that are ever present and discernible, and which incorporate the observer, undermine the feeling that one is alone in the world, or meaningless in it. The effort to know a place deeply is, ultimately, an expression of the human desire to belong, to fit somewhere.

The determination to know a particular place, in my experience, is consistently rewarded. And every natural place, to my mind, is open to being known. And somewhere in this process a person begins to sense that they *themselves* are becoming known, so that when they are absent from that place they know that place misses them. And this reciprocity, to know and be known, reinforces a sense that one is necessary in the world.

Perhaps the first rule of everything we endeavor to do is to pay attention. Perhaps the second is to be patient. And perhaps a third is to be attentive to what the body knows. In my experience, individual indigenous people are not necessarily more aware than people who've grown up in the modern culture I grew up in. Indigenous cultures, of course, are as replete with inattentive, lazy, and undiscerning individuals as "advanced" cultures. But they tend to value more highly the importance of intimacy with a place. When you travel with them, you're acutely aware that theirs is a fundamentally different praxis from your own. They're more attentive, more patient, less willing to say what they know, to collapse mystery into language. When I was young, and one of my traveling companions would make some stunningly insightful remark about the place we were traveling through, I would sometimes feel envious; a feeling related not so much to a desire to possess that same depth of knowledge but a desire to so obviously *belong* to a particular place. To so clearly be an integral part of the place one is standing in.

A grizzly bear stripping fruit from blackberry vines in a thicket is more than a bear stripping fruit from blackberry vines in a thicket. It is a point of entry into a world most of us have turned our backs on in an effort to go somewhere else, believing we'll be better off just *thinking* about a grizzly bear stripping fruit from blackberry vines in a thicket.

The moment is an invitation, and the bear's invitation to participate is offered, without prejudice, to anyone passing by.

BODIES IN MOTION AND AT REST

Thomas Lynch

So I'm over at the Hortons' with my stretcher and minivan and my able apprentice, young Matt Sheffler, because they found old George, the cemetery sexton, dead in bed this Thursday morning in ordinary time. And the police have been in to rule out foul play and the EMS team to run a tape so some ER doctor wired to the world can declare him dead at a safe distance. And now it's ours to do—Matt's and mine—to ease George from the bed to the stretcher, negotiate the sharp turn at the top of the stairs, and go out the front door to the dead wagon idling in the driveway and back to the funeral home from whence he'll take his leave—waked and well remembered—a Saturday service in the middle of April, his death observed, his taxes due.

We are bodies in motion and at rest—there in George's master bedroom, in the gray light of the midmorning, an hour or so after his daughter found him because he didn't answer when she called this morning, and he always answers, and she always calls, so she got in the car and drove over and found him exactly as we find him here: breathless, unfettered, perfectly still, manifestly indifferent to all this hubbub. And he is here, assembled on his bed as if nothing had happened, still propped on his left shoulder, his left ear buried in his pillow, his right leg hitched up over the left one, his right hand tucked up under the far pillow his ex-wife used to sleep on, before she left him twenty years ago, and under the former Mrs. Horton's pillow, I lift to show Matt, is a little pearl-handled .22 caliber that George always slept with since he has slept alone. "Security," he called it. He said it helped him sleep.

And really there is nothing out of order, no sign of panic or struggle or pain, and except for the cardiac blue tinting around his ears, the faint odor of body heat and a little early rigor in his limbs, which makes the moving of him easier, one'd never guess George wasn't just sleeping in this morning—catching the twenty extra winks—because maybe he'd been up late playing poker with the boys, or maybe he'd had a late dinner with his woman friend, or maybe he was just a little tired from digging graves and filling them, and anyway, he hadn't a grave to open this morning for one of the locals who was really dead.

But this morning George Horton is really dead and he's really being removed from his premises by Matt and me after we swaddle him in his own bed linens, sidle him on to the stretcher, tip the stretcher up to make the tight turn at the top of the stairs and carefully ease it down, trying to keep the wheels from thumping each time the heavier head end of the enterprise takes a step. And it's really a shame, all things considered, because here's George, more or less in his prime, just south of sixty, his kids raised, his house paid off, a girlfriend still in her thirties with whom he maintained twice-weekly relations—"catch as catch can," he liked to say. And he's a scratch golfer and a small business owner with reliable employees and frequent flier miles that he spends on trips to Vegas twice a year, where he lets himself get a little crazy with the crap tables and showgirls. And he has his money tucked into rent, and a daughter about to make him a grandfather for the first time, and really old George seemed to have it made, and except for our moving him feetfirst down the stairs this morning, he has everything to live for, everything.

And it is there, on the landing of the first floor, only a few feet from the front door out, that his very pregnant daughter waits in her warmup suit to tender her goodbyes to the grandfather of her baby, not yet born. And Matt's face is flushed with the lifting, the huffing and puffing, or the weight of it all, or the sad beauty of the woman as she runs her hand along her father's cheek, and she is catching her breath and her eyes are red and wet and she lifts her face to ask me, "Why?"

"His heart, Nancy," is what I tell her. "It looks like he just slept away. He never felt a thing." These are all the well-tested comforts one learns after twenty-five years of doing these things.

"But *why*?" she asks me, and now it is clear that how it happened is not good enough. And here I'm thinking all the usual suspects: the cheeseburgers, the whiskey, the Lucky Strikes, the thirty extra pounds we, some of us, carry, the walks we didn't take, the preventive medicines we all ignore, the work and the worry and the taxman, the luck of the draw, the nature of the beast, the way of the world, the shit that happens because it happens.

But Nancy is not asking for particulars. She wants to know why in the much larger, Overwhelming Question sense: why we don't just live forever. Why are we all eventually orphaned and heartbroken? Why we human beings cease to be. Why our nature won't leave well enough alone. Why we are not all immortal. Why this morning? Why George Horton? Why oh why oh why?

No few times in my life as a funeral director have I been asked this. Schoolchildren, the newly widowed, musing clergy, fellow pilgrims—maybe they think it was my idea. Maybe they just like to see me squirm contemplating a world in which folks wouldn't need caskets and hearses and the likes of me always ready and willing and at their service. Or maybe, like me, sometimes they really wonder.

"Do the math" is what George Horton would say. Or "Bottom line." Or "It's par for the course." Or "It's biblical." If none of these wisdoms seemed to suit, then "Not my day to watch it" is what he'd say. Pressed on the vast adverbials that come to mind while opening or closing graves, George could be counted on for tidy answers. Self-schooled in the Ways of the World, he confined his reading to the King James Bible, *The Wall Street Journal, Golf Digest,* the Victoria's Secret catalog, and the Big Book of Alcoholics Anonymous. He watched C-SPAN, The Home Shopping Network, and The Weather Channel. Most afternoons he'd doze off watching Oprah, with whom he was, quite helplessly, in love. On quiet days he'd surf the Web or check his portfolio online. On Sundays he watched talking heads and went to dinner and the movies with his woman friend. Weekday mornings he had coffee with the guys at the Summit Café before making the rounds of the half dozen cemeteries he was in charge of. Wednesdays and Saturdays he'd mostly golf.

"Do the math" I heard him give out with once from the cab of his backhoe for no apparent reason. He was backfilling a grave in Milford Memorial. "You gonna make babies, you've gotta make some room; it's biblical."

Or once, leaning on a shovel, waiting for the priest to finish: "Copulation, population, inspiration, expiration. It's all arithmetic—addition, multiplication, subtraction and long division. That's all we're doing here, just the math. Bottom line, we're buried a thousand per acre, or burned into two quarts of ashes, give or take."

There was no telling when such wisdoms would come to him.

But it came to me, embalming George later that morning, that the comfort in numbers is that they all add up. There is a balm in the known quantities, however finite. Any given year at this end of the millennium, 2.3 million Americans will die. Ten percent of pregnancies will be unintended. There'll be 60 million common colds. These are numbers you can take to the bank. Give or take, 3.9 million babies will be born. It's biblical. They'll get a little more or a little less of their 76 years of life expectancy. The boys will grow to just over 69 inches, the girls to just under 64. Of them, 25 percent will be cremated, 35 percent will be overweight, 52 percent will drink. Every year 2 million will get divorced, 4 million will get married and there'll be 30,000 suicides. A few will win the lotto, a few will run for public office, a few will be struck by lightning. And any given day, par for the course, 6,300 of our fellow citizens, just like George, will get breathless and outstretched and spoken of in the past tense; and most will be dressed up the way I dress up George, in his good blue suit, and put him in a casket with Matt Sheffler's help, and assemble the

2 or 3 dozen floral tributes and the 100 or 200 family and friends and the 60 or 70 cars that will follow in the 15-miles-per-hour procession down through town to grave 4 of lot 17 of section C in Milford Memorial, which will become, in the parlance of our trade, his final resting place, over which a 24-by-12-by-4-inch Barre granite stone will be placed, into which we will have sand-blasted his name and dates, one of which, subtracted from the other, will amount, more or less, to his life and times. The corruptible, according to the officiating clergy, will have put on incorruption, the mortal will have put on immortality. "Not my day to watch it" will be among the things we'll never hear George Horton say again.

Nor can we see clearly now, looking into his daughter Nancy's eyes, the blue morning at the end of this coming May when she'll stand, upright as any walking wound, holding her newborn at the graveside of the man, her one and only father, for whom her baby will be named. Nor can we hear the promises she makes to keep him alive, to always remember, forever and ever, in her heart of hearts. Nor is there any math or bottom line or Bible verse that adds or subtracts or in any way accounts for the moment or the mystery she holds there.

DRAFT NO. 4

John McPhee

Block. It puts some writers down for months. It puts some writers down for life. A not always brief or minor form of it mutes all writers from the outset of every day. "Dear Joel . . ." This is just a random sample from letters written to former students in response to their howling cries as they suffer the masochistic self-inflicted paralysis of a writer's normal routine. "Dear Joel . . ." This Joel will win huge awards and write countless books and a nationally syndicated column, but at the time of this letter he has just been finding out that to cross the electric fence from the actual world to the writing world requires at least as much invention as the writing itself. "Dear Joel: You are writing, say, about a grizzly bear. No words are forthcoming. For six, seven, ten hours no words have been forthcoming. You are blocked, frustrated, in despair. You are nowhere, and that's where you've been getting. What do you do? You write, 'Dear Mother.' And then you tell your mother about the block, the frustration, the ineptitude, the despair. You insist that you are not cut out to do this kind of work. You whine. You whimper. You outline your problem, and you mention that the bear has a fifty-five-inch waist and a neck more than thirty inches around but could run nose-to-nose with Secretariat. You say the bear prefers to lie down and rest. The bear rests fourteen hours a day. And you go on like that as long as you can. And then you go back and delete the 'Dear Mother' and all the whimpering and whining, and just keep the bear."

You could be Joel, even if your name is Jenny. Or Julie, Jillian, Jim, Jane, Joe. You are working on a first draft and small wonder you're unhappy. If you lack confidence in setting one word after another and sense that you are stuck in a place from which you will never be set free, if you feel sure that you will never make it and were not cut out to do this, if your prose seems stillborn and you completely lack confidence, you must be a writer. If you say you see things differently and describe your efforts positively, if you tell people that you "just love to write," you may be delusional. How could anyone ever know that something is good before it exists? And unless you can identify what is not succeeding—unless you can see those dark clunky spots that are giving you such a low opinion of your prose as it develops—how are you going to be able to tone it up and make it work?

The idea of writing "Dear Mother" and later snipping off the salutation had popped into my head years ago while I was participating in a panel of writers at the Y in Princeton. Jenny was the only member of my family there. She was ten. The bear got a big laugh, but cheerlessly I also served up the masochism and the self-inflicted paralysis, causing Jenny to tell me afterward that I was not sketching a complete picture.

"You know it isn't all like that," she said. "You should tell about the good part."

She had a point. It isn't all like that—only the first draft. First drafts are slow and develop clumsily because every sentence affects not only those before it but also those that follow. The first draft of my book on California geology took two gloomy years; the second, third, and fourth drafts took about six months altogether. That four-to-one ratio in writing time—first draft versus the other drafts combined—has for me been consistent in projects of any length, even if the first draft takes only a few days or weeks. There are psychological differences from phase to phase, and the first is the phase of the pit and the pendulum. After that, it seems as if a different person is taking over. Dread largely disappears. Problems become less threatening, more interesting.

Experience is more helpful, as if an amateur is being replaced by a professional. Days go by quickly and not a few could be called pleasant, I'll admit.

When Jenny was a senior at Princeton High School and much put out by the time it was taking her to start an assigned piece of writing, let alone complete it, she told me one day as I was driving her to school that she felt incompetent and was worried about the difficulty she was having getting things right the first time, worried by her need to revise. I went on to my office and wrote her a note. "Dear Jenny: The way to do a piece of writing is three or four times over, never once. For me, the hardest part comes first, getting something—anything—out in front of me. Sometimes in a nervous frenzy I just fling words as if I were flinging mud at a wall. Blurt out, heave out, babble out something—anything—as a first draft. With that, you have achieved a sort of nucleus. Then, as you work it over and alter it, you begin to shape sentences that score higher with the ear and eye. Edit it again—top to bottom. The chances are that about now you'll be seeing something that you are sort of eager for others to see. And all that takes time. What I have left out is the interstitial time. You finish that first awful blurting, and then you put the thing aside. You get in your car and drive home. On the way, your mind is still knitting at the words. You think of a better way to say something, a good phrase to correct a certain problem. Without the drafted version—if it did not exist—you obviously would not be thinking of things that would improve it. In short, you may be actually writing only two or three hours a day, but your mind, in one way or another, is working on it twenty-four hours a day—yes, while you sleep—but only if some sort of draft or earlier version already exists. Until it exists, writing has not really begun."

The difference between a common writer and an improviser on a stage (or any performing artist) is that writing can be revised. Actually, the essence of the process is revision. The adulating portrait of the perfect writer who never blots a line comes Express Mail from fairyland.

Jenny grew up to write novels, and at this point has published three. She keeps everything close-hauled, says nothing and reveals nothing as she goes along. I once asked her if she had been thinking about starting another book, and she said, "I finished it last week." Her sister Martha, two years younger, has written four novels. Martha calls me up nine times a day to tell me that writing is impossible, that she's not cut out to do it, that she'll never finish what she is working on, et cetera, et cetera, and so forth and so on, and I, who am probably disintegrating a third of the way through an impossible first draft, am supposed to turn into the Rock of Gibraltar. The talking rock: "Just stay at it; perseverance will change things." "You're so unhappy you sound authentic to me." "You can't make a fix unless you know what is broken."

When Jenny was ten months out of college, she was beginning to develop some retrospective empathy for me on that day at the Y when she was ten. Now she was in Edinburgh, writing on a fellowship, and she told me in a letter of her continuing doubt and discouragement. Those were the days of paper airmail, and by paper airmail I replied.

With respect to her wish to become a writer, she said she was asking herself day after day, "Who am I kidding?"

I said, "I think I first started saying that to myself almost exactly forty years ago. Before that, when I was twelve, I had no such question. It just seemed dead easy—a rip, a scam—to tickle some machine and cause it to print money. I still ask myself, 'Who am I kidding?' Not long ago, that question seemed so pertinent to me that I would bury my head in my office pillow. I was undertaking to write about geology and the question was proper. Who was I to take on that subject? It was terrifying. One falls into such projects like slipping into caves, and then wonders how to get out. To feel such doubt is a part of the picture—important and inescapable. When I hear some young writer express that sort of doubt, it serves as a checkpoint; if they don't say something like it they are quite possibly, well, kidding themselves."

She said, "My style is always that of what I am reading at the time—or overwhelmingly self-conscious and strained."

I said, "How unfortunate that would be if you were fifty-four. At twenty-three, it is not only natural; it is important. The developing writer reacts to excellence as it is discovered—wherever and whenever—and of course does some imitating (unavoidably) in the process of drawing from the admired fabric things to make one's own. Rapidly, the components of imitation fade. What remains is a new element in your own voice, which is not in any way an imitation. Your manner as a writer takes form in this way, a fragment at a time. A style that lacks strain and self-consciousness is what you seem to aspire to, or you wouldn't be bringing the matter up. Therefore, your goal is in the right place. So practice taking shots at it. A relaxed, unselfconscious style is not something that one person is born with and another not. Writers do not spring full-blown from the ear of Zeus."

Jenny said, "I can't seem to finish anything."

I said, "Neither can I."

Then I went back to my own writing, my own inability to get going until five in the afternoon, my animal sense of being hunted, my resemblance to the sand of Gibraltar.

It is toward the end of the second draft, if I'm lucky, when the feeling comes over me that I have something I want to show to other people, something that seems to be working and is not going to go away. The feeling is more than welcome, but it is hardly euphoria. It's just a new lease on life, a sense that I'm going to survive until the middle of next month. After reading the second draft aloud, and going through the piece for the third time (removing the tin horns and radio static that I heard while reading), I enclose words and phrases in penciled boxes for Draft No. 4. If I enjoy anything in this process it is Draft No. 4. I go searching for replacements for the words in the boxes. The final adjustments may be small-scale, but they are large to me, and I love addressing them. You could call this the copyediting phase if real copy editors were not out there in the future prepared to examine the piece. The basic thing I do with college students is pretend that I'm their editor and their copy editor. In preparation for conferences with them, I draw boxes around words or phrases in the pieces they write. I suggest to them that they might do this for themselves.

You draw a box not only around any word that does not seem quite right but also around words that fulfill their assignment but seem to present an opportunity. While the word inside the box may be perfectly OK, there is likely to be an even better word for this situation, a word right smack on the button, and why don't you try to find such a word? If none occurs, don't linger; keep reading and drawing boxes, and later revisit them one by one. If there's a box around "sensitive" because it seems pretentious in the context, try "susceptible." Why "susceptible"? Because you looked up "sensitive" in the dictionary and it said "highly susceptible." With dictionaries, I spend a great deal more time looking up words I know than words I have never heard of—at least ninety-nine to one. The dictionary definitions of words you are trying to replace are far more likely to help you out than a scattershot wad from a thesaurus. If you use the dictionary after the thesaurus, the thesaurus will not hurt you. So draw a box around "wad." Webster: "The cotton or silk obtained from the Syrian swallowwort, formerly cultivated in Egypt and imported to Europe." Oh. But read on: "A little mass, tuft, or bundle . . . a small, compact heap." Stet that one. I call this "the search for the mot juste," because when I was in the eighth grade Miss Bartholomew told us that Gustave Flaubert walked around in his garden for days on end searching in his head for *le mot juste*. Who could forget that? Flaubert seemed heroic. Certain kids considered him weird.

This, for example, came up while I was writing about the Atchafalaya, the huge river swamp in southern Louisiana, and how it looked from a small plane in the air. Land is growing there as silt arrives from the north. Parts of the swamp are filling in. From the airplane, you could discern where these places were because, seen through the trees, there would be an interruption of the reflection of sunlight on water. What word or phrase was I going to use for that reflection? I looked up "sparkle" in my old Webster's Collegiate. It said: "See 'flash.'" I looked up "flash." The definitions were followed by a presentation of synonyms: "flash, gleam, glance, glint, sparkle, glitter, scintillate, coruscate, glimmer, shimmer mean to shoot forth light." I liked that last part, so I changed the manuscript to say, "The reflection of the sun races through the trees and shoots forth light from the water."

In the search for words, thesauruses are useful things, but they don't talk about the words they list. They are also dangerous. They can lead you to choose a polysyllabic and fuzzy word when a simple and clear one is better. The value of a thesaurus is not to make a writer seem to have a vast vocabulary of recondite words. The value of a thesaurus is in the assistance it can give you in finding the best possible word for the mission that the word is supposed to fulfill. Writing teachers and journalism courses have been known to compare them to crutches and to imply that no writer of any character or competence would use them. At best, thesauruses are mere rest stops in the search for the mot juste. Your destination is the dictionary. Suppose you sense an opportunity beyond the word "intention." You read the dictionary's thesaurian list of synonyms: "intention, intent, purpose, design, aim, end, object, objective, goal." But the dictionary doesn't let it go at that. It goes on to tell you the differences all the way down the line—how each listed word differs from all the others. Some dictionaries keep themselves trim by just listing synonyms and not going on to make distinctions. You want the first kind, in which you are not just getting a list of words; you are being told the differences in their hues, as if you were looking at the stripes in an awning, each of a subtly different green. Look up "vertical." It tells you—believe it or not—that "vertical," "perpendicular," and "plumb" differ each from the two others. Ditto "plastic, pliable, pliant, ductile, malleable, adaptable." Ditto "fidelity, allegiance, fealty, loyalty, devotion, piety."

I grew up in canoes on northern lakes and forest rivers. Thirty years later, I was trying to choose a word or words that would explain why anyone in a modern nation would choose to go a long distance by canoe. I was damned if I was going to call it a sport, but nothing else occurred. I looked up "sport." There were seventeen lines of definition: "1. That which diverts, and makes mirth; pastime; diversion. 2. A diversion of the field." I stopped there.

> His professed criteria were to take it easy, see some wildlife, and travel light with his bark canoes—nothing more—and one could not help but lean his way. I had known of people who took collapsible cots, down pillows, chain saws, outboard motors, cases of beer, and battery-powered portable refrigerators on canoe trips—even into deep wilderness. You set your own standards. Travel by canoe is not a

> necessity, and will nevermore be the most efficient way to get from one region to another, or even from one lake to another—anywhere. A canoe trip has become simply a rite of oneness with certain terrain, a diversion of the field, an act performed not because it is necessary but because there is value in the act itself. . . .

If your journey is long enough in wild country, you change, albeit temporarily, while you are there. Writing about a river valley in Arctic Alaska, I was trying to describe that mental change, and I was searching for a word that would represent the idea, catalyze the theme. "Assimilate" came along pretty quickly. But "assimilate," in the context, was worse than "sport." So I looked up "assimilate": "1. To make similar or alike. 2. To liken; to compare. 3. "To . . . incorporate into the substance of the appropriating body."

> We sat around the campfire for at least another hour. We talked of rain and kestrels, oil and antlers, the height and the headwaters of the river. Neither Hession nor Fedeler once mentioned the bear.
>
> When I got into my sleeping bag, though, and closed my eyes, there he was, in color, on the side of the hill. The vision was indelible, but fear was not what put it there. More, it was a sense of sheer luck at having chosen in the first place to follow Fedeler and Hession up the river and into the hills—a memento not so much of one moment as of the entire circuit of the long afternoon. It was a vision of a whole land, with an animal in it. This was his country, clearly enough. To be there was to be incorporated, in however small a measure, into its substance—his country, and if you wanted to visit it you had better knock.

I was left, in the time that followed, with one huge regret. In three years of Alaska travel, research, and writing, it never occurred to me to wonder why the Arctic was called Arctic. I never thought about it until a few years after the book was published. If only I had looked in the dictionary, I would have incorporated the word's origin into the substance of the writing. This is how "Arctic" is defined: "Pertaining to, or situated under, the northern constellation called the Bear."

It was William Shawn who first mentioned to me the "irregular restrictive 'which.'" Mr. Shawn explained that under certain unusual and special circumstances the word "which" could be employed at the head of a restrictive clause. Ordinarily, the conjunction "that" would introduce a restrictive clause. Nonrestrictive: This is a baseball, which is spherical and white. Restrictive: This is the baseball that Babe Ruth hit out of the park after pointing at the fence in Chicago. The first ball is unspecific, and the sentence requires a comma if the writer wishes to digress into its shape and color. The second ball is very specific, and the sentence repels commas. There can be situations, though, wherein words or phrases lie between the specific object and the clause that proves its specificity, and would call for the irregular restrictive "which."

Confronting this memory, I cannot say that it kicks old Buddha's gong. Yet it has sent me through the entirety of two of my books on a computer search for the irregular restrictive "which." In well over a hundred thousand words, I found three:

> In 1822, the Belgian stratigrapher J. J. d'Omalius d'Halloy, working for the French government, put a name on the chalk of Europe which would come to represent an ungainly share of geologic time.

> Oakmont uses a *Poa annua* of its own creation which bears few seeds and therefore results in what golfers describe as a "less pebbly" surface.

> Dominy had risen to become U.S. Commissioner of Reclamation, the agency in the Department of the Interior which impounds water for as much as two hundred miles behind such constructions as Glen Canyon Dam, Grand Coulee Dam, Flaming Gorge Dam, Hoover Dam.

As it happens, those excerpts are not from the Shawn era but are all from pieces published in the twenty-first century. *The New Yorker,* in other words, has by no means forgotten the irregular restrictive "which," or the regular earth from which it springs.

In the same books, incidentally, I also quoted Thoreau and Leviticus, and may have winced in Shawn's honor.

> Four hundred yards above the interstate bridge, we came to Carthagina Island, standing in a flat-water pool. Thoreau doesn't call it by name, but he describes it as "a large and densely wooded island . . . the fairest which we had met with, with a handsome grove of elms at its head."

Nothing irregular there, H.D.T. It was the fairest island that you met with.

> Leviticus: "And the Lord spake unto Moses and to Aaron, saying unto them, Speak unto the children of Israel, saying, These are the beasts which ye shall eat among all the beasts that are on the earth."

Actually, Mr. Shawn was just another spear-carrier in the hall of usage and grammar. The dais was occupied for more than half a century by Eleanor Gould, "Miss Gould," who was Mrs. Packard, and whose wide reputation seeped down even into the awareness of apprentice writers everywhere. I was scarcely eighteen, and already collecting rejection slips, when I heard or read about a twenty-two-year-old Vassar graduate named Eleanor Gould, who, in 1925, bought a copy of the brand-new *New Yorker,* read it, and then reread it with a blue pencil in her hand. When she finished, the magazine was a mottled blue on every page—a circled embarrassment of dangling modifiers, conflicting pronouns, absent commas, and overall grammatical hash. She mailed the marked-up copy to Harold Ross, the founding editor, and Ross was said to have bellowed. What he bellowed was "Find this bitch and hire her!"

In reality, Eleanor Gould was nine years old when Ross invented *The New Yorker.* She grew up in Ohio, went to Oberlin

College, and graduated in 1938. Seven years later, she sought a job at *The New Yorker,* and in her application she mentioned one or two examples of the sort of help she felt she could provide. For example, something is not different *than* something else; it is different *from* something else. It was Shawn who hired her. He was the managing editor. There is no compact or simple title for what she did across the following fifty-four years. She was not an editor—not, at any rate, on the higher levels of holding writers' hands. She was not a fact-checker, although she would surely mention any fact that struck her as suspect. What she did was read the magazine in galley proofs and mark up the proofs. Each galley had a *New Yorker* column running down the middle and enough margin on either side to park a car. She filled the margins with remarks about usage, diction, indirection, word choice, punctuation, ambiguities, and so forth. Her completed product was sent on to the writer's editor, who read the marginalia and later brought up selected items with the writer, or just handed the writer the Gould proof, as it was known, and let the writer soak it up. Robert Bingham always passed the Gould proof along to me, almost always saying, "When she says 'Grammar,' sit up!"

On a highly competitive list, her foremost peeve in factual writing was indirection—sliding facts in sideways, expecting a reader to gather rather than receive information. You don't start off like an atmospheric Hedonist: "The house on Lovers' Lane was where the lovers loved loving." A Gould proof would have asked, "What house?" "What lovers?" "Where is Lovers' Lane?" In short, if you are introducing something, introduce it. Don't get artistic with the definite article. If you say "a house," you are introducing it. If you say "the house," the reader knows about it because you mentioned it earlier. Mr. Shawn was influenced by Miss Gould far more than vice versa. He was a bear on indirection.

Her suggested fixes did not always rise into comparison with invisible mending. Some writers developed reactions in the tantrum range. Nothing, though, was being forced upon the prose. If the writer wished to ignore a salient comment from Miss Gould instead of slapping the forehead and feeling grateful, that was up to the writer. It was the writer's signed piece. If the writer preferred warts, warts prevailed. A Gould proof rarely endeavored to influence in any manner the structure or thesis of a piece, and was not meant to. Its purpose, according to Miss Gould, was to help a writer achieve an intent in the clearest possible way. She sat you up, let me tell you. And not only did you not have to accept her suggested fixes but also—of course—you were free to fix the fixes according to the sound of things in your own head.

The general term for all this—from "house style" to a Gould-like proof—is "copyediting." Miss Gould accepted the title "grammarian" for several decades, but grammar was only the base of things she reacted to as she monitored the magazine. House style was actually dealt with by others before she saw anything. House style is not a reference to the canard that an entire magazine can be made to sound as if it were written by one writer. House style is a mechanical application of things like spelling and italics. In *The New Yorker,* "travelling" is spelled with two "l"s. Book titles are framed in quotation marks. The names of magazines are italicized, and if the names are in the possessive—*TV Guide's, National Geographic's*—the "s" is italicized, too. The names of ships are not italicized. It is house style to put the two dots over a second consecutive identical vowel because the house does not coöperate in deëmphasizing diaereses. In articles in *The New York Times* the name of everybody mentioned is preceded by Mr., Ms., or Mrs. (if not by a lofty title like President, Senator, General, or Cardinal), and, traditionally, if a *Times* reporter got into a skin boat with an Eskimo in the Chukchi Sea no personal pronoun was ever going to get into that boat. "A visitor" got into that boat. *The Chicago Manual of Style* is a quixotic attempt at one-style-fits-all for every house in America—newspapers, magazines, book publishers, blogishers.

Copy editors attend the flow of the prose and watch for leaks. Whatever else she was called, Eleanor Gould was a copy editor. She was one of several in a developing tradition that became a legacy. For a single closing issue, today's copy editors read *New Yorker* proofs so many times and in so many ways that they variously subtitle their own efforts. The five incumbents call themselves copy editors, page OK'ers, query proofreaders, and second readers. They all do all of it, and that's four job descriptions each for five people—twenty functionaries at five desks. They also do what Eleanor Gould did, and to this day when they finish working on a galley proof they say that it has been "Goulded." If they live in her shadow, they lengthen it.

They can be rarefied. Reading a sentence like "She didn't know what happened to the other five people travelling with her," they will see that what the writer could mean is that the traveller was one of eleven people on the trip. This is high-alloy nitpicking, but why not? There is elegance in the less ambiguous way. She didn't know what happened to the five other people who were travelling with her.

To linger in the same thin air, what is the difference between "further" and "farther"? In the dictionary, look up "further." It says "farther." Look up "farther." It says "further." So you're safe and can roll over and sleep. But the distinction has a difference and OK'ers know what's OK. "Farther" refers to measurable distance. "Further" is a matter of degree. Will you stop pelting me with derision? That's enough out of you. You'll go no further.

Getting into an authentic standoff with this multitalented, multifaceted, proofreading, query-proofing, copyediting, grammar-wielding corps is difficult to do, and in fifty years I have done so twice. One standoff, which shall not be elaborated here, had to do with my flippant use of scholarly parenthetical in-text citations (Mourt, 1622) in a piece in which the works cited did not appear on what scholars call the works cited list. There was no works cited list. The other standoff—related to the issue of February 23, 1987—had to do with the possessive of the word Corps. It was the piece about southern Louisiana, the Atchafalaya River, the vast swamp, and the levees, spillways, and navigation locks of the U.S. Army Corps of Engineers. It approached twenty thousand words in length and, as you can imagine, the word Corps was all over the text like an eruption of measles. Often, the word occurred in the possessive. When I was in the eighth grade, Miss Bartholomew told us that a noun ending in "s" could be rendered possessive by an apostrophe alone or by an apostrophe followed by an additional "s," tie goes to the writer. Now, in the Louisiana piece, I had written Corps' for each and every possessive Corps, and the copy editors said that the possessive of Corps should be printed as Corps's. I thought I was in a morgue. I said so. The copy editors phalanxed—me versus the whole department. They said that *The New Yorker* did not use the naked "s" apostrophe except with classical names like Jesus, Aeschylus, and Socrates; and even French names ending in a silent "s" were given the apostrophe "s," as in "Francois's," "*les jeunesses's,*" "Epesses's"—also as in "Amiens's hidden cache" and "*le français's* frank mustache." With regard to Corps's, the copy editors were uncharacteristically unbending. I said that if Corps's had to be the form printed, I would have to stop all forward motion and rewrite every sentence in which that possessive occurred—in ways that would avoid using it, in ways that would get rid of "all those corpses." I'm sure I spluttered about "slabsful of recumbents" and said it would be "as if every one of those Corps's was wired to a cold toe." This threat was not considered persuasive, but eventually it led to someone's remarkable suggestion. Why not call the U.S. Army Corps of Engineers and ask what they do when they need to express themselves in the possessive? I hadn't known that the Army Corps of Engineers was steeped in Fowler's Modern English Usage or Merriam-Webster's unparalleled English Usage or the flexibilities of grammar. How would the Corps write it? Corps', said the Corps. Never Corps's. Never the geminal "s"s.

Copy editors seldom stray into the realms of others, but when they do, their suggestions and comments are not unwelcome. Mary Norris, who joined *The New Yorker* in 1978 and has worked on untold numbers of my pieces, is a verbal diagnostician I would turn to for a first, second, or third opinion on just about anything. She doesn't mind when friends call her the Pencil Lady. A blog she began on *The New Yorker*'s website, mostly about copyediting, evolved into the best-selling book *Between You & Me: Confessions of a Comma Queen* (Norton, 2015). In 2003, we were closing the piece that retraced the journey made in 1839 by Henry David Thoreau and his brother, John, down the Concord River to the Merrimack and up the Merrimack through and beyond Manchester, New Hampshire. In manuscript and in the initial galley proofs, there was a sentence (odd out of context) that said:

> In bed at night for three or four months I'd been listening to Manchester laughing—a chorus of Manchesterians sitting on those steps convulsed by us on the way uphill with our canoe.

Mary Norris wrote on the proof, "Would you like 'Mancunians'?"

It was as if she had handed me a rare gold coin. Five years later, when I happened to be writing about lacrosse in Manchester, England, I worked in the word "Mancunian" three times in one short paragraph. It was the second-best demonym I'd ever heard, almost matching Vallisoletano (a citizen of Valladolid). The planet, of course, is covered with demonyms, and after scouring the world in conversations on this topic with Mary Norris I began a severely selective, highly subjective A-list, extending Mancunian and Vallisoletano through thirty-five others at this writing, including Wulfrunian (Wolverhampton), Novocastrian (Newcastle), Trifluvian (Trois-Rivières), Leodensian (Leeds), Minneapolitan (Minneapolis), Hartlepudlian (Hartlepool), Liverpudlian (you knew it), Haligonian (Halifax), Varsovian (Warsaw), Providentian (Providence), and Tridentine (Trent).

One can do worse than pretend to be a copy editor. In my role as my students' editor, I go through their papers with them privately a comma at a time. Much of what I tell them I have learned by osmosis from those OK'ers at *The New Yorker,* not to mention a range of others, from Miss Bartholomew, of Princeton Junior High School, to Carmen Gomezplata, of Farrar, Straus and Giroux. The students, picking up the parlance, sometimes go off and copyedit their roommates. This has led to disputes, and I have been asked to settle the disputes. My name isn't Strunk. I'm just another editee. But I do what I can, as, for example, after two such people recently got into a squabble over—imagine this—the possessive plural of "attorney general." The question came to me in an email: "If more than one attorney general possess a number of cars, how would you fill in the blanks (if at all) in the following sentence: 'the attorney[] general[] car[] were all parked next to one another'?"

Both Web. II and Random House say flatly that the plural of "attorney general" is both "attorneys general" and "attorney generals." That being so, I put on my robe, rapped the gavel, and said from the bench, "If you accept that the two forms are equal, I think you would write attorney generals' cars and not attorneys general's cars—for obvious reasons (a sense of the sight and sound of words has to kick in somewhere or the writer is missing one or two marbles)." What would I personally do? None of the above. I would refer to "the cars of the attorneys general." But that's just a matter of choice.

I work in a fake medieval turret on the roof of a campus building. When I come out and walk around, bumping into friends, they tend to ask me, "What are you working on?" I always feel like a parrot answering that question, and a nervous ill-humored parrot if I am writing a first draft. A few years ago, I had the luxury of a one-word reply.

"What are you working on?"

"Chalk."

"Chalk?"

"Chalk."

That did it. That seemed to be one more syllable than anyone wished to pursue.

But when the question comes in a note from one of your own daughters it is wise not to wax monosyllabic. Jenny, for example, was an assistant editor at Alfred A. Knopf when she innocently asked what I was working on, and got this reply:

"Dear Jenny: What am I working on? How is it going? Since you asked, at this point I have no confidence in this piece of writing. It tries a number of things I probably shouldn't be trying. It tries to use the present tense for the immediacy that the present tense develops, but without allowing any verb tense to become befouled in a double orientation of time. It tells its story inside out. Like the ship I'm writing about, it may have a crack in its hull. And I've barely started. After four months and nine days of staring into this monitor for what has probably amounted in aggregate to something closely approaching a thousand hours, that's enough. I'm going fishing."

FAILURE: A MEDITATION
ANOTHER ITERATION
(WITH INTERRUPTIONS)

Ander Monson

If there is form, then there must be failure of form
and there must always be further failures
for there always are
in the cellar

some personal, inevitable
some cultural, beautiful

with the beets and the other wrecks of last year's canning

stored in jars
for years.

The Museum of E-Failure, a collection of ghost websites
collects websites that, for one reason or another
have gone dead between 1998 and 2003

I have always thought a good project
would be to catalogue and pedigree
the thousands of dead literary magazines

the cast of signs and defunct ISSNs
smoke traces of what there was

.
what was, was here before this wreck, .
in this gap, this yawning space, this wasteland .
this Butte, Montana, world .
where sinkholes fill with rain and mining chemicals .
leach into the water, and birds land on the surface of these pools .
sicken, turn, and die, and bob there .
like leftover bits of punctuation .

.

.

.

. . . some magazines more recently deceased—like *Partisan Review*
. . . . or *Story,* or the *Prose Poem*—and some . . . .
. . . . dead for many years: *Godey's Lady's Book* (1830s) . . . .
. . . *Dennie's Portfolio* (1801, as *The Port Folio* through the 1820s)
. . . .
. . . . The *Gentleman's Magazine* . . . .
. . . . (renamed as *Graham's Magazine* in 1841) . . . .
. . . .
. . . . gone now . . . .
. . . . but somehow lodged. . . . .
. . . . in our cultural memory. . . . .
. . . . or, more likely, in archives . . . .
. . . . where the dead . . . .
. . . . live on . . . .
. . . . as noble gases caught in beakers. . . . .
. . . . forever ranging . . . . . .
. . . . and waiting for our call . . . .
. . . .
. . . . Bruce Sterling, sci-fi writer and visionary . . . .
. . . . (he collaborated with William Gibson of *Neuromancer* and cyberpunk fame on *The Difference Engine*—one of the progenitors of the "steam punk" literary genre). . . . .
. . . .
. . . has started a project to catalogue . . . .
. . . . forms of Dead Media—the phonograph . . . .
. . . . the eight-track, the telegraph . . . .

. . . . and all those wired creations with futuristic names. . .
. . . .
. . . .
. . . . and how many times have we heard pundits complaining, proclaiming . . . .
. . . . the book's death . . . .
. . . . whether online or in print, but yet . . . .
. . . the book—as form, as technology, as pleasure, as this—persists
. . . .
. . . .
. . . . and we love it . . . .
. . . even as we love our complaints about it, its unsuitability for these digital days . . . .
. . . . the growing population . . . .
(a mold, a monolith, a spread in space) of published books each year, each one special, each one a new voice, an original talent with something to contribute to our world of information . . . . .
. . . . and we love to see books and authors (almost celebrities) brought down, hence our fox hunt with James Frey, our exposure and excoriation of the plagiarists, our own homemade mission to search and love, talk about and destroy . . . .
. . . .
. . . We love wrecks . . . . . we fear / we cause / we are wrecks . . . .
. . . .
. . . .
. . . The writer Dame Rose Macaulay loved the wreck, ...
. . . see her near-archaeological/near-anthropological book . . . . .
. . . . *Pleasure of Ruins* . . . .
. . . .
. . . and the Web—ruined, scattered as it is—loves it too . . . .
. . . *see also* the website *Welcome to Heart Failure Online* . . . . . .
. . . .
. . . . as if the heart's stop and double-clutch . . . . .
. . . . is something more personal—a nightmare. . . . .
. . . café with its electric lights gazing . . . .
. . . . out—pseudo-Edward Hopper—to the street . . . .

. . . .

. . . . (the website's subtitle: "The Website Dedicated to the Patient with Heart Failure"—seems at the least a strange dedication considering those patients' prognosis) . . . .

. . . .

. . . . The HFSA—Heart Failure Society of America— . . . . .

. . . .

. . . is also quite creepy . . . though doubtlessly its mission—to disseminate information about this brought-on-by-fat, constant American threat . . . .

. . . is good and necessary . . . .

. . . .

. . . . The celebration of the failure of the central organ of the body seems a strange project, but now all sickness is a culture, is a club—*see* Barbara Ehrenreich's 2001 essay in *Harper's,* "Welcome to Cancerland," on the wonderful world of breast cancer . . . .

. . . .

. . . .

.

.

.

sometimes I just feel played splayed out or spread .
spaced in the face of it .
the impossible burst of everything .
punctuating everything .

.

.

.

. . . .

. . . .

. . . . *Failure is impossible*—the final . . . . . .
. . . . words of Susan B. Anthony to the National . . . .
. . . . American Woman Suffrage Association . . . .

. . . .

. . . . I would argue failure is inevitable . . . .
. . . . and obsolescence a kind of accomplishment . . . .

. . . .
. . . . and www.failure.com . . . .
. . . . .leads you to *Exponent,* a technical . . . .
. . . . engineering firm—an interesting domain name choice, the failure of the domain to lead you to what you expected—it is a pointer to a ghost . . . .
. . . . an empty box. . . . . . red herring . . . .
. . . or something more sinister (think whitehouse.com . . . .
. . . . that URL that led countless grade-school students unintentionally to porn . . . .
. . . . [this redirection a sinister, ...
effective marketing strategy] . . . .
. . . . —this whitehouse.com website even claims to have "been featured on *ABCNews, CNN, C|Net, MSNBC, NBC-Dateline,* and *Newsweek,*" and this is doubtless true, though it was featured as the most famous URL sham in history [any press is good press, especially notoriety] It was visited by over 85 million people—a McDonald's boast equivalent—crows the front page . . . .
. . . .
. . . . and each new crappy movie tells us it is this week's #1 [crappy] movie in America . . . .
. . . .
. . . popularity a sort of endorsement; the failure of critique . . . .
. . . . to stick . . . .
. . . .
. . . . like the prefab nineties British pop group the Spice Girls who, on their first exposure to the public, attracted the media's ire: . . . the British press mockingly labeled the five girls sporty, posh, ginger, baby, and scary; and then the Spice Girls simply appropriated those nicknames . . . .
. . . . and grew . . . .
. . . . into the media megalith they became before they too returned to dust . . . .
. . . .
. . . . and we'll return. . . . .
. . . . .to failure analysis & engineering. . . . .
. . . .

. . . . the failure of form to support innovation . . . .
. . . to support the content—potential outcome of this essay . . . .
[always a possibility . . . .
. . . and always this self-referentiality, a buffer against critique . . . .
. . . . a cushion against the fall]— . . . . . .
. . . .
. . . . the pressure that any literary thing exerts . . . .
. . . against its scaffolding as it is . . . .
. . . . constructed . . . .
. . . . raised up, bit by bit . . . .
. . . . above the ground . . . .
. . . . . . this pressure that builds until . . . .
. . . . the scaffolding is removed . . . .
. . . . .and the language stands . . . .
.
.
.
as is .
if it does .
or else returns to dust, to rust, a passing .
and extinguished lust .
ashes and .
the pizza crusts decomposing in the trash .
.
.
.
. . . .
. . . .
. . . . My failure to report an accident to the police—inexplicable now; certainly it occurred to me to do so after I backed into a gas pump at nineteen: my passenger friend yelled at me to drive, motherfucker, drive . . . .
. . . . and I did . . . .
. . . .(being 19 and a dumbass) . . . .
. . . and this ended as you'd think, in a frenzy of ticketing . . . . . .
. . . . . though it could have been worse—suspended license. . . . .
. . . .(one of the worst American failures) . . . .
. . . . instead of hospital or jail . . . .

. . . . my own highway failure . . . .
. . . . failure to segue successfully to .
. . . .
. . . *Highway failure* . . . .
. . . . *Failure of the road pavement—deflectograph* . . . .
. . . .
. . . . *Investigating road pavement failure*. . . . .
. . . .
. . . . *Pavement structural failure* . . . .
. . . .
. . . . *determining cause of road pavement failure*. . .
. . . . *Trial holes and their failures* . . . .
. . . .
. . . .
. . . . —all these engineering sites devoted . . . .
. . . . purely. to failures. . . . . . .
. . . . of forward thinking . . . .
. . . .
. . . . failures of structure. . . . . . (again the attraction . . . . .
. . . . to force and to form) . . .
. . . .
.
.
.
is this form a failure .
does it get traction against the page .
the subject the language does it get action .
or its opposite .
or does it wilt and fold .
in on itself, .
require resuscitation, radical surgery, or a eulogy .
.
.
.
. . . .
. . . . Consider antiobesity drugs and surgery options—only (typically) tried . . . .
. . . after "failure of lifestyle modifications" though increasingly

as you've noticed, it's all about the weight loss without the work
... (which will undoubtedly lead to some body failure ....
some wrench thrown in the body's gearworks & columns of steam)
....
....
....
....
.... "poverty as a failure of lifestyle" .
....
..............."failure of lifestyle evangelism"..........
....
....
.... and I celebrate all failures political: ....
... witness the *Mondale/Ferraro* bumper sticker ....
on my Mazda Protegé ....
....
.... (if I could find one ....
.... I would absolutely drive an Edsel) .....
....
.... or the *Dukakis/Bentsen* ....
.... campaign signs on my dried-up, dying lawn in 2004...
....
.... (designed to aggravate my neighbors ....
.... and as a no-doubt useless charm ....
................against the political ....
.... climate and the 2000 and 2004 reported failures ......
................of due process and election) ....
....
.... and there are websites that chatter at each other, address this failure—the WWW (itself a failed, retired term—who still calls it the World Wide Web, or that other chestnut, the Information Superhighway, thankfully dismembered and disposed of for what we hope will be forever) ....
.... the Web one big museum of the dead..............
.... the period after the period after the period ....
.... and the discarded ....
....
.... —why does the vast distributed space of the Internet

lend itself to the accumulation, the cataloguing of detritus, the feeding of the glob, the increase, conglomeration of failures: witness all the discussion groups and fansites devoted to canceled shows, devoted to erotic stories featuring the characters of canceled shows now somehow finding new life as semi-sexy ficto-zombies? . . . .
. . . .
. . . Maybe there is something in the makeup of the Web, maker of its own dissolving. . . . .
. . . that rewards the obsession with uselessness, with esoterica—
I used to run a website devoted to Elva Miller, a musician (in a loose
. . . sense of the word, or more accurately a singer) known as . . . .
. . . "Mrs. Miller" who was either terrible or great . . . .
. . . . —it was hard to tell— . . . .
. . . . who did covers of classic songs, but who couldn't . . . . .
. . . . exactly . . . .
. . . . sing . . . .
. . . . (she sounded like a warbling something in the mud) . . . .
. . . .
. . . . .the notes on the back of the LP . . . .
. . . .(I have mono and stereo versions both) toed the line . . . .
. . . between satire and seriousness—they never quite admitted . . .
. . . . that they were mocking her, and you couldn't be . . . . . .
. . . . .sure they were or weren't . . . .
. . . . thus her fame . . . .
. . . . as a liminal space . . . .
. . . . between praise . . . . . .
. . . . and infamy . . . .
. . . .
. . . . (evidently she appeared . . . .
. . . . on *The Ed Sullivan Show* a couple times . . . .
. . . . possibly as a sideshow or car wreck . . . .
. . . . .though one hopes not) . . . .
. . . .
. . . . and Capitol Records later re-released her work in their "Ultra-Lounge: Wild, Cool, and Swingin'" series that I highly recommend you check out, though her weirdo marijuana-themed album, the gem of her work, still goes without remastering or

reissue, hidden in the dusty stacks that dot the booths at record-collector shows ....

....

............I would occasionally get people who would come across my Mrs. Miller website and send me ecstatic emails, pleased to find another body in the void, pleased to join the club, the teeming masses of self-flagellating dorks, enthusiasts, these visits doubtlessly the result of some lucky online use of the search engine.........................

....

..... (great leveler, great connector for geeks to find each other....
.... exult and sneer and cluster) ....

....

....

... so I know something about the constituency of failure geeks

....

....

—as does L. Ron Hubbard, who has an article: “The Anatomy of Failure” ....
................(of course he does)...................

....

....

and motivational speakers swing from the rafters of possible failure ...... as spoofed by Despair.com’s “Failure” faux-motivational poster with an image of a runner, head in hands, and a caption: “When Your Best Just Isn’t Good Enough” ....

....

....

... or think of Wendell Berry’s essay ....
.....“The Failure of War”..........................

....

.... I love the idea of failure in art—the failed experiment...
................the beautiful wreck, the stalled fragment....

....

....

............all the broken chunks of the Greeks ....
... not failures of art but failures of preservation—archeological
.... and inevitable.......................

. . . . our inability to get the whole . . . .
. . . . story . . . .

.

.

.

a kind of intermittence .
a breaking up of radio wave .
of electronic wash .
and signal .
meaning itself winking out .
against a background of stars and static .

.

.

.

. . . . —but there's mystery there. . . . .
. . . which sometimes means loveliness . . . .
. . . .
. . . .
. . . (other times it just means continuing mystery). . . . .
. . . .
. . . .
. . . .
. . . . I didn't fail any class in any school that I actually attended—though there was a slough of failed tests due to disciplinary difficulties, and minor instances of plagiarism. . . . .
. . . .
. . . that now I regret, since plagiarism is the writer's greatest failure
. . . .
. . . . —a plagiarized book report, copied from the back of a Hardy Boys book, which was my first official publication . . . .
. . . . .in the *Daily Mining Gazette* . . . .
. . . . .the daily paper of Houghton, Michigan . . . .
. . . . .(land of closed-down mines and ghost towns . . . .
land of the industrial wrecks—the buried, angled dredge sticking out of the Portage. . . . .
. . . . . . the thousands on thousands of broken-window . . . . . .
. . . . indeterminate and no longer functional. . . . .

.... buildings ......
.... sites of danger, absolutely ....
.... and sites of fascination, ...
.... contemplation of loss, of gone....
.... of over now and passed).....
....
....
....
.................—a plagiarized line from a story..........
....
.... in my high school fiction class ....
....
....
.... my minor Brad Vice, Jayson Blair moment....
....
.
.
oh come on .
you've taken it too far .
whatever pain you have is not worth .
all this: leave it, let it list and drift, jut out .
into open space .
or subsist if it must .
and go down .
in a cloud of doubt .
.
.
.
....
....
....

So, from the BBC's *Institute of Failure* (a performance and theory collective ....
.... based of course in Britain) ....
....
.............the Types of Failure are: ....
....
....

....
....
.................*Accident, Mistake, Weakness, Inability*.....
Incorrect Method, Uselessness, Incompatibility, Embarrassment
...*Confusion, Redundancy, Obsolescence, Incoherence*.......
.*Unrecognizability, Absurdity, Invisibility, Impermanence*.....
..*Decay, Instability, Forgettability*.........................
.......*Tardiness, Disappearance, Catastrophe, Uncertainty*....
.........*Doubt, Fear, Distractibility*....................
.....................(a kind of anti–Boy Scout creed)....
....
....
.......but they left out Falsehood and Misrepresentation....
.....................the sad-eyed dog of Plagiarism......
......................or does *Redundancy* cover it?.....
............................or *Weakness*?..........
......................maybe the redundancy of form....
..................which this essay takes, after the snow essay
..........in the collection—is this a failure of invention....
.........or a growing of the concept? Does it break.......
....
.....apart?....................................
....
.......prefigure collapse?.............................
....
.........Is it a crutch on which the essay................
.......or the author..............................
...............perches.........................
..............................a treading of water, an
uneasiness to submit itself to analysis?....................
....
....
...Failure analysis is a branch of Materials Engineering......
.......and what a great term—both failure analysis........
............and materials engineering—a loveliness.......
...........of language moving unfettered through space—...
.........suggests..............................
.............a methodology, a mindset...............

....
.............our hundred connotations for the words.......
...our terrifying slash exhilarating college classes ....
....
.... “The Failure of Sex Education” ......
.
.
is this both analysis .
and anatomy .
or the failure of anatomy .
a geography .
a graph, connect the dots .
a plot, a plotting of points across the sky .
.
.
.
.... —failure as the ultimate criticism .....
...... we can lever against a policy or subject, that it failed ....
.... but again this is perhaps instructive ....
.... failed to do what? failed to guarantee results? .....
...already I am lapsing into business-speak ....
....
.... and failure as a rhetoric ....
.... as a personal rhetoric ....
...............is absolutely useful....................
....
....
....
...On weather and its importance in accidents and failures: ....
....
....
....
...*Some effects are quite well known, such as: Ice and snow leading to increases in traffic accidents*...................
....
.............*High winds leading to structural failures* ......
...*Low temperatures leading to freezing and bursting pipes*....
.... *High temperatures leading to pavement buckles* ....

. . . . . *Persistent rains leading to floods* . . . .
. . . .
. . . . . *Other effects are not as well known. For example:* . . . . . .
. . . *Increasing the water content of some soils leads to a decrease in shear strength* . . . .
. . . .
. . . . . *As a result, heavy rains* . . . .
can lead to sudden soil subsidence and damage to overlying structures
. . . .
. . . *Some clays swell dramatically* . . . .
. . . . . *when moistened, leading to foundation and roadway damage*
. . . .
. . . . *The impact strength and fracture toughness of many steels undergo a sharp decline at low temperature. This can lead to a brittle fracture in cold weather under loads that could otherwise be supported without failure* . . . .
. . . .
. . . *Bituminous materials (pitch, tar, asphalt) can soften in hot weather and, under load, can slowly flow and deform out of their original shape* . . . .
. . . .
. . . .
. . . . —there is a lovely mass . . . . a morass. . . . .
. . . . of language . . . .
. . . .
. . . .
. . . .
. . . . . The effects of my education's early bottom-out. . . . .
. . . before I would have gone on to engineering goodness and a high-paying job . . . .
. . . . (my life gone technical) . . . .
. . . . . as my parents would have had it . . . . (this
. . . . a failure in itself . . . .
. . . . .of living up to parental, parenthetical . . . . . .
. . . . expectations . . . .
. . . .
. . . .

....
.....Possible failure as a son ....
....
(my stepmother blamed her anxiety attacks on my bad behavior
....
which, while in some ways fair, seems—in retrospect—excessive)
....
....
....
... I like to think that I have not failed too often as a friend ....
.... though my former friends may want to disagree ....
....
....
but maybe these are *necessary* failures—failures to keep in touch
... or to keep up with high school friends as distance grows....
.....and as there become fewer reasons to do so ....
....
....
....
and no essay about failure could be complete without the sauciness
............of sexual failure—or its mention ....
.... though this is not purely confession— ....
....
....
....
... certainly American men have sexual failure on the brain....
... or the ad execs presume we do ....
...... judging from the constant bombardment at the back....
.... of *Rolling Stone* or *Maxim* or on television ......
....
... I like to think of these as material—the meter, the métier—of
future ruins ....
.... sites of excavation............
....
....
.
.

.
penis pumps, herbal supplements .
the drugs, the drugs, the drugs .
these sorts of scaffolding for our nether regions .
we must get pumped up .
jacked up .
maxed out, ripped .
erect and architected .
.
we need to stiffen .
pry things open .
arc and make it come to something .
.
.
.

....
.... in the way that cigarette ads from the '70s ....
..... seem bizarre and quaint, overt and overwrought ....
.... (could we have ever lived like that, we wonder?) ....
.... so this is my tiny arsenal of antiquated failure ....
.... embedded here for you ....
....
..... Failure, choking, chunking it; lack of success, as noun: ....
....
.... *abortion, bankruptcy, bomb, botch, breakdown, bummer, bungle, bust, checkmate, clinker, collapse, decay, decline, defeat, deficiency, deficit, deterioration, dog, downfall, dud, failing, false step, faux pas, fiasco, flop, frustration, implosion, inadequacy, lead balloon, lemon, loser, loss, mess, misadventure, miscarriage, misstep, no go, nonperformance, nonsuccess, overthrow, rout, rupture, sinking ship, stalemate, stoppage, total loss, turkey, washout, wreck* ....
....
.... as noun/as person: ......
....
....
.... *also-ran, bankrupt, beat, bomb, born loser, bum, cast-*

away, dead duck, deadbeat, defaulter, derelict, disappointment, dud, flop, flunky, good-for-nothing, has-been, incompetent, insolvent, loafer, loser, lumpy, might-have-been, moocher, ne'er-do-well, no-good, nobody, nonperformer, prodigal, stiff, turkey, underachiever, washout . . . .

. . . .

. . . .

. . . .

. . . . This essay as a failure in itself . . . . . .

. . . . an aborted exercise . . . .

. . . .

. . . . .if essays have a stated purpose. . . . .

. . . . and if this essay has a thesis . . . .

. . . . then it has failed to reach it. . . . .

. . . .

. . . . absolutely! . . . . . .

. . . . and you go, girl! . . . . .

. . . .

. . . .

. . . . .it has shown a demonstrated lack of success. . . .

. . . .

.

.

.

has it borne its load .
has it given birth .
to an entertaining anything .
has it prised, apprised you .
of the important world .
is it now a prize .
or should we raze it .
start again, and let it disappear .

.

.

.

. . . Call it a burn . . . . a bum . . . .

. . . . .a doldrum literary creation . . . .

....
....
................but again the wreck suggests the vase ......
.... the fragment evokes the once-whole torso ....
... the car glass scattered on the road, the flash and burn ......
tire-squeal, whiplash, and fire.............................
....
..... and it is maybe better to have failed at this ....
............than to have poured it all out on the page.......
.............simple, whole, unmediated, all too easily ......
....
....
....
....
....
....
....
....
....
....
....
....
....
....
....
....
....
....
....
....
....
....
....
....
....
....
....
....

LIVE THROUGH THAT?!

Eileen Myles

I just want to be frank about what you will be really living through.

You'll be living through flossing. Years of it, both in the mirror and away from it, both with girlfriends and alone. Girlfriends will be really excited that you floss your teeth, because they should and they think it's really inspiring that you do that and they will ask you if they can do it with you because it's easier that way, bumping their hips and thighs against you while you keep peering at yourself under the shitty bathroom light. They will even talk glowingly over drinks with their friends about the really diligent way you have of flossing and then the little brushes and even how you rinse and you'll look at their friends who look kind of weirded out and you'll be thinking you're just making me sound really old. I mean why do you think I floss my teeth for like fifteen minutes every night. My father lost his teeth at forty and then he died at forty-four. Before I decided I also wanted to live I was utterly convinced that I would never lose my teeth and I have had tooth loosening and tooth loss dreams all my life, so in my twenties when I had never gone to therapy I decided that I would always privilege the dentist over the therapist and that I was really getting a two-in-one service when I went to the dentist but still when I drank I would often pass out before I could floss. Then I stopped drinking. I found myself in my thirties leaning into the mirror one night cleaning away and I thought: fuck, is this what I lived for—to floss.

Well, yeah. I mean I don't know about anyone else but when I found myself at the age of thirty-three no longer spending the majority of my days getting sort of hammered I was to say the least perplexed. I never thought I wanted to DIE. That was not the point of my constant drinking. It wasn't a thought at all. Because there was such a thing as drunkenness I aspired to it. I took it, it was there. Moderate friends would wince and even suggest I was "self-destructive" but that didn't sound right to me. Things would happen, that's all. I didn't mean them to be. It was surrounding circumstances—to alcoholism. Which was what my entire family life was too. My father didn't mean to make me watch him die. It just happened. But this next act, the living, this was conscious. This was a choice. Or that's what I grappled with for a very long time. Do I want this. Being sober made me want to die. Cause I was swarming with feelings. About being a dyke. About being poor. About aging. About my inability to connect. About what a great poet I was, but what if—I don't know, first what if I can't write anymore, then what if no one will publish my work. None of these worries are particularly interesting or unique but I found myself in a state of endless worry. And who is this who can't turn the faucet of anxiety off with a drink or a drug. And yet I had a simple urge to preserve what I've got.

To tell you the truth if I am feeling ANXIOUS at night I sometimes think it's a good idea to go to bed without brushing my teeth. No face washing, nothing. It feels kind of wild. And I've slept with women and I've been friends with people who have shared that their secret decadence is the occasional tumble into the sack without brushing or flossing. So I do that too. But you know what, it's more interesting to floss. Because I face my face, myself, and I spend about seven minutes—first flossing, then the little brushes, then brushing the backs of the four molars, then the insides of up and down, then the front and the sides on the outside. I examine my gums. And uncannily at some point during this ritual I begin to feel better. It's like washing my car and I never wash my car. It's the most intimate expression of care I know. And if I don't do it my teeth hurt the next day. Because get this: when you age your teeth spread a little so food gets caught in the cracks and if you have bone decay (and I do) the food gets jammed down there and almost instantly it produces pain. And miraculously though that pain produces panic and I begin to fear I will lose a tooth what actually happens is after I do a really good flossing and brushing the next night and maybe a little gargling (with peroxide which is really kind of a trip—your mouth gets sudsy and greasy! Don't worry. It goes away) the pain subsides. And I did it. Me! To tell you the truth, good tooth care is more like repairing a bike which I also can't do. Okay so in all these years of tooth care some other things have happened, and I mean I have a mouth full of caps. I have fallen, and teeth have cracked of their own accord—well usually I bit a cherry pit, or a date. Or a kernel of corn, or a chicken bone—snap! A tooth cracks and now you have just dropped a thousand bucks. So my mouth is full of these perfectly stained off-white piano keys that I meticulously clean every night. But still in all these years of care, through a squadron of dentists—all in New York and in New York still—I will not go to a California dentist. I'm not having it. All of the dentists have said for years—one day you're going to have to go to a periodontist. That seemed like the end. Yet my mother who is in her eighties and has ALL HER TEETH, *she* has gone to a periodontist. How was it, Mom. Awful she says. But then I watch her biting into some food. We are usually eating when we talk and our love of food is certainly part of the issue here. Biting and eating, that's the story. Luckily when the day came—and really the day comes when you have the money—I began to explore going to a periodontist. I've gone several rounds of meet and greets and one guy up there in La Jolla was a monster. He made an obscene video of me with my lips pulled back and the damage revealed in that fashion which was worse than the most humiliating pornography, worse than dead, and even while he was giving me the instructions to get my lips and jaw into the horrifying poses, he said—what did he say—good girl, or that a girl, something that sounded like I was an animal. And it was going to cost thousands of dollars. So much money. And he would be pulling. And restoring. I would have a mouth full of living, false, not "teeth gone" but something cold. This is kind of the end of my story or the beginning of the next—a second act or maybe the third—live through that and that and that—because I did something I'd never done before. I am not middle class. I don't have sharp perceptions about personal investment and bourgeois self-esteem, or I didn't then. But I had heard about this thing which is getting a second opinion. I don't even know how I approached it. I guess I went to my dentist in New York, who I love, Michael Chang on Second Avenue across from the movie theater on Twelfth Street. I had another dentist before Michael Chang in the exact same location. It was Chuck. And he was great too. And Chuck sold Michael Chang his practice. So I stayed with the building and the view from that particular dental chair. I allowed myself to be part of someone's practice that was sold. I am trying to give you sort of an extended picture of what I am living through. And Michael Chang recommended another man, Michael Lanzetta.

I will only say that I enjoy these men and I trust them—with my mouth and my body. They are sweet guys. Incidentally I am fifty-seven. I just want to say something different has happened about living in the past few years. Not only am I not "self-destructive" nor am I ambivalent about wanting to live, nor am I unaware that this, all the time I've spent telling you about toothbrushing, this is actually *my life,* my time. One's life is literally that, their duration. And I've seen friends die young, much younger than me, and they keep dying my friends and one day I will too. And how I feel right now about that is a little sad because now I want to live so much and have all my time and do so many things. So I have to attend to the thing in front of me because if I am not focused I can get overwhelmed by my desire to do *everything* STILL, yet as they say the clock is ticking and I won't get to it all, I can't. And the impossibility of that choice, of the everything when I was young, that choice made me a poet because I could have some purchase on everything and do a little bit of it all the day. Just chipping away. And it's essentially the same now and I've made the same choice again, when I decided to do what's in front of me but I probably can do other things too and I will. I just don't need to talk about them here. So—

Dr. Lanzetta quoted me a price like one quarter of what the

animal doctor in La Jolla charged, and he was much less invasive in his plan and I was impressed that I had in my life held out for something simpler and more comfortable. It was a unique choice in my life. And I celebrate that today.

To hold out, as if I could be like that. To trust my own—no, I think I'll wait. So in the face of the mountain of time I've lived, and in the eye of the mystery of what remains I feel quietly smart and open my mouth widely and slowly tonight and I brush. I examine, I grin. I grin like a skull, but it's cool. Examine, grin again. I'm a mechanic now, doctor, friend. This skull is my friend.

EXCERPT FROM *THE ARGONAUTS*

Maggie Nelson

There are people out there who get annoyed at the story that Djuna Barnes, rather than identify as a lesbian, preferred to say that she "just loved Thelma." Gertrude Stein reputedly made similar claims, albeit not in those exact terms, about Alice. I get why it's politically maddening, but I've also always thought it a little romantic—the romance of letting an individual experience of desire take precedence over a categorical one. The story brings to mind art historian T. J. Clark's defense of his interest in the eighteenth-century painter Nicolas Poussin from imaginary interlocutors: "Calling an interest in Poussin nostalgic or elitist is like calling the interest one has, say, in the person one cares for most deeply 'hetero- (or homo-) sexist,' or 'exclusive' or 'proprietorial.' Yes, that may be right: those may be roughly the parameters, and regrettable; but the interest itself may still be more complete and human—still carry more of human possibility and compassion—than interests uncontaminated by any such affect or compulsion." Here, as elsewhere, contamination *makes deep* rather than disqualifies.

Besides, everyone knows that Barnes and Stein had relationships with women besides Thelma and Alice. Alice knew, too: she was apparently so jealous upon finding out that Stein's early novel *Q.E.D.* told the coded story of a love triangle involving Stein and a certain May Bookstaver that Alice—who was also Stein's editor and typist—found all sorts of weasely ways to omit every appearance of the word *May* or *may* when she retyped Stein's *Stanzas in Meditation,* henceforth an unwitting collaboration.

By February I was driving around the city looking at apartment after apartment, trying to find one big enough for us and your son, whom I hadn't yet met. Eventually we found a house on a hill with gleaming dark wood floors and a view of a mountain and a too-high rent. The day we got the keys, we slept together in a fit of giddiness on a thin blanket spread out over the wood floor of what would become our first bedroom.

That view. It may have been a pile of rough scrub with a stagnant pond at its top, but for two years, it was our mountain.

And then, just like that, I was folding your son's laundry. He had just turned three. Such little socks! Such little underwear! I marveled at them, made him lukewarm cocoa each morning with as much powder as can fit in the rim of a fingernail, played Fallen Soldier with him for hours on end. In Fallen Soldier he would collapse with all his gear on—sequined chain mail hat, sword, sheath, a limb wounded from battle, tied up in a scarf. I was the good Blue Witch who had to sprinkle healing dust all over him to bring him back to life. I had a twin who was evil; the evil twin had felled him with her poisonous blue powder. But now I was here to heal him. He lay there motionless, eyes closed, the faintest smile on his face, while I recited my monologue: *But where could this soldier have come from? How did he get so far from home? Is he badly wounded? Will he be kind or fierce when he awakens? Will he know I am good, or will he mistake me for my evil twin? What can I say that will bring him back to life?*

Throughout that fall, yellow YES ON PROP 8 signs were sprouting up everywhere, most notably jabbed into an otherwise bald and beautiful mountain I passed each day on my way to work. The sign depicted four stick figures raising their hands to the sky, in a paroxysm of joy—the joy, I suppose, of heteronormativity, here indicated by the fact that one of the stick figures sported a triangle skirt. (*What is that triangle, anyway? My twat?*) PROTECT CALIFORNIA CHILDREN! the stick figures cheered.

Each time I passed the sign stuck into the blameless mountain, I thought about Catherine Opie's *Self-Portrait/Cutting* from 1993, in which Opie photographed her back with a drawing of a house and two stick-figure women holding hands (two triangle skirts!) carved into it, along with a sun, a cloud, and two birds. She took the photo while the drawing was still dripping with blood. "Opie, who had recently broken up with her partner, was longing at the time to start a family, and the image radiates all the painful contradictions inherent in that wish," *Art in America* explains.

I don't get it, I said to Harry. Who wants a version of the Prop 8 poster, but with two triangle skirts?

Maybe Cathy does, Harry shrugged.

Once I wrote a book about domesticity in the poetry of certain gay men (Ashbery, Schuyler) and some women (Mayer, Notley). I wrote this book when I was living in New York City in a teeny, too-hot attic apartment on a Brooklyn thoroughfare underlined by the F train. I had an unusable stove filled with petrified mouse droppings, an empty fridge save for a couple of beers and yogurt peanut honey Balance bars, a futon on a piece of plywood unevenly balanced on milk crates for a bed, and a floor through which I could hear *Standcleartheclosingdoors* morning, noon, and night. I spent approximately seven hours a day lying in bed in this apartment, if that. Mostly I slept elsewhere. I wrote most everything I wrote and read most everything I read in public, just as I am writing this in public now.

I was so happy renting in New York City for so long because renting—or at least the way I rented, which involved never lifting a finger to better my surroundings—allows you to let things literally fall apart all around you. Then, when it gets to be too much, you just move on.

Many feminists have argued for *the decline of the domestic as a separate, inherently female sphere and the vindication of domesticity as an ethic, an affect, an aesthetic, and a public*. I'm not sure what this vindication would mean, exactly, though I think in my book I was angling for something of the same. But even then I suspected that I was doing so because I didn't have a domestic, and I liked it that way.

I liked Fallen Soldier because it gave me time to learn about your son's face in mute repose: big almond eyes, skin just starting to freckle. And clearly he found some novel, relaxing pleasure in just lying there, protected by imaginary armor, while a near stranger who was quickly becoming family picked up each limb and turned it over, trying to find the wound.

Not long ago, a friend came over to our house and pulled down a mug for coffee, a mug that was a gift from my mother. It's one of those mugs you can purchase online from Snapfish, with the photo of your choice emblazoned on it. I was horrified when I received it, but it's the biggest mug we own, so we keep it around, in case someone's in the mood for a trough of warm milk or something.

Wow, my friend said, filling it up. *I've never seen anything so heteronormative in all my life.*

The photo on the mug depicts my family and me, all dressed up to go to the *Nutcracker* at Christmastime—a ritual that was important to my mother when I was a little girl, and that we have revived with her now that there are children in my life.

In the photo I'm seven months pregnant with what will become Iggy, wearing a high ponytail and leopard print dress; Harry and his son are wearing matching dark suits, looking dashing. We're standing in front of the mantel at my mother's house, which has monogrammed stockings hanging from it. We look happy.

But what about it is the essence of heteronormativity? That my mother made a mug on a boojie service like Snapfish? That we're clearly participating, or acquiescing into participating, in a long tradition of families being photographed at holiday time in their holiday best? That my mother made me the mug, in part to indicate that she recognizes and accepts my tribe as family? What about my pregnancy—is that inherently heteronormative? Or is the presumed opposition of queerness and procreation (or, to put a finer edge on it, maternity) more a reactionary embrace of how things have shaken down for queers than the mark of some ontological truth? As more queers have kids, will the presumed opposition simply wither away? Will you miss it?

Is there something inherently queer about pregnancy itself, insofar as it profoundly alters one's "normal" state, and occasions a radical intimacy with—and radical alienation from—one's body? How can an experience so profoundly strange and wild and transformative also symbolize or enact the ultimate conformity? Or is this just another disqualification of anything tied too closely to the female animal from the privileged term (in this case, nonconformity, or radicality)? What about the fact that Harry is neither male nor female? *I'm a special—a two for one,* his character Valentine explains in *By Hook or By Crook.*

When or how do *new kinship systems mime older nuclear-family arrangements* and when or how do they *radically recontextualize them in a way that constitutes a rethinking of kinship*? How can you tell; or, rather, who's to tell? *Tell your girlfriend to find a different kid to play house with,* your ex would say, after we first moved in.

To align oneself with the real while intimating that others are at play, approximate, or in imitation can feel good. But any fixed claim on realness, especially when it is tied to an identity, also has a finger in psychosis. *If a man who thinks he is a king is mad, a king who thinks he is a king is no less so.*

Perhaps this is why psychologist D. W. Winnicott's notion of "feeling real" is so moving to me. One can aspire to feel real, one can help others to feel real, and one can oneself feel real—a feeling Winnicott describes as the collected, primary sensation of aliveness, "the aliveness of the body tissues and working of body-functions, including the heart's action and breathing," which makes spontaneous gesture possible. For Winnicott, feeling real is not reactive to external stimuli, nor is it an identity. It is a sensation—a sensation that spreads. Among other things, it makes one want to live.

Some people find pleasure in aligning themselves with an identity, as in *You make me feel like a natural woman*—made famous by Aretha Franklin and, later, by Judith Butler, who focused on the instability wrought by the simile. But there can also be a horror in doing so, not to mention an impossibility. *It's not possible to live twenty-four hours a day soaked in the immediate awareness of one's sex. Gendered self-consciousness has, mercifully, a flickering nature.*

A friend says he thinks of gender as a color. Gender does share with color a certain ontological indeterminacy: it isn't quite right to say that an object *is* a color, nor that the object *has* a color. Context also changes it: *all cats are gray*, etc. Nor is color *voluntary*, precisely. But none of these formulations means that the object in question is *colorless*.

The bad reading [of Gender Trouble*] goes something like this: I can get up in the morning, look in my closet, and decide which gender I want to be today. I can take out a piece of clothing and change my gender: stylize it, and then that evening I can change it again and be something radically other, so that what you get is something like the commodification of gender, and the understanding of taking on a gender as a kind of consumerism. . . . When my whole point was that the very formation of subjects, the very formation of persons, presupposes gender in a certain way—that gender is not to be chosen and that "performativity" is not radical choice and it's not voluntarism. . . . Performativity has to do with repetition, very often with the repetition of oppressive and painful gender norms to force them to resignify. This is not freedom, but a question of how to work the trap that one is inevitably in.*

You should order a mug in response, my friend mused while drinking her coffee. *Like, how about one that features Iggy's head crowning, in all its bloody glory?* (I had told her earlier that day that I was vaguely hurt that my mother hadn't wanted to look at my birth photos; Harry then reminded me that few people ever want to look at anyone's birth photos, at least not the graphic ones. And I was forced to admit that my past feelings about other people's birth photos bore out the truth of this statement. But in my postpartum haze, I felt as though giving birth to Iggy was such an achievement, and doesn't my mother like to be proud of my achievements? She *laminated* the page in *The New York Times* that listed me as a Guggenheim recipient, for God's sake. Unable to throw the Guggenheim placemat away [ingratitude], but not knowing what else to do with it, I've since placed it below Iggy's high chair, to catch the food that flows downward. Given that the fellowship essentially paid for his conception, each time

I sponge tidbits of shredded wheat or broccoli florets off of it, I feel a loose sense of justice.)

During our first forays out as a couple, I blushed a lot, felt dizzy with my luck, unable to contain the nearly exploding fact that I've so obviously gotten everything I'd ever wanted, everything there was to get. *Handsome, brilliant, quick-witted, articulate, forceful, you.* We spent hours and hours on the red couch, giggling, *The happiness police are going to come and arrest us if we go on this way. Arrest us for our luck.*

What if where I am is what I need? Before you, I had always thought of this mantra as a means of making peace with a bummer or even catastrophic situation. I never imagined it might apply to joy, too.

In *The Cancer Journals,* Audre Lorde rails against the imperative to optimism and happiness that she found in the medical discourse surrounding breast cancer. "Was I really fighting the spread of radiation, racism, woman-slaughter, chemical invasion of our food, pollution of our environment, the abuse and psychic destruction of our young, merely to avoid dealing with my first and greatest responsibility—to be happy?" Lorde writes. "Let us seek 'joy' rather than real food and clean air and a saner future on a liveable earth! As if happiness alone can protect us from the results of profit-madness."

Happiness is no protection, and certainly it is not a responsibility. *The freedom to be happy restricts human freedom if you are not free to be not happy.* But one can make of either freedom a habit, and only you know which you've chosen.

The wedding story of Mary and George Oppen is one of the only straight-people stories I know in which the marriage is made more romantic by virtue of its being a sham. Here is their story: One night in 1926, Mary went out on a date with George, whom she knew just a little from a college poetry class. As Mary remembers it: "He came for me in his roommate's Model T Ford, and we drove out to the country, sat and talked, made love, and talked until morning. . . . We talked as we had never talked before, an outpouring." Upon returning to their dorms in the morning, Mary found herself expelled; George was suspended. They then took off together, hitchhiking on the open road.

Before meeting George, Mary had decided firmly against marriage, considering it to be a "disastrous trap." But she also knew that traveling together without being married put her and George at risk with the law via the Mann Act—one of the many laws in U.S. history ostensibly passed to prosecute unequivocally bad things like sexual slavery, but which in actuality has been used to harass anyone whose relationships the state deems "immoral."

So in 1927, Mary got married. Here is her account of that day:

> Although I had a strong conviction that my relationship with George was not an affair of the State, the threat of imprisonment on the road frightened us, so we went to be married in Dallas. A girl we met gave me her purple velvet dress, her boyfriend gave us a pint of gin. George wore his college roommate's baggy plus-fours, but we did not drink the gin. We bought a ten-cent ring and went to the ugly red sandstone courthouse that still stands in Dallas. We gave my name, Mary Colby, and the name George was using, "David Verdi," because he was fleeing from his father.

And so Mary Colby marries David Verdi, but she never precisely marries George Oppen. They give the state the slip, along with George's wealthy family (who by this point had hired a private eye to find them). That slip then becomes a sliver of light filtering into their house for the next fifty-seven years. Fifty-seven years of baffling the paradigm, with ardor.

I have long known about madmen and kings; I have long known about feeling real. I have long been lucky enough to *feel* real, no matter what diminishments or depressions have come my way. And I have long known that the *moment of queer pride is a refusal to be shamed by witnessing the other as being ashamed of you.*

So why did your ex's digs about playing house sting so bright?

Sometimes one has to know something many times over. Sometimes one forgets, and then remembers. And then forgets, and then remembers. And then forgets again.

As with knowledge, so too, with presence.

If the baby could speak to the mother, says Winnicott, here is what it might say:

I find you;
You survive what I do to you as I come to recognize you as not-me;
I use you;
I forget you;
But you remember me;
I keep forgetting you;
I lose you;
I am sad.

HOMESCHOOL

Meghan O'Gieblyn

For most of my childhood—from kindergarten until tenth grade—I did not attend school. *Homeschooled* is the term I used as a kid, the term I still use today for expediency, though it has always seemed misleading, since schooling is what my mother meant to spare us from by keeping us at home. We lived during those years on a farm in Vermont that sat thirty miles outside the nearest functional town and was, in a lot of ways, autonomous. We ate eggs from our own chickens, heated the house with a wood-burning stove, and got our water from a local spring, which was just a PVC pipe extending from the side of a mountain next to a sign warning that the county could not guarantee the quality of the water. I spent most mornings doing the chores I shared with my brothers: feeding the chickens, stocking the woodbin, hauling hay bales out to the sheep pasture. After that, the day was my own. Sometimes I read alone in my room, or sat at the kitchen table drawing comics in my sketchbook. As the oldest, I was often responsible for the younger kids, but like most children in large families they were easy—hungry for attention, game for whatever task I invented. We made baroque concoctions of flour and spices in the mixer and played with the bottle-fed lambs that slept in the kitchen in a baby hamper and wobbled freely around the house all day. We were always trying to teach them to sit or roll over, as if they were dogs.

My mom was usually outdoors, tinkering with something in the barn or traipsing around the pasture, examining the sheep for hoof rot. It was just her and us. Our dad left when I was eight—first for inpatient treatment for what in those days was called "manic depression," then the following year for good, when he returned to the small Oregon town where he'd grown up. At the time my mom was pregnant with her fourth child. Even though we lived in a remote area, with no other adult in the house, she insisted on giving birth naturally, at home. The night her labor started, I was the one who called the midwife, who instructed me to fetch a heating pad and rubbing alcohol; she'd be there in forty minutes. When she arrived, I helped ferry towels back and forth from the bathroom, and was allowed to stay in the room for the birth.

This was, according to my mom, "an experience"—one of many things I would never have learned at school. The sole purpose of schools, she often said, was to teach children to stand in lines. They were places people sent their children to do "busy work"—one of her favorite phrases, a catchall for all manner of scholastic activity, from the pointless tasks contrived to habituate children to following rules (worksheets, self-assessments) to the required subjects she considered vehicles for the state's ideological agenda (sex education, evolutionary biology). My mom had been sent as a teenager to a boarding school in the South, a missionary reform academy that liberally practiced corporal punishment and from which she fled, sneaking out at night and hitchhiking back home to Michigan. Her animosity toward institutions must have stemmed from that experience, but she rarely mentioned it—and anyway, she rejected all forms of schooling: public and private, religious and secular.

Learning was something else. It was happening all the time, whether we were conscious of it or not, like breathing. In a letter to the state department of education, she referred to her pedagogy as "delight-directed integrated study," a term I believe she made up. She was required to write these letters every year, one for each child, detailing how she would teach the core subjects. I read them for the first time a couple years ago and was awed by their expansive, often creative notion of what qualifies as education. On the topic of Comprehensive Health, she wrote: "Meghan had a great introduction to the health care system this past spring when she spent four days in the hospital having her appendix out." On Citizenship, History, and Government: "We hope to have contact with a family of Russian immigrants through friends of ours who will be sponsoring them. This should help make real to Meghan some of the freedoms we enjoy in this country." All the letters were written in the same shrugging, breezy tone that was her primary mode of defense, and barely concealed her hostility toward state intervention. On sex education: "Presently she is gaining a good base of information by being involved with the life cycles in our barn, and some sheep we will breed this fall."

My mom considered music the most important part of our education. Each of us kids played at least one instrument, and the only time she interfered with our day was when the house was quiet for more than an hour. "I don't hear any practicing!" she'd call out. She also placed a disproportionate emphasis on memorization. By the age of ten I could, if prompted, recite entire chapters of the King James Bible. My mom would turn to me while we were weeding the garden or waiting in line at the supermarket and say, "Let's hear Luke 2." We did, technically, have textbooks; they came in the mail each August from a Christian education wholesaler in Texas. Occasionally, my mom would flip through one and comment on something, but they remained for the most part untouched, stacked on the kitchen sideboard. Subjects that didn't interest her were more or less neglected. I went for years without doing formal arithmetic. Until tenth grade, my knowledge of earth sciences began and ended with Genesis. Every few months my mom would recognize the lapse and try to remedy it with an outsize gesture. Once, she returned from a walk with a dead painted turtle she'd found on the side of the road, placed it on our backyard picnic table, pulled out a makeshift assortment of surgical tools—a screwdriver, dinner forks, a butcher knife—and announced we were having "science class."

But the vast majority of our day was spent doing nothing. My mom talked about the importance of "hayloft time," her term for idle reflection. Children needed to think, she was always saying. They needed to spend a lot of time alone. She believed that extended bouts of solitude would cultivate autonomy and independence of thought. I did hole up many afternoons atop the ziggurat of hay bales, reading, or sometimes just lying there in silence, watching the chaff fall from the rafters. I also spent a lot of time in the woods, which I called "exploring." Behind the sheep pasture was a dirt road that led up the mountain to a network of abandoned logging trails that were, for all I could tell, limitless. I walked them every day and never saw another person. It wasn't uncommon to stumble on a hidden wonder: a meadow, an overgrown pasture, tiered waterfalls that ran green over carpets of algae. In those moments I experienced life as early humans might have, in a condition not unlike the one idealized by the Romantics, my mind as empty and stark as the bars of sunlight crossing the forest floor. I walked until I was tired, or until the shadows grew long and the sun dipped below the mountains, and then I headed home.

To raise a child of nature—a child who is truly free—you must first remove him from society. Take him out of the city, with its vanities, its hierarchies, its parades of status, and away from the village, where he might learn the vices of peasants. Give him a wide stretch of land where he can wander wherever he wishes. Give him a tutor who does not teach but simply serves as a model. The overprotected child will grow up to be weak. Let him discover the limits of his freedom, learning from his own mistakes. Exercise his body, but keep his mind idle for as long as possible. When he grows older, he will read what he chooses to read, and will teach himself whatever he finds useful. By then, he will be a true freethinker, and approach every idea as a skeptic.

This is more or less the pedagogy laid out by Jean-Jacques Rousseau in *Émile, or On Education*, the vade mecum of modern homeschooling. Perhaps that's going too far. No homeschooler I've known has acknowledged its influence, but the book was the first to present a systematic argument that supports parents pulling their children out of schools and rearing them at home. If you were to trace the basic philosophical precepts of the American homeschooling movement back through the tributaries of history in search of their source, you would find them all in Rousseau: society and its institutions degrade the natural inclinations; spontaneous action is superior to habit; children are malleable and must be cultivated carefully and deliberately, like plants.

In the beginning, modern American homeschoolers called themselves "unschoolers," a nod to the Rousseauian idea that true education is naturalistic and self-directed. The term was coined by John Holt, a school reformer who'd gradually lost faith in reform. Holt believed that America was "a sick society" obsessed with violence, luxury, and power, and that public life rewarded groupthink and totalitarian consensus. During the free school movement of the 1960s, he wrote books outlining how schools could give children more freedom and autonomy, but he eventually became disillusioned with the charade of formal education. Schools could never be changed because they were inextricably linked to the corporate workforce; their sole task was to prepare children to be docile employees. "It was becoming clear to me that the great majority of boring, regimented schools were doing exactly what they had always done and what most people wanted them to do," he writes in his book *Teach Your Own:* "Teach children about Reality. Teach them that Life Is No Picnic. Teach them to Shut Up And Do What You're Told."

In the late 1970s, Holt began arguing that parents were perfectly capable of educating their own children. He started a newsletter, *Growing Without Schooling,* to connect his growing band of disciples, most of whom were hippies—back-to-the-landers, people living on communal farms—who believed unschooling was an ancient, intuitive way of raising children. Parents wrote in to share that their kids were "flowering" at home: a child of barely two had learned to cook meals for himself, using knives and a stove; a child of three had taught himself to read without instruction, and was so immersed in nature he could recognize and name every kind of tree. "By the time he was five," the father wrote, "he was so used to getting up in the morning with the ecstatic prospect of learning all day long that I hated to disabuse him of the notion that learning was natural by sending him to school."

But if you read the newsletter carefully, it's clear that not everyone maintained this laissez-faire approach. One father claims he has "eminent domain" over his children, which gives him the right "to rear and to train them according to the dictates of my own conscience before God." A mother, who describes her family as "churchgoing Catholics," writes that with her children at home, she and her husband can better oversee their socialization, their television viewing, and their sugar consumption. It turns out the hippies were not the only ones reading Holt's newsletter. His subscribers included a number of religious conservatives—evangelicals, Catholics, Seventh-day Adventists—who shared his belief that state education was a form of mind control, though for quite different reasons. For them, schools were not brainwashing children with capitalist values, but with the agenda of the radical left, which, according to the rhetoric, included evolutionary biology, sex education, and secular humanism.

In the second issue of *Growing Without Schooling,* Holt acknowledged that his disciples were "mixed allies" whose grievances about schools varied dramatically. He saw this diversity as a strength, proof of the movement's potential to transcend political and religious lines. It's hard not to wince at his naivete. In the coming decades, homeschooling would become almost entirely dominated by fundamentalist Christians, who had a more ambitious social agenda, massive organizational wealth, and—perhaps most crucially—a large contingent of mothers who were willing to forgo careers and stay home with their children. In those early, heady days of utopianism, it was perhaps difficult to grasp a truth that is all too plain now: that countercultural ideals like freedom, individualism, and antiauthoritarianism can be commandeered by the very institutional powers they were contrived to fight.

But perhaps the problem lies closer to the source, with the Enlightenment notion of absolute freedom. Rousseau speaks passionately of liberating children, and yet his pedagogy involves highly specific prescriptions for how a child should be bathed (in ice-cold water), where he should be raised (in a temperate climate, like France), how he should be fed (sparsely; too much food will disrupt his digestion). Émile cannot have contact with other children, or see doctors or priests during his early years.

"You will not be master of the child if you cannot control every one about him," the author warns. It is this contradiction in Rousseau—what Jacob Talmon called the "transition from absolute freedom to absolute necessity"—that led cold-war critics like Talmon and Isaiah Berlin to argue that his philosophy led, logically, to totalitarianism and other forms of social control. Like Rousseau, Holt believed true liberty was not merely the absence of unjust restraint, but the absence of all possible restraint. And from there it is only a short leap to the insistence that one must vigilantly maintain this freedom at any cost—and, finally, to the gnawing paranoia that there are subtle forces, everywhere and invisible, conspiring to constrict it.

My childhood was, in many ways, a walled garden constructed in accordance with nineteenth-century notions of innocence and autonomy. I was aware on some level that there was a broader culture from which we had deliberately exempted ourselves. My mother called it the World, which was neither the planet nor the cosmos, but a system of interlocking ideologies that were everywhere and in everything. Sometimes the World was capitalism, as when she complained that Christmas had been co-opted by the World's consumerism. Other times it was socialism, which was synonymous with the state, a vast and elusive force that had the power to take children from their parents. The World was feminism, environmentalism, secular humanism—ideologies that sprang from a single source and reinforced one another. We were to be in the World but not of it, existing within its physical coordinates but uncontaminated by its values. "Schoolkids," according to her, were hopeless products of the World. They could not think for themselves, but simply mimicked behavior they'd seen on television. ("Stop popping your gum," she would say. "You look like a schoolkid.") Media made for children was naturally suspect. My mom once pronounced an animated film about dinosaurs Darwinian propaganda, and marched us out of a community sing-along because a folk song espoused new age pantheism. I have more than once considered the brilliance she would have achieved as a critic, so relentless she was in deconstructing any artifact and reducing it to its essential message. Of all the things she taught me, this was the most formative: that life concealed vast power structures warring for control of my mind; that my only hope for freedom was to be vigilant in recognizing them and calling them by name.

Everyone we knew was like us. In those dark ages before chat rooms and social networks, my mom maintained some mysterious sonar for locating like-minded people: fundamentalists who shopped at cooperative groceries, strained their own yogurt, and spoke in tongues at the dinner table. For several years, our social life orbited around a weekly Bible study we attended at the house of a large extended homeschool family who took us into their fold. While the adults met upstairs, my siblings and I were abandoned to the other children, all cousins, who were less a peer group than a kind of child gang. The leaders were the two oldest boys, who wore matching fox-tooth necklaces and led us on long treks through the acres of swampland behind their house. Sometimes we were supposed to be looking for something—candle quartz, which they called crystals, or a fisher-cat that had been spotted in the area—but the expeditions were more often a hazing ritual, a test to see how far we would follow them into the darkened woods, crossing thin ice, crawling through the live wires of electrical fencing, climbing into abandoned deer blinds. I lagged at the back of the group, making sure my brothers, who were among the youngest, didn't get lost.

The girls all wore their hair long, grazing the backs of their knees. They were slightly older than me, and though they were kind—teaching me crochet stitches and braiding my hair—I was never sure whether I was their equal or their charge. During the coldest months, the boys gave up on their treks and we all hung out in the basement, occupying ourselves with a variety of homemade distractions that I am embarrassed to reproduce here. For a year or so, we were very into puppetry. We were once disciplined for "playing" Communion, passing around plates of broken saltines and Welch's grape juice. (Apparently this was sacrilege.) When I think back on those evenings, all I can think of is all that blood in close quarters, edging up on puberty. Most of the girls were in love with their cousins, and spoke of it wistfully, as a kind of romantic tragedy. "I'm sure Sean likes you," one of them confessed to me, sighing. "He'll never love me, because I'm his cousin."

We did occasionally have contact with larger groups. We went to church on Sundays, and in summer attended a missionary camp on Lake Michigan. In September, we sometimes went to Six Flags, which had a "homeschool day" discount to capitalize on the back-to-school lull. It was there, more than anywhere, that one could glimpse the movement in its entirety. The Christian Reconstructionists were easiest to spot (patriotic T-shirts), as were the macrobiotic hippies, who overlapped somewhat with the anti-vaxxers, the anarchists, and the preppers. There were the rich suburban kids whose parents had pulled them from school to better facilitate backpacking trips to Mongolia, and Mennonite girls in long denim skirts, plus the occasional Quiverfull family numbering twelve, fifteen, twenty-five. The full spectrum, in other words, of American private dissent. But even then, it didn't feel like a community so much as a summit of isolated tribes. Families came and left together, and remained as units throughout the day. The kids didn't talk. Concessions were a graveyard; everyone brought packed lunches.

Earlier this year, while going through some files my mom gave me, I came across a homeschool newsletter on the topic of socialization. I expected the authors would rehearse the arguments I'd heard as a child—that schools did not have a monopoly on social life; that there were plenty of other ways to meet people—and was surprised to find something else. The first article was by Sue Welch, a Christian homeschooling advocate. "The world says that our children need to spend large amounts of time with many of their own age-mates," she wrote. "This produces the desired effect of conformity." She went on to argue that socialization was a myth, devised by the state and their coterie of child psychologists to woo children away from the ideology of their parents. (The first definition of *socialize,* she pointed out, was "to place under government or group ownership or control.") Parents who accepted this wisdom were themselves victims of false consciousness: "Our own socialization has conditioned us to accept current opinion or psychological studies over God's revealed truth." The other authors more or less reiterated her argument: socialization was not only overblown, it was actively detrimental to children.

Poring over these documents, my first instinct was to dismiss these ideas as the fringe of the fringe. Like many adults who have left extremist religious backgrounds, I long ago came to terms with the fact that I was raised in a culture whose defining ethos was fear. But I always believed that fear was subliminal, and that the restrictions it spawned were carried out in a kind of dream-state by parents who had fallen under the sway of talk radio and the ambient alarm of the culture wars. I had a difficult time believing that isolation was systematically prescribed by homeschooling leaders, and that my own cloistered childhood was the result of my mother heeding their advice. Some additional research proved the breadth of my ignorance. This view of socialization appears in all the landmark homeschooling literature, including the work of Holt, who claimed that kids benefited from a limited number of friends and recommended that children spend substantial time alone. It reaches poetic heights in the books of Raymond Moore, a frequent guest on James Dobson's radio program *Family Talk* who popularized homeschooling among religious conservatives. In his 1981 book *Home Grown Kids,* "peer dependency" among children is referred to as "a social cancer" again and again.

Then there's this, from one of the most famous homeschooling advocates: "Thus the oversocialized person is kept on a psychological leash and spends his life running on rails that society has laid down for him. In many oversocialized people this results in a sense of constraint and powerlessness that can be a severe hardship. We suggest that oversocialization is among the more serious cruelties that human beings inflict on one another." OK, I lied. That one's Ted Kaczynski.

The Enlightenment idea that humans are infinitely malleable naturally has a dark side. If children can, as Rousseau claimed, be perfected through careful observance and social control, they can also be ruined if these methods are faulty or perverted. An entire strain of Counter-Enlightenment thought stemmed from this idea, the most well-known example being Mary Shelley's *Frankenstein*. Although the novel is often read as a parable about technological hubris, Shelley herself envisioned it as a drama about child-rearing, and wrote it, in part, as a critique of Rousseau's pedagogy. Victor's monster is born good and begins his life, like Émile, in the state of nature: he roams the countryside and educates himself by reading in isolation. But because his "parent" abandons him without completing his education, the child is unable to fully integrate himself into human society. When he finally emerges from nature and enters a village, people find him hideous and regard him as a monster. He is forced to retreat back into isolation, and eventually his alienation transforms him into a murderer.

In March 2018, Mark Conditt, a twenty-three-year-old man better known as the Austin package bomber, blew himself up in a Ford Ranger on the side of Interstate 35 outside Austin, Texas. Over the previous three weeks, Conditt had shipped homemade bombs in FedEx packages to various homes in the Austin area, all of them sent from the cryptic alias Kelly Killmore. While the attacks were initially believed to be racially motivated—the first two victims were people of color—later targets were white and lived in an upper-middle-class suburb. Conditt's motivations became even more puzzling after police recovered a twenty-five-minute confession video that did not mention anything about terrorism or hate. The interim police chief described the video as "the outcry of a very challenged young man talking about challenges in his personal life."

The lone eccentricity of Conditt's background was that he had been homeschooled. A local newspaper managed to reach Jeremiah Jensen, a friend of Conditt's, who alluded to the social struggles his friend faced as a homeschooler. "It's just very difficult for a lot of [homeschooled] kids to find a way to fit in once they are out in the real world," he told the paper. "I have a feeling that is what happened with Mark. I don't remember him ever being sure of what he wanted to do." Perhaps because there was no clear motive, Conditt's homeschooling seemed increasingly suspicious. BuzzFeed reported that in high school, Conditt had belonged to a Christian homeschool group called RIOT. The article cited a former group member who said that in addition to studying the Bible, RIOT members shot guns at a range and carried knives. She also noted that the kids were "very into science" and did experiments with chemicals.

A friend of mine who knew I was homeschooled sent me a link to the story the day it was published: "Ever heard of this homeschool Riot group?" He was under the impression—one that the article did not discourage—that the group was a radical nationwide cell network of Christian terrorists. I pointed out that RIOT was actually an acronym—Righteous Invasion of Truth—and the title of a 1995 album by Carman, who is basically the Barry Manilow of Christian contemporary music. Not exactly a figurehead of violent dissent. I linked a response article from HuffPost that excerpted a RIOT brochure, which was written in sunny, sociable language and interviewed one of the RIOT mothers, who spoke of the group in similarly benign terms. "Water balloons, cream pies, frisbee, etc.," she said. "That's what it is." By then, it was a moot point. People on Twitter were already proclaiming RIOT a neo-Nazi group and comparing it to ISIS.

I didn't rule out the possibility that homeschooling had contributed in some way to Conditt's sense of alienation. But the notion that he had been "radicalized" struck me as hysterical. It attributed to homeschooling the same vaguely conspiratorial powers of mind control that my mom ascribed to the World, and fell in line with some of the more outrageous assumptions people harbored about homeschoolers (how many times have I been asked if my parents kept us in cages or forbade us to leave the house?). My mother once pointed out that these stereotypes revealed how much people feared homeschoolers, which in turn revealed their own fear that they themselves were not free.

But after a while, I regretted defending the group to my friend. Why, after all, do I find it necessary to make these distinctions? Why, when I hear stories like these, do I immediately think of what my mother would say? It's difficult to account for why I still occasionally find myself defending homeschooling, despite everything I know about its detrimental effects and my own enduring alienation.

When I was eleven, my mom sold the farm, which had become untenable, and moved our family back to the Midwest. Her family lived in Michigan, and we moved, in part, to be closer to them, but our life there was, in some sense, as itinerant and isolated as it had been in Vermont. For several years we moved between seemingly identical towns in Illinois and Michigan, where we ate at the same chain restaurants, shopped at the same big-box stores, and attended nondenominational churches that were so similar to one another in their worship style and theology that they, too, seemed like franchises. We were closer to civilization but still resisting its pull, circling the outskirts of communities, protected by the dull scrim of suburban anonymity. Everything changed when my mother got remarried, to a man she'd met at church. He had a daughter, which brought another child into our family, and soon after the wedding we all moved to a lakeside town in Wisconsin, a place that was, unavoidably, a community. Neighbors came by to introduce themselves and invited us to picnics and block parties. My parents began hosting dinners at our house. That fall, my mom suggested that if we ever wanted to try school, this would be a good time.

After all her years of embattled opposition to schooling, I'm still unsure what led to her change of mind. It's possible she was simply exhausted by the stress of raising five children and wanted us out of the house, but it might have had something to do with the cultural shift taking place in those years. By the late 1990s, the countercultural Jesus People fundamentalism to which my mother subscribed had been absorbed by the megachurch movement—a brand of evangelicalism that was more suburban and upbeat, concerned with engaging the culture rather than resisting it. I was then fifteen years old, approaching what would have been the tenth grade. Although I maintained some misgivings about attending school, I suspected this was my one shot, and my siblings had agreed to go without hesitation. I said yes.

The school itself was a kind of nightmare: a large public institution with two campuses and a multimillion-dollar hockey rink that had been endowed by one of the parents. The football team was the Division I state champion, and on Fridays all the popular girls wore red tartan kilts to class to announce the weekend's field hockey match. The whole place smelled like an Abercrombie. My academic performance that first year was predictably uneven. I failed chemistry and barely scraped by in algebra. In music theory, I found the curriculum so elementary that the teacher eventually gave me a private desk in the corner and said I could use the hour to study for other classes. Things should have evened out over time, but my problem was not a dearth of knowledge but of discipline. I could not bring myself to concentrate on subjects that bored me. The one time I was formally reprimanded, it was for forging a note to get out of sociology so that I could work in the studio on a video production assignment. The principal, once the situation was sorted out, was baffled. "This is the first time I've sent someone to detention for doing homework," he said. I didn't understand what I'd done wrong. Why should I have to sit in a classroom where I was learning nothing useful, when there were things I wanted to do just down the hall?

I wish I could say I maintained the same aristocratic indifference in my social life, but I wanted desperately to be liked, and this made me painfully self-conscious. At lunch, I had a difficult time following conversations. Everyone seemed to be pantomiming, with great exaggeration, awe, affection, disgust. In retrospect, the problem was very simple: I was wholly ignorant of the social scripts that governed large groups of females. All my mental energy was devoted to deciphering codes, analyzing unfamiliar words, and unpacking innuendo. I often felt the other girls looking at me, wondering why I was so quiet, but I never contributed anything because I was always a couple steps behind, still processing the last thing that had been said.

Over time, my curiosity gave way to bewilderment, and eventually to boredom. I became fatigued whenever I was forced to talk to more than one person at a time, overcome with a weariness that felt at times like mental blankness, and at others like acute physical exhaustion. I began eating my lunch in the library, under the pretense that I was catching up on homework, not realizing that this simple act of independence would damn me to full social opprobrium. Rumors made their way back to me—that I picked my nose in class, that I wore the same pants for ten days straight—which led me to retreat further. As a homeschooler, I had never felt lonely, even though my life consisted largely of solitude. It wasn't until I entered school that I understood for the first time the ache of seclusion and personal failure. We read *Frankenstein* that year in English. I didn't know then that the novel was in conversation with Rousseau, but I remember identifying with the monster's alienation. "Everywhere I see bliss, from which I alone am irrevocably excluded," he cries out in one monologue. "I was benevolent and good; my soul glowed with love and humanity: but am I not alone, miserably alone?"

I wish I could say that all of this passed like a bad trip, the way high school does for so many people. But to this day, it's rare that I end a social interaction without retracing the steps of those long walks home from school: convinced that everything I said was false, that authentic communication is impossible within the confines of social norms. I suppose I might be an angry person had I not, in the end, found my way back to Nature, or its closest analogue. It was during high school that I began writing. I transcribed conversations I'd overheard at school, observations about people, insights about the books I was reading. It became a habit that I came to depend upon, like nourishment, in the same way I craved solitude. The world was pulsing forward at a relentless pace, but the page was infinitely slow, infinitely patient. My first-person voice became my primary sense of identity—an avatar of words and air that I constructed each day and carried in my backpack like a talisman. Its private sustenance was less like a pastime than like the wilderness I explored as a child with total freedom, never exhausting its limits.

Émile, of course, is not really a childcare manual. It's a philosophical treatise that explores an intractable problem: how can one maintain freedom from society while also existing within it? Many of Rousseau's first readers missed this point and took his prescriptions at face value. In the years after *Émile* was published, parents frequently wrote to Rousseau claiming that they were raising their children in the manner he'd outlined. To one such father he replied, "So much the worse, sir, for you and your son, so much the worse."

Rousseau knew that the state of nature was a lost Eden where no person could return. Society put humans in a state of disunity: one's natural inclinations were always at war with one's social duties. But isolating a child would only heighten that sense of disunity. "He who in the civil order wants to preserve the primacy of the sentiments of nature does not know what he wants," Rousseau writes in the early pages of the book—a user warning for anyone tempted to try his methods at home. "Always in contradiction with himself, always floating between his inclinations and his duties, he will never be either [natural] man or citizen. He will be good neither for himself nor for others. . . . He will be nothing."

I suppose this state of "contradiction," or disunity, sums up my position today. I left my family's ideology somewhat late—in my early twenties, after two tortured years of Bible college—which ultimately made the exit more difficult. I wasted a lot of time mourning the loss, drinking, working lousy jobs. But despite everything I now know about the ideologies that informed homeschooling, I maintain mostly good memories of those years I lived in innocence. I sometimes credit homeschooling with the qualities I've come to value most in myself: a capacity for solitude and absorption, a distrust of consensus. It is tempting, even, to believe that my childhood inadvertently endowed me with the tools to escape it—that my mother's insistence that the World was conspiring to brainwash me cultivated the very skepticism that I later trained on my family and their beliefs. But this is circular logic, like someone saying they are grateful for their diabetes because it forced them to change their eating habits. Its wisdom resembles the hollow syntax of rationalization. If I've often found it difficult to speak or write about this ambivalence, it's because it's impossible to do so without coming to interrogate my motives and doubt my own independence of mind.

Last summer, I came across Tara Westover's memoir *Educated,* a story that in many ways held a mirror to my own experience. Westover grew up in rural Idaho in a family of radical Mormon survivalists who forbade their children to attend school or see doctors. In her book, she recalls working alongside her father in his junkyard, where she sustained several injuries that were treated homeopathically; listening to his conspiratorial rants about the Feds; and helping her parents prep for the end of days. The story hinges on the process by which she educated herself, in secret, so that she could go to college—first at Brigham Young University, then at Cambridge, where she got a doctorate in history. The manuscript was bought for six figures within twenty-four hours of hitting the market, and has since been published in twenty countries.

The whole idea of the book—its publicity budget, its book-club sheen—struck me from the beginning as evidence of bad faith. Americans maintain a voracious appetite for child-isolation narratives (*The Wolfpack, Room*). Unlike the readers of *Émile,* who delighted in the fantasy of native innocence, for Americans the allure of these cloistered children lies in the belief that they have been brainwashed; their entrance into society is not a loss of innocence, but a drama of liberation. Throughout her media tour, Westover was celebrated as a feral child who had crossed over, a symbol of American autonomy and self-governance who had, by dint of will, clawed her way out of a family that, incidentally, held fast to those same American virtues. Magazine profiles reiterated how "normal" she seemed. In interviews, she spoke of "psychological manipulation" and "reality distortions" with the authority of someone who had completed years of therapy. "All abuse is foremost an assault on the mind," she told *Vogue*.

Still, these talking points did not quell the collective anxiety that Westover maintained some confusion about her upbringing, and I suppose this is what interested me most about her story. Several critics found it unsettling that her parents were occasionally characterized, in her memoir, with a note of affection, and that the descriptions of her childhood landscape were undergirded by a sense of longing. One interviewer wondered "if Westover only really comprehended the difficulty of her childhood when she sat down to write." Reviewers noted this too, but dismissed it as an aesthetic choice. That she refused to "demonize" her family was not evidence of sympathy, but the result of her "matter-of-fact lyricism" and "characteristic understatement," a writerly restraint contrived to lend the darker moments of her story even more power.

Westover once hinted that the early iterations of her book had a lighter tone. When she first began writing, she confessed in one interview, she regarded her family's behavior as harmless and eccentric: "I don't think I had really appreciated how extreme bits of it were. I would write about the injuries a lot of times like comedies, and my friends thought, 'this undermines my trust in you because it doesn't seem like you understand the situation.'" One might argue that Westover understood her situation better than anyone, having lived it, but her authority as a narrator—and more fundamentally, as a witness to her own life—was for many readers discounted by the brainwashing she'd experienced as a child. The most popular comment on the book's Goodreads page spells out what many readers found troubling: "I do not understand why an educated and worldly individual would have difficulty understanding the horrible and violent upbringing that she experienced." In the end, Westover, who has described her life as a process of regaining "custody of my own mind," was subjected, again and again, to the insistence that she did not actually know her own mind.

This is the predicament of people who were raised in highly controlled environments: any ambivalence about your upbringing is proof of its success, a sign that you are not yet completely free. Homeschoolers, after all, are not the only ones preoccupied with autonomy. All of us in America are Rousseau's children: obsessed with liberty, terrified of those who would put restraints on our thinking. If stories like Westover's are unsettling, it's because they reflect the larger disunity all of us know to be our fate—that none of us live completely off the ideological grid, impervious to malicious systems of thought. We are all like Frankenstein's monster, victims of our own miseducations, a motley patchwork of the influences that have shaped us, sometimes without our awareness or consent.

It is impossible to anticipate how a person will interpret the lessons of her childhood, whether she will find in them an impetus for violence or a source of creative inspiration. In my own family, my siblings and I have proved the outcomes of my mother's pedagogy wildly unpredictable. Despite her best efforts to raise us deliberately, each of us has negotiated, in idiosyncratic ways, the legacy of our childhood, and our lives have veered down such divergent paths that when we are all together, it is difficult to imagine we were reared under the same roof. My mother raised a writer, a musician, a missionary, a hotel manager, and an accountant; a progressive, a centrist, two moral conservatives, and a libertarian. I do not have children, but my siblings have collectively produced half a dozen. All of them go to school.

A VISIT TO SAN QUENTIN

Joyce Carol Oates

We came to San Quentin on a chill sunny morning in April 2011. The visitor to San Quentin is surprised that, from a little distance, the prison buildings are very distinctive. The main building is likely to be warmly glowing in sunshine and more resembles a historic architectural landmark, or a resort hotel, than one of the most notorious prisons in North America. Beyond the prison compound, to the south, are hills as denuded of trees as the rolling, dreamlike hills in a Grant Wood painting; to the north, blue-sparkling San Francisco Bay and beyond it the glittering high-rise buildings of the fabled city of San Francisco several miles away.

San Quentin Point is one of the most valuable real estate properties in the United States, and so it's ironic that the prison, first built in 1852, the oldest prison in California, takes up 275 acres of this waterside property. Almost you would think that some of the inmates must have spectacular views from their cell windows—except you will learn that San Quentin's cells, arranged in densely populated "cell blocks" in the interior of buildings, like rabbit warrens, don't have windows.

On the morning we drove to San Quentin from Berkeley, the sky was vivid-blue and the air in continual gusts. The hills beyond the prison were vivid-green from an unusually wet and protracted Northern California winter.

Is that the *prison*?—a first-time visitor is likely to exclaim.

But this is from a distance.

I had visited a maximum-security prison once before, in Trenton, New Jersey, in the 1980s. It had not been a pleasant experience nor one I had ever anticipated repeating, and yet, on this day, I was scheduled to be taken on a guided tour through San Quentin with approximately fifteen other individuals of whom the great majority were young women graduate students and their female professor from a criminology course at a university in San Francisco.

Waiting in line for the guided-tour leader to arrive, the young women—(you would have to call them girls in their behavior, appearance, mannerisms)—talked loudly and vivaciously together, as if oblivious of their surroundings, and eager for an entertaining adventure; once the tour began, they fell silent; and when the tour led us into the very interior of the prison, where the fact of what a prison is becomes viscerally evident, they were very silent, abashed, and intimidated. That is always the way with the guided tour into a maximum-security prison: you are not being taken on a mere tour but "taught a lesson." And you are not quite the person emerging whom you'd believed yourself to be, entering.

In the parking lot, in the trunk of our car, we'd had to leave behind all electronic devices, as well as our wallets, from which we'd taken our IDs. In San Quentin you are forbidden to bring many things designated as "contraband" and you are forbidden to wear certain colors—(primarily blue, the prisoners' color). Even men must not wear "open" shoes, i.e., sandals. Your arms must be covered, and clothing "appropriate."

Despite the warning beforehand, one of our group, an older man, was discovered to be wearing sandals and had to acquire proper footwear from one of the guards before he was allowed into the facility.

Our tour guide was late. From remarks told to us, the man's "lateness" was a matter of his own discretion: he was not often "on time." There was the sense, communicated to us subtly by guards, that civilians were not particularly welcome in the facility; it was a "favor" to the public, that guided tours were arranged from time to time. And so we were made to wait in the sunny, gusty air outside the first checkpoint, which was both a vehicular and a pedestrian checkpoint manned by a number of guards.

In the imagination a prison is a remote and lonely place but in reality, a prison is a place of business: a busy place. Delivery vehicles constantly arrived to move through the checkpoint. Corrections officers and other employees arrived. When at last our tour leader arrived, a lieutenant corrections officer, we were led singly through the pedestrian checkpoint and along a hilly pavement in the direction of the prison, some distance away; to our left, beautiful San Francisco Bay reflecting the sun; to our right, the rolling hills of a pastoral landscape. The visitor is tempted to think, *This is a magical place. This is not an ugly place.*

Now through the second checkpoint, where we signed into a log and where, when we left, we had to sign out; otherwise, the prison would go into "lockdown"—the assumption being that a visitor was unaccounted for inside the facility.

Our wrists were stamped with invisible ink. Grimly we were told that if we forgot and washed our hands, and washed away the ink, we would precipitate another "lockdown"—the assumption being that there was a visitor unaccounted for inside the facility.

Corrections officers were passing through the checkpoint, as we prepared to go through. It was prison protocol to allow them to go first. The guards were both female and male—the females as sturdy-bodied as the males, sexless in their dun-colored uniforms. They did not greet us, smile at us, acknowledge us at all.

The lieutenant led us into a spacious sun-filled courtyard. Here were extensive flower beds, planted by prisoners. There was not a prisoner in sight.

"The flag always flies at half-mast here."

We stared at a memorial stone as the lieutenant spoke of COs who'd "died in the line of duty" at San Quentin, a double column of names dating back to the nineteenth century. The lieutenant recounted for us how as a young CO he'd been on duty during the "most violent ten minutes" in the prison's history: in 1969 a Black Panther defense attorney had smuggled a firearm into the prison to give to his client, who hid it inside his clothing until, as he was being escorted back to his cell block, he suddenly began shooting, killing several COs and fellow prisoners before tower guards shot him dead.

We were aware now of tower guards. We were aware of high stone walls strung with razor wire like a deranged sort of tinsel. We were told that if a siren sounded, if the commandment *All down! All down!* was broadcast, we were to throw ourselves down to the ground without question. If we remained standing, we would be in danger of being shot down by guards in the towers. They would be training their rifles on us, invisibly.

Did we understand?

My old unease, which had begun at the first checkpoint, quickened now. For always you think, too late—*I have made a mistake coming here. Why did I come to this terrible place!*

The answers are idealist: to learn. To learn more about the world. To be less sheltered. To be less naive. To *know*.

Americans imprison—and execute—so many more individuals in proportion to our population than any other country in the world except China, one is compelled to *know*.

The lieutenant was saying that a CO's family doesn't know if he or she will be returning home from the prison. Inside, anything can happen, and it was likely to happen suddenly and unexpectedly and irrevocably.

"Irrevocably" was not the lieutenant's exact word. But this was his meaning.

He led us across the square and into the prison chapel, which was nondenominational. At the front of the room, which had seats for perhaps 150 people, was, not a crucifix, but a large cross in the shape of a T.

At a pulpit stood an inmate in prison attire, to address the tour group. He was in his thirties perhaps, with Hispanic features. Like one who has given a presentation many times before he told us with disarming frankness of his life: how he'd belonged to a gang, how he'd killed his own sister in a moment of panicked confusion, how he'd been sentenced to thirty-years-to-life—meaning that he was a "lifer," who might be granted parole sometime, if he didn't jeopardize his chances inside the prison.

The inmate wore blue: blue shirt, blue sweatpants, loose clothing. Down the sides of the trouser legs were letters in vivid white:

P

R

I

S

O

N

E

R

The inmate prayed, he said. Every day of his life he prayed for his sister, his mother, his family, himself. His manner was eager, earnest. He was due to meet with the parole board that very afternoon, he said. (He'd been turned down for parole at least once; inmates are typically turned down many times before being granted parole, if ever.) You could see that this was a San Quentin inmate who had accrued the approval of the prison authority and would not ever risk losing it: once a gang member, now he was one of *theirs*.

One of *ours*. Someone like *ourselves*.

Obviously he'd been "rehabilitated" in prison. And this was the goal of the enlightened prison—of course.

Abruptly then the session ended. The inmate was escorted from the pulpit by guards, and the tour group was led out of the chapel by the lieutenant.

Now we were being led into the interior of the prison—the "real" prison. We were led from the picturesque courtyard along a hilly paved walk, in a chilly wind. Around a corner, and into the "Yard."

That is, we stepped onto the edge of the "Yard." Here was a vast windswept space, part pavement and part scrubby grassland. We stared. Hundreds—could it really be *hundreds*?—of inmates in the Yard under the supervision of what appeared to be, to the casual eye, a dismayingly few guards.

Of course, there were the guard towers: the armed guards.

The prison population was somewhere beyond 5,000 inmates though the "design capacity" was for 3,082. Clearly just a fraction of these inmates were in the Yard at this time but their numbers seemed daunting.

We were led relentlessly forward, skirting the edge of the Yard. We were surprised to see a number of older inmates, several with long white beards, like comic representations of elderly men; they walked with canes, on the dirt track, while younger inmates jogged past them or, elsewhere in the Yard, tossed basketballs at netless rims, lifted weights and did exercises, or stood together talking, pacing about. You had the impression of rippling, seething, pulsing energy and restlessness, and you had the impression that the nearer of the inmates were watching us covertly, intensely. Everyone in the guided tour was very quiet now. The young women visitors were quiet now. The fact of the prison and what it contained was beginning to become real to us, not merely an idea. For there were no fences between the inmates and us, only just open space.

The lieutenant advised us not to look at the inmates. Not to stare.

"No 'eye contact.' No 'fraternizing' with inmates." The lieutenant explained how the prison population was divided into gangs, primarily; and these gangs—African Americans, Hispanics, Mexicans (Northern California, Southern California), "whites"—with now, in recent decades, "Chinese" (Asian)—had territorial possession of particular parts of the Yard that were off-limits to non-gang-members. There were desirable areas of the Yard dominated by Hispanics and "whites"—(Aryan

Brotherhood)—and less desirable areas, near the urinals, where African Americans gathered. (Why? Because Californian African Americans are so divided into warring gangs, they can't make up their differences in prison.)

We were shocked to see, not many yards away, open urinals in a row, against a wall. We were warned—*If anybody is using a urinal, don't look.*

It was a protocol of the Yard: *Don't look, don't stare. A man using one of the open-air urinals was invisible, and to cause him to feel visible is to invite trouble.*

The lieutenant led us past the single-story wooden structure that held classrooms. He led us into a dining hall—a vast, double dining hall—with rows of tables—empty at this time of day. You could not imagine this enormous dining hall filled with men—the noise, the restlessness; the food smells, the smells of men's bodies. The lieutenant spoke of the murals on the walls, which had been painted by an inmate named Alfredo Santos in the 1950s: striking, bizarre, a collage of renderings of newspaper photos and more ordinary individuals including a heroin addict (Santos himself). This art called to mind the slickly illustrative work of Thomas Hart Benton but also the matter-of-fact distortions of Hieronymus Bosch.

The lieutenant meant to entertain us by summoning a food worker, to provide us with food samples from the kitchen—"Any volunteers?"

Two members of the tour volunteered: a man and one of the young criminology students, who took bites of what resembled chicken nuggets, burritos, French fries, something that resembled cornmeal, and bravely pronounced them "Good"—"Pretty good."

The lieutenant told of the feat of "feeding" thousands of men three times a day. There was something disconcerting in the word "*feeding*": you had a vision of a cattle or a hog trough into which "feed" was dumped.

The lieutenant spoke proudly of the fact that the prison was mostly inmate-staffed—"Otherwise, there couldn't be a prison."

The original San Quentin had been built by prisoners, in fact. It had housed only sixty-eight inmates. Prior to that, California's first prison had been a 268-ton wooden ship anchored in San Francisco Bay and equipped to hold thirty prisoners.

But the prison facility was now badly overcrowded, like all prison facilities in the economically stressed state of California. Where there is overcrowding, three men to a cell, men quartered in places meant for other purposes, like a gym, there is likely to be more trouble.

The lieutenant told of uprisings in the dining hall, sudden riots, gang killings. At any meal there is the possibility of violence, with so many men crammed into so relatively small a space. The lieutenant showed us a cache of homemade weapons: a toothbrush sharpened to a deadly point, a razor blade attached to a papier-mâché handle, a metal hook fashioned out of paper clips, a spike, a nail, a pencil. . . . In the Yard, buried in the ground in certain places, were similar weapons, which gangs controlled; as soon as guards discovered the weapons and confiscated them, more weapons appeared and were buried in the ground.

Ingenious! The wish to harm others is a stimulant to the most amazing creativity and patience.

Wasn't it likely, most of the contraband to be fashioned into weapons was smuggled into San Quentin by guards—COs? For there was a drug trade here, and there were forbidden cell phones—how otherwise could such things be smuggled into the facility except by COs?

(The California corrections officers union is one of the strongest unions in the state. Much stronger, and its members much better paid, than the members of the teachers' union. The prison authority could not risk antagonizing such a powerful union.)

At no point in the tour did I think it would be prudent to ask questions about smuggled contraband. No one else asked, either.

During our visit in the dining hall, sirens erupted. Bells clanged. For a terrible few seconds it seemed to us that the prison was after all going to go into "lockdown"—(whatever precisely that meant: we had a vague, ominous sense of its meaning); but, fortunately, the sirens turned out to be a false alarm.

Maybe it was a suicide attempt, the lieutenant said. Adding laconically, or a suicide.

Next, the lieutenant led us to another grim building; and

another time, we went through a checkpoint. The invisible ink on our wrists was examined by frowning guards in ultraviolet light.

I was trying to imagine a plausible scenario in which an individual who had not been officially admitted to San Quentin as a visitor was now discovered in the very interior of the prison, somehow having managed to attach him- or herself to a tour group, who would be identified as an impostor or an intruder through this scrutiny, but I could not imagine this scenario.

He was taking us to Cell Block C, the lieutenant said. Into the very bowels of the prison, he might have said. Until now, the visit to San Quentin had been bearable. It had not provoked anxiety or even much unease, I think. If there was unease, I had resolved not to think about it, at least not yet. I had come here to be educated and illuminated and not entertained. And the others in our group must have felt more or less the same. For nothing threatening had happened to us, except the temporary alarms in the dining room, which had turned out to be false alarms. Our only firsthand experience of an inmate had been the speaker in the chapel, who had seemed to want to please us, like an earnest student. In the Yard, we'd seen men at a distance—it had seemed a safe distance.

But now in Cell Block C there was a very different atmosphere. The air was tense as the air before an electrical storm. A powerful smell of men's bodies. There was a high din as of the thrum of a hive—if you brought your ear close to the hive, you would be shocked at the myriad angry-sounding vibrations that never sleep. We would see now the typical inmates of San Quentin, in their own habitat.

These were "new recruits" in Cell Block C. Their gang identifications had not yet been determined. They were younger than the typical San Quentin inmate, and more "restless." This was the population that was most susceptible to suicides, the lieutenant said, as well as "other kinds of violence."

The lieutenant introduced us to cell block guards, who barely nodded at us. We were of no interest to them and if they felt anything for us, it was likely to be contempt. What the criminology students were thinking by this time, I could only guess. I knew, from my experience at the Trenton prison, that any close confrontation with prison inmates, though there are bars between you and them, is not going to be a pleasant one and still less is it a pleasant experience for women.

As the lieutenant was telling us about the history of the cell blocks—and of their present-day overcrowding—a movement overhead attracted my attention and I looked up to see, on a catwalk about fivc feet above the lieutenant's head, a uniformed guard with a rifle resting in the crook of his arm. The guard did not so much as glance down at me. He was indifferent to the guided tour as to the recited words of the tour guide. The barrel of his rifle did not seem quite aimed at anyone in the cell block, but it was clearly in readiness of being aimed. On a wall nearby was the ominous sign NO WARNING SHOTS.

Three inmates had been taken from their cells and were standing in the narrow passageway, not far from us. We could not help but stare—as they stared at us, in turn—for these were prison inmates of a kind you would find in a Hollywood action film. Two Hispanics, and a "white" man—husky, muscled, beefy, deep-chested, with thick necks. The white man had a shaved head and was covered in tattoos of a lurid sort: Nazi swastikas primarily. I had never seen anyone with a scalp tattooed in Nazi tattoos. The man had had to be a member of the notorious Aryan Brotherhood, a prison gang. Yet this man had been taken from his cell, and he stood quietly in the aisle among guards as if in an easy sort of fraternization; apparently he was no threat to the guards or to us. For as it turned out, he and the other two inmates had been paroled—or had served their full sentences—and would be now escorted out of the prison.

I thought *But who would hire a man covered in Nazi tattoos?*

The answer could only be *Another man covered in Nazi tattoos*.

The lieutenant now said, as I'd been hoping he would not, that it was time for a "walk-around-the-block."

In Trenton, something of the same phraseology had been used. But the inmates we'd seen had not been confined to a cell block, but to a large grim windowless space like an animal pen. They'd been loose, milling and pacing about, restless, edgy, staring in our direction as we'd looked down at them from a raised platform, at a height of about five feet.

The situation is different here, I thought. Yet I felt a stab of panic, for perhaps the situation would come to the same thing. It had been a nightmare I'd more or less managed to forget, or had pushed out of my mind. I told myself, *It won't be the same thing again. I am prepared this time.*

I was safer here in the cell block because of the abundance of other, younger women in the group. To the inmates, some of whom had already glimpsed them, the criminology students must have looked like high school girls. Their presence in this grim place was a kind of outrage, a provocation; it would arouse excitement, frustration, incredulity, wrath. Adroitly I'd maneuvered myself to the front of the line, just behind the lieutenant. I would walk just behind him "around the block"—I would not make the mistake of holding back and coming late in the line. For, at the start of the walk, the inmates whose cells we passed wouldn't quite grasp the situation, as we walked quickly by; but, by the time the fourth or fifth visitor passed a cell, all the prisoners would have been alerted to the tour by shouts and whistles. There would be a nightmare, but it would be a contained nightmare and it would not be mine this time.

The lieutenant warned: "Walk fast—move along. Don't stare into the cells. Don't get too close to the cells. Walk as far to the left as you can. If they can reach you, if they grab you, you might be seriously hurt. And the prison might go into lockdown."

Several of the criminology students were asking if they could stay behind. If they could just wait, and rejoin the group after the walk-around-the-block. Their voices were plaintive and pleading, but the lieutenant explained that this was not possible.

"The tour takes us through Cell Block C. We are all going to 'walk around the block' together."

Quietly enough the walk began along a walkway that spanned the full length of the first tier of cells. I was close behind the lieutenant and I was not going to look into the cells, for I did not want to make "eye contact" with an inmate whose desire at that moment might be to reach grunting through the bars and grab me and not let go until guards swarmed to his cell. I did not have that sort of curiosity—I was determined to walk fast, and to keep in motion. And so, as I passed the cells, one after another after another, the men inside had but a blurred awareness of me, as at the periphery of my vision, they were but a blurred presence to me, though I glimpsed enough to be aware of the cramped living conditions: bunk beds so close to the wall, inmates would have to pass sideways between the bunks and the walls; and a cell size of about nine by twelve feet. I was very nervous, and I was perspiring; and I could hear, behind us, the uplifted voices of men, shouts, whistles, whooping noises of elation, derision. I would have liked to press my hands over my ears. I did not glance back, at the terrified young women, forced to walk this gauntlet as close as possible to the wall, away from the prison bars. I knew what they were feeling, as I'd had to run a gauntlet of a kind, in Trenton.

But I'd been alone in my misery, in Trenton. For there, by chance I'd been the single female in the guided tour, a much smaller group than that at San Quentin, only about five or six people. The Trenton prison had not seemed so "secure" as San Quentin, and the tour guide not so experienced; but that might have been a misconception.

In a haze of discomfort, I followed the lieutenant in the "walk-around-the-block." I did not inflame any inmate by passing too near his cell, or looking overtly into it; but I was aware of the rippling, rising excitement in my wake, as the young women were forced to march past the cells, one by one by one. The slumberous hive was being roused, shaken; the buzzing hum rose to crude shouts, whistles, whoops. *But I am spared, this time.*

When we left the cell block, to return to the outside air, the tour group was abashed, shaken. What relief to get outside, to *breathe*! Especially the young women had been made to realize how little their *femininity* was valued, in such a place; to be *pretty* here, to suggest *sexual empowerment* here, was to invite the most primitive and pitiless violence, as in an atavistic revenge of the male against the female. Civilization protects the female against the male, essentially: this is a hard, crude truth to ponder if you hope to transcend the rigid gender-limits of sexism.

The meaning of the walk-around-the-block is to make a

woman understand this simple biological fact, that may be mistaken as a feminist proposition.

The meaning of the walk-around-the-block is to make both men and women understand: you must be protected from your fellow man by high walls, bars, razor wire, and high-powered rifles manned by guards in the service of the State. And if you don't think so, you are very naive, or a fool.

This is not the sunlit rationalist world of the Enlightenment, still less an evolving America envisioned by liberal intellectuals. It is very far from the affable mysticism of California's New Age. In San Quentin we recognize the starkly familiar dead end of Thomas Hobbes's *Leviathan* (1651) in which life is defined as "nasty, brutish, and short"—unless it is a highly controlled, defined, and subjugated life not unlike a maximum-security prison.

We were exhausted by the cell block gauntlet and we were eager for the (interminable) tour to end, but there was a final destination awaiting.

Not Death Row: "We don't take visitors to Death Row."

Our guide led us past a tall fortress-like building—the "Condemned Unit"—which housed over seven hundred men awaiting execution. (Condemned women, of whom there are far fewer, are housed at the Central California Women's Facility in Chowchilla.) With a sort of grim boastfulness the lieutenant spoke to us of the famous inmates who'd been executed at San Quentin: Caryl Chessman, William Bonin (the "Freeway Killer"), Clarence Ray Allen (at seventy-six, the "oldest person ever executed in California," in 2006), among many others. And there were those awaiting execution: pregnant-wife-killer Scott Peterson, serial killer–sadist Charles Ng, Richard Ramirez, the "Night Stalker" of the 1980s. In a perverse way the San Quentin authority appeared to be proud of its list of executed and condemned prisoners and proud of its distinction as the sole Death Row for men in the state of California.

When I asked the lieutenant which part of San Quentin he most liked to work in, without hesitation he said Death Row.

This was a surprise to me. I asked why and he said that the Death Row inmate was "more settled."

Death Row inmates had "come to accept" that they were going to die and some of them had acquired "wisdom."

Of course, some of these inmates were hoping for reprieves. Many were involved with Legal Defense lawyers and anti–capital punishment volunteers working to get their death sentences commuted. But the ones the lieutenant had liked to work with, he said, were the older men, who were "settled" in their minds.

The lieutenant had not spoken at such length to anyone else on the tour, or so warmly, as he was speaking now to me.

The lieutenant led us now to a nondescript building that housed the execution chamber. With a flourish of an old-fashioned key he unlocked the door that led directly into the chamber; it was noted that we did not have to pass through another checkpoint. ("No prisoners enter here except if they are going to be executed. And then, they do not return.") No one in our group was very enthusiastic about entering the execution chamber, but there was no escape: you could see that this was a ritual of the San Quentin tour, not to be avoided.

"When the death warrant is signed, the clock starts ticking for the condemned man. When it's time, the Death Team comes for him and brings him here."

There was a particular horror to these matter-of-fact words, that had surely been uttered many times in this somber place.

The room was not large, windowless and dimly lighted. There was a feeling here of *underground*. Plain straight-back wooden chairs arranged in a semicircle in an incongruously ordinary space except that, at the front of the room, was a bathysphere.

A bathysphere! Painted robin's-egg blue.

The lieutenant explained to his surprised charges that the San Quentin authority had purchased a "deep-sea diving bell" from a marine carnival some years ago, in an era when execution was by cyanide gas. The diving bell was airproof, and efficient.

Slowly we shuffled inside. There was a sour, sad odor here. The young women had lost all remnants of their initial vivacity, and the men in the group were looking grimly stoic. Like an MC on a TV reality show the lieutenant was hoping to seat some of us in "witness's chairs" at the front of the room—"C'mon! These are great seats." The hardback chairs provided an intimate look through the slotted Plexiglas windows of the diving bell into the interior at what appeared to be a hospital gurney, outfitted with straps.

"In the days when there was gas, it was practical to execute two at a time. Now, with lethal injection, they don't do that. And when we had an electric chair, they had just the one chair, not two."

"Two men executed at once?"

"Yes, sir. When there was gas."

But now, the lieutenant explained, gas had been declared *cruel and unusual punishment*. So there was just lethal injection—"People think it's some easy way to die. But it ain't."

A few of the young women students were sitting, weakly. But not at the front of the room; no one wanted to sit in these chairs, which brought witnesses within mere inches of the diving-bell windows. (The chairs were so bizarrely close, a witness's knees would be pressed against the exterior of the diving bell. Unless you shut your eyes, you would be staring at a dying man's contorted face from a distance of about twelve inches.) Most of us shrank from sitting down at all, as if to remain standing might be to accelerate the visit, and escape.

The plain wooden chairs so arranged suggested amateur theatrics—very amateur, as in a middle school. The (somewhat dingy) robin's-egg blue diving bell suggested sport, recreation, carny fun. But inside the bell, the death apparatus with its sinister black straps suggested a makeshift operating room, as in a cheap horror film.

I thought of, but did not mention, Franz Kafka's "In the Penal Colony," one of the great prophetic surrealist tales of the twentieth century, by a writer who might very likely have perished in a Nazi death camp if he had not died prematurely of tuberculosis in 1924.

The lieutenant was indicating those front-row chairs reserved for "family members of the victim." Beside these were chairs for the warden and other prison officials and law enforcement officers who'd apprehended the inmate; in the second row were chairs for other professionals and interested parties; in the back row, chairs for the "press."

Someone asked if executions were televised or recorded. The lieutenant shook his head with a frown, as if this were a foolish question—"No, sir."

I was wondering how the family of the victim could bear to sit so close to the diving bell, to peer through the narrow windows at the writhings of a dying man only inches away. Was this a way of assuaging grief, horror? Was this a way of providing "closure"? I thought rather it must be another element of nightmare, a stark and irremediable image to set beside other, horrific images of loss and degradation. *Eye for an eye, tooth for a tooth.* Was that a gratifying sort of folk justice?

Yet it certainly seemed to be an honored custom that the family of a murderer's victim was invited to the execution. The somber way in which the lieutenant spoke of the "family of the victim" and the special seats reserved for them suggested the importance of such witnessing—this was a gift, perhaps the only gift law enforcement could provide, to the families of victims.

Perhaps in older, less civilized societies the murderer's heart or severed head was also given to the victim's family, to do with it what they would.

But then I thought, it isn't given to us to understand, who have not suffered such losses. The appetite for blood, for revenge, for a settling of "injustice," that so fueled ancient Greek tragedies as well as the great revenge tragedies of the Renaissance, amid which Shakespeare's *Hamlet* is the surpassing model.

Yet I don't think I would want to "witness" such a horrific sight. Probably, I could not forgive—(I certainly could not forgive in place of someone who'd been murdered)—and I could not forget; but I would not want to witness another's death, even for the sake of revenge.

The lieutenant was telling us that no one had been executed at San Quentin since 2006—"There's some court case pending." But, he said, in a neutral voice that nonetheless suggested optimism, that was going to change soon—"In another year or two, executions will be resumed."

In the meantime, the "backlog" of the condemned was increasing in the Condemned Unit.

"Now ladies, gentlemen—how would *you* choose to die?"

It was a jaunty friendly question posed to us by the tour guide. Of course, it was a ritual question: you could assume that the lieutenant had asked it many times before.

"Gas, or lethal injection? Or—electrocution, hanging, firing squad? All were approved methods at one time."

At first no one spoke. It was a disconcerting question, and there seemed no good answer.

More fancifully the lieutenant said: "Or maybe—hit by a truck? Jump off Golden Gate Bridge?"

There were hesitant answers. Reluctant murmurs of "lethal injection."

The criminology students and their female professor concurred: "lethal injection."

The newest way of execution must always seem the most humane, I supposed. At one time, hanging. Or firing squad. Then, electrocution. Then gas. And now, with its suggestion of hospital care gone just slightly wrong—"lethal injection."

I said, I would start with one way of being executed and if I didn't like it, I'd switch to another.

It was an awkward sort of joke. It was the sort of joke a bright, brash ninth-grade boy might make, to startle and impress his teacher. Why I said this, when I was feeling in no way like joking, I have no idea.

Except I resented the tour guide quizzing us in this way. I resented the tour guide punishing us for our civilian status.

No one laughed at my joke. The lieutenant frowned at me. "But you have to choose," he said. "Gas, electrocution, lethal injection, hanging—"

I could not seem to reply. My awkward joke had been a surprise to me. Did I hope to alleviate the mood?—the mood of an *execution chamber*? Did I wish to appear naive, that I might not be revealed as agitated, angry, indignant?

One of the men in the group said that he would refuse to

choose—he would not participate in his own death. Triumphantly the lieutenant objected, if you don't choose, the warden will choose for you, but the man persisted: he would not participate in his own death.

This was a good answer, I thought. But a depressing answer.

For really there is no good answer to the lieutenant's question.

It is said that, if you are resolutely against capital punishment, you should not educate yourself in the sorts of crimes for which the "condemned" are executed. "An eye for an eye, a tooth for a tooth"—originally, this was a liberal principle, to discourage disproportionate punishments, and punishments against relatives of the alleged criminal. It was not considered harsh but rather a reasonable and equitable punishment.

By this time I'd begun to feel very strange. I had been staring at the gurney for too long.

My sense of myself was shrinking like a light made dim, dimmer—about to be extinguished. In a panic I thought, *Not here! I can't faint here*.

Somehow I made my way outside, into fresh air. Or maybe the tour was ending now. I was careful not to trip and fall, lose my balance and fall, for I did not want to attract attention, and I did not want to be "weak." It was my impression that the women in the group did not want to appear "weak." We had managed to get through the tour, and we were all still standing, though exhausted, and light-headed. A prison facility will suck the oxygen from your brain: you are left dazed and depleted and depressed, and the depression will not lighten but in fact increase for several days as you think back over the experience; then, the depression will begin to fade, as even the worst memories will fade.

The execution chamber was the last stop at San Quentin. The lieutenant led us around a maze of buildings to the inner checkpoint (where we were as carefully monitored as we'd been on our way in; and where our signatures in the logbook were checked against our previous signatures) and through the courtyard where the American flag flew at perpetual half-mast and so to the first, outer checkpoint (where we were again as carefully monitored as we'd been on our way in) and to freedom outside the gates. We dispersed, we were eager to be free of one another, hurrying in the parking lot to our vehicles, wind whipping our hair.

I felt the surge of relief and joy I'd felt in Trenton, exiting the much smaller prison there after what had seemed several hours of misery but had been only a little more than a single hour. *Never again!*

On San Francisco Bay sunlight glittered in dazzling ripples in slate-blue water. In the distance was the great city like a vision or a mirage you might hallucinate from within the walls of San Quentin, improbably beautiful.

BUSTED IN NEW YORK

Darryl Pinckney

How long had it been since I'd been out late on the Lower East Side? Back in the New Wave bohemian days of the late 1970s and early '80s, the Lower East Side was the capital of mischief. The low life was still literary. I could be persuaded to go anywhere in search of an authentic urban experience. But then my friends grew up, and I moved far away, as Europe seemed to me at the time. Because I don't drink and run wild anymore, because I now live down a dirt track in the English countryside, a Manhattan room of the young and the smooth can be intimidating.

But the reggae club the summer before last was known as a chill lounge. Rona let her hair hang over the beat. We were waiting for Billie. I was telling myself not to have a hard time waiting. I was looking forward to my session with that inner-child finder, marijuana. The reggae swelled around me. My head bobbed like a duck when there's bread on the water. I saw what looked like a ballet dancer's leg. Billie, and a Billie who knew the score. Her opening drink would not take long. We were going to step outside. We couldn't smoke pot in this reggae club. Not even in a reggae club? That's how long it had been since I'd been out late on the Lower East Side.

Streetlamps threw a spotlight over pedestrians crossing Second Avenue. Killer taxis left unpleasant gusts. I leaned into the summer heat. Soon we three were alone in the dark of Sixth

Street. Rona checked behind her. Then, like backup singers on the downbeat, Billie and I snapped glances over our right shoulders. Maybe some people wouldn't have bothered, but we were pros. We were veterans of the streets. Rona fired one up and passed it. We were chatting. I hogged it. We were drifting toward midnight. Billie handed it back to Rona. Three shapes in front of a doorway decided to heckle us. "You're having a good time." They sounded like unappetizing old kids. We moved to the curb. "We know what you're doing." Rona pushed her hand against the air to let them know that the joke, whatever it was, had to stop. "Smoke it." We shook our heads at their being so boisterous when they were maybe getting high themselves, and in a doorway, of all places. We should have looked ahead instead of behind.

We saw the corner, and we saw the big man in white-guy plaid shorts cutting a pigeon-toed diagonal from across the street. Everything about him was aimed toward us. His bright white sneakers continued to rise and fall in our direction. A huge meat-packing arm was held out to us, and a big voice was coming at us, too. His other arm came out of his undershirt with a square of ID. We had to keep moving toward him, like something swirling down a drain. There now seemed to be enough light for a film crew's night shoot. How could we have missed the blue unmarked van parked on the other side of Sixth Street?

"Been smoking something?" No answer. "Put your hands flat on the trunk of this car." The women, my friends, were side by side at the back of the car. I was on the sidewalk and had to bend over. Other undercovers quickly appeared. "We're going to empty your pockets." A woman had taken up position behind Rona and Billie. I felt a hand go into my pocket. My total financial assets held by a faded money clip hit the trunk of the car. "Did you all just meet tonight?" a new voice demanded. "No." My own voice was thin and completely lacking in the authority of outrage. The money clip was followed by a pack of menthol cigarettes, a disposable lighter, a case containing reading glasses, a John Coltrane–Johnny Hartman CD—"You listen to some good music," a head of hair said—and a mobile phone. "Where's your beeper?" He patted me down. "You got a beeper?" "No," came the thin reply.

The detectives murmured. They'd found the smallest stub of weed in a matchbook in Rona's pockets. The woman detective left. The detective with the hair asked the ladies to step over to the sidewalk. Where Plaid Shorts had, like me, the beginnings of his father's stomach, this one had pecs and biceps flowing out of a magenta tank top. He looked like a television actor in the role of maverick cop. The rest of him was in the suburban version of casual: crisp blue jeans and clean sneakers.

"So you guys just met tonight?" Tank Top asked. It was my turn. He was going to compare answers. Plaid Shorts said he was going over to check something. "How do you know each other?" Tank Top demanded. "School." If he identified us as middle class, wouldn't he have to watch himself? Maybe I was trying to prick some white blue-collar resentment, anything to turn the tables a little. When he asked about my beeper, I thought maybe he hoped he'd interrupted something good, criminally speaking, such as a black dude giving two white chicks a taste of the street herb they were about to buy or get ripped off for. But if he saw that we were okay, then the paperwork on the citation that they gave out in these cases would speed up. One black guy with gray in his beard and one and a half white girls, not two, because by that time they must have figured out that Billie's honey skin and the Asian cast to her eyes and her Church of England accent were some weird Caribbean story. Yes, Officer, I wanted to explain, the one with the henna highlights is a famous Jewish scientist, the daughter of the British Commonwealth is a banker, and I'm a black guy who needs two pairs of glasses and won't be on your computer lists, not even a credit rating.

Billie and Rona had shown no emotion until Plaid Shorts brought the handcuffs. They gave out soft, pastel exclamations. Plaid Shorts led them, affronted and vulnerable, across the street to the side door of the van. I thought, Rona's daughter walks just like her. I felt my watch being removed. Tank Top put my arms behind me and pushed my hands high up my back. I felt the metal around my wrists. I thought of my parents and how they would hurl themselves into this situation if they found out. I felt and heard the handcuffs lock. I thought of my parents and their lawsuits. Back in the good old days, they'd sued our hometown police department to force it to desegregate, and when that worked, they sued the fire department—things they did in their spare time, as good citizens, as blacks of their generation, members of the NAACP rank and file. Injustice had only to ring their doorbell, and they were off to the poorhouse. And here was frivolous me letting a white man put me in handcuffs for something other than protest. I remembered what my father had said to my tears at my sister's memorial the year before: keep it together.

But I was in shock. "I'm going to be sick." I was starting to list from side to side. "Have you been drinking?" "No." I was going deaf. "I'm going to pass out." Tank Top gripped me just below my right armpit, and we started off, but my feet waited before they followed my legs. The world broke into silent, colorful particles. I got to the door and fell flat into the van. Rona's face floated. I began to hear her. I concentrated on finding her face in one place, something I could get up for and move toward, even if only on my knees. "Don't hurt him," Rona and Billie called. "I'm trying to help him," Tank Top countered.

Keep it together, I chanted to myself. Not because I was a black man in handcuffs in front of two white guys; not because I was powerless, which made it all the more necessary at least to imitate the examples of dignity in confrontations with police I'd witnessed; and not because I was a grown man losing it in front of two women who, though in handcuffs, were trying to defend me. But because they were my friends. They were the ones with children at home. I crawled over to my friends in the seatless, windowless rear of the van, dripping sweat on them.

Plaid Shorts yanked the van into the street. Because we couldn't grab, and there was nothing to grab on to, we rolled into Alice-down-the-rabbit-hole positions and rolled again when Plaid Shorts hit the gas. "This is such bullshit," Billie said to the ceiling. "This sucks," Plaid Shorts said. But he wasn't talking to us. He looked across to Tank Top. "You got that right." "A big one," Plaid Shorts added. "Hate it," Tank Top said to his window. "Total bullshit." Rona had dusted off her repertoire of apt facial expressions. This one said, "Are these guys for real?" "Five more years, man, and then I'm out," Plaid Shorts said. "I can't wait to just do my band." He did a near wheelie around the corner. We shouldered back up into sitting positions pretty expertly after two corners. Tank Top took some gum from the dashboard and said he had to keep at this bullshit until he could pay off his wife. He told Plaid Shorts that instead of alimony he was offering his wife a once-in-a-lifetime, can't-refuse lump sum. "It's like a buyout."

The acid-driven power chords of Pink Floyd took over the van. Rona's expression said, "These guys are too much." "They're wild," Billie's eyes said as she looked for the place behind her where the music was blaring from. Maybe the detectives were trying to tell us something. Not that they were nice guys who, regrettably, had to do their job but that they were better than the job they'd been reduced to doing, and that they, too, had aspirations. The Rolling Stones came on next, and Plaid Shorts sang along. The music was perhaps meant to say that they weren't uncool, redneck cops having a blast at the expense of the liberal, the black, and the in-between.

I was too ashamed to be sympathetic. Being addressed as "sir" by Tank Top only after I had shown weakness and fear—that was humiliating. A cop could go off at any time. I'd thought of that and been afraid, and there was no way to take it back. And for what had I lost my self-respect? For an offense the detectives thought beneath their training. What did you do last night? Oh, I was picked up for a reefer, and I fainted like a man. The van went up one street and down another. We couldn't see much, but most likely we were driving around and around as various undercover operations didn't work out. On one dark corner we waited so long in the van by ourselves that we almost slept.

The van door slid open, and in the shaft of light Tank Top was helping a Hispanic woman, maybe in her fifties, climb aboard the bummer bus. "Hey, Officer," she said when we were under way. "My hand's too hot." The detective parked and helped Rona and Billie out. Tank Top said, "I'm going to loosen these tight cuffs, like you asked." Then he turned off the lights, slammed the door, and left me with this woman who made unsavory sounds in the dark. I thought she was trying to ditch her vials of crack, and the detectives would then claim that they were mine. I went over on my side, practicing my I-was-asleep defense. They put Rona and Billie back in the van, turned on the lights, drove off, stopped again, and got out by themselves. As soon as the doors closed, the Hispanic woman, who'd freed her hands, whipped out a big bag of heroin, snorted it on her knee, and deftly worked her hands back into the cuffs. Rona was laughing in disbelief. Quietly, the Hispanic woman zoned sideways. The detectives, when they got back in, firmly looked straight ahead.

The next time the van door opened, a Hispanic man, maybe also in his fifties, climbed in. A dark Rasta youth was pushed in after him. "Ooh," the Hispanic guy said, and he tried to shift himself. He nodded greetings of solidarity. What he'd been oohing about hit Rona's hygiene radar first. It made delicate Billie draw in her legs. The gleaming Rasta youth sprawled before us had matted dreadlocks that looked like what comes from the back of a furnace when its filter is changed. Maybe I should have thought harder about this being someone's son, but the stench was overpowering. Meanwhile, he kept up a stream of Babylon *raasclaat* denunciations of the police. He shouted curses on the white man. I thought, Rasta, my brother in Garvey, you are on your own. The detectives paid him no mind. They'd made their quota for the shift.

We'd been smoking a joint right around the corner from the local precinct house—that's how hip we were. The detectives took us inside, and the handcuffs came off. After three hours, it was a relief to see my fingers. Tank Top took me and the Rasta youth upstairs to a grotty corridor, and the strip search began. He made the Rasta youth wait in the shadows at the end. He ordered me to hand him my clothes item by item. I was to turn around, bend over, and drop my shorts. He said quickly that that was enough. I was to take off my socks and turn them inside out. "Get dressed." He asked if I'd ever been arrested. No. He said he would try to tell me what was going to happen. I thought I understood. He motioned to the Rasta and sent me downstairs. He and the Rasta followed moments later. Tank Top had returned my property, except for the phone and the CD. Such stuff had to go over to the lockup at Central, he explained. If that was the case, then the Rasta youth had a prayer shawl and a Torah for Central to deal with. Tank Top tried to talk when he took my fingerprints. "So, what kind of things do you write?" After that, he had paperwork to finish. Now and then he would dial a telephone number, mutter, hang up, and shrug. A clock kept vigil over a wall of "Most Wanted" leaflets.

When Plaid Shorts announced that we were moving, around five o'clock in the morning, the Hispanic man asked how much money I had on me. I'd covered the money clip with my hand when Tank Top passed it to me, but, clearly, I hadn't been quick enough. The Hispanic man said I couldn't bring in anything where we were going, because it would get taken off me. He informed Plaid Shorts, who agreed that I'd get robbed. Rona put my belongings, even my glasses, in her pocket. My property would be safer in the women's section, the Hispanic man advised as we were put back into handcuffs and then linked to one another. I was made to lead our daisy chain of handcuffs through the precinct's main room. As Plaid Shorts increased the pace, two officers by the front door erupted into grunting song. "Working on the chain gang, uh."

Downtown, we hopped out of the van into a street that was still dark. A semicircle of light waited for us to approach. This was the Tombs, that place I'd heard about, read about. Two more daisy chains of prisoners joined ours as Tank Top, having rung twice, banged on the metal grating over the entrance. It rolled up. Plaid Shorts and Tank Top surrendered us in a series of rapid clipboard signatures. When I realized that they intended to abandon us at this concrete threshold, I wanted to ask them when they planned to read us our rights. I'd begun to think of them as our undercovers. They were responsible for us. But they were gone, and we were across the line, and the metal grating was coming down.

I followed a black female corrections officer's rump up some stairs. A black male corrections officer unhooked everybody. My eyes stayed on Rona and Billie when they were ordered to move to the other side of the corridor. The women went in one direction, the men in another. Green bars streamed along either side of me as I hurried to keep up with the corrections officer who was now taking us down to the basement, and to keep ahead of someone whose footsteps menaced my heels.

The Rasta youth and I were directed into the last cell of the long jail. I insinuated myself onto the narrow metal bench that went from the bars of the cell to the rear wall, where it made a right angle toward the partition that hid the toilet. Nine mute, tired faces emphasized how cramped and stuffy the tiny cell was. One man was curled up asleep under the bench.

I didn't want to look too intently at the other men in judicial storage, in case to do so meant something I could not handle the consequences of. I also didn't want to look away too quickly when my gaze happened to meet someone else's. However, no one was interested in hassling the new arrivals. Men were waking up, and their banter competed with the locker-room-type noise coming from the corrections officers' oblong station desk. A short white girl with thick glasses and a rolling lectern called my name. She said the interview was to determine who was eligible for bail, but the questions also separated the wheat from the chaff, socioeconomically speaking. Some guys probably had no job, no taxable weekly income, no address, no mother's address. She lost patience with the Rasta youth's decent background. "Education? How far did you get in school?" A community-college degree. Her head was tilted up toward the spectacle of his hair. "We'll say grade fifteen."

Sometime later, the Rasta youth and I were summoned again. But again we were going only a few yards. A black corrections officer shooed aside someone blocking the door of the new cell, which was large and, sneaked glances told me, held some huge dudes. Fresh apprehension was bringing my body to something like exocrine parity with the Rasta youth's. I didn't know what to expect and so tried to prepare for the worst. We were shoulder to shoulder on a metal bench, like crows shuffling on a telephone wire. The move to this restless population had to be the final, dangerous descent, the reason I'd crammed my watch into my glasses case and handed everything off to Rona.

A black youth with his hair in tight braids called out to a new arrival, my Hispanic comrade. "Come on in." The black youth's knuckles looked as big as Mike Tyson's. "They took the murderers out early." He slapped five with a couple of his hulking neighbors and concerned himself with what he could see of his reflection in the metal bench between his thighs. He said something more. I didn't hear what he said, but it must have been wicked.

A black corrections officer reversed himself and glared through the green bars. "What?" "Nothing, Mo," the black youth said loudly, evenly. Only one of his neighbors giggled. "Say what, chump?" He was going for the keys at his hip. "You say something?" He was so agitated that he couldn't get the key in. He was as tall as a basketball power forward. Everything he said was a variation of "You want to say something?" The cell door flew open, and in a few steps the corrections officer was over the massive head of twinkling braids. "A real man would say something now." He waited for an answer. I could see him shaking. The black youth wasn't going to feed him any lines or provocation. The corrections officer pivoted toward the door. He had a baton on his belt but no gun. He made a satisfied noise with his keys.

It was not an impressive performance. I knew that. The corrections officer hadn't come up with any good lines. He just kept repeating himself. I could tell that all twenty-four of my cellmates were thinking how off the hook the corrections officer had been to raise up—the lingo was coming to me—on somebody like that. I was getting excited, feeling that I was on the verge of bonding with the other guys in our high and hip judgment against the corrections officer. He didn't meet our rigorous standards when it came to "reading" someone in the street manner. The black youth with the oiled, sparkling braids delivered our verdict: "Definitely bugging behind something."

The black corrections officer flung the metal door so hard, it bounced against the cell bars and rode back some. Giant steps put him in a place that blocked my view of the black youth. Spit was dancing from his head, pinwheel fashion, as he roared, "If I started to kick your black ass now, where would your black ass be next week?" I couldn't remember when I'd seen such sudden rage. It stopped all other activity in the basement. The tendons in his neck were ready to explode. I couldn't begin to think what his nostrils might be doing. Maybe our survival molecules were not the only ones to have been put on alert. Some of his colleagues had come by to monitor the situation. They turned back in a way that indicated they'd respect some code not to interfere. The cell was very still as the corrections officer made his exit. The street judgment was in his silence. Nobody wanted to look at him until he'd turned the lock. He'd made his point. He'd shown how dangerous was his longing to have a reason to lose control.

The corrections officer's brown skin looked glazed, as though it had been fired in a kiln. He didn't seem to know how to finish his scene and stood wheezing by the bars. I almost thought he was going to mellow into the dispersal-of-balm-and-poultice phase of tough love. The mask of the shock-tactics practitioner would drop. He'd apologize, give advice, tell the young brothers how he was once on his way to being where they were. The black corrections officer said, "Remember, I'll be going home at four o'clock. You'll still be here. You're in jail. I'm not." Maybe I should have taken into account the possibility that he had seen and had a lot of trouble doing his job. Maybe he and the black youth already had a story going, and I'd missed what started it. But that didn't matter. Only what he'd said about four o'clock mattered. It wasn't even nine o'clock in the morning yet. My Hispanic comrade was looking at me. He took his eyes heavenward and clasped his hands. Then he shot me an inaudible laugh.

Jail was going to get me over my fear of saying the obvious, because there was no way to ignore all morning the fact that everyone in the cell was either black or Hispanic. The irony, for me, was that an all-black gathering usually meant a special event, a stirring occasion. I thought back to some black guys I used to know who enjoyed telling me that black guys like me ought to hang out with black groups like theirs. It flattered me to believe that I flattered them with my yearning for instruction in the art of how to be down with it. But this was not what they had in mind. The mood in the cell was like that of an emergency room in a city hospital: a mixture of squalor, panic, boredom, and resentment at the supposed randomness of bad luck.

Some guys, the Rasta youth among them, had elected to slip down onto the concrete floor. They were opting out of consciousness. Our cell had no television, no radio, no newspapers. There was a water fountain, a disgusting toilet, and two pay phones from which collect calls could be made. I don't know how those guys knew when the corrections officers had their backs turned, or how they'd held on to the contraband of drugs and matches they'd been thoroughly searched for, or how they knew who in which cell had what, but at one moment, as if by secret signal, paraphernalia went flying through green bars from cell to cell. The next thing I knew, guys were taking turns smoking crack behind the waist-high partition of the raised open toilet of our cell. Right there in the Tombs. I guess they figured there was no chance of the crack outsmelling the toilet. I'd switched seats and, as a result, was too near the burning funk. I saw my Hispanic comrade casually walk away from the hot spot, and soon, I, too, got up and crossed the cell. His look of approval after I'd eased in somewhere else told me that I'd made the right move.

A black guy with broken teeth, dressed in a torn car coat, emerged from behind the toilet. He ambled around and then seized the floor. "You remember Lucky Lou Diamond? I had twenty thousand dollar over to Jersey City." I tuned in, eager for a jailhouse Richard Pryor who could turn the cell into something else. "Nineteen seventy-five? Bunny hat on my head? Your Honor. There's no mouth on the girl he touched." His free association promised much, but it gutter-balled into such incoherence that the black youth with braids spoke for everyone when he barked, "Sit down."

It was quiet for a while, but then the Rasta youth snapped to attention. Something jerked him to his feet and set him standing squarely in front of the cell door, his right knee pounding out a steady rhythm. I thought, Just when things were manageable, my brother in Selassie has to flip out. I braced myself for his rap. But he was ready for his lunch. He was first in the line we were commanded to make; first to march out of the cell toward stacks of chalk-colored squares on long, low trolleys that looked like what bricks are transported on at a building site. We were to pick up a sandwich, turn, take a plastic cup of grape juice from another low trolley, and then march back to the cell.

A black guy in an orange jumpsuit—a trusty—called after me to let me know that I'd missed my allotted sandwich. Something about being urged to march rendered me unable to lift anything other than a cup of juice. Very soon the cell was strewn with sandwich remnants. Leaking sachets of mustard and mayonnaise found their way under the bench. A wedge of cheese crowned one of the pay phones. Lunch added to the odors of incarceration. However, there was plenty of room, because some of the men whose size so alarmed me when I first entered the cell had dived to the floor. I counted nine guys asleep in the grime, six of them in the fetal position, their wrists between their knees. Heads had to loll down some broad shoulders before they could touch concrete. A young, crack-thin guy woke and, using his palms for locomotion, crawled along on his stomach to the trash can, where he reached up to extract sandwich remains.

I overheard some of the guys say a little while later that the police had arrested so many people in the sweep of the previous evening that two special night courts had been set up to process the haul. They would start to call names at four o'clock. Waiting might have been easier had there been no clock. At the appointed hour, the only official movement came from the black corrections officer who'd flipped out that morning. I'm sorry to report that he went through all the transparent maneuvers of rubbing it in. He paraded by us on his way to the oblong station desk, ostensibly laughing at himself for forgetting something. And just in case the black youth with braids was pretending to take no notice of him, the corrections officer brought over a white officer holding a clipboard and pointed at the youth. His colleague tapped him a have-a-good-night. "I told you when you got here not to give me any problems." The black youth looked toward the bars, at last, his arms hugging his chest. The black corrections officer flicked a salute.

"Yo, Pops," I heard the black youth say once the air had calmed down again around us. "Pops," he called again in my direction. I couldn't believe that he was talking to me. Pops? Everybody in the cell who spoke to someone he didn't know said, "Yo, G." I pointed to myself. Who, me? "Mind my asking what you're in for?" I made a smoking gesture with two fingers of my right hand. "Uh-huh. You dress Italian. But." A neighbor of his wanted to give him five for that observation, but he just looked at him hard. It was true. The soundtrack of brotherhood in my head was nearly all Marvin Gaye. It had finally happened: I was older than a cartoon father on television. I was older than Homer Simpson.

I wasn't sure if Old Four Eyes in the Robert Hayden poem fled to "danger in the safety zones" or "safety in the danger zones." It was important to me, sitting there in my concrete elsewhere, which seemed dirtier and dimmer the longer I had to wait.

As the cell emptied, it got eerier. The few new guys, dressed in their garrulous night selves, were out of sympathy with the general tone of exhaustion and passivity. One new guy ranted about calling his girlfriend to tell her to hook up a plane to Canada, because after he made bail he was going to step off, boy. Another, the lone white, clung to a pay phone. He suggested to a friend that they deceive his brother-in-law. "Don't tell him it's for me." He could press telephone numbers with amazing speed. He insisted to the next friend that she had to get the bail money out of her mother, because he could not, he said, shooting his eyes across us, the nonwhite, do Rikers.

My name was called, the cell door gapped open, and I floated out. Neither my Hispanic comrade nor the Rasta youth followed. I regretted that I would not have the chance to thank the man who had watched my back. Very soon I found myself upstairs in a new cell that had an iron-lattice screen. Beyond it was the outside world. I heard the voices of what I supposed were women corrections officers, and then over the walls I heard Billie and Rona in their interview cells. They heard me; we heard one another.

The public defender on the free persons' side of the barrier was a heavyset white woman. She went from cubicle to cubicle, guiding us toward a plea: Adjournment in Contemplation of Dismissal, or ACD. If we didn't get picked up for the same offense within a twelve-month period, then the charge would be dropped, ACD.

I told the PD that I'd used the pay phones. I knew that that afternoon a friend of mine had come zooming down with newspapers and a criminal lawyer and had been denied access. She said they were entitled to hold us for at least twenty-four hours before they had to do anything with us. I said that being in custody was the punishment. I said prosecution of so-called quality-of-life crimes was a form of harassment. She explained that under the circumstances they didn't have to read us our rights. I was about to compare such offenses to civil disobedience, but the last thing this calm and capable PD was interested in was anybody's vanity. She said that high arrest figures justified the large increase in the number of police on the streets. It was that simple.

In the courtroom, I felt as though we were guest speakers at a high school, the offenders with us behind the court reporter looked so tadpole, so young. We stood when the judge entered. "He's not that kind of judge," a black bailiff said. Maybe because I was minutes and a plea away from getting out, tenderness got the better of me. I thought of my older sister and her practice in defense of juvenile offenders valiantly conducted from files in shopping bags in the trunk of her car. Our case was called, and we sat some rows back from the attorneys' desks, where we were unable to hear the grim PD, even if we could have concentrated enough.

God bless the old-hippie souls who still believed in public life and social responsibility, I thought, but the PD had no time for effusive thanks. I'd been so hypnotized by green bars that the marble floor outside the courtroom was dazzling. The white clerks behind the counter in a payments-and-records office were accustomed to a stressed-out public and were rude back. Down in the lobby, Rona and Billie ran for the door marked women. I rushed over to a rickety blue booth for my fix of those former slave crops—tobacco, sugar, coffee.

Perhaps our elation on Rona's rooftop was unearned, but we felt like released hostages. We made jokes as soon as we had an audience of friends. Even the squalid bits, when told the right way, got laughs. Maybe we were defending ourselves against our deeper reactions to what had happened to us. Rona's husband said that now that his little boy was old enough to play in the street, he had had to tell him what to do should the police ever stop him. Don't move; do exactly what they say; take no chances; give no lip. We wondered how popular these sweeps would be after more white people had been caught in the net.

We'd been abruptly deprived of our liberty, and that would always make for a chilling memory. And as I'd learned sitting in the cell with all those guys whose stories I didn't know and couldn't ask for: the system exists, the system—for the nonwhite young, the poor—is real. New arrest records had been created, but we were out, and friends were standing in wreaths of smoke, savoring the night view of fire escapes, water tanks, and lights in distant windows.

Six days after my release, I was back on the Lower East Side. I understood what Rona meant when she said that she fell in love with New York the day she realized that she could get a candy bar on every corner. But jail worked; it won. I thought, I'm not doing that again. The romance was over. For me, the changes in the streets went with everything else. Once upon a time, people moved to New York to become New Yorkers. Then people moved to New York and thought it perfectly okay to remain themselves. Goodbye, Frank O'Hara.

"Yo, Papi," I heard. I was astonished. It was my Hispanic comrade. They'd given him five days on Rikers Island for possession of a crack pipe. He was selling vinyl records on the sidewalk before he got moved off that bit of Second Avenue. Could I help him out? It would be my privilege. He said he remembered what the black youth with braids had said when they took him out of that cell in the Tombs. "Kidnapped by the mayor, y'all."

AGAINST "GUNMETAL"

Lia Purpura

June. Cape May, NJ. Boardwalk.

Rain coming harder. People hurrying. People jumping boardwalk puddles with bright sand-centers. Avoiding the spume of passing cars. Ingraytensifying the soft dunes with neon rain gear, all the ponchos calm and isoscelate, then blown scalene in wind. Now it's more to watch, the dodging and pitching. More, maybe, "fun." Of interest. "Human interest," because rain alters people in unexpected ways. And the unexpected makes people so human.

Remember that.

Out there on the boardwalk, they're absolutely dedicated to being human, and though not one of them has a choice, many variations come forth. All the ways are recognizable, but some are more precise in cast and tensity, saturation and value, and take patience to see and to name.

Outside's thunderclap, its tonnage and stipple. The toilet in the room above's flush. Extended, deepening thunder sounds. The picture window's darkening glaze. Except for the mother with her hood pulled tight, a sporty family neverminding the rain, laughing, carrying big, wet cups of coffee. A runner tendon-stretching, braced against a stop sign. An old-salt type in a long, yellow slicker, waving to someone, or directing the deluge. More cars than usual heading north to the parkway, as goes the decision through many heads at once to leave the shore earlier than planned. Methods of resignation abound: one on a gearless softseater pitches into the weather headfirst, a sack of oranges hooked on his arm. Four pedaling a surrey remain committed to their rented hour. The sky brightens. The clouds shift. The cars slow and their numbers decrease. Runners come out, had they ducked under awnings. Outside our window, a gaslamp-style streetlight's on; it must have self-lit at the first hint of dark. Walkers wearing long sleeves and sweatshirts, who must have tested (head out a window, arm out a door) the temperature before emerging.

Various pitched rumbles, filling, ablating. A rough sound, that otherwise might be silk tearing, but for now is tires parting puddles. All headlights on. Sky darkening again. Those choosing to be out or having been caught, somewhere on those bodies in the noisy rain: shiny, cicatricial spots of damp. Wet shoulders where clothing is sticking. Abrasions on ankles where sockless shoes rub. Itchy tags. Rings of sweat. Objectwise, sunglasses in bags or hooked at collars. Loose, jangling change. Newspapers rolled and stuffed in back pockets. Some lightning now, but candescent, not the sky-ripping variety. Some darkness lifting at the horizon, baring a strip between sea and sky, like a hem rising over a sock.

Now the umbrellas, now that the walkers have figured it out: rainy not rain. Dark as any November day, late in the afternoon. Blue turned to its compounds and alloys, its milkier elements, whitened and hardened. On Beach Drive, the activity increases: Doppler riffs. Gutters surging. Thunder yanked like special-effect sheets of aluminum, behind the scenes. A jogger who can't economize movements, whose legs seem strapped on and lack propulsion, whose elbows angle too far from his body, seems wetter than others. Bending in wind, heavy with rain, some hardy beach roses suggest a boat tethered and scuffed against unseen pilings.

One species of sleeping person can sense rain and somehow knows to stay abed, undisturbed in their summer rental, up and down the beach. An announcement such as this won't jar them: *May I have your attention, please. Lightning is on the beachfront. Lightning is on the beachfront. Clear the area for your safety.* It sounds not at all canned: the voice of a real and excited someone, red-faced, soaked and bringing the news. At the horizon where ocean meets sky, a mist congests and erases perspective. Rain threshes the sand. The sky darkens further. The sky turns, toward or into. The sky now. The sky is—what *is* the shade, gradient, hue, tint I'm seeing? The __________ sky. That sense of searching, fingertips tapping, calling forth terms. Sifting, anticipating: the something sky. Something. Something pushes in. It draws up to full height.

It blots out any other sky, *gunmetal,* does.

How irksome. *Gunmetal*. What a cliché.

Strike me down if I use it again. If I don't, right now, erase this method, by which we impart, those of us who know nothing about guns, drama to a sky, pressure to a scene, hardness, know-how, coldness to a description, glad for its hint of treachery, its sidelong, thanatotic meanness.

Why erase, though? Why deny the relief of a shared, common phrase—novelistically charged, not the worst imaginable? You know gunmetal and *I* know gunmetal: why not meet there? Pretend it's a bar of the same cool name, "Gunmetal's" (brushed steel, understated track lighting) and relax, converse, affirm each other's positions on many Big (or breezy and minor) Life Issues. Since I had nowhere to go this evening and you were free, and isn't that better than staying home? Even if I know where the conversation's headed? And really, you're perfectly decent company, *you* aren't at fault. But after an evening like this, I'm way more antsy and hardly refreshed, since I'm not at all changed or challenged or stretched. And neither are you.

And yes, the *coldness* of a gun pertains. A gun is, when you first hold it, very cold, and way heavier than you'd think—say a .22, hitched right up against the shoulder. At least the one I shot weighed more than I expected, made as it was, of . . . I don't know what. Gunmetal, I guess. I hardly have anyone to ask about this. One strictly seasonal pheasant-hunting friend, who will answer modestly and not say one thing beyond what he knows. Another who fought in the Iran-Iraq War, and though that's long ago now for him, I hesitate. Because maybe it's not so long ago, the way rogue scenes slide in when you're making a sandwich, washing your hair, touching your sleeping child's face. . . . Also, I've seen that tree, in the photo in his living room, the tree he's standing so uprightly next to (he in his uniform, and both so thin they look related) and *something* came just before the photo and *something* happened just after it, to the side of the tree, or behind it—it's that the tree's starkness is a point of reference. There is, I think, a lot more he knows, for example, on the subject of grenades, that I don't want to ask about either, there being no "grenade blue" I'm harrying here. Though there's a sky for that, too. A misty tint, a haze indicating surprise detonation, rain turned to hail, very suddenly.

But I want to know what "gunmetal" means, and found the perfect guy to ask, a friend of a friend, a gunmaker out west, who's currently working on a matchlock from 1510 ("older than all my friends combined" he says).

My questions, of course, are embarrassingly basic.

And yes, I do need to start at the beginning.

Jim writes: *Glocks are made of plastic with metal inserts in the receiver or frame (the part you hang on to), the slide and barrel are metal and the color is determined by the options you choose.* (He's seen pink as well as sky-blue ones.) *The basic metal a .22 is made of varies but it is always shiny silver, what we in the trade call "in the white." This reflects that it has not been colored or coated yet. The coloring (whether it be bluing, Frenching, coating, or browning) is put there to keep the metal from corroding or oxidizing in an undesirable manner. "Gunmetal" as a color is usually a gray, more technically called "French gray." Think of the dark ash on charcoal, only shiny.*

The shiniest guns would be chrome or nickel-plated, the blackest ones would be the black epoxy-coated; black chrome is black beyond belief, but is shiny like a mirror. These coatings can be applied to any firearm. I have examples of almost anything you would like. . . .

Almost anything I would like . . . as, too, this sky is variously compounded, concussive, concupiscent, and oh, could be layered with names transfinitely: it's the rivery color a silver spoon turns when held in a flame. It's the color of a well-used plumber's wrench. A perfectly battered railroad tie. I try on: *A burnt-spoon sky. Below a sky where we sat down, under wrench-colored clouds. Before the sky opened and a rain as hard as railroad ties fell . . .* It's the color of a cataract (which, very like "promontory," is not much in use, ever-nailed as they are to the nineteenth century, provenance of the Lake District poets). It's a kinked intestine-gone-bloodless-pale sky. Translucent, unfeathered, fallen-chick silver. Powdered zinc. Stripped olive pit. Dirty-kid water in a porcelain tub. Farinaceous. Clayey. Grime in pressed tin. So why *gunmetal*? If it's something about the act of smithing, why not things from the worlds of cooper, tinker, wainwright, glazier? I suppose the throwback quality's engaging—the forging, the shine, the bluing, blacking, and browning—but mostly, I think, it's rugged and hip to suggest with this phrase you know something about guns; enough at least to toss likeness around. You have to like a likeness to toss it (note: kids running, jostling, outshouting each other as they race to a car will call "*shotgun*!" not "*side saddle*!" not "*the seat next to my mom*").

If you're really set on naming a sky by way of armaments, try a breech-loading carbine's pencilly softness, or another from the Civil War (see the excellent display at the Gettysburg Visitor Center), a Harpers Ferry musket whose mottling looks like winter rain. Try a cannon's smoothbore, or case shot, the spherical or precisely penile munitions, pocked, blackened, and smutted by all the ways they ruined a body, rolled, muddied and were gathered up again for duty. Try the brass coat buttons, buckles, and plates identifying cavalry, riflemen, musicians, artillery, infantry, engineers, and the tarnish spots there, *that* color, where the salts in blood wore away the finely wrought eagles, lyres, and flags. A mess cup's the color of the Potomac in winter. A bayonet's black as a rasping crow. And "rust," it turns out, is a complicated blood-dew-gunsmoke amalgam.

"Battleship gray" is also a problem; consider the monstrous snout of a ship, fastened with rivets the size of plates, unyielding and lithic—does a sky intend to communicate this? To bear down, to invade? Can't we come up with something other than a destroyer's brutal, flat gray to signal a presence that hovers over with steady nerves and conviction? In Farsi, my friend offered

Ghamangeez, "a saddening sky," and his wife refined it: "a sky that brings on sadness."

Okay. Now we're getting somewhere.

It's quick, gunmetal is, and efficient. I'll give it that. It speeds the scene. So you can get on to something else. It's a term that makes you feel part of a team. A baton you hold firmly and pass down the line. The way a party icebreaker works: let me introduce you to X. Now you're friends. Now the two of you can have coffee together. Then *you* introduce. To one of *your* friends. They go for a drink (you know where). Now so many of us have something in common. We're cozy. We know what the other means when we say . . .

Skies change, thankfully, and grays complicate—unfurl, turn smoky, egressive, specular. A few hours later, the sky in Cape May has taken a turn that stymies. It stumps me. Car base coats, the flat ones, rally to help. Giorgio Morandi knew, and applied to the bottles and humble plates in his paintings a range of opacities, the soft, cool creams of unspeckled eggs, of froths and dunes. Of dusty, white Neccos (whose flavor is cinnamon, and surprisingly spicy, almost fireball hot, but muted and sweeter, so the shock spreads more evenly over the tongue, with no ping, no ache, nothing tornadic). *This* sky is more oatmeal, ashed incense, clamshell. It's the color of shit in its calcified state, though this likeness is not much in use, alas, our palette's not very broadly accepting, and shit is not aesthetically easy; it won't stay domed. Won't stay chapeled, as it is when left alone to dry into earthy, roadside temples. Fat white gulls and snowy egrets disappear against this sky, which makes its color more erasure than presence. Ghosted. Palimpsistic.

Birds can't sink into gunmetal skies.

"Gunmetal," on the comportment family tree, is close to "steely." Steely eyes. Steely wills. Ramrod posture. (And ramrods, of course, pack down charge in muzzle-loading guns; thus a body fit to load munitions, push explosives, shoulder them in, so straight and stiff, it must have been trained. *To fight, to serve and never to yield,* its motto might be. A body like that. A sky like that. Mission-bound. Single-minded.)

"Gunmetal," deployed, delivers a payload of routine. And routine is a much sought-after commodity. I get that. The best of us succumb at times. About McDonald's, for instance, the Cape May guidebook confirms, "You can't live on gourmet food alone. So it's comforting to have Mickey D's right here! There are few things in life more reliable or comforting than a Happy Meal. There is something to be said about knowing EXACTLY what you're getting EVERY TIME. No worrying if your steak is going to be cooked enough, or if the clams are bad. The only thing to worry about at McDonald's is whether to get your meal small, medium, or large." "Gunmetal" as Happy Meal. It's compact, the phrase "gunmetal sky," as reliable a delivery system as any Big Mac, withtwoallbeefpattiesspecialsaucelettucecheesepicklesonionsonasesameseedbun. (How cleverly that little jingle—I can still hear the tune—indicates both precision and overabundance.) And though I won't go on with this point, research shows there are 380 seeds on each sesame-seed bun, "give or take a few."

So when I say the word to myself, for a sky's particular depth and hue, "gunmetal," which precisely means "dark gray with blue or purple tinge" (but you knew that, didn't you), a third, nictitating lid comes down and though I *see* the sky—more accurately, the real seeing stops. The little path meandering out, where I went hunting all this time for other colors the sky might be, fuzzes up. It bombs the path, "gunmetal" does. I'm trying to locate it in my body (say at the spot where clavicle and shoulder meet, where the rifle kicked hard and knocked a week-long bruise into place) so I can say the word "gunmetal" and mean it. But I don't feel it. I just join with. I fall in. I get phalanxed with the staters. Heads of Statement all start talking. All agreeing, nodding, yessing. Settling. I feel I've been given one of those ovoid bumper stickers, alerting all to my vacation spot—that mysterious "OBX" (Outer Banks Crossing, I learned at a stoplight, eye level with an SUV's bumper). Or in Cape May it's "Exit Zero." Very in-clubbish. The longer I stay in a place, the more okay the decals seem. I'm hustled in with the locals and after a while—we've been coming here for years—I begin to feel pretty local myself. Happy to be readable. Glad to be part of.

At luminous moments I have wanted to say, "How blessed I

have been"—but can't. My problem is accepting a gift so weirdly, singularly bestowed: why me? why not them? I'm better with gratitude that's more diffuse: late afternoon in the middle of my life, cooking dinner, the window open, sun releasing the scent of pine floors into a solitude still and light-scoured. I'm more at home with moments beflecked with goodness, than I am with the handed-down-from-on-high kind. Things like plumbing and clean hot water, hard, tart apples, and well-sharpened knives best set my gratitude in motion. "Gunmetal" would make a follower of me; using it, I'd have to say a thing I've been taught to say. Believe a thing about the sky I've been given to believe. As I'd have to take "blessed" to mean: I have been chosen, marked, held right in the center of some kind, crosshaired sight. Which is nice. But doesn't the universe also fix on falling sparrows, lend its attention to spectacular disaster, train its very steady eye on accidents, suffering, diminishment—and not intercept, help out, bless them?

I want such a sky to quiet me (not "strike me dumb"—that's a rod drawn up, enforcing awe, and one is "smote"). And I want, in that quiet, to search out my terms. And what I decide on, I want to be more than a firearm's alloy. Harder to come by. Stronger. Chromatic. I want to turn to oyster and mouse, tide pool and tin, and then tank those and reconfigure if the gray they offer is not worthy, if associations gained are not surprising, of a distance previously unreachable, and intimately roomy. Freshening and new.

Or let's not play Name That Color at all: goodbye to Keystone, Gauntlet, Cloak, Summit, Uncertain, Vast, and Repose (from the neighborhood paint store's line of gray offerings) and take up geography and spatial relations—how far, in what way, for how long did the sky lift away from sea, hunch in close, or variegate.

Or activate good old "gray" as a suffix, but hitch it to actions like *torque-*, *welter-*, and *brim-*. *Coruscate-*, *grizzle-*, *rave-*, *solder-*, *convulse-*.

Or consider that which disappears into the sky—bottle-nosed dolphins that leap-because-they-can, their play, research shows, both useless and necessary—in other words, restorative. Dolphins leap because muscles want flexing, because the air at Cape May in June is warmer than water and the change is pleasing, the shift between elements tickles them. In fact, I just learned, dolphins mate up to eight times a day—even when not in heat.

To disappear into an endless, dolphin sky.

To sift and sift and sift words—and not find. And in the face of not-finding, to not-rely-on. To turn away usual corollaries. To maybe just sit before such a gray sky and give up, until strength returns and possibilities rise. Or maybe just watching is enough. To unburden in that way. To unwind. Take it out of your pocket, your holster, that sky. Lay down your gunmetal. It's the sky buy-back program. The sky amnesty plan. Turn it in, buddy. Hand it over, right now, while you can, and you won't be charged with theft.

And now you're free to find your own term.

BEEPER WORLD

Karen Russell

The jellyfish life cycle, we were taught in school, involves a sessile state and a period of radiant flight. As polyps, jellyfish are rooted to the seafloor by fleshy stalks. As medusae, they swim freely, contracting the bright umbrellas of their bodies to whoosh around the ocean, migrating by luminous conjunction: *and and and*. In this anchorless state, the jellies are labeled adults.

But there is also an intermediate stage: the ephyra. Ephyrae are goofy, adolescent beings. They develop at the tops of polyps; for a while, it looks as though the organism is dreaming of a baby jellyfish. Then they detach, like mutinous mushroom caps. Away they float, disk-shaped and aglow. This is sometimes referred to as "blooming." Newborn zeros, they are tumid with light. They swarm into fleets—hundreds of thousands rising through the dark sea—but their movement is wobbly, desultory; their trajectory has a temporal, and not a spatial, destination: the future, when they will be old enough to mate with one another. Just by virtue of swimming forward through time—and avoiding the mouths of predators—they develop into medusae. They locomote in the dark via golden pulsations.

For my fourteenth birthday, I got a purple Motorola beeper. It was a twinkling cartridge, the trendy fluorescent model. It cost sixty dollars at the Beeper World kiosk at South Florida's Dadeland Mall. Other colors were played out, we were told by the persuasively disdainful concierge, a friend's terrifying older brother, on whom we all had dutiful crushes. He wore silver jewelry on parts of his face that did not strike one as load-bearing—there was a green gem levitating on his chin scruff, for example. He didn't have to work hard to convince us that we needed those beepers.

The beeper, for a certain kind of Miami teenager in the nineties, was an essential evolutionary adaptation. You simply couldn't survive, socially, without one. A visit to Beeper World became a retail rite of passage. It usually occurred around the time that your older friends obtained their driver's licenses and thus achieved vehicular autonomy, budding off the polyp of a South Florida carport. Somewhat motile, you sought liberation from the terrible bondage of your parents' landline. So you lassoed your eyes and your lips in spooky-dark pencil, you strapped on Miami's regulation platform heels, with cork soles that added five inches to your height, and you queued up at Beeper World to receive your tiny occult device.

The beeper is a palm-size plastic grenade set to detonate anytime someone punches your ten-note conjuring spell into a telephone keypad. When this happens, your beeper shakes and emits two staccato squeaks. Unlike a ringing phone, you cannot answer it; the beeper merely alerts you to the fact that someone, somewhere, is bent on communicating something to you. It's an antique magic, of course, in the era of the Android. The beeper is a primitive thinker: it contains only the rudiments of its successors' intelligence. Numbers, not words, appear on its screen. A secret message squints itself into view.

You return the page from a landline. If you're out with us teenagers, in 1996, in Coconut Grove, you return the page from a pay phone mere feet away from the gusting mist of a pink mall waterfall, so close to this cascade that your arm hairs shine with chlorinated dew. To stand inside the phone booth makes you feel like the vibrating needle at the center of a compass—on a weekend night, all Grove traffic will be moving in a chrome blur around this booth. Cars shake with bass like lovesick bullfrogs.

Whoever beeped you will have to shout into their phone to be heard over Ini Kamoze.

I was always amazed by the line at this booth. On a Saturday night, it could be forty minutes long. This made trying to use the greasy public phone feel like waiting for Space Mountain. Queued up with my doppelgangers, other Miami girls wearing Gap perfume samples and the diaphanous ghosts of clothes (shirts that looked like pure foam with zippers, white thong-revealing denim), I read and reread the message on my beeper and rehearsed what I was going to say when it was finally my turn at bat. I remember the wait as a happy one, albeit nerve-racking: we stood shoulder to shoulder in the Florida heat, perspiring even at midnight, cupping the glowing screens of our pagers like little haunted limes.

The sonic burr of a beeper on our teenage flesh was exotic. It was the purr of someone wanting you. It was violent: a spur digging into your side. The most common message came loaded with potential, an opaque command behind the glass window: "423" ("Call me"). I'm sure it was no accident that we all carried these things in our pockets, or clipped against our pelvic bones.

To those messages you added your own tag, a sort of self-chosen varsity number—mine was 22—to identify yourself. "423-123-22" = "Call me, I miss you, it's Karen." The argot of the beeper was not subtle. In its concision, Miami beeper-speak resembled the dialogue of Hemingway, or a Spanish parody of the dialogue of Hemingway, or a terse, perverted robot. Much of what we beeped to one another was either blunt declarations of love or blunt declarations of horniness.

Recently, I asked my best friend, Karina, for the codes she remembered:

123 I MISS YOU

143 I LOVE YOU

193 MISS ME?

23 TE AMO

26 TE QUIERO

42 FUCK ME

43 FUCK YOU

423 CALL ME

07 JUST KIDDING

303 STOP PLAYING

606 BITCH

345987 I'M HORNY

99 NIGHT NIGHT

45 GOODNIGHT

56 SWEET DREAMS

911 EMERGENCY/CALL ME NOW!

77 FRIENDS FOREVER

477 BEST FRIENDS FOREVER

And then there were the codes that resembled words when held upside down:

07734 HELLO

14 HI

50538 BESOS

7735 SELLOUT

35006*17715 SILLY GOOSE

304 HOE

Apparently there were regional variations to the beeper code, numeric dialects that evolved in Los Angeles and Houston, where kids used slightly different numbers to candy-heart each other affectionate demands ("Come over"; "Kiss me"). Now the code strikes me as innocent, even at its lewdest—a refuge from the frightening flexibility of the English alphabet. We had a system that let us reduce a thousand streaming, volatile feelings into these digitized grunts: paint-by-number insults and flirtations, heat-and-serve proposals. Punch a few buttons, and you could kiss anyone goodnight, or tell him off. It was a common lexicon, and it also saved you from the real burden, at that age, of having to know what you felt, what you might actually want.

If text messages have permitted today's youth to write out their fantasies with Joycean bloat, 1996 was another era entirely—strange days populated by characters out of Cormac McCarthy, when your avatar might be "8," and what you could say, as "8," was limited to autistic haikus. Yes. No. Fuck You. So much ungovernable longing got compressed into integers.

One day, I'd love to write a story about two goony guys, ZP and JP, who are accidental savants of the beeper code. They are Florida boys in Clorox-white ball caps and black jeans with pant legs the width of tepees. Friday looms, and the phone banks are silent. No girl they've beeped is calling them back. None of the plans they've suggested, possibilities that were in turn suggested to them by the prix fixe menu of the beeper code, seem at all likely to come to fruition. "This buffet needs more options," ZP complains.

Even though they are both failing out of precalculus, they start fiddling around with numbers, swapping 2s and 4s, dividing by pi, using weird functions on that ninety-dollar graphing calculator we were all forced to buy. Eventually, JP and ZP invent an entirely new code—a programming language for teenagers who want to design alternate realities together. Maybe something wild happens next, something far in excess of any of the finite set of Saturdays that the old beeper code could generate: people gather and drink on the beach, people gather and drink in a club, people stay home and drink in a cloud of self-pity and confused arousal. It's a real breakthrough in the tropical science of coming of age. ZP and JP's codes show up on beeper screens across South Dade and spontaneously combust in their classmates' brains. Entirely new vistas appear—places to go that make the mall seem like a tomb. Minds are daisy-chained together, all of them translating ZP and JP's numbers into the strangest pictures. If the former beeper code was a tram tour with twelve stops, this new code goes *off road*.

ZP and JP, sitting goggle-eyed in JP's bedroom, staring at the telephone and then the sapphire-blue Motorola pager, share an Alexander Graham Bell moment of nerdy euphoria. The boys bump fists. Maybe they chest bump, maybe they risk a hug. Who knows? Maybe they can now beep each other something that is a more efficient relay of astonishment and joy than any of these gestures. Verbs that never occurred to these kids suddenly rear before them in their imagination—verbs that make the typical Saturday routine of ingesting fruit-flavored poisons and attempting to undress one another seem timid by comparison. Teenagers all across America begin to beep one another messages with this rogue code.

Say "143" to anyone from Miami who came of age in the nineties, and watch a strange glow flood his or her eyes. Today the beeper is a tech shibboleth for me, in much the same way that velocipedes and gramophones and Betamax videocassettes must have been for our forebears. "What was your beeper code?" I'll ask if I want to find others of my generation: the first wave of South Floridian high schoolers (and the last) for whom the beeper played a critical role in courtship, aggression, the coordination of liquor-store runs. We were crude engineers, clumsily trying to input emotions into one another. The futures that we were actually trying to create? These were too grandiose to admit to one another aloud, or even to ourselves. We wanted to make strangers fall in love with us, we wanted to perfume distant rooms with our absence, to launch our loneliness into suburbs as remote as Davie and West Kendall. In fact, what we wanted as fourteen- and fifteen-year-olds must have been largely unutterable. Who knows what dangerous confessions we might have wound up making without the corset of this script? "45," we could beep a stranger, and be done with it.

True confession: I never wanted a beeper. I feared the telephone, and other humans. The beeper confirms the presence of another mind in the roaring universe and summons you to it. You would think this would be a reassuring compliment. Somebody is thinking of you, wishing for the uniquely fricative properties of your voice. Yet in my experience, to be beeped by a non-parent was dreadful. Decoding the numbers was a stressful affair, and I brought a level of fear to the translation project that would have made my Navy father roll his eyes. Friends could beep you, but so could total strangers. "Call me, hoe!" an unknown number might request of you, from the wilds of Broward County, and how would you respond?

Before acquiring a beeper, I spent most nights hidden in my bedroom, barricaded from the unpredictable voices of the living by big square books. I communed with the dead and the imaginary, to whom I drafted responses that were always wordless, and absolutely private. During the day, I was an anxious kid who liked to disappear into Miami's mangrove jungles on my bicycle, alone. By fourteen, I was beginning to understand, to my horror and elation, that I would have to figure out a way to stay "in touch" with other people. Solitude of the kind I'd enjoyed in the deep July of childhood had already gone extinct—and I can remember staring at a white heron from my bicycle seat along Biscayne Bay, feeling my beeper go off. Using the beeper code, I found that I could actually program certain desires into myself. "555," I punched into the keypad: "I want you." Somehow the mechanical act of entering these codes into the phone increased the strength of my ambivalent wish, and suddenly I did want a friend to call me back or a boyfriend to come visit.

My female friends beeped and responded to beeps with the same efficient urgency as the surgeons at Baptist Hospital. Now we could always be on call for one another. Our telepathic net was externalized, formalized. "911!" Carla or Alexis would beep me. I will spare you a description of the situations that, at fourteen, we deemed emergencies.

We were tidaling ephyrae: translucent bubble creatures, cartwheeling through space, illuminating in electric pulses our own quietly panicked trails as we drifted through the black seas of nocturnal Miami. Back then, I clipped the beeper to my belt loop and read it like a tiny glowing book. 50538-69-07. I'm cringing now, remembering all the messages I had stored on that miniature record—it housed my first love letters, it was the closest thing I had to a high school diary. You could scroll through them backward, those algebraic proofs of longing, and all our ridiculous and earnest declarations composed of 7s and 1s. I really believed I'd save them for all time, encrypted on a shitty Motorola pager, the black box of adolescence. 123,143, 56, Miami.

THIS OLD HOUSE

David Sedaris

When it came to decorating her home, my mother was nothing if not practical. She learned early on that children will destroy whatever you put in front of them, so for most of my youth our furniture was chosen for its durability rather than for its beauty. The one exception was the dining room set my parents bought shortly after they were married. Should a guest eye the buffet for longer than a second, my mother would jump in to prompt a compliment. "You like it?" she'd ask. "It's from Scandinavia!" This, we learned, was the name of a region, a cold and forsaken place where people stayed indoors and plotted the death of knobs.

The buffet, like the table, was an exercise in elegant simplicity. The set was made of teak and had been finished with tung oil. This brought out the character of the wood, allowing it, at certain times of day, to practically glow. Nothing was more beautiful than our dining room, especially after my father covered the walls with cork. It wasn't the kind you use on bulletin boards, but something coarse and dark, the color of damp pine mulch. Light the candles beneath the chafing dish, lay the table with the charcoal textured dinnerware we hardly ever used, and you had yourself a real picture.

This dining room, I liked to think, was what my family was all about. Throughout my childhood it brought me great pleasure, but then I turned sixteen and decided that I didn't like it anymore. What changed my mind was a television show, a weekly drama about a close-knit family in Depression-era Virginia. This family didn't have a blender or a country club membership, but they did have one another—that and a really great house, an old one, built in the twenties or something. All of their bedrooms had slanted clapboard walls and oil lamps that bathed everything in fragile golden light. I wouldn't have used the word "romantic," but that's how I thought of it.

"You think those prewar years were cozy?" my father once asked. "Try getting up at five A.M. to sell newspapers on the snow-covered streets. That's what I did, and it stunk to high heaven."

"Well," I told him, "I'm just sorry that you weren't able to appreciate it."

Like anyone nostalgic for a time he didn't live through, I chose to weed out the little inconveniences: polio, say, or the thought of eating stewed squirrel. The world was simply grander back then, somehow more civilized, and nicer to look at. And the history! Wasn't it crushing to live in a house no older than our cat?

"No," my father said. "Not at all."

My mother felt the same: "Boxed in by neighbors, having to walk through my parents' bedroom in order to reach the kitchen. If you think that was fun, you never saw your grandfather with his teeth out."

They were more than willing to leave their pasts behind them and reacted strongly when my sister Gretchen and I began dragging it home. "The *Andrews* Sisters?" My father groaned. "What the hell do you want to listen to them for?"

When I started buying clothes from Goodwill, he really went off, and for good reason, probably. The suspenders and knickers were bad enough, but when I added a top hat, he planted himself in the doorway and physically prevented me from leaving the house. "It doesn't make sense," I remember him saying. "That hat with those pants, worn with the damn platform shoes . . ." His speech temporarily left him, and he found himself waving his hands, no doubt wishing that they held magic wands. "You're just . . . a mess is what you are."

The way I saw it, the problem wasn't my outfit, but my context. Sure I looked out of place beside a Scandinavian buffet, but put me in the proper environment, and I'd undoubtedly fit right in.

"The environment you're looking for is called a psychiatric hospital," my father said. "Now give me the damn hat before I burn it off."

I longed for a home where history was respected, and four years later I finally found one. This was in Chapel Hill, North Carolina. I'd gone there to visit an old friend from high school, and because I was between jobs and had no real obligations I decided to stay for a while, and maybe look for some dishwashing work. The restaurant that hired me was a local institution, all dark wood and windowpanes the size of playing cards. The food was OK, but what the place was really known for was the classical music that the owner, a man named Byron, pumped into the dining room. Anyone else might have thrown in a compilation tape, but he took his responsibilities very seriously and planned each meal as if it were an evening at Tanglewood. I hoped that dishwashing might lead to a job in the dining room, busing tables and eventually waiting on them, but I kept these aspirations to myself. Dressed as I was, in jodhpurs and a smoking jacket, I should have been grateful that I was hired at all.

After getting my first paycheck, I scouted out a place to live. My two requirements were that it be cheap and close to where I worked, and on both counts I succeeded. I couldn't have dreamt that it would also be old and untouched, an actual boardinghouse. The owner was adjusting her Room for Rent sign as I passed, and our eyes locked in an expression that said Hark, stranger, you are one of me! Both of us looked like figures from a scratchy newsreel, me the unemployed factory worker in tortoiseshell safety glasses and a tweed overcoat two sizes too large, and she, the feisty widow lady, taking in boarders in order to make ends meet. "Excuse me," I called, "but is that hat from the forties?"

The woman put her hands to her head and adjusted what looked like a fistful of cherries spilling from a velveteen saucer. "Why, yes it is," she said. "How canny of you to notice." I'll say her name was Rosemary Dowd, and as she introduced herself I tried to guess her age. What foxed me was her makeup, which was on the heavy side and involved a great deal of peach-colored powder. From a distance, her hair looked white, but now I could see that it was streaked with yellow, almost randomly, like snow that had been peed on. If she seemed somewhat mannish, it was the fault of her clothing rather than her features. Both her jacket and her blouse were kitted out with shoulder pads, and when worn together she could barely fit through the door. This might be a problem for others, but Rosemary didn't get out much. And why would she want to?

I hadn't even crossed the threshold when I agreed to take the room. What sold me was the look of the place. Some might have found it shabby—"a dump," my father would eventually call it—but, unless you ate them, a few thousand paint chips never hurt anyone. The same could be said for the groaning front porch and the occasional missing shingle. It was easy to imagine that the house, set as it was on the lip of a university parking lot, had dropped from the sky, like Dorothy's in *The Wizard of Oz,* but with a second story. Then there was the inside, which was even better. The front door opened onto a living room, or, as Rosemary called it, the "parlor." The word was old-fashioned but fitting. Velvet curtains framed the windows. The walls were papered in a faint, floral pattern, and doilies were everywhere, laid flat on tabletops and sagging like cobwebs from the backs of overstuffed chairs. My eyes moved from one thing to another, and, like my mother with her dining room set, Rosemary took note of where they landed. "I see you like my davenport," she said, and "You don't find lamps like that anymore. It's a genuine Stephanie."

It came as no surprise that she bought and sold antiques, or "dabbled" in them, as she said. Every available surface was crowded with objects: green glass candy dishes, framed photographs of movie stars, cigarette boxes with monogrammed lids. An umbrella leaned against an open steamer trunk, and, when I observed that its handle was Bakelite, my new landlady unpinned her saucer of cherries and predicted that the two of us were going to get along famously.

And for many months, we did. Rosemary lived on the ground floor, in a set of closed-off rooms she referred to as her "chambers." The door that led to them opened onto the parlor, and when I stood outside I could sometimes hear her television. This seemed to me a kind of betrayal, like putting a pool table inside the Great Pyramid, but she assured me that the set was an old one—"My 'Model Tee Vee,'" she called it.

My room was upstairs, and in a letter home I described it as "hunky-dory." How else to capture my peeling, buckled wallpaper and the way that it brought everything together. The bed, the desk, the brass-plated floor lamp: it was all there waiting for me, and though certain pieces had seen better days—the guest chair, for instance, was missing its seat—at least everything was uniformly old. From my window I could see the parking lot, and beyond that the busy road leading to the restaurant. It pleased Rosemary that I worked in such a venerable place. "It suits you," she said. "And don't feel bad about washing dishes. I think even Gable did it for a while."

"Did he?"

I felt so clever, catching all her references. The other boarder didn't even know who Charlie Chan was, and the guy was half Korean! I'd see him in the hall from time to time—a chemistry major, I think he was. There was a third room as well, but because of some water damage Rosemary was having a hard time renting it. "Not that I care so much," she told me. "In my business, it's more about quality than quantity."

I moved in at the beginning of January, and throughout that winter my life felt like a beautiful dream. I'd come home at the end of the day and Rosemary would be sitting in the parlor, both of us fully costumed. "Aha!" she'd say. "Just the young man I was looking for." Then she'd pull out some new treasure she'd bought at an estate sale and explain what made it so valuable. "On most of the later Fire King loaf pans, the trademark helmet is etched rather than embossed."

The idea was that we were different, not like the rest of America, with its Fuzzbusters and shopping malls and rotating showerheads. "If it's not new and shiny, they don't want anything to do with it," Rosemary would complain. "Give them the Liberty Bell, and they'd bitch about the crack. That's how folks are nowadays. I've seen it."

There was a radio station in Raleigh that broadcast old programs, and sometimes at night, when the reception was good, we'd sit on the davenport and listen to Jack Benny or *Fibber McGee and Molly*. Rosemary might mend a worn WAC uniform with her old-timey sewing kit, while I'd stare into the fireplace and wish that it still worked. Maybe we'd leaf through some old *Look* magazines. Maybe the wind would rattle the windows, and we'd draw a quilt over our laps and savor the heady scent of mothballs.

I hoped our lives would continue this way forever, but inevitably the past came knocking. Not the good kind that was collectible, but the bad kind that had arthritis. One afternoon in early April, I returned from work to find a lost-looking, white-haired woman sitting in the parlor. Her fingers were stiff and gnarled, so rather than shake hands I offered a little salute. "Sister Sykes" was how she introduced herself. I thought that was maybe what they called her in church, but then Rosemary walked out of her chambers and told me through gritted teeth that this was a professional name.

"Mother here was a psychic," she explained. "Had herself a tarot deck and a crystal ball and told people whatever stupid malarkey they wanted to hear."

"That I did." Sister Sykes chuckled.

You'd think that someone who occasionally wore a turban herself would like having a psychic as a mom, but Rosemary was over it. "If she'd forecast thirty years ago that I'd wind up having to take care of her, I would have put my head in the oven and killed myself," she told me.

When June rolled around, the chemistry student graduated, and his room was rented to a young man named Chaz, who worked on a road construction crew. "You know those guys that hold the flags?" he said. "Well, that's me. That's what I do."

His face, like his name, was chiseled and memorable and, after deciding that he was too handsome, I began to examine him for flaws. The split lower lip only added to his appeal, so I moved on to his hair, which had clearly been blow-dried, and to the strand of turquoise pebbles visible through his unbuttoned shirt.

"What are you looking at?" he asked, and before I had a chance to blush he started telling me about his ex-girlfriend. They'd lived together for six months, in a little apartment behind Fowlers grocery store, but then she cheated on him with someone named Robby, an asshole who went to UNC and majored in fucking up other people's lives. "You're not one of those college snobs, are you?" he asked.

I probably should have said "No" rather than "Not presently."

"What did you study?" he asked. "Bank robbing?"

"Excuse me?"

"Your clothes," he said. "You and that lady downstairs look like those people from *Bonnie and Clyde,* not the stars, but the other ones. The ones who fuck everything up."

"Yes, well, we're individuals."

"Individual freaks," he said, and then he laughed, suggesting that there were no hard feelings. "Anyway, I don't have time to stand around and jaw. A friend and me are hitting the bars."

He'd do this every time: start a conversation and end it abruptly, as if it had been me who was running his mouth. Before Chaz moved in, the upstairs was fairly quiet. Now I heard the sound of his radio through the wall, a rock station that made it all the harder to pretend I was living in gentler times. When he was bored, he'd knock on my door and demand that I give him a cigarette. Then he'd stand there and smoke it, complaining that my room was too clean, my sketches were too sketchy, my old-fashioned bathrobe was too old-fashioned. "Well, enough of this," he'd say. "I have my own life to lead." Three or four times a night this would happen.

As Chaz changed life on the second floor, Sister Sykes changed it on the first. I went to check my mail one morning and found Rosemary dressed just like anyone else her age: no hat or costume jewelry, just a pair of slacks and a ho-hum blouse with unpadded shoulders. She wasn't wearing makeup either and had neglected to curl her hair. "What can I tell you?" she said. "That kind of dazzle takes time, and I just don't seem to have any lately." The parlor, which had always been just so, had gone downhill as well. Now there were cans of iced tea mix sitting on the Victrola, and boxed pots and pans parked in the corner where the credenza used to be. There was no more listening to Jack Benny because that was Sister Sykes's bath time. "The queen bee," Rosemary called her.

Later that summer, just after the Fourth of July, I came downstairs and found a pair of scuffed white suitcases beside the front door. I hoped that someone was on his way out—Chaz, specifically—but it appeared that the luggage was coming rather than going. "Meet my daughter," Rosemary said, this with the same grudging tone she'd used to introduce her mother. The young woman—I'll call her Ava—took a rope of hair from the side of her head and stuck it in her mouth. She was a skinny thing and very pale, dressed in jeans and a Western-style shirt. "In her own little world," Sister Sykes observed.

Rosemary would tell me later that her daughter had just been released from a mental institution, and though I tried to act surprised I don't think I was very convincing. It was like she was on acid almost, the way she'd sit and examine something long after it lost its mystery: an ashtray, a dried-up moth, Chaz's blow-dryer in the upstairs bathroom. Everything got equal attention, including my room. There were no lockable doors on the second floor. The keys had been lost years earlier, so Ava just wandered in whenever she felt like it. I'd come home after a full day of work—my clothes smelling of wet garbage, my shoes squishy with dishwater—and find her sitting on my bed or standing like a zombie behind my door. "You scared me," I'd say, and she'd stare into my face until I turned away.

The situation at Rosemary's sank to a new low when Chaz lost his job. "I was overqualified," he told me, but, as the days passed, his story became more elaborate, and he felt an ever-increasing urge to share it with me. He started knocking more often, not caring that it was 6:00 A.M. or well after midnight. "And another thing . . . ," he'd say, stringing together ten separate conversations. He got into a fight that left him with a black eye. He threw his radio out the window and then scattered the broken pieces throughout the parking lot.

Late one evening he came to my door, and when I opened it he grabbed me around the waist and lifted me off the floor. This might sound innocent, but his was not a celebratory gesture. We hadn't won a game or been granted a stay of execution, and carefree people don't call you a "hand puppet of the Dark Lord" when they pick you up without your consent. I knew then that there was something seriously wrong with the guy, but I couldn't put a name to it. I guess I thought that Chaz was too good-looking to be crazy.

When he started slipping notes under my door, I decided it was time to update my thinking. "Now I'm going to die and come back on the same day," one of them read. It wasn't just the messages, but the writing itself that spooked me, the letters all jittery and butting up against one another. Some of his notes included diagrams, and flames rendered in red ink. When he started leaving them for Rosemary, she called him down to the parlor and told him he had to leave. For a minute or two, he seemed to take it well, but then he thought better of it and threatened to return as a vapor.

"Did he say 'viper'?" Sister Sykes asked.

Chaz's parents came a week later and asked if any of us had seen him. "He's schizophrenic, you see, and sometimes he goes off his medication."

I'd thought that Rosemary would be sympathetic, but she was sick to death of mental illness, just as she was sick of old people, and of having to take in boarders to make ends meet. "If he was so screwy, you should have told me before he moved in," she said to Chaz's father. "I can't have people like that running through my house. What with these antiques, it's not safe." The man's eyes wandered around the parlor, and through them I saw what he did: a dirty room full of junk. It had never been anything more than that, but for some reason—the heat, maybe, or the couple's heavy, almost contagious sense of despair—every gouge and smudge jumped violently into focus. More depressing still was the thought that I belonged here, that I fit in.

For years the university had been trying to buy Rosemary's property. Representatives would come to the door, and her accounts of these meetings seemed torn from a late-night movie. "So I said to him, 'But don't you see? This isn't just a house. It's my home, sir. My home.' "

They didn't want the building, of course, but the land. With every passing semester, it became more valuable, and she was smart to hold out for as long as she did. I don't know what the final offer was, but Rosemary accepted it. She signed the papers with a vintage fountain pen and was still holding it when she came to give me the news. This was in August, and I was lying on my floor, making a sweat angel. A part of me was sad that the house was being sold, but another, bigger part—the part that loved air-conditioning—was more than ready to move on. It was pretty clear that as far as the restaurant was concerned, I was never going to advance beyond dishwashing. Then, too, it was hard to live in a college town and not go to college. The students I saw out my window were a constant reminder that I was just spinning my wheels, and I was beginning to imagine how I would feel in another ten years, when they started looking like kids to me.

A few days before I left, Ava and I sat together on the front porch. It had just begun to rain when she turned, and asked, "Did I ever tell you about my daddy?"

This was more than I'd ever heard her say, and before continuing she took off her shoes and socks and set them on the floor beside her. Then she drew a hank of hair into her mouth and told me that her father had died of a heart attack. "Said he didn't feel well, and an hour later he just plunked over."

I asked a few follow-up questions and learned that he had died on November 19, 1963. Three days after that, the funeral was held, and while riding from the church to the cemetery Ava looked out the window and noticed that everyone she passed was crying. "Old people, college students, even the colored men at the gas station—the soul brothers, or whatever we're supposed to call them now."

It was such an outmoded term, I just had to use it myself. "How did the soul brothers know your father?"

"That's just it," she said. "No one told us until after the burial that Kennedy had been shot. It happened when we were in the church, so that's what everyone was so upset about. The president, not my father."

She then put her socks back on and walked into the parlor, leaving both me and her shoes behind.

When I'd tell people about this later, they'd say, "Oh, come on," because it was all too much, really. An arthritic psychic, a ramshackle house, and either two or four crazy people, depending on your tolerance for hats. Harder to swallow is that each of us was such a cliché. It was as if you'd taken a Carson McCullers novel, mixed it with a Tennessee Williams play, and dumped all the sets and characters into a single box. I didn't add that Sister Sykes used to own a squirrel monkey, as it only amounted to overkill. Even the outside world seems suspect here: the leafy college town, the restaurant with its classical music.

I never presumed that Kennedy's death was responsible for Ava's breakdown. Plenty of people endure startling coincidences with no lasting aftereffects, so I imagine her troubles started years earlier. As for Chaz, I later learned that it was fairly common for schizophrenics to go off their medication. I'd think it strange that the boardinghouse attracted both him and me, but that's what cheap places do—draw in people with no money. An apartment of my own was unthinkable at that time of my life, and even if I'd found an affordable one it wouldn't have satisfied my fundamental need to live in a communal past, or what I imagined the past to be like: a world full of antiques. What I could never fathom, and still can't, really, is that at one point all those things were new. The wheezing Victrola, the hulking davenport—how were they any different from the eight-track tape player or my parents' Scandinavian dining room set? Given enough time, I guess anything can look good. All it has to do is survive.

DIFFERENCES: SEX, SEPARATENESS & MARRIAGE

Shifra Sharlin

I used to scorn carpeting for the same reason that I would rather squint than wear sunglasses. The late Russell Hoban put it best: "I don't want anything to come between me and It." While I doubt that religion and flooring have anything in common, I am certain that I was reaching for the same thing as Hoban. I'm not sure what to call it. Truth? Authenticity? Unmediated experience? Or did Chase and Phillips in *A New Introduction to Greek* put it best? *Chalepa ta kola:* difficult things are beautiful. I used to think that Chase and Phillips meant that things are beautiful because they are difficult. Authentic encounters were difficult ones: a hard floor, the sun making my eyes water, my beloved and me.

Everything I was afraid to ask about sex I learned from neighbors. Thin walls make the best classrooms. I was a reluctant student. Nothing, let alone the framed and stretched Marimekko purchased for its sound-insulating properties, could prevent those lessons from reaching me. I was newly married and living in Berkeley then.

Reading the Marquis de Sade reminds me of my Berkeley

neighbors, but that is not why I am reading him. I am out to prove that Michel Foucault was wrong about modern life. In his 1966 book, *The Order of Things: An Archaeology of the Human Sciences,* Foucault argues that the Marquis de Sade marks the "frontier" into the modern world. "After him, violence, life and death, desire and sexuality will extend, below the level of representation, an immense expanse of shade. . . ." Why should death and sadism define the modern world? Why does being hidden and violent have to be its most salient feature?

My motives for pursuing this line of inquiry are selfish. I do not want a Marquis de Sade kind of life. My husband and I met in a Biblical Hebrew class. By the end of the first class I had formed my opinion of him based on three things: his beautiful hands, his receptiveness to my delight that squirrels were entering the building opposite via its ivied walls and an open window, and his *Biblia Hebraica*. In her book on Sade, Simone de Beauvoir wrote, "If ever we hope to transcend the separateness of individuals, we may do so only on condition that we be aware of its existence." I got married believing that I always could, probably would, get a divorce: the bride-to-be as wannabe libertine.

I got married in a Marquis de Sade kind of world. Foucault's claim that Sade marked the frontier into the modern world is plausible if the modern world begins, more or less, with the publication of *The Order of Things*. Apollinaire, who championed Cubism and other avant-garde art, rediscovered Sade at the beginning of the twentieth century. The Surrealists adopted him next. By mid-century, Sade had become such a fixture of modern intellectual life that Frances Ferguson in a 1991 article, "Sade and the Pornographic Legacy," observed "writing about Sade was almost a predictable stage in establishing an intellectual career; what the writing of pastorals and epics had classically done to demonstrate poetic seriousness, writing about Sade did for writers like Klossowski, Blanchot, Bataille, Beauvoir, Barthes, Lacan, and Foucault."

When pornography replaced pastoral and epic, the naked body took center stage. Sade's seriousness is a form of striptease. Clothing is only the first and easiest thing to go. Sade teases most in stripping away everything else; exactly what is stripped and why occupies those demonstrating their poetic seriousness. The desire for stripping occupies me. That impulse seems as romantic as any happy pastoral. Or archaeological dig.

Stripping away proved rewarding for Gideon Algernon Mantel of Oxford. In 1790, several years after Sade had finished *The 120 Days of Sodom or the School for Libertines,* Mantel became the first to unearth dinosaur bones. Sade was not so lucky. Not content with stripping away their victims' clothes, his libertines kept going until they hit blood and guts. The failure of their excavations to yield more than a passing thrill led Foucault to conclude that there are no lasting thrills to be had between one person and another. In the hope of finding something more, Foucault looks down, digging beneath the surface; Beauvoir looks up, hoping to transcend what both see as mere surface obstacles to desire's perfect consummation.

Not only French intellectuals were searching high and low for the naked truth. Wikipedia has an entry, a long entry, "Marquis de Sade in Popular Culture," which lists all of the movies, plays, and novels that feature or refer to Sade. The majority of them came out between 1966 and 1977. For instance, eight movies about Sade appeared in that period. At about the same time that *The Order of Things* appeared in Paris, my parents could not stop talking about the critically acclaimed film (based on the 1960s Peter Weiss play) that they had seen in Ames, Iowa: *The Persecution and Assassination of Jean-Paul Marat as Performed by the Inmates of the Asylum of Charenton Under the Direction of the Marquis de Sade*, or *Marat/Sade*. Twelve was too young to see it, but just the right age to learn that mad, persecuted, libidinous, subversive, anti-authoritarian rebellion was serious.

And that I was not. Sade's popularity signaled that his form of seriousness was everywhere, including my bookshelves. Sade fit the profile of the then-reigning countercultural hero. Any reckoning of Sade's cultural presence has to list all of the books, movies, plays, and television shows where he did not appear by name but was nonetheless present: Kurt Vonnegut, Ken Kesey, Jack Kerouac, Lenny Bruce, Yukio Mishima, and Russell Hoban. Hoban's quip about religion, for instance, echoes the line uttered by a fifteen-year-old Brooke Shields about wearing Calvin Klein jeans: "Nothing comes between me and my Calvins." In those days, everybody was scorning whatever came between themselves and their It of choice.

Sade was an equal-opportunity libertine: women were admitted to the ranks. His own Juliette, the eponymous heroine of thousands of pages of relentless libertinage, could be considered a precursor, if not exactly a role model, for the women of Erica Jong, Anne Roiphe, Alison Lurie, Marge Piercy, Margaret Atwood, and Angela Carter, women all of my friends emulated. I could never manage to be more than a wannabe. Maybe that is the reason I was a wannabe libertine bride-to-be: wannabes never run the risk of becoming disillusioned. Or maybe I was ahead of my time.

The modern world at whose frontier Foucault had placed Sade ended well before my tenth anniversary. A world at whose frontier stands Ronald Reagan and AIDS is not the kind of world I am happy to live in either, much less to have prefigured, however unintentionally. But Lionel Trilling, in an essay he was working on at the time of his death in 1975, suggests another start date and another kind of world. In that essay, "Why Read Jane Austen?" Trilling tries to understand the shift in taste among his students from William Blake to Jane Austen. I would like to think that shift signals a greater, cultural shift, from the world of Sade to the one of his near-contemporary, Austen.

Two books by Angela Carter show that Austen stood for everything Sade opposed. In her solitary book of cultural criticism, *The Sadeian Woman,* Carter celebrates Sade; in her novel *Wise Children,* she imagines a woman at the start of a revolution burning a copy of *Mansfield Park*. Austen cherished what Sade tried to strip away. The truth of her characters does not lie either below or above the surface. Austen takes the fully clothed body seriously. Her characters are never naked. Why bother? Even if they had been, they would have been nonetheless attired in their social selves.

As Sade's cultural presence dwindled, Austen's took off. In her excellent book, *Why Jane Austen?,* Rachel Brownstein traces the rise of "Jane-o-mania." While there were only a few television adaptations of her work in the early 1970s, since the 1990s and

Amy Heckerling's *Clueless,* an *Emma* transported to contemporary Los Angeles, adaptations of Austen's novels and life continue to appear regularly. The membership of the Jane Austen Society of North America has exploded. And, just as with Sade, Austen is often present even when she is not named. In the HBO series *Sex and the City* friendship trumps sex. The true Sadean woman would not get together with her girlfriends to discuss courtship, clothing, and apartments. Wikipedia owes Austen her own popular culture entry. What does the modern world look like when we think of Jane Austen as defining its frontier? What does sex look like? What about my marriage?

Marriage is like the *Biblia Hebraica.* As a critical edition of the Hebrew text, the *Biblia Hebraica* prints both the editor's version of the text in two columns and, arranged horizontally at the bottom of the page in the scholarly apparatus, the variations from different versions that have appeared in the thousands of years of the text's transmission and translation. Like marriage, the *Biblia Hebraica* is subject to an unending process of interpretation.

My husband thinks the comparison is apt. He laughed when I told him. He laughs rarely and when he does, it sounds forced as if he never learned how to do it properly. He did not. Apparently, laughter is not something that can be self-taught like vocabulary and grammar. This was one of his better laughs; its spontaneity and delight surprised me. In response to my email asking for an explanation, he wrote: "Just as we recognize the text as being the Bible, however many variations there might be, so we recognize a particular marriage as being that singular marriage no matter the permutations and reconfigurations." Nobody understands me the way he does.

Our marriage was founded on a key principle of biblical interpretation: *lectio difficilior potior:* the difficult reading is more likely. This means that in choosing among alternative readings, the difficult one is more likely to be correct because a scribe would have been more inclined to err by making the text easier to understand than in inventing yet another textual difficulty. Difficult things are not only beautiful; they are true.

True? Now I think this is a Sadean principle. Foucault might agree, because it dates from the same period as Sade. The

Lutheran pietist clergyman Johann Albrecht Bengel arrived at the principle about the truth in difficult readings in 1725. Like Gideon Mantel in Oxford, he was also digging deep for origins. Bengel dreamed of divining an original of the Greek New Testament based on textual evidence alone. Philologists, like libertines, search for a perfect match.

Meaning seeks embodiment in words as desire seeks embodiment in fornicating. Sade's libertines fail to find what they are looking for. They are compelled to keep up their relentless fornication because they never find that single person who could realize their singular desire. This is the reason that, in Foucault's account, desire persists in dark, hidden, and violent ways. Thwarted and frustrated, it turns twisted.

Difference troubles Sade and his libertines. Sade's libertines demand a match that is as instantaneous as it is perfect. What they cannot strip away, they transform. Sade turns his women into men. Sodomy is the preferred form of intercourse. When the vagina is not superfluous, it rarely has intercourse with a penis. A female libertine has an elongated clitoris that functions as a miniature penis when aroused. Differences denied are nonetheless differences that enrage. Torture is courtship for the impatient.

Enter Jane Austen. Austen and Sade have different approaches to the resolution of differences. In contrast to Sade, Austen's courtship plots expand on the complications and complexities that intervene before two people can realize their singular desire for one another. Before the happy ending, they must first learn how unlikely it is. They must discover just how different they are. Mr. Darcy can moderate his pride enough to propose marriage to the prejudiced Elizabeth Bennet, but not enough to prevent him from revealing his pride's persistence and depth. Elizabeth Bennet, her prejudices confirmed and inflamed, angrily refuses him. And the novel is only half over.

Fortunate reader. The complications arising from their differences lie at the heart of the novel's drama, wit, and romance. Differences are not an obstacle to marriage; they make marriage both possible and necessary. They make courtship entertaining. How dull Mr. Darcy and Elizabeth Bennet would be if they agreed on all things. Their differences, both of social background and temperament, keep the plot moving. Austen's truths are dynamic not naked.

Austen's modern world was not that of the proto-archaeologist, Gideon Mantel, let alone the Marquis de Sade. Hers was more like the one of those Birmingham inventors and industrialists who called themselves the Lunar Men. Among them was James Watt, who was working on improvements to the steam engine at about the time that Jane Austen was born. By the time she was writing her novels, the engines he had designed were moving the machinery of the Industrial Revolution. Austen, like Watt, did not excavate; she made things work.

The differences between Mr. Darcy and Elizabeth Bennet are personified in their friends and family, the very people who, by taking sides, have dramatized those differences all along. In spite of their role in impeding the courtship, or perhaps because of it, Austen's novels always end with a complete report of their fates and locations, usually somewhere nearby. Their friends and family remain to remind them of their differences. The courtship plot does not end with a happy couple alone.

Our favorite biblical romance does not end that way either. It became our favorite on our road trip to California from Chicago in a so-called drive-away, a car that was being repossessed by a bank. The white Mercury Cougar came with a large knife under the driver's seat and idled at thirty mph. We took turns driving and reading out loud to one another from the *Biblia Hebraica*. He was driving across the Great Salt Lake as I read about the patriarch Jacob and his beloved, Rachel, in the book of Genesis. "And Jacob worked for Rachel for seven years, but in his eyes those years felt like a few days because of his love for her." In Hebrew, the verse scans as poetry.

Nothing in the scholarly apparatus could resolve my Sade-like incomprehension: if Jacob had truly loved Rachel, seven years would have felt like forever. My husband did not try to change my mind. Not like the time, decades later, when he begged me to be his soul mate, because I had wanted to give up on living with him, a person who seemed most animated by rage. Instead we reconfigured ourselves by the kind of work I cannot explain except by saying that I finally understood Jacob's patience.

The scholarly apparatus now functions differently than it once did. No scholar thinks that there is a correct reading, because there is no such thing as an original, true, and authentic version. That belief belonged to a world where the authority of the Septuagint, the Greek translation of the Bible, rested on the story that seventy translators arrived at a single, identical version, proving dictation as divine as that of Moses at Sinai. Now scholars think that those are not competing voices buried in the scholarly apparatus; they are the sounds of different versions making themselves heard. Differences do not mean error.

I no longer prefer difficult things. My husband and I are newly arrived in Manhattan. Here our downstairs neighbors are the problem, complaining about noise from us. We are almost flattered. We put down carpeting at their request. The once-scorned carpeting both insulates and amplifies. Our neighbors' needs are always underfoot. What separates also joins. The friction of differences keeps things moving.

INFORMATION SICKNESS

David Shields

I love all forms of taxonomy: lists, categories, compartments, containers, boundaries. When I went to the famous Amsterdam sex shops, I was struck mainly by the arrangement of movies and magazines into exceedingly minute subdivisions of pleasure and pain. I love doing errands, and what I especially love about doing errands is crossing things off my errand list. When making phone calls, running errands, or performing ablutions, I always begin with what seems to me the least personal item and conclude with what seems to me the most personal item.

(Pre-email, pre-texting) I used to be happy to play phone tag for weeks on end in order to avoid actually talking, let alone meeting, with someone. The sound of static on the car radio is, to me, reassuring, sensuous, even beautiful. At the market, I always choose self-service checkout over human interaction.

The moment I walk into a hotel room, I turn on my laptop and the TV (the latter as wallpaper), which I turn off when I go to sleep. The worst drunk I know—twelve-ounce tumblers of scotch at eight in the morning—leaves CNN on all night downstairs as a sort of lifeline in his sleep. (He's always talking about "black": black air is considered the ultimate sin; he can't tolerate black; "they went to black"; the famous six minutes of black—

he's obsessed with black, afraid of it, secretly thrilled by its suggestion of depth.) I don't ordinarily drink coffee, but once, in order to stay up all night, I drank twelve cups in eight hours; the next morning, I walked into a Chec Medical Center and said, "Please, you've got to do something to turn my brain off." When I'm nervous and need to calm down, I chew blank three-by-five cards like a woodchuck.

I once ate a half-gallon carton of ice cream in a single sitting. Ditto a bag of sixty-four cookies. I know no purer joy than residence in the throes of sugar shock: the exact moment, just before you crash, when your brain turns off and you leave the planet. Before seeing friends I haven't seen for a long time, I go on a diet because I want people to think, *He doesn't seem to seek solace in overeating; he must be happy and focused.*

Once, immediately after the breakup of a relationship, I managed to lose my wallet, checkbook, and address book within the space of a week. I find that if I'm having trouble remembering something—the name of a movie, say, or a friend's phone number—I often inadvertently trigger memory by holding the item (such as a video guide or my phone) housing the information.

I prefer previews to the movie, the "about the author" notes in the back of literary magazines to the contents of the magazine, pregame hype to the game. If I'm reading a book and it seems truly interesting, I tend to start reading back to front in order not to be too deeply under the sway of forward progress.

Once, a movie marquee's misspelling of the word "nominations" irritated me so much that when the punkette in the booth outside expressed zero interest in my correction, I bought a ticket for the movie, which I'd already seen, in order to be able to go inside and urge someone to do something about the error. On the other hand, in sixth grade I "liked" a girl named Connie Cummings; classmates wrote in chalk on the playground "DS + CC = Dog Shit + Cow Crap," which, to their surprise and perhaps Connie's as well, didn't bother me in the least: it seemed, simply, clever.

I never saw my mother, whose maiden name was Hannah Bloom, giddier than when she noticed that the *New York Times* crossword puzzle clue for 5-across was "Hard-hearted girl" and the clue for 7-across was "Claire of films." And yet my parents hoped so strongly that my sister and I would never "become part of the system" that they were honestly chagrined when, at age fifteen, I received my Social Security number, whereas my main response when I recently got audited by the IRS and saw my TRW credit report was a kind of relief that my existence could be confirmed by outside sources.

When I used to jog, I would pick up my pace and really run if I thought someone was watching me, but when no longer being watched, I'd go back to jogging. In conversation I feel little compunction about asking people extremely intimate questions but tend to balk when someone asks me even the most moderately personal question. In social situations in which it would be to my disadvantage to appear heterosexual, I attempt to give the impression that it's not beyond my ken to be bisexual. At a Halloween party many years ago, costumed as a pirate, I was flirting with a woman dressed as a lioness until she told me to take off my sunglasses, then said, "Oh, you're Jewish!"; my eyes were Jewish.

If a new song grabs my heart, I'll typically play it over and over again until it's completely robbed of all significance, beauty, and power. At a museum bookstore I bought dozens of postcards, none of which had any human figures on them, and the cashier said, "You know, you might be saying something here about yourself." I was: I'm drawn to affectless people whose emptiness is a frozen pond on which I excitedly skate.

I have a persistent yearning that I don't have to live, exactly, anywhere. When I lived for several years in New York, I'd go out every night at eleven and come back with the next day's *Times* and a pint of ice cream, then eat the whole carton while reading the paper, which had the odd but, I suppose, desired effect of blotting out tomorrow before it had even happened. My nightmares—an endless network of honeycombs, a thousand cracks in a desiccated lake—are always about the multiplying of chaos. Two questions constantly occur to me: What would this look like filmed? What would the soundtrack be? I grew up at a very busy intersection, and to me aesthetic bliss was hearing the sound of brakes screeching, then waiting for the sound of the crash.

GRAY AREA: THINKING WITH A DAMAGED BRAIN

Floyd Skloot

I used to be able to think. My brain's circuits were all connected and I had spark, a quickness of mind that let me function well in the world. I could reason and total up numbers; I could find the right word, could hold a thought in mind, match faces with names, converse coherently in crowded hallways, learn new tasks. I had a memory and an intuition that I could trust.

All that changed when I contracted the virus that targeted my brain. More than a decade later, most of the damage is hidden.

My cerebral cortex, the gray matter that MIT neuroscientist Steven Pinker likens to "a large sheet of two-dimensional tissue that has been wadded up to fit inside the spherical skull," is riddled instead of whole. This sheet and the thinking it governs are now porous. Invisible to the naked eye but readily seen through brain imaging technology are areas of scar tissue that constrict blood flow. The lesions in my gray matter appear as a scatter of white spots like bubbles or a ghostly pattern of potshots. Their effect is dramatic; I am like the brain-damaged patient described by neuroscientist V. S. Ramachandran in his book *Phantoms in the Brain:* "parts of her had forever vanished, lost in patches of permanently atrophied brain tissue." More hidden still are lesions in my Self, fissures in the thought process that result from this damage to my brain. When the brain changes, the mind changes—these lesions have altered who I am.

Neurologists have a host of clinical tests that let them observe what a brain-damaged patient can and cannot do. They stroke his sole to test for a spinal reflex known as Babinski's sign or have him stand with feet together and eyes closed to see if the ability to maintain posture is compromised. They ask him to repeat a set of seven random digits forward and four in reverse order, to spell *world* backward, to remember three specific words such as *barn* and *handsome* and *teach* after a period of unrelated conversation. A new laboratory technique, positron emission tomography, uses radioactively labeled oxygen or glucose that essentially lights up specific and different areas of the brain being activated when a person speaks words or sees words or hears words, revealing the organic location for areas of behavioral malfunction. Another new technique, functional magnetic resonance imaging, measures increases in brain blood flow associated with certain actions. The resulting computer-generated pictures, eerily colorful relief maps of the brain's lunar topology, pinpoint hidden damage zones.

But I do not need a sophisticated and expensive high-tech test to know what my damaged brain looks like. People living with such injuries know intimately that things are amiss. They see it in activities of daily living, in the way simple tasks become unmanageable. This morning, preparing oatmeal for my wife, Beverly, I carefully measured out one-third cup of oats and poured them onto the pot's lid rather than into the bowl. In its absence, a reliably functioning brain is something I can feel viscerally. The zip of connection, the shock of axon-to-axon information flow across a synapse is not simply a textbook affair for me. Sometimes I see my brain as a scalded pudding, with fluky dark spots here and there through its dense layers, and small scoops missing. Sometimes I see it as an eviscerated old TV console, wires all disconnected and misconnected, tubes blown, dust in the crevices.

Some of this personal, low-tech evidence is apparent in basic functions like walking, or accurately sitting in the chair I'm approaching, or breathing if I am tired. It is apparent in activities requiring the processing of certain fundamental information. For example, no matter how many times I have been shown how to do it, I cannot assemble our poultry shears or the attachments for our hand-cranked pasta maker. At my writing desk, I finish a note and place the pen in my half-full mug of tea rather than in its holder, which quite obviously teems with other pens. I struggle to figure out how a pillow goes into a pillowcase. I cannot properly adjust Beverly's stereo receiver to access the radio; it has been and remains useful to me only in its present setting as a CD player. These are all public, easily discernible malfunctions.

However, it is in the utterly private sphere that I most acutely experience how changed I am. Ramachandran compares this to harboring a zombie, playing host to a completely nonconscious being somewhere inside yourself. For me, being brain damaged also has a physical, conscious component. Alone with my ideas and dreams and feelings, turned inward by the isolation and timelessness of chronic illness, I face a kind of ongoing mental vertigo in which thoughts teeter and topple into those fissures of cognition I mentioned earlier. I lose my way. I spend a lot of time staring into space, probably with my jaw drooping, as concentration disintegrates and focus dissolves. Thought itself has become a gray area, a matter of blurred edges and lost distinctions, with little that is sharp about it. This is not the way I used to be.

In their fascinating study *Brain Repair,* an international trio of neuroscientists—Donald G. Stein from America, Simón Brailowsky from Mexico, and Bruno Will from France—reports that after injury "both cortical and subcortical structures undergo dramatic changes in the pattern of blood flow and neural activity, even those structures that do not appear to be directly or primarily connected with the zone of injury." From this observation, they conclude that "the entire brain—not just the region around the area of damage—reorganizes in response to brain injury." The implications of this are staggering; my entire brain, the organ by which my very consciousness is controlled, was reorganized one day fourteen years ago. I went to sleep here and woke up there; the place looked the same but nothing in it worked the way it used to.

If Descartes was correct, and to think is to be, then what happens when I cannot think, or at least cannot think as I did, cannot think well enough to function in a job or in the world? Who am I?

You should hear me talk. I often come to a complete stop in midsentence, unable to find a word I need, and this silence is an apt reflection of the impulse blockage occurring in my brain. Sitting next to Beverly as she drives our pickup truck through Portland traffic at 6:00 P.M., I say, "We should have gone for pizza to avoid this blood . . ." and cannot go on. I hear myself; I know I was about to say "blood tower traffic" instead of "rush hour traffic." Or I manifest staggered speech patterns—which feels like speaking with a limp—as I attempt to locate an elusive word. "I went to the . . . *hospital* yesterday for some . . . *tests* because my head . . . *hurt*." Or I blunder on, consumed by a feeling that something is going wrong, as when I put fresh grounds into the empty carafe instead of the filter basket on my coffee maker, put eye drops in my nose, or spray the cleaning mist onto my face instead of the shower walls. So at the dinner table I might say "Pass the sawdust" instead of "Pass the rice," knowing even as it happens that I am saying something inappropriate. "Crown the soup" is, I think, a more lovely way to say "Garnish the soup" anyway. So too, a "kickback" is a more resonant name for a "relapse." *I'm having a kickback*. I might announce that "the shore is breaking" when I mean to say "the shower is leaking," or call a bookmark a placemat. There is nothing smooth or unified anymore about the process by which I communicate; it is dis-integrated and unpredictably awkward. My brain has suddenly become like an old man's. Neurologist David Goldblatt has developed a table that correlates cognitive decline in age-associated memory impairment and traumatic brain injury, and the parallels are remarkable. Not gradually, the way such changes occur naturally, but overnight, I was geezered.

It is not just about words. "Dyscalculic," I struggle with the math required to halve a recipe or to figure out how many more pages are left in a book I'm reading. If we are on E. Eighty-Second and Third in Manhattan, staying with Larry Salander for the week, it is very difficult for me to compute how far away the

Gotham Book Mart is over on W. Forty-Seventh between Fifth and Sixth, though I spent much of my childhood in the city.

Because it is a place where I still try to operate normally, the kitchen is an ideal neurological observatory. After putting the leftover chicken in a plastic bag, I stick it back in the oven instead of the refrigerator. I put the freshly cleaned pan in the refrigerator, which is how I figure out that I must have put the chicken someplace else because it's missing. I pick up a chef's knife by its blade. I cut off an eighth of a giant white onion and then try to stuff the remainder into a recycled sixteen-ounce yogurt container that might just hold the small portion I set aside. I assemble ingredients for a vinaigrette, pouring the oil into an old olive jar, adding balsamic vinegar, mustard, a touch of fresh lemon juice, and spices. Then I place the lid on upside down and shake vigorously, spewing the contents everywhere. I stack the newspaper in the woodstove for recycling. I walk the garbage up our two-hundred-yard-long driveway and try to put it in the mailbox instead of the trash container.

At home is one thing; when I perform these gaffes in public, the effect is often humiliating. I can be a spectacle. In a music store last fall, I was seeking an instruction book for Beverly, who wanted to relearn how to play her old recorder. She informed me that there were several kinds of recorders; it was important to buy exactly the right category of book since instructions for a soprano recorder would do her no good while learning on an alto. I made my way up to the counter and nodded when the saleswoman asked what I wanted. Nothing came out of my mouth, but I did manage to gesture over my right shoulder like an umpire signaling an out. I knew I was in trouble, but forged ahead anyway, saying, "Where are the books for sombrero reporters?" Last summer in Manhattan, I routinely exited the subway stations and led Beverly in the wrong direction, no matter which way we intended to go. She kept saying things like "I think west is that way, sweetie," while I confidently and mistakenly headed east, into the glare of the morning sun, or "Isn't that the river?" as I led her away from our riverside destination. Last week, in downtown Portland on a warm November morning, I stopped at the corner of Tenth and Burnside, one of the busiest crossings in the city, carefully checked the traffic light (red) and the traffic lanes (bus coming), and started to walk into the street. A muttering transient standing beside me on his way to Powell's City of Books, where he was going to trade in his overnight haul of tomes for cash, grabbed my shoulder just in time.

At home or not at home, it ultimately makes no difference. The sensation of "dysfunctional mentation" is like being caught in a spiral of lostness. Outside the house, I operate with sporadic success, often not knowing where I am or where I'm going or what I'm doing. Inside the house, the same feelings sometimes apply and I find myself standing on the top of the staircase wondering why I am going down. Even inside my head there is a feeling of being lost, thoughts that go nowhere, emptiness where I expect to find words or ideas, dreams I never remember.

Back in the fall, when it was Beverly's birthday, at least I did remember to go to the music store. More often, I forget what I am after within seconds of beginning the search. As she gets dressed for work, Beverly will tell me what she wants packed for lunch and I will forget her menu by the time I get up the fourteen stairs. Now I write her order down like a waiter. Sometimes I think I should carry a pen and paper at all times. In the midst of preparing a salad, I stop to walk the four paces over to the little desk where we keep our shopping list and forget "tomatoes" by the time I get there. So I should also have paper handy everywhere. Between looking up a phone number and dialing it, I forget the sequence. I need the whole phone book on my speed dial system.

Though they appear without warning, these snafus are no longer strange to me. I know where they come from. As Dr. Richard M. Restak notes in *The Modular Brain,* "A common error frequently resulting from brain damage involves producing a semantically related word instead of the correct response." But these paraphasias and neologisms, my "expressive aphasias," and my dyscalculas and my failures to process—the rapids of confusion through which I feel myself flailing—though common for me and others with brain damage, are more than symptoms to me. They are also more than what neurologists like to call "deficits," the word of choice when describing impairment or incapacity of neurological function, as Oliver Sacks explains in his introduction to *The Man Who Mistook His Wife for a Hat.* These "deficits" have been incorporated into my very being, my consciousness. They are now part of my repertoire. Deficits imply losses; I have to know how to see them as gains.

Practitioners of neuroscience call the damage caused by trauma, stroke, or disease "an insult to the brain." So pervasive is this language that the states of Georgia, Kentucky, and Minnesota, among others, incorporate the phrase "insult to the brain" in their statutory definitions of traumatic brain injury for disability determinations. Such "insults," according to the Brain Injury Association of Utah, "may produce a diminished or altered state of consciousness, which results in an impairment of cognitive abilities or physical functioning." The death of one Miles Dethmuffen, front man and founding member of the Boston rock band Dethmuffen, was attributed in news reports to "an alcoholic insult to the brain." The language used is so cool. There is this sentence from the website NeuroAdvance.com: "When there is an insult to the brain, some of the cells die." Yes.

"Insult" is an exquisitely zany word for the catastrophic neurological event it is meant to describe. In current usage, of course, insult generally refers to an offensive remark or action, an affront, a violation of mannerly conduct. To insult is to treat with gross insensitivity, insolence, or contemptuous rudeness. The medical meaning, however, as with so many other medical words and phrases, is different, older, linked to a sense of the word that is some two or three centuries out of date. *Insult* comes from the Latin compound verb *insultare,* which means "to jump on," and is also the root word for "assault" and "assail." It's a word that connotes aggressive physical abuse, an attack. Originally, it suggested leaping upon the prostrate body of a foe, which may be how its link to contemptuous action was forged.

Though "an insult to the brain" (a blow to the head, a metal shard through the skull, a stroke, a viral attack) is a kind of assault, I am curious about the way "contempt" has found its way into the matter. Contempt was always part of the meaning of *insult* and now it is primary to the meaning. Certainly a virus is not acting contemptuously when it targets the brain; neither is the pavement nor steering wheel, nor falling wrench, nor clot of blood, nor most other agents of insult. But I think society at large—medical scientists, insurers, legislators, and the person-on-the-street—does feel a kind of contempt for the brain damaged with their comical way of walking, their odd patterns of speech or ways in which neurological damage is expressed, their apparent stupidity, their abnormality. The damage done to a brain seems to evoke disdain in those who observe it and shame or disgrace in those who experience it. I know I referred to a feeling of humiliation when I expose my aberrant behaviors in public.

Poet Peter Davison has noticed the resonant irony of the phrase "an insult to the brain" and made use of it in his poem "The Obituary Writer." Thinking about the suicide of John Berryman, the heavily addicted poet whose long-expected death in 1972 followed years of public behavior symptomatic of brain damage, Davison writes that "his hullabaloos / of falling-down drunkenness were an insult to the brain." In this poem, toying with the meaning of the phrase, Davison suggests that Berryman's drinking may have been an insult to his brain, technically speaking, but that watching him was, for a friend, another kind of brain insult. He has grasped the fatuousness of the phrase as a medical term, its inherent judgment of contempt, and made use of it for its poetic ambiguity.

But I have become enamored of the idea that my brain has been insulted by a virus. I use it as motivation. There is a long tradition of avenging insults through duels or counterinsults, through litigation, through the public humiliation of the original insult. So I write. I avenge myself on an insult that was meant, it feels, to silence me by compromising my word-finding capacity, my ability to concentrate and remember, to spell or conceptualize, to express myself, to think.

The duel is fought over and over. I have developed certain habits that enable me to work—a team of seconds, to elaborate this metaphor of a duel. I must be willing to write slowly, to leave blank spaces where I cannot find words that I seek, compose in fragments and without an overall ordering principle or imposed form. I explore and make discoveries in my writing now, never quite sure where I am going but willing to let things ride and discover later how they all fit together. Every time I finish an essay or poem or piece of fiction, it feels as though I have faced down the insult.

In his book *Creating Mind,* Harvard neurobiologist John E. Dowling says, "The cerebral cortex of the human brain, the seat of higher neural function—perception, memory, language, and intelligence—is far more developed than is the cerebral cortex of any other vertebrate." Our gray matter is what makes us human. Dowling goes on to say that "because of the added neural cells and cortical development in the human brain, new facets of mind emerge." Like the fractured facet of a gemstone or crystal, like a crack in the facet of a bone, a chipped facet of mind corrupts the whole, and this is what an insult to the brain does.

Though people long believed, with Aristotle, that the mind was located within the heart, the link between brain and mind is by now a basic fact of cognitive science. Like countless others, I am living proof of it. Indeed, it is by studying the behavior of brain-damaged patients like me that medical science first learned, for example, that the brain is modular, with specific areas responsible for specific functions, or that functions on one side of the body are controlled by areas on the opposite side of the brain. "The odd behavior of these patients," says Ramachandran, speaking of the brain damaged, "can help us solve the mystery of how various parts of the brain create a useful representation of the external world and generate the illusion of 'self' that endures in space and time." Unfortunately, there is ample opportunity to observe this in action since, according to the Brain Injury Association, more than two million Americans suffer traumatic brain injury every year, a total that does not include damage by disease.

No one has yet explained the way a brain produces what we think of as consciousness. How does the firing of electrical impulse across a synapse produce love, math, nightmare, theology, appetite? Stated more traditionally, how do brain and mind interact? Bookstore shelves are now filled with books, like Steven Pinker's brilliant 1997 study *How the Mind Works,* which attempt to explain how a three-and-a-half-pound organ that is the consistency of Jell-O makes us see, think, feel, choose, and act. "The mind is not the brain," Pinker says, "but what the brain does."

And what the brain does, according to Pinker, "is information processing, or computation." We think we think with our brain. But in doing its job of creating consciousness, the brain actually relies on a vast network of systems and is connected to everything—eyes, ears, skin, limbs, nerves. The key word is "processing." We actually think with our whole body. The brain, however, takes what is shipped to it, crunches the data, and sends back instructions. It converts, it generates results. Or, when damaged, does not. There is nothing wrong with my sensory receptors, for instance. I see quite well. I can hear and smell, my speech mechanisms (tongue, lips, nerves) are intact. My skin remains sensitive. But it's in putting things together that I fail. Messages get garbled, blocked, missed. There is, it sometimes seems, a lot of static when I try to think, and this is the gray area where nothing is clear any longer.

Neurons, the brain's nerve cells, are designed to process information. They "receive, integrate and transmit," as Dowling says, receiving input from dendrites and transmitting output along axons, sending messages to one another across chemical passages called synapses. When there are lesions like the ones that riddle my gray matter, processing is compromised. Not only that, certain cells have simply died, and with them the receiving, integrating, and transmitting functions they performed.

My mind does not make connections because, in essence, some of my brain's connectors have been broken or frayed. I simply have less to work with and it is no surprise that my IQ dropped measurably in the aftermath of my illness. Failing to make connections, on both the physical and metaphysical levels, is distressing. It is very difficult for me to "free-associate"; my stream of consciousness does not absorb runoff or feeder streams well, but rushes headlong instead. Mental activity that should follow a distinct pattern does not, and I experience my thought process as subject to random misfirings. I do not feel in control of my intelligence. Saying "Pass me the tracks" when I intended to say "Pass me the gravy" is a nifty example. Was it because gravy sounds like grooves, which led to tracks, or because my tendency to spill gravy leaves tracks on my clothes? A misfire, a glitch in the gray area that thought has become for me, and as a result my ability to express myself is compromised. My very nature seems to have altered.

I am also easily overloaded. I cannot read the menu in a crowded, noisy restaurant. I get exhausted at Portland Trailblazers basketball games, with all the visual and aural imagery, all the manufactured commotion, so I stopped going thirteen years ago. My hands are scarred from burns and cuts that occurred when I tried to cook and converse at the same time. I cannot drive in traffic, especially in our standard transmission pickup truck. I cannot talk about, say, the fiction of Thomas Hardy while I drive; I need to be given directions in small doses rather than all at once, and need those directions to be given precisely at the time I must make the required turn. This is, as Richard Restak explains, because driving and talking about Hardy, or driving and processing information about where to turn, are handled by different parts of the brain, and my brain's parts have trouble working together.

I used to write accompanied by soft jazz, but now the least pattern of noises distracts me and shatters concentration. My entire writing process, in fact, has been transformed as I learned to work with my newly configured brain and its strange snags. I have become an avid note taker, a jotter of random thoughts that might or might not find their way together or amount to anything, a writer of bursts instead of steady work. A slight interruption—the movement of a squirrel across my window view, the call of a hawk, a spell of coughing—will not just make me lose my train of thought, it will leave me at the station for the rest of the day.

I have just finished reading a book about Muhammad Ali, *King of the World*, written by David Remnick. I anticipated identifying a bit with Ali, now suffering from Parkinson's disease, who shows so strikingly what brain damage can do, stripped as he is of so many of the functions—speech, movement, spontaneity—that once characterized him. But it was reading about Floyd Patterson that got me.

Patterson was a childhood hero of mine. Not only did we share a rare first name, we lived in neighboring towns—he was in Rockville Centre, on Long Island, while I was five minutes away in Long Beach, just across the bridge. I was nine when he beat Archie Moore to take the heavyweight championship belt, almost twelve when he lost it to Ingemar Johannson, and almost thirteen when he so memorably won it back. The image of Johannson's left leg quivering as he lay unconscious on the mat is one of those vivid memories that endures (because, apparently, it is stored in a different part of the brain than other, less momentous memories). That Floyd, like me, was small of stature in his world, was shy and vulnerable, and I was powerfully drawn to him.

During his sixty-four professional fights, his long amateur career, his many rounds of sparring to prepare for fights, Patterson absorbed a tremendous amount of damage to his brain. Now that he is in his sixties, his ability to think is devastated. Testifying in court earlier this year in his capacity as head of the New York State Athletic Commission, Patterson "generally seemed lost." He could not remember the names of his fellow commissioners, his phone number or secretary's name or lawyer's name. He could not remember the year of his greatest fight, against Archie Moore, or "the most basic rules of boxing (the size of the ring, the number of rounds in a championship fight)." He kept responding to questions by saying, "It's hard to think when I'm tired."

Finally, admitting "I'm lost," he said, "Sometimes I can't even remember my wife's name, and I've been married thirty-two, thirty-three years." He added again that it was hard for him to think when he was tired. "Sometimes, I can't even remember my own name."

People often ask if I will ever "get better." In part, I think what they wonder about is whether the brain can heal itself. Will I be able, either suddenly or gradually, to think as I once did? Will I toss aside the cane, be free of symptoms, have all the functions governed by my brain restored to smooth service, rejoin the world of work and long-distance running? The question tends to catch me by surprise because I believe I have stopped asking it myself.

The conventional wisdom has long been that brains do not repair themselves. Other body tissue, other kinds of cells, are replaced after damage, but we have as many brain cells at age one as we will ever have. This has been a fundamental tenet of neuroscience, yet it has also long been clear that people do recover—fully or in part—from brain injury. Some stroke victims relearn how to walk and talk, feeling returns in once-numb limbs. Children, especially children, recover and show no lasting ill effects from catastrophic injuries or coma-inducing bouts of meningitis.

So brain cells do not get replaced or repaired, but brain-damaged people occasionally do regain function. In a sense, then, the brain heals, but its cells do not.

There are in general five theories about the way people might recover function lost to brain damage. One suggests that we do not need all our brain because we only use a small part of it to function. Another is that some brain tissue can be made to take over functions lost to damage elsewhere. Connected to this is the idea that the brain has a backup mechanism in place allowing cells to take over like understudies. Rehabilitation can teach people new ways to perform some old tasks, bypassing the damaged area altogether. And finally, there is the theory that in time, and after the chemical shock of the original injury, things return to normal and we just get better.

It is probably true that, for me, a few of these healing phenomena have taken place. I have, for instance, gotten more adept at tying my shoes, taking a shower, driving for short periods. With careful preparation, I can appear in public to read from my work or attend a party. I have developed techniques to slow my interactions with people or to incorporate my mistakes into a longer-term process of communications or composition. I may not be very good in spontaneous situations, but given time to craft my responses I can sometimes do well. But I still can't think.

A recent development promises to up the ante in the game of recovery from brain damage. *The New York Times* reported in October 1998 that "adult humans can generate new brain cells." A team at the Salk Institute for Biological Studies in La Jolla, California, observed new growth in cells of the hippocampus, which controls learning and memory in the brain. The team's leader, Dr. Fred Gage, expressed the usual cautions; more time is needed to "learn whether new cell creation can be put to work" and under what conditions. But the findings were deemed both "interesting" and "important."

There is only one sensible response to news like this. It has no personal meaning to me. Clinical use of the finding lies so far in the future as to be useless, even if regenerating cells could restore my lost functions. Best not to think about this sort of thing.

Because, in fact, the question of whether I will ever get better is meaningless. To continue looking outside for a cure, a "magic bullet," some combination of therapies and treatments and chemicals to restore what I have lost, is to miss the point altogether. Certainly if a safe, effective way existed to resurrect dead cells, or to generate replacements, and if this somehow guaranteed that I would flash back or flash forward to "be the person I was," it would be tempting to try.

But how would that be? Would the memories that have vanished reappear? Not likely. Would I be like the man, blind for decades, who had sight restored and could not handle the experience of vision, could not make sense of a world he could see? I am, in fact, who I am now. I have changed. I have learned to live and live richly as I am now. Slowed down, softer, more heedful of all that I see and hear and feel, more removed from the hubbub, more internal. I have made certain decisions, such as moving from the city to a remote rural hilltop in the middle of twenty acres of forest, that have turned out to be good for my health and even my soul. I have gained the love of a woman who knew me before I got sick and likes me much better now. Certainly I want to be well. I miss being able to think clearly and sharply, to function in the world, to move with grace. I miss the feeling of coherence or integrity that comes with a functional brain. I feel old before my time.

But in many important respects, I have already gotten better. I continue to learn new ways of living with a damaged brain. I continue to make progress, to avenge the insult, to see my way around the gray area. But no, I am not going to be the man I was. In this, I am hardly alone.

CASSANDRA AMONG THE CREEPS

Rebecca Solnit

The story of Cassandra, the woman who told the truth but was not believed, is not nearly as embedded in our culture as that of the Boy Who Cried Wolf—that is, the boy who was believed the first few times he told the same lie. Perhaps it should be. The daughter of the king of Troy, Cassandra was cursed with the gift of accurate prophecies no one heeded; her people locked her up before Agamemnon took her as a spoil of war who was casually slain along with him.

I have been thinking of Cassandra as we sail through the choppy waters of the gender wars—because credibility is such a foundational power in those wars and because women are so often accused of being categorically lacking in this department.

Not uncommonly, when a woman says something that impugns a man, particularly one at the heart of the status quo, especially if it has to do with sex, the response will question not just the facts of her assertion but her capacity to speak and her right to do so. Generations of women have been told they are delusional, confused, manipulative, malicious, conspiratorial, congenitally dishonest, often all at once.

Part of what interests me is the impulse to dismiss and how often it slides into the very incoherence or hysteria of which women are routinely accused. It would be nice if, say, Rush Limbaugh, who called Sandra Fluke a "slut" and a "prostitute" for testifying to Democrats in Congress about the need to fund birth control and who apparently completely failed to comprehend how birth control works—Limbaugh the word-salad king, the factually challenged, the eternally riled—got called hysterical once in a while.

Rachel Carson was labeled thus for her landmark work on the dangers of pesticides, *Silent Spring*. Carson had put together a book whose research was meticulously footnoted and whose argument is now considered prophetic. But the chemical companies were not happy, and being female was, so to speak, her Achilles' heel. On October 14, 1962, the *Arizona Star* reviewed her book with the headline "*Silent Spring* Makes Protest Too Hysterical." The preceding month—in an article that assured readers that DDT was entirely harmless to humans—*Time* magazine had called Carson's book "unfair, one-sided, and hysterically overemphatic." "Many scientists sympathize with Miss Carson's . . . mystical attachment to the balance of nature," the review allowed. "But they fear that her emotional and inaccurate outburst . . . may do harm." Carson was a scientist, incidentally.

Hysteria derives from the Greek word for "uterus," and the extreme emotional state it denotes was once thought to be due to a wandering womb; men were by definition exempt from this diagnosis that now just means being incoherent, overwrought, and maybe confused. In the late nineteenth century, it was a commonly diagnosed condition. Women diagnosed with hysteria whose agonies were put on display by Sigmund Freud's teacher Jean-Martin Charcot appear, in some cases, to have been suffering from abuse, the resultant trauma, and the inability to express its cause.

The young Freud had a succession of patients whose troubles seemed to spring from childhood sexual abuse. What they were saying was unspeakable, in a sense: even today the severest traumas in war and domestic life so violate social mores and the victim's psyche that they are excruciating to articulate. Sexual assault, like torture, is an attack on a victim's right to bodily integrity, to self-determination and self-expression. It's annihilatory, silencing. It intends to rub out the voice and rights of the victim, who must rise up out of that annihilation to speak.

To tell a story and have it and the teller recognized and respected is still one of the best methods we have of overcoming trauma. Freud's patients, amazingly, found their way to telling what they had suffered, and at first he heard them. In 1896, he wrote, "I therefore put forward the thesis that at the bottom of every case of hysteria there are one or more occurrences of *premature sexual experience*." Then he repudiated his findings. If he believed his patients, he wrote, "in all cases, the father, *not excluding my own*, had to be accused of being perverse."

As the feminist psychiatrist Judith Herman puts it in her book *Trauma and Recovery:* "His correspondence makes clear that he was increasingly troubled by the radical social implications of his hypothesis. . . . Faced with this dilemma, Freud stopped listening to his female patients." If they were telling the truth, he would have to challenge the whole edifice of patriarchal authority to support them. Later, she adds, "with a stubborn persistence that drove him into ever greater convolutions of theory, he insisted that women imagined and longed for the abusive sexual encounters of which they complained." It was as though a handy alibi had been constructed for all transgressive authority, all male perpetrators of crimes against females. She wanted it. She imagined it. She doesn't know what she is saying.

Silence, like Dante's hell, has its concentric circles. First come the internal inhibitions, self-doubts, repressions, confusions, and shame that make it difficult to impossible to speak, along with the fear of being punished or ostracized for doing so. Susan Brison, now chair of the philosophy department at Dartmouth, was raped in 1990 by a man, a stranger, who called her a whore and told her to shut up before choking her repeatedly, bashing her head with a stone, and leaving her for dead. Afterward she found various problems in talking about the experience: "It was one thing to have decided to speak and write about my rape, but another to find the voice with which to do it. Even after my fractured trachea had healed, I frequently had trouble speaking. I was never entirely mute, but I often had bouts of what a friend labeled 'fractured speech,' during which I stuttered and stammered, unable to string together a simple sentence without the words scattering like a broken necklace."

Surrounding this circle are the forces who attempt to silence someone who speaks up anyway, whether by humiliating or bullying or outright violence, including violence unto death. This region is now notably populated by the victims of high school and college rapes. In many cases, these young women have been hounded and threatened for speaking up; some have become suicidal as a result; the potential crimes go uninvestigated or unprosecuted; and many American universities appear to be graduating numerous unpunished rapists these days.

Finally, in the outermost ring, when the story has been told and the speaker has not been silenced directly, tale and teller are discredited. Given the hostility of this zone, you could call the brief era when Freud listened to his patients with an open mind a false dawn. For it's particularly when women speak up about sexual crimes that their right and capacity to speak come under attack. It seems almost reflexive at this point, and there is certainly a very clear pattern, one that has a history.

That pattern was first comprehensively challenged in the 1980s. We have at this point heard way too much about the 1960s, but the revolutionary changes of the 1980s—in toppled regimes around the world and in the bedroom, the classroom, the workplace, and the streets, and even in political organizing (with the feminist-inspired rise of consensus and other anti-hierarchical, anti-authoritarian techniques)—are mostly neglected and forgotten. It was an explosive era. The feminism of that era is often dismissed as grimly anti-sex because it pointed out that sex is an arena of power and that power is liable to abuse and because it described the nature of some of that abuse.

Feminists didn't just push for legislation but from the mid-1970s on defined and named whole categories of violation that had previously been unrecognized. In doing so, they announced that abuse of power was a serious problem, and that the authority of men, of bosses, husbands, fathers—and adults generally—was going to be questioned. They created a framework and support network for stories of incest and child abuse, as well as rape and domestic violence. Those stories became part of the narrative explosion in our time as so many of the formerly silent spoke up about their experiences.

Part of the messiness of that era was that no one quite knew how to listen to children, or how to question them, or in some cases how to sift through their own memories or those of adult patients in therapy. The infamous McMartin Preschool abuse trial, one of the longest and most costly in this country's history, began in 1983 when a Los Angeles area mother claimed her child was molested there. The authorities not only jumped on the situation but asked parents to ask their children leading questions and employed a therapist to interview hundreds of children with more leading questions, rewards, puppets, and other tools and techniques to help them construct wild stories about satanic abuse.

The results of the McMartin trial's chaotic interrogations are sometimes cited as evidence that children are unreliable, delusional liars, but it might be useful to remember that it was the adults who were the problem in that case. Law professor Doug Linder writes that the prosecutor gave an interview in which he "acknowledges that children began 'embellishing and embellishing' their stories of sexual abuse and said that, as prosecutors, 'we had no business being in court'" and added that potentially exculpatory evidence was withheld. Even so, the accused in that long trial and a subsequent one were not found guilty, though this is seldom remembered.

On October 11, 1991, a law professor was called to testify before the Senate Judiciary Committee. The occasion was the confirmation hearing for Clarence Thomas, nominated to the Supreme Court by George H. W. Bush; the speaker was Anita Hill. When asked in a private interview and then, after that interview was leaked to the press, in Senate hearings, she recounted a list of incidents in which Thomas, then her boss, made her listen to him talk about pornography he'd watched and his sexual fantasies. He also pressured her to date him. When she declined, she said, "He would not accept my explanation as being valid," as though *no* were not itself valid.

Though she was criticized for doing nothing about his conduct at the time, it's worth remembering that feminists had only recently articulated the concept and coined the term *sexual harassment,* and that only in 1986, after the incidents she described had taken place, had the Supreme Court recognized such behavior in the workplace as a violation of the law. When she did speak up about it in 1991 she was attacked, extravagantly and furiously. Her interrogators were all men, the Republicans in particular jocular and incredulous and jeering. Senator Arlen Specter asked one witness, who on the basis of a couple of fleeting encounters testified that Hill had sexual fantasies about him, "Do you think it a possibility that Professor Hill imagined or fantasized the things she has charged him with?" It was the Freudian framework all over again: When she said something repellent happened, she was wishing it had, and maybe she couldn't tell the difference.

The country was in an uproar and a sort of civil war, as many women understood exactly how ordinary harassment is and how many unpleasant consequences there can be for reporting it, and many men didn't get it. In the short term, Hill was subjected to a humiliating ordeal, and Thomas won the appointment anyway. The loudest accusations came from conservative journalist David Brock, who published first an article and then a whole book smearing Hill. A decade later he repented from both his attacks on her and his alignment with the right, writing, "Doing everything I could to ruin Hill's credibility, I took a scattershot approach, dumping virtually every derogatory—and often contradictory—allegation I had collected on Hill from the Thomas camp into the mix. . . . She was, in my words, 'a little bit nutty and a little bit slutty.' "

In the long term, "I Believe You, Anita" became a feminist slogan, and Hill is often credited with launching a revolution in recognition of and response to workplace sexual harassment. A month after the hearings, Congress passed the Civil Rights Act of 1991, part of which allowed sexual-harassment victims to sue their employers for damages and backpay. Harassment claims skyrocketed as people were given a way to address workplace abuses. The 1992 election was nicknamed "The Year of the Woman," and Carol Moseley Braun, still the only African

American woman ever elected to the Senate, won office along with more female senators and congresswomen than ever before.

Still, even now, when a woman says something uncomfortable about male misconduct, she is routinely portrayed as delusional, a malicious conspirator, a pathological liar, a whiner who doesn't recognize it's all in fun, or all of the above. The overkill of these responses recalls Freud's deployment of the joke about the broken kettle. A man accused by his neighbor of having returned a borrowed kettle damaged replies that he had returned it undamaged, it was already damaged when he borrowed it, and he had never borrowed it anyway. When a woman accuses a man and he or his defenders protest that much, she becomes that broken kettle.

Even this year, when Dylan Farrow repeated her charges that her adoptive father, Woody Allen, had molested her, she became the most broken kettle around. A host of attackers arose. Allen published a tirade, asserting he could not have molested the child in the attic room where she said he did because he didn't like that room, proposing that his daughter had been coached and "indoctrinated" by her mother, Mia, who might have ghostwritten the accusation Dylan Farrow published, and adding that Mia had "undoubtedly" gotten the idea from a song about an attic. There was another gender divide, in which many women found the young woman credible, because they'd heard it all before, while many men seemed focused on false accusations and exaggerated the frequency of such occurrences. The ghost of the McMartin Preschool trial was raised, by people who seemed to have a false memory of the trial and its outcome.

Herman's *Trauma and Recovery,* which addresses rape, child molestation, and wartime trauma together, notes:

> Secrecy and silence are the perpetrator's first line of defense. If secrecy fails, the perpetrator attacks the credibility of his victim. If he cannot silence her absolutely, he tries to make sure that no one listens. . . . After every atrocity one can expect to hear the same predictable apologies: it never happened; the victim lies; the victim exaggerates; the victim

> brought it on herself; and in any case it is time to forget the past and move on. The more powerful the perpetrator, the greater is his prerogative to name and define reality, and the more completely his arguments prevail.

They don't always prevail in our time. We are still in an era of battles over who will be granted the right to speak and the right to be believed, and pressure comes from both directions. From the men's rights movement and a lot of popular misinformation comes the notion that there is an epidemic of groundless accusations of sexual assault.* The implication that women as a category are unreliable and that false rape charges are the real issue is used to silence individual women and to avoid discussing sexual violence, and to make out men as the principal victims. The framework is reminiscent of that attached to voter fraud, a crime so rare in the United States that it appears to have had no significant impact on election outcomes in a very long time. Nevertheless, claims by conservatives that such fraud is widespread have in recent years been used to disenfranchise the kinds of people—poor, non-white, students—likely to vote against them.

I'm not arguing here that women and children don't lie. Men, women, and children lie, but the latter two are not disproportionately prone to doing so, and men—a category that includes used-car salesmen, Baron von Münchhausen, and Richard Nixon—are not possessed of special veracity. I am arguing that we should be clear that this old framework of feminine mendacity and murky-mindedness is still routinely trotted out, and we should learn to recognize it for what it is.

---

*False accusations of rape are a reality, and a relatively rare one, though the stories of those convicted falsely are terrible. A British study by the Crown Prosecution Service released in 2013 noted that there were 5,651 prosecutions for rape in the period studied versus only 35 prosecutions for false allegations of rape. And a 2000 U.S. Department of Justice report cites these estimates for the United States: 322,230 annual rapes, resulting in 55,424 reports to police, 26,271 arrests, and 7,007 convictions—or slightly more than 2 percent of rapes counted and 12 percent of rapes reported resulted in jail sentences. Of which the number that were false is undoubtedly not colossal.

A friend of mine who works in sexual harassment training at a major university reports that when she gave a presentation at the business school on her campus, one of the older male professors asked, "Why would we start an investigation based on only one woman's report?" She has dozens of stories like this, and others about women—students, employees, professors, researchers—struggling to be believed, especially when they testify against high-status offenders.

This summer, antediluvian columnist George Will claimed that there is only a "supposed campus epidemic of rape," and that when universities or feminists or liberals "make victimhood a coveted status that confers privileges, victims proliferate." Young women replied by creating the Twitter hashtag #survivorprivilege, posting remarks such as "I didn't realize it was a privilege to live with PTSD, severe anxiety & depression" and "#ShouldIBeQuiet because when i spoke out everyone said it was a lie?" Will's column hardly even constitutes a twist on the old idea that women are naturally unreliable, that there's nothing to see in all these rape charges, and that we should just move along.

I had a tiny scale model of that experience myself earlier this year. I had posted on social media a slice of an essay I'd published a few years ago about the 1970s in California. Immediately, a stranger—a man of affluence and culture—denounced me on Facebook in response to its two paragraphs about incidents in my life back then (being hit on by grown-up hippie dudes when I was embarking on my teens). Both his fury and his baseless confidence in his ability to render judgment were remarkable; he said in part, "you are exaggerating beyond reality with no more 'proof' offered than a FOX news reporter. You 'feel' it's true so you say it's true. Well I call 'bullshit.'" I should have offered proof, as though proof were possible about a host of incidents decades ago. I am like bad people who distort facts. I am subjective but believe I am objective; I feel but confuse feeling with thinking or knowing. It's such a familiar litany and a familiar rage.

If we could recognize or even name this pattern of discrediting, we could bypass recommencing the credibility conversation every time a woman speaks. One more thing about Cassandra: in the most famous version of the myth, the disbelief with which her prophecies were met was the result of a curse placed on her by Apollo when she refused to have sex with the god. The idea that loss of credibility is tied to asserting rights over your own body was there all along. But with the real-life Cassandras among us, we can lift the curse by making up our own minds about who to believe and why.

ERIC GARNER AND ME

Clifford Thompson

Please permit me a crude analogy. The fall of 2014 was like an unforeseen rainstorm, a cracking open of a heretofore cloudless sky of the kind that used to occur on bad sitcoms of years gone by: everyone who was caught unprepared—i.e., everyone—scrambled for the nearest cover, these people heading to that awning, those people to another. The rain, in this analogy, is the non-indictment of the police officers who choked Eric Garner to death, as shown on the videotape seen by the entire world—this, close on the heels of the non-indictment of the police officer who shot Michael Brown to death, and sixteen months after the nonconviction of the self-appointed public guardian who shot and killed Trayvon Martin. The awnings, in this analogy, are our ready-made opinions about it all. From the crowd under one awning: *This is the kind of justice blacks can expect in a white society, which is no justice at all.* From the other side of the street: *The so-called victims must have been doing something wrong.*

And then there were those of us, few at first glance, caught in the middle of the street. I am not merely trying to seem different or special, like the kid who answers "Present" instead of "Here" when the teacher takes attendance. And I don't mean to suggest that I was neutral in the debate. In fact, I was one of those shutting down traffic on Broadway in New York while chanting, in an echo of Eric Garner's last words, "I can't breathe!" But to stretch this analogy possibly further than it will go, I went out to protest in the falling rain, the squall blinding me to what I had long believed, perhaps blinding me to the existence of others who, just maybe, were getting drenched along with me.

I am black. The unpunished killings of men with skin like mine got me angry enough to voice an unequivocal statement—*This must stop!*—of the kind I seldom seem able to make. I lack ideological cover. For many, that cover is merely being black; for many, blackness, like a press secretary, determines their responses to life and events, externally if not internally. My own press secretary has long cowered under his desk, driven there by others' anger at his words, by his own lack of faith in what he says, by his occasional struggle even to form a statement, by new information that would make that statement obsolete.

I am mixing metaphors, usually a sign of confusion, of a need to simplify, step back, breathe deeply, start at the beginning.

The beginning is the family I was born into fifty-two years ago now, becoming its seventh member, joining my parents, three (much) older siblings, and my maternal grandmother in an entirely black, lower-middle-class/working-poor neighborhood of Washington, D.C. Everyone can complain about his childhood, but I have no more complaints than anyone else, and fewer than most. I was cared for, loved. I was raised, though not purposely, to see the world in neutral terms. Our small, semidetached red-brick house did not have an abundance of space (for years I slept in a room with three other people), but we had a basement and a backyard, where the view of a housing project, in which my friends lived, reminded me that I was not actually poor. It's not that I thought I was rich; rich was what you saw on TV. But seeing that most of the TV-rich were white did not lead me to any conclusions, since not all of the TV whites were rich, and, hell, the black family on *The Jeffersons* had their own maid. Maybe the twin pillars of the neutrality with which I viewed the world were the things missing from my little corner of it: (1) discussion of white people—my family simply never talked about them; and (2) white people themselves. In those formative years, I had no scarring experiences, in fact very few experiences of any kind, with whites—unless you count my being told, by classmates, that I talked like one. I knew, of course, about slavery—everyone knew about slavery—but I also knew, or at least sensed, that a new day had come. There were still racists, of course, but racism as the law of the land had ended. Maybe, once, most white people had been evil. But that was over. The clock had been reset.

And so, in the early 1980s—in this new era for which Martin Luther King, Jr., had died—when I went away to a rather prestigious, mostly white college in the cornfields of Ohio (the reward for my nerdy, studious ways), a surprise awaited me, though it wasn't white racism. Instead, when a black student circulated a pamphlet about the need to address the prejudice and discrimination we blacks suffered, I honestly did not know what he was talking about. I felt like I had landed in a 3-D movie house where I alone was without glasses. Weren't we all allowed to enroll in the same classes, live in the same dorms? Any segregation, it seemed to me, was voluntary: in the cafeteria, black students tended to eat together, and many if not most of them lived in African Heritage House, a dorm I had seen listed as I filled out housing forms but had not chosen. That decision did not reflect any disdain; I simply didn't see the need. I was proud of my heritage—as an elementary school student I had turned in unassigned reports based on entries in my Afro-American history book—but my pride did not require a whole dorm. So I was assigned to a residence where (another surprise) I turned out to be the only black male. Not that it bothered me, not particularly. I befriended some of the whites around me; I dated one (for far too long), and then, later, another. It was after moving into a different dorm my sophomore year, and making a couple of black friends, that I learned how much contempt a lot of black students had for me. And that's when the philosophy my family had implicitly passed on to me hardened into a creed, an emotional armor: I would judge people as individuals, if I had to judge them at all. I would befriend, date, marry whomever I wanted. If you didn't like it, to hell with you.

Let us fast-forward to 2014, when I found myself somehow no longer in my college years but deep in that hazily defined period called middle age. I have two daughters, one newly grown, one nearly so. My wife is white. So is, for the most part, the Brooklyn neighborhood where I have lived for longer than two decades. Over the years, as I've gotten farther physically from the black community (wherever that is), I've come to understand more about what plagues it. There was never a movie-style "Aha!" moment; more a piecemeal gathering of information, a gradual putting-together of a puzzle with a few areas still to be filled in. (I am always suspicious of those who see the puzzle as child's play.) I've learned some things just by walking around with brown skin—getting followed out of stores, having someone call the police after seeing me leave my own residence. I've learned other things studying history over three decades, such as the Southern practice of convict leasing, or arresting men essentially for the crime of being black and then hiring them out as (unpaid) prison labor until they died, a system that extended slavery, in all but name, into the twentieth century; incidents including the epidemic of lynching and the Tulsa race riot of 1921, in which whites burned the nation's wealthiest black community to the ground; and the exclusion of blacks, during the post–World War II boom, from housing loans of the kind that allowed whites to accumulate and pass on property and wealth, which contributes to disparities to this day. All of it adds up to a more detailed version of what I already knew about, what everyone knows about: the terrible abuse blacks have faced in America, and—allow me to drop the past perfect tense—continue to face, from harsher prison sentencing, to the placing of toxic waste near poor (i.e., black and Hispanic) neighborhoods, to the congressional stonewalling of the country's first black president, to things that, no doubt, we aren't even aware of.

And yet what other country do we have? Most of us, for all the kente cloth we like to wear, have never been to Africa. While learning more about blacks' often miserable experience in these United States, I have learned more, too, about what we've accomplished in spite of it all, which includes giving this nation its sound as well as large parts of its culture. The pride I felt even as a boy reading his Afro-American history book has only grown, and I cannot feel that the black American story has been a wholly bad one. Through it all—my marriage attests to this—I've maintained my faith, above all else, in assessing people for who they are, not what they look like. It is, simply, the right thing to do.

Oh, I get angry. Sometimes I talk to other blacks who seem to think—they never come out and say so, but I can tell—that I just don't get it, "it" being the hard kernel at the center of things, the undeniable, fundamental unfairness of our situation, the one proper starting point for any discussion of race; if I did get it, I would feel the other "it," the anger that is like an unscratchable itch, one as difficult to put into words as the effect of a child's death, one that a nonblack person will never understand. Oh, but I get "it." I get the feeling that comes with living in a place where so many in the dominant group, if not purposely or consciously racist, don't seem to have a clue. I get it when a nonblack person asks me what it was like to grow up in an entirely black neighborhood, the implication being that I was raised by monkeys or wolves; I get it when someone wants to know whether my hair would be straight, i.e., normal, if I combed it out. I get why a lot of black people feel that life's too short to expose yourself to this crap and that it's easier to simply avoid white people whenever possible.

What I don't get, and never have, is why I'm *supposed* to feel that way. I once read a quote from a black person about Clarence Thomas, a quote that I don't have in front of me but that was very close to, "The fact that he gets in bed with a white woman every night tells me all I need to know about him." I want to make it clear that I am no fan of Clarence Thomas, but his sins, to my mind, do not include getting in bed every night with a white woman—or else, obviously, I am a sinner, too. What might this sin of Clarence Thomas and Clifford Thompson be? Thinking so little of ourselves as black men—and, by extension, thinking so little of other blacks—that we share a bed with a representative of the oppressor? This logic holds only if you consider one person of a given skin color to be as good as another, i.e., if you consider any white person a stand-in for all racist whites, which is the opposite of the creed I adopted in my youth. And this old creed of mine has taken a beating over the years, but it has never given out or—at least before 2014—even threatened to. For every white person who has asked me an idiotic question like those mentioned above, there has been another who has listened to my problems, who has shared his or her own, who has laughed and joked with me, who has, simply put, loved me. (And black friends have done the same.) Is part of what they love the idea of having a black friend? You'd have to ask them, but assume for a moment that the answer is yes, and consider that in some integrated situations, blacks have approached me in friendship *for the same reason*. There are nonblacks I can't stand the sight of, and there are blacks I love, and the reverse is also true. It is that simple.

Well, nearly. There are those depressing moments when it seems there is a black way of looking at things and a white way of looking at things and never the twain shall meet. One day several years ago I was on a fairly crowded Brooklyn-bound subway train whose passengers included a white mother and her inconsolable toddler. What the little girl needed consoling over was not clear, unless it was that her mother—if their display was at all representative—was incapable of impressing on this child that nothing was actually wrong and that therefore the child should, for others' sake if not her own, relax and stop her damn shrieking. Then a man sitting near the two began playing his acoustic guitar and singing to the child, who, surprised into forgetting she was supposed to be upset, stopped her racket and actually smiled. I watched the other whites on the train smile too, as they gazed at one another in shared appreciation of the moment; and then my eyes met those of a black woman, and we shook our heads, registering the same thought: This child is being taught to whine with dissatisfaction until she gets her way or the next shiny thing comes along; she is being taught that she is the center of the universe; and we are watching it happen. And in our exchange was an unspoken judgment on the ways of white folks.

Whites, of course, have their judgments on the ways of black folks, too. Often these judgments are wrong. Much of what ails blacks is not our fault. Blacks are at an economic disadvantage in this country for reasons including some I've already mentioned, and this puts us at an educational disadvantage: poor neighborhoods do not have the tax base for well-funded public schools and do not have parents contributing extra educational resources, the way, say, Park Slope does, and this educational disadvantage only reinforces the economic one. And blacks are, there is no denying it, victims of discrimination—conscious or unconscious—in myriad areas of life, from housing to criminal justice to employment. Also true: we do not always help ourselves. Two-thirds of births among black women are out of wedlock, compared with one-quarter for white women, and according to the research organization Child Trends, "Among Hispanic and white women, 68 percent of all nonmarital births [occur] within cohabiting unions, compared with only 35 and 45 percent, respectively, among black and Asian women." I have nothing but respect and admiration for black single mothers—and there are a lot of them—who work two jobs to try to hold their families together; I feel a bit differently toward black men who bring children into the world and can't be bothered to raise them, who populate poor neighborhoods with children whose role models are out on the corner. Am I airing dirty laundry? To paraphrase the now-despised Bill Cosby, our dirty laundry gets out every weekday at two forty-five. Am I blaming the victim? Yes, I am, because the truth—not a black or white but a human truth, as timeless as it is unfair—is that the sympathy people feel toward victims turns to contempt when those victims appear to be contributing, to whatever degree, to their own problems. No less a black symbol than Louis Farrakhan called, some twenty years ago, for black men to atone—his word—for their failures in their own communities; no less a civil rights icon than Jesse Jackson admitted years ago, with regard to black crime, that he was weary of hearing footsteps behind him outside at night and being relieved on discovering that they belonged to a white person.

(That said, a small, irrational part of me—let's call him Eldridge—knowing how much whites fear strange black men, thinks: *Good. That is the price you pay for everything else.*)

Where does all this leave us? I can say only where it leaves me: with a finger to point at everyone, I point it with total conviction at no one; unable to fit the crowns of guilt or innocence securely on the head of any whole race, I am back where I started at the age of nineteen, judging people—I say it once more—as individuals. I was back there, at any rate, until the events of 2014.

Twenty-twelve and 2013 had been horrific enough, with young Trayvon Martin followed because he was black and wearing a hoodie and then shot to death by a man who then went free. As outrageous as Martin's death was, there was some small uncertainty as to what took place between him and George Zimmerman in that land of Stand Your Ground, and even the event at the center of the 2014 Ferguson episode, for all of the ugliness surrounding it, was not entirely clear. Uncertainty, though, was entirely—and painfully—absent in the video showing Eric Garner's death, for which, once again, no one was punished. It was less that incident than what it demonstrated—the blatant lack of justice for black Americans in matters involving the police and the courts—that made me question the way I had operated in the world all these years. Was my credo—my overriding concern for treating people as individuals, in a society tilted against people who looked like me—the mark of a fool? Was it the equivalent of saying "Come on, guys, play nice" in the middle of a war? Or would the abandonment of my core principles in the face of doubt have meant that I lacked integrity? "Integrity," of course, and ironically, is the state achieved by the process of integration, or forming an undivided whole, and from that point of view, I was not in danger of losing my integrity, since I'd never had any. Undivided? Me, the man who never encountered an issue of which he could not see at least two sides? Even in the face of the blatant horror that was Eric Garner's killing, I had conflicting thoughts—not about the sheer wrong of the police response to a man helplessly repeating "I can't breathe" while his head is pressed to the pavement, but about my own response. I felt something like horror at myself, living as possibly the least upscale member of an increasingly upscale, increasingly white community, basking in my superiority to those ever-engaged in making their petty racial distinctions—this, while the Eric Garners of our nation were being taken from their families and neighborhoods to prison or the grave, largely if not entirely because they were black. I am friends on Facebook with a young black woman I barely know, whose posts suggest that she has spent as large a proportion of her life around whites as I have: in the thick of the events of 2014, one of her posts read simply, "I love you, black people." I understood, oh, I understood perfectly, the feeling behind that post. I had a similar impulse—to run with my arms outstretched to a black neighborhood, shouting, "I'm sorry! Take me back!" A number of things prevented my doing that, however, of which a couple are relevant here.

First: sorry for *what,* when we get right down to it? For having deprived the black community of my (nonexistent) wealth? For having denied my people my gifts? (The one day I spent teaching classes in an inner-city neighborhood convinced me, as if I had needed convincing, that that is not where my talents lie.) For having withheld my preternaturally desirable self and the fruits of my grade-A gene pool from a black woman? (Which woman? Or is there, somewhere, one who embodies all black women, a kind of sub-Christ? What's Her email address?) *I love you, black people.* And, actually, I do, in a sense of loving: I love the way, in the face of everything, understanding what we understand, exchanging a knowing glance here and there, we carry on with our lives; I love that in any field of endeavor you care to name, you can find at least one of us, his or her presence representing an improbable journey; I love the selflessness with which so many of us care for each other. But that kind of love is distinct from its in-the-flesh counterpart. I cannot claim to love black people, for the simple reason that I will never meet the vast majority. I love *some* black people, just as there are some white people I love. All of which left me, once again, where I started, older but no wiser, if anything more confused than before.

My wife, watching me brood, suggested that I participate in a rally that was about to take place in Manhattan; it would help, she said, to be around like-minded people. I wasn't sure there was another mind like mine out there—if so, God help the person it belonged to—but I took her advice anyway. She was not able to go to the first rally I attended, which got under way near City Hall as the sun was going down, but there was no shortage of people in the park, black and white and Asian and Latino, shouting slogans into the chilly air—"Black lives matter," "No justice, no peace, no racist police"—in preparation to marching up the middle of Broadway, making the cars and buses go around us. But at another rally, on a late morning in Union Square, where it was colder but sunnier as we took to the streets, my wife joined me. Our voices were two among thousands, indistinguishable but adding to the roar—fittingly, since, as I finally, finally understood, none of this was about my little life. And yet it confirmed for me the rightness of what I had always believed, as people of every shade came together, their color less important than their desire to see the right thing done.

WE OUT HERE

Wesley Yang

A few years back, I wrote an article about Aaron Swartz, a hacker and activist who killed himself while under indictment for the unauthorized downloading of millions of academic-journal articles from an online archive. Swartz was devoted to an ethic of candid introspection, which he had practiced even at the age of seventeen, on a blog he kept as a freshman at Stanford University, in 2004. In September of that year, Swartz published a short post confessing to something that few take the time to consider. "However much I hate prejudice at a conscious level, I am nonetheless extremely prejudiced," he wrote:

> At my CS class, my eyes just passed over the large number of foreign and Asian students to land on mostly white ones (black ones too, occasionally). My Asian neighbor tried to make conversation with me and even though he had no accent, because of his face I imagined that he did. Had he been white, there is no question I would have started talking to him about stuff, but instead I brushed him off. I begin to wonder how many people I've skipped over.

There's no term that quite captures what Swartz is describing here. He is admitting to an assumption that results in no act of visible hostility or hatred. He simply declines to extend to the Asian man who is seated next to him in class the same degree of friendliness and regard that he would extend to a white man. Perhaps Swartz's classmate asked himself later that day whether Swartz was merely a rude jerk, or whether there was a specifically racial component to what had happened. Maybe he didn't pause to wonder if the latter was the cause; maybe, as an Asian person living in the most Asian region of America, in a classroom full of others of his kind, at a school where Asians were strongly represented, he had no reason to think that anyone would treat him unkindly because of his race.

Or maybe the nameless Asian man came away from that incident inwardly torn, uncertain whether he had encountered subtle racism, his own social ineptitude, or the intrinsic hardness of the world. Maybe he suspected that all these things were factors—knowing all the while that to make an issue of it would seem an excessive response to an easily deniable claim about an event of small importance with many possible explanations.

If Swartz had thought more deeply about the reflexive aversion he felt toward the Asian man sitting next to him, he might have said something like this: "This person is likely to be a bore. This person is likely to be a grind. This person is likely to be lacking in emotional resonance, presence, humor, individuality, spontaneity, energy, imagination, and warmth. This person is likely to be passive, obedient, submissive, a hardworking nonentity, a nobody, a nullity, one of those mute lugubrious bespectacled glum-faced inscrutable spiky-haired presences haunting the library behind a stack of books, who gaze impassively into a column of figures or drool onto the table while napping in the wee hours." But it's doubtful he would have compiled that list. The whole point of living in a culture is that much of the labor of perception and judgment is done for you, spread through media, and absorbed through an imperceptible process that has no single author. Perhaps you, too, can envision being surrounded by Asian faces, all of them merging into one another in their meek self-effacement.

What we know for certain is that had he gotten to know Swartz, who would soon drop out of Stanford to help found the startup Reddit—that is to say, had Swartz not brushed him off because of his race—that nameless Asian man's life would have been changed for the better.

How do you quantify the effects of things that don't happen to you? I thought of this question when I glimpsed a picture of protesters at Yale University last fall, many of them black and female, bearing a sign with the following message:

WE OUT HERE

WEVE BEEN HERE

WE AINT LEAVING

WE ARE LOVED

It was unclear to what extent the tension between insisting that you aren't leaving (presumably in defiance of someone or something that would prefer otherwise) and declaring that you are loved (presumably in solidarity with others who might doubt that this was true about themselves and others like them) was intentional. But the slogans testified to the sad but unmentioned fact that seemed to be at the core of these campus protests: that while you can prohibit the use of racial slurs through rules and norms, no administration or law can force someone to befriend you, or to love you, or to see you as a person who matters, or to notice you at all.

I should confess here to the biases that influence my thinking. At the YMCA camp I attended when I was nine—the first (and, as it happens, the last) setting in which I was subjected to daily racial slurs—my father asked the counselors to ensure fair odds in the physical confrontations between me and the tormentors that he made clear were to be expected. It would not have occurred to him to demand that the administration protect me from bullies. Growing up meant forsaking the frightened victim in yourself, which had a way of sliding into disdain for the category of frightened victims in general.

I don't mean to suggest that I endured a tough upbringing or that my father was a hard man. My upbringing in a small New Jersey suburb was soft—especially when compared with the life, for instance, of my mother. The suffering she endured was squarely in the median range of what people born in Korea in the 1930s experienced. It was not unusual for American bombers to destroy your family's house during the Korean War. It was not unusual for your brother or father or sister to be killed by friendly fire. It was routine for proud and ancient families like my mother's to be reduced to a destitute rabble living off the charity of American missionaries. But her struggle did and does make most of the challenges that you are likely to face as the child of Americans in a part of the country where most of the kids assume they are headed to college seem fantastically trivial in comparison.

The theory of microaggression can't help but seem to me mostly an indicator of how radically devoid of other threats our lives in America have become—at least in the fortunate part of the country where people go to college. But maybe I've grown habituated to conditions that today's young people feel entitled to reject. And maybe I escaped the role of frightened victim by finding others to victimize. When I think back to those years when all my attitudes were formed, I think also of the only black girl in the gifted-and-talented programs where I first made friends. Her name was Shakina, and she was different in many respects from the suburban Jewish and Asian male wiseasses who were the norm in those classes (if not in the general population of their own schools). What an odious term, "the gifted," to describe a group whose gifts mainly consisted of being the children of lawyers and dentists and professors and bankers—but let's not deny that there was a certain facility we possessed or that it was a source of pride to be segregated into a place where our need for instruction tailored to our superior abilities would be honored. It should not surprise anyone that being bullied during our school days made us not lovers of humanity but victimizers of others the moment we had the numbers on our side. And I guess it goes without saying that we abused Shakina mercilessly, and that even if our teachers had done more to forbid us from mocking how she talked, as they sometimes tried to do, to little effect, no one could force us to see her as our equal.

In later years, in those same gifted classes, I encountered omnicompetent, hyperarticulate black teenagers who seemed on the fast track to world domination. They could code-switch from street vernacular to the smooth diction of the lecture hall, using each idiom to swell the power and persuasiveness of the other. They had forged in the crucible of their souls the resources necessary to survive and triumph in a world that wasn't inclined to believe in their existence until they had proved it. Everyone wanted to know them. Adversity, and the strength to meet it with forbearance and grace, had made them more interesting and complex than anyone who hadn't been exposed to the same stimulus that adversity ends up becoming for those who aren't destroyed by it. These people were cool.

They were also exceptional. The campus protests remind us that any system that requires exceptional fortitude from certain categories of people is an unjust one. The jargon that tried to name this injustice and serve as a tool in the struggle against it—white privilege, microaggression, safe space, etc.—caught on so fast because it named something that people recognized right away from their own lives. Like any new language that seeks to politicize everyday life, the terms were awkward, heavy-handed, and formulaic, but they gave confidence to people desiring redress for the subtle incursions on their dignity that they suspected were holding them back. The new vocabulary provided confirmation of what young people have always had reason to suspect—that the world was conspiring to strip them of their dignity and keep them in their place—and elevated those grievances to the status of a larger political project. Of course, the terms could easily become totalizing and portray the world as an "iron cage" in which crude identity categories determine everyone's fate in a way that is demonstrably false. In practice, the protesters wound up appealing to college bureaucrats to wipe away the accretions of the world's violent history.

And yet they also gave voice to an aspiration that people of my generation and older, who had grown up more isolated in a whiter America, had not thought could be expressed as a collective demand rather than as an individual wish: that all of us, even the unexceptional, could claim as a matter of right an equal share of existential comfort as those who had never had cause to think of themselves as the other. This still seems to me an impossible wish, and, like all impossible wishes, one that is charged with authoritarian potential. But those of us who have grown inured to life's quotidian brutalities—the ones we accept for ourselves and the ones we unthinkingly impose on others—should not be surprised that the young have a different sense of the possible than we do, or forget too readily what it was like before we were so inured.

PERMISSIONS

Grateful acknowledgment is made to the following for permission to reprint previously published materials:

"I Am the Happiness of This World" by Hilton Als. Copyright © 2013 by Hilton Als. Reprinted by permission of The Wylie Agency LLC.

"One Summer" from *The Way the World Works: Essays* by Nicholson Baker. Copyright © 2012 by Nicholson Baker. Reprinted by permission of Simon & Schuster, Inc. and Melanie Jackson Agency, LLC. All rights reserved.

"Portrait of the Bagel as a Young Man" from *How to Be a Man: Scenes from a Protracted Boyhood* by Thomas Beller. Copyright © 2005 by Thomas Beller. Reprinted by permission of W. W. Norton & Company, Inc.

"Brave Face" by Sven Birkerts. Copyright © 2003 by Sven Birkerts. Originally published in *The Boston Globe* on February 2, 2003. Reprinted by permission of the author.

Excerpt from *On Immunity: An Inoculation* (pages 12–17) by Eula Biss. Copyright © 2013 by Eula Biss. Reprinted by permission of The Permissions Company, LLC, on behalf of Graywolf Press, www.graywolfpress.org.

"Tactless" from *Awkward: A Detour* by Mary Cappello. Copyright © 2007 by Mary Cappello. Reprinted by permission of Bellevue Literary Press, New York.

"Decreation: How Women Like Sappho, Marguerite Porete and Simone Weil Tell God" from *Decreation: Poetry, Essays, Opera* by Anne Carson. Copyright © 2005 by Anne Carson. Reprinted by permission of Alfred A. Knopf, an imprint of the Knopf Doubleday Publishing Group, a division of Penguin Random House LLC. All rights reserved.

"Home Alone" from *The Professor and Other Writings* by Terry Castle. Copyright © 2010 by Terry Castle. Reprinted by permission of HarperCollins Publishers and Janklow & Nesbit Associates.

"Girl" from *How to Write an Autobiographical Novel: Essays* by Alexander Chee. Copyright © 2018 by Alexander Chee. Reprinted by permission of Houghton Mifflin Harcourt Publishing Company, Bloomsbury Publishing Plc, and The Wylie Agency LLC. All rights reserved.

"Black Body: Rereading James Baldwin's 'Stranger in the Village'" by Teju Cole. Originally published in *The New Yorker* on August 19, 2014. Copyright © 2014 by Condé Nast. Reprinted by permission of Condé Nast.

"Greedy Sleep" by Bernard Cooper. Copyright © 2018 by Bernard Cooper. Reprinted by permission of ICM Partners.

"The Doctor Is a Woman" from *Look Alive Out There: Essays* by Sloane Crosley. Copyright © 2018 by Sloane Crosley. Reprinted by permission of HarperCollins Publishers Ltd. and Farrar, Straus and Giroux. All rights reserved.

"Loitering" by Charles D'Ambrosio. Copyright © 2014 by Charles D'Ambrosio. Reprinted by permission of Tin House, LLC. All rights reserved.

"Matricide" from *The Unspeakable: And Other Subjects of Discussion* by Meghan Daum. Copyright © 2014 by Meghan Daum. Reprinted by permission of the author and Farrar, Straus and Giroux. All rights reserved.

"Joyas Voladoras" from *One Long River of Song* by Brian Doyle. Copyright © 2019 by Brian Doyle. Reprinted by permission of Little, Brown, an imprint of Hachette Book Group, Inc.

"Otherwise Known as the Human Condition (with Particular Reference to Doughnut Plant Doughnuts)" from *Otherwise Known as the Human Condition: Selected Essays and Reviews* by Geoff Dyer. Copyright © 2011 by Geoff Dyer. Reprinted by permission of Canongate Books Ltd. and The Permissions Company, LLC, on behalf of Graywolf Press, www.graywolfpress.org.

"CID–LAX–BOG" by Lina Ferreira. Copyright © 2017 by Lina M. Ferreira Cabeza-Vanegas. Reprinted by permission of the author.

"Doing No Harm: Some Thoughts on Reading and Writing in the Age of Umbrage" from *Romance of Elsewhere* by Lynn Freed. Copyright © 2017 by Lynn Freed. Reprinted by permission of Counterpoint Press.

"The Case of the Angry Daughter" by Rivka Galchen. Copyright © 2019 by Rivka Galchen. Originally published in *The New York Times Magazine* on December 17, 2019. Reprinted by permission of the author.

"Scat" from *The Book of Delights* by Ross Gay. Copyright © 2019 by Ross Gay. Reprinted by permission of Algonquin Books of Chapel Hill and Coronet, an imprint of Hodder and Stoughton Limited. All rights reserved.

"On Revenge" from *American Originality: Essays on Poetry* by Louise Glück. Copyright © 2017 by Louise Glück. Reprinted by permission of Farrar, Straus and Giroux, and Carcanet Press Limited. All rights reserved.

"Faculty Wife" from *Book of Days: Personal Essays* by Emily Fox Gordon. Copyright © 2010 by Emily Fox Gordon. Reprinted by permission of the author and Spiegel & Grau, an imprint of Random House, a division of Penguin Random House LLC. All rights reserved.

"Other People's Secrets" from *I Could Tell You Stories: Sojourns in the Land of Memory* by Patricia Hampl. Copyright © 1999 by Patricia Hampl. Reprinted by permission of Marly Rusoff Literary Agency and W. W. Norton & Company, Inc.

"The Aquarium" from *The Book of My Lives* by Aleksandar Hemon. Copyright © 2013 by Aleksandar Hemon. Reprinted by permission of Farrar, Straus and Giroux. All rights reserved.

"The Terror of Love" from *Meaty: Essays* by Samantha Irby. Copyright © 2013, 2018 by Samantha Irby. Reprinted by permission of Vintage Books, an imprint of the Knopf Doubleday Publishing Group, a division of Penguin Random House LLC. All rights reserved.

"The Empathy Exams" from *The Empathy Exams: Essays* by Leslie Jamison. Copyright © 2014 by Leslie Jamison. Reprinted by permission of The Permissions Company, LLC, on behalf of Graywolf Press, www.graywolfpress.org.

Excerpt from *Negroland: A Memoir* by Margo Jefferson. Copyright © 2015 by Margo Jefferson. Reprinted by permission of Pantheon Books, an imprint of the Knopf Doubleday Publishing Group, a division of Penguin Random House LLC, Granta Books, and The Wylie Agency LLC.

"Domestic Gulags" from *Against Love: A Polemic* by Laura Kipnis. Copyright © 2003 by Laura Kipnis. Reprinted by permission of Pantheon Books, an imprint of the Knopf Doubleday Publishing Group, a division of Penguin Random House LLC. All rights reserved.

"Ann; Death and the Maiden" from *I'll Be Your Mirror: Essays and Aphorisms* by David Lazar. Copyright © 2017 by the Board of Regents of the University of Nebraska. Reprinted by permission of the University of Nebraska Press.

"Dear Friend, from My Life I Write to You in Your Life" from *Dear Friend, from My Life I Write to You in Your Life* by Yiyun Li. Copyright © 2017 by Yiyun Li. Reprinted by permission of Random House, an imprint and division of Penguin Random House LLC. All rights reserved.

"Experience Necessary" from *After Montaigne: Contemporary Essayists Cover the Essays*, edited by David Lazar and Patrick Madden, by Phillip Lopate. Copyright © 2015 by Phillip Lopate. Reprinted by permission of the author.

"The Invitation" by Barry Lopez. Copyright © 2015 by Barry Lopez. Originally published in *Granta* on November 18, 2015. Reprinted by permission of SLL/Sterling Lord Literistic, Inc.

"Bodies in Motion and at Rest" from *Bodies in Motion and at Rest* by Thomas Lynch. Copyright © 2000 by Thomas Lynch. Reprinted by permission of the author and W. W. Norton & Company, Inc.

"Draft No. 4" from *Draft No. 4: On the Writing Process* by John McPhee. Copyright © 2017 by John McPhee. Reprinted by permission of Farrar, Straus and Giroux. All rights reserved.

"Failure: A Meditation, Another Iteration (with Interruptions)" from *Neck Deep and Other Predicaments* by Ander Monson. Copyright © 2007 by Ander Monson. Reprinted by permission of The Permissions Company, LLC, on behalf of Graywolf Press, www.graywolfpress.org.

"Live Through That?!" from *The Importance of Being Iceland: Travel Essays in Art* by Eileen Myles. Copyright © 2009 by Eileen Myles. Reprinted by permission of Semiotext(e).

Excerpt from *The Argonauts* (pages 9–16) by Maggie Nelson. Copyright © 2015 by Maggie Nelson. Reprinted by permission of The Permissions Company, LLC, on behalf of Graywolf Press, www.graywolfpress.org.

"Homeschool" by Meghan O'Gieblyn. Copyright © 2019 by Meghan O'Gieblyn. Originally published in *n+1* (Winter 2019). Reprinted by permission of Meghan O'Gieblyn.

"A Visit to San Quentin" from *Soul at the White Heat* by Joyce Carol Oates. Copyright © 2016 by *The Ontario Review, Inc.* Reprinted by permission of HarperCollins Publishers.

"Busted in New York" from *Busted in New York and Other Essays* by Darryl Pinckney. Copyright © 2019 by Darryl Pinckney. Reprinted by permission of Farrar, Straus and Giroux. All rights reserved.

"Against 'Gunmetal'" from *Rough Likeness: Essays* by Lia Purpura. Copyright © 2011 by Lia Purpura. Reprinted by permission of The Permissions Company, LLC, on behalf of Sarabande Books, www.sarabandebooks.org.

"Beeper World" by Karen Russell. Copyright © 2014 by Karen Russell. Originally published in *Harper's Magazine* (December 2014). Reprinted by permission of the Denise Shannon Literary Agency, Inc. All rights reserved.

"This Old House" by David Sedaris. Copyright © 2007 by David Sedaris. Originally published in *The New Yorker* and *When You Are Engulfed in Flames* (Little, Brown and Company, 2008). Reprinted by permission of Little, Brown, an imprint of Hachette Book Group, Inc. and Don Congdon Associates, Inc.

"Differences: Sex, Separateness & Marriage" by Shifra Sharlin. Copyright © 2013 by Shifra Sharlin. Originally published in *Salmagundi*. Reprinted by permission of the author.

"Information Sickness" from *Other People: Takes & Mistakes* by David Shields. Copyright © 2017 by David Shields. Reprinted by permission of the author and Alfred A. Knopf, an imprint of the Knopf Doubleday Publishing Group, a division of Penguin Random House LLC. All rights reserved.

"Gray Area: Thinking with a Damaged Brain" from *In the Shadow of Memory* by Floyd Skloot. Copyright © 2003 by Floyd Skloot. Reprinted by permission of the University of Nebraska Press.

"Cassandra Among the Creeps" from *Men Explain Things to Me* by Rebecca Solnit. Copyright © 2014 by Rebecca Solnit. Originally published by Haymarket Books in 2014. Reprinted by permission of Hill Nadell Literary Agency.

"Eric Garner and Me" by Clifford Thompson. Copyright © 2015 by Clifford Thompson. Originally published in the *Los Angeles Review of Books* on November 18, 2015. Reprinted by permission of the author.

"We Out Here" from *The Souls of Yellow Folk: Essays* by Wesley Yang. Copyright © 2018 by Wesley Yang. Reprinted by permission of W. W. Norton & Company, Inc.

ALSO BY

PHILLIP LOPATE

THE ART OF THE PERSONAL ESSAY

An Anthology from the Classical Era to the Present

For more than four hundred years, the personal essay has been one of the richest and most vibrant of all literary forms. *The Art of the Personal Essay* is the first anthology to celebrate this fertile genre. By presenting more than seventy-five personal essays, including influential forerunners from ancient Greece, Rome, and the Far East, masterpieces from the dawn of the personal essay in the sixteenth century, and a wealth of the finest personal essays from the last four centuries, editor Phillip Lopate, himself an acclaimed essayist, displays the tradition of the personal essay in all its historical grandeur, depth, and diversity.

Literary Criticism/Essays

THE GLORIOUS AMERICAN ESSAY

One Hundred Essays from Colonial Times to the Present

The essay form is an especially democratic one, and many of the essays Phillip Lopate has gathered here address themselves—sometimes critically—to American values. We see the Puritans, the Founding Fathers and Mothers, and the stars of the American Renaissance struggle to establish a national culture. A grand tradition of nature writing runs from Audubon, Thoreau, and John Muir to Rachel Carson and Annie Dillard. Marginalized groups use the essay to assert or to complicate notions of identity. Lopate has cast his net wide, embracing critical, personal, political, philosophical, literary, polemical, autobiographical, and humorous essays. Americans by birth as well as immigrants appear here, famous essayists alongside writers more celebrated for fiction or poetry. The result is a dazzling overview of the riches of the American essay.

Essays

THE GOLDEN AGE OF THE AMERICAN ESSAY
1945–1970

The three decades that followed World War II were an exceptionally fertile period for American essays. The explosion of journals and magazines, the rise of public intellectuals, and breakthroughs in the arts inspired a flowering of literary culture. At the same time, the many problems that confronted midcentury America—racism, sexism, nuclear threat, war, poverty, and environmental degradation among them—proved fruitful topics for America's best minds. In *The Golden Age of the American Essay*, Phillip Lopate assembles a dazzling array of famous writers, critics, sociologists, theologians, historians, activists, theorists, humorists, poets, and novelists. Here are writers like James Agee, E. B. White, A. J. Liebling, Randall Jarrell, and Mary McCarthy, pivoting from the comic indignities of daily life to world peace, consumerism, and restaurants in Paris. Here are Norman Mailer on Jackie Kennedy, Vladimir Nabokov on *Lolita*, Martin Luther King, Jr.'s "Letter from Birmingham Jail," and Richard Hofstadter's "The Paranoid Style in American Politics." Here are Gore Vidal, Rachel Carson, James Baldwin, Susan Sontag, John Updike, Joan Didion, and many more in a treasury of brilliant writing that has stood the test of time.

Essays

ALSO AVAILABLE
Waterfront